RENAISSANCE ESSAYS

Portrait of Principal William Robertson by Raeburn, in the Senate Room, Edinburgh University. Among the books Robertson chose to be displayed in his portrait is Muratori's *Annali* (see Plate 3) *(By kind permission of Edinburgh University's Pictures and Galleries Committee)*

RENAISSANCE ESSAYS

———

DENYS HAY

THE HAMBLEDON PRESS

LONDON AND RONCEVERTE

Published by The Hambledon Press, 1988

102 Gloucester Avenue, London NW1 8HX (U.K.)

309 Greenbrier Avenue, Ronceverte WV 24970 (U.S.A.)

ISBN 0 907628 96 6

British Library Cataloguing in Publication Data

Hay, Denys
    Renaissance essays.
    1. Europe – History – 476-1492
    2. Europe – History – 1492-1648
    I. Title
    CB 940.2'1   D202

Library of Congress Cataloging-in-Publication Data

Hay, Denys
    Renaissance essays.

    Selected essays originally published 1951-1983.
    1. Renaissance. 2. Renaissance – Historiography.
    I. Title.
    CB361.H32   1988   940.2'1   87-18158

Printed and bound by Billing and Sons, Worcester

CONTENTS

vi   *Contents*

LIST OF ILLUSTRATIONS

ACKNOWLEDGEMENTS

The articles in this volume initially appeared in the following places. They are here reprinted by the kind permission of the original publishers.

1   *Studies in Church History* (1982), pp. 1-18.

2   *Scottish Historical Review*, xxx (1951), pp. 15-29.

3   *Proceedings of the British Academy*, xlv (1960), pp. 97-128.

4   *Bulletin of the Institute of Historical Research*, xxxv (1962), pp. 111-27.

5   *L.A. Muratori Storigrafo: Atti del Convegno Internazionale di Studi Muratoriani* (Olschki, Florence, 1975), pp. 323-39.

6   *Il Rinascimento: Interpretazioni e Problemi* (Laterza, Rome-Bari, 1979); *The Renaissance* (Methuen, London, 1982), pp. 1-32.

7   *Renaissance Studies in Honor of Hans Baron*, edited by A.Molho and J.A. Tedeschi (Sansoni, Florence, 1971), pp. xiii-xxix.

8   *From the Renaissance to the Counter-Reformation: Essays in Honor of Garrett Mattingley*, edited by C.H. Carter (Random House, New York, 1965), pp. 113-44.

9   *Itinerarium Italicum*, edited by H.A. Oberman and T.A. Brady (Brill, Leiden, 1975), pp. 305-67.

10   *History*, liii (1969), pp. 35-50.

11   *Rendiconti dell' Accademia Nazionale dei Lincei*, 175 (1972), pp. 3-17.

12   *Transactions of the Royal Historical Society*, 5th series, 4 (1954), pp. 91-109.

13   *Transactions of the Dumfriesshire and Galloway Natural History and Antiquarian Society Transactions*, xxxi (1954 for 1952-3), pp. 145-66.

14   *Transactions of the Royal Historical Society*, 5th series,
      25 (1975), pp. 77-92.

15   *Renaissance and Reformation in Scotland: Essays for
      Gordon Donaldson*, edited by I. Cowan and D. Shaw
      (Scottish Academic Press, Edinburgh, 1983), pp. 114-24.

16   *Società, Politica e Cultura a Carpi ai Tempi di Alberto
      III Pio* (Antenore, Padua, 1981), pp. 189-206.

17   *Italian Renaissance Studies*, edited by E.F. Jacob
      (Fabers, London, 1960), pp. 48-68.

18   *Florilegium Historiale: Essays Presented to Wallace
      Ferguson*, edited by J.G. Rowe and W.H. Stockdale
      (University of Toronto Press, 1971), pp. 3-17.

19   *Per Federico Chabod (1901-1960), I (Lo Stato e il
      Potere nel Rinascimento)*, Annali della Facoltà di
      Scienze Politiche, Perugia (1980-1), pp. 129-36.

20   *Studies in Medieval History Presented to R.H.C. Davis*,
      edited by H. Mayr-Harting and R.I. Moore (Hambledon
      Press, London, 1985), pp. 297-307.

21   *Printing and the Mind of Man* (Cassell, London, 1967),
      pp. xvii-xxxvi.

PREFACE

It will be evident from the contents of this book that the 'Renaissance' of the title refers to a period of time rather than a cultural change in European style, which was what the word used mainly to mean. For the rest how may one excuse the assembling of such a miscellany of pieces, chosen by the publisher from my scattered writings? Perhaps I may be allowed a semi-autobiographical approach.

I mention below that as an undergraduate I was forcibly discouraged from taking the Renaissance option, and as a result concentrated on medieval history; but my reason for interest in especially Italian history in the period between Petrarch and the Sack of Rome goes back to school days. I had the great good fortune to go to the Royal Grammar School at Newcastle upon Tyne. Among several good history masters was a remarkable teacher called R.F.I. Bunn, who later moved on to Manchester Grammar School. I think it was he who urged me to read Burckhardt's *Civilization of the Renaissance in Italy*. I was lucky enough to get as a school prize in 1933 a copy (remaindered!) of the beautifully illustrated Middlemore translation (1929) which has been with me ever since. Read at first with devotion, re-read in fury, I finally accepted it for its seminal character.

If the chauvinistic direction of my Oxford tutor V. H. Galbraith headed me off the Renaissance it was he who suggested I might consider Polydore Vergil, when I was looking around for a research topic. And so I did, with interruptions due to the War, until I finally edited a text of the most recent part of his original MS, now in the Vatican Library. My work on this began with the 'Rome transcripts' in the P.R.O. and then was based (fortunately) on photostats of the MS. I say fortunately because when I first saw the MS after the War I was shaken to see the crumbling state of the paper. The photostats which I obtained, paid for by a fund administered by Sir Maurice Powicke, are now in the Bodleian Library.

During the War I was for a time seconded to Cabinet Office as a War Historian, which involved me in a fresh interest in historiography, reflected in some of the pieces reprinted here. I once had the ambition to write a big book on the history of historiography. It has alas been my fate to write little books on big subjects, partly the result of a great deal of time spent in teaching, much of it to undergraduates, of which I am by no means ashamed and from which I have learned a lot.

One joy, ever since I haunted the book barrows in the exciting covered market at Newcastle, has been books. This has left a residual interest in printing and publishing. The nearest I have ever been to expressing this obsession was when Stanley Morison asked me, I have often wondered why, to write a preface to the remarkable catalogue of the exhibition he and others organised called 'Printing and the Mind of Man'. The IPEX exhibition of 1963 of the craft of printing and some of its most influential productions from the fifteenth century onwards was mounted at the B.M. (as it was still called) and at Earl's Court and Olympia. For me it meant some exhilarating sessions with Stanley Morison in London and Chicago; it was champagne in mid-morning, not coffee, and sometimes acrimonious debates on Sex and the Scriptures.

Another off-shoot of this enterprise was my getting to know John Carter, whose extraordinary exposure of Thomas J. Wise was published in the latter's lifetime. The book he wrote about it with Graham Pollard (1934) once kept me awake all night in a sleeper from London to Edinburgh. Unfortunately I've had no opportunity to write of Renaissance forgery, a subject less studied than forgery in the medieval period. But I touch on two odd characters – Annius (or Nanni) of Viterbo and Trithemius (below pp. 382, 419). Their activities are still shrouded in learned controversy. Thomas J. Wise's deceits are more or less unveiled by now.

To explain some of the other essays is really to catalogue men who have been friends and whose work has often been very relevant to my interests. Wallace Ferguson, whom I recall with pleasure in London, Ontario, and here in Edinburgh was the author of a remarkable *vade mecum* for all students of the Renaissance, a model of useful historiography. More original are the works of Paul Oskar Kristeller, philosopher and collector of bibliographical information on a colossal scale. My contribution to one of the four, I believe, volumes dedicated to him reflects my own indebtedness; his own magisterial *Iter Italicum* goes marching on, now in volume 3. His flat in Amsterdam Avenue looks out at Columbia University and is near the headquarters of the Renaissance Society of which for years he has been a guiding light. With him I must link Hans Baron, my colleague when I was a research fellow at the Newberry Library in Chicago: a marvellous Library and a man to whose work, especially the articles published in the immediate pre-war period, I owe an entirely new understanding of the current of thought we incapsulate in the term Renaissance. I know he intends to reprint them. I hope he does so soon.

Baron and Kristeller are members of that diaspora of German scholarship from which the Anglo-Saxon world has benefited. But the indigenous contribution (if we may thus term it) in this area of scholarship is not restricted to Wallace Ferguson: Garrett Mattingly, to whom I made a pilgrimage when he was a visiting professorial fellow at Balliol. I remember him warmly; I also recall the dry Martini he 'engineered' for me, and the warm inscription in his book on the Armada which he gave me.

Italians too have made notable contributions. First must be mentioned Eugenio Garin. He is often regarded as a Doppelgänger of Baron, but his output over the years, as editor, translator and commentator on humanist texts is prodigious. Another Italian of outstanding merit was Federico Chabod. My essay in this volume, edited by Sergio Bertelli, is an inadequate testimony to my esteem and indebtedness to Chabod and the deep sympathy he inspired in me from the first time I met him in Paris in 1961.

I cannot find any further umbrellas to cover the other pieces in this volume. The Border and the Anglo-Scottish frontier are part of my inheritance, since I was brought up by my grandfather who came originally from the Scottish side of the Border Line. And, again, I must revert to Mr. Bunn who once startled a class by writing on the blackboard 'A.D. 410. Foundation of the Newcastle Society of Antiquaries'. This shocking remark (his métier was to shock) being interpreted meant that when Rome withdrew from Britain the Roman Wall fell into ruins, to be dug up and cherished by the learned of our own days. From that frontier to others is a short step: to Italians and Barbarians, to ecclesiastical differences such as that between Gallicanism and Anglicanism, to the hazy no-man's land between politics and principles, touched on here in the discussion of More's *Utopia*, a lecture I gave in the superb ambience of the Farnesina beside the Tiber in Rome. And touched on also in the essay I contributed to Ralph Davis's *Festschrift*: does history have relevance for public life? This is a perpetual conundrum for me. And age does not bring a solution any nearer.

Edinburgh, October 1987

These essays are dedicated in affection and
respect to the names of my grandfather
THOMAS WAUGH
and my uncle
HERBERT WAUGH

1

SCHOLARSHIP, RELIGION AND THE CHURCH

IN choosing this subject (on which many speakers have touched in talking to this Society) I started by intending to be more precise in my topic, as well as to introduce the question of church reform. The scholarship I had in mind was classical scholarship and all that went with it in eloquence, enjoyment and understanding of ancient authors. Against this I wished to pit those proponents of a religious life who rejected antiquity and all it stood for. Not of course *all* of either kind, but some representative examples drawn from the later Middle Ages. In the event the task I had chosen proved much more intricate that I had supposed it would be, the emerging picture more blurred. This, as we all know, is a fairly familiar phenomenon. And as for reform it figures, I am afraid, rather incidentally in what follows.

I was also impressed at a recent committee meeting by the remark of a former president—a very just remark, I believe. He simply pointed out that our society is the *ecclesiastical* history society and not the *religious* history society, and hinted gently that some of us tended to forget this. Of course it is true that while the church, the *ecclesia* of our title, is distinct from religion, the two overlap and mingle. The institutions of the church are often the framework within which the faith and its manifestations operate. Yet the fact remains that faith, devotion, prayer, exaltation and despair—religion, in short—are *not* institutionalised in any obvious way and are, indeed, both difficult to identify and to define. The church as a machine can offer opportunities and consolations, as when it enables sinners to confess and depends upon its priests to administer effective sacraments and to absolve, even when such priests are themselves not in a state of grace. But even the greatest and most solemn moments in life have no need of the intervention of church and clergy. Birth, marriage and death are part of the natural order. No priest is needed to baptise, to marry or to throw a handful of earth on the corpse in the grave. Anyone can baptise in an emergency; in matrimony the priest is a mere witness until in the sixteenth century he becomes a registrar as well; and, to repeat an injunction we expensively forget now: 'let the dead bury their dead'.

Yet my quotation comes from St Matthew and it was written in a language (soon available in Greek or Latin versions) which was unknown to the rapidly multiplying Christian communities of the early middle ages. Since my modest abilities are confined to the Latin West let me rephrase the last sentence and enlarge it: in the West the Bible was a Latin book and if one wanted to penetrate to the sort of mysteries I have hinted at in the last few minutes—the picture of religion as expounded in the Old and New Testaments—one had to have the ability to read Latin, and, if possible, the great theologians of the early centuries. Moreover for priest and people there was the celebration of Mass and, at least annually, the celebration of the Eucharist. All this in Latin too, as well as the regular prescribed hours of the priest. To preserve and propagate a mandarin language amidst hordes of people speaking dozens of vernaculars (many of course derived from Latin) and dialects of vernaculars, was a herculean task, performed with very indifferent success in the medieval and early modern period. We may well suspect that the task was complicated in that the faithful confessed, again annually if at all, in their own language and were given penance in like manner; if they heard a service, and this became commoner in and after the thirteenth century, it was often a queer charade of gestures, a queer macaronic mixture of Latin and whatever of the local vernacular the preacher could command. But it too *did* make the preacher different from the priest rapidly and expertly going through the motions at the altar and reciting (or mumbling) the Latin service.

It would be interesting to speculate on the effects of this split minded classical world of the pre-Reformation period. But this evening I invite you to reflect with me on the much more familiar and easy problem of Latin and the clergy as a problem facing the hierarchy in order to fulfill what by the early middle ages had become regarded as the role of the church: the performance at due times and places of the rites of the liturgy. There is no doubt that most parish priests were, if not self-educated, at least given their basic instruction by a priest with no training in teaching, and came to their career if not their vocation by a kind of apprenticeship. Scraps of information suggest that many priests (perhaps some in early days manumitted bondsmen) were barely literate and so ill paid and provided for that they were little different in manners or morals from the rural and perhaps sometimes the urban population of small towns, among whom they moved. If this, I believe, was the training that most young men got, how did they survive examination for ordination? The answer is, of course, that this was perfunctory in many cases. The general acceptance by bishops and their chanceries that there *must* be ministers to serve altars must have made senior clergy less than particular as to all the statutory requirements save the basic one of a title—of a source of income from church or family or (in the case of regulars) an Order, so that the young man would not join the wandering priests and religious who brought disrepute on their cloth. Of these parochial clergy, those whom (I suppose) most men saw, occasionally at least, I do not propose to treat. They were not educated and so in no recognisable way encountered in an embarrassing form the dilemmas I wish briefly to discuss in what follows.

Do you remember the fierce story in the *Speculum Perfectionis* in which the Saint rebukes the young brother who asks permission to have his own psalter? Here is a bit of it.

> On another time a certain brother novice who knew how to read the psalter, though not well, obtained from the Minister-General leave to have one; yet, because he heard that blessed Francis wished his bretheren not to desire knowledge and books, he was not content to have it without the leave of blessed Francis. When therefore blessed Francis had come to the place where that novice was, the novice said: 'Father, it would be a great solace to me to have a psalter, but though the General has conceded it to me, yet I wish to have it, Father, with thy knowledge'. To whom blessed Francis answered: 'Charles the Emperor, Roland and Oliver, and all the Paladins and strong men, being mighty in war chasing the infidels with much travail and sweat to the death, had over them notable victory, and at the last themselves did die in battle, holy martyrs for the faith of Christ; but now there are many who would fain receive honours and human praise for the mere telling of the things which those others did. So also amongst ourselves are many who would fain receive honours and praise by reciting and preaching only the works which the saints did'. (As if he would say: 'Books and science should not be esteemed, but rather virtuous labours, since knowledge puffeth up, but charity edifieth'). But after a few days, when blessed Francis was sitting at the fire, the same novice spoke to him again of the psalter. And blessed Francis said to him: 'After you have a psalter, you will desire and wish to have a breviary.

Then you will sit in your chair, like a great prelate and say to your brother: "Bring me the breviary"?'[1].

Of course we know that the Dominicans flocked to the Universities as the Franciscans did a little later. But there has always been a profound suspicion among religious folk (and I mean by religious not members of Orders but men and women of devout disposition) to regard learning and especially book learning as a very suspicious activity. 'Of making many books there is no end and much learning is a weariness of the flesh', so says Ecclesiastes. 'Knowledge', to come to the New Testament, 'puffeth a man up'. Indeed, broadly speaking, books and learning come rather badly out of the Book, the texts gathered in the Bible. The paradox is that these condemnations of books come from *the* book.

Yet from Christian antiquity onwards Christian books multiplied—commentaries, works of devotion, of history, the whole gamut of literature including sacred poetry and even prose fiction if we include the early *Acta Sanctorum*. And behind these productions of the patristic period lay the surviving works of classical antiquity, which were to be called the 'classics'. These were written in a style which was exempt from any criticism of later Latin and if a scholar in the middle ages wished to master his Christian texts he had to begin by being familiar with the non-Christian writers of an earlier period. Please observe that I do not say 'pagan' writers. I avoid this expression for two reasons. First, it would have utterly bewildered the ancient writers themselves. For Vergil, Cicero, Horace, Livy and so on did not regard themselves as pagan in large measure because of their cultivation and practice of literature. Second with a few rare exceptions the Latin writers of antiquity were not pagan in the pejorative sense of that term. I mean they were not dealing in wicked or unholy or irreligious matter, let alone concerning themselves with strange gods. I say this deliberately, excluding some Greek authors and realising there are smutty or suggestive passages in Ovid and Martial who, despite that (or because of it?) were to be very influential in the Middle Ages and Renaissance. On the contrary, as if to balance the indiscretion of one or two poets, I would readily concede that most Latin prose writers are ineffably

---

[1] The subject treated in this brief lecture has, it must be stressed, been the subject of many books and articles.; I shall mention only one of what would otherwise have become an unmanageable bibliography: Charles Norris Cochrane, *Christianity and Classical Culture* (Oxford rev. ed. 1944, repr. 1972). *Speculum perfectionis* trans. R. Steel (London 1903). For a brief note on this work see Moorman p 596.

boring, being pompous to please their pompous readers. Yet it was to these writers of prose and poetry that the neophyte clergyman, who aspired to more than a barnyard in a decrepit village, were directed as formal education of the clergy was, however ineffectually, decreed by the Councils of the Lateran in 1179 and 1215, when bishops were directed to provide free education for priests.

We are, of course, at the beginning of the *universitates*, those guilds of experts in grammar, logic and style, which were to dominate European education until the eighteenth century[2]. The curriculum, whether mastered earlier at a grammar school or at the University in the Faculty of Arts, depended on the grammarians of late antiquity and the literary texts to which their gristly manuals were intended to be a guide. Uncouth the manuals were. Uncouth, or at any rate spiritually irrelevant, as most of the classical texts were, that was what the aspiring clergyman was exposed to: perhaps one should say ambitious rather than aspiring. For the successful graduates, as they emerged as such in the thirteenth century, had the ball at their feet. They were (as K. B. McFarlane put it) masters of their world, as well as M.A.'s[3]. Their future lay in running the establishment. They had been warned, one might say, by St Bernard. 'It is not argument that comprehends them [the essential elements of God], but holiness, if at least that can anyway be comprehended which is incomprehensible'[4]. Lawyers (if I may presume to paraphrase Bernard, writing at much the same moment as Gratian) are lousy.

Lawyers, however, were there to stay, and so were universities, with their M.A.s, and doctorates of medicine and law, above all of theology. Willy-nilly the clerk met the classics and so elaborated the debate, destined to last for centuries, between the poet and the prophet. As you know, the contradiction was, in a sense, resolved by saying that the poet *was* a prophet.

In reviewing the history of the educated clergy, whether regular or secular, it is important to remember that their scholarship and the learning they were exposed to as novices, or at a later date university students, was down to the twelfth century not in any meaningful sense

---

[2] H. Rashdall, *Medieval Universities*, ed. Powicke and Emden, 3 vols (Oxford 1936).

[3] 'Like their lay counterparts . . . churchmen were divided into two nations, of masters and men. The masters were the masters of arts'. K. B. McFarlane, *John Wycliffe and the Beginnings of English Nonconformity* (London 1952) p 14.

[4] *De consideratione*, V.xiv in *PL* 182 p 805; trans George Lewis (Oxford 1908).

directly derived from the Scriptures. The colossal, the incredible
edifice of theological and philosophical learning which dominates the
early middle ages was derived from the fathers of the church as a
result of their knowledge of the philosophies of the ancients. At first
this was above all Plato and the neo-Platonic writers like Plotinus, as
well as those mysterious works by Hermes Trismegistus, Orpheus,
Pythagoras and so on which have latterly been much studied because
of the revived interest in them at the end of the fifteenth century. On
the basis of Platonism and its related 'schools', on the basis of the
grammar and dialectic associated with antiquity, was reared the vast
erudition which dominated the western world down to the thirteenth
century and beyond, and which may even have penetrated to a handful
of laity, otherwise unlearned, who were prepared to ask a question or
two as they looked in marvel at a window or statue or walked on the
lovely marble floor at Siena Cathedral and wondered why the Sybils
were there as well as Hermes Mercurius Trismegistus, 'contemporary
of Moses' as the Latin inscription adds. (The depictions of Religion,
Faith, Hope and Charity, we may note, have no words of identification
or explanation.)

The late twelfth and thirteenth centuries were to see a much more
radical influence exercised by the ancient world. As Aristotle's works
were translated into Latin they swept the older Platonic scheme of
things away and, despite the works of Ficino, Pico della Mirandola
and some of their contemporaries in the Florence of the decades round
1500, Aristotelian concepts of method were dominant for centuries as
we can see from much recent work, including Father McConica's
recent contribution to the *English Historical Review* on 'Humanism and
Aristotle in Tudor Oxford'.[5]

This last observation has brought me to the point on which in this
brief survey I wish to dwell longest. When the revival of letters (as the
Renaissance used to be called) occurred, what were the reactions it
provoked among men brought up in older ways? Of these, as I have
suggested, there were two types: the large group of parochial clergy
who were virtually devoid of intellectual interests (to whom I believe
we should add the bulk perhaps of regulars, at any rate outside the Order
of Preachers), and the much smaller number of men who had been
exposed to university training, at Oxford, Paris, Cologne or at one or
two Dominican convents even in Italy. The clash between the 'old

---

[5] James McConica, EHR 94 (1979) 291–397, with many references to current literature.

learning' and the new respect for the moral philosophy inculcated by the Latin masters from Cicero to Seneca, was from time to time sharp. If we are dealing admittedly with a kind of *querelle des livres*, with a 'battle of the books', with an esoteric argument among the intellectual elite, that does not detract from its significance. I cannot, of course, deal with all the tensions of the intellectuals in this field between Petrarch and Erasmus; other contributors to this conference will, I hope, fill in some gaps. For my own part I shall touch on the beginning and the end (so far as the Reformation ended the controversy) and more rapidly from Petrarch to Erasmus. And I shall concentrate on one or two very well-known episodes:

1. Petrarch's 'On his own ignorance' and related writings.

2. Giovanni Dominici's *Lucula noctis* with its background among the writings of disciples of Coluccio Salutati;

3. Valla, including what might fairly be called the 'new criticism' of the Scriptures.

4. Erasmus—at least some of his moods or attitudes, and especially the *Antibarbari*.

I realise that this is a preponderantly Renaissance collection, leaning heavily on the Italian side. It is not necessarily totally unrepresentative of the intelligentsia of the later Middle Ages, but to keep the boat on a more level keel, may I start with a few words on two northerners, Thomas à Kempis and Nicholas Cusanus?

Now that we can talk with confidence of the author of the *Imitatio Christi*, as we surely can after the remarkable work of the late Dr Delaissé, the collection of meditations which took form in the famous book have a new poignancy: one, if I may suggest it, of simplicity.[6] Again, as in so many writers who censure intellectual complexity, Thomas denies that learning has any connection with devotion:

> What good can it do you to discuss the mystery of the God the Trinity in learned terms if you lack humility and so displease that God? Learned arguments do not make a man holy and righteous, whereas a good life makes him dear to God. . . . If you know the whole Bible off by heart and see all expositions of scholars, what good would it do you without the love and grace

---

[6] L. M. J. Delaissé, *Le manuscrit autographe de Thomas à Kempis et 'L'imitation de Jesus Christ'*, Publications de *Scriptorium* 2, in 2 vols (Paris-Bruxelles 1956).

of God? (I.i) . . . The highest and most profitable form of study is to understand one's inmost nature and despise it (I.ii).[7]

For Thomas à Kempis holiness and humility are preferable to scholarship. 'A humble ignorant man who serves God is better than a proud scholar'. And so on; there is no need to labour the point. Yet we have known for a long time that Thomas constructed his prose on a rhythmical basis, as argued by Hirsche in 1874 and amply demonstrated in Delaissé's careful reproduction of the punctuation in his diplomatic edition.[8] In this last edition we can also see that the author lovingly revised and revised again his collection of meditations—*labor limae* literally and with a devout purpose.

This paradox of writing well in order to disclaim the importance of good writing, of being concerned to be convincing, even in one's Augustinian cell, is, I suppose, an aspect of the *Nova devotio* which links it with earlier reform movements. It also tempts one to rechristen the *Imitatio Christi* as the *Docta ignorantia*, and the product of the same milieu, by another alumnus of the Bretheren's school at Deventer.[9] And here, of course, one is positively overwhelmed by Nicholas Cusanus's erudition. The *Docta ignorantia* was dedicated to Cardinal Giulio Cesarini; Cusanus himself was soon to be a cardinal. But in everything he wrote there is a mystical tint which is almost obscured, it seems to me, by the invocation of Platonic and neo-Platonic mysteries, even in his sermons, even in his commentary on the Lord's Prayer,[10] a task which usually brought even the great stylists to simplicity.

There is then, just about the time when the humanities are about to triumph in parts of Italy, a markedly ambivalent medievalism in trans-Alpine Europe. In his book *Petrarch and the Renascence* (1943) Professor J. H. Whitfield at one point wrote 'The first step from a medieval to a civilised society lies in the re-establishment (he means by Petrarch) of the link between man and man by means of ideas and

---

[7] Delaissé II. 181, 182. The most recent trans. into English is by Betty Knott (London 1963) with a useful introduction which unaccountably neglects to refer to the work of Delaissé.

[8] Delaissé I. 103n; Knott, intro. 34–6.

[9] See in general Albert Hyma, *The Christian Renaissance*, 2nd ed. (Hamden, Conn. 1965) *passim;* and Ernst Cassirer, *The Individual and the Cosmos in Renaissance Philosophy.* (Oxford 1964).

[10] A useful anthology in French, trans. and ed. M. de Gandillac, *Oeuvres choisies de Nicolas de Cues* (Paris 1942); the commentary on the Lord's Prayer (1442), pp 106–171, was, despite its erudition, composed in German and presumably intended for a wider audience than the books.

reflection'.[11] What I invite you to observe in this sentence is the contrast drawn by Whitfield between a 'medieval world' and a 'civilised society'. It says something for the continued domination of humanist values almost to our own day that a learned man could make such an observation.

And so I am come to Petrarch—a little earlier than Thomas à Kempis and Cusanus—but one of the first Renaissance scholars to exhibit a full awareness of the problems presented by the study of ancient literature. Again he wrote a book which might well be renamed *Docta ignorantia*, that savage grumble about his young critics which we know as *De sui ipsius et multorum ignorantia*. This essay is, I suppose, nearer in spirit to Thomas à Kempis than to Cusanus, despite Petrarch's admiration for Plato, whom he did not know very well, for he irritably and repeatedly disclaims any virtue in learning in itself. 'It is safer to strive for a good and pious will than for a capable and clear intellect'.[12] Or to paraphrase the sentiment in the verse written (I find the author surprising) by Charles Kingsley: 'Be good, sweet maid, and let who can be clever'. But, despite some works of devotion, which Professor Whitfield finds stodgy and insincere, and which I have, I confess, never read carefully, there is no doubt that Petrarch relished his fame as a scholar, his laureation, his comfortable pluralism, the company of low women and the idealisation of Laura.[13] And above all he enjoyed the admiration of men of learning. Not the lawyers or the smart Averroists from Padua who had dismissed him as an old fuddy-duddy (if they *were* Averroists). In his most important Latin book, the great dialogue with Augustine which we call the *Secretum*, he brilliantly displays his Ciceronian roots and his preoccupation with the world. When Augustine loses patience with him, we can sympathise with the Saint: it is that sort of book. There is no Renaissance dialogue to match it.

Petrarch was well aware of the tensions between poetry and revealed truth, or at any rate of the potential dangers. And to meet the criticism he resorted to the medieval solution of the problem: allegory. This is how he interpreted Vergil; this is how he expected his contemporaries to understand the mysteries enshrined in the hexameters of his own poem, the *Africa*. And an exactly similar defence of poetry was made by Boccaccio. The difference between the medieval and those early

[11] Whitfield, *Petrarch and the Renascence*, p 63.
[12] Ed. L. M. Capelli (Paris 1906); trans. Hans Nachod in *The Renaissance Philosophy of Man*, ed. Cassirer, Kristeller, Randall (Chicago 1948) p 105.
[13] Whitfield, *Petrarch*, cap. iii.

Renaissance arguments for the study of ancient writers is not that they differ in substance, nor that they really change the arguments put forward by the Fathers themselves. The point is that they are spilling over into the lay arena. The medieval scholar who struggled to master Latin was a clerk. Many, and soon I suppose most, of those who read Boccaccio's *Genealogie deorum gentilium libri* were not in any true sense clergy.[14] His arguments in the last two books of the *Genealogy of the Pagan Gods* are the old ones, but the elaborateness of the treatment was novel. A century ago critics often found Boccaccio's apologia quite unconvincing. In the shadow of the great Romantic poets of the nineteenth century it seemed absurd to defend poetry as versification, as word play, as needing all the devices of interpretation so that beautiful fables became transformed into religious truths.[15] But this 'moralisation' of the ancient classics was too deeply embedded in medieval tradition to be ignored, too convenient a bulwark of orthodox Christians resisting the attacks of austere critics such as Cardinal Giovanni Dominici, the devout author of the *Lucula noctis* and the celebrated letter to a mother on how to educate a child according to Christian principles. His dates are 1356-1419.[16]

If Boccaccio, like his predecessors as far back as St Jerome, claimed that the scriptures were saturated with poetry, that they too had to be interpreted, so Dominici stressed the anti-intellectualism which is the overwhelming characteristic of the New Testament. Dominici's *Lucula noctis* disputed the points advanced in a letter written by an admirer of Coluccio Salutati and did so in true scholastic fashion. He first set out the arguments *for* reading the ancient classics before refuting them. It is by far the most elaborate destruction, despite momentary confusion, of the relevance of the classics to a Christian which was composed before it ceased to be a real issue, with the spread of humanist education all over Europe. This diatribe by the learned Dominican did provoke a reply from Salutati, although it was unfinished owing to the great humanist's death and not published until about a century ago. Much of the controversy cannot fail to seem like logic-chopping and perhaps a simpler and more convincing picture of

---

[14] A convenient summary of the patristic arguments in the first chapter of E. Harris Harbison, *The Christian scholar in the Age of the Reformation* (New York 1956); and see n. 1 above. For Boccaccio see the ed. by Vincenzio Romano in 'Scrittori d'Italia', 2 vols. (Bari 1951), ii pp 679–785.

[15] See, for example, Edward Hutton, *Giovanni Boccaccio* (London 1910) pp 246–7.

[16] The *Lucula noctis*, ed. E. Hunt (Notre Dame 1940); convenient extracts from the *Regola del governo* in Claudio Varese, ed. *Prosatori volgari del quattrocento* (Milan 1955), pp 24–40.

the position of Dominici is to look at his *Regola del governo di cura familiare*. The texts he there prescribes are: the psalter and holy doctrine (presumably he means the basic material of the New Testament): Cato, Aesop, Boethius, extracts from St Augustine, Prudentius, Hugh of St Victor and the versification of the Bible by Theodulus. Ovid is dismissed as poisonous and Jupiter and Venus must never even seem to compete with Father, Son and Holy Ghost. He who spares the rod spoils the child.

This last point of Dominici's, that discipline must be inflicted on children ('debbono essere battuti, e battuti spesso') was perhaps associated dimly with discipline of a specified sort, though Dominici's reasons are that children are naturally wicked. But it was a pedagogic technique which, like so much I have touched on, spans the middle ages, the Renaissance and comes down to our own day, although in recent decades I do not think a sculpture of a professor of *humanity* would carry his birch; he could assume that Latin had been beaten into boys at school. But the need to beat Latin into young people became much more urgent with the onward march of neo-classical Latin. Latin becomes harder to learn; you won't find *Lucula* in Lewis and Short; it is not to be found in the Vulgate even, let alone in the works of Valla.[17]

In turning now to Lorenzo Valla I am, however, going to draw your attention not to his *Elegantiae* but rather to his *De libero arbitrio* and *De voluptate*, which are in a way the application of his skills as a latinist to the demolition (at any rate in part) of the moral value and philosophical integrity and importance of ancient literature and especially philosophy. These treatises in dialogue form are, of course, very difficult to handle and Valla has over the centuries been classified as a Stoic, an Epicurean, and, needless to say, a godless pagan. Recent scholarship has, in my view, shown that, whatever the varieties of arguments which Valla put in the mouths of his disputants he himself was unquestionably a Catholic though, in a curious fashion he reminds me more of the sort of position which, in Northern terms, suggests Ockham and nominalism, faith rather than reason. The belief in God,

---

[17] *Lucula noctis*=firefly. The classical word for this is *lampyris;* see Francesco Novati, ed., *Epistolario di Coluccio Salutati* in 'Fonti per la storia d'Italia', vol. iv (Rome 1905) p 209n; for a further discussion of Salutati's notes on the Dominici text see B. L. Ullman's paper in *Medievalia et humanistica* (1943) reprinted in *Studies in the Italian Rennaissance* (Rome 1973) pp 255–275. Cf. Hunt's ed. p. vxi n. The allusion is to John i.5: 'And the light shineth in darkness and the darkness comprehended it not'.

of course, is not to be regarded as incompatible with scepticism.[18]
Here, for example, is a remark by Valla in line with earlier quotations
in my short survey.

> But why have the poets, the greatest men, attributed such things
> to the gods? You must concede one or the other, either the poets
> have said the truth about the gods, or they themselves have been
> what they wished the gods to be. There is no middle course . . .

Professor Trinkaus describes his position in the classics *versus* Christianity debate as 'empiricism'; more helpfully, I believe, he described
his deliberate policy as placing 'his rhetoric in the service of theology'.[19]
And it is in this sense, as I am treating the question this evening, I
regard him as a turning point, for at the crudest level those clergy—
there were only a handful of them before the end of the sixteenth
century—who did get formal instruction in the few available seminaries did so because they had rhetoric hammered into them, and had at
their disposal a kind of Latin to carry exposition and exegesis which
positively demanded a close attention to the classics at which they
personally looked askance. There is, admittedly, something illogical
about this. After all Petrarch read Cicero for moral inspiration, while
Valla is critical of 'the dogmatic and rigid character of classical moral
systems'.[20] One is tempted to go on quoting from this remarkably
original man; I shall content myself with one more. This comes from a
rather later work, *De professione religiosorum* of about 1440 (more
celebrated works belong to an earlier decade). In this Valla debates
with a friar, and stands on its head the remark attributed to St Francis
with which I began. When the friar advances the virtue of his poverty,
this is how Lorenzo deals with him. 'I've said I used money to buy books.
If you behave differently and give to the poor you are a fool (stultus)
not loving yourself as you love your neighbour'. We may think
this an odd application of the Sermon on the Mount, but some
mendicant libraries were, of course, in the top flight, and not only the
Dominicans'.[21]

But Valla is a turning point in two other ways, I judge. First his
religious position, which attracted such sympathy among reformers
like Luther and Calvin; and of this I shall not speak more. Second

---

[18] On the varying reactions to Lorenzo Valla see most recently Charles Trinkaus, *In our
Image and Likeness*, 2 vols (London 1970).
[19] Trinkaus, I p 128.
[20] *Ibid.*
[21] Conveniently in E. Garin, ed., *Prosatori latini del quattrocento* (Milan 1952) pp 578–9

because by his *Adnotationes in Novum Testamentum* (1448), which Erasmus was to publish in 1505 and which led him on to the new versions[22] in Greek and Latin of the New Testament, which might have been Erasmus's greatest work had not the Reformation crushed any attempts, by Protestants or Catholics, to emend the Vulgate text. It must, of course, be remembered that revision of the Latin bible was almost continuous in the Middle Ages.[23] It is curious to read Erasmus's introduction in the dedication to Christopher Fisher; it consists, one must feel perversely, in defending emendation of great authors in antiquity by other great authors of antiquity—Aristotle's criticism of others, for instance, Jerome's criticism of Augustine, and so on. This may be excused as more a justification of Valla than of attempting to improve the text of the Scriptures and Erasmus turns in conclusion to placing grammar in the service of theology, and of removing from the Bible the 'sin of corruption' (*magis nefas est depravare*).[24]

In his *Erasmus* (1923) Preserved Smith describes 'the Dutchman' as 'the Italian's truest disciple'.

> For Valla was an incarnation of the intellectual Renaissance, a critic and iconoclast of the calibre almost of Voltaire, unparallelled as yet in modern learning for the daring, acumen, irreverence and brilliancy of his attack on religion.[25]

It is, we must admit, true that Erasmus shared in Valla's contempt for scholasticism and respect for the Fathers, but (lucky man) the latter cannot be accused of laying eggs for Luther to hatch.

Before Luther began hatching reformation eggs Erasmus delivered what was to be his fiercest attack on the old ideas regarding literary values. It is with a brief discussion of this that I wish to end my talk. The *Antibarbari* had been written about 1487-8, although it was not published until 1520 and then in a mutilated form as the first book only survived in the author's possession.

The *Antibarbari*, which has recently appeared in the Collected Works of the Toronto series translated by Margaret Mann Phillips,[26] is a

[22] P. S. Allen, ed., *Opus Epistolarum* (Oxford 1906) ep. 1; 'Complete Works of Erasmus Translated into English', vol. 2, ed. and trans. R. A. B. Mynors, D. F. S. Thomson and W. K. Ferguson (Toronto 1975), p 89.
[23] See Beryl Smalley, *The Study of the Bible in the Middle Ages* (Notre Dame 1964); Raphael Loewe, 'The medieval history of the Latin Vulgate', in G. W. H. Lampe, ed., *Cambridge History of the Bible 2* (Cambridge 1969).
[24] Toronto version, vol 23. ed, and trans. Margaret Mann Phillips (Toronto 1978) p 95.
[25] Preserved Smith, p 15.
[26] See above, n. 24.

positive anthology of all the criticisms of ancient learning and literature
that I have touched on earlier. The defence of reading the literature of
antiquity is put into the mouth of Erasmus's friend Batt (Jacob Batt,
town clerk of Bergen) who developed the point that education has got
into the wrong hands (the clergy) and is aiming to stifle true learning
rather than encourage it. We must remember in all this that Erasmus
was, or had been, a monk and that he had been exposed to the old
training of the old centre of theology, the University of Paris. It is so
easy now to read Erasmus's dialogue in Mrs Phillips' translation that I
need only point to a few passages. It is, in a special sense, another
approach to *docta ignorantia*, only this time it is ignorance which
impedes *doctrina* rather than transcending it. The devout are 'jealous,
sluggish creatures'.[27] He puts into the Augean stable the followers of
Francis, Dominic and Elijah (by the last he means the Carmelites). He
lists the Fathers who were steeped in the classics; he derides the holy
who are ignorant of letters. To St Paul's 'knowledge puffs up' he
retorts 'ignorance puffs up too', and urges that Pauline charity em-
braces scholarship; he can even take Christ's entry into Jerusalem on a
donkey as an excuse for his curious interpretation: 'Jerome and
Augustine were donkeys for Christ', and so on. Above all, he returns
to the old trick of confuting authorities with authorities and, like many
before him, advances the texts assembled and commented on in
Gratian's Pars Ia *Distinctio* xxxvii.[28] (May I here interpolate the observation that Gratian's collection of texts, in the *Distinctiones* as elsewhere in
the *Decretum* were among the best known texts not only in the Middle
Ages but also in the Renaissance—so well had the church inculcated its
senior clergy with canon law that they became expert—or should I say
non expers?—in the platitudes of patristic thought). Gratian's distinction
was entitled 'Episcopi et ecclesiastici literas seculares sciant ad necessi-
tatem'. The authorities are overwhelming that they should, that they
must, indeed, if they are to understand adequately the scripture, which
is the subject of *Distinctio* xxxviii.

Erasmus's dialogue, read rapidly, has a disappointingly cheap
flavour. He makes points, one might say, like a bright school boy and
not like a serious thinker. Was he the first, I wonder, who claimed that
sainted martyrs were two a penny and did nothing for the Church
while sainted doctors were rare (were there more than twenty?) and

---

[27] *Ibid.* pp 46–48, 61.
[28] It is customary to refer to the ed. by E. Friedberg, i (Leipzig 1879), but of course the
citations are in all the numerous editions.

would influence their own and countless generations? I am rather cruelly paraphrasing. But not too cruelly.

> The martyrs died and so diminished the number of Christians; the scholars persuaded others and so increased it. In short, the martyrs would have shed their blood in vain for the teaching of Christ unless the others (that is the scholars) had defended it against the heretics by their writings.[29]

This, of course, is not Erasmus's last word on literature and devotion. He took, as I have said elsewhere, a different line in the *Ciceronianus* (1528). But in broad terms it represents the accepted doctrine of the new grammarians, who felt that their labours were in tune with the infinite—whether they taught in a Lutheran, a Presbyterian or a Jesuit school.

As this was to last until well into the nineteenth century, the age of what, in our provincial way, we call the public schools dare I tease you with another quotation which may (or may not) make my point? It is from a book by a curious genius called Thomas Love Peacock and comes from what I personally regard as his most entertaining work, *Crotchet Castle* (1831). I refer especially to the ordering by Mr Crotchet, senior, of 'Venuses of all sizes and kinds' which he displayed all over his public rooms.[30] The reverend Dr Folliott, broadminded as he was, in all conscience, as well as positively drenched in the classics, was shocked, and here is a portion of the ensuing dialogue:

> Mr Crotchet, on reading this order in the evening paper [that no plaster of Paris Venuses should appear in the streets without petticoats], which, by the postman's early arrival, was always laid on his breakfast-table, determined to fill his house with Venuses of all sizes and kinds. In pursuance of this resolution, came packages by water-carriage, containing an infinite variety of Venuses. There were the Medicean Venus, and the Bathing Venus; the Uranian Venus, and the Pandemian Venus; the Crouching Venus, and the Sleeping Venus; the Venus rising from the sea, the Venus with the apple of Paris, and the Venus with the armour of Mars.
>
> The Reverend Doctor Folliott had been very much astonished at this unexpected display. Disposed, as he was, to hold, that what-

[29] Ed. Margaret Mann Phillips, p 83.
[30] Ed. R. W. Chapman, *The Misfortunes of Elphin and Crotchet Castle* (Oxford 1924) pp 192–201.

ever had been in Greece, was right; he was more than doubtful
of the propriety of throwing open the classical *adytum* to the
illiterate profane.

Dr FOLLIOTT

Now, sir, that little figure in the centre of the mantlepiece—as a
grave *paterfamilias*, Mr Crotchet, with a fair nubile daughter,
whose eyes are like the fish-pools of Heshbon—I would ask you
if you hold that figure to be altogether delicate?

Mr CROTCHET

The Sleeping Venus, sir? Nothing can be more delicate than the
entire contour of the figure, the flow of the hair on the shoulders
and neck, the form of the feet and fingers. It is altogether a most
delicate morsel.

Dr FOLLIOTT

Why, in that sense, perhaps, it is as delicate as whitebait in July.
But the attitude, sir, the attitude.

Mr CROTCHET

Nothing can be more natural, sir.

Dr FOLLIOTT

That is the very thing, sir. It is too natural. . . . But to return to
the point. Now these two large figures, one with drapery on the
lower half of the body, and the other with no drapery at all; upon
my word, sir, it matters not what godfathers and godmothers
may have promised and vowed for the children of this world,
touching the devil and other things to be renounced, if such
figures as those are to be put before their eyes.

Mr CROTCHET

Sir, the naked figure is the Pandemian Venus, and the half-
draped figure is the Uranian Venus; and I say, sir, that figure
realises the finest imaginings of Plato, and is the personification of
the most refined and exalted feeling of which the human mind is
susceptible; the love of pure, intellectual beauty.

Dr FOLLIOTT

I am aware, sir, that Plato, in his Symposium, discourseth very eloquently touching the Uranian and Pandemian Venus: but you must remember that, in our Universities, Plato is held to be little better than a misleader of youth; and they have shown their contempt for him, not only by never reading him (a mode of contempt in which they deal very largely), but even by never printing a complete edition of him; although they have printed many ancient books, which nobody suspects to have been ever read on the spot, except by a person attached to the press, who is therefore emphatically called 'the reader".

Mr CROTCHET

Well, sir?

Dr FOLLIOTT

Why, sir, to 'the reader' aforesaid (supposing either of our Universities to have printed an edition of Plato), or to any one else who can be supposed to have read Plato, or indeed to be ever likely to do so, I would very willingly show these figures; because to such they would, I grant you, be the outward and visible signs of poetical and philosophical ideas: but, to the multitude, the gross carnal multitude, they are but two beautiful women, one half undressed, and the other quite so.

Mr CROTCHET

Then, sir, let the multitude look upon them and learn modesty.

Dr FOLLIOTT

I must say that, if I wished my footman to learn modesty, I should not dream of sending him to school to a naked Venus.

Mr CROTCHET

Well, sir, the Greeks; why do we call the Elgin marbles inestimable? Simply because they are true to nature. And why are they so superior in that point to all modern works, with all our greater knowledge of anatomy? Why, sir, but because the Greeks, having no cant, had better opportunities of studying models.

Dr FOLLIOTT

Sir, I deny our greater knowledge of anatomy. But I shall take the liberty to employ, on this occasion, the *argumentum ad hominem*. Would you have allowed Miss Crotchet to sit for a model to Canova?

Mr CROTCHET

Yes, sir.

'God bless my soul, sir!' exclaimed the Reverend Doctor Folliott, throwing himself back into a chair, and flinging up his heels, with the premeditated design of giving emphasis to his exclamation: but by miscalculating his *impetus*, he overbalanced his chair, and laid himself on the carpet in a right angle, of which his back was the base.

I fear I have been frivolous. It cannot be otherwise in this company to upset a reverend doctor. But my point is that the antithesis between the ancient classics and the scriptures was a continuing story. Nor was it really wiped off the blackboard by centuries of education which assumed an essential compatability; nor by centuries in which the laity, like Mr Crotchet, were prepared to press the dilemma to its angular conclusion. And on that angular conclusion I too will end.

2

THE HISTORIOGRAPHER ROYAL
IN ENGLAND AND SCOTLAND

THE following pages are intended to suggest how the office of Historiographer Royal may be used as evidence for past attitudes to historical writing and thinking. Before dealing with this, a short explanation of the origin of the appointment is given, together with an analysis of the nebulous rights and duties of the Historiographer. A list of the Historiographers and a brief Bibliography are provided in the appended notes.

PREHISTORY

At all times rulers have been concerned with contemporary annalists. The ruler, of course, sets the pace, while the historian only narrates what is over and done with. Chronicles must come after Kings (as they do in an inspired quarter), but kings are never tired of trying to mould the myth. Hot news, we may say, is malleable. Ancient history would furnish many examples of the process, but it will be more to the present purpose to recall the close connection between the great monastery of St. Denis and the Capetians and the similar link between the English crown and St. Albans. Over and above a patronage of scholars and literary men, the kings of France and England maintained a direct interest in the national chronicles, at once a quarry for precedents and an instrument of propaganda: Matthew Paris was a friend of Henry III, while Edward I bolstered his Scottish pretensions from the St. Albans' as well as other chronicles. Such a direct connection between action and the recording of action is a necessity of government; but in the middle ages it was erratic in its operation. Barbour at the Scottish Court and Froissart in England were by no means the servants of particular princes or policies. For the origins of such a rigid association we must turn to renaissance Italy.

The medieval Latin word ' historiographus ' meant at first a painter of historical paintings. Later it re-acquired its meaning of historian. Finally it came to apply to the paid historian, as a result of the tendency in Italian courts of the late fourteenth and the fifteenth centuries to employ official apologists. The tradition was not originally a product of tyranny. Republican Florence started the practice of employing humanists before the papacy and the other principalities of the peninsula. But the dynasties had more reason than the republics to justify themselves; and Milan, Mantua, Naples and other courts were soon equipped each with its official historiographer, writing narratives designed to display the genius of the ruling family. The aim was to sweep away any doubts as to the matter by the virtuosity of the manner in which the story was composed. When Platina turned from writing the history of the Gonzaga family to his *Vitae Christi ac omnium pontificum*, the greatest court in Europe had its historiographer and it was to be expected that trans-Alpine rulers would hanker after this novel type of diplomacy. The orator, the Latin Secretary, the historiographer became indispensable instruments of a civilized government. By the end of the fifteenth century Italian humanist historians could rely on employment among the Barbarians. This process of exporting Italian historical scholarship could be illustrated from half a dozen countries where Italians were directly employed, or where Italian influence guided native historians. In this brief paper we will consider only the evidence of England and Scotland, but in view of later developments it will be as well to start by indicating what happened in this connection in France.

Humanism developed slowly in France, and it was not until the end of the fifteenth century that a native historian appeared who could make a plausible claim to reflect the new culture in his work. This was Gaguin, Minister-General of the Trinitarians, whose *Gesta regum francorum* was published in 1495. Patron of the humanists in Paris (and of Erasmus in particular), member of the court circle and envoy to England in 1489, Gaguin had ambitions to supersede those earlier official historians, the monks of St. Denis, whose historical work had been moribund for half a century. Yet Gaguin did not come up to the standards which humanism demanded of a historian. He was not disinterested, but a violent partisan ; he was not sceptical, but reproduced the legends of Francus and Pharamond; and his Latin scarcely passed muster. One can therefore understand why the French court, in about 1500, turned to an Italian, Paulus Aemilius. Paul-Émile (Paolo Emilii as he was called in his native Verona)

had been the domestic scholar of Cardinal Charles of Bourbon
and in that capacity had written a history of the Gauls which is a
monument of oratorical narrative.   Here clearly was a fitter
candidate than Gaguin for the duty of showing the favourable
aspects of the houses of Capet and Valois.   For the first twenty
years of the sixteenth century Paul-Émile, now a canon of Notre
Dame de Paris, laboured at his *De rebus Gestis Francorum Libri X*.
His taste was finicky, his methods slow; and though the crown
put at his disposal such narrative sources as it controlled, the final
book was not in print when he died in 1529.   Appearing posthumously in 1539, however, its success was immediate and its
influence profound.   With continuations by du Tillet and Le
Ferron it was frequently reprinted in the sixteenth century—
perhaps as many as fourteen editions of the fat Latin folio
appearing up to 1601, besides a bewildering number of more or
less unacknowledged translations.   Possibly the success of Paul-
Émile may be regarded as one reason for the early recognition
of the need for an official historian in France; certainly from at
least as early as 1550 we find Historiographers Royal at the
French court.

   In England the story up to this stage is curiously similar.
The first humanist historian employed by the Tudors was
Bernard André, a Frenchman whose humanism was as inferior to
the genuine article as Gaguin's had been.   André seems to have
composed annals fairly regularly, but partly in his somewhat
vague office as poet laureate.   He could not compete with the
Urbino scholar Polydore Vergil who arrived in 1502, and who
was already the author of a historical work, *De rerum inventoribus*,
which was destined to become one of the sixteenth century's best-
sellers.   From about 1506 Vergil was at work on a history of
England; and if this was only published in 1534, we know that
a draft of it was completed twenty years earlier. Vergil cannot be
blamed (as Paul-Émile was) for lack of diligence.   The *Anglica
Historia* of Polydore Vergil was perhaps not as successful as
Paul-Émile's history of France—though it was reprinted a score
of times.   Unquestionably, however, it was more influential.
His account of the period 1399 to 1509 was virtually translated
by Hall in his *Chronicle*, and, transmitted ultimately by Shakespeare, created an important section of the national myth.   Moreover Vergil did not merely describe a heroic Henry V and a
malignant Richard III; his influence extended beyond the
invention of a picture gallery of monarchs to the establishment of

a historical method which was too seldom emulated by his English plagiarists. The fifteenth century theorists of historiography had exalted aims: lack of bias, scrupulous adherence to truth, and rigorous criticism of the legendary, the magical, and the miraculous. Vergil, writing in Latin of a country for which he had no innate affection, succeeded far better than native historians in viewing the English past with freshness and detachment. Brutus and Arthur, idols of Tudor society and Tudor princes, were politely relegated to the limbo of the non-proven. This, as Sidney was quick to point out, made for pedantry; but poetry was in the end to be discredited as a vehicle for historical truth.

When we turn to Scotland a very different picture meets us. The historians were not Italians, and some of them were scarcely humanists. Was it poverty at court, or distance from Italy, or pure indifference to the need that led Scottish kings (and especially James IV) to ignore Italians and to rely on native talent? We know that Vergil's offer to incorporate Scottish material in his history was rejected: perhaps the mere existence of an Italian at the English court was good enough ground for avoiding such a situation in Scotland. At all events the works produced by John Major and Hector Boece compare badly with the histories of Paul-Émile and Vergil. John Major was an inadequate Latinist; Boece swallowed whole the most implausible tales of Scottish antiquity, in some cases adding romantic episodes out of his own head. Was it not Hector Boece who invented the *jus primae noctis?*

The merits of the French, English and Scottish histories I have touched on vary enormously both as humanist exercises and as historical essays. They are relevant here because they were all produced under the aegis of kings and they were all addressed to foreign—Latin reading—audiences. This second point may perhaps be insisted on. Major's book was published at Paris in 1521; Boece's at the same place in 1526; Vergil's history was printed at Basle. Works disseminated in this way at important publishing centres were aimed at the world of international learning, and, if their authors were not Historiographers Royal, they undoubtedly had an official and quasi-diplomatic function.

Then the world of learning was torn into two by the Reformation. Princes symbolized the religions of their peoples and, as the expropriated papal sovereignty resolved itself into a dozen national absolutisms, the kings of Europe developed a vested interest in controlling not merely the external propaganda (or foreign policy) of their countries, but also the internal propaganda. The consumption of print by comparatively unlearned sections of the community was in any case increasing in the fifteenth and sixteenth centuries. In some countries, notably in England and Scotland, the Reformation went hand in hand with educational advances which increased the need for kings to determine as far as possible the political literature offered to their subjects. We are mostly familiar with the negative means to this end, the apparatus of the royal privilege, the censorship of books and (in England) registration with the Stationers' Company. The positive means—support of official apologists, subvention of sympathetic bodies, in a word the distribution of retainers to counsel—this is not so well known; the patronage of literature by Tudor sovereigns, for example, might repay investigation.[1] Defence of the religious settlement and of the dynasty were tasks readily undertaken in England by native historians and especially by Londoners. From Hall to Holinshed the English vernacular chroniclers regarded this as their principal aim. Scotland too was well served. The defects of Major and Boece were more than compensated for by the erudition and skill of George Buchanan's *Rerum Scoticarum Historia*, published (in Edinburgh, be it noted) in 1582. And did not Knox himself compose a history of the Reformation?[2] Compared with such *ipsissima verba* the patronage of scholarship by Archbishop Parker, and the tentative idea of an ' academe roiall ' in Elizabeth's last years are insignificant. But is that not to say that in Scotland the Reformation was more bitter than in England? In France also the Reformation involved civil war: and possibly that helps to account for the early appearance of the court apologist there. England had her dynastic troubles before 1485 (which Vergil dealt with so devastatingly and so permanently), and she had her religious troubles in the mid-sixteenth century: the two did not coincide, as they tended to do in France. It is, therefore, to the violence of French political life in the third quarter of the century that I feel inclined to attribute the permanence of the office of Historiographer Royal in France.

[1] Since the above was first written an admirable essay along these lines has been published by W. Gordon Zeeveld, *The Foundations of Tudor Policy*, Harvard University Press, 1948.

[2] Buchanan's book, it might be noted, was reprinted again as soon as 1583. Note also the more or less official historical works of David Calderwood and Archbishop Spottiswoode in relation to the struggle over episcopacy.

Admittedly the French court in the seventeenth century was a hive of titular dignities; and if the office had not existed it would perhaps have been invented by Louis XIV. It is none the less remarkable that French Historiographers Royal run in an unbroken line up to the Revolution of 1789;[3] at least seventy-three can be identified, some being historians of repute, which, as we shall see in a moment, is a matter for surprise. Boileau and Racine adorned the office, and so did André Duchesne and the brothers Sainte-Marthe (who started *Gallia Christiana*); the eminent scholars included Mézeray, Daniel and Voltaire. Yet from our point of view it is of less importance that many French historiographers were intrinsically brilliant; the cardinal point is that such an official was a part of the court of ' le roi soleil '.

It is true that in the circumstances of the revolution of the 1640's a situation existed in both England and Scotland where, as in Medicean France, control over opinion aimed at the establishment of a government-dictated version of events. In 1649, for example, the Scots parliament proposed to appoint ' some able and sufficient man for drawing up, compiling, and writing the history, records and chronicles of the time ', because in times of troubles ' history hath been many times unfaithfully transmitted to after ages and the posterity abused '. But apparently the proposal did not materialize. In England we have cause to be grateful that an ordinance of 1643 created a commission (which included Selden and Simonds d'Ewes) ' for the preservation for the public use of such books, evidences, records and writing ' as had been sequestered; nor were they to be sold, since that might have been ' much more disadvantageous and prejudicial to the public (both for the present and for posterity) than the benefit of their sale can in any way recompense '. The commonwealth was cautious and conserved. The office of Historiographer Royal was a careless Stuart importation from France.

THE OFFICE IN ENGLAND AND SCOTLAND

The first Historiographer Royal in England was appointed in 1661.[4] This was James Howell and the letter in which he urged

---

[3] Occasionally more than one person held the title, and drew the pension, at the same time.

[4] I do not include the name of G. Dempster (?1579-1625) among the English Historiographers, although he seems for a brief space to have had some official recognition from James VI and I (see *Dict. Nat. Biog.*, s.v.).

the need for the office and advanced his own claim to it is quoted below. It is not certain when the first Scottish Historiographer was appointed, but it was probably after 1661, and perhaps after 1663, for in the latter year the first holder, William Turner, unsuccessfully applied for the Chair of Humanity in Edinburgh University. From the appointment of Howell the office in England was continuously filled until it lapsed at the accession of Victoria; even then the holder, G. P. R. James, was not formally deprived. In Scotland the office continues to the present day, though there appears to have been a gap from 1736 to 1763.

The terms of appointment may best be studied in the full records available in the Scottish Register House. The Scottish Historiographer was appointed by an instrument under the Great Seal. The patent conferred the *munus et officium* on the holder (on account of his merits and outstanding virtues) during the pleasure of the Sovereign, together with all fees, casual revenues, privileges and immunities pertaining to his office or which should in future be deemed to pertain thereto; together with the right to fulfil and exercise his office as freely as any predecessor therein and, with this in view, to have right of access to the archives and histories, whether printed or in MS., from the king's public offices for his information in compiling the history of the kingdom; and in general to enjoy all things what-soever pertaining to the fulfilment of the said duty and office. The early patents end by stipulating the remuneration.

This document varied slightly from time to time, but later alterations were significant only in four respects:

(*a*) With the appointment of D. Crawford in 1704 the office was for the holder's life, and was no longer terminable at the will or by the death of the sovereign.

(*b*) With the appointment of Robertson in 1763 the reference to the compilation of a history of Scotland was omitted. Robertson had in fact secured the office because he had already written a history of Scotland.

(*c*) Remuneration was at first £40. Robertson received £200. John Hill Burton was given £184, and at that figure the stipend has remained.

(*d*) All patents were in Latin until the appointment of the first professor (D. Masson) in 1893; from that time the instrument was drawn in English. The operative section of the patent appointing Professor Masson runs

' to have, hold, exercise and enjoy the said office during
the natural life of the said David Masson, together with
all rights, liberties, privileges, benefits and advantages
whatsoever pertaining and competent to the said office,
used or wont or which did at any time bygone pertain
to the same.'

But what were the rights and duties of the office? They were
in fact indeterminate. Unquestionably the Historiographer was
expected to give general support to the government which had
put him into office; but naturally this was not stated in the patent.
It has been argued that Dryden attempted to give that support;
it is certain that G. P. R. James composed a pamphlet or two as a
defence of government policy. In Scotland, where the office
survives, the Historiographer Royal is occasionally consulted by
government departments on questions with a historical background. But, in general, the duties of the office were and
remained small and insignificant. In 1870, indeed, the Treasury
Commission (Camperdown Commission) declared that the
historiographer had no duties.

The rights of the Historiographer Royal were and are equally
vague. The most significant was, of course, the right of access
to archive material; but this has little importance today when
records are generally available to the public, though presumably
the Historiographer could, if he wished, claim to see papers not
yet accessible to unprivileged scholars. In 1689 Christopher
Irving pleaded his patent when prosecuted for non-payment of
taxes to the city of Edinburgh; but the courts dismissed his plea.

SIGNIFICANCE OF THE OFFICE

Here then is an office with virtually no rights or duties and
with only a small pension. If the reader will glance at the
appended list of holders of the two appointments he will notice
that, up to the date when the English office expires in 1837, only
Rymer, Madox and perhaps Clarke could by any stretch of the
imagination claim the title of historian, and, among the Scots,
only Robertson and perhaps Gillies. Only five historians out of
eighteen Historiographers Royal is a remarkably low proportion.
There seem to be two main explanations for this—the contemporary attitude to history and the machinery of patronage.

In the seventeenth and eighteenth centuries we have no lack of
definitions of what historians should regard as their province.

Here it may be best if we ignore the great pundits like Bolingbroke and Chesterfield and attend to the Historiographers
themselves. When Howell applied for the position in 1661 he
wrote:

> 'The prudentest and best policy'd states (i.e. France) have a
> Minister of State appointed and qualified with the title historiographer
> general . . . to digest in writing and to transmit to posterity the actions
> and counsels of that state as also to vindicate them.' Such an officer
> should disdain to make his history a mere diary; he should be prepared
> to make research into past causes of present problems; he should have
> right of access to state papers current as well as ancient; and he should
> be allowed 'a liberal allowance out of the public stock'.

In 1714 when Swift memorialized Queen Anne on the office
(which he had coveted from 1710 onwards) he wrote :

> 'The change of ministry about four years ago, the fall of the duke
> of Marlborough and the proceedings since in relation to the peace and
> treaties, are all capable of being very maliciously represented to
> posterity, if they should fall under the pen of some writer of the
> opposite party, as they probably may.
> 'Upon these reasons, it is necessary, for the honour of the Queen,
> and in justice to her servants, that some able hand should be immed-
> iately employed to write the history of her majesty's reign, that the
> truth of things may be transmitted to future ages, and bear down the
> falsehood of malicious pens.
> 'The Dean of St. Patrick's is ready . . . desiring her Majesty will
> please to appoint him her historiographer not from any view of the
> profit (which is so inconsiderable, that it will hardly serve to pay the
> expense of searching offices) but from an earnest desire to serve his
> queen and country ; for which that employment will qualify him by
> an opportunity of access to those places where papers and records are
> kept, which will be necessary to any who undertake such an history.'

The history which Howell and Swift were urging was partizan
but it was also contemporary or very recent history. There is
plenty of evidence that this was the normal attitude to the word
history at the time. Consider the titles of some of the periodicals:
The Historian (1712), *The Historical Register* (1716), *Historical
Lists of Horse Races* (1729), *Historical Journal* (1732), *Historical
and Political Mercury* (1759). These journals were all (except the
horse-racing paper) concerned with current politics. If a Briton
from the Augustan age could survey our modern literature he
would be astounded at the rubric in the *English Historical Review*
which excludes from review 'works dealing with current

politics '; on looking through the *Scottish Historical Review* he
would be surprised that its title was not the *True Scottish Historical
Review*. Broadly speaking, for the seventeenth and eighteenth
centuries history was not past politics but present politics.

The origin of this use of the word history to cover an interest
in current politics can be traced in all likelihood to a renaissance
distinction between *historia* and *annales*. This distinction deep-
ened during the two centuries after 1500 as works of great learning and little popular appeal were produced by historians who
were primarily annalists. The concept of the ' antiquary ' helped
the process further, and in the England of Queen Anne the
difference between historians and antiquaries was rather one of
function than, as it is today, one of quality and scale.[5] Madox,
for example, was proud to be an antiquary. One result of this
process was that history became polite and fashionable, preoccupied with markedly unscholarly problems. Along with
modern languages and travel, it went to the construction of the
eighteenth-century gentleman. This is the significance of the
establishment of the chairs of Modern History founded by
George I at Oxford and Cambridge in 1724. King and government intended the professors (who also supervised instruction in
modern languages) to provide a supply of tutors for the nobility
on their foreign tours—in the words of Sir Charles Firth, ' English
bear-leaders for English bears '. The aim was to avoid dependence on foreigners, especially in the training of young diplomats.
It is worth remarking that Rymer's *Foedera* originated in the
desire, not for medieval erudition, but for a currently useful
corpus of diplomatic instruments. This attitude to history altered
during the course of the eighteenth century and it is of interest
that of the three great names associated with the change two
were Scots and one a Historiographer Royal. It was effected by
Robertson, Gibbon and Scott in Britain, following a similar trend
in continental historiography, associated in its early stages with
Voltaire. Voltairean rationalism and the learned academies were
already influential by the early eighteenth century, and it is today
a matter for astonishment that the British government ignored the
request of Leibnitz, in 1714, to be given the post of Historiographer Royal.

Yet, when all is said and done, by explaining how for a time
history tended to be regarded primarily as contemporary history,

[5] Cf. also Paul Hazard, *La crise de la conscience Européenne, 1680-1715* (Paris,
1935), esp. 30-53, for a wider view of historiographical problems at this time.

we scarcely account for the absence among our historiographers
of more than a handful of true historians. From Thucydides to
Machiavelli most of the great historians were in fact contemporary historians, and it is hard to see why the English and Scottish
Historiographers Royal were so blighted in this respect. We
must turn to the other part of our argument.

Prior to the nineteenth century the post of Historiographer
Royal was regarded as a sinecure. Like any other sinecure, it
was given to the candidate whose patron had influence at the
critical moment. A brief résumé will indicate the monotonously
depressing effects of the system. In England Howell was given
the position to keep him quiet; Dryden because his stipend as
laureate was not enough; Shadwell because he acquired Dryden's
positions when the latter was disgraced; Rymer and Madox
because of the enlightened benevolence of Lord Somers; Philipps
because he was tutor to George II's children; Stonehewer because the Duke of Grafton wanted a place for his friend and
private secretary; Louis Dutens had equally aristocratic connections, while J. Stanier Clarke enjoyed the protection of the
Prince of Wales; G. P. R. James bombarded the royal family
with dedications and ministers with endless memoranda before
he wore down what can only be construed as indifference. The
Scottish story is no different, though the participants are smaller
fry: no Swift or Leibnitz ever coveted the Scottish post. I
cannot say why the first occupant was chosen. The second, J.
Fall, had been a tutor in the household of the Duke of Queens-
berry ; he rose with the Duke and, when the Duke fell in 1686,
Fall was deprived of his office. The post was then given to an
upstart schoolmaster and army doctor called Irving, whose un-
savoury reputation was outweighed by loyalty to James VII.
When Irving died in 1693 Carstares (Presbyterian chaplain to
William III and his adviser on Scottish affairs) secured the post
for his cousin William Dunlop, for whom he had earlier obtained
the principalship of Glasgow University *vice* Fall.[6] David
Crawford obtained the office not because he was a bad dramatist,
but because he was a good anti-Covenanter; David Sympson
obtained it because he was librarian at Holyrood. Then comes a
gap in the Scottish series of Historiographers Royal. I suggest

[6] This conjunction on two occasions of the Glasgow principalship with the post
of Historiographer Royal led one of Wodrow's correspondents into thinking that
the two positions were always linked—a measure of the failure of the Historiographer to attract attention.

that the office had died, in much the same way as it was later to
do in early nineteenth century England. Its resumption in 1763
is, I think, a matter of considerable importance.

Bute revived the position for Principal Robertson, whose novel
historical scholarship was impressing his contemporaries. Bute
was no doubt intent on helping Robertson; but he was equally
interested in the exercise of that drab patronage which produced
the calamitous effects I have just outlined. 'Most of our best
authors are wholly devoted to me,' wrote Bute, 'and I have laid
the foundation for gaining Robertson.' This link between party
and patron by no means died out in the eighteenth century. For
instance, Patrick Fraser Tytler was promised the post in Gillies's
lifetime, and he was undoubtedly the most accomplished Scottish
historian at the time. But Gillies died in 1836 and the post went
to Brodie, who was a reliable Whig. When Skene died in
January 1893 *The Scotsman* in a special article complimented
Gladstone on his choice of Skene although Skene had been a
Tory, and implored him to be equally disinterested in the appointment of his successor.

The Lord Chamberlain when questioned about Shadwell's
appointment as Historiographer Royal and Poet Laureate is
supposed to have remarked, 'I do not pretend to say how great
a poet Shadwell may be, but I am sure he is an honest man'. In
short, it was complete luck if a historian, let alone a scholar, got
the post. Hence the importance of Robertson's appointment.
Robertson was a fully fledged historian of the modern sort when
he was appointed; there can be no doubt of his determination to
be an active historiographer.[7] His long and productive reign
associated the office with what the nineteenth century came
unanimously to regard as history. Hence the office in Scotland
survived the 1830's when its equivalent in England was swept
away. It became, in fact, the first public and official recognition
of the new method of historical composition and learning. The
metamorphoses of the regius chairs at Oxford and Cambridge
come considerably later than this; in Scotland the academic
recognition of history dates only from about 1900. So we may
be grateful to Bute for his self-interest, to Robertson, and to the
historians who so ably followed his lead. The Historiographers
after Gillies were all both researchers and editors on the one hand,
and popularizers of history on the other, thus exemplifying the

----

[7] This is clear from an interesting letter he wrote to Bute, 9 April 1763, published
by N. S. Jucker, *The Jenkinson Papers 1760-1766* (London, 1949), pp. 136-9.

two functions which are regarded today as the complementary tasks of the historian.[8]

BIBLIOGRAPHY

Scottish Records: MS. Register of the Great Seal and MS. Establishment List 1707-1820, in the Register House, Edinburgh; Laing MSS., Edinburgh University Library. *Dictionary of National Biography*; E. K. Broadus, *The Laureateship* (Oxford, 1921), Appendix i, 219-222; R. G. Ham, ' Dryden as Historiographer Royal ', in *Review of English Studies*, xi (1935), 284-98 ; *The Scotsman*, 28 January 1893 and (article by W. Forbes Gray) 7 July 1930; *Early Letters of R. Wodrow* (ed. L. W. Sharp, Scot. Hist. Soc.), 63; James Howell, *Familiar Letters* (ed. J. Jacobs, 1892), 687-9; J. Swift, *Works* (ed. Temple Scott), v (1907), 477, and *Correspondence* (ed. F. Elrington Ball), i (1910), 190, ii (1911), 161, 184, 188, 196, 419; R. Klibanski, 'Leibnitz's Unknown Correspondence ', in *Medieval and Renaissance Studies*, i (1941-3), 142, 148-9.

Two useful studies of similar phenomena are: G. P. Gooch, ' Cambridge Chair of Modern History ', in *Studies in Modern History* (1931), 289-326; C. H. Firth, ' Modern History at Oxford, 1724-1841 ', in *English Historical Review*, xxxii (1917), 1-21.

THE HISTORIOGRAPHERS ROYAL IN ENGLAND AND SCOTLAND

England

Date of
appt.

George Dempster (supra, p. 20, *note* 4).

1661   **James Howell** (1594?-1666): Dodona's Grove, 1640; Instructions for Foreign Travel, 1642; Survey of the Signory of Venice, 1651; Epistolae Ho-Elianae, 1655; (ed.) Cotgrave's French-English Dictionary, 1650; (ed.) Sir R. Cotton's Posthuma, 1657; English-French-Italian-Spanish Dictionary, 1659-60; Poems, 1663.

1670   **J. Dryden** (1631-1700): (Main works up to deprivation of laureateship and office of H.R. in 1688) Heroic Stanzas, 1658; Astrea Redux, 1660; Panegyric, 1661; Wild Gallant, 1663; Annus Mirabilis, 1666; Essay on Dramatic Poesy, 1668; Amboyna, 1673, and many other plays including Aurungzebe, 1675, All for Love, 1678; Absalom and Achitophel, 1681; Medal, MacFlecknoe, 1682; Hind and the Panther, 1687.

1689   **T. Shadwell** (1642?-1692): Sullen Lovers, 1668; Enchanted

[8] I have to thank Dr. H. W. Meikle, the Historiographer Royal, who replied most courteously to my enquiries.

Island, 1673, and many other plays; Tenth Satire of Juvenal, 1687.

1692   T. Rymer (1641-1713): Short View of Tragedy, 1678; Edgar or the English Monarch (a play), 1678; Foedera, 1704-35; Of Antiquity, Power and Decay of Parliaments, 1714.

1714   T. Madox (1666-1727): Formulare Anglicanum, 1702; History and Antiquities of the Exchequer, 1711; Firma Burgi, 1722; Baronia Anglica, 1736.

1732   J. T. Philipps (d. 1755): Discours touchant l'origine et le progrès de la religion Chrétienne parmi la nation Britannique, 1716; Dissertationes Historicae Quatuor, 1735; (ed.) A Compendious Way of Teaching Ancient and Modern Languages, 1723; Religions, etc. of People of Malabar, 1717; Essay towards a Universal Grammar, 1726; Fundamental Laws and Constitutions of European Countries, 1752.

1755   R. Stonehewer (1728?-1809).

1810   L. Dutens (1730-1812): (ed.) Leibnitz's Opera Omnia, 1768; Mémoires d'un voyageur qui se repose, 1806.

1812   J. S. Clarke (1765?-1834): Progress of Maritime Discovery, 1803; Historical Memoirs of Shipwrecks, 1805; Life of Lord Nelson, 1809; Life of James II, 1816.

1837   G. P. R. James (1801-1860): Richelieu, 1829, and 56 other novels; Life of Edward the Black Prince, 1836; Life and Times of Louis XIV, 1838; Brief History of the U.S. Boundary Question, 1839.

Scotland

(For the better known historiographers, only the main books are noticed. The works of recent historiographers are not given.)

Date of
appt.

W. Turner (fl. 1663, d. 1682).

1682   J. Fall (1647-1711): (ed.) Archbishop Leighton's Works, 1693.

1686   C. Irving (c. 1625-1693): Bellum Grammaticale, 1658; (trans.) Anatomia Sambuci, 1655; Medicina Magnetica, 1656; (ed.) J. Wallaei Medica Omnia, 1660; Historiae Scotiae Nomenclatura, 1665, 1682.

1693   W. Dunlop—the elder (1649-1700): (MS. history of Renfrewshire, published by the Maitland Club).

1704   D. Crawford (1665-1706): Courtship à la Mode, 1700; Ovidius Britannicus, 1703; Love at First Sight, 1704; Memoirs of the Affairs of Scotland, 1706.

1708   D. Sympson (d.? 1736): A Genealogical & Historical Account of the Illustrious Name of Stuart, 1712; A True Account of the Life of J. Sharpe, 1723.

1763 **W. Robertson** (1721-1793): History of Scotland, 1759; History of Charles V, 1769; History of America, 1777.

1793 **J. Gillies** (1747-1836): History of Greece, 1786; Frederick II of Prussia, 1789; History of the World (to death of Augustus), 1807; (trans.) Lysias and Isocrates, 1778; Aristotle's Ethics and Politics, 1787, and Rhetoric, 1823.

1836 **G. Brodie** (1786?-1867): History of the British Empire from 1625 to 1660, 1822; (ed.) Stair's Institutes of the Laws of Scotland, 1826-31.

1867 **J. H. Burton** (1809-1881): (early and pseudonymous writings omitted) Manual of Law, 1839; Bentham's Works (ed.), 1843; Benthamiana, 1843; (ed.) Athole Papers, 1840, Darien Papers 1849; Life of Hume, 1846; Hume's Letters, 1849; Manual of Political and Social Economy, 1849; Narratives from Criminal Trials in Scotland, 1852; Law of Bankruptcy in Scotland, 1853; History of Scotland, vol. i, 1852 (completed 1870); (ed.) A. Carlyle's Autobiography, 1860; Bookhunter, 1860; Scot Abroad, 1864; Reign of Queen Anne, 1880.

1881 **W. F. Skene** (1809-1892): The Highlanders . . . Origin, History and Antiquities, 1837; Four Ancient Books of Wales, 1868; Coronation Stone of Scone, 1869; (ed.) Chronicles of Picts and Scots, 1867, Fordun, 1871, Liber Pluscardensis, 1876, Adamnan, 1874; Celtic Scotland, 1876-80; Gospel History for the Young, 1883-4.

1893 **D. Masson.**

1908 **P. Hume Brown.**

1919 **R. S. Rait.**

1930 **R. K. Hannay.**

1940 **H. W. Meikle.**

1958 **J. D. Mackie**

1979 **Gordon Donaldson***

---

*When I first began my enquiries into the Office of Historiographer Royal in Scotland Mr. Meikle told me that 'the remuneration had varied from 20 pounds scots a month to £180 per annum paid to R. K. Hannay. He himself was appointed without salary.' Professor Donaldson, who has been as helpful as his predecessor Meikle, tells me that in the letter inviting him to accept the appointment it was expressly stated that the office carried no emoluments. On the other hand, the Historiographer Royal is a member of the royal household in Scotland and expected to contribute to a wedding present to the Prince of Wales; he recalls that earlier Hannay had been asked for two guineas on the marriage of the late Duke of Kent. This is now limited to presents only for the heir apparent.

1   Engraved portrait of Flavio Biondo, from Paolo Giovio's *Elogia virorum literis illustrium* (Basel, 1578). In his life of Fra Angelico, Vasari says this was saved by Giovio from the destroyed chapel of the Sacrament.

3

FLAVIO BIONDO AND THE MIDDLE AGES

ONE of the paradoxes of historical writing is that even its
ablest practitioners are soon neglected. Indeed, where their
ability has been literary they suffer at the hands of posterity
even more than their fair share of oblivion, ending up (in our
own day) in the limbo of the prescribed books for public exami-
nations or the pit of postgraduate theses. Yet, even unread,
certain historians exert an influence over later ages which en-
sures them a kind of anonymous immortality. Their immediate
successors transmit an interpretation which, in the hands of later
exponents, is divorced from its first begetters. This is particularly
true of historiography prior to the second half of the nineteenth
century, prior to the monograph and the learned journal.
Nowadays we are all obsessed with our indebtedness to others
and ransack the scholarly literature of our immediate predecessors for parallels to observe and precedents to quote. And we are
as suspicious of literary graces as earlier critics were offended by
their absence: it can become almost insulting to say that a contemporary writes well. It is, in short, easier far to assure oneself
a niche in a bibliographical Pantheon by a gnarled and ungracious investigation into some small and intricate historical
problem than by a survey, however delightful, of a big subject.

These reflections are pertinent to a consideration of the writer
on whom I am privileged to lecture today. Flavio Biondo in a
sense stands at the threshold of a world where, for the first time,
history could be presented either as art or as science. His reputation in his own day was to some degree determined by his
response to this question; and more recently he has been singled
out for praise because he is supposed to have chosen erudition at
the expense of artistry. My purpose in what follows will be to
examine in some detail Biondo's most famous work, the *Decades*,
a history covering the period from the fall of Rome to the middle
of the fifteenth century. It can be stated confidently that it is
talked about more often than it is read, as is the case with the
works of all the main Renaissance historians.

Historical writing was extraordinarily luxuriant in medieval
Italy. It provides evidence of an interest in the past on the part
both of scholars and, with the emergence of vernacular narratives, of an ever widening lay public. It may well be that this
was one of the features of Italian cultural life most propitious
to the development of the new values of humanism. Certainly
humanism encouraged further extensions of historical activity in
Renaissance Italy, although in ways which have seemed to
many to be unfortunate. If one compares a fine example of the
vernacular chronicle with a fine piece of humanist history—
Villani with Bruni, for example—there does seem to be a frigi-
dity in the latter, an air of unreality and artifice, absent from
the earlier writer. But the gains offered by the new methods
were great. In an accomplished historian like Bruni or Poggio
we find first of all a commendable concentration on the form
and style of presentation foreign to the earlier Tuscan writers,
whose felicities are accidental. More important still, we sometimes find an anxiety to display motives which is not often seen
in the rambling narration, however picturesque and lively, of
less sophisticated writers: the humanist historian, in short, often
had an axe to grind; he was a publicist, and his work was
addressed to men of affairs. In any event the vernacular writers
continued to thrive, picturesque as ever; even if we neglect them
their contemporaries did not.[1] Both sources, the humanist Latin
and the vernacular, contributed to the formation of the historiography of Machiavelli and Guicciardini.

The analysis of Renaissance historical writing which is accepted
at large today owes much to a short chapter in Burckhardt's
book.[2] Starting from this Fueter elaborated a sharp distinction
between what he called the Rhetorical school, stemming from
Bruni, and the Scholarly school. The first was, he argued, by
far the more influential since it placed humanism at the service
of the city and the dynasty. At its best it was brilliantly apologetic, at its worst it was a feeble imitation of the Livy so admired
by all its practitioners. For the rhetoricians the first aims were
to persuade and to please, and stylistic brilliance and purity was
a necessary condition of success, for the histories of cities or
princes were not meant to convince within the area of the
writer's loyalty but at large in Italy. Bruni, Poggio, Accolti were
Florentine chancellors; Sabellico was a pensioner of the Vene-

[1] See V. Rossi, 'Storia litteraria d'Italia', *Il Quattrocento*, new ed., Milan,
1938, pp. 182–8 and refs.
[2] *Civilization of the Renaissance in Italy*, part III, ch. viii.

tian state; Pontano was a servant as well as the historian of King
Ferrante, as Crivelli and Simonetta were successively secretaries
as well as biographers of Francesco Sforza.[1] Opposed to the
rhetorical historians were the laborious disciples of erudition, of
history for its own sake, whose scientific interests transcended
loyalty to a state: of these the luminaries were Calchi at Milan,
Valla the critic of the Donation of Constantine, Pomponio Leto
the Roman antiquary; their master was Flavio Biondo.[2]

This Burckhardt–Fueter interpretation has been very widely
accepted, for few of us have had the occasion to read carefully
the old editions where most of this literature is still enshrined.
We take on trust the truth of what has entered the canon of
Renaissance interpretation, and see the game being played
according to the rules determined for us by Fueter. These rules
can be summarized in his own words: the imitation of classical
models (especially in respect of a rhetorical approach), and a
'secularization of history' which involved jettisoning a providential view of history and all that went with it, notably the outmoded universals of empire and papacy, and the miraculous.
These characteristics were approved of by Fueter, but he argued
that with the excessive regard to style went a neglect of chronology, a distortion of institutional realities, and a perverse glori-
fication of men and states.[3] Recent studies of Leonardo Bruni
have disputed some of these strictures:[4] the present paper may
show that an examination of the founder of the 'learned school'
leads to other modifications in hitherto received opinions.

Before we examine Flavio Biondo's place in the traditional
picture we must look for a moment at his life, which has some
light to throw on his writings. It is a life devoid of much excitement.[5] Born at Forlì in November or December 1392, educated

[1] E. Fueter, *Geschichte der neuern Historiographie*, 1911; later editions, so far
as the matters discussed here are concerned, seem to add nothing to the
second which appeared revised as a French translation by E. Jeanmaire
(Paris, 1914), which I accordingly use; the relevant pages are 10–60.

[2] Fueter, pp. 128–36.

[3] Ibid., pp. 10–18.

[4] E. Santini, intro. to *Leonardi Aretini historiarum Florentini populi libri xii*,
RR. II. SS., xix pt. 3, pp. i–vi; B. L. Ullman, in *Studies in the Italian Renaissance*, Rome, 1955, pp. 321–44.

[5] The introduction to B. Nogara's *Scritti inediti e rari di Biondo Flavio*, 'Studi
e testi', no. 48, Vatican 1927, supersedes all earlier biographical accounts of
which the most valuable was the short study of A. Masius, *Flavio Biondo, sein
Leben und seine Werke*, Leipzig, 1879. Unless otherwise noted the following
account is based on these authorities. There is an extended notice of Nogara's
book by A. Campana in *La Romagna* (Imola), xvi (1927), 487–97, and a

at Cremona, he and his family were buffeted by all the political
storms which raged in the Romagna. One of his earliest memories was being held in his father's arms to see the comet which,
as it soon emerged, betokened the fall of Gian Galeazzo Visconti.[1]
When he was thirty a revolution in Forlì led to his exile. By this
time he was already, it seems, occasionally employed by his city
and already on intimate terms with Guarino da Verona. The
next years are filled by a series of posts significant of the openings
increasingly available to the humanist-trained scholar: secretary
of the Venetian Francesco Barbaro at Vicenza and Bergamo, of
Pietro Loredano at Brescia, of Capranica (governor at Forlì)
and, in 1432, of Vitelleschi then governor of the March of
Ancona. From Vitelleschi's service Biondo passed, early in 1433,
to the service of the pope: in 1434 he was appointed to the papal
secretariat. So far his career gave promise of an active participation in public life, with high promotion as its natural end. And
for a time this must have seemed likely not only to Biondo but
to his fellow administrators. He was charged with important
negotiations on behalf of the pope in Romagna and at Venice
in 1434. He followed Eugenius IV to Florence, when the pope
escaped from Rome in that year, and he was then involved in
negotiations with Sforza.

His biographers, following a lead given by Paolo Giovio,[2]
make this year a turning point in Biondo's life: from now on he
is supposed to have abandoned interest in a political career,
realizing that his marriage, which had occurred in 1423, would
preclude the very highest ecclesiastical responsibilities and rewards. Yet there are some grounds for doubting this, or at any
rate for arguing that too little has been made of Biondo's public
importance after 1434. In the first place, in 1437, when Leonardo
Bruni despaired of securing a proper reward from Humphrey
Duke of Gloucester for his Latin version of Aristotle's *Politics* and
wished to give it to Eugenius IV, he chose Biondo as his agent—
presumably because the latter had the pope's ear.[3] Second, he
was fairly prominent in the negotiations with the Greeks at
Ferrara and Florence which culminated in the ill-fated union of

valuable review by R. Sabbadini in the *Giornale storico della letteratura italiana*,
xciii (1929), 182–6.
  [1] *Decades*, ed. Basle 1531 (the edition hereafter quoted for this work and
the other main books by Biondo), p. 392, a corrupt passage in printed texts;
see Nogara, p. xxiv and note.
  [2] Quoted Nogara, p. lxxiv, note.
  [3] Cf. R. Weiss, *Humanism in England during the XVth Century*, Oxford, 1941,
pp. 48–49.

July 1439. In fact he was one of those who attested the act of union[1] which he quotes verbatim in his history.[2] Third, when Thomas Bekynton, anxious to secure a bishopric, was distributing gifts to influential members of the Curia in 1441 he was advised to include Biondo among the recipients, which he did.[3] And fourth, in 1449, two years after the election of Nicholas V, Biondo was forced to leave the Curia, to which he did not return until early in 1453. What led to this fall from favour we do not know. Biondo referred to the machinations of an enemy unnamed.[4] Aeneas Sylvius explained it as the common fate of favourites of the old pope in the early years of his successor: this can be supported, though Pius II may not have known this, by the careful way Biondo removed from the master copy of his *Italia illustrata* flattering references to Nicholas V after the latter had died. Nogara, Biondo's most recent and most scholarly biographer, has the flattering explanation that in the flippant milieu of *abbreviatores* like Poggio, Biondo's purity led to his victimization. Whatever the truth in all this, it remains clear enough that Biondo, as late as 1449, was important enough to have important enemies. In my judgement we should date his withdrawal from active participation in papal politics from 1450 rather than from 1434. What is clear is that for the rest of his life he played only a very small part in public affairs. He was in the papal secretariat until his death in June 1463. 'He died a poor man, as was proper for a scholar', commented Pius II. He was buried in S. Maria in Aracoeli on the Capitol, heart of that Rome which formed the centre of so much of his writing.

To his writings we must now turn.[5] All are of interest, but I shall only pause here to indicate those of directly historical content. These are in fact more substantial than his treatises on philology, education, or crusades, which are paradoxically better understood than the major books, for they have been printed or reprinted with all the aids of modern scholarship and typography. The four big books—*Roma instaurata* (1444-6), *Italia illustrata* (1448–53), the *Decades*, and *Roma triumphans* (1456–60)

---

[1] Nogara, p. lxxxii. [2] *Decades*, pp. 550–1.
[3] *Correspondence of T. Bekynton*, ed. G. Williams, Rolls Series, i. 169–72, 241–2. This is not mentioned by Nogara.
[4] Quoted Nogara, p. cxiv.
[5] A brief chronology of composition and publication is attempted below in Appendix I (pp. 64-5), as this is not to be found in Nogara or elsewhere.

—have all to be studied in sixteenth-century folios, where the pages of dense type, the absence of paragraphs, the frequent errors of the printer, and the absence of adequate lists of contents and indexes are all formidable obstacles to ready comprehension, let alone pleasurable reading. (This is often the penalty of a certain amount of popularity in the late fifteenth and the sixteenth century: a manuscript by a relatively unimportant and uninfluential Renaissance writer has more chance of being published critically in our own day than the work of an author, however important, who achieved print in or near his own time.)

The *Italia illustrata* has naturally been given more attention than the others, for in it Biondo achieved a new and fruitful combination of geography and history, of antiquities and contemporary observation. This was undoubtedly the inspiration of the larger and better-written surveys of Aeneas Sylvius, and leads on to the scholarly geographers of the next century. It has been made the subject of a short essay;[1] this has been outmoded, however, by the publication of additional material.[2]

A proper understanding of the *Roma instaurata* and *Roma triumphans* must wait, as Professor Momigliano has pointed out, until we find someone willing to write a history of antiquarian thought in Italy.[3] In a sense they were the most rapidly superseded of all Biondo's books, for they stimulated a host of other topographers and antiquaries who were better equipped. As we shall see, they throw some light on the general aims of their author as historian.

The biggest and probably the most important of Biondo's works was the *Decades*. How may this be briefly described? It consists of forty-two books, running from the seizure of Rome by Alaric in A.D. 410 down to the peace of Cavriana in the autumn of 1441. Arranged in decades of books, the first ten extend to January 754; the second ten to the election of John XXIII in 1410; the third, beginning with a retrospect to the death of Gian Galeazzo in 1402, goes down to November 1439; the fourth contains two books, the first covering 1440 and the

[1] Johann Clemens Husslein, *Flavio Biondo als Geograph des Frühhumanismus*, Würzburg, 1901.

[2] Such as Nogara prints from two manuscripts, one at Florence (Riccardiano 1198) and one at the Vatican (Ottoboniano 2369), op. cit., pp. 219–39; and A. Campana discusses Cod. Classense 203 at Ravenna in 'Passi inediti dell' "Italia illustrata" di Biondo Flavio', *Rinascita* (Florence), i. (1938), 91–97.

[3] A. Momigliano, *Journal of the Warb. and Court. Institutes*, xiii (1950), 289 n.

second (which was not in the early printed editions)[1] covering 1441. It will be observed that far more space is devoted to the forty years of the fifteenth century than would seem to be justified by the broad aim of the author: furthermore one should note that the fourteenth century is practically concentrated into one book, II. x, of thirty-five pages.[2] But these dates and proportions tell us nothing. What is the book about? To answer that question we must consider how it was composed.

In the late 1430's Biondo, an established member of the papal Curia, an author recognized by the scholars of Florence and Venice, turned to writing history. From the first reference to this, in a letter of 1440 to Francesco Barbaro, we must infer that he was drawn to contemporary history, the scope of his work being described as being 'mainly the changes in the Italian scene', *maximis quae Italiam agitant rerum varietatibus*.[3] The four books here referred to began in 1417, circulated in manuscript among the author's friends and were subsequently added to until, revised, and now beginning at 1402, they had reached twelve books and the final terminus of the whole work by some point in 1442. Eleven of these were in fact circulating and had attracted favourable comment. In 1443 the Italian content of this portion of the work is expressly stated by Biondo in a letter to Alfonso of Aragon: *quae . . . ubique in Italia sunt gesta*.[4] But at this stage a bigger plan had emerged: the author sends Alfonso the first eight books of a new section, beginning with the fall of Rome, and explains that he deliberately wrote the contemporary portion first and only later turned back to the earlier centuries.

That in fact the author had had the whole work before him when he began writing in 1439 has reasonably been doubted. But besides the letter of 1443 to Alfonso there is another piece of evidence that by about 1442 he had extended the work back to

[1] A portion of IV. ii was printed by G. Williams in *Bekynton Correspondence*, ii. 327–38, from Corpus Christi College, Cambridge, MS. 205; Nogara, who printed the whole of IV. ii from two Vatican manuscripts, was not aware of this text, which contains, in an illuminated initial on f. 1, what appears to be a portrait of Biondo, much defaced. See further below, p. 42.

[2] See below, Appendix II, for a sketch of the periods covered by each book. In a letter to Francesco Sforza written at the end of his life Biondo summarized the chronology as follows: 'La mia prima deca, longa de anni CCCC, uene fino ad VIIJ^c ab incarnatione. La seconda ariua al MCCCC; la tertia, piena di geste de annj XLIJ, dal MCCCC uene fin a la pace . . . a Martinengo . . .', Nogara, pp. 211–12.

[3] Nogara, p. 103, and cf. intro. pp. lxxxiii–lxxxiv.

[4] Nogara, p. 148.

the fall of Rome. I have mentioned that Bekynton sought his friendship with a gift. This produced from Biondo a letter, dated from Florence on 18 June 1442, in which he writes that Bekynton's present has given him great pleasure and that he hopes to reciprocate very soon by sending something which, since his English correspondent lacks nothing in the material sense, shall be for his solace and enjoyment.[1] What Biondo in fact sent was a copy of the twelve completed books of his history, the volume now being in the library of Corpus Christi College, Cambridge.[2] Now there are several manuscripts which contain the third decade and one or both books of the fourth. But this copy can be assigned with confidence to the months immediately after June 1442 and it already contains in the opening words of decade III a reference to the earlier sections of the work. So precise in fact is the reference to the author's joy in having completed his task of resuscitating a thousand years in twenty books[3] that we can hardly question that some kind of draft of the earlier decades was indeed completed by about 1442, even if only eight books of the first decade were fit to be sent to Alfonso early in 1443. Biondo himself gives us a clue when in the first pages he indicates that his work covers a thousand and twenty years—*in praesens tempus* (which would be 1442).[4] Certainly it was later polished: he tells us this himself in a letter of 1444 which refers to the work being in the hands of copyists;[5] and events of November 1443 are mentioned in decade I, ix.[6] Early in 1444 we find him

[1] *Bekynton correspondence*, i. 241–2: '... quae jocunditatem offerat at aliquod ornamentum'.

[2] MS. 205; G. J. Vossius, *De historicis latinis libri iii*, Leyden, 1651, p. 585; *Bekynton Correspondence*, i, p. xxxii; M. R. James, *Descr. Cat. of the MSS. in ... Corpus Christi College*, i. 494–5. I have to thank Mr. R. Vaughan for arranging for me to consult this manuscript.

[3] Corpus Christi MS. 205, f. 1r: 'Laetanti iam mihi et exultanti non obscuram magis quam sepultam mille annorum historiam uiginti librorum uoluminibus in lucem, certumque ordinem reduxisse....' Cf. ed. Basle, 1531, p. 392, where the same words occur.

[4] See passage quoted below, p. 43, n. 4; as noted below, p. 52, Biondo put the fall of Rome in A.D. 412.

[5] 'Historiae meae, quibus limandis hactenus insudavi, in librariorum manibus sunt, quarum exemplum ut habeas curabo....' Nogara, p. 154.

[6] Nogara, p. ciii. It would be useful as a check to find other unequivocal indications in the first two decades of events in the 1430's and 1440's. But the only other such points that I have noted—a reference to Bruni's version of Procopius early in the first decade and another to Eugenius IV's escape from Rome in book iv of the second decade—are not helpful: the first could have been written at any point in or after 1441 and the second in or after 1434 (*Decades*, pp. 43, 236).

anxious to have an earlier draft returned so that only one version may circulate.[1] By October 1453 Biondo himself claims that his work is now dispersed through all Europe. We may fairly summarize all this by saying that by 1442 the whole work existed in draft and that the final version was circulating by 1452, if not considerably earlier.[2]

The account I have given of the composition of the *Decades*, which differs a little from those previously accepted,[3] was proffered as preliminary to an attempt to define the scope of what, in its contemporary aspect, Biondo had defined as 'Italian history' when discussing decade III. He hardly tells us in the work itself what precisely he intends to cover in the earlier portions. It is, he says at the start, to cover the deeds of the thousand and thirty years since the Goths captured the city.[4] It is from the fall of Rome that a new epoch must be dated: Livy's history was called 'ab urbe condita'; and his (we may infer) *ab inclinatione imperii*.[5] But the Roman empire was a bigger affair than Italy itself. And so the story is at first filled by 'those things which happened in the former provinces of the empire beyond the Alps and outside Italy',[6] where, he laments later on, the rule of Rome

[1] Nogara, p. 161. Nogara dates this letter 1446: but advances as his reason the congratulations with which it begins, which he says arise from E. Barbaro's promotion to the see of Verona (16 November, 1443, cf. Eubel, ii. 265, and not October, as in Nogara, p. civ, n. 127). In 1446 he may perhaps have felt so dissatisfied with the second decade as to refer to it as unwritten save for the first book; but this letter is undated in the original and parts of it are evidently corrupt: Nogara, p. 162.

[2] I do not think the undated letter asking Sforza for details of Visconti origins, *c.* 1450–1 (Nogara, p. cv), suggests that the work was still unwritten in its fourteenth-century parts—though the fourteenth-century portion is a hurried piece of writing (above, p. 41) ; any more than that may be inferred from the letter of December 1454 (Nogara, p. 168) asking for materials for Genoese history.

[3] Nogara's interpretation is neatly digested by V. Rossi in the revised version of his *Quattrocento*, as cited above, p. 36 n. I differ in considering that the *Decades* were to all intents finished by the mid-1440's.

[4] *Decades*, p. 3: 'Visum est itaque operaeprecium a me factum iri, si annorum mille et trigenta quot ab capta a Gothis urbe Roma in praesens tempus numerantur, ea inuolucra et omni posteritati admiranda facinora in lucem perduxero.'

[5] Ibid., p. 10: 'Annus . . . qui et salutis Christianae duodecimus et quadringentesimus fuit, nobis primus erit ab inclinatione imperii constitutus'; see the whole passage of which this is the end, and below, p. 52.

[6] Ibid., p. 55: 'Haec quidem in Romanis quondam prouinciis Transalpinis et extra Italiam tunc fiebant'; and cf. the letter to Barbaro of (?)1444: 'praeclara optabiliaque in Romano olim imperio, in Italia, in Venetis, in Liburnis inserta sunt gesta', Nogara, p. 161.

is a thing of the past.[1] The scope of the first eight books of the first decade (i.e. down to about A.D. 600) may fairly be described as an account of the former provinces of the empire, with the stress laid on events in Italy.[2] He summarizes this himself by saying he has described not only the decline of the empire, but also the devastation of Rome and Italy.[3]

Soon, however, we may detect a change in the author's aim. Already in book ix of the first decade he explains that much could be written of the former provinces—Gaul, Spain, England, and the rest. But they all continue in independence, and his prime task is the decline of Rome.[4] Yet Rome was now the heart of another kind of universal state: the *orbis christianus* is mentioned—very significantly he abandons the dating *ab inclinatione imperii* at this point—in 'the year of the incarnation of our Lord 700'. And the first decade ends with a frank disclaimer of any intention of a general account of the Franks.[5] Later on we are told that the deeds of Otto I outside Italy are beyond his scope.[6] Thereafter, though we have references to the provinces, the wider horizon might be described as Christian rather than imperial: it is as an extension of Christendom that Charlemagne's campaigns are presented;[7] it is for this reason that the relief of the Holy Land is described as the finest deed of any pope;[8] and this explains the very full account of the Crusades in the Middle East and elsewhere. From the fourth book of the second decade to the end of the eighth book, from the Council of Clermont to

[1] *Decades*, p. 100: '. . . quod neque in Galliis, neque in Hispaniis, aut Germania, siue in insula Britannia, et prouinciis quae Danubium adiacent, aliqualis ultra fuit Romano imperatori aut Romanae reipublicae iurisdictio'. And compare the passage p. 365 where, on Petrarch's authority, Cola di Rienzi's reinvocation of ancient Rome is described as causing favourable comment in the non-Italian provinces of the old Empire.

[2] Cf. ibid., pp. 111, 115–16; and the remarks on Africa and Spain in the last book of the first decade, pp. 136–7.

[3] Ibid., p. 150.

[4] Ibid., p. 133.

[5] Ibid., p. 148. On the dating see further, below, p. 52.

[6] Ibid., pp. 182–3: 'Multa interim maximaque, et quidem praeclarissima in regnis Franciae et Germaniae Otho gesserat, quae nostrae intentioni parum accommoda omittimus.'

[7] Ibid., p. 161: 'Erant autem tunc in Romani olim imperii Europae prouinciis res turbulentissimae. . . . Dumque tot in locis rem bene gererent Christiani. . . .' In so far as the older area is referred to at this stage it is only the European provinces which are involved, e.g. p. 176: '. . . cum multis Europae prouinciis, tum Italiae. . . .'

[8] Ibid., p. 207: '. . . facinus . . . maximum excellentissimumque omnium quae fuerint pontificis Romani cuiuspiam ductum.'

the fall of Acre in 1291, the non-Italian material is virtually restricted to accounts of the Crusades.[1]

Before Biondo reaches the third decade and the events of the fifteenth century he has, of course, begun narrowing his interest to that intensive concentration on Italy which, as we have seen, he himself recognized as his aim in the later books. How did he view Italy? What is the range of his interest in Italian affairs? There are some tantalizing glimpses of a general interpretation of Italian history. In an early passage of the *Decades* Biondo consoles himself for the shame of the fall of Rome by contemplating the rise of a new Italy: let us be encouraged by narrating the beginnings of the new cities, the glory of a splendid people, which were to restore to Italy her lost dignity: Venice, Siena, Florence, and the rest re-establish for Italy the glory of fallen Rome.[2] But this proves a dead end. Biondo does not deal adequately with any city save Venice, whose origins (not surprisingly in view of his intimacy with Venetians) are discussed at some length.[3] The rest are merely mentioned, if at all, in a perfunctory line or two. Another theme, rather more substantial this time, is the need for peace in Italy. He seems to have accepted that the barbarian invaders of Italy soon became Italians:[4] thereafter Italy is disturbed either by foreign attack —by aggressive Greeks under Justinian, later by Germans and French[5]—or by domestic warfare. This deep-rooted desire for *pax in Italia* accounts, of course, for the panegyric on Theodoric[6] which Machiavelli later helped to form into a significant strand in Italian historiography. Popes are praised for their efforts to secure peace in the peninsula: so Honorius III[7] and so, in his

---

[1] Ibid., pp. 215–332. Note here *passim* the use of 'nostri' for 'Christiani'. And note the references, pp. 267–8, to crusading in Spain, and pp. 318–19 to Louis IX in Tunis.

[2] Ibid., p. 30: '. . . sed dedit animos, et ut omni absterso pudore scriberemus, nos pulit spes proposita narrandae originis nouarum urbium, praestantissimorumque populorum decus, quorum et nouae sobolis excellentia, non parua ex parte Romanam restituit Italis dignitatem. Videmus nanque dei nostri rebus Italiae indulgentissimi benignitate, multum creuisse Venetam, Senensem, Ferrariensem . . . ciuitates . . . per quarum opes, uirorumque qui in illis coaluerunt uirtutem, et dignitas adest et gloria Italiae Romana reipublica destitutae.'

[3] Venetian origins are discussed on pp. 41–42.

[4] Ibid., p. 95: after 72 years the Goths are now *omnes in Italia geniti et nutriti*.

[5] Ibid., p. 389: Alberico da Barbiano praised for driving the *externam militiam* from Italy.

[6] Ibid., pp. 33 ff.

[7] Ibid., p. 276.

own day, Martin V, who attempted to pacify the papal states
when he failed to secure a more general settlement;[1] Benedict
XII on the other hand is rebuked for having legitimized the
tyrants of Lombardy—however wise it may have seemed at the
time.[2] The schism of 1378 is stated to be a disaster for Italy as
well as for the whole of Christendom.[3] The poisonous rivalries
of Guelf and Ghibelline call forth a stinging passage: *ea infausta
rebus Italiae nomina*. The scourge continues to our own day,
Biondo goes on, and Italians treat each other worse than they
had formerly been treated by the barbarians: town against
town, region against region, one section of the population
against another group—only Venice has been spared this cause
of division.[4]

Yet such passionate moments do not represent a steady argument and when Biondo comes to the events of his own day in
the third and fourth decades alarums and excursions become
his theme. As we shall see, the third decade represents a different
kind of history in more ways than one compared with what
goes before, and I shall have occasion to suggest that it is more
stylishly composed, more 'humanist'.[5] But we should be wrong
to think that the concentration on war was a product of Biondo's
humanist aspirations. It was, unhappily for him and his contemporaries, the true condition of his times in the Italy which
was now his main theme. 'Italy was now quiet', he writes of the
peace of April 1428, 'and this had happened seldom enough in
previous centuries'.[6] But the peace lasted only four months and
later on Biondo describes such a period as 'rather an interval
between upheavals', and noted that the lull corresponded to
winter months when campaigning was suspended.[7] The whole
work ends with the peace of Cavriana in the autumn of 1441.[8]
But this terminus represented nothing very significant for Biondo.

One can, of course, feel disappointed that the political scene
in early fifteenth-century Italy is treated by Biondo in strictly
inter-state terms. The internal history of the cities is hardly
touched on. For example, the rise of the Medici is very cursorily
treated[9] and the affairs of Forlì are given a prominence which,

[1] *Decades*, p. 458.   [2] Ibid., p. 362.
[3] Ibid., p. 375.   [4] Ibid., p. 288.
[5] Below, p. 51.
[6] *Decades*, p. 446: 'quiescebat Italia, quod multis anteactis seculis raro
contigisse constabat.'
[7] Ibid., p. 562: 'uel quies, uel ea erat a motibus uacatio.'
[8] Nogara, p. 28.   [9] *Decades*, p. 489.

though natural, is disproportionate: for the rest, only Bologna's internal politics are discussed with any fullness,[1] and Rome's in so far as they impinged on papal action. Yet to critics who accused him of not seeing the trees because of the wood Biondo could have replied fairly enough—'how else could I have done it?' No general history of the peninsula could have displayed the detailed internal history of Florence or Genoa or Naples. As it was Biondo again and again[2] bemoans the difficulty of organizing this material in his third decade. Anyone who has tried to write or lecture on Italian history in the early fifteenth century will sympathize with his embarrassment.

The account given above of what the *Decades* are about does not end up with any simple picture. But it seemed worth while demonstrating the varieties and changes in the scope of various parts of the work because some rather ambitious claims have been made for it. An Italian critic has seen in it a picture of the final stage in Orosius's doctrine that world monarchy had moved from the East to Carthage, from Carthage to Rome—the eternal nature of the final *translatio imperii* being secured by the Christian religion.[3] That pagan Rome was justified for Biondo by becoming the centre of Christianity we cannot doubt. A passage of great eloquence comes at the end of his survey of the antiquities of the ancient city in the *Roma instaurata*. He sweeps away the legionaries and the temples and proclaims a new Rome: Christ is *imperator*, the city now the seat of an eternal religion, its citadel and dwelling place: of old men feared the name of Rome, now they worship it.[4] My point is that such a view does not colour

[1] Ibid., p. 446. At p. 497 Biondo rejects the possibility of writing succinctly of the internal history of Naples, or even of mastering adequately the factions, 'qui ter quaterque diuersa secuti sunt studia'.

[2] Ibid., p. 459: 'Distrahent uero scribentem, tam diuersae inter sese, quam frequentes ac propemodum continuae rerum Italiae agitationes . . .'; p. 514: '. . . nihil est operosius, quam cum gesta in regione una scribere aggressi fuerimus, ita dicendi cursum moderari, ut eodem tempore alibi gestorum ratio habita uideatur.'

[3] L. Colini Baldeschi, *Studio critico sulle opere di Flavio Biondo*, Macerata, 1895, p. 8, or (more accessibly, perhaps) in *La Nuova Rassegna* (Rome), 1894, pp. 1024–37.

[4] *Roma Instaurata*, p. 271: 'Viget certe uiget adhuc, et quanquam minori diffusa orbis terrarum spacio solidiori certe innixa fundamento urbis Romae gloria maiestatis. Habetque Roma aliquod in regna et gentes imperium, cui tutando augendoque non legionibus, cohortibus, turmis et manipulis, non equitatu peditatuque opus, nullo nunc delectu militum, qui aut sponte dent nomina, aut militare cogantur eductae Roma et Italia copiae in hostem ducuntur, aut imperii limites custodiuntur. Non sanguis ad praesentem

the *Decades*, though at one point it is reflected there. 'Then', he writes of the conversion of the English, 'Rome again began to rule Britain and this was accomplished by the use of a better kind of warfare than of old, the preaching of Christ's servants and the authority of the pope.'[1] This view of a transcending Christian mission is elsewhere in the *Decades* only suggested in Biondo's account of the Crusades.[2]

Another kind of erroneous judgement falsifies the range of Biondo's book. Fueter writes: 'Italy is in the foreground, but the history of other countries is always summarised'; 'this man without a native land had written the history of the whole of Christendom'.[3] This is just not true. Let us glance at the glimpses of English history in the *Decades*. There are references, and not much more, to St. Augustine's mission of conversion,[4] to Cnut's visit to Rome,[5] to Henry II's reconciliation with the pope after the murder of Becket,[6] to John's submission to Innocent III,[7] to Henry III's quarrel with de Montfort (apropos the intervention of Clement IV),[8] and (apropos the career of Albergati) to papal efforts at Arras to heal the Anglo-French war.[9] From these fugitive points one could hardly construct even the briefest account of English history. It is true only in a very limited sense that the *Decades* are a general history of medieval Europe: we should note that Biondo himself complains when discussing the tenth and eleventh centuries that his sources deal too much with the former provinces of Rome, and tell him far too little about 'the Roman empire, the popes of Rome and even less about affairs in Italy'.[10] One reason for these shifts in emphasis is laid bare

seruandam patriam effunditur, non mortalium caedes committuntur. Sed per dei nostri et domini nostri Iesu Christi imperatoris uere summi, uere aeterni religionis sedem, arcem, atque domicilium in Roma constitutum, ductosque in illa ab annis mille et quadringentis martyrum triumphos, per dispersas in omnibus aeternae et gloriosissimae Romae templis, aedibus, sacellisque sanctorum reliquias magna nunc orbis terrarum pars Romanum nomen dulci magis subjectione colit, quam olim fuit solita contremiscere. Dictatorem nunc perpetuum non Caesaris, sed piscatoris Petri successorem, &c.'

[1] *Decades*, p. 110: 'Tuncque coepit urbs Roma per arma solito feliciora, seruorum scilicet Christi praedicationem et summi pontificis autoritatem, Britanniae insulae et eius incolis Saxonibus Anglicis denuo imperare.' Cf. Bede's praise of Ethelbert, who had learned that 'seruitium Christi uoluntarium, non coacticium esse debere', ed. Plummer, i. 47.

[2] It is, of course, also revealed in Biondo's Crusading treatises written between 1452 and 1454; see below, Appendix I, no. 5.

[3] Fueter, pp. 128, 132.   [4] *Decades*, p. 110.
[5] Ibid., p. 192.   [6] Ibid., p. 252.   [7] Ibid., p. 275.
[8] Ibid., p. 313.   [9] Ibid., p. 493.   [10] Ibid., p. 177.

when we turn to the two related problems of Biondo's sources and the construction and style of exposition he adopted.

The first of these questions—his sources—must not detain us long. Decades I and II were analysed from the viewpoint of the sources in a brief dissertation published in 1881.[1] It may be summarized and supplemented as follows. Biondo used a number of general historical compendia: the Liber pontificalis, Sigebert of Gembloux, Martinus Polonus, Vincent of Beauvais, Giovanni Villani are the most important; and with these we may link the crusading writers, notably William of Tyre and Jacques de Vitry. To these he added certain sources more limited in scope and often more valuable historically: Paulus Diaconus, Jordanes, Gregory the Great, the *Gesta regum Francorum*, Einhard, are his main authorities for the period up to the ninth century. For the tenth to the thirteenth he depended greatly on the general chronicles I have mentioned, as well as on Ptolemy of Lucca and the great Venetian chronicle of Andrea Dandolo. In his early fourteenth-century passages good use is made of the works of Dante (including valuable references to letters which are otherwise not known)[2] and for the mid-fourteenth century Biondo draws very freely on Petrarch's letters.[3] Events in the third decade are, of course, those for which Biondo is himself a first-hand witness, but we are sometimes very conscious of his dependence on information provided by correspondents: there can be no doubt that Biondo's narrative of the defence of Brescia in 1438 and 1439 depended on the account of its Venetian hero, Francesco Barbaro, in whose service Biondo began his career.[4]

In addition to narrative sources and the letters of Dante and Petrarch, Biondo made occasional use of documents and archaeological material. Papal privileges are quoted,[5] so is Gratian's *Decretum*,[6] papal registers,[7] and other documents.[8] The third decade contains among other things references to letters by Eugenius IV,[9] the bull of union between the Latin and Greek

[1] Paul Buchholz, *Die Quellen der Historiarum Decades des Flavius Biondus,* Naumburg, 1881.

[2] On this see M. Barbi, 'Sulla dimora di Dante à Forlì', *Bull. della Soc. Dantesca,* ser. 1, no. 8 (Florence, 1893), 21–28.

[3] *Decades,* pp. 329, 334, 364–70 *passim.*

[4] Ibid., pp. 528 ff.

[5] Ibid., p. 165.

[6] Ibid., p. 184; cf. p. 280.

[7] Ibid., pp. 193, 198, 200, 203.

[8] Ibid., pp. 313, 387.

[9] Ibid., p. 475.

churches which is given *in extenso*,[1] while the terms of the settlement with the Armenian church are fully rehearsed.[2] That the
author of *Italia illustrata* and *Roma instaurata* should include frequent references to old buildings is hardly surprising and a long
list could be drawn up of such passages. They are particularly
full for the north of Italy[3] and frequent for Rome,[4] though they
contain disarming anachronisms which warn us of Biondo's
limitations as an historian of art.[5]

Such a list is, I think, impressive, and rightly so. But I have
introduced it at this point in order to finish what I have to say
about the scope of the *Decades*, which, as we have seen, shifts
gradually from a large view of the old Roman world at the start
to a narrow concentration on Italy at the end. The reason for
this is that, whatever Biondo's merits as a critic (and to these I
shall devote a word shortly) he was in the last resort the victim
rather than the master of his sources. He does not take all his
materials and spread them out in a fundamentally reconstructed
story. Rather he has one main source and sticks to it, using other
writers for supplementing his narrative. Thus Paulus Diaconus
supplies the skeleton of his narrative of the fifth century.[6] The
account of the Goths comes from Procopius, largely it seems
from the version of Leonardo Bruni.[7] Then he reverts again to
Paulus Diaconus down to the mid-eighth century.[8] From the
ninth century down to the Crusades his main account is drawn
out of Ptolemy of Lucca, who, with Villani, is the basis for the
rest of the second decade.[9] These main sources partly account
for the emphasis which the history of Biondo has from time to
time; we may reflect that, doubtless involuntarily, he thus transmitted fairly truly the changing horizons of earlier periods.

The composition, style, and structure of the *Decades* demand
a moment's consideration: they have been neglected from this
point of view and here again, under the influence of Fueter, we
have regarded Biondo's book as all of a piece. It is, in fact, very
far from being that and, just as we have seen that the content

---

[1] *Decades*, pp. 550–1; cf. Hefele-Leclercq, *Histoire des Conciles*, VII. ii. 1038–40.

[2] *Decades*, p. 559; Hefele-Leclercq, VII. ii, 1079–80.

[3] e.g. *Decades*, pp. 14, 44 (Ravenna), 167 (Venice).

[4] e.g. ibid., pp. 97–98, 123, 275–6, 280, 325, 373.

[5] Theodolinda's church at Monza, p. 113; cf. *Italia illustrata*, p. 364.

[6] *Decades*, pp. 14–38.

[7] Ibid., pp. 38–98. Biondo himself points out that Bruni's *De Bello Italico
adversus Gothos* is just a version of Procopius: ibid., p. 43; on Biondo's use of
Bruni cf. Buchholz, pp. 33–38.

[8] *Decades*, pp. 98–149.　　　　　　　　　　　　[9] Ibid., pp. 174–392.

changes, so, but much more drastically, we can observe a sharp transition in Biondo's manner of exposition. There is a tremendous difference between the third decade (and what he added of a fourth) and what goes before. The contemporary part, written first, betokens far greater attention to stylistic preoccupations. This strikes a reader of the work as a whole very forcibly. The differences are as follows. First, there is an avowed concern with style. Decade III begins with a long passage describing the anxieties of an historian from the viewpoint of linguistic propriety.[1] How can an historian of the post-Roman world deal with a vocabulary which has no exact parallels in the writers of antiquity? As Biondo points out, the Romans had no artillery of a modern kind and war in particular is full of terminological pitfalls. The other great field of embarrassment is found in place-names, and here he refers us to what he has written on this in his *Italia illustrata*.[2] We are used to accepting such an awareness of stylistic problems in Leonardo Bruni and in what Fueter called the 'school of Bruni': but we have been led to suppose that Biondo is free of it.[3] There is, however, more to it than that. I think one must admit that he was not a writer of sparkling Latin; but one must note on the other hand that on occasions he tried very hard to be fashionable[4] and that once or twice he produces very gripping and lively passages: such as, for example, his account of his own adventurous journey from the Curia to Venice in the summer of 1434[5] and the dramatic escape of Eugenius IV from Rome shortly afterwards, so vividly described that Biondo has (wrongly) been regarded as an eye-witness.[6]

In all these points Biondo is, we might say, of 'the school of Bruni'. And so he is in three other features of the third decade. There is an almost total absence of precise chronological statements: 'at the same time, just after this, meanwhile';[7] these are the conjunctive phrases which lead us on from one point of time to another. In the whole of this part of the work, covering as it does a period of forty-two years, there are only two dates—at the start of each of the two books of the fourth decade. It is true that

[1] Ibid., pp. 393–6.
[2] Ibid., p. 395. Cf. *Ital. illus.*, p. 294.   [3] Fueter, p. 129.
[4] See e.g. the Ciceronian diction on p. 407: *regina . . . orat, obsecrat, obtestatur*, &c.
[5] Ibid., pp. 479–80 (cf. Nogara, pp. lxvi–lxvii).
[6] Ibid., pp. 481–4.
[7] 'interea, quo tempore, non multi intercesserunt dies', &c.

the attentive reader will observe that from the seventh book of the third decade the author gives in effect a book to a year;[1] prior to that he must not let his attention wander or he will be lost indeed. Second, like Bruni and the classical models admired at the time, the third decade is full of set battle pieces; their bulk obtrudes itself as disproportionate even granted that the period was full of wars.[2] And, finally, the modern part has many speeches: about a tenth of the pages devoted to the years 1400–42 are filled by direct speech.[3]

When we compare this with the first two decades we can see how differently they were composed. There is no indication of concern over vocabulary or style; there are no extended descriptions of famous actions, bellicose or otherwise; there are some speeches, but very few and much shorter.[4] And (praise be) there are plenty of dates. At first Biondo ambitiously tried to construct a chronology from the fall of Rome and up to the year 1000 we occasionally meet an *annus ab inclinatione imperii*,[5] a rather uncertain indication as Biondo put his catastrophe in the year A.D. 412. But soon this affectation is discarded. Once, in the year 700, he gives us the year of the Incarnation,[6] and from A.D. 1000 it is invariably used by him, to the great solace of the reader. I have noted seventy-two dates,[7] or on average one in every five or six years from 1000 to 1400. Here again we must attribute these practices to the sources Biondo was using.[8]

The composition and style of the various parts of Biondo's *Decades* thus reflect in many ways the authorities on which he depended, and in particular the moment when he passes from a dependence on others to the description of the events of his own lifetime. The change in manner between the first two

[1] See Appendix II.

[2] e.g. *Decades*, pp. 456–7, 462–3, 488–9, 494, 497–9, 528–42, 572–4.

[3] Ibid., pp. 402, 405, 421–31, 437, 475, 477, 484, 503, 518, 573; Nogara, p. 20.

[4] I have noted only the following: pp. 47, 78–79, 84–85, 197, 207–8. Cf. p. 216 where Biondo announces that 'the speech which Robert the Monk (of St. Remy) puts into Bohemund's mouth may be omitted'.

[5] *Decades*, pp. 10, 13–14, 25, 26, 30, 43, 120, 133, 170, and in the titles of books *passim*; cf. above, p. 43.

[6] Ibid., p. 136.

[7] These are mostly (but not completely) shown in marginalia in the Basle edition of 1531.

[8] And so also the use of regnal year of pope and emperor, p. 101. If the third decade is devoid of dates of years, it is fairly liberally provided with months and days: among these we may note a number referring not to the Roman calendar but to saints' days: pp. 485, 490, 498, 537.

decades and the contemporary portion may have a further explanation. Aulus Gellius had recalled a distinction made between *annales* and *historia*;[1] and this was referred to, at about the time Biondo was at work, by his friend Guarino da Verona.[2] *Historia* differed from *annales* both in being the work of an observer of the events in question and in laying bare motives[3] which would account for the great space which, as already pointed out, is allotted to speeches in the third decade. There is, however, no evidence that Biondo himself was aware of these differences in approach and in general there seems little reason to suppose that the structure of the work has much significance. There seems to me to be little behind the division into decades, though we know that this is in fact how he saw the books himself, for so he refers to them on several occasions.[4] If it was to Livy's work he tacitly compared his own[5] his model's decades did not offer much encouragement to treat the division as significant; for Biondo a decade, we may be sure, meant only ten books, whatever it had meant to Livy. Nor can one find much behind the division into books. Perhaps this absence of sharply defined endings also stems from Livy. However that may be, the books in Biondo's *Decades* end and begin for the most part without much obvious necessity. Again and again a book stops with some indication that a new subject demands a fresh start, but the new book belies this.[6] Even when, in the modern part, virtually a whole book is devoted to one subject (as in III. ii which really deals entirely with the great debate at Venice in 1425 on the Florentine alliance), the author seems unconscious of it, though he gradually becomes aware that after 1437 he is giving a book to a year and ending at the autumn hibernation of the armies.[7] If one lists the main dates covered by each book[8] one can get the

[1] *Noct. Att.* v. xviii.

[2] R. Sabbadini, *Il Metodo degli umanisti*, Florence, 1922, p. 79: letter to Tobia del Borgo, 1446.

[3] Aulus Gellius, loc. cit.: 'Historiam ab annalibus quidam differre eo putant, quod, cum utrumque sit rerum gestarum narratio, earum tamen proprie rerum sit historia, quibus rebus gerendis interfuit is, qui narret.' He then quotes Sempronius Asellio on the need for a historian 'quo consilio quaque ratione gesta essent, demonstrare'.

[4] 'Tres historiarum mearum decades' (1453), Nogara, p. 167; 'la mia prima deca' (1463), ibid., pp. 211–12; the manuscripts enumerate thus: *Quartae decadis liber secundus incipit*, &c.

[5] Biondo refers to Livy's decades as such, Nogara, p. 211.

[6] Ibid., p. 238; '. . . ut liberiore animo ampliorique spacio narrare possimus'; cf. pp. 255, 276, 304, 481.

[7] Ibid., p. 561.   [8] See Appendix II.

impression of a kind of symmetry which in reality is absent. Most books end with a cluster of insignificant events and yet this effect of a dying fall reflects no conscious artistry but only the annalistic framework within which Biondo worked. He called it *ratio temporis*.[1] And chronology makes him mince up what look like being indestructible historical units. His elaborate and lengthy account of the first crusade[2] is sawn in half to insert a comment on affairs in Italy;[3] his very full account of the war between Venice and Genoa in 1378–80 is interrupted by a sentence dealing with the obedience of the schismatic popes.[4] And so with all the central events of his own day, though in this contemporary section (as we have seen) he frequently bemoans his inability to organize his material.[5] We cannot blame Biondo for making an *Odtaa* of the past: it was what most of his contemporaries were doing, what their revered classical exemplars did, and it was what the medieval chronicler had done, in that interval the history of which Biondo had set himself to write. Nor can we discern in Biondo any novel view as to the historian's mission. He subscribes to the conventional attitude: that history is the means by which the great man's fame is handed down to posterity.[6]

I have spent some time in a criticism of Biondo (and, by implication, of those who have given him extravagant praise). In turning by way of conclusion to estimate his value and his influence I shall have occasion to sing his praises. And in the first place we must recognize him as being the first medieval historian. He takes this place by virtue of the book which I have laboriously considered, which runs from the fall of Rome to the Renaissance. 'All who cherish literature know', he wrote to Alfonso of Aragon in 1443, 'that for twelve hundred years the Latins have had few poets and no historians. From Orosius onwards events are obscure. Today we have many who interest themselves in verse, speeches and letter-writing, translating a great deal from Greek into Latin and popularising some of the mysteries of knowledge in an elegant manner, but not under-

---

[1] e.g. on pp. 296, 481, 550.   [2] Ibid., pp. 217–230.
[3] Ibid., p. 228.   [4] Ibid., pp. 378–84.
[5] See above, p. 47 and n. 2.
[6] Nogara, pp. 150–2 (letter to Alfonso, 1443); pp. 185–9 (second letter to Galeazzo Sforza, 1458); p. 211 (letter to Francesco Sforza, 1463): 'La quale gloria sempre ha habuto questa conditione in ciascuno grande et uirtuoso homo, che tanto è durata e amplificata, quanto ha habuto bone et sollide historie scripte, etc.'

taking the large historical work which is called for.'[1] Biondo, in short, realized on the one hand that there was a gap to be filled, and on the other that to fill it would not be a particularly fashionable activity, and so (as he says elsewhere himself) not likely to bring him any material rewards.[2] He thus at any rate tried to get outside his own period and is entitled to our esteem on that account. It was probably a more difficult step to take than merely to realize, as he did, that the *studia eloquentiae* were again flourishing in Italy.[3] The revival of letters is not equated by him with a brave new world: he had the future of his ten children to think about and no patron to relieve him of the embarrassments of the active life so praised by Florentine 'progressives'.

Recognizing and chronicling the *medium aevum*, even if not using the phrase, constitutes a major claim to the esteem of posterity. There are other aspects of the *Decades* that are meritorious: while it is true that many of the errors in his sources are transmitted uncorrected by Biondo,[4] it is also true that he frequently subjects them to criticism: his discussion of Procopius,[5] of the Liber pontificum,[6] of the chronology of Vincent of Beauvais and other thirteenth-century writers,[7] of the uncritical use made of Martinus Polonus,[8] are only a few examples of the sharp asides in which this critical acumen is displayed. Equally significant is his awareness that his sources have greater authority when they are dealing with events of their own time: thus he remarks on Ptolemy of Lucca's closeness to the diffusion in Italy of Guelf-Ghibelline rivalries;[9] for the same reason Dante

---

[1] See the full passage, summarized above, in Nogara, p. 148.

[2] To Giacomo Bracelli, 10 December 1454: 'sed quicquid et qualicumque iudicio dignum sit, quod dicturus sum, uelim credas me, qui nulla ad scribendum spe pecuniaria sim adductus; nullam ab auaritia et ingratitudine iniuriam existimare': Nogara, p. 168; cf. Masius, p. 30.

[3] Biondo's concern with humanism as such deserves separate treatment. It is briefly discussed by Wallace K. Ferguson, *Renaissance in Historical Thought*, New York, 1948, pp. 22–23. The key text is the long passage in *Italia illustrata*, pp. 345–8, which surveys the men of letters stemming from John of Ravenna: cf. G. Voigt, *Wiederbelebung des classischen Alterthums*, 3rd ed., Berlin, 1893, i. 219–220, 245. In the *De Verbis Romanae Locutionis*, Nogara, p. 125, Biondo describes the barbarous Latin of some of his colleagues in the Curia, 'Gallos, Cimbros, Teutonos, Alamannos, Anglicos, Britannos, Pannoniosque . . . qui . . . illiterati et penitus idiotae dici possint.'

[4] Buchholz, p. 6.   [5] *Decades*, pp. 43, 64–65.

[6] Ibid., p. 140.   [7] Ibid., p. 180.

[8] Ibid., p. 237.

[9] Ibid., p. 289; on Paulus Diaconus's authority see below, p. 56, n. 3.

is frequently advanced both as actor and source.[1] Nor are we entirely dependent on the internal evidence of the *Decades* for our knowledge of Biondo's care over his authorities. Several letters have survived which show him asking for help: to Alfonso of Aragon for Spanish sources, to Giacomo Bracelli for a Genoese chronicle, and to Francesco Sforza for details of early Visconti history.[2] Even more interesting are three manuscripts at the Vatican which show Biondo at work gathering his materials. The first is the history of Paulus Diaconus which contains many annotations in the hand of Biondo.[3] Another has particular relevance for an English historian, for it is the *British History* of Geoffrey of Monmouth.[4] There is no case here of Biondo annotating the text: it contains only one devastating final comment on the utter waste of time it had caused him:[5] 'I have never come across anything so stuffed with lies and frivolities.' Another manuscript seems to contain a sheet of notes made from a copy of the *Liber Pontificalis*.[6]

Biondo's decision not to classicize the terminology of his sources has been much admired[7] and undoubtedly it had a certain boldness about it at a time when Bruni and Poggio were both his contemporaries and fellow graduates of the Curia. Some of the modern admiration is, however, due to an attitude of censure taken towards the 'rhetorical' writing of humanist historians, which has been much exaggerated.[8] If we are grateful to Biondo for giving us words like 'Manganellae et bricolae', 'feudatarius', 'barchae', 'gonzardi', 'banderesii', 'bombardae',[9] we must accept in him equally a neglect of the beautiful, and an indifference to good taste which might have deprived him of merit had not the vernaculars come to the rescue. Indifference justly describes his attitude to literature, for he was not unaware of the felicities of good writing, as we may see from his praise of

---

[1] *Decades*, pp. 331–2, 338, 342.

[2] Nogara, pp. 147, 168, cv and n.

[3] Cod. Vat. Lat. 1795. Cf. Nogara cvii and n., where the impression is unintentionally conveyed that Biondo's animadversions are mostly hostile. Most of the annotations in the manuscript are in fact summaries or notes drawing attention to a passage. On fol. 49ᵛ Biondo identifies the author as an Italian because he says *nostrum Adriaticum*; fol. 66ᵛ: *Nota auctor proximus fuit his temporibus*.

[4] Cod. Vat. Lat. 2005.　　　　　　　　　　[5] Ibid., fol. 69.

[6] Cod. Urb. Lat. 395, fol. 231ᵛ, *ex priuatis scriptis blondi*.

[7] Fueter, p. 129; Nogara, p. cviii.

[8] See above, p. 37, n. 4.

[9] *Decades*, pp. 264, 275, 373, 377, 378, 383. There are many others.

Bruni, whom he calls *scriptor aetate nostra clarissimus*.[1] In any case we must not exaggerate Biondo's stylistic ineptitude. As already observed, he makes intermittent efforts to polish his style in the third decade and succeeds there in attaining some passages of sustained effect. In any event, judged by the standards of fourteenth-century Latin, he wrote well. Even among practitioners of what Fueter would have us regard as the 'rhetorical school' he found admirers of his competence. For example, Cardinal Prospero Colonna invited Biondo, as well as Bruni, Poggio, and other admitted stylists, to suggest emendations to his Livy,[2] and he was praised as a writer by Leodrisio Crivelli, the first of the Sforza humanist historians.[3]

Careful handling of sources, concentration on a new and significant period of time, these are major titles to recognition as an important scholar. But Biondo's sense of the conjunction of events, of the causal element is less impressive, because very much less in evidence. The chronicling pattern of writing, of course, hardly lends itself to elaborate analysis of motive. But none the less in a work which it has been claimed inaugurated scientific history,[4] an historian whom his admirers have compared with Vico,[5] in the event seldom uncovers the springs of human action. It is not that Biondo shelters behind the providential view of history, to which he would have subscribed, as we may see (*pace* Fueter) from the frequent record he gives of both miracles and saints.[6] God is occasionally invoked as a cause but

---

[1] Ibid., p. 43. Cf. above, p. 51.

[2] Giuseppe Billanovich e M. Ferraris, 'Le "emendationes in T. Livium" del Valla, e il Codex Regius di Livio', *Italia medioevale e umanistica*, i (1958), 248.

[3] Leodrisio Crivelli 'de vita Sfortiae vicecomitis', Muratori, *Scriptores* (1731), xix. 629: '. . . vir in scribendo aeque exercitatus ac doctus, . . . multa . . . felici stylo complexus est.'

[4] P. Villari, *N. Machiavelli e i suoi tempi*, 2nd ed., 3 vols., Milan, 1895-7, i. 143; cf. iii. 203.

[5] L. Barozzi e R. Sabbadini, *Studi sul Panormita e sul Valla* (R. Istituto di Studi Superiori . . . in Firenze), Florence, 1891, p. 222.

[6] Fueter, p. 131: 'As with other humanists, he finds no place for legends and miracles'. Miracles: *Decades*, pp. 24, 52, 85, 108, 131, 191, 220–1, 252 (St. Thomas of Canterbury), 281 (St. Francis), 297 (St. Stanislaus), 323 (St. Gregory X); other canonizations: ibid., pp. 283 (St. Dominic, St. Anthony of Padua, Queen Elizabeth of Hungary), 297 (St. Edmund of Canterbury), 309 (St. Clare), 313 (Aquinas and Bonaventure), 335 (St. Louis), 348 (Celestine V); with these may be linked the translation of St. Augustine's remains to Pavia, p. 142, and the translation of St. Mark to Venice, pp. 172–3. See p. 172 for a criticism of J. de Voragine and other hagiographers; and cf. *Roma instaurata*, pp. 271–2, for a list of the holy places in Rome.

seldom (and this is the point) in an avenging or rewarding capacity: the galaxy of splendid cities which rose in Italy after the fall of Rome is attributed to the grace of God:[1] and so is the universal devastation of the Black Death.[2] But I have only observed two occasions when the wrath of God is advanced—for barbarian attacks on Italy[3] and for the loss by Heraclius of the Asiatic provinces of the empire.[4] Fortune makes even rarer appearances than God.[5] Human nature, grasping, superstitious, always ready to take risks, sometimes appears in Biondo's pages: Saladin is driven by ambition,[6] Sforza overplays his hand.[7] But there are besides these explanatory moments a few passages where political situations are analysed in political terms.

'No cause for the overthrow of the declining empire appears more effective', writes Biondo in what is really his only general comment on the coronation of Charlemagne in 800, 'than the conflict now begun between Rome and Constantinople'.[8] This is an important observation, and later he has other notes on the disastrous effects of the rivalry of Greek and Latin.[9] Again, he sees justly the consequences for northern Europe of the division of the Empire after Charlemagne's death,[10] just as later he rightly attributes the Angevin connexion with Naples to the abiding fear inspired in the papacy by Frederick II.[11] I have already mentioned his account of the Guelf-Ghibelline distractions of thirteenth-century Italy: he does not see their social origins in the Italian communes; but he does see their prolonged deleterious effects.[12] To the long vacancy between the death of Nicholas IV in 1292 and the election of Celestine V in 1294 he attributes the failure of the union of the churches agreed on at Lyons and the continued war between England and France, with all the evil results that flowed from both events.[13] A very interesting passage examines the difficulties in securing a Venetian-Florentine alliance in 1425: ancient hatreds were exacerbated by trade rivalries and in particular by competition from Pisa in the Eastern trade.[14]

[1] *Decades*, p. 30: *dei nostri . . . benignitate* (see above, p. 45, n. 2).
[2] Ibid., p. 365: 'ut omnes una deus ruina populos prostraturos uideretur.'
[3] Ibid., p. 108.   [4] Ibid., p. 125.
[5] Ibid., pp. 477, 483.   [6] Ibid., p. 256.
[7] Ibid., p. 477; and cf. other instances, pp. 333, 401.
[8] Ibid., p. 166: cf. pp. 163–4.
[9] Ibid., p. 309.   [10] Ibid., p. 175.
[11] Ibid., p. 313.
[12] Above, p. 46; cf. *Decades*, pp. 315, 353, 374.
[13] Ibid., p. 333.   [14] Ibid., p. 421.

These passages suggest that Biondo was a sufficiently shrewd commentator on politics. Why, then, does he exercise his talents so rarely? Aside from his own disinclination, and it must be conceded that reflecting about the past is a more exacting occupation than baldly narrating it, there is one reason which springs to mind. Biondo was a servant of the pope, writing his history at a time when the papacy was more involved than ever before in shifting political alignments. Properly to comment on either the past or the present might have involved Biondo in censure or dismissal. In all the welter of factional history Biondo's work has, in fact, a kind of detachment which is both rare and salutory; in particular he frequently gives us a view which is in striking contrast with the victorious versions embodied in what might be called the Whig tradition of the Florentines.[1] And by detachment should not be meant a Guelf or pro-papal attitude to the past. A student of Biondo has claimed that he had 'l'animo profondamente religioso e Guelfo'[2] on the grounds that he was hostile to Lombards, and to German emperors. This does not seem evident from a reading of the *Decades*. The popes play a very small part in the early *Decades*[3] and there is, significantly, no reference to the Donation of Constantine, the genuineness of which Valla had just attacked, and no moralizing on Canossa.[4] It is true that we know from Biondo's other writings[5] that he saw Christian Rome as the shining successor of the old empire. But this did not provoke him into a blind defence of the papacy: it would be hard to say whether his picture of Frederick II is harsher than that of Boniface VIII,[6] and he is capable of criticizing, albeit indirectly, the Italian prelates of his own day.[7] It is true that he hardly supported the conciliar programme and from his pages no just appraisal of the debates at Constance or Basle can be made. We should perhaps discriminate, however, between his treatment of Basle and Constance. He deals with neither in any detail, but against the bitter remarks he makes about the fathers at Basle we should place the much more

[1] Cf. *Decades*, p. 374, on the attitude to the papacy of the Florentines, *populi in res nouas semper procliues*.

[2] Colini Baldeschi, *Studio critico*, p. 5.

[3] Popes are mentioned only on pp. 24 and 36, in the first three books. Cf. the sketchy treatment of Innocent III, pp. 275–6.

[4] Ibid., p. 200.

[5] Above, pp. 47-8, and Colini Baldeschi, pp. 8–10.

[6] Cf. the unflattering picture of Urban VI, *Decades*, p. 385.

[7] Ibid., p. 435: Albergati praised as a saintly man, 'cui ecclesia rarissimos aetate nostra habuerit praelatos adsimiles'.

sympathetic account he gives of Constance, and note that he quotes (somewhat incorrectly) the terms of the decree *Frequens*.[1]

He was not a publicist. He had no argument to press; it is this which really distinguishes him from a good many of his humanist contemporaries and which led to a somewhat disparaging view of him among some of them. Biondo himself regarded his work as successful and applauded, and reported in 1443 to Leonello d'Este that he had received the praises of Francesco Barbaro and Pier Candido Decembrio, and had heard that Leonardo Bruni was also favourably impressed by it.[2] Note the approval of Bruni, which Biondo had heard about, he says, through mutual friends: the point is worth mentioning for Fueter wrote 'a humanist like Bruni found it distasteful to be compromised by a public acknowledgement of this too well-informed historian', and others have only too glibly repeated what Fueter almost literally invented.[3] His work was thus in good repute with leading humanists at Venice, Milan, and Florence. But his reputation extended beyond Italy. In 1453 Biondo says that copies of the *Decades* are distributed throughout Europe, and ten years later he says there are copies in England, Spain, France, as well as Italy, more than fifty copies being sold.[4] Yet these signs of esteem are recorded for us by Biondo himself, and very soon we have less flattering judgements from other sources. Pius II wrote of him:

He wrote a universal history which is a painstaking and useful work. Blondus was by no means a good stylist. He did not revise carefully what he had written and took pains to write a great deal rather than the essential truth. It would be most valuable if some learned and stylish author would polish and emend his works.[5]

[1] *Decades*, pp. 399 (Constance), 477, 514, 527 (references to Basle).

[2] Nogara, pp. 146–7.

[3] Masius, p. 33, drew attention to the letter in which Biondo reported the reaction of his friends: from the fact that Bruni had not written to Biondo (up to that point) and (I suppose) from the phrase '. . . eamdem historiam, ut amici retulerunt, aliis *me absente* laudaverit' constructed his theory of Bruni's squeamish repugnance. I can see no other grounds for the statement in Fueter, p. 132. For an example of glib repetition I can refer to my introduction to *Anglica Historia of P. Vergil*, Camden Society 1950, p. xxvii.

[4] 'Tres Historiarum mearum decades, quae iam disseminatae in omni Europa sunt . . .', Nogara, p. 167; '. . . disseminate per Anglia, Spagna, Franza, quanto per Italia . . . chè per la christianitate in ogni natione e prouintie sono molti uolumi de mie historie, de quali oltra cinquanta sono gosti a chi li a uoluti oltra ducati quaranta per uno', ibid., p. 212.

[5] See the full passage, *Commentarii*, Frankfurt, 1614, p. 310, quoted Nogara, p. cxi, n. This judgement is echoed by Voigt, ii. 492.

And even a minor poetaster like Cleofilo could write equivocally of the man and the historian.[1]

If imitation is flattery, Biondo had little enough of it. Among the very numerous contemporaries of his who were composing apologia his lack of party spirit was itself an irritation. Crivelli, whose praise of Biondo's style has been referred to already, found him sadly lacking as a source of information on the history of the Sforza;[2] Platina as apologist of the Gonzaga of Mantua is even sharper in his strictures.[3] The point, however, is that he was widely used. Pius II put his own advice into practice by making an abridgement of the first two decades[4] and this work had considerable influence, not least because in this form Biondo became one of the prime sources of Platina's *Lives of the Popes*,[5] the most generally influential and long-lived of all humanist Latin histories. What may be described as the most influential of the vernacular Italian histories, Machiavelli's *Florentine History*, equally depends greatly on the *Decades*.[6] Practically every sixteenth-century scholar must have turned to the *Decades* for factual information[7] and when Pius II's epitome appeared in the Italian translation of Lucio Fauno[8] Biondo's work was made available to a much wider public.

[1] As the epigram is unprinted I give it from Cod. Vat. Lat. 5763, fol. 36ᵛ.

De Blondo historico

Blonde Latinarum scriptor celeberrime rerum
    Æmiliae splendor, gloria, fama, decus,
Te Liui superat tantum facundia, quantum
    Res tua Romana distat ab historia.

On Cleofilo, Francesco Ottavio of Fano, d. 1490, see Tiraboschi, vi. 925. For a few other judgements of Biondo see Apostolo Zeno, *Dissertazioni Vossiane*, Venice, 2 vols., 1752, i. 233–4.

[2] Muratori, xix. 629.   [3] Ibid., xx. 815.

[4] See Appendix I below, no. 2. It is to be noted that Pius did not correct the mistakes of fact which he had earlier stigmatized.

[5] G. Gaida discusses Platina's indebtedness fully, *Platynae historici liber de vita . . . omnium pontificum*, R.R. II, SS., III. i, intro., pp. liv–lvii.

[6] Villari, *Machiavelli*, iii. 206–73 passim and, for nature of the borrowings in book i, L. La Rocca, *Il primo libro delle 'Istorie florentine' di N. Machiavelli e del parallelismo con le 'Decadi' di F. Biondo*, Palermo, 1904.

[7] The following are given as instances, not as a complete list—Bartolomeo Scala, Wimpfeling, Meisterlin: Fueter, pp. 30, 227, 242; Sabellico: Nogara, p. cxi, n. 142; Donato Giannoti: Villari, *Machiavelli*, iii. 223; Giambullari: Colini Baldeschi, p. 5; Paulus Aemilius: doctoral dissertation on 'Gaguin and Aemilius', by Miss K. Davies, Edinburgh (1954); Polydore Vergil: D. Hay, *P. Vergil*, pp. 56, 86; Girolamo della Corte: M. Barbi, *Bull. della Soc. Dantesca*, no. 8 (1893), pp. 24–25. Cf. M. Bandello, *Novella* IV. viii.

[8] Venice, 2 vols., 1543–4, repr. 1547. Fauno translated Pius II's epitome

In this way Biondo may justly be said to have laid his imprint
on the writing of history in subsequent centuries: his digest of the
materials became the common property of the much more exact
scholars who followed him. Sigonius, Muratori in the *Annali
d'Italia*, Sismondi in the *Républiques italiennes* follow more or less
a path hacked out by their unassuming predecessor. They do so,
of course, from the sources themselves; but then so did Biondo,
and many of the authorities quoted for the events of the early
fifteenth century by Sismondi for instance are sixteenth-century
historians like Scipio Amirati, or even fifteenth-century writers
such as Poggio or Simonetta, who had used Biondo in their turn.
Here I am, of course, referring to the third decade covering
Biondo's own lifetime which has been unduly neglected as a
primary source.[1] There are even some nourishing morsels to be
found in the second decade where the author calls on family
memories, such as his grandfather's account of the effects of the
Black Death in 1348,[2] or the picture he was given by old men of
the wretched remnants of Louis of Anjou's army straggling home
across the Romagna in 1384, naked and unarmed.[3]

At the start of this paper the point was made that Biondo stood
at a moment when it was possible to choose between writing
history as a form of artistic literature and writing history without
such pretensions. I do not think Biondo made such a conscious
choice, nor do I think all contemporaries attributed as much
importance to it as we have been led to suppose. I trust it will
also be agreed that so far as Biondo himself is concerned he fits
ill into a rigid antithesis between rhetoric and learning: there
are moments when he is consciously rhetorical, more frequent
moments when he is careless of this and reflects the carelessness
of his sources, those writers of the Middle Ages whose epoch his
own work helped to define. Yet whether or not we can call the

of the first two decades, and himself epitomized as well as translated books
xxi–xxxi. (The work includes Italian versions of R. Volaterrano 'delle cose
d'Italia' and Sabellico 'dell' antichità' d'Aquileia'). For another sixteenth-
century translation of the first decade in a MS. at Forlì, see F. Cavichi, 'La
prima delle "Historiarum Decades" di F. Biondo volgarizzata da A. Numai',
Atti e memorie della R. deputazione di storia patria per le provincie di Romagna, ser.
iv, vol. viii (Bologna, 1918), 281–96.
    [1] For praise of Biondo's accuracy see P. Partner, *The Papal State under
Martin V*, 1958, p. 90, n. 4: 'not only the fullest, but the most reliable historian
of these events' (at Bologna in 1428).
    [2] *Decades*, p. 366.
    [3] Ibid., p. 385.

pedantic and ungracious researchers of the sixteenth and seventeenth centuries Biondo's 'school', there is no doubt that at that time a division developed between the antiquarian and the more popular writer of history. However cherished Biondo may have been by the former, he was out of favour with the latter, whose subjects were either nationalistic or confined to contemporary affairs. Yet his own theme in the *Decades* had a celebrated reincarnation. It was appropriate that, when scholarship and literary artistry came together again in the eighteenth century, one of the resulting masterpieces was another *Decline and Fall of the Roman Empire*.

Additional Note

The biographical element in the above account lacked the recent study by Riccardo Fubini in the Dizionario *Biografico Italiano*, vol. 10 (1968), with an admirable bibliography.

APPENDIX I

Dates of Composition and Publication of Flavio Biondo's Principal Writings

NOT included in this list are the letters, of which there are not many and of which a good account is given by Nogara (above, p. 37, n. 5). Two of these are in effect short treatises: Nogara, pp. cxlvi–cxlvii, 170–89. Biondo's first recorded scholarly work is a transcription of the *Brutus* (Cicero *de Oratore*), Nogara, p. xxxvi. I note manuscripts in British libraries.

1. 1435. *De uerbis Romanae locutionis*: a treatise on whether there had been two Latins, one literary and one popular. Ed. prin., Rome, ?1470 (with no. 3); reprinted by G. Mignini, *Propugnatore*, vol. 23 (1890); and by Nogara, pp. 115–30.

2. 1439 onwards (see above, pp. 40 ff.). *Historiarum ab inclinatione Romani imperii decades III, libri xxxi.*[1] Ed. prin., Venice, 1483; Venice, 1484 (with Pius II's epitome); Basle, 1531 (with nos. 3, 4, 6); Basle, 1559 (with nos. 3, 4, 5*d*, 6). Pius II's epitome, Rome, 1481; in *Opera Omnia*, Basle, 1551 and 1571; Helmstadt, 1700; L. Fauno's translation of the epitome, Venice, 1543–4; Venice, 1547.[2] Book xxxii printed in part in G. Williams, *Bekynton's Correspondence* (Rolls Series), ii. 327–38, and in full by Nogara, pp. 3–28.

3. 1444–6. *Roma instaurata.*[3] Three books on the topography of ancient Rome. Ed. prin., Rome ?1470 (with no. 1); Verona, 1481–2 (with nos. 4, 5*d*);[4] Venice, 1503 (with nos. 4, 5*d*); Venice, 1510 (with nos. 4, 5*d*); Turin, 1527 (with no. 4); Basle, 1531 (with nos. 2, 4, 6); Basle, 1559 (with nos. 2, 4, 5*d*, 6). L. Fauno's Italian translation (and of no. 4), Venice, 1543, 1548, 1558.

4. 1448–53. *Italia illustrata.*[5] A description of Italy, province by province. Ed. prin., Rome, 1474;[6] Verona, 1481–2 (with nos. 3, 5*d*); Venice, 1503 (with nos. 3, 5*d*); Venice 1510 (with nos. 3, 5*d*); Turin, 1527 (with no. 3); Basle, 1531 (with nos. 2, 3, 6); Basle, 1559 (with nos. 2, 3, 5*d*, 6).[7] L. Fauno's Italian translation (and of no. 3), Venice, 1543, 1548, 1558.

[1] Corpus Christi College, Cambridge, MS. 205 (see above, p. 42).

[2] See above, p. 61, n. 8.

[3] Brit. Mus., MSS. Harl. 4913, Add. 21956, Add. 17375 (incomplete; a coat of arms on f. 1 suggests that this manuscript belonged to a member of the Becchi-Nettoli family of Florence—I have to thank Mr. M. Maclagan for help in connexion with this).

[4] A variant noticed in M. Pellechet, *Catalogue général des incunables des bibliothèques publiques de France*, ii. 17.

[5] Brit. Mus., Sloane MS. 2456; Balliol College, Oxford, MS. 286.

[6] A variant noticed in Pellechet, ii. 16.

[7] A few extracts in G. B. Pio's miscellanea on Rome (P. Victor, P. Laetus, &c.), Bologna, 1520, sig. II i–kkiv.

5. 1452–4. Writings advocating a crusade:

    (*a*) *Oratio . . . coram imperatore Frederico et Alphonso Aragonum rege*: O. Lobeck, *Programm des Gymnasiums zum heiligen Kreuz*, Dresden, 1892, pp. xvii–xxii; Nogara, pp. 107–14.

    (*b*) *Ad Alphonsum Aragonensem . . . de expeditione in Turchos*: Nogara, pp. 31–51.

    (*c*) *Ad Petrum de Campo Fregoso . . . Genuae ducem*: Nogara, pp. 61–71.

    (*d*) *De gestis Venetorum* or *Consultatio an bellum uel pax cum Turcis magis expediat reipublicae Venetorum*.[1] Ed. prin. Verona, 1481–2 (with nos. 3, 4); Venice, 1503 (with nos. 3, 4); Venice, 1510 (with nos. 3, 4); Basle, 1559 (with nos. 2, 3, 4, 6); and in J. G. Graevius, *Thesaurus* (1722 ff.), V. i.

6. 1456–60. *Roma Triumphans*. Ten books on the religion, government, armies, and customs of ancient Rome. Ed. prin. Mantua ?1472; Brescia, 1482; Brescia, 1503; Venice, 1511; Basle, 1531 (with nos. 2, 3, 4); Paris, 1533; Basle, 1559 (with nos. 2, 3, 4, 5*d*). L. Fauno's Italian translation, Venice, 1544; Venice, 1549.

7. 1459–60. *Populi Veneti historiarum liber i*. An incomplete account, ending in the early sixth century: Nogara, pp. 77–89.

8. 1460. *Borsus, siue de militia et iurisprudentia*. A treatise dedicated to Borso d'Este: Nogara, pp. 130–44.

    [1] Bodleian Library, MS. Laud Misc. 718.

APPENDIX II

The Decades: Periods Covered by each Book

I. i. A.D. 412–23
  ii. to 476
  iii. to 536
  iv. to 538
  v. to 541
  vi. to 546
  vii. to 575
  viii. to 602
  ix. to 685
  x. to January 754

II. i [xi]. to 806
  ii [xii]. to 961
  iii [xiii]. to October 1097
  iv [xiv]. to 1123
  v [xv]. to 1177
  vi [xvi]. to 1215
  vii [xvii]. to 1240
  viii [xviii]. to 1291
  ix [xix]. to 1332
  x [xx]. to 1410

III. i [xxi]. to February 1424
  ii [xxii]. to January 1426
  iii [xxiii]. to September 1429
  iv [xxiv]. to autumn 1431
  v [xxv]. to May 1434
  vi [xxvi]. to August 1435
  vii [xxvii]. to December 1437
  viii [xxviii]. to March 1438
  ix [xxix]. to April 1439
  x [xxx]. to November 1439

IV. i [xxxi]. to autumn 1440
  ii [xxxii]. to October 1441.

HISTORY AND HISTORIANS IN FRANCE AND ENGLAND
DURING THE FIFTEENTH CENTURY[1]

IN THE TWO millennia which comprise our era the political connexions between France and England have usually been close and have often been intimate. Likewise cultural developments in each region have acted on one another so that there are centuries at a time when one is faced by a past which is Anglo-French rather than English or French, when one must study the history of one area largely through the writers of the other, and when the kind of historical writing being composed on both sides of the Channel is strikingly similar. These parallels and similarities are particularly notable in the thirteenth and fourteenth centuries and again in the seventeenth and eighteenth. The fifteenth century—although it was a time of intense mutual involvement, especially down to the fourteen-sixties—sees surprising differences in the historiography of the two countries. The following pages try briefly to establish what these differences were.

The remarkable similarity in the writing of history north and south of the Channel in the early and central Middle Ages goes even deeper than might have been expected as the result of the common ancestry of medieval historical writing in Orosius and Bede, in a liturgical preoccupation with chronology and the resulting Easter Tables. Such influences are admittedly basic, for they were in time to produce those *annales* which, bodied out into chronicles such as that of Sigebert of Gembloux, underlie all twelfth- and thirteenth-century historiography in western Europe. All of this gave a frame of reference and of periodization (or, in later terms, of absence of periodization), just as it gave a body of historical information which subsequent writers could if they wished elaborate, but from which they had to begin. For the striking thing about the medieval chronicler in the palmy days of the twelfth and thirteenth centuries is that for the

---

[1] Originally a paper read to the Franco-British Conference of Historians in Cambridge in September 1961. I gratefully incorporate a few points made in the subsequent discussion. An indebtedness of much longer standing, increased on this occasion, must be expressed to Mr. C. A. J. Armstrong.

most part he was writing contemporary history. When he dealt with epochs earlier than his own he was content to take over the hallowed scheme and trace the past from the Creation along lines familiar to him, from sources (if one can use the word) no less familiar, to which he merely added or subtracted in accordance with his ambitions and his knowledge. His creative activity came when he reached his own times. Matthew Paris, who conscientiously and critically rewrote the St. Albans' chronicle down to 1235, then went on to treat the period from 1235 to 1259 with a detail so great that his narrative for this quarter-century is as copious as that devoted to the previous two millennia. 'His primary object', says Dr. Richard Vaughan, 'was the recording of contemporary events.'[1] The essentially contemporary nature of the history composed by the medieval chronicler is, of course, not always so strikingly illustrated. But it holds good of most French writing as of most English. It is, for instance, to be seen in the chronicles composed at Saint-Denis, which were assembled bit by bit over the years, by men who witnessed the events they were recording. Thus what both the French and the English were accustomed to, by the mid-thirteenth century, were pictures of the past put together in two parts: a background, based on the old masters, and a foreground, painted from the life. It is worth insisting on this, for the nonsensical claim is sometimes advanced that the medieval chronicler wrote *sub specie aeternitatis*.

Besides sharing this aim of keeping earlier narratives up-to-date, French and English historians in the thirteenth century exhibit a further common trait: the encouragement of national mythology. This was perhaps most evident on the French side. Here, for example, is an early passage from the *Grandes Chroniques*:

Li commencemenz de ceste hystoire sera pris à la haute lignie des Troiens, dont ele est descendue par longue succession.
  Certaine chose est donques que li roi de France, par les quex li roiaumes est glorieus et renommez, descendirent de la noble lignie de Troie. Glorieus furent en victoires, noble en renommée, en la foi crestienne fervent et devot. Et ja soit ce que cele nacion soit fort et fiere et cruel contre ses anemis, selonc ce que li nons le senefie, si est ele misericors et debonaire vers ses sougez et vers ceus que ele souzmet par bataille.[2]

The Trojan myth had been long a-growing. By the thirteenth century it was fully developed in England as in France and in both countries it was associated with the dynasty. That is shown clearly enough in the passage just quoted from the *Grandes Chroniques*, which, it has been plausibly argued, were put together in this form at the request of Louis IX himself.[3] As for England, we should recall the way Edward I turned to the chronicles during his preparation of the Scottish claim.

[1] R. Vaughan, *Matthew Paris* (Cambridge, 1958), p. 125.
[2] *Les Grandes Chroniques de France*, ed. J. Viard (Soc. de l'hist. de France, 1920–53), i. 4.
[3] J. Viard, introduction, *ibid.*, i, pp. xix–xxiv.

In one respect France was strikingly ahead of England by 1300: she had a prose vernacular chronicle, the self-same *Grandes Chroniques*. No such virtuosity was to be found on this side of the Channel, despite the previous existence of the Anglo-Saxon Chronicles. Perhaps because there were two vernaculars of an unrelated kind—Anglo-Norman and English—literary development, outside the serious Latin scholarship of the monk and clerk, was retarded. We have Langtoft and, almost at the turn of the century, we have the start of the *Brut of England*; but they are both in Anglo-Norman, and when Langtoft was translated, by Robert Manning, he was translated not into prose but into English verse. The matter of Troy, the implied and explicit support of a dynastic view of the past, these are all here: but their appeal is to the clergy and the upper strata in society.

This rapid backward glance at historical writing in England and France before the Hundred Years War must now lead on to a somewhat fuller picture of fourteenth-century developments. These were in some ways to bring the historians of the two countries together, in other ways to intensify differences.

There was in all conscience plenty of reason for similarity if only because of common language and political pressures. French or Anglo-Norman was demonstrably still a living vernacular in England in the fourteenth century, used by all literate groups and not only by the nobles and gentry.[1] It was encouraged by mutual involvement in war and diplomacy, the presence of numerous French and Breton exiles in England, the English soldiers in France, and the merchants following the flag here and there and notably in the one English acquisition of Edward III, the town of Calais. In the fluctuating fortunes of war many a Frenchman 'became English' (to use contemporary phraseology) and many an English subject in Gascony 'became French'. Moreover the war provided a dominant theme and its course could not but form the staple of any narrative of either kingdom. Beyond that the monarchs of the two countries positively competed with each other in striking the social attitudes we call 'chivalrous': the Garter of 1348 is followed by the Étoile of 1351, both of them, as M. Renouard has shown, reflecting the politics of dynasty and nation.[2] Vows and devices and perilous adventures were indulged in not only by young gentlemen but also by their seniors; the tournament became decorative and, despite its profit and loss side, war was treated by the gentry as a kind of joust.

There are, of course, anticipations of all this in fact and in literature. Joinville had turned Louis IX into a sort of Paladin, even if as an old man he viewed such royal escapades overseas as bad for government at home;

[1] Helen Suggett, 'The use of French in England in the later middle ages', *Trans. Roy. Hist. Soc.*, 4th ser., xxviii (1946), 61–83.
[2] Yves Renouard, 'L'ordre de la Jarretière et l'ordre de l'Etoile', *Moyen âge*, lv (1949), 281–300.

if Edward I did not get married in 1299 in Arthurian style, he certainly
in 1306 held the 'feast of the Swans' and 'informed the proceedings of
chivalry with political significance'.[1] The literary encouragement for
such behaviour was abundant and grew all the more influential as men of
noble and knightly rank began to read for themselves in prose instead of
listening to the rhymes of professional bards and reciters. By the fourteenth
century the harvest of romance, sown so richly in the twelfth, was gathered
in. In no literary field was this more evident than in historiography.
England produced the works of Sir Thomas Gray of Heton and the
Chandos herald. The first of these, the *Scalacronica*, was composed in
1355; the second, the *Life of the Black Prince*, about 1386. The first is
in Anglo-Norman and Chandos herald wrote in French verse. In France
there is another work primarily English in content: the *Chronique de
Jean le Bel*, written between 1357 and 1361. Ten years later the deeds of
Bertrand du Guesclin were commemorated by Cuvelier, in what has been
described as the last of the *chansons de geste*.

At about this time, the early thirteen-seventies, was published the first
version of the most remarkable of the chivalrous historical works of the
fourteenth century, the chronicle of Jean Froissart. The very popularity
of this has deprived us of a complete scholarly edition in our own day, so
complex are the textual problems of the various recensions. His narrative
covered, it will be remembered, the European scene from about 1326 to
the end of the century and reflected, more than any other contemporary
work, the mutual involvement of England and France:

Afin que les grans merveilles et li biau fait d'armes, qui sont avenu par les grans
guerres de France et d'Engleterre et des royaumes voisins, dont li roy et leurs
consaulz sont cause, soient notablement registré et ou tamps present et à venir
veu et cogneu, je me voel ensonniier de l'ordonner et mettre en prose selonch
le vraie information que j'ay eu des vaillans hommes, chevaliers et escuiers, qui
les ont aidiés à acroistre, et ossi de aucuns rois d'armes et leurs mareschaus,
qui par droit sont et doient estre just inquisiteur et raporteur de tels besongnes.[2]

Written in prose (it is significant that the author had earlier composed a
metrical chronicle), Froissart's great work not only charmed his contemporaries by its masterly narrative style, but established itself as a
repository of authenticated deeds of *noblesse*—a kind of *Who's Who* or
Almanach de Gotha—so that there was positive anxiety on the part of
gentlemen to secure the immortality of a reference in his pages.

Yet, despite the Anglo-French wars and the Anglo-French truces and
treaties, despite the shared chivalry and even despite Froissart, the historiography of England and France steadily drew apart during the fourteenth
century. Monastic history was written in both countries but activity at
St. Albans, which had rivalled Saint-Denis in the thirteenth century as a

[1] F. M. Powicke, *The Thirteenth Century*, pp. 514-5 and nn.
[2] J. Froissart, *Chroniques*, i, ed. S. Luce (Soc. de l'hist. de France, Paris, 1869),
p. 1.

centre of great chronicles, dwindled almost to vanishing point. The St. Albans' chronicle was revived by Thomas Walsingham in the thirteen-seventies but the resulting works are thin indeed compared with the steady stream of writings at Saint-Denis which culminated in the large scale work of the anonymous monk who covered the years for 1380 to 1420. The standard historical work of fourteenth-century England was produced by the Chester Benedictine, Ranulph Higden. His *Polychronicon*, written in mid-century and continued by other hands, became in Trevisa's English translation of 1387 the nearest English equivalent to the *Grandes Chroniques*. A work destined to be hardly less influential was the *Brut of England*, which, in its original French form, goes back to the early fourteenth century,[1] and which also was put into English at the start of Richard II's reign.

The narrative sources for the two countries in the fourteenth century are, of course, not restricted to the books just mentioned: very many other works will be found listed in the reference books and manuals. But it is important to stress the absence in England of an official historio-graphical centre such as was provided for France at Saint-Denis. This was to lead to important consequences in the next hundred years, and so was the emergence in England of the town chronicle.

In turning now to the fifteenth century we must first appreciate the sharp decline in the writing of Anglo-Norman. Although the French language was still a viable vernacular in fourteenth-century England, it was, despite politics, declining in importance. There are plausible tales in Froissart of some of the linguistic difficulties on the field of battle.[2] Under Henry IV and Henry V the decline was rapid; it seems fair to say that by the middle of the century it was rare to use Anglo-Norman save on formal occasions. Doubtless the war with France, which under Henry V and his brother had a bitterness it had lacked under Edward III, encouraged this change: the language of the 'natural enemy' must have incurred some of the odium attracted by all alien things in those xenophobic days. Many a travelled Englishman must have also found it hard not to laugh, with Chaucer, at French as spoken at Stratford atte Bowe and to feel the folly of mastering Anglo-Norman, which was for all practical purposes now not as good as English.

Since most Englishmen who could read now stopped bothering with French, this at once made it unlikely that Froissart would be influential in England, even if his treatment of the last years of Richard II had not been unsympathetic to the new régime. It is nevertheless astonishing how

[1] See J. Taylor, *Eng. Hist. Rev.*, lxxii (1957), 423–37.
[2] Froissart, ix. 258–9. These difficulties become much greater in the fifteenth century: Rymer, ix. 656–9; T. Walsingham, *Historia brevis* (1574), pp. 412–13, quoted by L. Douët-d'Arcq in his edition of E. de Monstrelet, *La Chronique* (6 vols., Soc. de l'hist. de France, 1857–62), i. 81; *Letters and Papers illustrative of the Wars of the English in France* (Rolls Ser., 1861–4), ii. 676–7.

uninfluential he was, despite the importance his chronicle had for Englishmen and for their history and the existence of a fair number of manuscripts
on this side of the Channel. As for a translation, we have to wait until the
version of Lord Berners, printed by Pynson from 1523 to 1525, and reprinted in 1545. There is then silence until 1812.[1] It is true that through
Polydore Vergil and the early Tudor chronicles portions of Froissart's
narrative became imbedded in historical tradition even before Berners'
version came out. But the absence of any chivalrous strain in English
historians is striking. Not one English writer before Berners can be said to
have drawn inspiration from the most remarkable writer of French historical
prose in the fourteenth century, save perhaps the so-called 'heralds' who
have left accounts of ceremonies at Yorkist and early Tudor courts.[2]

It was very different in France. Apart from a number of smaller works
such as *Le livre des faits du maréchal Boucicaut* and *La chronique du bon duc
Loys de Bourbon*, a great series of chronicles stemming from Froissart
spans the fifteenth century: Enguerrand de Monstrelet, Georges Chastellain, Olivier de la Marche. Whatever their faults, whatever their novelties,
these writers were as historians direct descendants of Froissart. That some
French critics have dismissed them as Burgundians is a matter referred
to below.

This, then, is the first and most striking difference between English and
French historiography in the fifteenth century: chivalrous history is found
flourishing across the Channel; in England it is not found at all. But there
are other differences hardly less pronounced: the continued vitality of
French official and semi-official historians; the emergence in France of
the memorialist; the flowering in England of the London town chronicle;
and the influence in both countries of the Italian Renaissance.

The whole subject of the official element in French history seems
mysterious and our ignorance of its origins is regrettable. In the fifteenth
century it was less vital than it had been, but the main point is that it was
far from finished; the French king still paid a monk of Saint-Denis as
'chroniqueur de France'; and the Crown intermittently derived propaganda support from other clerks and scholars in its service. As far as the
fourteenth and fifteenth centuries are concerned we must accept Monsieur
Bossuat's argument that works by officially sponsored or employed writers
should be related to the political aims of the French crown: 'Le chroniqueur
est bien un agent d'information, mais il doit renseigner le public dans un
sens déterminé et il ne doit conserver d'objectivité que la dose suffisante
pour donner à ses écrits un minimum de vraisemblance.'[3] Hence the

[1] J. Froissart, *Chronicles of England*, transl. Lord Berners (2 vols., London,
1812). An epitome translated from Sleidan was published in 1608 and again in
1611, *S.T.C.*, 2nd ed., nos. 11396-11400.
[2] C. L. Kingsford, *English Historical Literature in the Fifteenth Century* (Oxford,
1913), pp. 178-9. Cf. also John Leland, *Collectanea*, ed. T. Hearne (2nd edn.,
6 vols., 1770), iv. 185-300, v. 352-81.
[3] André Bossuat, 'Jean Castel, chroniqueur de France', *Moyen âge*, lxiv (1958),
300.

increasing importance of writing in French. The Religieux de Saint Denis, whose impressive Latin chronicle ends at 1420 and whose identity has recently been the subject of the conjectures of Monsieur Charles Samaran,[1] was apparently succeeded by Jean Chartier. Jean Chartier's *French* chronicle, covering the reign of Charles VII, is well known.[2] His *Latin* chronicle, written earlier and running from 1422 to 1450, is a continuation of the work of the Religieux.[3] Jean Chartier died in February 1464 and it is not apparently till then, shortly after the accession of Louis XI, when many changes occur, that a break came in the Sandionysian tradition. From 1463 to 1476 the 'chroniqueur de France' was Jean Castel, monk of Saint Martin des Champs and later abbot of Saint Maur des Fossés, a grandson of Christine de Pisan.[4] It has recently been argued[5] that he was more active as a chronicler than used to be supposed, and this perhaps restored royal faith in monastic writers. At all events the Saint-Denis connexion was revived at Castel's death. The chronicles he had been using were returned to the *trésor* at Saint-Denis and in 1482 we have a fugitive glimpse of a monk of that house apparently resuming the task of chronicler; his name was Mathieu Levrien.[6] The future, however, was not to lie with monks. Already in the life-time of Jean Castel there occurs the appointment of Guillaume Danicot as *historian*. Danicot was, it is true, a Benedictine, but a *gyrovagus* who finally became in 1472 a papal penitentiary. He described his task as that of a 'historian, to gather and search for the histories and legends dealing with events in this kingdom', that is, not as 'chroniqueur' to add to a continuous pre-existing narrative. He died in 1472 or 1473 with nothing accomplished, it seems, save a few minor translations with no bearing on his job as an official historiographer.[7] It was following on his death and that of Jean Castel a little later that Robert Gaguin wrote his letter to the royal chancellor, Pierre Doriole,[8] suggesting that he might be nominated. But with Gaguin we come to the problem of Renaissance influence to be discussed in a moment.

[1] 'Etudes sandionysiennes', B[*ibliothèque de l'*]E[*cole des*] C[*hartes*], ciii (1943), 40–8.

[2] J. Chartier, *Chronique de Charles VII*, ed. Vallet de Viriville (3 vols., Paris, 1858).

[3] J. Chartier, *La Chronique latine inédite*, ed. C. Samaran (Paris, 1928).

[4] C. Samaran in *Mélanges . . . offerts à Antoine Thomas* (Paris, 1927), pp. 395–404.

[5] Bossuat, 'Castel', *ubi supra*, pp. 285–304, 499–538. Prints Vat. Cod. Reginensis Lat. 499, fos. 1–6.

[6] C. Samaran, 'Un ouvrage de Guillaume Danicot, historiographe de Louis XI', *Mélanges d'archéologie et d'histoire de l'école française de Rome*, xlv (1928), 8; Samaran, 'Mathieu Levrien, chroniqueur de Saint-Denis', *B.E.C.*, xcix (1938), 125–31.

[7] J. Lesellier, *Mélanges . . . de l'école fr. de Rome*, xliii (1926), 1–42; Samaran, *ibid.*, xlv (1928), 8–20; and Samaran, *B.E.C.*, xcix (1938), 125–31.

[8] R. Gaguin, *Epistole et Orationes*, ed. L. Thuasne (Paris, 1903), i. 252–5 and intro. p. 38.

It is right to consider the memorialist in close association with the official historian, for it was because of his proximity to a prince that such a writer gained both his knowledge of the facts and his concern with central political issues. These are essential ingredients in the new historical awareness of such commentators and it is because of his combination of official knowledge and urgent political awareness that one must place Thomas Basin among the earliest members of this group. His career was, in a sense, the opposite of that of his successor Commynes, for Basin, having served the French crown, in the end took refuge with Burgundy. Certainly his aim (complicated, perhaps, rather than clarified by Italian influences) was much the same as Commynes's. Basin explained his purpose as '. . . duorum Francorum regum . . . res gestas, quas magna ex parte vel ipsi vidimus vel talibus consecuti sumus auctoribus, de quorum fide minime foret ambigendum, litteris, ad posterum utilitatem et cautelam, digerere et mandare'.[1] And Commynes's avowed intention was '. . . escrire et mettres par memoire ce que j'ay sceu et cogneu des faictz du roy Loys unziesme . . .'[2] Originality lies, of course, not in the announcement of a programme but in its performance. Both writers were remarkably successful. Basin is politically conscious and so is Commynes. Both are intent on drawing on experience for general rules of public behaviour (though this is much more the case with Commynes, perhaps because he is in the last resort a more sentimental and conventional personality than Basin); both are concerned with government in a new and imaginative way, totally foreign to earlier historians.[3] There are indeed massive differences, and not merely due to Basin's choice of Latin, Commynes's of French. Basin is a spokesman for the forces in France which resented and resisted the slowly growing machinery of royal centralization. As can now be seen, he was swimming vainly against the tide of history; he believed in a France where the magnates, led by the peers of France, were the natural sources not merely of counsel but of power, above all of military power, and he was prepared to carry his principles into practice by supporting the campaigns of the League of the Commonweal. Commynes, while not unaware of the advantages of the old order, or rather perhaps while not ignoring the very real dangers of the new order, was, in the last resort, convinced that only a strong king

---

[1] T. Basin, *Hist. de Charles VII*, ed. C. Samaran (Paris, 1933–44), i. 4.

[2] P. de Commynes, *Mémoires*, ed. J. Calmette (Paris, 1924–5), i. 1.

[3] There is no need to cite examples from Commynes. As for Basin v. *Hist. de Charles VII*, i. 192–7 (reflections on the Peace of Arras), i. 292–301 (truce of 1444 and especially pp. 298–9, the marriage of Margaret of Anjou to Henry VI), ii. 24–47 (the famous reflections on Charles VII's military reforms), ii. 222–3 (a king does not intervene between a town and its overlord), ii. 278–311 (concluding reflections). The impressive evidence of *Hist. Louis XI*, as of the *Apologia*, might also be advanced, but in view of the partisanship they display I leave them for separate discussion: they are printed by J. Quicherat, *Hist. des règnes de Charles VII et de Louis XI* (4 vols., Soc. de l'hist. de France, Paris, 1855–9), ii, iii; and now by Samaran, 3 vols. (1963-72), and *Apologia* (1974).

could save France from internecine strife; only by having a sovereign above the battle could one hope for domestic peace.[1] Basin is a politician; Commynes is a *politique*.

From the point of view of this short survey the works of these men raise two questions: first, what were the differences between them and the other French chroniclers of the fifteenth century ? and second, why did contemporary England,fail to produce such historians ?

As far as the first matter is concerned, one may be tempted to ascribe the differences between Basin and Commynes on the one hand and on the other hand writers like Monstrelet and Chastellain, to the existence of the so-called 'Burgundian School', with its concentration on old-fashioned panoply and unscrupulous propaganda. Yet it needs a very strong imagina-tion to discern a 'Burgundian School'. Its existence seems to be due largely to Auguste Molinier. Molinier, without whose splendid volumes on *Les sources de l'histoire de France* no one would be able to find a way through the labyrinth of French historiography, was a man of 1900. That is, he wrote in the dark days when Alsace and Lorraine lay in the hands of the new 'natural enemy' and, to my mind, this colours his whole attitude to the nature of the Burgundian contribution to French and indeed to European history. He introduces his discussion of 'Les écrivains de l'école bourguignonne' thus:

. . . ils ont non seulement raconté les annales de leur temps, mais, bien plus, ils ont présenté les faits sous un certain jour et ont cherché à imposer leurs opinions à leurs lecteurs. En protégeant les littérateurs de leur temps, les princes de Bourgogne satisfaisaient leurs goûts personnels et obéissaient à une haute pensée politique; il existait dès cette époque une opinion publique. Jean-sans-Peur, Philippe le Bon et plus tard les premiers Bourgogne-Habsbourg ont su s'adresser à cette opinion, en appeler au jugement plus ou moins clairvoyant de la foule. . .. C'est peut-être la première fois qu'on trouve en France ce qu'on appelle aujourd'hui une campagne de presse; les résultats en furent extraordinaires; il subsista des partisans des ducs de Bourgogne longtemps après le traité d'Arras, et ce vieux levain d'opposition ne disparut entièrement que sous Louis XI.[2]

The detailed analysis is in keeping with this. Molinier groups them all under 'chroniques étrangères' (iv. 186). Monstrelet is 'Bourguignon dans l'âme, et d'autant plus dangereux qu'il est un Bourguignon honteux' (iv. 193); Wavrin is 'dévoué à la cause bourguignonne' (iv. 196); Chastellain 'est bourguignon' but (to his credit) 'c'est presque inconsciemment' (iv. 199); Olivier de la Marche was 'trop dévoué à la maison de Bourgogne pour juger équitablement les hommes et les choses' (iv. 202).

The dukes of Burgundy were lavish patrons and their protégés naturally

---

[1] On Commynes's reluctant support of a powerful monarchy cf. W. J. Bouwsma, 'The politics of Commynes', *Jour. Mod. Hist.*, xxiii (1951), 315–28.

[2] A. Molinier, *Les sources de l'histoire de France des origines aux guerres d'Italie* (6 vols., Paris, 1901–6), v, Introduction, pp. cxliv–cxlv.

saw events from a Burgundian angle; this may even have been part of ducal policy, like the assiduous care devoted to the ducal archives.[1] And in so far as these writers were the disciples and advocates of a Burgundian idea it did, of course, commit them to what M. Bonenfant has rightly called 'un archaïsme parfait'[2]; but their archaic nature stems from a genuine inability to detach themselves from older attitudes to both politics and the writing of history more than from the support they may have given to what, in the end, was to be a lost cause. As Molinier himself has pointed out, a great many of the writers of the earlier fifteenth century were adherents of Burgundy:

Si on voulait réunir tous les chroniqueurs d'âme bourguignonne, il faudrait joindre aux grands écrivains indiqués ici une foule d'autres, moins connus sans doute, mais presque aussi importants, les uns de Paris, les autres de Rouen; tel le prêtre parisien auteur du *Journal*, le normand Pierre Cochon, l'anonyme auquel on doit la chronique dite des Cordeliers, ou encore le religieux de Saint-Denis, biographe de Charles VI.[3]

There were, after all, good political grounds for such sentiments.

Among the so-called 'Burgundian School', only Chastellain rises above the general level—both as a prose writer and as a recorder of the events of his own day. It is no accident that Molinier found it difficult to fit him in as a 'Burgundian', for he explicitly denies his membership of the 'School': 'Doncques qui Anglois ne suis, mais François, qui Espagnol, ne Ytalien ne suis, mais François, de deux François, l'un roy, l'autre duc.'[4] But Chastellain lacks the ability to extract a political message from his experience and his observation, and in his chronicle we find here and there examples of a purely chivalrous historiography[5] which would be grotesque in Basin or Commynes. He was, in a word, incapable of looking at events as a statesman.

If, as it appears, fifteenth-century French writers may not be rigidly divided into royalists and Burgundians, it must nevertheless be admitted that the schism in French politics did stimulate reflective temperaments and develop the intellectual maturity of Basin and Commynes. They were original at any rate largely because they were faced with a novel situation, which invited them to a fresh appraisal of the political situation. Likewise, the war with England encouraged the composition of French chronicles under royal auspices, designed to fortify the morale of the nation. But a not dissimilar situation existed in England. There too there was a schism

[1] Cf. J. Richard, 'Les archives et les archivistes des ducs de Bourgogne', *B.E.C.*, cv (1944), 123–69.
[2] P. Bonenfant, *Philippe Le Bon* (Bruxelles, 1955), p. 119.
[3] Molinier, iv. 187.
[4] G. Chastellain, *Oeuvres*, ed. Kervyn de Lettenhove (1863–6), iv. 21; cf. J. Huizinga, 'L'état bourguignon', *Moyen âge*, 3e sér., i (1930), 171–93; ii (1931), 11–35, 83–96.
[5] E.g. Book iv, chaps. lxxxix and xcii.

in the monarchy and there too there was a war with France. Why was there no English Commynes and why was the official historian in England practically unknown?

One can reply, of course, to the first question briefly by saying that there is no French Dante and no Italian Shakespeare or Molière: genius has its own times and places. The tensions of fifteenth-century France were, however, much greater than those in England. The civil war in England was a war between rival dynasties and their adherents—not between the whole principle of monarchy and the whole notion of the provincial power of territorial magnates. There is thus no competition between Lancastrian, Yorkist and Tudor historians, for all are supporters of the Crown. No English duke sought to gain permanent power outside England (in Scotland, for instance, or France) so that he could preserve his rights and secure his influence inside the kingdom: the rivals wanted the crown, their adherents wanted the spoils of royal administration. In France, which is not an island, both the monarchy and its opponents were more powerful. What English equivalent is there of the financial machinery of Charles VII? We can scarcely compare 'the duke of Lancastre, that warred the Kynge off Spayne'[1] or Gloucester in Hainault with great feudatories like Orleans at the beginning of the century or Brittany at the end—let alone Burgundy.

But the English scene nevertheless boasts one figure who is nearer to Commynes than to any other of his contemporaries: Sir John Fortescue. His career, with its sharp change of allegiance in 1471 after the fall of the Lancastrians, is faintly like Basin's and, like Basin, he turned to literature because he was more or less excluded from active politics; he was in turn a councillor to Henry VI and then to Edward IV—as Commynes served Charles the Bold and Louis XI; and if he wrote no history, he was more ready than the rest of his English contemporaries to digest his experience for the benefit of government and posterity. His two main works are wrapped up in Aristotelian diction but this must not mislead us, for the result is not the conventional *de regimine principum* but an original contribution to political philosophy and one, it has recently been argued,[2] which is anything but 'medieval' in the traditional or McIlwain sense. Fortescue deserves to be remembered here for his extraordinarily shrewd and apt use of contemporary history to point his argument, his preoccupation with the French scene and analysis of French problems and his concern to secure a maximum of authority and a maximum of liberty—in real, not theoretical terms. Again and again he speaks with the voice of Commynes and often voices the same sentiments.

As for the absence of an official historiography in fifteenth-century England, this too must not be pressed too far. As Professor Galbraith has

[1]Sir J. Fortescue, *The Governance of England*, ed. C. Plummer (Oxford, 1885), p. 130.
[2]R. W. K. Hinton, 'English constitutional theories from Sir John Fortescue to Sir John Eliot', *Eng. Hist. Rev.*, lxxv (1960), 410–25.

shown, Thomas Walsingham is hard at work at St. Albans from the thirteen-seventies down to 1420,[1] and his last work is the *Ypodigma Neustriae*, which, if it is in fact an abbreviated history of England, is conceived as an Anglo-Norman story and dedicated to Henry V as conqueror of Normandy. Hardyng's rhymed chronicle and his Scottish forgeries were all highly tendentious. The English versions of the *Polychronicon* and of the *Brut* paint a picture of English antiquity as fanciful as anything in the *Grandes Chroniques*. But all of this (and more[2]) was churned out with little or no royal encouragement and this does contrast sharply with what happened in France.

In this brief review of fifteenth-century historiography in the two countries pride of place has hitherto been given to France. We have seen that the official history at Saint-Denis was still active in the early fifteenth century; and we have seen how the chivalrous tradition of Froissart merged into the elaborate chronicles of Monstrelet and his successors, while a new type of memorialist appears, at first in rudimentary form with Basin and then in completer form with Commynes. In all these genres England had little of significance to offer. It is now time to turn to a type of history in which England had the advantage, the town chronicle. This new kind of historiography was, of course, far from being peculiar to England. From the twelfth century in Italy, from the late thirteenth in Germany, the annals of towns are put together by men of bourgeois outlook and interest—bourgeois even when they are technically clerks. In their most rudimentary form such annals consist of lists of annually elected magistrates and officials. To such entries are gradually added brief observations of a more general kind. In fact the birth of this civic history has striking resemblances to the birth of the monastic chronicle in the annotated Easter Tables.

Such a chronicle appears in London in the thirteenth century in Latin; a second London chronicle in Latin follows in the early fourteenth century; these two are the only surviving early examples of London annals but others are known to have existed for this period.[3] In the fourteenth century we also find chronicles for London written in French. With the early fifteenth century, however, begins the series of London chronicles written in English, which were to have such a remarkable popular appeal that it has been reckoned that about forty fifteenth-century London chronicles have survived, representatives doubtless of an even larger number. Moreover, the enormously popular *Brut* was, for the period of Richard II onwards, a city chronicle. A version of this was published by Caxton in 1480. These town chronicles lead on to Robert Fabyan's large work, printed in 1516; he is presumably the author of the *Great Chronicle*

---

[1]V. H. Galbraith, *The St. Albans Chronicle 1406–1420* (Oxford, 1937). After Walsingham the St. Albans writers are unimportant and concerned with local matters. See Kingsford, pp. 150–4 for Amundesham and Whethamstede.

[2]Pseudo-Elmham, Capgrave.

[3]Kingsford, p. 71 and n. 4.

which was not published till 1938.[1] With Fabyan we enter the sixteenth century, when the town chronicle tradition began to assume new forms.

C. L. Kingsford, to whom most of our knowledge of town chronicles is due, considered the London annals as the 'primary Chronicle source of the period'[2] and he devoted many years to discriminating between the 'dozen more or less distinct recensions', into which he divided them. Into this complicated matter there is no need to enter here. It is sufficient to note that the chronicles, more or less full, more or less up to date, were clearly a regular item in the houses of well-to-do citizens and gentlemen and were equally clearly popular items in the stock of the scrivener and bookseller. The Londoner liked reading about his town; he accepted gladly a background of history usually based on the *Brut*; but he was mainly interested in the events of his own day and in those of the immediately preceding generation. Needless to say, the resulting narratives display the voluntary chauvinism of other English fifteenth-century writings. Nor was this historical interest entirely confined to London. Civic records are given greater prominence and permanence in many places from the later fourteenth century and such municipal activity could border on the chronicle as in the *Diary of the Corporation of Reading*, begun in 1431.[3] The most impressive, and the earliest, of the genuine town chronicles is Robert Ricart's *Maire's Calendar* of Bristol. Ricart was town clerk from 1479 to 1503 and wrote—apparently without reliance on the London chronicles—a series of annals which are relatively full from 1447 to 1497.[4] Such local histories multiply in the sixteenth and seventeenth centuries until they merge with the antiquarianism of a later age.

When, however, France is looked at, what is striking is the absence of such works. Molinier records civic chronicles in three places only: Béziers (the work of the *escudier* Mascaro); Montpellier (*Le petit Thalamus*); and Bordeaux ('La chronique des coutumes de Bordeaux').[5] On examination, however, the Bordeaux record ceases to count: it is a miscellaneous series of jottings which should properly be described as a commonplace book or *livre de raison*.[6] Mascaro's chronicle, however, is very definitely a civic chronicle. From 1336 to 1390 are recorded regularly the names of the consuls and other officials of Béziers, and brief notes on regional and general history.[7] The *Petit Thalamus* of Montpellier is likewise a true

---

[1] *The Great Chronicle of London*, ed. A. H. Thomas and I. D. Thornley (1938).
[2] Kingsford, p. 70.
[3] R. Flenley, *Six Town Chronicles* (Oxford, 1911), p. 12.
[4] Flenley, p. 29; Kingsford, p. 111.
[5] Molinier, v, § 189 (p. cxxxii); iv. 34, 37, 38 (nos. 3145–6, 3159, 3161).
[6] See Germain Lefèvre-Pontalis, 'Petite chronique de Guyenne jusqu'à l'an 1442', *B.E.C.*, xlvii (1886), 53–79. The title *livre de raison* is given here for want of a better term; it seems to be used in this sense, as well as in its more precise meaning of a book of family accounts and records.
[7] Published by C. Barbier, 'Le Libre de Memorias de Jaeme Mascaro', *Revue des langues romanes*, xxxiv (1890), 36–100, 515–64.

town chronicle, listing the consuls and inserting notes of other events.[1] We thus have only two French town chronicles and it is of some significance that they both come from the Midi; one is tempted to associate them with Italy, rather than with France.

Above all it is odd that there is no chronicle tradition in Paris. We know now that the size of Paris was some 80,000 souls, nearly twice as big as London.[2] Kingsford was inclined to attribute the flourishing historiography of London in the early fifteenth century to the revolution of 1399[3]; certainly that event and the victories of Henry V in France, which bulk large in the chronicles where contemporary ballads are imbedded in the texts, were enough to start men scribbling and demanding a history book from the stationer. But Paris saw upheavals no less catastrophic: a darkening feud between Burgundy and Orleans, an English intervention in French civil disturbances and Paris the object of all parties down to 1435. Moreover Paris produced, and London did not, both statesmen and demagogues of real significance: there are no Londoners like Étienne Marcel or Simonnet Caboche.

Bourgeois writers there were in Paris, and not least the author, a clerk, who conceals his anonymity under just that title.[4] But the *Journal d'un bourgeois* differs profoundly from the civic chronicles in London. In its way it is even more remarkable than they are for it is a diary, written by the author for himself alone, not, like the civic annalists' works, a matter of public property. Nor does the Bourgeois concern himself with the magistracy; only the recurrent pageantry of the ecclesiastical year gives a pattern to his writing. Like the city chroniclers in London, his pen follows popular emotion: he begins as a supporter of the Burgundians and gives his applause to the English; he ends by hating them and acclaiming the treaty of Arras and the return of Charles VII; just as the Londoners veer from Lancaster to York. But that, and his concern with bread and butter matters, 'the dere yere, and the great frost', end the similarity. One is left to speculate on the reasons for the absence of a specifically Paris town chronicle. Was it because the municipal officers were of less account there ? Was it because the royal *prévot* at the Châtelet, reflecting the attitudes and the power of central government, had reduced the importance of the *prévot des marchands* and the town authorities ? Was it because the politics of the university and the clergy bulked larger than the politics of the genuinely mercantile groups ? One further contrast between London and Paris was obviously to influence historical writing in the two cities: even after Paris had again come into royal hands in 1435, the king seldom resided in the capital. Fifteenth-century Parisians seem to

[1] At least the passage (1204–1253) printed in C. de Vic and J. J. Vaissete, *Histoire de Languedoc* (new edn., Toulouse, 1872–1904), viii, cols. 212–4.
[2] P. Dollinger, *Rev. historique*, ccxvi (1956), 35–44.
[3] *Chronicles of London*, ed. C. L. Kingsford (1905), intro. p. viii.
[4] *Journal d'un bourgeois de Paris*, ed. A. Tuetey (Soc. de l'hist. de Paris, Paris, 1881); trans. Janet Shirley, Oxford 1968.

have been content to read their history in the *Grandes Chroniques*, although they were proud enough of their city, as can be seen from the testimonies gathered together by Le Roux de Lincy and Tisserand, in the lavish volume misleadingly entitled *Paris et ses historiens aux XIVe et XVe siècles*.[1] *Elogia* such as these are, of course, common at this time, not least in Italy.

The final development to which attention should be drawn is the influence in both countries of the Italian Renaissance. Thanks to much recent work, not least by Roberto Weiss and Franco Simone, we know far more than before of the contacts between England and France and Italy. These were much richer and more continuous than used to be supposed and some writers, including probably the two scholars just mentioned, would be inclined to reverse the traditional picture and make the northern Renaissance date from the fifteenth century. My own view is the opposite of this. Granted the extraordinarily frequent and sustained connexions maintained especially between Italy and France from the fourteenth century onwards, it seems astonishing that so little of the new Italian values had taken root in France before 1500. Indeed in the field of historiography one may doubt whether there is anything of substance to be found in either England or France.

England had certainly an early encouragement to rewrite her history in the new Italian manner. Tito Livio Frulovisi was employed by Humphrey duke of Gloucester to write the biography of his brother Henry V; and Professor Weiss has announced the discovery of a further work by the same hand, a metrical celebration of Humphrey's own activities in 1435 and 1436.[2] On top of that, Flavio Biondo sent a copy of part of his *Historia ab inclinatione Romani Imperii* to the royal secretary Beckington, a splendid volume which is now in Cambridge in the library of Corpus Christi College.[3] Other men displayed some sympathy: there are a few English laymen, besides Humphrey, who were interested in the novelties of Italy; and some clerks came back with humanist manuscripts. But there is little to show for all this. Frulovisi's life was copied and adapted into an English version and so was another similar work by the 'pseudo-Elmham'; they were used in the sixteenth century and thus have a certain influence. But they do not change the current of English historiography.

The picture is not very different in France. Chastellain's rhetorical style is based, no doubt, on Roman models—but on models familiar enough in earlier centuries, and the form of his work is not affected. Basin, who had lived in 1438 and 1439 in the Florence of the Renaissance (though he surely thought of it as the Florence of Eugenius IV and the Council), undoubtedly, in both form and language, reflects something of the new

[1] A. J. V. Le Roux de Lincy and L. M. Tisserand, *Paris et ses historiens aux XIVe et XVe siècles* (Histoire Générale de Paris, 1867).

[2] *Fritz Saxl . . . Memorial Essays*, ed. D. J. Gordon (1957), pp. 218–27.

[3] MS. 205, see M. R. James, *A Descriptive Catalogue of the Manuscripts in the Library of Corpus Christi College, Cambridge* (1912), i. 494–5.

historiographical style but so thinly and faintly as not to influence anyone else along the same path. He was in any case precluded from a full employment of Renaissance techniques, for he was against the government whereas humanist historians were always for it. Monsieur Samaran compares Basin's 'humanism' to Robert Gaguin's,[1] and this is not to say much. Gaguin had unquestionably a taste for literature and *litterati* in the Italian manner; and he used one or two recent Italian works in compiling his *Compendium de origine et gestis Francorum*. In style and critical awareness Gaguin is not as good as Basin, but he was writing a general history of France, and he was concerned to set it under princely patronage.

Thus in neither France nor England before the end of the fifteenth century can we find any native writer thoroughly influenced by Bruni, Biondo or Platina, or their many Italian emulators. Thereafter the scene changes, and in an impressive way. Paolo Emili of Verona, at work in France after 1494, produced the earlier books of what was to be an enormously influential history. And in England Polydore Vergil of Urbino was likewise at work from 1505. What had made the difference was at any rate in part the conviction in high places that apologists in the neo-Latin of the humanists, writing the history of a dynasty in a modern and convincing way, were as indispensable as neo-Latin writing diplomats and secretaries. The word 'neo-Latin' must be stressed, for royal secretaries in the fifteenth century had, both in France and England, acted as propagandists.[2] The international scene of the early decades of the sixteenth century demanded humanist Latin: Paolo Emili and Polydore Vergil were imported and encouraged because native scholars were not capable at first of producing the desired effect.

The great differences in historical writing between the two countries are, one may feel, of some significance as illustrations of diverging paths of political evolution. It was suggested earlier that one may partly account for the absence of a town chronicle in Paris in the greater authority wielded there by a royal official. In the dominant position of the official historian have we not a further reflection of a kind of selfconscious monarchy which is absent in England? The London chronicles, which spill over into all forms of popular history by the late fifteenth century, are also perhaps an indication of the growing political influence of the members of that middle group in the country—the gentry and prosperous burgesses—who in parliament were beginning to be coherent and vocal. Such a development is not witnessed in France. There there was no parliament and, in the English sense, no Commons. One can even detect such pressures at work in the sixteenth century, for in France the humanist innovations of Paolo Emili and others often develop into rhetorical works, while in

[1] Basin, *Hist. de Charles VII*, i, intro. p. xx.
[2] A. Bossuat, 'La littérature de propagande au XVᵉ siècle: le mémoire de Jean de Rinel, secrétaire du roi d'Angleterre, contre le duc de Bourgogne (1435)', *Cahiers d'histoire*, i (Grenoble, 1956), 131–46; instances, besides Rinel, are Beckington, Jean de Montreuil, Alain Chartier, Noël de Fribois.

England they are more or less absorbed into the homespun of Hall and Holinshed.

The preceding pages have brought the outlines of the story down to the sixteenth century. In conclusion one may add that there are several other aspects of the fifteenth-century problem not touched on above; and one must indicate that logically the analysis should be carried further—at least until the seventeenth century.

As to matters not discussed two questions may serve to show what may be worth investigation. In England we see in the fifteenth century the start of a native antiquarian movement, owing nothing to Italian examples, a good deal to patriotic sentiment. One calls to mind Fastolf's secretary, William Worcester,[1] and John Rous of Warwick. This was to develop in the sixteenth century, with John Leland, until it combines with continental scholarship in men like Camden to form one of the characteristic features of seventeenth-century scholarship. Was there anything like this in fifteenth-century France? Did some of the Trojan experts discussed by M. André Bossuat[2] ever collect the physical memorials of early Frankish times? And is one right to think that in France in the fifteenth and sixteenth centuries more *livres de raison* are to be found than in England, where there seems to be a relative scarcity of commonplace books, 'collections' and so on?

As to the further story, it would show how historical techniques and styles in France and England came together again, mainly under the influence of humanist scholars. By the seventeenth century the uniformities of earlier days were largely re-established in a Europe where the Republic of Letters was stronger than it had ever been before. There are still important differences. The long series of memorialists in France, from Guillaume du Bellay to Saint-Simon, cannot be matched in England; nor can the official historiographer, though we find a half-hearted imitation of this in Restoration England and in Scotland (where it still exists).[3] We cannot parallel in England or elsewhere in Europe the astonishing series of French historical scholars adorning the age of Louis XIV. France, on the other hand, has no equivalent to the extraordinary development—due to a conjunction of the influences of the miracle play, the town chronicle and Polydore Vergil—which made the matter of England a subject for the Elizabethan dramatists. Corneille and Racine avoided even the mythical parts of French history. Shakespeare was to be the greatest single force in establishing for the Englishman the traditional picture of his past.

---

[1] K. B. McFarlane, 'William Worcester: a preliminary survey', in *Studies presented to Sir Hilary Jenkinson*, ed. J. C. Davies (1957), pp. 196–221.

[2] A. Bossuat, 'Les origines Troyennes, leur rôle dans la littérature historique au XVe siècle', *Annales de Normandie*, viii (1958), 187–97.

[3] I have discussed this briefly above, pp. 20-33.

2   Engraved portrait of L.A. Muratori in his study at Modena

5

MURATORI AND THE BRITISH HISTORIANS

I

I must begin by apologising for a change in the title of my paper. On your programme it is stated to be about ' Il Muratori e gli storici inglesi '. Now it should have been ' Muratori and the *British* historians' or perhaps, ' Muratori and the historians of England and Scotland '. I am myself partly to blame for this. I am so used in Italy to hearing all people from Britain described as ' Inglesi ', and to having letters from Italy addressed to me at ' Edimburgo, Inghilterra ', that I did not at first notice how peculiarly inappropriate the title was. Of the historians to be mentioned three were Scottish by birth and domicile, Hume, Robertson and Sir Walter Scott. Moreover I believe that it was no accident that history made such remarkable progress in Scotland in the later eighteenth century, but rather that there were particular features of the Scottish intellectual scene which favoured a reception of ideas from the Continent. In many ways the century running from 1750 to 1850 in Britain was dominated by Scottish intellectuals, many of whom left Scotland for the south of England, where (for example) they were extremely prominent as printers and publishers in London. Let us remember that the *Encyclopaedia Britannica* was originally edited by a ' society of gentlemen in Scotland ', and was first published at Edinburgh in 1771.[1]

I shall therefore begin with a few brief observations on the likenesses and differences in the England and Scotland of the decades follow-

---

[1] Gibbon's publisher was a Scot by then domiciled in London, William Strahan. In the late eighhteenth nad nineteenth centuries Scotsmen were very prominent in London as printers and publishers. The various titles Hume gave to his *History* as it came out reflect his and his contemporaries' awareness of the differences which it was hoped that the union might obliterate: *The History of Great Britain (under the House of Stuart)*, Edinburgh, 1754-57; *The History of England under the House of Tudor*. Edinburgh, 1759; *The History of England from the Invasion of Julius Caesar to the Accession of Henry VIII*, London, 1761.

ing Muratori's death.[2] Of the overall situation one must recall that the Union of the two countries, enacted in 1707, had survived the second and final attempt of the Stewart exiles to overthrow it in 1745. The failure of the Young Pretender demonstrated that Scots did not want to break up the English partnership; the savage repression which followed the failure of the rebellion led, though painfully, to the penetration of the Highlands by Lowland civilization. Not only did Scotland adhere to England, she was thus to become for the first time herself one country. The British were governed by a constitution which we would nowadays regard as corrupt but which was, as you will remember, admired by Continental observers as representative, just and tolerant. The Hanoverian kings are not regarded as Enlightened Despots. At any rate they were not despots, yet, if not enlightened, they had established in 1737 the university of Göttingen where at this very time were being laid the foundations of the 'German historical school' which was to influence so profoundly the European scholarship of the nineteenth century.[3]

Within the United Kingdom contrasts of an important kind survived, as in large measure they still do. The most important contrast was in religion. The Anglican reformation in the end produced a church which admitted wide doctrinal variations, but was hierarchical – the Roman church (it has been said) without the Pope. In Scotland Calvinism prevailed, sometimes in forms as rigid as anywhere in Europe. Further contrasts lay and lie in law and education. In Scottish law there was a marked 'reception' of the principles of Roman jurisprudence in and after the sixteenth century, and in many ways the Scottish legal system contrasts markedly with the common law tradition in England. As for education, the Scottish reformers had postulated in 1560 a scheme which would have established a school in every parish, grammar schools in all the bigger towns, topped off by universities, of which there were four by 1600. This programme was not implemented to any extent at the parochial level. But the standards of the town grammar schools was as high as that of similar schools on the Continent and there is no doubt that in the eighteenth century a much higher proportion of young men went to the University in Scotland than in England. Furthermore, the Scottish University contrasted sharply with the moribund institutions at Oxford and Cambridge, whose defects are so witheringly exposed by Edward Gibbon in his autobiography. St. Andrews was admittedly

---

[2] Three recent works on Scottish history may be mentioned which, though dealing with periods longer than than touched on in this paper, are all especially authoritative for the century 1750-1850; R. MITCHISON, *A History of Scotland*, London, 1970; W. FERGUSON, *Scotland, 1689 to the Present Day*, Edinburgh, 1968; T. C. SMOUT, *A History of the Scottish People 1560-1830*, London, 1969.

[3] H. BUTTERFIELD, *Man on his Past*, Cambridge, 1955.

pretty decrepit, but Glasgow, Aberdeen and Edinburgh contained some of the most adventurous philosophers, scientists and scholars of the eighteenth and early nineteenth centuries. In addition, many members of the gentry who were aiming at professional careers also went to study at Continental universities, especially at the University of Leyden.

History and historians in Scotland were bound to be affected by this intellectual ferment. A centre like Edinburgh was more receptive to new ideas than was perhaps even London and certainly offered more resources to the student and the professor. In London the British Museum Library did not open until 1759, the first significant public library in the capital. But already in the year of Muratori's death there were three great public libraries in Edinburgh – the University library (whose history we can chart in some detail since we have manuscript catalogues from the middle of the eighteenth century),[4] and the libraries belonging to two groups of lawyers – the Advocates and the Writers to the Signet (senior solicitors). Both these last were large collections and in due time the Advocates' Library was to become the National Library of Scotland. Indeed I am sure that Edinburgh had the best library facilities in Britain until that great Modenese emigré Sir Anthony Panizzi by about 1850 turned the British Museum Library into the greatest research library in the world. I stress the point for this reason: by the end of the eighteenth century there were in Edinburgh three collections available to the serious scholar in each of which he would find a set of Muratori's main works. The number is truly astonishing. Besides the *Annali*, all three Edinburgh collections had the *Antiquitates* in Latin or Italian or both and the *Scriptores* were available at both the Signet and the Advocates libraries.[5] The most remarkable collection was in the Advocates' Library where, besides *Annali*, *Antiquitates* and *Scriptores*, there were copies of thirteen other works by Muratori. May

---

[4] Edinburgh University Library MS. Da.1.11, the earliest (circa 1750) catalogue, with subsequent MS. additions. A printed catalogue of the University Library came out in 3 vols., Edinburgh, 1918-23. MS. ' receipt books ', in which borrowings are recorded, have survived. Some of Robertson's borrowings are recorded for the period when he was writing *Charles V, inter alia*, VOLTAIRE, *Histoire generale*, 8 vols.; PASQUIER, *Recherches de la France*, Graevius. See MSS. Da. 2.2-3.

[5] ' Part the first ' of a printed *Catalogue of the Library of the Faculty of Advocates*, edited by Thomas Ruddiman (on whom see *Dict. Nat. Biog.*), came out at Edinburgh in 1742; pts. 2 and 3 appeared respectively in 1776 and 1807. This enables one to chart approximately the arrival of particular books in the Library. All the main works by Muratori were present in 1776. Mr. Alan Bell, of the National Library of Scotland, kindly tells me that the Curator's Accounts (MS.F.R. 118) show the acquisition of the *Scriptores* (£ 27), the *Antiquitates* (£ 5.11s) and the *Novus Theasaurus Inscriptionum* (£ 3.6s) on 10 July 1744, i.e. *before* Hume's tenure of the librarianship. The first printed catalogue of the Library of the Writers to H. M. Signet was published in 1805, by which date the Library had *Scriptores* and *Antiquitates*; the *Annali* are not in the Supplement (1826) but they are in the next supplement (1833). There were, of course, other libraries in late eighteenth-century Edinburgh, but of less moment: e.g. that of the Society of Antiquaries.

I remind you that from 1752 to 1757 the librarian here was David
Hume? We can conclude that this massive total of 17 works, in all 65
volumes, represent remarkable Scottish interest in the manifold learning
of Muratori.[6]

The riches of Scottish scholarship and of Scottish libraries tended
to be concentrated in the late eighteenth century in Edinburgh. But
such a concentration did not mean that they were not influential in the
whole island. Scots came from all over Scotland to study in the newest
but best endowed of the four universities. And there was (and there
still is) a steady stream of students from England. It is important to
recall that religious tests were imposed at Oxford and Cambridge so
that many non-conformists or sceptics came to Edinburgh. Finally many
prosperous English people, accustomed to the gaiety of foreign travel,
came to Edinburgh during the Revolutionary and Napoleonic period,
so that Edinburgh society was diverse and influential during the period
when it was the intellectual capital of the United Kingdom.[7]

In that milieu history had important functions, literary, political
and social. Muratori's historical writings accordingly had great relevance. It seems to me that his influence on British historiography can
be usefully treated under three heads: his editorial work, his analytical essays and his narrative *Annali*.[8]

II.

Of these three topics the first two are, I suppose, aspects of the
history of antiquarianism. Now this is a subject which has been relatively neglected. In Fueter's *Storia della Storiografia moderna* Mura-

---

[6] For Hume's connection with the Advocates Library see E. C. Mossner, *The Life
of David Hume*, Edinburgh, 1954, esp. pp. 250-55; cfr. G. GIARIZZO, *David Hume politico e storico*, Torino, 1962.

[7] Among the many pictures of this epoch in the history of Edinburgh an attractive
contemporary account is provided in Henry Cockburn, *Memorials of his Time*, Edinburgh,
1856 but written between 1821 and 1830; for a recent evocation of the city, extended
vastly and beautifully at this time, see A. J. YOUNGSON, *The Making of Georgian Edinburgh*, Edinburgh, 1966. On the ' Scottish Enlightenment ' (Illuminismo Scozzese), which
is now a thriving industry, see e.g. G. BRYSON, *Man and Society: The Scottish Inquiry
of the XVIII Century*, Princeton, 1945; D. DAICHES, *The Paradox of Scottish Culture*,
London, 1964; N. T. PHILLIPSON and R. MITCHISON (eds.), *Scotland in the Age of Improvement*, Edinburgh, 1970.

[8] Muratori's direct connections with Britain and British scholars are not of moment.
The British Museum Library has the following Muratori items in its manuscript collections: Egerton 50, Add. MSS. 26081, 12110, 22881. These are letters to and from Muratori which are printed in Càmpori's edition of the *Epistolario*; Acton had copies of those
in Add. MS. 26081; Cambridge University Library Add. MS. 4890, fos. 453-6. So far as
I can see the only English correspondent of Muratori was Bodley's Librarian, John Hudson
(see *Dict. Nat. Biog.*), who approached Muratori regarding a Josephus in the Ambrosian
Library in Milan: see *Epistolario* iii, no. 1017; iv, no. 1397. The Muratori letters in the
Bodleian Library Western MS. 17364 are to J. P. d'Orville.

tori's vast *Scriptores*, parts of which we all still use, are passed over in complete silence. It is curious that there is no synoptic work on European antiquarianism, for the great works of the seventeenth and early eighteenth centuries – the *Acta Sanctorum* of the Bollandist fathers, the innumerable volumes of the Maurists, Ducange, Leibniz, Dugdale and Rymer have been discussed (if at all) partially and not as soldiers in the same army, attacking ignorance of the past, ' demythologising' what had passed for history down to the Counter Reformation.[9] It is, incidentally, a pity that Italy lacks any general survey of the rich scholarship of this period; there is not even a good study of Ughelli, although his *epistolario* could readily be assembled from manuscripts in the Vatican Library.[10]

In the history of antiquarianism I distinguish between editorial work and analytical essays, partly because a well-edited text has often a usefulness to scholars irrespective of the ability of the editor. (Thomas Rymer, whose *Foedera* English historians still depend on, was intellectually negligible – a playwright *manqué*). In this regard Muratori forms a link in the chain which begins with Pithou, Bongars and the Duchesnes in France, Archbishop Parker in England, Schardius and Goldast in Germany, but he however was at work after Mabillon and Leibniz and the link he forged in the great chain of learning has proved very strong indeed.[11] As far as England is concerned the *Scriptores Rerum Italicarum* were an inspiration, as they were everywhere in Europe, although it was to be long before results were achieved.[12]

In the year 1818 a meeting of noblemen and gentlemen, interested in historical literature, and conscious of the inadequacy of all previous attempts, was convened at Spencer House. It resolved to recommend to the government, through the Earl of Liverpool, a complete collection of our annals and other historical documents commencing with the earliest notices of Britain, and ending with the Reformations to be published at the expense of the government.[13]

---

[9] There are several recent works of value on French antiquarian and historical thought in the sixteenth century notably J. H. FRANKLIN, *Jean Bodin and the Sixteenth-century Revolution in the Methodology of Law and History*, New York, 1963 and D. R. KELLEY, *Foundations of Modern Historical Scholarship*, New York, 1970; for the English antiquaries of the seventeenth century see D. C. DOUGLAS, *English Scholars*, London, 1939.

[10] A start has been made on this most important task by Dr. Giorgio Morelli.

[11] The only synoptic view of this enormous field of European scholarship with which I am familiar is the brilliant but not comprehensive work by P. HAZARD, *La crise de la conscience Européenne*, Paris, 1935; attractive essays on the Bollandists and the Maurists are to be found in D. KNOWLES, *Great Historical Enterprises*, Edinburgh, 1963.

[12] See the introduction by Sir T. D. HARDY to PETRIE's *Monuments Historica Britannia*, Record Commission,, London, 1948.

[13] Sir T. D. HARDY, introduction to *Descriptive Catalogue of Materials Relating*

The editor appointed was called Petrie; he had been an archivist.
He did not live to see the publication of a truncated, but huge, first
volume in 1848. Significantly it was entitled *Monumenta Historica
Britannica.* Please notice the dates. The project began in 1818; in 1826
appeared the first volume of the *Monumenta Germaniae historica* –
another descendant of Muratori – and the title of the abortive English work reflects the extraordinary prestige of Pertz and his colla-
borators.[14] The successful venture in Britain was to be the series of
volumes issued under the authority of the ' Master of the Rolls ' (hence
usually called the ' Rolls Series ').[15] The first of these volumes appeared
in 1858 and the last in 1897: in all there were 237 volumes and medieval history was established as an academic discipline in the course
of this half century. You will observe that in this editorial development
Muratori's influence was exercised (in my opinion) through the media-
tion of Pertz and the German *Monumenta*. In a sense this was inevitable. National self-respect demanded a national series. Muratori's
collection could not be directly imitated in the United Kingdom; furthermore medieval technical scholarship was raising the standards of
the critical reader. Muratori would have been hard put to it to produce
unaided his 25 folios a century later; Petrie's difficulties seem to prove
the point.

By Muratori's ' analytical essays ' I refer chiefly to the *Antiquitates*,
that remarkable group of learned disquisitions which appeared later in
a shortened Italian version. In most ways I suspect that these studies
are the most important work of Muratori – in the sense that in the long
run (and it was to be a very long run) they helped to produce a new
and more sophisticated historiography. Here again, of course, Muratori
had predecessors. Perhaps the greatest of them was Étienne Pasquier
in his *Recherches de la France* and some of his letters. The tradition
is carried on in seventeenth century literature in all parts of Europe,
and most typically is reflected in the activities of the learned societies
and clubs where gentlemen of scholarly inclinations and scholars with
the right connections read papers to each other. And, indeed, some of
the *Dissertazioni sopra le antichità italiane dei secoli di mezzo* began
in this way.[16] Muratori's *Antiquitates* constitutes the biggest and most

to the History of Great Britain and Ireland to the End of the Reign of Henry VII (Rolls
Series, 1862), i, p. xlvi.

[14] For Pertz and his influence, see G. P. Gooch, *History and Historians in the
Nineteenth Century*, London, 1913, pp. 64-75; Knowles, *Great Historical Enterprises*,
pp. 65-92.

[15] The Master of the Rolls was the judge (at that time a member of the government of the day) with overall responsibility for the public records, many of which had
immediate legal relevance. On the Rolls Series, see Knowles, *op. cit.*, pp. 101-34.

[16] *Dissertazioni sopra le antichità italiane*, 3 vols., Milan, 1751. G.-F. Soli Muratori ' ai lettori ' with reference to diss. XIV. I do not pretend in this paper to deal

important collection of such historical essays and it both encouraged other historians to do likewise – to write about problems rather than narrating the public activities of public persons – and it provided them with a digest of his own vast work on medieval Italy not arranged as a continuous story (that was the function of the *Annali*) but under topics. ' Le mie ricerche ', says Muratori, offer ' vari prospetti dell'Italia e Nazione Italiana, in quella guisa appunto che fanno quei che prendono a discrivere qualche grande Città, o alcun splendido regio palazzo . . . Ho scelto e trattato vari principali argomenti spettanti all'Italia dell'età media '. Classical Rome was well served by existing books. Not so the ' Antichità de i tempi barbarici ' for which materials were scarce and scattered. To penetrate ' cotesta Erudizione non sempre amena ' the archives are essential. So that the *Dissertazioni* digested not only the *Scriptores* but a vast range of other materials – charters, coins, medals, seals, ' ed altri frammenti di Antichità '.[17]

The Scotish historians of the eighteenth century went to Muratori's works to learn their craft. Fueter ranges them under the rubric ' School of Voltaire '.[18] However that may be (and to a non-expert like myself ' school of Montesquieu ' would seem more appropriate) there was one feature of Voltaire's historical technique which they did not emulate. Voltaire followed humanist tradition in writing in a fine prose style in which there were no excrescences such as ugly quotations in barbarous languages, and no abrasive elements such as footnotes or other references to his sources. Robertson remarks on this in the final footnote to his ' View of the Progress of Society in Europe ', (in his *Charles V*, 1769) in which he explains one of the principles which have guided his own ' proofs and illustrations '.

In all my inquiries and disquisitions . . . I have not once mentioned M. de Voltaire, who, in his Essay sur l'histoire genérale, has reviewed the same period and treated of all these subjects. This does not proceed from inattention to the works of that extraordinary man, whose genius, no less enterprising than universal, has attempted almost every different species of literary composition . . . But as he seldom imitates the example of modern historians, in citing the authors from whom they derived their information, I could not, with propriety, appeal to his authority in confirmation of any doubtful or unknown fact . . .[19]

---

with Muratori himself, on which subject I have consulted with profit S. BERTELLI, *Erudizione e storia in L. A. Muratori*, Naples, 1960.

[17] *Antichità*, pref., sig. b5.

[18] E. Fueter, trans. A. SPINELLI, *Storia della storiografia moderna*, Milano-Napoli, 1970, pp. 429 ff. The whole matter is also, of course, discussed by F. MEINECKE, *Historism*, trans. Anderson, London, 1972.

[19] W. ROBERTSON, *The History of the Reign of the Emperor Charles the Fifth*. I refer to the edition in two vols., London, 1809, i.574. There is now an attractive reprint of the ' View ' edited with an introduction by F. GILBERT as *The Progress of Society in Europe*, Chicago, 1972; but this omits all but three of the ' proofs and illustrations '.

And Robertson goes on to say that had Voltaire's practice been different his own annotation would have been lighter and Voltaire's readers would have realised that he was not only witty but learned too.

Hume's ' dissertations ' or ' disquisitions ' are, you will recall, scattered through the *History of England* as ' appendices '. This undoubtedly reflects the continuing dichotomy between learning and literature, between the antiquary and the historian, which had developed from the mid-sixteenth century and reached its fullest development during the seventeenth century. Then the *eruditi*, the Maurists, the Bollandists and so on, in all European countries were doubtless often *bought* by the gentry and nobility for the private libraries which were now *de rigueur*, but there for the most part they remained unread. The history which was currently read was either the work of the memorialists, or the smooth and undemanding narratives of men like Mézeray and Daniel.[20] It is important to insist on the prominence of this type of historical literature all through the seventeenth and also the eighteenth centuries. When reading histories of historiography it is all too easy to suppose that by the 1730's and 1740's everyone was reading Voltaire. It was because, even for Voltaire, erudition was not polite that he avoided parading it. And for similar reasons Hume and Robertson make a sharp distinction between their art prose and its scholarly props and supports.

Nevertheless both Hume and Robertson do use both footnotes and extended ' appendices ' or ' disquisitions ' in which authorities are adduced and compared. At first sight Hume seems less developed in this regard. This is partly because Robertson is so much better a historian than Hume, so much more learned and penetrating – so much more a historian's historian – and was destined to exert over the next century a profounder influence. But the difference is a little less marked if we take into account Hume's *Essays* in which we occasionally encounter the digested materials of the past in a form virtually the same as that of a ' dissertazione '. I am thinking for example of the long Essay ' of the populousness of ancient nations '.[21]

In thus placing scholarship alongside narration Hume and Robertson were taking an immensely important step towards a more sophisticated and mature history. The future, the long distant future, lay with the analysis of past societies, with the history of institutions, of economic relationships, cultural change and so forth. As I wrote twenty years ago in connection with Polydore Vergil: ' the future of historiography was to lie precisely in the discursive treatment of

---

[20] HAZARD, *op. cit.*, i.40-4.

[21] *Essays,* ed Green and Grose, London, 1882, i. 381-443; for Hume's views on the importance of history (all educated persons should know the history of the Greeks, the Romans and their own native land) see *Essays,* ii.390.

particular issues rather than in the chronological enumeration of events '.[22] Hume and Robertson in their learned, non-narrative, passages are dealing with problems and not with personalities. And in their notes and dissertations the whole of modern erudition is displayed. In this world of learning Muratori occupied a most prominent place. This is much clearer from Robertson than from Hume, not only (I believe) because Robertson has occasion to turn to Muratori's writings frequently since he was dealing with aspects of European history but also because he had a vivid awareness of the importance for modern history of the centuries in which the nations of Europe had been formed.

If we look at the annotation of Robertson's famous panorama of medieval European history, which he prefaced to his *Charles V*, we will find that Muratori's name occurs more often than that of any other single scholar. They are all there – Ducange, Mabillon, the *Acta Sanctorum*, Dugdale, Spelman and the other stars in that brilliant constellation of erudition. But Muratori is, I think, the most frequently quoted name. The reason is not far to seek. A rapid survey of the references shows that for every reference to his other works (*Scriptores, Antichità Estensi, Annali*) there are six or seven to the *Antiquitates*. It is no accident that in his portrait by Raeburn, among the books he has chosen to surround himself we can read the title *Antichità italiane*.[23] This is not by any means to say that Muratori is the only modern Italian author to influence Robertson; Sarpi remains important and so – to a greater degree but perhaps also because of his attitude to the Roman church – does Giannone, whose ' boldness and discernment ' are expressly commended by Robertson [24] and from whom both Hume and Robertson derived their views about the rise and influence of Roman law.[25] Robertson himself explains the function of his ' proofs and illustrations ':

The chief intention of these notes was to bring at once under the view of my readers, such facts and circumstances as tend to illustrate or confirm what is contained in that part of the history to which they refer. When these lay scattered in many different authors, and were taken from books not

---

[22] *Polydore Vergil*, Oxford, 1952, p. 100.

[23] The picture hangs in the Senatus Hall of Edinburgh University, and is reproduced hare by courtesy of the University and with the help of Miss Sheila Fletcher. The mace symbolises Robertson's role as Principal of the University. The other authors whose books are shown are: ROBERTSON'S own *History of Scotland*, Tacitus, Zurita and St. Jerome. Robertson, it must be remembered, was a minister of the Church of Scotland.

[24] *Charles V*, i. 513.

[25] *Ibid.*, i. 57, 515; GIARRIZZO, *Hume*, pp. 261-62. On Robertson see in general *W. Robertson als Geschichtsschreiber des Europaischen Staatensystems*, an ' Inaugural-Dissertation ' for the doctorate at Marburg (1953) by Manfred Schlenke; G. FALCO, *La Polemica sue medio evo* i, Biblioteca della società storica subalpina, Torino, 1933; Fueter and MEINECKE, *ubi supra* n. 18.

generally known, or which many of my readers might find it disagreeable to consult, I thought it would be of advantage to collect them together.[26]

The very phrases recall Muratori's preface to the *Antichità* and ' cotesta Erudizione non sempre amena ' although they do not reach that exciting moment when Muratori invites others to improve on his work: ' Tra quegli argomenti che ho preso a trattare, ve ne sono molti, che a un uomo erudito porger potrebbero materia, onde farne un competente volume '.[27]

I must not give you the impression that all of Hume's and Robertson's historical researches are as elaborate or as technically satisfactory as many of Muratori's.[28] Hume, one feels, frequently compiled references rather than digested them and too often the philosopher in him led to Man in the abstract rather than to the observation of the activities of the men and women which constitute the historian's province. Many of Robertson's ' proofs and illustrations ' are brief enough and only about 13 of the first 30 (that is, those dealing with medieval European history) are comparable to the essays of Muratori and while the analytical approach to problems was the way nineteenth-century history was to take, it took a long time to become the dominant mode of academic history. Politics retained its primacy; narrative remained basic.

III.

I turn now to the third of the triumvirate of historians on whom Muratori laid his imprint, Edward Gibbon – surely the greatest of the narrative historians of recent centuries. This brings us to the influence of the *Annali* but before I say something of this may I remind you of two matters? First, that national history became the dominant form, governing both erudite and popular history, and often coloured by romantic attitudes, as a result of the French revolution and the Napoleonic occupation of much of continental Europe. National histories were, of course, not new, and the notion of a Balance of Power was one of the assumptions which antedates the Revolution. But the chauvinism of Latin and Teuton and their branches and subdivisions gave lurid undertones to much nineteenth-century historiography. Second, we must not suppose that Muratori, gentle, liberal, humane and intellectually cosmopolitan as he was, displayed a strong sense of *Italianità* only

---

[26] *Charles V*, i. 518.

[27] *Antichità*, pref., sig. b3vo.

[28] The study of the *technical* scholarship of both writers would be a useful undertaking. This aspect of historiography is almost entirely neglected for all periods.

in the *Annali.* The conception and execution of the *Scriptores* and of the *Antiquitates* equally reflect a profound love of Italy and a desire to illustrate its past. Looking at the erudition of the period of *La crise de la conscience européenne* Paul Hazard writes: ' L'Angleterre (he means Britain!) s'interessait plus volontiers peutêtre aux études grecques, la Hollande aux études latines, la France à l'hagiographie; et l'Italie a son propre passé '.[29] Of the many *érudits* of Italy (Muratori names them in his prefaces and they fill columns in the various ' Methods ' and bibliographies currently available in his day, such as that of Langlet du Fresnoy)[30] the majority dealt with regional history, as was to be expected of historians living in a land which was divided up into a number of small states. Muratori's work for the Este family illustrates this. But he always had Italy in mind: witness the title of his *Antichità Estensi e Italiane,* which came out in 1717. And the design of and intention behind the *Antiquitates* was the scientific study of the institutions of the Italian nation in the Middle Ages, ' Re, Duchi, Marchesi, Conti ed altri magistrati . . . i vari riti del governo politico, ed i costumi . . . privati. La libertà e Servitù . . ., i giudizi, la milizia . . ., le Città . . . Finalmente la Religione . . .'.[31] And, in this form, the *Antiquitates* did constitute a topical or analytical survey of medieval Italy.

But it was, of course, the *Annali* to which readers went who wanted the history of the peninsula. In the *Annali* Italy had unquestionably the fullest and most scientifically documented narrative of any European country,[32] a remarkable matter considering the absence of central government and (compared to London, Paris, Madrid) a capital city. Nor was the work restricted in its, scope to the Middle Ages. Professor Franco Venturi has recently demonstrated how valuable the *Annali* are for the author's own lifetime.[33]

Robertson, as I have mentioned, used the *Annali* but it was, of course, Edward Gibbon who gave the work its British *imprimatur,* so to speak. This was not only by using it, but by explicit commendation. In the survey of medieval Rome given in chapter LXIX Muratori was described as a basic authority. Gibbon writes: ' The dates of years in the margin may, throughout this chapter, be understood as tacit references to the Annals of Muratori, my ordinary and excellent

---

[29] HAZARD, i. 65.

[30] The English adaptation of this by R. Rawlinson (London, 1728) was made from the Italian version of S. Coleti, with a preface to Maffeo Farsetti (1716); the bibliographies of Italian history and of the regions of Italy are accordingly very full and still of some use.

[31] *Antichità,* loc. cit.

[32] F. VENTURI, *Settecento riformatore,* Torino, 1969, p. 716.

[33] *Ibid.,* p. 66.

guide. He uses, and indeed quotes, with the freedom of a master, his great Collection of the Italian Historians, in xxviii volumes; and, as that treasure is in my library, I have thought it an amusement, if not a duty, to consult the originals '.[34] At the end of chapter LXX Gibbon lists the authorities he has used in dealing with Rome and the papacy in the fourteenth and fifteenth centuries. They are mostly ' in the Collections of Muratori, my guide and master in the history of Italy '. After listing Muratori's main works Gibbon adds that ' In all his works Muratori proves himself a diligent and laborious writer, who aspires above the prejudices of a Catholic priest '.[35]

The paradox of Gibbon's admiration for Roman Catholic scholars has repeatedly engaged the interest of critics. Giorgio Falco wrote that he ' accoglie e concilia ragione e Rivelazione '.[36] Christopher Dawson, himself a Roman Catholic, found it curious that the inheritor of the devout and self-effacing Tillemont should be not some latter-day Bossuet ' but the infidel Gibbon . . . who used the· material which Tillemont had so laboriously collected in order to explain away Christianity and to rationalise the history of the Church '.[37] But Giuseppe Giarrizzo has rightly stressed the character of Muratori's disposition so far as religion and history are concerned: ' Moderato e penetrante, Muratori ama più la giustificazione che la condanna; e però la storia tutta, e l'ecclesiastica e la profana, egli intende come storia civile, in cui l'uomo, e non Dio, sta al centro del quadro '.[38] This ' moderatismo ' was profound in Muratori and it obviously appealed to the cool and detached attitude which Gibbon attained, ' all passion spent ', in the late 1760s. And Giarrizzo has also pointed out how congenial to Gibbon was Muratori's attitude to the question of the Italian nation, which derived partly from his desire to oppose an Italian consciousness as a bulwark against the temporal ambitions of the popes and partly from the need to explain the reception of Italian values outside Italy despite the all but universal repugnance inspired by the Roman church at all times.[39]

---

[34] *Decline and Fall*, ed. Bury, London, 1902, vii, 216, n. 17. For the *Annali* and the *Scriptores* in Gibbon's library at Lausanne see G. KEYNES, *The Library of Edward Gibbon*, London, 1940, but reissued by the Bibliographical Society, 203-4, where other works by Muraotori are listed. The best recent discussion of this side of Gibbon is by G. GIARRIZZO, *Edward Gibbon e la cultura europea del settecento*, Napoli, 1954; see also C. Dawson, ' Edward Gibbon ', « Proc. Brit. Acad. », XX (1934), 159-80, and in general Falco, Fueter and Meinecke.

[35] *Decline and Fall*, vii, 299-300; for Gibbon's praise of Muratori's impartiality, *ibid.*, 263 n.

[36] FALCO, p. 201.

[37] DAWSON, p. 167.

[38] GIARRIZZO, *Gibbon*, p. 459. Robertson might also be so described.

[39] *Ibid.*, pp. 461-2.

It is easy to see why Gibbon preferred Muratori to Maffei; his own explanation for his preference was wrapped up typically enough in social terms: Maffei wrote as a proud noble, Muratori as a plebeian.[40]

It would be pleasant to be able to argue that Gibbon derived his original inspiration from Muratori. But it would not be true. He was fired by history through Hume. His theme went back to Poggio, to Flavio Biondo, to Sigonio: in short, he and Muratori shared a common ancestry so far as the *Decline and Fall* are concerned.[41] That is not to say that in many important matters Muratori did not exercise a substantial influence, beyond merely that of providing texts. For example, Gibbon adopted Muratori's picture of the Italian nation being a product of the Middle Ages, and he also followed him in his admiration for the Lombards (Langobardi).[42]

What Gibbon did was to bridge the gap between erudition and history which, as I said earlier, had developed early in the seventeenth century. He was steeped in the learned authors of the seventeenth century [43] and at the same time he was a man of letters, intent on providing a gripping account of a tremendous historical process. He was not the first British historian to be influenced by the new scholarship. We have seen that Hume and Robertson were both anxious to profit from it. But they failed (and this is especially true of Hume) to integrate their erudition with their exposition; the two were juxtaposed, not amalgamated. The ' philosophic spirit ' to that extent dominated the ' historical spirit ' as it was to emerge in Gibbon, let alone in the new history which was being born in his day at Göttingen. With Gibbon history detached itself finally from ethics.[44] This led to a work which did not elevate or improve the mind and Fueter clearly finds this distasteful: ' non mirava ad altro successo che alla gloria letteraria '.[45] But that indeed he achieved and in countless reprints throughout the nineteenth century *The Decline and Fall* was read by all manner of men and thus generations of Britons became acquainted at any rate with the *name* of Muratori. My grandfather, who brought me up, told me

---

[40] *Decline and Fall*, iv. 194, n. 34; cfr. GIARRIZZO, *Gibbon*, 450 n.

[41] Cfr. DAWSON, pp. 163-64 It is surprising that Gibbon did not apparently have F. BIONDO's, *Decades* in his library; he had Sigonio's works (see KEYNES, *sub nomina*).

[42] GIARRIZZO, *Gibbon*, pp. 457-63.

[43] Cfr. Dawson, *passim*; and J. W. SWAIN, *Edward Gibbon the Historian*, London and New York, 1966, p. 106, where Gibbon's defence of the *érudits* in the *Essai sur l'étude de la littérature* is discussed.

[44] In general see A. MOMIGLIANO, *Ancient History and the Antiquarian*, reprinted from « Journ. Warburg & Courtauld Institutes », 13 (1950), in *Studies in Historiography*, London, 1966, pp. 1-39 and *ibid.*, pp. 40-55, ' GIBBON's, *Contribution to historical Method* '.

[45] FUETER, p. 474.

when I was a little boy that ' Gibbon read like a novel ' and family tradition had it that he had read *The Decline and Fall* in its entirety on his honeymoon. Now my grandfather was not a scholar. He was a businessman. You will not be surprised to learn that he was a very unsuccessful businessman.

IV.

By the nineteenth century academic history at last established itself, even in Britain. There was then no need to defend or excuse the learned writers whose erudition had nurtured but whose lack of ' philosophy ' had embarassed the writers of the so-called Enlightenment. Even the new generation of novelists and poets respected the sort of verisimilitude which could be extracted from chroniclers like Giovanni Villani. It is interesting to note how romantic impulses embraced the pedantry and precision of Mabillon, Ducange and Muratori. Sir Walter Scott had the *Annali* on the shelves of his large library, still happily preserved in the mansion house he built at Abbotsford.[46] How much Muratori's writings provided material for his imagination to work on we can hardly guess. But at any rate on one occasion we can see an exact reference: in *Count Robert of Paris* Scott refers to Muratori for material referring to the Varangian Guard.[47]

By the time of Scott, Sismondi was the established and popular *cicerone* to medieval Italy. Much admired in Britain, Sismondi transmitted Muratori yet again, this time in a post-Revolutionary guise. Late in the nineteenth century a remarkable scholar called Boulting was to produce an English digest of Sismondi in which he refreshed that somewhat weary work with copious draughts drawn (with exact references) from Muratori's *Scriptores*. ' Boulting's Sismondi ' remains the best available history of medieval Italy in English.[48] It has been out of print for half a century, while smaller and less demanding manuals have tried to take its place.

It was fortunate that the *academic* renaissance of history in Britain (I should really say its birth, for it had never earlier been an academic subject) was to be largely dominated by the cosmopolitan

---

[46] J. G. COCHRANE, editor, *Catalogue of the Library at Abbotsford*, Bannatyne Club, Edinburgh, 1838.

[47] I am obliged for this reference to Mr. Philip Bradley, F. L. A., who has studied various aspects of Scott's allusions.

[48] William Boulting's substantial work appeared about September 1906. (This information was kindly provided by Messrs. Routledge and Kegan Paul.) It has the great merit (as has L. Simeoni's manual) of accepting that there cannot be a unified history of Italy for this period.

figure of Lord Acton, whose largest monument, I suppose, is the *Cambridge Modern History*. Acton had learned his history from Döl-linger, who came out of that remarkable German tradition which has been christened the ' Göttingen school '. Members of this ' school ' at the same time had criticised the superficialities of the Enlightenment and yet had at the same time inherited the ambition to carry history ' to higher levels of generalisation '.[49] Döllinger had learned his business by mastering the erudite writings of the XVII and XVIII centuries and in turn Acton did the same, rating Muratori very high.[50] I say Acton's European interest was ' fortunate ' because the other two pil-lars of British scholarship at the time, Bishop William Stubbs and Frederick Maitland, both wrote the history of Britain – indeed, more precisely, the history of England.

This is an important point, for Acton's influence helped to ensure that in British universities and grammar schools European history was taught more nearly on an equality with national history. I believe that did not happen on the Continent. I cannot pretend that this important development resulted solely from Muratori, who was only one of the stones on which Acton raised the edifice of sound learning. But Acton's influence was to ensure that medieval European history filled about half of my curriculum as a student at Oxford and that I, like very many others, came to meet the ' Old ' and the ' New ' Muratori in a way that (I am confident) Italian, French and German students did not and do not get to know the Rolls Series or the Calendars of Patent and Close Rolls as primary sources of British (or English!) history.

Acton's influence was partly due to his being a great European nobleman. He was born in Naples of a German mother; he even spent some reluctant time in Edinburgh. He also carried weight because he was the friend of important British public figures like Gladstone.[51] But it is interesting even if a coincidence that, like Muratori and like his master Döllinger, he was a liberal Roman Catholic at a time when, with the Vatican Council of 1870, shackles seemed about to be placed again on scholars of the old Church. Acton ,with his marvellous library,[52] his intense and unremitting reading, his collections of *fiches*, had a na-

---

[49] BUTTERFIELD, *op. cit.*, p. 8; cfr. p. 60.

[50] *Ibid.*, pp. 66, 69, 207-8.

[51] There is now a vast literature on Acton; a useful recent work on Acton as a historian is L. KOCHAN, *Acton on History*, London, 1954. Sir Herbert Butterfield makes extensive use of the Acton MSS at Cambridge in *Man on His Past*.

[52] Acton's books and papers are now in the Cambridge University Library. The books, by any reckoning a remarkable collection, in which the erudition of the continental scholars of the seventeenth and eighteenth centuries is well represented, have been cata-logued in a series of printed volumes: ' Acton Collection ', Cambridge University Library Bulletin, extra series, 4 volumes, Cambridge, 1908-10.

tural affinity with ' il Proposto Muratori ', although his ultimate and unrealised aim was a history of human liberty and not the history of a nation or even a continent. Perhaps in the end Gibbon's judgment was right, and that what was needed was ' L'esprit philosophique qui rassemble ' rather than ' L'esprit compilateur qui ramasse '.[53] What Acton's life does display is that, whether as ' rassembleur ' or ' ramasseur ', a Muratori was no longer possible by the end of the nineteenth century. Acton's *Cambridge Modern History* was to be a work of lofty and impartial *collaboration*, not the work of a single pen. But then the message of the ' New ' *Rerum Italicarum Scriptores* is the same and is doubtless not unfamiliar to you.

May I conclude by stressing again the remarkable character of the *Annali* and the *Antiquitates*. In the first we have an honest attempt to document the history of a nation which, as I have said, lacked until the nineteenth century any express political cohesion. Recent historians, it seems to me, often falsify the medieval picture of Italy by resorting to a catastrophic view of the Italian past, not unlike the stressing of ' Revolution ' by the historians of the Enlightenment. This means placing undue emphasis on ' foreign policy ', if one can apply that expression to the Middle Ages. Now to this distortion, which has bedevilled Italian historiography since Machiavelli, Muratori offers a wonderful corrective. Muratori was convinced that the peace of his own day was a *summum bonum*.[54] His story is not a unified picture. The *Annali* are old-fashioned chronology (as compared with the *Antiquitates*) but they are true to the messy reality. Muratori still offers a model for that unattained end – a history of the Italian people before 1871.

As for the *Antiquitates*, the tradition they belong to, and of which they are the best early example, was to lead in the end to the analytical history of the professional historians of the later nineteenth century. It would be a fascinating task to illustrate the emergence of a new historiographical technique, but it would lead us too far afield, even if restricted to Britain. I suspect that Muratori's *Antiquitates*, though still a direct inspiration to men like Hallam,[55] had ceased to be influen-

---

[53] Quoted by GIARRIZZO, *Gibbon*, p. 98.

[54] *Annali* ix; cfr. my *Profilo storico del rinascimento italiano*, Firenze, 1966, p. 54.

[55] The historical scholarship of H. HALLAM (e.g. *A View of the State of Europe during the Middle Ages*, 1818-48; *The Literature of Europe during the 15th, 16th and 17th Centuries*, 1837-39); of H. W. LECKY (e.g. *Rise and Influence of the Spirit of Rationalism in Europe*, 1865) and of W. H. BUCKLE (e.g. *History of Civilization in England, France, Spain and Scotland*, 1866), which are still plundered by all of us, were based in large measure on the *eruditi*, and not least on Muratori.

tial by the early twentieth century. It is the fate of erudition to be superseded. That we are now celebrating Muratori here in Modena for the second time in a generation is an indication that he, more than many of the scholars to whom we owe so much, still retains a living interest.[56]

[56] I have to thank Mr. Roger Paxton for preparing the abbreviated Italian version of this paper which I read at Modena and my colleagues Professor G. F. A. Best, Mr. C. P. Finlayson, Dr. A. M. Freedman, Mr. B. D. Phillips, Dr. N. T. Phillipson and Professor A. J. Youngson for help of various kinds. My daughter Jenny Marchant kindly checked manuscripts for me at the British Museum.

ANNALI D'ITALIA

DAL PRINCIPIO

DELL'ERA VOLGARE

Sino all'Anno 1500.

COMPILATI

DA LODOVICO ANTONIO

MURATORI

Bibliotecario del SERENISSIMO

DUCA DI MODENA.

TOMO PRIMO

Dall'Anno primo dell'Era volgare fino all'Anno 221.

IN MILANO,

MDCCXLIV.

A spese di GIOVAMBATISTA PASQUALI

LIBRARO IN VENEZIA.

3   Title page of Muratori's *Annali*, vol. 1 (Milan, 1744)

6

HISTORIANS AND THE RENAISSANCE
DURING THE LAST TWENTY-FIVE YEARS

NYONE surveying the problem of the Renaissance in the last twenty or thirty years must be astonished at the tenacity with which the categories established by Jacob Burckhardt have survived criticism. *Die Kultur der Renaissance in Italien* came out in Basle in 1860 and over a century later its main argument remains virtually unchallenged. True, Burckhardt's synthesis had been built on foundations which went back to the Renaissance period itself, to Petrarch and his successors, long before Vasari gave 'Rinascita' its definition as applied to the fine arts. How the concept of the rebirth of classical norms began to take over education and literature, both in revived Latin and Greek as well as in the vernaculars, has been told in the authoritative pages of Wallace K. Ferguson's *The Renaissance in Historical Thought*.[1] What Burckhardt (and Georg Voigt at much the same time, though on a much narrower front)[2] did was to extend the concept of the Renaissance from the arts and belles-lettres to the wider world of society and of history in its broadest sense. Voigt explained how the humanities at the time of Coluccio Salutati were adopted by the Florentines; Burckhardt's essay began with a substantial survey of Italian history, which he entitled 'The state as a work of art' (though the phrase remains somewhat gnomic). In the rest of his modestly written book, Burckhardt applied as thoroughly as he could the aphorism invented by Jules Michelet: that the Renaissance witnessed 'the discovery of the world and of man'.[3] This meant for Burckhardt that the Renaissance ushered in attitudes

1 Cambridge, Mass., 1948. There is an elaborate bibliography, much wider in scope than the title of the book suggests, in Carlo Angeleri, *Il problema religioso del Rinascimento* (Florence, 1952), 163–203. See too the critical bibliography appended by Federico Chabod to his essay, 'The concept of the Renaissance', which I have used in the revised English translation, *Machiavelli and the Renaissance* (London, 1958), 201–47.
2 Georg Voigt, *Die Wiederbelebung des classischen Altherthums*, reprint (Berlin, 1960); there is a poor and unreliable Italian translation of this by Zippel (Florence, 1888).
3 The title of Part IV of Burckhardt's book and the section in which he touched, *inter alia*, on the natural sciences.

which would change the whole world, first of all in Italy and then elsewhere, to inaugurate that 'modern' world, with its attitudes to natural phenomena, moral and religious questions, as well as to public affairs and the creative work of artists and writers. In the main it is within the context of these ideas that students of the Renaissance still move; indeed it is probably true to say that the basic tenets of the Burckhardtian position are more dominant, more unchallenged, today than they were before the two World Wars.

It is not the intention of this study to analyse the evolution of Renaissance studies before 1939. Yet something must be said of the criticism encountered by Burckhardt and his disciples before then, if we are properly to appreciate the diminution, even the disappearance for all practical purposes, of such criticism in recent decades. However, in view of Professor Ferguson's full survey there is no need for an elaborate description of the attacks directed at Burckhardt's position. Perhaps the criticisms may be reduced to two broad headings. There were those who argued that the Renaissance which started in Italy in the fourteenth and fifteenth centuries was only one of several such episodes in the cultural development of Europe, so that 'Renaissance' should be regarded as a generic name for successive but disparate returns to, or recoveries of, Classical Antiquity. On the other hand there were some who denied that anything had happened in Italy which deserved to be regarded as special and important.

The first group of critics were in general the more impressive and productive. As a result of their labours medieval studies were greatly enriched by research into the 'Carolingian' renaissance and the 'twelfth-century' renaissance. The former was for long regarded, and rightly, as a somewhat fugitive moment in which a mere handful of scholars, following Alcuin's inspiration, were involved.[4] Unquestionably many of the men involved had some public influence; their activities led to the preservation of many ancient manuscripts; and the writing of the period was to inspire, albeit mistakenly, the belief that the clear minuscule lettering in which these texts were copied was antique, in this way leading them to be treated as models for the humanist hands of the fifteenth century and later.[5]

The 'twelfth-century' renaissance was only slightly more appealing

---

4 For a recent, if partial, study of the period, see Donald Bullough, *The Age of Charlemagne* (London, 1965, rev. edn 1972). When was the expression 'Renaissance' first applied to the scholars and scholarship of Carolingian times? Perhaps in G. Brunhes, *La foi chrétienne et la philosophie au temps de la renaissance carolingienne* (Paris, 1903)? Ferguson, op. cit., argues, p. 45, that the 'Carolingian' renaissance is a concept which goes back to Melanchthon.

5 B.L. Ullman, *Origin and Development of Humanist Script* (Rome, 1960); there is a big and growing literature on this topic.

to a wider public, and in some ways was to have less far-reaching consequences, at any rate so far as later cultural events in Italy were concerned. Associated with the schools of Chartres and Paris, with Latin
writers like Bernard and Theoderic of Chartres and with the English
prelate, John of Salisbury, we have the impression of a learned coterie
cultivating Latin letters for each other's benefit, detached from the
rough and tumble of real life as led by the mass of their contemporaries.
Charles Homer Haskins' admirable study, *The Renaissance of the
Twelfth Century*,[6] restricts its subject to the 'complete development of
Romanesque art and the rise of Gothic; the full bloom of vernacular
poetry, both lyric and epic; and the new learning and the new literature
in Latin'.[7] Haskins' book, however, ends with a chapter called 'The
beginnings of universities', and with Paris and Bologna and their multiplying offspring, we enter a new intellectual environment in the
thirteenth century. This has been characterized, most persistently and
ferociously by Giuseppe Toffanin, as a world of 'science' or legalism.[8]
The metaphysicians and the theologians, the teachers of the sacred text
and the professors of canon and civil law, came to dominate higher
education, and drove literature and the humanities into the by-ways of
education, into the most dingy and the most disreputable corners of the
groves of academe. The result (so runs the argument) was that the
emotional and moral solvent of the ancient classics was frozen for three
or four generations, inaccessible to serious and sensible men. That the
thirteenth-century university had little time for poetry and letters is
incontestable. Yet we should remember that – despite initial resistance
by the hierarchy in Paris – Aristotle was better known, if only in Latin
versions, in the thirteenth century than at any time before the
sixteenth; that the jurists of Italy in the thirteenth century were to form
the most influential of the admirers of Petrarch and the 'new learning' a
hundred years later; and that the notarial art and the *ars dictaminis*
secured the practice if not the idealization of good literature.[9]

The 'Carolingian' and ·'twelfth-century' renaissances were thus
supported by a very small, though influential, group, and so had little
widespread patronage, unless one includes (as Haskins did) the development of Gothic art and architecture. All in all, we must be grateful for
the useful distinction which Erwin Panofsky made between the 'Renaissance' and 'renascences' in western art in the book so titled.[10] He

6 Cambridge, Mass., 1947.

7 Reprint, New York, 1967, 6.

8 G. Toffanin, *Storia dell'umanesimo* (Naples, 1933), frequently reprinted
   and extended; and in many other works.

9 Paul Oskar Kristeller, *Studies in Renaissance Thought and Letters* (Rome,
   1956), 561–7, and in other writings.

10 E. Panofsky, *Renaissance and Renascences in Western Art* (Stockholm,
   1960).

applied his analysis to the arts but it seems to me equally relevant in the spheres of learning and literature. There were moments when classical motifs, ideas and texts attracted attention among a few *cognoscenti*, but these were relatively evanescent[11] and in no sense dispose of the originality, social relevance and influence, profound and long lived, of the cultural changes of the Italy of the fourteenth and subsequent centuries, destined to dominate the cultural values of the western world almost to our own day.

The faint criticisms encountered by Burckhardt reduced, or attempted to reduce, the concept of renaissance to a mere recurrent type of revived interest in the antique. The other criticisms, while they cannot be so neatly associated, all in the end denied in effect that there was an Italian Renaissance at all – or at any rate that it had any significance. This was partly attempted by stressing that the 'modern world', which Burckhardt had seen the Renaissance ushering in, was in practice permeated with medieval concepts. Such was the argument of literary critics like Douglas Bush and E.M.W. Tillyard,[12] parallel in its way to the argument advanced much earlier, that even in the thirteenth century 'humanism' was influential: it was argued by H. Thode that the key figure in the evolution of the Italian Renaissance and the modern world was St Francis of Assisi.[13] A different line was pursued by some historians of both the Roman and the Protestant persuasions. Almost from the start reformers had seen the striking innovations in teaching as a mere episode in the recovery of ancient purity, an incident only to be commemorated in the new (or old but revived) churches. That Melanchthon was a sound Latinist in the new manner and Calvin could be regarded as a humanist of stature seemed to clinch the matter. Who 'laid the egg that Luther hatched' but Erasmus himself, prince of the new learning? Besides, the great ages of Roman literature corresponded with the great ages of the early Church. For many a Protestant schoolchild, certainly down to my own day in Britain, the importance of the Renaissance lay in its being a prelude to the far more important

11 Some would add an 'Ottonian' renaissance. For F. von Bezold's and F. Schneider's works (1922, 1926), arguing a permanent 'continuity of the classical tradition through the medieval period', see Ferguson, op. cit., 333–4. And cf. also P. Renucci, *L'aventure de l'humanisme européen* (Paris, 1953), with copious references.

12 For Bush see Ferguson, op. cit., 355–6; E.M.W. Tillyard, *The Elizabethan World Picture* (Cambridge, 1944).

13 *Franz von Assisi und die Anfänge der Kunst der Renaissance in Italien* (Berlin, 1885). I avoid discussion here of L. von Pastor's tortuous distinction in his *History of the Popes* between a Christian renaissance (which was healthy) and a pagan renaissance (which was wicked and unhealthy), and of apologetic works such as that by Vladimir Zabughin, *Storia del rinascimento cristiano in Italia* (Milan, 1924). Cf. p. 16.

Reformation: witness the titles of the first two volumes of the *Cambridge Modern History*: I. *Renaissance*, II. *Reformation*. These came out in 1902. That they were planned by the Roman Catholic Lord Acton merely reinforces the hold that the connection I have outlined exercised in northern Europe at this time.

These assumptions were, however, less drastically opposed to the significance of the Renaissance than those which effectively sought to obliterate the concept or deny its validity altogether. Of those who were prepared to challenge the basic notion of individualism, or rather the cult of the individual as Burckhardt himself would have termed it, none was more persistent than that great French philosopher and man of letters, Etienne Gilson. His challenge was repeatedly delivered, but in no place more movingly than in *Héloïse et Abélard*, only the last of a series of criticisms.[14]

> Avant de trouver une formule pour définir le moyen âge, il faudrait en trouver une pour définir Héloïse. Je conseillerais ensuite d'en chercher une pour définir Pétrarque. Ceci fait, que l'on en cherche une troisième pour définir Erasme. Ces trois problèmes une fois résolus, on pourra procéder en toute sécurité à définir le Moyen Age et la Renaissance. Trois plus deux font cinq impossibilités.[15]

I will say a word later on Gilson's position.

The other main attack, less witty, less shrewd and, in my judgement, less relevant, came from the historians of science. If Gilson had in a sense produced a syllogism which sought to demonstrate the irrelevancy of categories by finding evidence (in a sense) for all attitudes at all times, so the historian of science presented the following argument:

> The Renaissance is supposed to lead to the Modern World;
> The modern world is based on physical science;
> There was no humanist interest in physical science;
> Therefore there was no Renaissance in Italy in the fourteenth and fifteenth centuries.

The most vociferous purveyor of such syllogistic propositions, if not perhaps the most subtle, was the late Lynn Thorndike, at length in his *History of Magic and Experimental Science*,[16] and more briefly on several other occasions. But he did not stand alone. Some similar presuppositions colour the large-scale work of Pierre Duhem.[17] George Sarton's view was that 'from the scientific point of view, the Renais-

14 Paris, 1938. For earlier essays by Gilson see Ferguson, op. cit., 335.
15 Op. cit., p. 180.
16 New York, 1923–41.
17 *Le système du monde* (Paris, 1913–17).

sance was *not* a Renaissance'.[18] And many other writers took a not
dissimilar line, or at any rate reinforced the view that medieval men
were as concerned with the 'discovery of the world' as their Renaissance
successors.[19] One has a lingering suspicion that with this approach the
writers have allowed the modern dominance of the natural sciences to
lead them to exaggerate the influence of the few professors at Paris,
Oxford and elsewhere who speculated on cosmological theory, the
concept of motion, and so on.

There is, clearly, an imperative need for historians not to become
tyrannized by their artificial abstractions. There is nothing God-given
about terms like 'Renaissance', 'modern', 'Risorgimento' or any similar
expressions. Historians should all be 'nominalists', to use medieval
scholastic terminology: and this is really the position adopted by Johan
Huizinga, which in its very different way is as subtle and sophisticated
as Burckhardt's.

> The soul of Western Christendom itself was outgrowing medieval
> forms and modes of thought that had become shackles. The Middle
> Ages had always lived in the shadow of Antiquity, always handled its
> treasures, or what they had of them, interpreting it [Antiquity]
> according to truly medieval principles: scholastic theology and
> chivalry, asceticism and courtesy. Now, by an inward ripening, the
> mind, after being so long conversant with the forms of Antiquity,
> began to grasp its spirit.[20]

After the Second World War these debates and doubts seem stilled and
the framework of Burckhardt, modified here and there, as it was to be
later, still held firm. Like a well-made ship, his survey survived the
winds of criticism.[21] But, before we consider the developments in
Renaissance historiography since 1950, it is essential to note some
very important works which fall just before, or in, or just after the war
years, and whose influence as a result had a delayed effect. They are
chiefly to be associated with three men, whom I name here in what I

---

18 Quoted by Ferguson, op. cit., 383. See also G. Sarton, *Appreciation of
   Ancient and Medieval Science during the Renaissance* (Philadelphia, 1955).
19 E.g. Emile Mâle, *L'art religieux du XIIIe siècle en France* (Paris, 1910); N.
   Pevsner, *The Leaves of Southwell* (London, 1945).
20 Johan Huizinga, *The Waning of the Middle Ages*; I quote from the English
   translation (London, 1937), 307.
21 The most ponderous contradiction (if that exactly describes it) of the view
   that the Renaissance was a critical episode is Hiram Haydn's *The Counter
   Renaissance* (New York, 1950), although he nevertheless regards it as 'a
   part of the historical period called the Renaissance', a good example of the
   confusions induced by allowing the periodic concept to get out of hand. A
   much shorter but more telling examination of some sceptical writers is
   Paul F. Grendler, *Critics of the Italian World* (Madison, 1969).

believe to be their order of seniority by age: Hans Baron, Paul Oskar Kristeller and Eugenio Garin. The first two had been German citizens and, when one notices with some astonishment the relative absence of significant German or Austrian Renaissance scholarship after 1945[22], as contrasted with the rich talent devoted to Reformation studies, one must recall that remarkable *diaspora* of scholars from these countries which has enriched scholarship in this as in other fields, especially in the USA. Some of the names of such writers will occur in what follows.

Baron's first major work on Bruni's history appeared in German in 1928, but to my mind even more influential were the pieces published in English in 1939–40. In many ways these revolutionized Renaissance scholarship by introducing a link, closer than that forged by Burckhardt or anyone else, between public life and public literature. Even more important than the essay on Bruni are 'Cicero and the Roman civic spirit' and 'Franciscan poverty and civic wealth', both peculiarly pregnant with ideas which were to enrich succeeding scholars. 'Civic humanism' in a very real sense derives from these essays its modern acceptance as a 'term of art', as one of those 'nominalist' concepts which we could nowadays ill dispose of – a term, indeed, which is being liberally appropriated for other periods and circumstances.[23] Baron's name will figure again below, but he deserves priority here, not only because of his age.[24]

Kristeller probably entered the arena of Renaissance scholarship somewhat later (1929) than Baron and his influence has been quite different. Far from offering a novel concept of 'civic humanism' he has proceeded with the double dedication of a philosopher and bibliographer who has concentrated his main interests on the fifteenth century. This had made its impact before the war: *Supplementum Ficinianum . . . Opuscula inedita et dispersa* came out in two volumes in Florence in 1937. His name, like Baron's, will occur later in this survey.

Finally, Eugenio Garin, to whose work this collection of essays bears witness, produced his study of *Giovanni Pico della Mirandola*, also in Florence, in 1937. Like Kristeller, his university function was to teach philosophy. Like Baron and Kristeller his prolific contributions continue; all three act as a bridge between the pre-war and post-war worlds

---

22 But not German Swiss, e.g. G. Kisch, W. Kaegi (his life of Burckhardt), R. von Albertini ; see below, p. 114.

23 For example, one finds recent research devoted to the 'civic humanism' of the Enlightenment. *Habent sua fata tituli*! Baron's papers are in the *Bulletin of the J. Rylands Library*, XX, and *Speculum*, XIII, both for 1938.

24 For some details see A. Molho and J. Tedeschi (eds), *Renaissance Essays in Honor of Hans Baron* (Dekalb, Ill., and Florence, 1971). His bibliography begins in 1924.

of Renaissance scholarship.[25]

In the last twenty-five or thirty years the continued leadership of the three scholars just mentioned has ensured inescapable continuities between pre- and post-war activity in Renaissance research. It is not as though 1939 and war had not been a troublesome possibility for years, and an emotional impact of fear or desperation had already begun, one suspects, to influence scholars long before the invasion of Poland. That so many Germans and Austrians were obliged to live abroad doubtless explains to some extent (as I have said) why post-1945 Renaissance scholarship is less evident in Germany than it had been earlier. A small indication of this is the absence, so far as I know, of any journal in German expressly devoted to the Renaissance, such periodicals being found in France (or Switzerland), America and Italy. That is not, of course, to say that the German Renaissance has been totally neglected. But significant works seem mainly to have been produced by scholars outside Germany – one thinks of the writings of Forster, Strauss and Spitz. The point is worth stressing, since Burckhardt had a thoroughly German training (he was a pupil of Ranke and Kugler) and the elaboration of his essay (*ein Versuch*, as he subtitled his book) by later Germans, for whose erudition he expressed little sympathy, suggested that Germany was likely to witness a continued development in this field of history.[26]

As I stated above, the survival of Burckhardt's main categories seems no longer at risk. The work of demolishing or denying them has been abandoned in favour of detailed analysis, criticism and correction, and above all elaboration. This has been made possible largely by adapting a view of the Renaissance as a fairly prolonged period in time. Despite his tendency to draw his evidence from three centuries somewhat indiscriminately, despite the lengthy historical Part I, which runs from Frederick II to Charles V, I do not believe that Burckhardt intended to view the Renaissance as a substantial period. He intended the cultural changes which he investigated and illustrated to constitute a watershed in time rather than an epoch in world history. The Renaissance inaugurated the modern world, made the Italian the 'first-born among

25 For a bibliography of Garin's writings as far as 1969 see p. 14. Kristeller's writings are listed in E.P. Mahoney (ed.), *Philosophy and Humanism. Renaissance Essays in honor of Paul Oskar Kristeller* (New York, 1976), 543–89. Note that Chabod in his bibliographical survey, above, n. 1, devotes section III (pp. 217–19) exclusively to Baron, Kristeller and Garin. In what I have written above I was tempted to add Chabod himself (1901–60), making him a fourth Colossus of the Renaissance field – as in so many of the other areas of his multitudinous interests.
26 At first glance it is paradoxical that the author of the *Cicerone* should have been so hostile to the *eruditi*; in the end he turned back to art history as his main professional concern, but not to erudition!

the sons of modern Europe'. Individualism, the cult of fame, the revival of Antiquity, 'the discerning and bringing to light' of 'the full, whole nature of man', the production of a new society, in which talent, intellectual or political, could enable anyone to rise into the upper classes – this I believe to be the essence of Burckhardt's picture of the Renaissance. As the English historian G.P. Gooch remarked in his *History and Historians in the Nineteenth Century*,[27] 'as Riehl loved the peasant, Burckhardt loved the *élite*'. The picture Burckhardt painted was, we should remember, far from optimistic. The exciting changes just mentioned went with, if they did not positively involve, a decline in religious sentiment. Yet if superstition increased, among a chosen few an enlightened pantheistic paganism developed. The book ends thus:

> Echoes of medieval mysticism here flow into one current with Platonic doctrines, and with a characteristically modern spirit. One of the most precious fruits of the knowledge of the world and of man here comes to maturity, on whose account alone the Italian Renaissance must be called the leader of modern ages.[28]

This brief summary of *Die Kultur der Renaissance in Italien*[29] and the quotation of its last lines will indicate to the reader how faithfully the areas of life and learning identified by Burckhardt have been further elaborated, and especially in recent decades. A glance at the contents of this very volume will provide easy confirmation that this is the case. They will emphasize also that the word is now, in practice, regarded as a period of time.

The Swiss historian has thus encouraged the acceptance by historians of a new epoch, which has, I suppose, had most influence in the United States, where every large university history department may be depended on to have one or more Renaissance specialists. So in the western world we have currently four eras: ancient, medieval, Renaissance, modern (all, indeed, but especially the latter, vulnerable to further subdivisions such as 'early modern', 'contemporary'). I do not propose to say more on the question of periodization, but to accept this treatment of the Renaissance as a fact. There have been many dis-

---

27 1913.
28 I quote the translation by G.C. Middlemore, 2 vols (London 1878), II, 383. The last phrase in the original runs '*die Renaissance von Italien die Führerin unseres Weltalters*' (ed. Goetz, Stuttgart, 1922), 416, which is perhaps not quite fairly rendered as 'modern ages' by Middlemore.
29 That we should be careful in equating *Kultur* with 'civilization' is demonstrated by Norbert Elias, *Über den Prozess der Civilisation* (Basel, 1939); vol. I of this is available in English as *The Civilising Process* (New York, 1978). I am grateful to Professor E. Midelfort for drawing my attention to this.

cussions of the matter, one of the best and most well-known being by Delio Cantimori.[30]

Thus we apply the term Renaissance freely, perhaps more outside Italy than inside that country, to everything that happened between about 1350 and 1600 – politics, science, and of course the fine arts, literature and learning. This can and sometimes does cause confusion between the older Vasari–Michelet–Burckhardt scheme, where the emphasis is on the inspiration of Classical Antiquity and innovation, and the new position. For example, it is hard to detect anything humanist in the bulk of the literature released by the printing press from the mid-fifteenth to the mid-sixteenth centuries; and one could say something similar about much northern European art and architecture. It is perhaps because there are difficulties like these that scholars have devoted themselves in the last generation to pursuing detailed researches rather than embarking on the reformulation of vast interpretative theories which in any case produce their own terminological quandaries. A Renaissance *convegno*, more particularly in the USA, usually issues in a collection of papers dealing with any aspect of the period, regardless of its connection with humanists or the humanities. The titles of books themselves (again this is best observed outside Italy) use Renaissance as a generic term for all the occurrences of several centuries.[31] Among the positive advantages of this is that non-Italian writers are not tempted to avoid the discussion of cultural change within the social and political context. One can read the whole of Luigi Simeoni's in many ways admirable *Le signorie*[32] without being allowed to admit that the massive changes in the Italian milieu which we describe synoptically as the Renaissance deserve a place in his text; in fact Simeoni at the very start of his book expressly dismisses the Renaissance as having any effect on the public life of the nation. The matter, however, deserves the sort of careful discussion Chabod gave it,[33] and in any case it is integral to any total view of Italy in the fourteenth and fifteenth centuries if only because many of the narrative sources are steeped in humanist style and impregnated with humanist assumptions of an ideologically significant kind. One must, however, not exaggerate the difference between Italian and non-Italian practice. If non-Italian historians regularly admit art and learning, science and

30 A *relazione* to the Tenth International Congress of Historical Sciences, Rome, 1955, reprinted in *Studi di storia* (Turin, 1959), 340–65 and in *Storici e storia* (Turin, 1971), 553–77.

31 For instance in the first volume of both the old and the new *Cambridge Modern History*. There is now an illustrated Italian translation of the new *CMH*.

32 In the series 'Storia politica d'Italia', 2 vols (Milan, 1950).

33 Chabod's views were first published in the *Actes du colloque sur la Renaissance 1956* (Paris, 1958).

philosophy, into their general surveys of the Renaissance it is often not as an essential element in the narrative, but somewhat peripheral, even merely decorative. Much the same criticism might be levelled at the treatment accorded to the Renaissance in the new *Storia d'Italia*, edited by Einaudi; there the issue is virtually ignored in the first, key volume, and it is discussed at length but in an entirely distinct section in the second volume.[34]

Despite Burckhardt's invitation to associate history *simpliciter* with cultural history the only outstanding exponent of this approach seems to me to be Hans Baron. This is apparent both in his pre-war essays and in even more explicit fashion in his *Crisis of the Early Italian Renaissance*,[35] in which he advanced the argument that it was the political threats to Florentine liberty, chiefly by the Visconti, which precipitated the conscious reception of the new style, in substance republican and in inspiration classical, by the ruling classes of the city on the Arno. There is no doubt of the influence this thesis has exerted; like all magisterial pronouncements it has been paid the compliment of severe criticism.[36] But besides those for whom Baron's arguments seem unpersuasive, there are in addition others who, quite independently, see no need to enlarge the concept of the Renaissance beyond the limits it had for Voltaire. I may instance my old friend Roberto Weiss who viewed the Renaissance and its humanist propagators as simply a story of recovering ancient texts, collecting classical manuscripts and so on, and not even to any significant extent drawing attention to the effects of the humanities on secondary-school curricula. Nor would Baron regard his work in this particular sense as breaking new ground. His *Crisis* is

---

34 1 (Turin, 1972); 2** (1974) has an essay by Paul Renucci (cf. above, n. 11) on 'la cultura', 1085–466 with, on the Renaissance as such, a subsection entitled 'L'Italia all'avanguardia (secolo xv)', 1210–69. One reason for the subordinate place accorded to the Renaissance in this (in many ways) original and exciting treatment of Italian history is the strong emphasis placed more or less throughout on economic factors, and of course the Renaissance coincided with a marked economic recession in Italy. Cf. Robert S. Lopez, 'Hard times and investment in culture', a lecture given in the Metropolitan Museum, New York, in 1953, and now reprinted in *Six Essays* (New York, 1962). I may perhaps be allowed immodestly to refer to my *Italian Renaissance in its Historical Background* (Cambridge, 1961), translated into Italian with a generous preface by Garin, as *Profilo storico del rinascimento italiano* (Florence, 1966); a new and revised edition of my book (Cambridge, 1977) has, I understand, been translated into Italian.

35 Princeton, 1955, in two vols, revised edn in one vol., Princeton, 1966; to be associated with the author's *Humanistic and political Literature in Florence and Venice at the Beginning of the Quattrocento: Studies in Criticism and Chronology* (Cambridge, Mass., 1955).

36 Note especially the book by J.E. Siegel, *Rhetoric and Philosophy in Renaissance Humanism* (Princeton, 1968); and the exchanges between Siegel and Baron in *Past and Present*, 34 and 36 (1966–7).

dedicated to Walter Goetz, 'who taught me that history should be a study of both politics and culture'. One of the most promising developments in this regard is the attention increasingly being paid to Italian political speculation at this time, or, to use Burckhardt's somewhat enigmatic words, 'the state as a work of art'.

This last phrase, with its suggestions of nineteenth-century pragmatism, hardly lends itself to the messy realities of Italian and European politics in the fifteenth or sixteenth centuries. But Nicolai Rubinstein, Felix Gilbert and William Bouwsma, among others, have shown how rewarding can be the investigation not only of what happened, but of what the best minds of the day thought ought to happen.[37] I name these three scholars not at random but because their works have, as it were, crossed my path; I am well aware that there are many others but obviously I cannot attempt a systematic bibliography of this or any other aspect of my subject. The new emphasis on political thought, while it naturally gravitates to individual thinkers such as Valla, Guicciardini and their theorizing contemporaries,[38] also leads to a straight discussion of political and administrative history.

Here the effort and the results in late times have been truly remarkable. It is almost invidious to single out single writers from the mass of researchers whose time has been devoted (without always specific reference to the Renaissance) to the fourteenth and fifteenth centuries. A large number are Americans, benefiting from generous support from foundations in the USA and abodes with and near good libraries at I Tatti and the American Academy in Rome. Perhaps the most stimulating work is one which crosses easily from speculation to action; certainly Chabod referred to it in such terms. I am speaking of Rudolf von Albertini, *Das florentinische Staatsbewusstsein im Übergang von der Republik zum Prinzipat*.[39] In this remarkable work the men of letters act, so the speak, as *metteurs en scène* for the play itself.

37 Of Rubinstein's many writings in this area I instance 'Florence and the Despots', *Transactions of the Royal Historical Society*, ser. v, 2 (1952), and 'Florentine constitutionalism and the Medici ascendancy', in *Florentine Studies*, ed. by Rubinstein himself (London, 1968); and see below n. 98. Felix Gilbert's rich researches may be represented by his masterly study of *Machiavelli and Guicciardini* (Princeton, 1965); W. Bouwsma, *Venice and the Defence of Republican Liberty* (Berkeley, 1968).

38 Cf. Gilbert's book referred to in the preceding note; Franco Gaeta, *Lorenzo Valla: filologia e storia nell'umanesimo italiano* (Naples, 1955). I renounce references to other studies of Machiavelli and his speculation save to say that in general I believe great reliance can be placed on Chabod, whose scattered essays on Machiavelli are now gathered together in *Scritti su Machiavelli* (Turin, 1964); cf. above, n. 1.

39 Published in Berne in 1955; there is now an Italian translation (Turin, 1970).

To the actors in the public drama a great deal of work has been devoted. The books and articles of so many Americans come to mind – Brucker, Becker, Martines, Molho, for example[40] – that an Anglo-Saxon like myself tends to forget the formidable activities of Italian political historians themselves, scholars such as Berengo, Cognasso, Ridolfi, Valeri, the contributors to the new collective histories such as Einaudi's venture and the substantial volumes devoted to the history of Milan, Naples and Padua.[41] Is it too much to say that co-operation on this scale would not have been easy to secure half a century ago? Would *stranieri* like the Florentine Garin or the Valdaostan Chabod have written substantial portions[42] of the Treccani degli Alfieri volumes on Milan? To an outsider this seems to be a wholesome development in Italian historiography, and one obviously not confined to the Renaissance period. If Italian political history at this time cannot be treated as a unified story (and here I stand whole-heartedly behind Simeoni), or only at the expense of reality,[43] then at least the experts can collaborate on a topical basis within a regional framework.

40 In several cases the works I cite could be supplemented by others by the same authors. G.A. Brucker, *Florentine Politics and Society 1343–1378* (Princeton, 1962), and *The Civic World of Renaissance Florence* (Princeton, 1977); M.B. Becker, *Florence in Transition*, 2 vols (Baltimore, 1967–8); L. Martines, *Lawyers and Statecraft in Renaissance Florence* (Princeton, 1968, and cf. below n. 50); A. Molho, 'Florentine public finances', in *The Early Renaissance 1400–33* (Cambridge, Mass., 1971).

41 M. Berengo, *Nobili e mercanti nella Lucca del cinquecento* (Turin, 1965); F. Cognasso, *Storia di Torino* (Turin, 1964) and *L'Italia nel Rinascimento* (Turin, 1965); Roberto Ridolfi, lives of *Savonarola, Machiavelli, Guicciardini* (Rome, respectively 1952, 1954, 1960); N. Valeri, *L'Italia nell'età dei principati* (Verona, 1950); Simeoni, above, n. 32; Piero Pieri, see, p. 22. Since the prestigious volumes of the *Storia di Milano* began to appear in 1953, many other Italian towns and regions have tried to follow suit. As an example I instance the elaborate *Storia di Napoli*, 13 vols (1967–71); others are found for Padua, Piedmont, Genoa and many other urban centres with their dependent areas: see the references in the Valsecchi–Martini volumes referred to below, n. 45. Of a different type is the very thorough and traditional *Storia di Roma*, which contains in its 22 vols an admirable survey, *Topografia e Urbanistica di Roma*, by F. Castagnoli and others (Bologna, 1958). It should again be stressed that the books and authors I have named here are but a fraction of those which would impose themselves if a complete critical bibliography of Italian historians of this period were intended; for one thing I have omitted dozens of important articles in central and regional Italian journals.

42 Garin's contributions are in vols VI and VII, and cover the literary side of Milanese culture in the fifteenth century; Chabod was charged with the composition of vol. IX, but did not live to complete it. His contributions were reprinted as *Storia di Milano nell' epoca di Carlo V* (Turin, 1971).

43 But of course it is sometimes so treated in other works, e.g. Valeri's, above, n. 41.

In this activity there is, perhaps, an undue emphasis placed on the history of Florence as the very type and model of Italian political and cultural evolution. Florence is in fact a most eccentric feature of peninsular political life, and indisputably has a critical place in the artistic changes of the early Renaissance and even perhaps keeps its interest into the mannerist period. There are the manuscripts in the Laurentian and dozens of other libraries, public and private and, above all, the town has in its Biblioteca Nazionale the biggest, best organized and most efficient of the scholarly 'public' libraries[44] of Italy. This it remains despite the terrible effects of the floods of 1966. (The absence of any other effective national library with complete holdings of all books published in Italy and of any library with all important works, not just on Italian history, published abroad, remains one of the disgraces of Italian academic provision and, if only incidentally, one of the main impediments to a rational survey of Italian history, cultural or otherwise.)

A rough and ready impression of the prominence of Tuscan and especially Florentine studies in recent Italian research may be obtained from the space allocated to it in *La storiografia italiana negli ultimi vent' anni*, in which Tuscany occupies about a fifth of the section devoted to regional studies in the later Middle Ages.[45]

Another reason for Florentine studies taking the lead in historical research is, of course, the existence of state and other archives. The former are vast and, despite damage over the years, including the floods mentioned above, comprise an astonishingly rich repository covering both the period of the commune and the principate. The *fonds* in the

44 The Nazionale at Florence has about twice as many printed volumes as the Nazionale at Rome. It must be remarked that the system of municipal public libraries which is found in the English-speaking world is virtually non-existent in Italy, outside Milan, although legally encouraged. The concept of 'public library' in Italy is really restricted to great scholarly collections. This is a most striking illustration of the persistence in Italy of humanist values, but one may speculate what effect this undoubted deprivation has had on the intellectual development of Italians; a systematic local provision of reference and general reading on an ever increasing scale, including recent fiction, biographies and 'popular' scholarship, has been a feature of Britain, for example, since about 1850.

45 Franco Valsecchi and Giuseppe Martini (eds), *La storiografia italiana negli ultimi vent'anni*, 2 vols (Milan, 1970). A long section of the regional history of the later Middle Ages by Gigliola Rondinini Soldi is appended to Martini's survey of the Basso medioevo. In order of the number of pages allocated to a region, the provinces order themselves thus: 1. Tuscany (52.5 pp.); 2. Veneto (30.6); 3. Lombardy (21.3); 4. Campania (21); 5. Liguria (21); 6. Sicily (19.5) . . . Rome and Lazio (12). I repeat that this essay does not cover art and architecture, topics which also powerfully draw students to Florence.

Archivio di stato, together with the many other public and private collections of papers in the city, as well as those in Lucca, Pisa, Siena, Prato and other towns of the region, act as magnets both for seasoned scholars, some of whose projects are of great importance,[46] as well as for younger men and women. These records were virtually unused either by Burckhardt, or by his contemporaries. Yet not very long after, in 1896, R. Davidsohn was to begin his demonstration of the riches to be mined in the records. The neglect of archival material was not due to its inaccessibility, especially in Tuscany. It was much more due to the deep-seated tradition that narrative history was based on narrative sources and the only additional matter regularly admitted (mainly through the practice and precept of Ranke) were those 'narrative' documents, diplomatic dispatches and *relazioni*, the latter particularly valuable in Venice from the early fifteenth century. Admittedly Italian state archives, extraordinarily varied and valuable as many of them were, were also often in a very confused condition and were only treated scientifically as the present century got under way.[47] The result was that Italian archives (as is more or less the case with those in other countries) were jungles penetrated by largely untrained antiquarian-minded persons, interested more in the details of some individual's biography or questions of the topography of estates than in the examination of political or social development as such.[48]

How dramatically this situation has changed! The advent of economic history as a sophisticated discipline in its own right has had profound effects on the use of archives, reinforced as it occasionally was and is (especially in Italy) by Marxist ideological assumptions, convincing researchers that their work was in some mysterious way encouraging the revolutionary process. The serried volumes of taxation records began to usurp the place of the serried volumes of diplomatic records in the priorities of historians. This can be illustrated in scores of works by Italians and foreigners. Elio Conti (for example) has devoted years of study to the cadastral records to explain rural Tuscan land-

---

46 We may instance the *Lettere* of Lorenzo de' Medici, under the general editorship of Nicolai Rubinstein. Three volumes of this have so far appeared (Florence, 1977), the first two edited by Professor R. Fubini, the third by Professor Rubinstein. Vol. IV (ed. Rubinstein) came out in 1981; vols V and VI (Michael Mallett), VII (H. Butters) and VIII (D. Bullard), are in an advanced state of preparation.

47 Cf. the useful survey by P. d'Angiolini and C. Pavone, 'Gli archivi', Einaudi *Storia d'Italia*, 5** (Turin, 1973), 1659-91.

48 The regional surveys already mentioned above (n. 45) illustrate these points, but only to a limited extent given the vast amount of trivial (as well as important) material printed in the numerous local Italian historical journals.

holding.[49] Scores of others have followed him to the records of the *catasti* , as for instance Lauro Martines in his survey of the income of humanists at the turn of the fourteenth and fifteenth centuries, or Richard Goldthwaite in his investigation of the wealth of four Florentine families.[50] In recent years increasing attention has been paid to the structure of the Italian family: for example, the work of David Herlihy and Christiane Klapish-Zuber, especially *Les Toscans et leurs familles*.[51] Many other scholars are at work in this field.

Economic history has been pursued, of course, all over the peninsula and not just in Tuscany. It is difficult to identify typical works without appearing to neglect others of equal value. Genoese trade and banking has been the province of Jacques Heers; Venetian shipping and trade have been studied pre-eminently by F.C. Lane and Alberto Tenenti; for Rome we turn to the masterly volumes of Jean Delumeau, centred on the mid-sixteenth century but ranging backwards in time.[52] But in this area surely Tuscany still has a lead. There are the successive studies of the late Raymond de Roover on the Medici bank and Bowski's work on Sienese public finance.[53] Economic considerations also play a large part in the 'straight' history, uniting political, social and cultural elements displayed in many of the writings of Gene A. Brucker.[54]

Many of these monographs are intricate and technical and assume a degree of sustained effort on the part of the reader, e.g. in the understanding of the credit and exchange arrangements of a world which dealt in money which was both paper (almost but not quite in our sense of the term) and metal (genuine metal needing to be assayed), and

---

49 Elio Conti, *I catasti agrari della repubblica fiorentina* (Rome, 1966, *et seq.*). On rural history see also many papers by P.J. Jones, e.g. *Cambridge Economic History*, I, 2nd edn (Cambridge, 1966), 340–431.

50 Lauro Martines, *The Social World of the Florentine Humanist 1390–1460* (London, 1963); Richard Goldthwaite, *Private Wealth in Renaissance Florence* (Princeton, 1968).

51 Paris, 1978.

52 Jacques Heers, *Gênes au XVe siècle* (Paris, 1961), a work flawed in my judgement by the relegation of the political narrative, without which the economic analysis becomes obscure, to a perfunctory final chapter; F.C. Lane's many works may be represented by his latest and most general, *Venice – A Maritime Republic* (Baltimore, 1973); Alberto Tenenti's writings on Venice include *Naufrages, corsaires et assurances maritimes à Venise* (Paris, 1959) and *Cristoforo da Canal. La marine venétienne avant Lepanto* (Paris, 1962); J. Delumeau, *Vie économique et sociale de Rome dans la seconde moitié du XVI siècle*, 2 vols (Paris, 1957–9) is also useful for earlier periods, especially on papal finances.

53 Raymond de Roover may be represented by *The Rise and Fall of the Medici Bank 1397–1494* (Cambridge, Mass., 1963); W. Bowski, *The Finances of the Commune of Siena 1287–1355* (Oxford, 1970).

54 *Renaissance Florence* (New York, 1969); *The Civic World of Early Renaissance Florence* (Princeton, 1977); cf. above, n. 40.

a mixture involving paper transactions based on the genuine gold and silver of the coins: all very hard for those of us who hardly recall a time when money was more than tokens. Fortunately some admirable general economic historians have surveyed the Renaissance era.[55] It is however fair in this context to stress that these writers on general economic history are not concerned in any direct sense with the Renaissance as such, as Lopez had been in his essay referred to above,[56] with the exception of Sapori, who contributed (albeit in an indirect manner) to the debate on periodization.[57] The fact is that in broad terms the flowering of Italian genius in the arts and in letters corresponded with a period of economic recession.

If economic historians have enriched our understanding of the background to the Italian Renaissance by investigating rural economy and mercantile practice, one must perforce be more cautious of the findings of those scholars who have moved from the known to the hypothetical in the ocean of figures afforded by Italian record material. One may describe this as a movement from the abacus to the computer, or as a signal tribute to the school of *Annales* and the influence of Fernand Braudel. I say a 'movement', for the outstanding figure in this world of calculation as far as Italy is concerned is the above-mentioned American, David Herlihy, whose earliest work was an extremely good account of the history of Pisa in the years of her decline as a great power.[58] This was written (as other admirable essays by him)[59] before the mirage of mathematical exactitude enveloped him as it did so many others. One has the impression that this odd phase is passing away and that at all events it had not attracted any significant Italian adherents; they remained content with older methods of dealing with figures. There is no evidence to suggest, for instance, that Beloch's population calculations, which become firm only as we move from the sixteenth to the seventeenth century, have been supplemented by modern research,

55 E.g. G. Luzzatto, *Storia economica d'Italia* (incomplete) (Rome, 1949); Armando Sapori, *Il mercante italiano nel medioevo* (Milan, 1941); *Studi di storia economica medievale* (Florence, 1946) and many earlier works; Yves Renouard, *Les hommes d'affaires d'Italie du moyen âge* (Paris, 1949).

56 Above, n. 34; also Lopez's chapter in *Cambridge Economic History*, II (Cambridge, 1952); having said that, it is fair to add that Christian Bec attributes the inspiration for his *Les marchands écrivains: affaires et humanisme à Florence 1375-1434* (Paris–The Hague, 1967) 'to a hypothesis formulated by Y. Renouard' in a contribution to *Il quattrocento. Libera cattedra di storia della civiltà fiorentina* (Florence, 1954).

57 See Delio Cantimori's contribution to *Studi in onore di Armando Sapori* (Milan, 1957), reprinted in *Storici e storia*, op. cit., 597–609.

58 *Pisa in the Early Renaissance* (New Haven, 1958).

59 E.g. 'Sancta Maria Impruneta: a rural commune in the Middle Ages', Rubinstein (ed.), *Florentine Studies*, 242–76.

however sophisticated.[60] Figures were compiled for specific occasions: they cannot usually be made to serve purposes other than those for which they were at first assembled.[61]

I have touched on some of the salient innovations of recent years, assuming that – although Italians have been slower to adopt the convention than others – we must accept the Renaissance now as a period of time, in which all that happens falls fairly under scrutiny. But, this accepted, it is remarkable how conservative what might be called 'Renaissance' scholarship has remained, faithful to its centuries-old association with the fine arts, education, belles-lettres and ethical problems, all in association with *Die Wiederbelebung des classischen Altherthums*, to use Georg Voigt's title (1859). This is very clearly seen in the work of Eugenio Garin himself. His prodigious output follows in the tradition of scholarship in which the recovery of Antiquity and the perfection of a revived Latin as a means of communication is firmly rooted; to these interests we must add philosophy, about which a word in a moment. His general study *L'umanesimo italiano: filosofia e vita civile nel Rinascimento*, first appeared in German (Berne, 1947), then in Italian (Bari, 1952). In 1957 there appeared *L'educazione in Europa* (also published in Bari), to be read with his large anthology of Renaissance texts on the subject.[62] *L'umanesimo italiano* has been his most influential book so far, not least in the English-speaking world, where a translation appeared in 1968 in Oxford. It is worth remarking that in this book he reached many conclusions similar to those of Hans Baron. But Garin's chief fame is, surely, the discovery of new texts and the meticulous editing of old ones. Here his signal contribution to the series

60 Karl Julius Beloch, *Bevölkerungsgeschichte Italiens*, II, 2nd edn (Berlin, 1965).
61 For reasoned criticism of what is usually called the *Annales* school, see Robert W. Fogel, 'The limits of quantitative methods', *American Historical Review*, 80 (1975); Alan Bullock, *Is History becoming a Social Science?*, Leslie Stephen Lecture (Cambridge, 1976); and most recently the judicious paper by Professor René Pillorget in *Durham University Journal* (1977), 'From a classical to a serial and quantitative study of history: some new directions in French historical research'. And see the recent work by L. Allegra and A. Torre, *La nascita della storia sociale in Francia: dalla Comune alle Annales* (Turin, 1977). The mention of recent criticism, partly perhaps arising from the tremendous bulk of *Annales*, in no way impugns the significance of all of the authors or all of their contributions, to which I for one have occasionally turned gratefully; the neatest illustration of its influence is the cover and contents of the *Revue historique* in recent years; or the popularity of the title *Annali* or its equivalent, which emphatically does not reflect the continued inspiration of Muratori!
62 Prior to Garin's *L'umanesimo italiano* he had published an anthology of texts on the subject, *Il Rinascimento italiano* (Milan, 1941). On education note also his collection of texts, *L'educazione umanistica in Italia* (Bari, 1949), and *L'educazione in Europa* (Bari, 1957).

'La letteratura italiana: storia e testi', *Prosatori latini del quat-trocento*,[63] has become indispensable to all teachers and students of the Renaissance. But it would be absurd to list Garin's editorial work, beyond reminding the reader that his influence in this sphere is very considerable as one of the joint editors of *Rinascimento* since 1962 (and now its sole editor). (The multitude of Garin's books, articles and reviews as a whole were listed down to 1969 in the *Bibliografia* published by Laterza in that year to mark his sixtieth birthday.) This insistence on textual scholarship is the most authentic inheritance of the Renaissance, taking us back to Poggio, Salutati, Niccoli and their peers. Garin's work in this type of scholarship is, I believe, not only in the *tradizione rinascimentale* but represents the interests of many scholars in Italy since the war. One thinks of scores of editors and commentators: Spongano, Branca, Bonfantini, Panigada and Perosa are names that spring to mind. Nor must we forget the foreign scholars who have contributed to editorial work on Italian Renaissance texts: B.L. Ullman's edition of Salutati's *De laboribus Herculis* (Zurich, 1951); Cecil Grayson's edition of L.B. Alberti's *Della famiglia* (Bari, 1960–6), Raymond Marcel's edition and translation of Marsilio Ficino's *Commentaire sur le banquet de Platon* (Paris, 1956). The moment one writes down a few names one is conscious that they are but a small sample of the many who have contributed. In the long list it is surely certain that here at least Italians are the most numerous, still maintaining the great tradition of textual criticism and publication that runs, almost unbroken, from Muratori to Remigio Sabbadini and onwards. All in all, we are now infinitely better provided with reliable texts of Italian authors from the mid-fourteenth to the mid-sixteenth century than was the case before the Second World War, and much of the credit for the work itself and for encouraging others to embark on it belongs to Garin. His philosophical interests are dealt with elsewhere in this volume, by Paul Oskar Kristeller. It may however be noted that they too include editorial work on Pico della Mirandola and other speculative writers of the period.

The preponderant literary (and artistic) emphasis of recent works on the Renaissance may also be seen by glancing at the contents of the three main journals devoted to Renaissance studies – *Rinascita* and its sequel *Rinascimento* (since 1950), *Bibliothèque d'humanisme et Renaissance* (since 1941) and *Renaissance Quarterly* (since 1967 and since volume 28 incorporating the annual *Renaissance Studies*).[64] It is, of course, the case

63 Milan, 1952.
64 The *Bibliothèque d'humanisme et Renaissance* was preceded (1934–40) by *Humanisme et Renaissance*; the *Renaissance Quarterly* was preceded by *Renaissance News* (1948–66). Of the non-specialist journals alluded to above perhaps the most important is the *Journal of the Courtauld and Warburg Institutes*.

that many important communications are made to other periodicals: the big national historical reviews, for example, and those exclusively devoted to the arts and literature. But specialization prevails: a trend found in every branch of knowledge, alas with many detrimental effects, such as a parochialism of scholarship, a narrowing of cultural horizons and an encouragement to pedantic points of marginal interest. But it exists and therefore many a paper which would have been published in the *Giornale storico della letteratura italiana* fifty years ago now appears in *Rinascimento*. I do not mean that its quality is thus diminished, only that the specialisms that bedevil our lives make it exceedingly hard to encourage even the attempt to take a sympathetic interest in a subject as a whole rather than some period or aspect of it. Perhaps I speak here as a benighted Briton, condemned to much teaching and never having enjoyed much leisure for research, but nevertheless Italian professors do *some* teaching (and many of them a good deal), and not all Americans get support for lengthy sojourns abroad. The problem of a narrowing of our general view of literature, the arts, society and politics is, therefore, I fear, a growing one.

The dichotomy is particularly noticeable in the field of culture and may be vividly illustrated by the relative neglect of the new humanist attitudes, and techniques of communication ('poetry'), in countries other than Italy. In a sense, as I said earlier, I believe it to be true that the late Roberto Weiss simply did not believe in any *generalized* spread of the humanities: he saw the collection of manuscripts, the schoolmaster, the sonnet even, as happening in the England of the fifteenth century, but did not ask why *then*, save that the missionaries, so to speak, came from Italy; the Renaissance spread like the pox – by contagion.[65] The approach of another student to another part of Europe was, I consider, much more fruitful. I refer to the many studies devoted to the humanities in France from the fourteenth to the seventeenth centuries composed with enormous erudition and no little wit by another old friend, alas also recently deceased, Franco Simone. His researches did try to establish, and in my view succeeded in establishing, which of Petrarch's works were 'digestible' in the France of the early Renaissance, and went on to establish norms for both literature and history, in their interreactions, over succeeding

65 Roberto Weiss, *Il primo secolo dell'umanesimo italiano. Studi e testi* (Rome, 1949), an elaboration and development of his inaugural lecture at London (1947). For his views on humanism in England, see *Humanism in England*, 3rd edn (Oxford, 1957), which is severely restricted to the fifteenth century. His *Spread of Italian Humanism* is entirely literary in a narrow sense and is somewhat disappointing; so too is his contribution on 'Learning and education in Western Europe from 1470 to 1520', *New Cambridge Modern History*, I (Cambridge, 1957), 95–126.

centuries.[66]

Greatly as social and political history has influenced the study of cultural history in the Renaissance period – and this could have been driven home much more forcibly by adducing more names of recent scholars who have made great use of documentary material[67] – there yet remain areas where intensive research is still needed. Perhaps the most significant of these is the cultural and spiritual history of the Church in Italy during the fourteenth and fifteenth centuries. Many of the great writers and artists were clergy and the bulk of their work one may guess was devoted either to moral issues or to ecclesiastical subjects. All were at any rate technically Christians, despite Burckhardt's conviction that the period saw a rise in scepticism and irreligion, a point to be heavily emphasized by Pastor in his distinction between the 'Pagan' and the 'Christian' Renaissance. Admittedly it is extremely difficult to know what are a man's innermost convictions. This is obviously the case with the creator of mute buildings and pictures. But it is far from being a great deal easier when one is dealing with written views. Obviously there are identifiable extremes. For cases in point one could instance the severe condemnation of the new styles and assumptions in Giovanni Dominici's *Lucula noctis* or the firm repetition of the old case for 'poetry', in Boccaccio's *Genealogia deorum gentilium*, or in Salutati, the specific object of Dominici's treatise. But it is often extremely difficult to determine when or whether a writer is expressing his own views, and this is especially so in dialogues, that favourite form of Renaissance literature based on a technique of exposition beloved by Antiquity. What exactly does Petrarch mean when, at the end of the *Secretum*, he admits the truth – the absolute truth – of St Augustine's strictures and then refuses to act upon them, at any rate for the foreseeable future? What exactly do we infer of Valla's own position from the views put into the mouths of interlocutors in his *De libero arbitrio*?[68] Or, to take what might appear at first sight a perfectly plain

66 Franco Simone's influence was of course exerted to a large extent through *Studi francesi* which he edited from Turin. In many ways his most remarkable work seems to me the early *La coscienza della Rinascita negli umanisti francesi* (Rome, 1949). The insights here displayed were developed further in his *Rinascimento francese* (Turin, 1961) and *Umanesimo, Rinascimento, Barocco in Francia* (Milan, 1968), as well as in many articles. Gilson's influence is evident in all of Simone's work. For his connection with Garin see the *premessa* to the last-named volume.

67 Rubinstein, above, n. 46; E. Fiumi, 'Fioritura e decadenza dell'economia fiorentina', three parts in *Archivio storico italiano*, vols 115–17 (1957–9) and *Storia economica e sociale di San Gemignano* (Florence, 1961). But there are scores more of important studies based on archival studies, as one sees in the titles listed in *La storiografia italiana*.

68 Charles Trinkaus grapples with this sort of problem at several points in his *In Our Image and Likeness*, 2 vols (London, 1970).

problem, what was Boccaccio's personal attitude to the question of sexual morality?[69] Was Platina's *vitae pontificum romanorum* a humdrum narrative or, at any rate occasionally, a deliberate attempt to urge the need for a reformed Papacy?[70]

Church history in Renaissance Italy has been neglected until recently. However, the *Rivista della storia della chiesa in Italia* has made a remarkable contribution since 1946; and other periodicals of great interest are springing up, such as the more episodic *Ricerche per la storia religiosa di Roma* (since 1977). But a good deal of work has also certainly been put into the edition of texts and we may cite as examples the splendid editions which have appeared of the sermons of Bernardino da Siena and Bernardino da Feltre.[71] There has also been much recent work done on the confraternities and movements of popular devotion prior to the sixteenth century[72] and such study is probably a more rewarding entrée into the religious milieu than the analysis of men of great devotion like the famous Observant preachers already mentioned, or even those friars whose political influence was demonstrably considerable, like the Dominican Savonarola. For the confraternities brought together both the simple and the learned, the rich and the poor. What we need, I feel, are more works such as the remarkably suggestive work of Alberto Tenenti, *Il senso della morte e l'amore della vita nel Rinascimento*[73], in which, as the reader will recall, he contrasts the literature and symbolism of death and of holy dying in Italy and northern Europe and, in greatest detail, in Italy and France. It is notable that Tenenti is a historian, not a literary critic. Quite apart from the largely 'un-literary' nature of his written evidence, he is less likely to fall into the trap which awaits the biographer, of assuming a coherence and continuity of position in his hero, a fault which flaws many studies of individual men of religion. The historian of religious sensibility must read between the lines; must try to see the effects of popular manifestations (here the great public spectacles of Italy, and especially of Rome, await a historian who is alive to their significance in the

69 John Charles Nelson, 'Love and sex in the Decameron', in the Kristeller *Festschrift* (above, n. 25) 339–51.
70 One of the conclusions which my graduate student Richard Palermino seems to be reaching : M.Litt. 1973, Ph.D. 1980.
71 The first edn by the Fathers of the College of St Bonaventure, 7 vols (Florence, 1950–9); the second edn by Father Carlo Varischi, OFM Cap., 3 vols (Milan, 1964).
72 Of many studies we may recall *Il movimento dei disciplinati nel settimo centenario dal suo inizio*, Convegno internazionale 1960, Deputazione di storia patria per l'Umbria, app. al *Bolletino*, no. 9.
73 Turin, 1957.

political and spiritual spheres)[74] and the influence of growing literacy and the printing press. On this last point it is worth repeating parenthetically the complaint voiced earlier regarding Italian libraries, here relating it to the absence of any adequate catalogues of Italian printed books, save what is provided by the *Indice generale degli incunaboli* and the *Gesamtkatalog der Wiegendrucke* (as far as they go) for incunables, and those catalogues which emanate from the only library with a complete catalogue, the British Library References Division, formerly the British Museum Library.[75] This is very sad considering how many incunables are to be found in Italian libraries, but the position is being redeemed: see additional note, below, p. 132.

If it seems that religion in its broadest sense – popular and learned piety, patronage, finance of buildings and church decorations and cult developments – is deserving of greater study than it has yet had from Italian and other scholars, there is one area where activity has been intense. I refer to the Italian reformers. Not only have Antonio Rotondò and Carlo Ginzburg recently produced important studies, but there is now an elaborate series, edited by Luigi Firpo and Giorgio Spini with the assistance of Rotondò and John Tedeschi, *Corpus reformatorum italicorum*.[76] This line of research had its 'first begetter' in Delio Cantimori, whose *Eretici italiani del Cinquecento* appeared first in the form of a collection of documents (1937) and elaborated as a book in 1939 (Florence). One of the most illuminating results of these enquiries shows how intellectual (or, if you will, non-popular) these devel-

---

74 Cf. Brian Pullan's remarks on processions in Venice in *Rich and Poor in Renaissance Venice* (Oxford, 1971). Contemporary accounts are probably fullest for Rome (where the Jubilee for long was a complication and an encouragement) but they are found everywhere and, it need be hardly said, not just in Italian towns.

75 The chequered career of the *Gesamtkatalog* came to an end with the Second World War; it has subsequently resumed to reach 'Federicis'; Garnaschelli *et al.* (eds), *Indice generale degli incunaboli delle biblioteche d'Italià*, began to appear (Rome) in 1943. After 1500 we move into a darker world but the British Museum's short title catalogue for *Italy* (London, 1958) is an immense help, although the Museum lacks a substantial proportion of known titles; cf. also F.J. Norton, *Italian Printers 1501–20* (Cambridge, 1924). The Italian *Primo Catalogo collettivo delle biblioteche italiane* began publication at Rome in 1962, but has not got beyond 'B', with a Dante volume ahead of schedule. The Italian incunables in the British Library are superbly presented in Parts IV to VII of the *Catalogue of Books Printed in the XVth Century now in the British Museum* (London, 1916–35), with the remarkable introduction by J.V. Scholderer in Part VII. This brief note does not by any means exhaust bibliographical aids for the post-1500 period, but over-all they remain sadly inadequate.

76 The first volume to appear, Camillo Renato, *Opere*, ed. A. Rotondò (Florence–Chicago, 1968), is to be followed we hope by many more.

opments were, in their attempts to establish widespread diffusion of heterodox views, despite the horrific activities of the Inquisition; and in following up the Italian reformers one is compelled to cross the Alps[77] as with Peter Martyr Vermigli (on whom Philip McNair has written a fine book).[78] The most characteristic form taken by this exported Italian reform was Socinianism, destined to have its full development in a more peaceful period than the stormiest days of the German Reformation, and in places far removed from Italy, notably (in what was to become known as Unitarianism) in Poland, Hungary and England.[79] One has the impression that the historians of the Reformation in Italy, even if in the end it was abortive, are pursuing a more coherent programme than students of the Renaissance as such.[80] This is all the more forcible since the Anglo-Saxon and German tradition is to treat the Renaissance as a kind of preliminary to the serious business of reform. It may be added that Italians are not merely concerning themselves with early evidence of Protestantism (the *Beneficio di Cristo*, B. Ochino and so on) but also with the effects in Italy of what we must learn to call not the 'Counter-Reformation' but the 'Catholic Reformation', which has prompted the excellent writings of Alberigo, Prodi and D'Addario, to name but a few.[81]

Another area which, it may be assumed, would repay detailed study is education. The admirably edited texts which Garin has produced are, like the studies of W.H. Woodward (which have stood the test of time well),[82] based mainly on theoretical expositions rather than on a study of practice. We know a great deal about Guarino and Vittorino, and we know what some of their contemporaries such as Vergerio and Pope Pius II regarded as ideal curricula. But what actually happened in the generality of schools? For educational history illustrating the diffusion of humanist principles we have to turn to students of teaching in

77 Two examples: the studies gathered in A. Rotondò's *Studi e ricerche di storia ereticale italiana del cinquecento* (Turin, 1974); Carlo Ginzburg, *Il Nicodemismo* (Turin, 1970); cf. *Eresia e riforma nell'Italia del cinquecento. Miscellanea I* (Florence–Chicago, 1974).
78 *Peter Martyr in Italy* (Oxford, 1967).
79 John Tedeschi (ed.), *Italian Reformation Studies in Honor of Laelius Socinus* (Florence, 1965).
80 Even the Waldensians are active. Cf. G. Gonnet, *Le confessioni di fede Valdesi prima della riforma* (Turin, 1967).
81 Among the many writings of these scholars I cite only G. Alberigo, *I vescovi italiani al concilio di Trento* (Florence, 1959); P. Prodi, 'Riforma cattolica o controriforma', *Nuove questioni di storia moderna*, ed. L. Bulfaretti (Milan, 1964); A. D'Addario, *Aspetti della controriforma a Firenze* (Rome, 1972). For a recent treatment and text of one of the most notable figures in the wake of these changes see now the *Opere* of Paolo Sarpi, ed. by Gaetano and Luisa Cozzi in the series 'Letteratura Italiana' (Milan, 1969).
82 Below, n. 92.

northern Europe, where (as in England) the transformation of the curriculum can be dramatically displayed.[83] I am not aware of any comparable work on the schools of Italy and of only a few partial studies of Renaissance universities.[84] The survey of the Italian grammar school in G. Manacorda's incomplete *Storia della scuola in Italia* (Milan, 1914) stops unfortunately before the Florentine Renaissance begins, but some treatment of this problem is to be found in Christian Bec's *Marchands écrivains à Florence 1375-1434*,[85] in his discussion of the 'Formation intellectuelle et culture des marchands'. Much more needs to be done if we are to perceive how the educational changes affected the peninsula as a whole. By the late fifteenth century nearly every Italian scholar wrote in a more or less neo-classical style, just as scholars did in the rest of Europe by 1600 or thereabouts. But how did this come about? Certainly not because the Council of Trent ordered seminaries in all dioceses for priests, for these took centuries to be erected; and certainly not because of the sporadic efforts of Jesuits and Barnabites.

Another gap, perhaps even more surprising, is the study of the effects of the Renaissance on Italian archaeology and historiography. This is, indeed, an area in which Europe as a whole is defective for the Renaissance period. In archaeology the only systematic and scientific work which has been done is concentrated on Rome and tends on the whole to look forward to the new city rather than examine the old: I think of the fine books by T. Magnuson and Redig de Campos.[86] But what is needed is an account of the progressive interest in, and understanding of, Italian classical buildings, from Flavio Biondo (or earlier) onwards. The task would be arduous, for this type of literature is constantly being rewritten generation by generation, and the task in

---

83 For some references to recent work see my contribution to H. Oberman and T. Brady (eds), *Itinerarium italicum* (essays in honour of Kristeller), (Leiden, 1965).

84 The standard authorities are W.H. Woodward, *Vittorino da Feltre and other Humanist Educators* (Cambridge, 1897), and *Education during the Renaissance* (Cambridge, 1906); and of course Garin's works (above, n. 62), especially *L'educazione in Europa*, 119-21, where he discusses the dispersion of the new methods and ideals in Italian education, but depends, as does Woodward, on the theorists. Yet every Italian town of any size must have had a grammar school by 1500, surely, *endowed* to secure for it more than a precarious existence.

85 Paris, 1967.

86 T. Magnuson, *Studies in Roman Quattrocento Architecture* (Stockholm, 1958); D. Redig de Campos, *I palazzi vaticani* (Bologna, 1967). Roberto Weiss may be consulted for the antiquaries in *The Renaissance Discovery of Classical Antiquity* (Oxford, 1969). But the most thorough and exciting survey is the unpublished Edinburgh doctoral dissertation of Peter Spring (1973), 'The topographical and archaeological study of the antiquities of the city of Rome 1420-7'.

Italy would be compounded by the multiplicity of places where local antiquaries were increasingly at work.

As for historiography, it is sad that we still have to depend, for an over-all view, on the work, admirable as it is in many ways, of Eduard Fueter.[87] Fueter is schematic and thorough and, apart from the stimulating survey in Felix Gilbert's *Machiavelli and Guicciardini: Politics and History in Sixteeth Century Florence*,[88] which is much wider-ranging than its title suggests (it includes, for example, a most useful analysis of Pontano's *Actius*), he has, I believe, no rival for the Renaissance period. There are, of course, large numbers of works on the major historians. To go back no further than the 1950s we have 'lives and times' studies by Roberto Ridolfi on *Machiavelli* (1954) and *Guicciardini* (1960). We have some admirable regional studies such as that edited by Agostino Pertusi for Venice.[89] But in general, works such as these tend to neglect the philological element which is surely the basis of the historian's task: his search for and evaluation of his source material, his attempts to date and criticize such material, to gain access to documentary matter and distinguish it from narrative evidence, written or oral. This aspect of historiography has almost entirely been neglected, and not only in Italy. Fueter, to quote a case in point,[90] does not quite ignore Baronius' discussion of sources but he is really concerned to show him as a polemical opponent of the Magdeburg centuriators, whereas his publication of source material surely deserves commendation. We should recall how Valla's celebrated 'De falso edita et ementita Constantini donatione declamatio' lacks anything which we would nowadays regard as historical criticism and we should not attribute the essay so much to his courage (as Fueter does) as to the enmity of his patron Alfonso V to Eugenius IV at that time.[91] Here Fueter falls victim to his quite unreal distinction between the 'schools' of Bruni and of Biondo: the first 'rhetorical', the second 'erudite'. No one who reads Biondo's *Decades* can be under any illusion regarding his erudition, for he merely followed a given source and seldom criticized or

87 Originally published in German in 1911, it was translated by A. Spinelli as *Storia della Storiografia moderna* (reprinted Milan, 1970); the Italian version is based on the third German edition (1928) which contains a very few additional notes by Fueter; those added by the translator are negligible.
88 Princeton, 1965.
89 *La storiografia veneziana fino al secolo XVI. Aspetti e problemi* (Florence, 1970), especially the contribution of Gaetano Cozzi; cf. also Hans Baron, 'Early Renaissance Venetian chronicles', in his *From Petrarch to Leonardo Bruni* (Chicago, 1968).
90 Ed. ital. cit., 340.
91 Ibid., 144–5.

compared.[92] It was (and this need surprise no one) in the careful attempts to compare physical remains with classical writings that erudition of the modern sort was to emerge, and with this Fueter is hardly concerned. His plan admits no place for scholarship as such. Mabillon, whose *De re diplomatica* (1681-1704) was surely the foundation of modern scientific historiography, forces his way into Fueter's survey by way of his *Annales ordinis S. Benedicti*, but of Muratori we hear only of the *Annali*, since this is regarded as narrative history; there is not a word of that massive monument, the *Rerum Italicarum scriptores*, which is still used today as a basic tool of research.[93] Admittedly historians, medieval as well as Renaissance, had an axe to grind. The Renaissance historian ground the big axes of powerful rulers: he was often a propagandist and as such played a major role in the studies already alluded to on Italian political thought in the Renaissance. Yet the future of historiography was at stake in the handful of men who published texts, even perhaps when these were forged.[94] Undoubtedly the classical scholars blazed the trail and the historiography of the ancient world was the first to be treated with distinction and sophistication. After all, it fell well within the humanist curriculum.

May I be permitted to add two further desiderata? The first is for a more deliberate and rounded study of Florence in the whole of the fifteenth century. In general, works like Baron's,[95] and Christian Bec's recent and most interesting *Les marchands écrivains: affaires et humanisme à Florence 1375-1434*, tend to end in the 1440s.[96] But works such as Brucker's[97] would be an enormous help if written for the fifteenth, and especially the later fifteenth and the early sixteenth centuries, when they would link up with von Albertini, Cochrane and others, forming a coherent cultural and political survey. There are, indeed, extremely important works such as Nicolai Rubinstein's on the period, but this is not concerned with cultural matters, nor even to any great extent with the political principles which the author had dealt

---

92 Cf. my lecture, 'Flavio Biondo and the Middle Ages', above, chapter 3, pp. 35-66.

93 Fueter, op. cit., 401, 409.

94 I refer to the curious activities of Annius or Nanni da Viterbo (1432-1502) who, so far as I know, still awaits proper study; on Trithemius, his contemporary in Germany, see now the study of Klaus Arnold (Würzburg, 1971).

95 Baron, of course, has concerned himself with later periods, e.g. his study of aspects of Machiavelli's works in *English Historical Review*, LXXVI (1961).

96 Cf. above, p. 127.

97 Above, n. 40.

with for earlier and later periods.[98] The absence of a general study of
Florence at this time is of particular importance, since it was during the
middle and later fifteenth century that the innovations in literature and
the arts spread so rapidly to the princely courts of Italy and, later still,
penetrated so deeply into the princely courts and societies of the rest of
Europe that their consequences, to some degree, are still an important
force in modern society. Until the day before yesterday – yes! as
recently as that – every scholar and many men of affairs had some
Latin, many a great deal, as a direct consequence of the extraordinary
elevation of the humanities (as defined by Kristeller) during the earlier,
republican, period of 'civic humanism'. It was only when the princes
and their courtiers took over the direction of culture from the
marchands écrivains that Florentine values could be exported.

My reference to Latin leads me to my second plea. It is of a very
different sort and perhaps it is now unattainable. I refer to the need for
rapid and effective protection and stimulation of the teaching of Latin in
all countries where medieval and Renaissance (let alone classical)
studies are regarded as significant regions in which to explore the mind
of man. Classical languages are in peril and, in this context, I naturally
refer to Latin. In Britain and the English-speaking world the decline in
the teaching of Latin is dramatic in most places. I understand that much
the same is true of even the Romance areas of Europe – France, Spain,
even Italy.[99] This is by no means all loss. If a series such as 'La
letteratura italiana: Studi e testi', with its facing Italian translations of
admirably edited originals, would have been inconceivable before the
war, at any rate at a level above the brief anthology, it nevertheless has
two good results. First, it makes available to a much wider public the
resources of a dead language. Second, the very act of translation
reinforces the critical attention the editor pays to his original: I speak

---

98 N. Rubinstein, *The Government of Florence under the Medici, 1434-1494*
(Oxford, 1966); see above, n. 37, and also the same author's 'Machiavelli
and the world of Florentine politics', in *Studies on Machiavelli* (Florence,
1972). There are a number of articles of great interest dealing with the
critical years 1378-1434, e.g. A. Molho, 'Politics and the ruling class in
early Renaissance Florence', *Nuova rivista storica*, 52 (1968), 401-20, in
which the concept of a 'political class' is usefully discussed, as it is also by
Dale Kent, 'The Florentine Reggimento in the Fifteenth Century',
Renaissance Quarterly, XXVIII (1975), 575-638. But the later fifteenth
century in Florence tends to be treated biographically, so to speak, as in the
works of Ridolfi ·(above, n. 41); cf. the very interesting book by D.
Weinstein, *Savonarola and Florence* (Princeton, 1970).

99 As I understand the matter the classical curriculum used in some countries,
including Germany, had statutory authority in secondary and higher education until fairly recently.

from harrowing experience.[100] But these benefits are not much to set against the inability of the average student to understand even the footnotes in the standard works of an older generation, where 'a classical education' could be assumed by writers of serious works.

For a balanced account of the period I have touched on so inadequately in the previous pages, the account of Giuseppe Martini[101] should be consulted, where he had space to summarize many of the works to which I have only been able to allude. In general I believe he is right to stress what he calls the 'linea Baron–Garin' as that which has dominated recent scholarship. In essence this means that students of humanism are finding themselves obliged to take into account the historical background, the political situation, the economic development of their world. One could instance many examples of the fruitful results of this conjunction; indeed many have been mentioned. To these may be added for good measure Garin's own studies (for example, of the chancellor historians of Florence)[102] and the work by Claudio Varese, *Storia e politica nella prosa del quattrocento*,[103] which, incidentally, is one of the relatively few books which makes a gallant attempt to deal with the mid-fourteenth century. In this connection I should like also to mention the most interesting and, I suspect, somewhat neglected social matters discussed by Piero Pieri in *Il Rinascimento e la crisi militare italiana*,[104] which does run down to the 1530s.

There is another reason for consulting the relevant pages in *La storiografia italiana negli ultimi vent'anni*. Both Martini and his collaborator Gigliola Rondinini Soldi deal with a great many *Italian* writers and thus give a more balanced picture than I can, limited as I am to my knowledge of works published outside Italy. Nevertheless the influence of non-Italians on the interpretation of the Renaissance has been profound in the last three decades and my references to non-Italian and especially American scholars could have been greatly extended. Some reasons for this I touch on above when referring to the leadership of Tuscany in the comparative table of research done. But there is, of course, more to it than that. Every country in the world has had a brief period of student trouble in recent years. Italy's universities are both perpetually in student trouble and desperately in need of academic and

---

100 Polydore Vergil, *Anglica Historia* (London, 1950); Aeneas Sylvius Piccolomini, *De gestis concilii Basiliensis libri ii* (with W.K. Smith) (Oxford, 1967).

101 See above, p. 116 note 45.

102 Now reprinted in *Scienza e vita civile nel Rinascimento* (Bari, 1965); but in the same collection the essay on 'La cultura fiorentina nell'età di Leonardo' does not introduce political factors.

103 Turin, 1961.

104 Turin, 1952.

administrative reform, with particular attention required to organize graduate schools. These as such are rare in the United Kingdom, and in the USA they are often bad. But at their best they prepare young graduates for research in a marvellously systematic way, both by course work and by detailed supervision by a senior teacher. Does it not strike an Italian as absurd that it needed an American, Paul Oskar Kristeller, in his great *Iter italicum*,[105] to identify the unpublished or badly published manuscripts of the Italian Renaissance?

What I am pleading for is an Italian academic system which will produce more men of genius like Garin and not make them so exceptional: my counsel is *reculez pour mieux sauter*. United Kingdom universities seldom run to 'research schools' in any meaningful sense, though we have a right to be proud of the Institute of Historical Research and the Warburg Institute and a few similar graduate centres.[106] But, it may be said, we do encourage students to study the history of *foreign* countries and it is surely a fact that for one Italian studying English or American history there are half a dozen Englishmen and two dozen Americans studying Italian history. The study of other cultures is built into the British and American undergraduate curriculum and extends to postgraduate work.

Yet without the excitements of Italian cultural and political history it is doubtful whether Italy would have attracted so much attention. The end of the ancient Roman world, the slow spread of Christianity, the rise of the communes, the emerging principates, the struggle of Florence with the 'tyrants', the cultural leadership of Italian letters, music and painting from the Renaissance onwards all through the epoch of the Grand Tour, and then the excitements of the Risorgimento and now the excitements of a disintegrating Italy, all make her a wonderful country to concentrate on.

As far as the Renaissance portion of this complicated story is concerned, the indefatigable work of Eugenio Garin gives him a central and commanding place, where his enormous learning is so wide as to deserve the various diverse contributions to this volume. And how many contemporary historians, as opposed to belle-lettristes, have earned in their lifetimes (see p. 121) the distinction of a separately printed bibliography? One knows that it is seriously out-of-date already.

105 Warburg Institute and Brill, I (1963), II (1967); a third volume   was published in 1983.
106 We must all look with admiration tinged with envy at the lavish resources available to French scholars for research at home and abroad in the Centre de recherches scientifiques, VIe section, of the Ecole Pratique des Hautes Etudes.

Additional Note (cf. p. 125, above). The British Library is organising an Incunable Short Title Catalogue (ISTC); see British Library Occasional Papers, 5 (1987).

7

THE PLACE OF HANS BARON
IN RENAISSANCE HISTORIOGRAPHY

Renaissance scholarship has been transformed in the course of the last thirty-odd years. Among those who have contributed most to the change Hans Baron is certainly to be numbered. What are the ways in which he has influenced the development of historical scholarship in this field?

To answer this question involves recalling the general state of Renaissance studies before the Second World War and this is far from easily done. I propose to meet the difficulty by using as a stalking horse the treatment of the subject in the two last volumes of the *Cambridge Medieval History*. In volume VII (published in 1932) and in volume VIII (1936) there are chapters by Arthur A. Tilley, dealing respectively with ' The early Renaissance ' and ' The Renaissance in Europe '[1]. By the 1930s Tilley, a French don at Cambridge who had written extensively on the Renaissance in France[2], was an elderly man but I believe that the synoptic chapters in the *Cambridge Medieval History* represent a fairly up to date (for the period) view of the subject. His bibliographies are not among the fullest in these uneven volumes[3], but one observes that he recorded Giuseppe Toffanin's *Che cosa fu l'umanesimo?* (1928) and clearly tried to keep abreast of the times. I shall now try to summarise his summary.

« The early Renaissance » begins, in effect, with Petrarch, who was « the first modern man » and was rightly

[1] VII, 751-776, VIII, 773-802.
[2] *The Literature of the French Renaissance: An Introductory Essay* (Cambridge, 1885); *The literature of the French Renaissance*, 2 vols. (Cambridge, 1904); *The Dawn of the Renaissance* (Cambridge, 1918).
[3] *Cambridge Medieval History*, VII, 966-8; VIII, 1004-6.

termed the first humanist, for he was the first to find in
ancient literature a larger measure than elsewhere of that
learning and training in virtue which are peculiar to man [4].
The resulting devotion to the Latin classics encouraged
the existing Italian impulse to discover new manuscripts
and form libraries. In this activity Petrarch was aided by
Boccaccio, who excelled him in Greek. Tilley records
Salutati's appointment as ' Latin secretary ' at Florence
and has a word on Luigi Marsili before touching on developments at Padua. There then follows a couple of pages
on the study of Greek before we encounter Leonardo
Bruni, whose « chief service to learning was the translation into Latin of works by Plato, Plutarch and
Aristotle » [5]. We have a few lines on a number of scholars — Marsuppini, Manetti, Traversari — before a rather
more elaborate account of Poggio and his discoveries,
which leads to a further discussion of libraries, this in
turn demanding some account of the manuscript book
trade. The description of Guarino's and Vittorino's educational programme comes next, explicitly based on the
works of Woodward. Some patrons are now put before
the reader: Nicholas V (with particular reference to
Filelfo, Biondo, who represented a ' higher ' type of
humanism, and Valla), Alfonso V (Fazio and Beccadelli).
The humanists' faults derived from that « inordinate desire for fame » which characterised the period, but on
the whole they were Christians except for Marsuppini.
The chapter concludes with a brief description of development in the arts at Florence — much less confident
than the rest of the section [6]. It leads on to the observation

---

[4] *Op. cit.* VII, 754.

[5] *Ibid.*, 760.

[6] *Ibid.*, 773: « The study of man ... leads to the study of individual
man and ... portraiture rapidly develops. Yet during the first half of the
fifteenth century avowed portraits of living persons were rare at Florence ».
In vol. VIII there is a separate chapter by W. G. Constable on the arts (down
to the beginning of the fifteenth century as far as Italy is concerned).

that secular art owed much to the way the « despots » had broken away from the « tutelage of the Church » in the cities of Northern Italy.

The contribution by Tilley to volume VIII begins abruptly with a catalogue of the popes after Nicholas V, and the affair of Pomponio Leto leads on to a description of the academies of Naples and Florence, the latter in turn involving a discussion of Ficino, Pico and Politian. Then, without warning, we are presented with the invention of printing and its diffusion in Italy. There then follows a brief description of Italian art in the fifteenth century [7] which ends with a couple of pages on « a third Renaissance feature of much of the Italian art of this time ... its scientific spirit » [8]; here Leonardo stands supreme. The author then deals *seriatim* with the spread of the Renaissance from Italy to other parts of Europe: France, the Low Countries and Germany, Hungary, Spain and England, taking the story down to the beginning of the sixteenth century, but not beyond; Reuchlin's quarrel with his obscurantist critics, « this memorable struggle between the forces of conservatism and those of progress, between medieval theology and humanism », belonged to modern history not to medieval [9]. In each of these national parts of the essay we are presented with the great figures of scholarship: « The restorer of classical studies in Spain was Antonio de Nebrija » is a not unrepresentative sentence [10].

It is, of course, easy enough to see the literary ancestry of Tilley's approach. This lay, as one would expect, in Voigt, Burckhardt and Symonds, that closely related group of scholars whose views, on the whole mutually compatible, had dominated learned discussion from the

[7] See previous note.
[8] *Cambridge Medieval History*, VIII, 779.
[9] *Ibid.*, 790.
[10] *Ibid.*, 795.

end of the nineteenth century onwards. This dependence is even more clearly revealed if Tilley's major generalisations are considered. The Renaissance is « the transition from the medieval to the modern world » which has « special features which distinguish it from other historical periods ». « If humanism is rightly defined as the cult of antiquity ... ». « These ardent humanists suffered from more than a touch of that pedantry which regards language and literature as having little relation to real life ». « Such was the Renaissance — not a rebirth, not a sudden transformation from darkness to light, but a gradual transition from the medieval to the modern world ... stimulated by the advent of a new spirit — a spirit of enthusiasm, of adventure, of pride in the dignity of man, a belief in individual effort, of criticism of old tradition, of search for new knowledge, a spirit guided and sustained by intercourse with the great writers of antiquity — poets, philosophers, historians — many of whom had been disinterred from dust-laden repositories, and who were all studied with a new reverence and a more enlightened understanding » [11].

Looking back on this presentation of the Renaissance the most striking feature is its desultory character. Scholarship since the 1880s was slotted unhappily into the Burckhardt framework with small regard for the logical, let alone the aesthetic, form of the master's work. The result tended to become an amalgam of assertions of broad principles with antiquarian observation of detail, in which the structure of society and politics was all but ignored and (for example) no distinction was drawn between the cultural developments to be found in republics, principates, monarchies. It is true that the « primacy » of Florence is mentioned by Tilley more than once [12]. It is also true that there are fugitive references in his pages to moral

---

[11] *Ibid.*, VII, 751, 769, 770, 775.
[12] *Ibid.*, VII, 771, VIII, 778.

or ethical questions [13]. But these hints do not provide an argument. They are not integral to an understanding of the individual scholars and artists who are successively dealt with. In short, the Renaissance is neither explained nor interpreted. It is treated as a collection of self-evident phenomena, ultimately requiring no justification.

If, with recent scholarship behind us, we find Tilley's account jejune, fragmented and detached from a solid social and political background, we should not be too severe on the author, nor reprove the editor's choice of a literary historian [14]. Looking at Tilley thirty-five years on, I find him more sophisticated than the actual teaching on the subject which I experienced in the 1930s when these Cambridge volumes were being prepared. At secondary school, where I read Burckhardt with great excitement in 1931, the Renaissance was firmly treated as the curtain-raiser to the drama of the Reformation. At Oxford, when I expressed a desire (I suppose this must have been in 1936) to study « The Italian Renaissance » as my « special subject », I was told by my tutor that only girls did that: I was to concentrate on the manly Middle Ages [15].

Now on what is our contemporary view of the Renaissance based? I suppose that most of us accept the Renaissance as a period which is worth studying in its own right rather than a lengthy « transition » from Middle

---

[13] *Ibid.*, VII, 754: « Petrarch ... was the first to find in ancient literature a larger measure than elsewhere of that learning and training in virtue which are peculiar to man ». VIII, 801: «... In England as in France the Renaissance at the close of the fifteenth century had a profoundly serious and ethical bias ... ».

[14] Cf. the account of the early Renaissance given at exactly the same time by E. P. Cheyney in the « Rise of Modern Europe » series: *The Dawn of a New Era* (New York & London, 1936). The next volume in the series is by Myron Gilmore. It appeared in 1952 and is called the *World of Humanism*. Note the syntactical consequences of emulating Michelet !

[15] That girls tended more than young men to study the Renaissance at Oxford in those days was, I suspect, because the subject was taught by a don at a woman's college, Miss Cecilia M. Ady.

Ages to modernity while we also have a distinctly more sceptical attitude to « periods » as such, realising their subjective quality. Beyond that we have lately grown accustomed to treating the changes which we summarise in the word « Renaissance » as serious factors in the public life of earlier times — matters (that is to say) to be digested by the « general » historian as well as by the art historian, or the historian of ideas. And if the Renaissance is to be treated seriously then it clearly revolves round the moral imperatives and the political urgencies of the period of its development. It was, at any rate in my own case, only when I read some of Hans Baron's articles published just before the War that I realised just how profoundly important the Renaissance had been in the evolution of the conscience and the consciousness of Europe [16].

There are a number of these papers prepared and published by Baron when he was in that unhappy interval between Germany and a new career in the States. I think in particular of two of them: the essay on «Cicero and the Roman Civic Spirit » and that on « Franciscan Poverty and Civic Wealth », both published in 1938 [17]. These articles were, of course, not the first indication of his novel approach. The edition of Leonardo Bruni's humanistic and philosophical works (1928) and the article in the *Historische Zeitschrift* (1933) on historical thought point forward, though perhaps more towards the post-war synthesis of the *Crisis* than expressly to the questions of morality raised in the essays to which I have referred. There is no need to provide a summary here of these two remarkable pieces of scholarship which are now part of

---

[16] I did not read these articles until just after the war, when preparing Edinburgh lectures on the later Middle Ages.

[17] « Cicero and the Roman Civic Spirit in the Middle Ages and Early Renaissance », *Bulletin of the John Rylands Library*, XXII (1938), 72-97; « Franciscan Poverty and Civic Wealth as Factors in the Rise of Humanistic Thought », *Speculum*, XIII (1938), 1-37.

the canon of Renaissance historiography[18]. To one reader at any rate they gave an entirely new dimension to the processes of intellectual change and went a long way to make plain why the Renaissance was important and why it developed in Italy as it did.

To begin with Baron was working within a framework which emphasised the chronological prominence and priority of Tuscany and above all of Florence in the evolution of new social and moral attitudes. This was a very important adjustment to the conventional Burckhardtian picture (part I of the *Civilization of the Renaissance in Italy* deals with tyrannies before it turns to republics), and it had parallels in the tendency discernible between the wars to relate the origins of the Renaissance to the development of capitalism. The principal result was the important distinction between « civic » humanism and its later princely manifestations. This basic notion has proved methodologically extremely rewarding and has been generally adopted in post-war surveys of the period and its problems[19].

Beyond that, Baron's interpretation was important in other ways. First of all he showed that a great mass of humanistic literature was to be taken seriously and not dismissed, as much of it had been by Burckhardt, Voigt and their successors, as empty vapourisings, stylish manipulation of Latin as an end in itself, the mere emulation of antiquity. The most immediately impressive feature of Baron's work was indeed the way in which it was solidly anchored in the literature of the period — these articles

---

[18] Cfr. Wallace K. Ferguson, *The Renaissance in Historical Thought* (Boston, 1948), pp. 231-38; Ferguson here discusses Baron briefly on pp. 228-9, but deals at greater length with his work in « The Interpretation of Italian Humanism: The Contribution of Hans Baron », *Journal of the History of Ideas*, XIX (1958), 14-25.

[19] For example E. Garin in his well-known work on Italian humanism which first appeared in a German version at Bonn in 1947. I have already pointed out the prophetic observation in G. Voigt's *Wiederb'lebung* (1859), that Salutati secured « Bürgerrecht », for humanism in Florence; cf. my *The Italian Renaissance in its Historical Background* (Cambridge, 1961), p. 121.

hardly refer to any secondary authorities, for the simple reason that the author could find little prior work that was relevant to his purposes, and knew his texts so well that he could with confidence base his argument on the original materials. Secondly, this acceptance of a basic seriousness in much of the literature, especially the Latin literature, suggested that there were good practical reasons lying behind the patronage of the humanist by the Florentine bourgeoisie. And this was even more strongly suggested by the argument that the humanist had justified a moral position (the compatibility of the active life and of wealth with the demands of Christian citizenship) which afforded a long overdue adjustment between the demands of official doctrine and the practical possibilities of ordinary life. The conscience of the literate citizen was gradually eased by a growing conviction that his normal pattern of life was not as offensive to God as he had been taught to think it was.

Moreover the urgencies of these readjustments involved looking at classical antiquity with new eyes, stripping away from the writers of Greece and Rome the garb which had clothed them in the Middle Ages, and which had in some ways been furbished up in the fourteenth century. If, as Baron argued, Aristotelian values were to be dominant in the successful acceptance of the Renaissance we are faced with the paradox that the century when Aristotle was most thoroughly studied in western Europe was the thirteenth. In fact the Aristotle and the Cicero of the schoolmen had been strangely transmogrified in earlier centuries. No passage in Baron's work is more telling than that in which he discussed Petrarch's discovery of Cicero's letters to Atticus and draws out its consequences for the poet and moralist, who « shrank back in horror » from the revelation of Cicero's profound and permanent interest in political power [20]. Later writers were to become

---

[20] « Cicero and the Roman Civic Spirit », pp. 16-17.

aware of an unavoidable distinction between their own days and the days of the ancient world. From this was to spring both the sense of identity with classical civilization and the sense of anachronism. These two elements in the cultural scene of the late fifteenth and sixteenth century were sometimes at war with one another. But that the first reinforced the new educational curriculum there can be no doubt, nor that the second was the mainspring in the evolution of a new historiography.

And, finally, this moral readjustment could easily be absorbed and applied in societies quite different from that of republican Florence, which had seen the new ideas emerge and had nourished them. If we substitute *subditus* for *civis* we are still left with the burden of the older tradition. Service of a prince, management of farms and estates was just as much involvement in the world as the activity of counting house and guild. But the arguments supporting the active life and wealth which had been evolved by humanists were not limited to republican situations but were equally applicable in the courts of popes, dukes and kings, in Italy and in the rest of Europe. Thus the educational innovations and the moral adjustments of the civic humanism of Florence could be readily received in the princely and monarchical parts of Italy and elsewhere, that is to say, in most of the Continent. As Baron said himself, in connection with the problem of wealth, « the internal connection between the new Aristotelianism and the spirit of the Renaissance becomes wholly evident when an attempt is made to look beyond the history of Italy » [21]. Had the innovations of the Renaissance been restricted to republics they would never have attained, as they did, the power to change the ethical, literary and artistic assumptions of the whole of Europe.

Burckhardt, product himself of an educational system which had its birth in the Renaissance, had scarcely felt

---

[21] « Franciscan poverty », p. 36.

the need to account in any chronological or narrative sense for the emergence of the new ideas but had sought rather to identify and analyse them. The notions of individualism, of modernity, of scepticism and *virtù*, of naturalism in art and the intellectual importance of the physical sciences were all as self-evident as a school curriculum based on Latin and Greek. « Causation », as Professor Wallace Ferguson sums it up, « was not his major interest » [22]. And in so far as Burckhardt fell back on Hegelian concepts such as the « spirit of Italy » he was both frustrating rational examination and inviting others to that vague impressionism of which he was seldom guilty himself. In writing in this way I do not mean to suggest an opposition which hardly exists. Baron would probably in the end be prepared to argue that Burckhardt's basic approach was correct and he has in fact suggested that, as sociology comes increasingly to influence historical research, so « the core of the Burckhardtian conception of the Renaissance ... may still prove superior to the competing views about the nature of the transition to the modern age » [23].

This last observation is taken from Baron's retrospective appraisal of Burckhardt which was published in 1960 on the centenary of the first publication of the *Civilization of the Renaissance in Italy* [24]. In this he stressed the existence long before Burckhardt of schemes of historical evolution which included the Renaissance, and argued that what Burckhardt contributed to this prior pattern was on the one hand a denial that the movement was to be received as an anticipation of the Enlightenment and on the other « rebuttals » of the « classicist belief » that the revival of ancient letters played a causal role. Likewise Burckhardt's

[22] *Renaissance in Historical Thought*, p. 189.
[23] Hans Baron, « Burckhardt's *Civilization of the Renaissance* a Century after its Publication », *Renaissance News*, XIII (1960), 222.
[24] *Ibid.*, pp. 207-222.

stress on individualism had a lengthy ancestry. None the less the synthesis had « solidity and vastness ». The main criticism to be levelled at its work (said Baron) was its neglect of « the rudimentary sociology of city-state life already prepared by the historians of the Enlightenment and of Romanticism » and this neglect was a consequence of Burckhardt's well-established aversion to « the rising democratic trend »[25]. When he wrote this Baron had already published in 1955 the *Crisis* with its supporting *Humanistic and Political Literature*[26]. The subtitle of the *Crisis* — « Civic humanism and Republican Liberty in an age of Classicism and Tyranny » — is one authoritative statement of the essence of these volumes. Another is to be found in the dedication of the *Crisis* to Walter Goetz, who taught the author « that history should be a study of both politics and culture ». In these volumes Baron expressly attempted the investigation of the connection between society and culture, between political situations and concomitant developments in historiography, political and educational theory.

It was, of course, the case that Burckhardt had treated the political situation in Italy as the background against which he placed his analysis of the spiritual and intellectual state of the peninsula. But it is also the case that he did not really discriminate between the moral and cultural pressures exerted by the different kinds of states to be found in Italy — republics, tyrannies and the two curious monarchies — the nonhereditary papacy and the kingdom of Naples, which was hereditary but with a tradition of dramatic dynastic fractures. Nor did Burckhardt really justify the title of the first section of the *Civilization of*

---

[25] *Ibid.*, p. 218.
[26] *The Crisis of the Early Italian Renaissance* (Princeton, 1955), 2 vols.; *Humanistic and Political Literature in Florence and Venice at the Beginning of the Quattrocento: Studies in Criticism and Chronology* (Cambridge, Mass., 1955). A completely revised and in part rewritten edition of the *Crisis* in one volume was published at Princeton in 1966.

the Renaissance in Italy, « The State as a work of art », as we can see when we look at the transition to the next section, part II « The development of the individual », where the first chapter begins « In the character of these states, whether republics or despotisms, lies not the only but the chief reason for the early development of the Italian ». Despotism, Burckhardt goes on to claim, particularly favoured individuality, in both the tyrant and his « tools » — ministers, courtiers and so on; but even in republics the precarious nature of governments meant that « the individual was led to make the utmost of the exercise and enjoyment of power »; while « the private man, indifferent to politics » but cultivating intellectual interests was thrown up in both tyrannies and republics [27]. This was to ignore the plain fact that the first clear statements of the new moral attitudes and the first novel creations in painting, sculpture and architecture are to be found, not in the tyrannies, but in republican Florence in the years adjacent to 1400.

Baron had long been working his way towards the position he was to take up in the *Crisis*. There is a bold indication of his future programme in 1938 [28], when the threat of Visconti conquest was advanced as the main reason for the emergence of a new outlook among Florentine patricians and humanists, in alliance with one another. What is equally important, he himself regarded this approach as continuing an existing, though weak, tradition, faintly discernible in the writings of David Hume and Adam Ferguson but with a more unequivocal spokesman in Paolo Emiliani-Giudici, who published his

---

[27] I quote from the Middlemore translation in the 1929 London edition, pp. 143-5. It is worth while pointing out that this handsome volume (published by Harrap) was the first time that an English version had appeared with illustrations. It was *remaindered* when I acquired my copy in 1933. The great *popular* interest in the Renaissance comes after the Second World War.

[28] « The Historical Background of the Florentine Renaissance », *History*, new ser. XXII (1938), 315-327.

Storia delle belle arti in Italia in 1844. This last book, « undoubtedly ... familiar to Burckhardt », certainly does contain some pregnant observations on the connections between politics and cultural changes in those quotations to which Baron draws our attention [29], but it seems a small and uncertain link between the hints of the Edinburgh philosophers of the eighteenth century and Baron's own confident and finely integrated thesis of 1955, with its re-examination of the composition and dating of many of the major texts.

Is Baron right in his interpretation of the cultural consequences of the Florentine-Milanese struggle at the time of Giangaleazzo, and the subsequent threat to Tuscan states of Ladislas of Naples and Filippo Maria Visconti? He has been criticised because, by making the Florence of Salutati and Bruni the turning point of the humanist story (as it so evidently is in the evolution of the arts), he has unduly depreciated the significance of Petrarch. To this he has himself replied [30]: Petrarch was more original, pointed more dramatically forwards, in his earlier than in his later days, and could not take the final step towards the New World of which he was in many ways the prophet. And in this same reply he goes on to indicate the telling fact that the political-cultural relationship had been successfully used as a framework for enquiry by other recent writers besides himself [31]. Further Baron's influence and the general acceptance of his interpretation are also witnessed by that form of flattery which consists in animadversion. The exchanges between Seigel and

---

[29] « Burckhardt's *Civilization* », p. 217.

[30] « Moot Problems of Renaissance Interpretation: An Answer to Wallace K. Ferguson », *Journal of the History of Ideas*, XIX (1958), 26-34, esp. pp. 28-9.

[31] Referring to his chapter on « Fifteenth-century Civilization and the Renaissance » in the *New Cambridge Modern History*, I (1957), 50-75 and the note on p. 73; he names Garin, von Albertini, Renaudet, Spongano, and Ferguson.

Baron in *Past and Present* are now matters of record, and it seems to the present writer that Hans Baron has the better of the debate [32]. What lies behind much of the hostile reaction is a pejorative view of classical rhetoric. This is, in many ways, a revival of the judgment of Burckhardt, Voigt and others, who were prepared to tolerate stylish Latin in poetry, oratory and letters, but who condemned it in serious prose; who regretted the urbanity (« how insipid and conventional ») of Bruni's history (for example) and compared it unfavourably with Giovanni Villani or Machiavelli writing history in the vernacular [33]. Classical rhetoric, which determined the structure of most of the serious Latin writing of the *quattrocento* and the *cinquecento*, came in time to dominate vernacular composition in Western European countries down to the nineteenth century. It is dangerous, therefore, to condemn classical rhetoric as such or regard as mere exercises the works written according to its rules. A work must be judged by its contents. « What so effectually proclaims the madman », asked Cicero himself, « as the hollow thundering of words — be they never so choice and resplendent — which have no thought or knowledge behind them? » [34]. Rhetoric is a means of communicating and of persuading. Modern vernaculars permit these functions still to be performed, though the rules have not been formulated.

Finally, it has been urged that the oligarchy of Florence in the period after the Ciompi rising was very narrow and lacked all « democratic » content, was, in short, little different from the personnel to be found in the princely courts. (This is an argument which harks back again to

---

[32] J. E. Seigel, « ' Civic Humanism ' or Ciceronian Rhetoric ? The Culture of Petrarch and Bruni », *Past and Present*, no. 34 (1966); Hans Baron, « Leonardo Bruni: ' Professional Rhetorician ' or ' Civic Humanist ' ? », *Past and Present*, no. 36 (1967). For other critics see P. J. Jones' review of the second edition (1966) of the *Crisis in History*, LIII (1968), 410-13.

[33] Burckhardt, *Civilization* (1929), pp. 247-8.

[34] Cicero, *De Oratore*, I. XII. 51; trans. Sutton, Loeb ed., I. 39.

Burckhardt). Here too Baron is well-enough aware of the manipulation of power by the great families in Florence, but, as Professor Molho has shown recently, the « political class » of Florence, called on to man not only the nine-man signoria every other month, but the many other commissions and offices of the state, was in fact a relatively large body: « one would not be too far wrong in asserting that the Florentine oligarchy during the last two decades of the Trecento numbered some 2000 men » [35]. Likewise Professor Rubinstein has shown how cautiously fifteenth-century Medici leaders had to move, how uncertain they sometimes were of getting their own way, how in basic structure Florence remained a republic until the sixteenth century [36].

Cataloguing Baron's writings and defending him from criticism in the way I have done above gives, of course, an unbalanced view of his place in Renaissance historiography. As for the criticism, he can take care of himself very well and needs no help from me or anyone else. It would, however, be absurd to suggest that in his generation his has been the only major reassessment of fundamental questions regarding the Renaissance. There has been a great deal of other, independent work of profound importance, notably in the field of educational and philosophical ideas: the names of Cassirer, Kristeller and Garin impose themselves. And in art history, in literary history and in history *simpliciter* there have been and are many other equally important and equally independent researches.

Yet it is my impression that the possibilities for synthesis afforded by Baron's thesis are attracting the

---

[35] Anthony Molho, « The Florentine Oligarchy and the Balìe of the Late Trecento », *Speculum*, XLIII (1968), 27; and see the same writer's paper on « Politics and the Ruling Class in Early Renaissance Florence », *Nuova rivista storica*, LII (1968), 401-420. Cf. also Lauro Martines, *Lawyers and Statecraft in Renaissance Florence* (Princeton, 1968), pp. 388-9.

[36] Nicolai Rubinstein, *The Government of Florence under the Medici, 1434 to 1494* (Oxford, 1966).

attention of scholars in many fields. After all the social
and political structures of our own day evidently affect
our cultural preoccupations and ambitions. There is every
reason to suppose that, at a few rare and exciting moments,
these social and political factors may induce innovations
in the moral and ideological pattern which in the long
run can transform art, letters and certain aspects of public
life. This enunciation of principle has to be expressed
with great circumspection if it is to avoid both Marxist
and other forms of determinism or the absurd conclusion
that such occasions involve total transformations of every
aspect of public life. I am myself not persuaded that those
cultural innovations we summarise in the word Renaissance had much consequence for the *spiritual* history of
the *quattrocento*. And the influence of humanism on government was not much greater: it helped on an existing
trend towards the employment by princes in administration and diplomacy of literate laymen rather than clergy —
an important but not a catastrophic development [37]. But
surely there is no doubt that in many other respects what
happened in Florence in the decades round 1400 was to
colour deeply the whole picture of Europe in the course
of the sixteenth century. This would have been impossible
at the level of mere ratiocination or decoration. It represents fundamental ethical, educational and cultural mo-
tivation in the governing classes of virtually the whole
continent which was largely supplied by the new attitudes
adopted in Florence in the days of Salutati, Bruni,
Masaccio, Brunelleschi and all the other heroes and their
patrons.

Now this irradiation of European life could only happen
when Florentine republicanism had ceased to be an enve-

---

[37] On this cf. F. Chabod's contribution to *Actes du colloque sur la Renaissance, Sorbonne 1956* (Paris, 1958). For diplomats see the book by Hans Baron's
great friend (the second edition of the *Crisis* is dedicated to his memory)
Garrett Mattingly, *Renaissance Diplomacy* (London, 1955).

lope round the fructifying ideas which were otherwise welcome in a society predominantly agrarian, where princes, courtiers and gentry were the cultural pace-setters. I am therefore sometimes inclined to feel that Hans Baron's careful investigation of the ethical world, of the gradual change from a formal acceptance of renunciation to a formal acceptance of the active life and of wealth, may in the end of the day prove to be a more enduring inspiration and influence than his equally careful investigation into the climate which encouraged such a development. At any rate I can only repeat my own sense of nourishment from both the rich feasts with which he has regaled us.

« Both the rich feasts ... » As I write this I realise how inadequately the figure two enumerates the Renaissance subjects with which Baron has passed so many creative years. There are his many studies of works of literature not directly related to the themes on which I have touched above — notably the major papers on Petrarch and Machiavelli — which are discussed elsewhere in this volume by Professor Buck [38]. And there are a whole series of investigations into Renaissance historiography ranging over a period of about forty years [39]. And what will he do next?

[38] See, *Renaissance Studies in Honor of Hans Baron*, edited by Anthony Molho and John A. Tedeschi (Dekalb, Illinois, 1971), pp. xxxi-lxiii.

[39] From the Bruni studies of 1928 and « Das Erwachen des historischen Denkens im Humanismus des Quattrocento », *Historische Zeitschrift*, CXLVII (1933), down to a volume of collected essays, *From Petrarch to Leonardo Bruni* (Chicago, 1968), especially those on Dati and the « Early Renaissance Venetian Chronicles ».

4 John Colet (1467?-1519), Dean of St. Pauls. Bust by Torrigiano
(National Portrait Gallery)

8

THE EARLY RENAISSANCE IN ENGLAND*

Lewis Einstein wrote in the preface of his *Italian Renaissance in England:* "The history of the Italian Renaissance in the countries of Europe outside of Italy still remains a subject half explored." He wrote this in 1902; sixty years later it is still broadly true for England and perhaps for other parts of Europe. There is no book to which one can turn for a general and authoritative survey of the Renaissance in England, apart from Einstein's own book, which has many of the structural faults of a pioneering venture and is marred by frequent errors of fact. It is true that what one may call the prehistory of the English Renaissance has been written, by W. F. Schirmer in 1931, and, even more completely for the fifteenth century, by Roberto Weiss (1940; new edition 1957). For a survey of the full flowering of the Tudor period we must consult Douglas Bush's little book, a quite remarkable performance if we remember it was composed of lectures delivered in 1939, but strongest on the Continental side and on Milton and in any case not pretending to be systematic or thorough. And ten years ago we had the brilliant, perverse volume contributed by the late C. S. Lewis to the Oxford History of English Literature, with its cumbersome title, *English literature in the XVI century excluding drama* (1954) —a title which conceals what by any reckoning is one of the finest pieces of critical writing of this century.

It is noteworthy that the authors cited are literary men: Schirmer, Bush, and Lewis are historians of English literature; Weiss is a professor of Italian. Now this monopoly of English Renaissance studies by scholars of literature is not quite entire: if we were to list monographic studies of various aspects of the Renaissance in England, various articles and books devoted to individual humanists, we would find a sizeable number of studies by historians of art, of

* A draft of this essay was read to the Renaissance Conference at Austin, Texas, in April, 1964.

ideas, of religion, of institutions. Even a few scholars who are historians *simpliciter* have made modest contributions. But they have done so, one might say, rather by the way, leaving any attempt at generalities to their literary colleagues. It is of course true that no one could accuse either Professor Bush or Professor Lewis of neglecting ideas. One can, however, accuse them fairly enough of neglecting the historical background and this, to my way of thinking, is a serious defect in their work. Lewis's history as such will be found on pp. 56–59: three and a half pages of the 558 pages of his text. Historians are more generous: Mackie's volume on the early Tudors has a whole chapter devoted to "The achievement of the Age," and so has J. B. Black in his volume on Elizabeth's reign. Oxford editors, it seems, have been firmer with their historians than with their *belles lettristes*. What is so depressing in all this is, however, the divorce between civilization and the changing public situation. The literary specialist and the historian each gives a guilty acknowledgment that his world is only part of the world, and then proceeds as if it were the world in its entirety.

If one compares this with the way the Renaissance in Italy has been treated the contrast is striking. One may feel (I do myself feel) that Burckhardt's history is somewhat oddly conceived, and that it fails in some respects to be integrated with the body of his book. But it is there, big and plain, as the first section of his book. Since then there has been a steady acknowledgment of the necessity of associating history pure and history cultural in discussions of the Renaissance in Italy—especially when written by non-Italians. You will hardly need to be reminded of the brilliant way politics and ideas have been woven together by Hans Baron. More recently others have followed the same path who are, or who would regard it as an honor to be, counted as his disciples.

A short essay is not the best occasion on which to try to remedy the position with regard to the English Renaissance, even when it is only the early period, down to 1535 or thereabouts, which is under review.[1] What follows is a mere sketch. I shall begin by a

---

1. Since writing this essay I have read the useful survey of P. O. Kristeller, "The European Diffusion of Italian Humanism," *Italica*, XXXIX (1962). Attention should also be drawn to R. Weiss, *The Spread of Italian Humanism*, which has just been published (London, 1964).

short assessment of the political and social scene in the fifteenth and early sixteenth centuries and then go on to consider this as a framework for the reception and development of Renaissance concepts and practices.

C. L. Kingsford characterized the Lancastrian and Yorkist period as one of "prejudice and promise" and at first sight one is inclined to regard the prejudice as more noticeable than the promise. It is traditionally regarded as an age of war: Henry IV seized the throne and murdered the deposed Richard II; similar brutal changes of monarch occurred in 1471, 1483, and 1485; Henry V died of camp fever and only Edward IV died in his own bed. The domestic strife engendered during Richard II's reign lasted till the invasion of France in 1415. Then there was war abroad till 1453. By that time the country was in the thick of the disorders, local and central, which are collectively termed the Wars of the Roses. These were to double the rate at which noble families were normally extinguished from natural causes and to encourage the gentry to the dubious and often fugitive loyalties of "bastard feudalism."

Yet it would be wrong to regard the fifteenth century in England as a period of anarchy. We can apply to the whole period the judicious judgment of Bishop Stubbs on the dark days of the 1440s and 1450s: "The kingdom . . . was exhausted, improverished, and in disorder, but it was not unconstitutionally ruled."[2] Much of the exhaustion and improverishment was, we should remember, the product not of kings and lords but of general economic processes which, from the early fourteenth century, had clouded the whole European scene. It can, indeed, be argued that the violence of aggressive Englishmen on the Continent under Edward III and, later, the bitterness of the civil war in the next century, reflect economic pressures on the gentry and nobles, who found it harder to live comfortably off their manors than they had in the boom days of Henry III and the Lord Edward.

At any rate, in all the troubles of the fifteenth century legitimism prevailed; the dynasty was never at stake, and so the Crown was, in an important sense, above the battle. More than that, the magnates and their supporters were now turning to the King in ways which would have seemed inconceivable a century earlier. From the King

2. *Constitutional History*, III, p. 155.

flowed the captaincies and the keeperships, the honors and the perquisites of government. And, in a paradoxical way, the very acts of rebellion and war against the King made a stronger man of his successor, for the attainders and forfeitures of his discomfited rival's party offered a cozy way of keeping them obedient—a cumulative process, from which the Tudors were greatly to benefit, as Dr. J. R. Lander has demonstrated.[3] Of one thing there can surely be no doubt: by the 1470s the English King was stronger than he ever had been before. If we compare Edward IV or Richard III or Henry VII with Edward III or even Edward I we can see that whatever else the Wars of the Roses did, they did not weaken monarchy.

The foreign wars and the domestic wars, together with the economic troubles which were their concomitants if not their causes, not only did not seriously hamper the developing authority of the King, but they may even have provoked some of the more interesting innovations of the period. Foreign war stimulated diplomacy; domestic war strengthened a more modern notion of the court, while the council, permanent and professional, buttressed the administration by even bigger bastions of paper. In each of these spheres—diplomacy, the court, and the council—we see, of course, the King, but we also see the secretary.[4] The major administrative developments, the main new factors in the constitutional scene of later medieval England, were the inventive use of household machinery for government, the chamber as an exchequer, the signet as the most lively of the seals, and, though dimly enough at first, the secretarial maid-of-all-work who was to become, by the middle of the sixteenth century, the chief dynamo in the administrative machine. The court, the council, and the secretary, whose operations constituted the basis of Tudor government, were all present in the fifteenth century.

There is no doubt of the cultural consequences of the mounting

3. J. R. Lander, "Attainder and forfeiture, 1453–1509," *Historical Journal*, 4 (1961), pp. 119–51.

4. J. Otway-Ruthven, *The King's Secretary and the Signet Office in the XV Century* (1923); J. F. Baldwin, *The King's Council in England during the Middle Ages* (1913); A. R. Myers, ed., *The Household of Edward IV: the Black Book and the Ordinance of 1478* (1959). In general, cf. S. B. Chrimes, *An Introduction to the Administrative History of Medieval England* (1952), pp. 241–70 and refs.

tide of conciliar activity under Henry VII and Henry VIII; equally
the diplomatic activity of the early Tudor Kings made imperative
demands on the country's intellectual resources. Why do we not find
an earlier adoption of Italian methods, manners, and attitudes which
were obviously capable of responding so admirably to the new
needs of government and which were to come in rapidly in the
sixteenth century? Why do we not find in the fifteenth century the
indigenous "professional" humanist (to use Roberto Weiss's useful
term)? Why is there no Thomas More at the court of Edward IV?
Part of the answer to this lies, I believe, in the inaccessibility of
early-fifteenth-century Italian innovations, enveloped as they were
in the bourgeois republicanism of Florence. It was not until the
second half of the fifteenth century that Italian courts adopted, and
to some extent modified, the message of Salutati, Bruni, and the
rest. It is significant that the Englishmen who were customers of
Vespasiano da Bisticci were for the most part aristocrats: Gloucester,
Tiptoft, Gray;[5] their tastes were for what was solid, old-fashioned
in Renaissance scholarship, and for what married most happily with
the established hierarchies of Church and State, with the moral and
educational traditions of Northern Europe. This leads to the real
reason for the sluggishness of the English: the relative success with
which the ancient arrangements coped with the slowly evolving
social and cultural situation.

The rise of the gentry in England, about which we have heard so
much in recent years in connection with the Elizabethan and Jacobean periods,[6] is a long story. Whether we can see it happening in
the twelfth century, as Professor R. W. Southern has recently argued,[7]

5. See Weiss, *Humanism in England*, pp. 58, 88, 115 and cf. the same
   author's article on Tito Livio Frulovisi's *Humfroidos* in *Fritz Saxl
   Memorial Essays*, ed. D. J. Gordon (1957), pp. 218–27. On Grey
   see now the excellent account by R. A. B. Mynors, *Catalogue of the
   Manuscripts of Balliol College* (1963), pp. xxiv–xlv.

6. R. H. Tawney, L. Stone, H. R. Trevor-Roper, J. H. Hexter. The
   bibliography to 1960 is referred to in Hexter's devastating essay,
   now in *Reappraisals in History* (1961). One of the most curious
   features in the whole curious affair is the starting date of 1540.

7. "The Place of Henry I in English History," *Proc. Brit. Acad.*,
   XLVIII (1962), pp. 127–69.

may be debated but there is no question about the fourteenth and fifteenth centuries. English public affairs at this time are incomprehensible if we do not take account of the thrusting ambitions of hundreds of small landowners, rising and falling like the handful of peers and, in much the same way, adding to their properties by marriage and purchase. They cling to the great, they throng Parliament, they climb the ladder of preferment in Church and State.[8] And, not least, they increasingly go to school and university.

One of the silent revolutions of the later Middle Ages is the way the old fabric of ecclesiastical education—song schools, grammar schools, universities—housed a new lay clientele with no intentions of pursuing the traditional curriculum to its logical end. Boys learned their letters not to become priests but in order to become more effective laymen, in order to enter the law or at any rate to have a smattering of law so useful in a litigious society where titles to property were nearly always confused and doubtful, in order to perform the arithmetic of trade, commerce and estate management, in order to staff the administration of King, nobles, and bishops who were turning now more and more to the literate laity and away from clerical servants. When I refer to a silent revolution I do not, of course, mean that no new schools and colleges were founded. They were, and in impressive numbers. I mean rather that new institutions did not seriously alter old practices. The only change we can really see is the development of the ideal of a devout laity alongside the educational ideal of a well-educated clergy; and even this is hardly evident before its explicit statement in Colet's foundation at St. Paul's in 1512. The provision of facilities for an instructed and religious laity was taken much further in other parts of Northern Europe in the fifteenth century and is best seen in the educational arrangements associated with the Brethren of the Common Life. In England, although we do not have any organized and self-conscious educational movement, just as we do not have any syste-

8. For their prominence by 1500, cf. the first chapter of Fritz Caspari, *Humanism and Social Order in Tudor England* (1954). I find it difficult, however, to go along with Dr. Caspari in his argument that the English gentry felt a natural sympathy with "the ideas of the humanists" because they were derived from an antiquity in which "there was a definite similarity between the Roman and the English aristocracy."

matic group mysticism, something of the same spirit prevails.

How literate were the laity? In London, where there was relatively plentiful provision of schools, Miss Thrupp reached the conclusion that in "the merchant class . . . all the men read English and most of them had some training in Latin";[9] a survey of a still bigger section of the London population in the mid-fifteenth century suggests that about 40 per cent of males were literate.[10] Later still, Thomas More's guess that "farre more than fowre partes of all the whole divided into tenne, coulde never reade englishe yet" suggests that something approaching 60 per cent could,[11] though we may suspect that reading did not take writing with it. As for the country at large, composed mainly of agricultural laborers, the literate were doubtless in a tiny minority—perhaps the fraction of one per cent of Bishop Stephen Gardiner's estimate in 1547.[12] This does not mean, of course, that no peasants acquired education, though we may suspect that those who did soon left the plough and that there were not many others like Robert Wyllyams, who, at the time Gardiner was writing his letter, demonstrated his literacy with an inscription in a book he read, "Keppynge Shepe uppon Seynbury Hill."[13] If literate shepherds were rare, however, it was quite a different matter with their masters. The papers of the Pastons, the Lelys, the Stonors show country gentlemen of an extremely articulate kind and C. L. Kingsford's judgment is well-founded:

> . . . Capacity to read and write was no longer an accomplishment confined to the clerical class. The wives and sisters of country gentlemen could often write as well as their husbands and brothers, and both they and their servants could and commonly did keep regular household accounts.[14]

9. Sylvia L. Thrupp, *Merchant Class of Medieval London* (1948), p. 161; cf. 157n3 for references to earlier studies.

10. *Ibid.*, pp. 156–57.

11. H. S. Bennett, *English Books and Readers 1475–1557* (1952), p. 28; J. W. Adamson, *The Illiterate Anglo-Saxon* (1946), chap. III, *passim*. The subject has more recently been surveyed in chap. XI of Raymond Urwin, *The Heritage of the English Library* (1964).

12. Bennett, *loc. cit.*

13. Denys Hay, *Polydore Vergil* (1952), p. 69.

14. *Prejudice and Promise*, p. 35.

Moreover, while a hack dominie was retained in such households to write letters and to teach the children, the menfolk of the family were sent seriously to school and to university, as we can see in the case of the Pastons, whose very rise was attributed by a malicious enemy to the borrowing of money by the husbandman Clement Paston to send his son, the future justice, to school. By the end of the century a Paston had gone to Eton, then in the process of becoming that mysterious English phenomenon, a public, that is a private, school.[15] Eton, Winchester, and other establishments had been intended for the middling gentry, and the middling gentry responded.

It is necessary to insist on the political, social, and economic background, because it goes far to explain the character of the English response to the new developments in Italy. There are many contacts between England and Italy in the fifteenth century but they are not really productive until the early sixteenth century, and even then seem gradual rather than dramatic.

Nonetheless there are some pointers in the fifteenth century to the course events later took. We find, for example, a few isolated cases of the royal secretariate responding to its duties in a novel way. In 1412 a diplomatic occasion provoked an English clerk to conscious effort at stylish Latinity as can be seen in two letters printed recently by Monsieur Pocquet du Haut-Jussé.[16] Much more impressive is the scholarship of Thomas Bekynton, who was royal secretary from 1438 to 1443 and who, we read, "conceived classical learning not only as an intellectual attainment but also as a thing of practical value."[17] Professor Weiss attributes to Bekynton's influence the "literary qualifications" of not fewer than six other royal servants and diplomats. In addition the secretaries of the fifteenth century number James Goldwell, later Ambassador to Rome and Bishop of Norwich,[18] whose remarkable collection of humanist manuscripts

15. See H. S. Bennett, *The Pastons and their England* (reprinted 1932), pp. 107–8.

16. "La Renaissance littéraire autour de Henry V," *Revue Historique,* CCXXIV (1960), pp. 329–38; cf. E. F. Jacob, "Verborum florida venustas," *Essays in the Conciliar Epoch* (second edition, 1953), pp. 185–206.

17. Weiss, *Humanism in England,* p. 74.

18. Secretary 1460, bishop 1472: Otway-Ruthven, pp. 175–76.

was bequeathed to All Souls.[19]

The secretaries demand scrutiny because it is obvious that theirs was a sphere of activity in which the Renaissance was relevant. The secretaries, even though they themselves were technically clergy, headed a department which was thoroughly lay: the signet clerks are laymen from 1437, "a change . . . in line with the general tendency of the period, but . . . the earliest and most complete example."[20] Lay professionalism like this involves continuities not least because it involved (as it did not do with the clergy who served the Crown) a notion of office as property. And in the secretaries and in the council to which they were more closely attached, continuity is what we find. A highly expert councillor was worth his weight in gold and we should not have been surprised, as perhaps some of us were, when Dr. Lander showed us how many men were common to the councils of Edward IV, Richard III, and Henry VII.[21] One such figure is Oliver King. King, a very well-educated man (Cambridge and Orléans), was French secretary (1475–80) and then secretary to both Edward IV and his son (1480–83) and to Henry VII (1487–95). He was the first secretary to become a bishop while in office and under him the office became in a sense one of state: it became "public."[22]

The last decade of the fifteenth century and the first decade of the sixteenth see these processes carried further and consolidated. The Poet Laureate is Bernard André, from early in the reign.[23] A Latin secretary makes his appearance in 1495.[24] Three years earlier we find the first appointment of a King's Librarian.[25] Oliver King is

19. Weiss, *Humanism in England,* pp. 176–77.

20. Otway-Ruthven, p. 129.

21. "Council, administration and councillors, 1461–1485," *Bull. Inst. Hist. Res.,* XXXII (1959), pp. 138–80.

22. Otway-Ruthven, pp. 140, 178–79.

23. W. Busch, *England under the Tudors* (1895), I, p. 393 (only Vol. I was published).

24. Otway-Ruthven, pp. 190–91: "a conscious creation to meet the needs of a new age."

25. G. F. Warner and J. P. Gilson, *Catalogue of Western MSS. in the Old Royal and King's Collections,* I (1921), p. xiii.

succeeded in 1500 by Thomas Ruthal, who could be described not only as a man of affairs, but as a man of letters, too, for he is (I think) the first secretary to be the subject of a dedication, by the Italian nuncio Pietro Griffo, of the oration he would have made to Henry VII if the King had not died.[26] The episode also shows how significant a figure the secretary had become by this date. Pietro Griffo's name reminds us that the Italians have come to town. Professor Weiss has listed them for the fifteenth century. By the early sixteenth they are establishing themselves: Henry VII makes Carmelianus his Latin secretary and invites Polydore Vergil to write the history of England. Even more important, the humanities are beginning to get into the schools. The first schoolmaster who can fairly be said to be a humanist is John Alnwykill, teaching grammar at Magdalen College School from about 1481,[27] the earliest of a remarkable series of teachers there.

This is not to suggest that with the Tudors there was a steady infiltration of Italians, bearing in their new civilization on platters, so to speak. Much that was both original and Continental came from Northern Europe: Erasmus directly owed little to Italy, and from his first visit in 1499 his was the most potent single influence on the humanities as such in England. The first two Royal Librarians were Flemings.[28] The Italians were in any case men of the second rank even when, like Vergil, they were pretty influential. What strikes one about the decades on either side of 1500 is a new mood of receptivity and an atmosphere propitious to the establishment of new ideas and practices. This can probably be positively demonstrated by the book-buying habits of libraries and private persons, a subject that has yet to be properly examined.[29] But that a fresh air

26. Printed by Pynson in 1509 (S.T.C. 12413). On Griffo see a jejune paper by the present writer in *Italian Studies*, II (1938-39), pp. 118-28.

27. Weiss, *Humanism in England*, pp. 168–69.

28. Quintin Poulet, 1492, and Giles Duwes, 1509: Warner and Gilson, *op. cit.*, pp. xiii-xiv.

29. We have no studies of English purchases of foreign books as such at the start of the sixteenth century, but cf. *Catalogue of the Library of Syon Monastery, Isleworth*, ed. Mary Bateson (1898), p. viii. The valuable collection of material in Sears Jayne, *Library Catalogues of the English Renaissance* (1956) marks a great step forward.

was blowing through England is surely evident from the emergence of three men whom we can reasonably describe as really important native humanists: Richard Pace, Thomas More, and Thomas Elyot. Each of these remarkable men was very largely the product of an English environment—More and Elyot were so almost completely; each was involved, because of his talents, in public service; and each was a man of the old order.

It is this more general spirit of receptiveness which makes itself felt by the end of the fifteenth century. Scholars and clergy had visited Italy for centuries; many of those who went there in the early and mid-fifteenth century had acquired a taste for the new humanities.[30] But in the Yorkist period to some extent, and much more under Henry VII, the aptitude and abilities of the new type of scholar found support and encouragement in high places, and notably from prelates like Morton, Fisher, and Fox. Above all they were fostered at court. This is seen not only in the Italians like Carmelianus and Vergil but in more permanent ways—especially in the new foundations at Cambridge, for it was the circle round Henry VII's mother that was responsible for changes which, whether intended so or not, began to "humanize" the universities. André and Linacre, appointed tutors to Prince Arthur, and Skelton, tutor to the future Henry VIII, are the first of a continuous series of humanist instructors for the royal children of Tudor England.[31] One must always take Erasmus with two grains of salt—one of the genuine problems of early Tudor scholarship is that one is compelled to see so much through Erasmus's spectacles—yet his enthusiastic picture of England at the turn of the century culminates with his meeting Prince Henry at Eltham, and it carries conviction. It must indeed have seemed to the humanists propitious that the Crown was to pass in 1509 into the hands of a boy brought up in the modern manner.

Henry VIII as King did not in fact spend much time in writing Latin exercises or conversing with elderly scholars: his personal letters and his spoken language were mostly "vulgar" in the techni-

---

30. Cf. George B. Parks, *The English Traveller to Italy*, I (to 1525), (1954).

31. For the career of another, John Palsgrave (tutor to Mary Tudor, 1513, and Henry Fitzroy, 1525), see *The Comedy of Acolastus*, ed. P. L. Carver (E.E.T.S. no. 202, 1937), pp. xi–xii, xxiv–xxxv.

cal sense of the term. Moreover, the humanists who had found favor in his father's court gradually found themselves squeezed out by a fresh group. But the new men were also humanists or humanist trained and the processes by which the humanities were integrated into the fabric of public life continued at an accelerated pace. In 1516 Richard Pace, trained by Langton and in Italy, experienced as secretary to Cardinal Bainbridge in Rome, became the first thoroughly trained humanist secretary of the King. At just the same time Bishop Richard Fox's creation, Corpus Christi College, opened its doors at Oxford—a *trilingue* on the same model as Busleyden's great institution which was to begin the next year at Louvain.

But the interesting point about developments under both Henry VII and Henry VIII is not their inherent originality. Colleges had been founded earlier and so had schools. Pace, as we have seen, had predecessors somewhat like him in background if less impressive as scholars. What *is* remarkable is the way that the new type of scholar found himself becoming indispensable. Colet's foundation of St. Paul's (1510) was in many ways an orthodox and conventional step: the devout dean had as his aim the promotion of Christian morality. But the men who became high masters there, from William Lilly onwards, were humanist grammarians on the Italian model and what struck one Italian writing in the 1530s was not that St. Paul's had produced devotion but that the youth of London who went there were "more civilized," *politior*,[32] fifteen years earlier Pace had referred to the school in the same way.[33] There was nothing particularly original about the statutes of Alcock's foundation of Jesus College at Cambridge, or Smith's of Brasenose at Oxford, though the same Italian linked them with Fisher's Christ's and John's and Fox's Corpus as part of the diffusion among the English of *bonarum artium ac disciplinarum studia*.[34] By the 1530s, one feels, the steps taken in Henry VII's

32. Vergil, *Anglica Historia* (Camden Series, 1950), p. 147 collation.

33. R. Pace, *De Fructu* (Basle, 1517), dedication to Colet, pp. 13–14; "Tanta praeterea eruditio ut extrusa pene omni barbarie (in qua nostri olim adolescentes solebant fere aetatem consumere, et longissimo tempore, ut nihil boni discerent, laborare) politiorem latinitatem, atque ipsam Romanam linguam, in Britanniam nostram introduxisse uideatur."

34. Vergil, *op. cit.*, pp. 145–46 collation.

reign and earlier seemed predestined to accomplish a revolution.[35] The Lady Margaret, one must say, looking at her severe face in St. John's hall, wrought better than she knew; and so, perhaps, did Fisher.[36]

Professor Zeeveld has underlined for us further consequences of these developments.[37] Not only did Wolsey, with the active support of his master, provide a further college at Oxford—and one intended in its way to be as innovating as Corpus—but in the household of his bastard Thomas Winter he supported on the Continent a number of young scholars, as did Henry VIII in the household of Reginald Pole. Wolsey, indeed, stands out well in any examination of the new learning at court. Ex-grammar schoolmaster as he was, he had the sense to admire and use Richard Pace, who repaid his master by a glowing page in the *De Fructu*,[38] and Wolsey (we sometimes tend to forget) picked out another man who had knocked about in Italy, Thomas Cromwell.

Pace's *De Fructu* came out of the press of Froben at Basle in 1516. The occasion for its composition is described by the author in his dedication to Colet. While traveling back from Rome some years earlier, he had met at dinner "one of those whom we call gentlemen (*generosos*)." This gentleman, hearing one of the party praise good education, burst into a tirade against scholarship. "What rubbish," he cried. "All learned men are paupers—even Erasmus complains of poverty. By God's body, I would rather my son was hanged than that he should be studious. Gentlemen's sons should be able to sound the hunting horn, hunt cunningly, neatly train, and use a hawk. The study of literature should be left to the sons of peasants." Pace is provoked into a sharp reply: when the King needs

---

35. Professor Lawrence V. Ryan, who was kind enough to read and comment on a version of this paper, pointed out to me the significance of the revised statutes for St. John's College (1524, 1530): cf. J. B. Mullinger, *The University of Cambridge from the Earliest Times to the Royal Injunctions of 1535*, pp. 622–25, where Fisher's borrowings from the statutes of Fox's and Wolsey's Oxford foundations are discussed.

36. For his nervousness, cf. Mullinger, *loc. cit.*

37. W. Gordon Zeeveld, *Foundations of Tudor Policy* (1948).

38. Pace, *op. cit.*, pp. 112–13.

someone to reply to a foreign ambassador, he will turn not to the horn-blowing gentleman but to the educated rustic.[39] As Mr. Fritz Caspari says, this is why gentlemen sought education;[40] the point has been stressed, in a wider context, by J. H. Hexter in his paper on the education of the aristocracy.[41] Pace wrote in Latin. In 1531 Thomas Elyot published his *Governour* in English.[42] One might say the battle was won, for in addition to summarizing, in an English context, the doctrines of learned public service, the notion of "true nobility" and so on, which come out of the earliest stages of the Italian Renaissance, its Florentine and republican matrix, Elyot did more. He introduced the gentlemen of England to the Courtier: to *Castiglione's* courtier in particular but in a larger sense to the whole complex of the Italian Renaissance in its late-fifteenth- early-six-teenth-century state, when it had moved into an ambience of popes and princes, an ambience obviously compatible with the social situation in Northern Europe.[43]

The moment that letters could take a man to fame and fortune, of course, there arose another set of problems and it is an interesting comment on the Wolsey period that at least one of the Cardinal's protégés felt that this had already happened. Thomas Lupset, writing in 1529, complained that the scholar's ambitions have become no different from those of other men of affairs: "The same confusion is with us scholers: for our first study is to get promotion, to get these goodis, to live welthily."[44] This observation comes from the

39. *Ibid.*, pp. 15–16. Pace's gentleman despising education existed: see Carver's introduction to *Acolastus,* pp. xxxi–ii: the competition be-tween the courtier-gentleman and the courtier-scholar could provoke tension round a prince.

40. Caspari, *op. cit.,* p. 137.

41. Now reprinted in *Reappraisals in History* (1961), pp. 45–70.

42. See Stanford E. Lehmberg, *Sir Thomas Elyot, Tudor Humanist* (1960).

43. Cf. Denys Hay, *Italian Renaissance in its Historical Background* (1961), pp. 179–201.

44. "An exhortacion to young men," in *Life and Works of Thomas Lupset,* J. A. Gee, ed. (1928), p. 240; for date of composition, *ibid.,* pp. 124–25.

man into whose mouth Starkey, about 1535, put the observations that "every honest man . . . ought . . . first to make himself perfit, and then to commune the same perfection to other"; and "whosoever . . . drawn by the sweetness of his studies . . . leaveth the cure of the common weal and policy . . . doth manifest wrong to his country and friends."[45]

I have tried to point out in this brief survey how the political and social structure in England during the fifteenth century gradually found in Italian experience matters and methods which could easily fit into a situation in which the royal court had a prominence it had lacked in earlier centuries; the gentry and nobles, flocking to the traditional schools and universities, were ready for doctrines which would justify both their increasing literacy and their concentration of interest in the court. Much of this had happened by the mid-1530s and I have chosen to stop there for several reasons. The next steps consisted, I believe, in the rapid establishment of the grammar or public school as an institution. Italian influences pure and simple come into their own in the later sixteenth century, in educational theory, in courtly doctrine, in the incipient mystique of the Grand Tour. The two major figures of the early Renaissance in England, More and Elyot, owe very little to direct contact with Italy. By the Elizabethan period Italy was a very potent force in literature, art, and scholarship.[46]

In this later stage, in the full flowering of the English Renaissance, we move into an essentially vernacular world. The "golden English" of Professor Lewis's periodization, it may be suspected, owed far more than he allows to the fundamental influence of Latin grammar. Are there any signs that "golden English" is on the way before More's death? There is plenty of evidence that the matter preoccupied authors. If Elyot thought that classical Latin writers had "incomparably . . . more grace and delectation" than English permitted,[47] More disagreed:

45. Thomas Starkey, *A Dialogue between Reginald Pole and Thomas Lupset*, Kathleen M. Burton, ed. (1948), pp. 22, 24.

46. George B. Parks, "The genesis of Tudor interest in Italian," *P.M.L.A.*, LXXVII (1962). I have to thank Professor Sears Jayne for drawing my attention to this.

47. *Governour*, I, p. 129. And cf. E. J. Sweeting, *Studies in Early Tudor Criticism* (1940), pp. 52–57.

For as for that our tongue is called barbarous, is but a fantasy: for so is, as every learned man knoweth, every strange language to other. And if they would call it barren of words, there is no doubt but it is plenteous enough to express our minds in anything whereof one man hath used to speak with another.[48]

More has, of course, been acclaimed with some justification as himself the first embodiment of a modern and effective prose, and when R. W. Chambers argues, as he does,[49] that More's style follows the lead of devotional writings of the previous two centuries this is further evidence of the influence of the literate laity of whom I have spoken. What can, however, surely not be denied is that More and others of his generation who wrote English with a fair degree of vigor, economy, and variety, were to a man the products of Latin scholarship. It is as and when the grammar school education of a new type permeates English letters in the middle decades of the sixteenth century that a generation emerges ready to produce and enjoy the vernacular Renaissance of the late Tudor and early Jacobean period. Insofar as this was anticipated before the mid-1530s it was because a few men had enjoyed the full experience of Latin. A recent illustration of this can be seen in Professor Sylvester's edition of More's *Richard III*.[50] One may suspect moreover that as much was done for the language by conscientious composition and translation at a level below that of a genius like Thomas More. In Elyot, for example, we find a deliberate attempt spread over a lifetime to make English prose adequate for its new task of being the omnicompetent vehicle for all literature. In his day history, science, and learned work generally could hardly be well or accurately written in English. Elyot's labors, and those of so many of his contemporaries, are not easy reading, but they are, as

48. *Dialogue concerning Tyndale*, W. E. Campbell, ed., introd. A. W. Reed (1931), p. 247.

49. *On the continuity of English Prose from Alfred to More and his School* (E.E.T.S.) (sep. reprint, 1950), pp. cxxi–cxli.

50. Yale edition of the Complete Works of Thomas More, 2, *The History of King Richard III*, Richard S. Sylvester, ed. (1963), see pp. lvi–lix.

Professor John Butt has demonstrated,[51] the bedrock of later prose.

Prose, then, was on the way to its later grandeurs by the middle of the reign of Henry VIII. Poetry largely slumbered in its "drab" dreariness. Yet even here the odd ray of hope was shed by a grammarian. Some years ago I was delighted to come on this Shakespearean couplet:

> Ther be many lordes that cannot pley the lorde,
> But I that am none can pley it rially.

This was written in the reign of Henry VII by the anonymous teacher at Magdalen College School, whose *vulgaria* have been printed by Professor William Nelson.[52] It is, of course, part of a piece of prose. But it is also part of an impetus to write English rhythmically and well which was released by the Latin pedagogues who were becoming a necessary part of the English scene.

51. "A plea for more English Dictionaries," *Durham University Journal,* n.s., XII (1951), pp. 96–102.

52. *A Fifteenth Century School Book,* W. Nelson, ed. (1956), p. 84 (no. 351).

9

ENGLAND AND THE HUMANITIES
IN THE FIFTEENTH CENTURY

The large subject of this study invites an answer, however tentative, to some questions which naturally arise in the mind of anyone reflecting on the matter. By the end of the fifteenth century we have in Thomas More (born 1478) the finest 'humanist' produced by England. Why had he no predecessor of stature? Why was he relatively isolated in his own day? How did the situation change so rapidly in the next generation? These queries are the more tantalising when we remember that the new learning had borne handsome fruit in Italy by 1400, and that traffic in men and ideas between England and Italy was more intense after the Schism (1378-1417) than it had been for a hundred and fifty years. The new ideas of the Italians were to be absorbed by the literate English (as by the literate among other European peoples) by the end of the sixteenth century, and it is worth pondering why the process of absorption took so long.

It is necessary to begin with some severe definitions if the argument is not to become vapid. Already the reader has encountered above two highly ambiguous expressions—humanist and literate. Any study which figures in a volume dedicated to Paul Oskar Kristeller must heed his strictures on the loose manner in which 'humanist' and 'humanism' are often used.[1] Humanist, either as noun or adjective, is less liable to abuse than humanism, at any rate by historians of the Renaissance period.[2] Certainly in the fifteenth and sixteenth centuries in both Italy and the North the word was applied primarily if not exclusively to the new type of Latin grammarian, the teacher of the humanities, the professor of 'humanity' as he was (and is) called in Scottish universities.[3] The new curriculum was geared to the 'cycle of scholarly disciplines, namely grammar, rhetoric, history, poetry,

---

[1] Kristeller has touched on these words and their meaning on several occasions. See especially *The Classics and Renaissance Thought* (Cambridge, Mass., 1955), 9-10 (reprinted as *Renaissance Thought*, New York, 1961).

[2] Note the temptation (especially in America?) to lengthen the adjective 'humanist' to the unnecessary Germanic 'humanistic'.

[3] Cf. below p. 230.

and moral philosophy' studied through the 'reading and interpretation' of the 'standard ancient writers in Latin and, to a lesser extent, Greek'.[4] When the slang Italian word *humanista* is recorded at the end of the fifteenth century it is clear that it is equivalent in meaning to the old term *artista*.[5] By a permissible extension we may apply the word also to those patrons of the practitioners of *literae humaniores* who themselves would have hardly stooped to teach or who only taught when driven to do so by dire necessity. We may therefore admit as a humanist one who practised, taught, promoted or comprehended with sympathy and approval the new educational and moral programme. 'Humanism' has, however, reasonable meaning for the Renaissance period only if it is similarly restricted, and is not used as a blanket term to cover every aspect of *quattrocento* life and learning. As a generic term for a system of education it is useful; as an invitation to confused assumptions about 'the dignity of man', of the 'humane' or 'human-centred' in anything approaching a modern connotation, it is best avoided. (I shall return shortly to the word 'literate').

That these remarks are not entirely superfluous may be seen when we turn to the standard and indispensable work by Roberto Weiss, *Humanism in England during the Fifteenth Century* (1940; 2nd ed., 1957; 3rd ed., 1967). Although the author begins with a statement not so very different from that given above he soon (as it seems to me) slips momentarily into a vaguer and more dangerous identification of 'humanism' as a 'cultural movement' which 'offered several advantages over scholasticism'. Provided we accept that the writer here alludes to two different pedagogical techniques we need not demur at the statement, even if it arouses our suspicions. But in fact Roberto Weiss immediately makes it clear that for him humanism was indeed an emotional or intellectual position affecting a man's total view of the world.

> In its attempts to unify all knowledge within a system of logic, scholasticism lacked flexibility and powers of adaptation, was difficult of application in particular instances, and left no room for romanticism [*sic*]. Humanism on the other hand with its leaning toward Platonism displayed a wider scope, greater elasticity, and less dogmatism and adherence to formulae, so that all this combined with its emergence

[4] Kristeller, *loc. cit.*

[5] Cf. P. O. Kristeller, *Studies in Renaissance Thought and Letters* (Rome, 1956), 553-583, and esp. 564-574.

as a distinct system at a time when scholasticism had practically ceased to produce original speculation, rendered it very attractive to those scholars who came into contact with it.[6]

It is exceedingly difficult to make sense of this passage but it should be remembered when reading the detailed studies of patronage and book collecting which form the substance of the book, for it would have led one to expect some discussion of education in England in both school and university, some analysis of social pressures. These are not given by Weiss and obviously they cannot adequately be covered in a short account such as this. But there does seem to be a need for a brief response to the plan Weiss tries to sketch at the beginning of his study, but did not really execute.

> Therefore in approaching English humanism it is important to consider the possible influence exercised not only by its scholarly, but also by its economic, political and social backgrounds, and to bear in mind the peculiarities common to intellectual movements in the making.[7]

In what follows I shall begin by comparing the Italian and the English scene—social, political and cultural—at the turn of the fourteenth and fifteenth centuries. I shall then briefly examine Italian cultural changes in the first half of the fifteenth century, treating this as a critical period in the Italian Renaissance, when the major innovations (some of which had been made much earlier) firmly established themselves. I shall then examine the contacts of Englishmen with Italy at this time and try to piece together the degree to which they were aware that change was in the Italian air. Finally I shall turn to the later fifteenth and early sixteenth centuries. In the decades from 1470 onwards the pace at which Renaissance values were accepted in

---

[6] The revisions in this fundamental work are appended to the text in the second and third editions; pagination is therefore not affected. In these addenda Weiss refers to an important article by Kristeller, but he does not seem to have accepted its relevance. He would have been the first to admit that he was primarily concerned with the development of classical studies as such and not with the 'Renaissance', a concept of which he certainly talked latterly in somewhat sceptical terms. For all the implied criticism my dependence upon and respect for his work will be apparent in what follows. His work entirely supersedes Walter F. Schirmer, *Der Englische Frühhumanismus* (Leipzig, 1931). It will be long before Weiss's book is superseded, but some useful additional material will be found in the catalogue of the Bodleian Library exhibition, *Duke Humphrey and English Humanism in the Fifteenth Century* (1970), with substantial introduction and notes by Dr. Richard Hunt and Miss Tilly de la Mare.

[7] *Op. cit.*, p. 5.

the North quickened, not least because of minor but nonetheless influential changes in Italy.

I. ITALY AND ENGLAND: DIVISIONS AND UNITIES

Such a plan, it must be admitted, accepts in broad terms a contrast between Italy and the trans-Alpine world. Such a contrast can and must be drawn. But it will be apparent in what follows how profound also were the similarities. Indeed had they not been so it is impossible to imagine the ultimate transplantation of so much of Renaissance Italy to other parts of Europe: the transplantation took long to be effective, perhaps, but it could not have been effective at all had there been a fundamental opposition between Italy and her neighbours. And of course there was in the purely political sense no 'Italy' at all. If one talks of a European 'States-system' then the Italian participants are Milan, Florence, Venice, Naples, the Papacy and so on. A gulf separated Sicily from Piedmont far greater than that which separated the north of England from the South, or even those dividing England from Scotland or France.

This internal division in Italy, this absence of a centralised government comparable to those found in England, France, Castile and Aragon, was an old story and it was to persist for centuries to come. It perplexed and obsessed observers like Machiavelli and Guicciardini in the early years of the sixteenth century. It continues to bother, even torment, many Italian historians today—witness their approach in the monumental *Storia d'Italia* which has recently begun to appear from the publishing house of Giulio Einaudi in Turin.[8] Of course it is easy to exaggerate both the disunity of Italy and the unities of other countries. There had been a *rex Angliae* since 1200, but the *Angli* of of his earlier title were quite capable of tearing themselves in pieces—under Henry III, Edward II, Richard II, Henry VI, Charles I. In France, the *regnum Franciae* of the thirteenth century had to suffer not merely English attack, but devastating civil war in the fifteenth, sixteenth and seventeenth centuries—wars which had a markedly regional or provincial ingredient.[9] Moreover, if in Italy we find ourselves ignoring large areas—the south hardly enters the Renaissance story in the *quattrocento*, nor does Piedmont—so likewise in any ac-

---

[8] At the time of writing four volumes have appeared, 1, 2 and 5 in two parts (1972-73). See especially the contributions in vol. 1 by G. Galasso and Corrado Vivanti. The latter's title is 'Lacerazione e contraste'.

[9] Cf. Giulio Einaudi's shrewd remarks, *op. cit.*, I, xxii-xxiii.

count of 'pre-humanism' in England we find ourselves gravitating to the south and east of the country, and we would do this whatever aspect of change we were investigating. To that extent 'England' is almost as arbitrary or unreal a concept as 'Italy', although the natives of each region had no such hesitations in identifying those who came from the other. To that extent there were Italians even if there was no Italian state, and there were English even if their state was often weak and divided.

To a great extent the reception of Italian humanist and artistic methods and values occurred in northern Europe at about the same time and in somewhat similar ways. It is therefore helpful to keep in mind parallel developments in Germany (a land even more divided than Italy), France and other neighbouring countries. Among these must be included Scotland, and this not because from that day to this the foreigner confuses the component parts of the United Kingdom, but because in some ways the Renaissance had a more favourable climate in Scotland. The fifteenth century marks a high point in Scottish vernacular literature; and there were ecclesiastical, legal and educational changes which were conducive to the admission of new ideas. It was a Scottish king, James VI, who in 1603 became King also of England. In good humanist fashion James VI and I tried to name the new amalgam Great Britain.[10]

II. ANGLO-ITALIAN CONTRASTS

Any comparison of Italy and England in the age of Salutati and Chaucer must begin with the social scene, before proceeding to political institutions and practice, and the intellectual and artistic background. I shall start with the dissimilarities, as these have usually been stressed in earlier analyses.

At first sight society in Italy was dramatically different from what it was in England. Italy was a world of towns, big and little. The big towns, despite plague and prolonged economic recession, were much bigger and the small towns were infinitely more numerous than in England. Florence, Milan, Venice and Naples were all at least twice as populous as early-fifteenth century London, which had about 40,000 souls; and London was by far the biggest centre,

---

[10] Cf. S. T. Bindoff, 'The Stuarts and their Style', *English Historical Review*, LX (1945), 192-216; and my paper on 'The use of the term "Great Britain" in the Middle Ages', now reprinted in *Europe: The Emergence of an Idea*, 2nd ed. (Edinburgh, 1968), 128-144.

after which one dropped to a mere 10,000 at a few other important centres, York, Norwich, Coventry and Bristol. This was a reflection of the greater population and urban wealth of Italy and of the basically agrarian and village life of England. A distinction between town and country, between urban and bourgeois on the one hand and peasant and country gentleman on the other, marks this situation, even allowing that in Italian cities (as in cities everywhere) there were then large parks and gardens, long since built over. With this, perhaps even as a consequence of it, we must note a commercial and industrial activity in Italy which could not at the time be even remotely paralleled elsewhere. Admittedly this economic ferment was not universal in the peninsula. Florence, Milan, Venice and Genoa were in the fifteenth century, even if past their apogee, hardly typical of a land where the most numinous centre, Rome, was a collection of shabby ruins and the trade of Naples was largely controlled by Florentine bankers. Nevertheless the sophistication of the Italian businessman and his resources both technical and material made him appear a different animal to his northern counterpart, still pooling his slenderer capital, when engaged in long-distance trade, and with primitive methods of accounting. And the northern merchant in his Hanse was well aware of the difference, for the bankers of Tuscany were familiar figures, indeed rapidly becoming essential elements, in northern commerce. The English, especially in London and the bigger towns, had already exhibited their xenophobic sentiments.

In the English parliament there was a clumsy but unavoidable instrument through which much government had to operate and which, like the Crown, lent an air of unity to the public scene. Parliament by now an assembly with two houses, the lower consisting of elected gentry (lesser nobles in continental terms) and elected burgesses, the upper of the greater magnates (lords) and the greater clergy (prelates) passed statutes and voted money grants to the king. Apart from his irregular feudal revenue and the customs dues, the king was dependent on taxes voted in parliament and on subsidies voted by the clergy in their own assemblies. Constitutionalists like Fortescue and Commynes greatly admired the English parliament, but it undoubtedly prevented the king from tapping, as rulers did in France (and the Italian states), the real income of his subjects. This perhaps led to a certain sophistication in England. Budgeting a year ahead was important; it was scarcely found in the Italian hand-to-mouth financial arrangements. And we should not readily equate the Commons and Lords of England with the Estates (clergy, nobles, townsmen) of continental assemblies. Some elected representatives, the cream of the 'political class', governed in the Italian republics. Elsewhere the *parlamento* in Italy was a vestigial reminder of olden days, without real power and with no future. In one other field the contemporary observer might have detected a further political difference. The professional paid armies of France and England were larger and perhaps more loyal than the professional armies of the peninsula. This was perhaps a consequence of the Hundred Years War. It certainly derived strength from the stability of French and English dynasties; an element of allegiance entered the northern military situation which an Italian general like Francesco Sforza could scarcely feel for any of his employers; the sentiment was not even produced by two generations of Sforza rule as dukes of Milan. This military contrast was diminishing in the later fifteenth century, when many Italian states had standing armies of some kind—although this did not provide an 'Italian' force comparable to that of France.[11] And finally there is no doubt that the clergy outside Italy were subservient to their secular masters, and obedient to princely bidding. In Italy princes also tried to insist on control of the clergy but the pope was another prince with whom one sometimes had to make a deal.

This leads one to a consideration, necessarily somewhat longer, of the differences of a cultural kind between England and early Renaissance Italy. If religion may be subsumed under the rubric culture we may here notice at once the fire and colour of Italian devotion. The monastic life, withdrawn from the world, dependent on decent endowment and honest administration, was doubtless still practised with more success in England and the north than it was in Italy, where very many monasteries had collapsed into corruption and physical ruin. Episcopal control of diocesan discipline was likewise hardly to be found south of the Alps. Against this must be set the passionate devotion to the Holy Family (especially the Virgin) and the saints, the splendour of public worship in procession and at the great festivals, the repetition of mendicant excitement in the emergence in the 1360s of the Franciscan Observants.

---

[11] Cf. now Michael Mallett, *Mercenaries and their Masters: Warfare in Renaissance Italy* (London, 1974).

There is a tepidity about English religion in the later Middle Ages which makes the Italian seem perhaps unduly spiritual. There are no Bernardinos in London. There is little enough evidence even of Third Orders in England and even the quiet Brethren of the Common Life did not cross the North Sea. Parish rivalries in England were muted, compared with the violent polarisation of Mediterranean devotion. The Cathedral did not dominate so many cities; the Baptistery as such was unknown. With these differences, and closely related to them, was the relative wealth of the English secular clergy. This is most readily measured in episcopal income, but it covered the whole gamut of benefices. A fat clerical career was readily available in England and there was never difficulty in finding a poor curate or vicar to serve parishes which had lost most of the priests' stipend. In Italy there were parishes too poor to maintain any sort of priest; there were bishoprics with virtually no endowed income at all.

Probably more clergy in England (though still a small minority of the clerical order as a whole) went to universities than was the case in Italy, even allowing for the smaller English population. The universities to which they went were predominantly their own, Oxford and Cambridge. The days were nearly over when there was a substantial English nation in the Faculty of Arts at Paris; that had been killed by the long war, and it came to be called the German nation. Oxford and Cambridge not only educated clergy, which had been their main function from the start, but also an increasing number of laymen, anxious (as we shall see) for a little grammar and a year or two away from home, but not intending to put their university training to serious professional use. The courses were lengthy and, from a layman's point of view, singularly arid or inappropriate. We shall have to consider aspects of the scholastic scene later but it may be recorded here that to reach a bachelor degree at Oxford at the end of the fourteenth century the student usually spent four years in the schools; about three more years took him to a master's degree; if he aspired to the highest degree of all, the doctorate in Divinity, another seven or eight years were needed. Even if one began at the age of fifteen it was unlikely that one could finish before one was thirty. Wycliffe was over forty when he got his D.D. in 1372. Doctors of Divinity were at the apex of the educational ladder. In the English universities, as at Paris, theology was the senior discipline and the faculty of theology the senior faculty. For those who merely successfully survived the arts curriculum, a lush career opened out: 'churchmen, like their lay counter-parts, were divided into the two nations of masters and men. The masters were the masters of arts'. [12]

Such a prolonged education needed money, so that in general it was the well-to-do clergy (apart from monks and friars) who were university trained. And the same can be said of the Italian university, save that the component of men in religious orders was conspicuously smaller: friars got their Divinity in one or other of their own convents; there were virtually no faculties of theology there in 1400. The prestige accorded in northern universities to theology was given in Italy to law and, to a much lesser degree, to medicine. Here again courses were long and expensive, young lawyers (as opposed to humbler notaries) tended to come from well-to-do families. How else could one afford a degree which, if one wished to be *Doctor utriusque juris*, doctor in both canon and civil law, took ten years—assuming one had adequate arts preparation to enter for a higher degree? Since young men reading law at the better Italian universities were about seventeen when they started they were often in their late twenties when they finished; there were, even at Bologna, short cuts but these were even more expensive. As with the northern doctor, the D.U.J. had the world at his feet.[13]

There is no disputing that we have here a difference between England and Italy which is of some cultural significance. The hier-archies of the professional élites were distinct. The young patrician on the road to high office and political prominence in Italy was trained in law, above all in Roman law. In England the practising lawyer was a common lawyer, trained not in Oxford or Cambridge but by a mixture of apprenticeship and teaching in the Inns of Court in London. Moreover, as we should notice in passing, this preemi-nence of the civil law was to pass from Italy to other northern coun-tries, including Scotland, with the steady reception in these areas of Roman law. This did not in the end occur in England. There some canon law was taught at the universities until the Reformation, and a good deal of Roman law as well; the latter never had as much status at Oxford and Cambridge as Divinity, and we find a number

---

[12] K. B. McFarlane, *John Wycliffe and the Beginnings of English Nonconformity* (London, 1952), 14. And see *ibid.*, 19-21, for a succinct account of the Oxford university curriculum in the fourteenth century.

[13] A useful survey in Lauro Martines, *Lawyers and Statecraft in Renaissance Florence* (Princeton, 1968), 28-91.

of ambitious Englishmen reading civil law there as well as heading for the schools of Bologna and Padua.[14]

The Latin formation of the M.A.s and theologians in the north and of the lawyers in Italy was doubtless much the same in the thirteenth and early fourteenth centuries: a solid foundation of grammar and rhetoric. Already in the fourteenth century in Italy we find some scholars inveighing against the law. Petrarch's aversion to the legal training of his youth is well known, and this has a slightly paradoxical air when one recalls how closely associated with an interest in the classics were many lawyers of the time, many indeed who were Petrarch's own admirers and correspondents.[15] Certainly by the end of the century the number of lawyers and others who had a higher command of classical Latin and a deeper understanding of its possibilities for scholarship and art had begun to produce a new situation in Italy, one which is not paralleled north of the Alps. The D.D.s and B.D.s of the highest faculty in both Paris and Oxford are still active as theologians and metaphysicians, but they are not concerned to civilize their means of communication as the humanist in Italy was. Nor should we place too much emphasis on university training as a factor in promoting classical studies in Italy. It was far more the way in which boys were taught Latin before going to the university or in their training for the profession of notary. Coluccio Salutati was a notary and had never been to a university. One cannot find anyone remotely like him in the England of the 1380s and 1390s.[16]

Before the *Studia humanitatis* flowered after 1400 there was thus far more evidence of changed attitudes to Latin literature to be observed in Italy than elsewhere in Europe. Equally striking is the extraordinary advance in the vernacular literature there during the *quattrocento*. Dante, Petrarch and Boccaccio wrote much in Latin, and much that was intensely original, but they were known to the public in their own day and have been household words in Italy ever since because of their Italian verse and prose. Only in England have we two poets—Langland and Chaucer—who can (however

---

[14] See for students and for other English visitors, G. B. Parks, *The English Traveller to Italy*, I (Rome, 1954).

[15] Roberto Weiss, *Il primo secolo del umanesimo italiano* (Rome, 1949).

[16] That is, no fourteenth-century product of an English 'business-school', as such establishments have come to be called (*dictamen* in Latin and French, with related drafting of conveyances, etc., and some accountancy), emerged as a good scholar.

different their works are) bear comparison with the authors. of the *Divine Comedy* and the *Trionfi*. No northern country could at the time match the prose of Boccaccio; we must remember that sophistication in prose is more demanding than in verse. It is surely not accidental that the three great Tuscans had each a remarkable talent in Latin composition. This cannot be said of the two English poets, and it is salutory to recall the gristly prose of *The Book of the Astrolabe* or 'The Persones Tale'. There seems little doubt that the more polished language of the Italian writers owed much to their better schooling in the classics.

There is thus a sharp enough contrast on the educational and literary fronts between Italy and England, or any other northern land. The same is true in art and architecture. The German or North French pilgrim to Rome or Palestine left behind him as he crossed the Alps a land of church spires and rural castles, and he entered a land where, despite the inroads of Gothic, the ancient basilica remained the basic pattern for a great church—indeed many of the cathedrals and collegiate churches were ancient enough in Italy— and where the magnate still had his town house as his fortress. So much has often been done later to destroy or remodel medieval Italian buildings that we may be in danger of overstressing differences: there is no doubt that the architects of Siena and Milan cathedrals were confidently copying French or Burgundian styles, and the same is true of scores of other thirteenth and fourteenth century churches. Medieval travellers seldom conveyed their reactions to novelties of an artistic kind, save in the case of curiosities such as the pavement in the Duomo in Siena. Yet the pervasive Romanesque and Byzantine survived, the coloured marble outside and the darkness within, and must have made the northern visitor conscious more of dissimilarity than of similarity even when he encountered churches expressly emulating styles with which he was familiar. And this must have been all the more the case when his eye fell on the painted decoration of altar or chapel or pulpit. Giotto and the Pisani have no contemporaries elsewhere on the Continent, let alone in England, who could match their accomplishments as painters and sculptors respectively, although it is arguable that the independent panel portrait was found in France before it emerged in Italy. Yet in the visual arts the late fourteenth century witnessed the dispersion all over Europe, Italy included, of the manner known to modern scholars as 'International Gothic'. Hence our comparison of England and Italy about

1400 has produced an area of shared experience. An Englishman who had admired the Wilton diptych would have found Lorenzo Monaco a sympathetic painter, or so it appears to one little qualified to generalise in the field of art history.

III. ANGLO-ITALIAN SIMILARITIES

There are many other similarities to record, many activities and assumptions common to the two countries. In turning to them now I shall deal with them, as before, under topics, economic and social, political, and those more general features of common culture to which we have been led by International Gothic. If Italy was a land of towns in some of which commerce and manufacturers had developed to an extent not found in other areas, it was also a country where, difficult as it may be to appreciate the fact, the vast majority of the population were peasants working in the fields and the hills. Moreover, one can see, though we seldom regard them, a rural 'aristocracy', who enter the records of the Romagna, or the Ligurian hinterland, or the kingdom of Naples as brigands and mercenary thugs, although for much of the class and for much of the time they cannot have been very different in their ambitions and enjoyments than the gentry and squirearchy of rural England. At all events their literary pleasures cannot have been very different—bawdy and lachrymose tales, many of them derived from the heroic cycles of Charlemagne and Arthur, and destined to provide, both in Italy and England, material for Renaissance epic. At a higher educational level, while the relative academic ratings of theology and law were undoubtedly as described above, there were of course many Italian theologians, the most able of whom often followed in the steps of Aquinas and Bonaventure to Paris. Likewise there were canonists and civilians in England: of the twenty-two archbishops of Canterbury and York whose pontificates fell in whole or in part into the fourteenth century, eight were doctors of civil law, four were doctors of both civil and canon law; only three were doctors of theology, two were M.A.s and four apparently had no degrees at all.[17]

---

[17] Figures taken, as later in this essay, from the new ed. of John Le Neve, *Fasti Ecclesiae Anglicanae 1300-1541*, 12 vols. (London, 1962-67). For comparison we may look at the degrees for which there is evidence held by cardinals created by the popes at Avignon: of the 66 for whom details are available (about half the total) 18 were theologians, 21 were canonists, 18 were civilians, and 7 D.U.J.s. Bernard Guillemain, *La cour pontificale à Avignon* (Paris, 1966), 217.

Again it is true that there was a unified central government in England, and in the fourteenth century war with Scotland and France did much to intensify the loyalties of his subjects to the king. English culture was gravitating ineluctably to a court and London was becoming a capital where litigation, administration and pleasure attracted nobles, gentry and burgesses from the whole land. Yet much of this political homogeneity is somewhat illusory. Great families dominated many country areas and the reign of the young king Richard II was to see a popular rebellion confined to the more advanced agricultural areas of south and east, and it was to culminate in his deposition and murder by magnates outraged by what they regarded as his high-handed and arbitrary rule. Italian politics may have been precarious at that time but none of his subjects deposed Giangaleazzo Visconti. If royal power existed throughout the realm of England it was often in practice exercised by, and to the advantage of, local potentates. So powerful is the model of monarchic unity that we forget these things, we forget Ireland, we assume that Edward I's conquest of Wales was at once effective and ignore the continuing independence or unruliness of the Marcher lords of the west and the north. All of this was reflected in the emergence of a mercenary or 'bastard' feudalism which has striking parallels with the *condotte* of Italy: a prince bought the services of soldiers for regular wages.

Nor can it be overlooked that, despite the different structures of the university curricula and despite the differing places occupied by the higher faculties of divinity and law, the substructure of fourteenth-century education was much the same everywhere. Basic Latin grammar was taught from Donatus and Priscian and from the glosses, commentaries and versifications derived from these authors, most pervasively the *Doctrinale* of Alexander de Villedieu. However wildly the pronunciation of language may have varied, Italians and Englishmen shared the same Latin grammar and more or less the same collections of authors—I refer to the run-of-the-mill scholar and student. Accidence and syntax do not lend themselves to regional variations and are resistant in the main to any fundamental alteration. What was to characterise humanist education was not the structure of elementary instruction in Latin, but the use to which it was put.

Italians, then, with the rest of the inhabitants of Western Europe, shared much the same economy, had much the same social and political arrangements, and were not too sharply distinguished by cultural attitudes. Even at the level of the vernacular a common substratum of *motifs* and traditional tales permeated all areas of Europe. Differences indeed there were, but an intellectual, Bishop Richard of Bury, diplomat author of the *Philobiblon*, could happily encounter Petrarch while he was on a mission to Avignon in 1333, as Geoffrey Chaucer seems to have done at Padua forty years later. Such contacts have sometimes been used to urge that there were men who belonged in some sense to the same 'movement'. It would be absurd to compare either of the Englishmen with Petrarch. Bury was an avid book-collector and admirer of scholarship, but his views on life and literature were conventional. Chaucer was a great poet, but entirely lacked Petrarch's philosophical and speculative interests, or his mastery of Latin. Nor can one regard as early 'humanists' the group of English mendicants about whom Miss Beryl Smalley has written so entertainingly in her *English Friars and Antiquity in the Early XIVth Century*.[18] What one can say is that in the fourteenth century there was a shared experience of religion, society and culture upon which subsequent development was to be based.

It is indeed this situation which makes the different routes taken in literature and the arts in England and Italy after about 1400 so very remarkable. That the two roads were later to join in the highway of early modern civilization makes the *quattrocento* contrasts all the more interesting and deserving of exploration.

IV. FIFTEENTH CENTURY CHANGE: ITALY AND ENGLAND

There is no doubt that Italy witnessed first the changes which we summarise in the term 'Renaissance'. It is, however, important to remember that the Renaissance, despite all its dramatic innovations was only gradually an Italian phenomenon, that is one affecting the peninsula more or less as a whole. It is necessary at the outset to set down the main stages in the development of new approaches in Italy so that they may be set against the time-table in England. I hope I may be forgiven for here summarising an argument which I have set out elsewhere at greater length.[19]

Perhaps it is as well to recall in broad outline the political scene.

---

[18] Oxford, 1960; see my review in *English Historical Review*, LXXVII (1962), 530-532.

[19] *The Italian Renaissance in its Historical Background* (Cambridge, 1961); the Italian translation has a revised bibliography. I do not repeat annotation in what follows.

The years of papal residence at Avignon (1305-78) had enabled or provoked the development of strong *signorie* in north Italy and the papal states. After the Schism (1378-1417) the re-established papacy managed with some set-backs to establish itself firmly in Rome, making the city a political centre of significance for the first time since the early thirteenth century. This precipitated a prolonged struggle for power in the Papal States, in turn involving Venice, Milan and Florence, to whose outcome rulers of the Kingdom of Naples, of whatever race, could not be indifferent. Until the 1450s there was a period of prolonged and bloody conflict. After 1454 and the establishment of the Italian League a period of uncertain equilibrium followed, to be ended by the death of the ruler of Naples in 1494 and the French invasion which followed. By the early sixteenth century the major powers of continental Europe had armies and political ambitions in the peninsula. It was against this background that there emerged the novel approaches to cultural and ethical problems which were in the end to be of such interest to the world at large.

The period of 'pre-humanism' in Italy contained some remarkable scholars and personalities. Petrarch was by far the greatest although Boccaccio in his Latin works was probably more accessible to other students, a more consistent exponent of new trends, and more immediately influential on scholarship. This period came to an end in the 1370s when Petrarch and Boccaccio both died and when Coluccio Salutati, notary and administrator, was appointed to be Chancellor of the republic of Florence. He it was (and again I use Voigt's extraordinarily perceptive phrase) who secured for humanism the right of citizenship in Florence. The 'new learning', one might say, had found an environment in which it was cherished—cherished, we must admit, for good reasons and for bad: because it was a weapon in the Florentine diplomatic armoury; because it was a comforting thing for worldly men to be told that they might be comfortable without being offensive in the eyes of God; because classical ideas chimed in with the art of Masaccio and Ghiberti, with the architecture of Brunelleschi; because it soon became chic to patronise the *studia humanitatis* even if one was not necessarily an adept.

With Coluccio and his successor, the chancellor Leonardo Bruni, we enter a remarkable period in Florentine history. The early decades of the fifteenth century see Florentines rewriting their history and rebuilding and redecorating their city. Much of this activity was provoked, it seems, by a desire to justify the cruel expense and prolonged efforts to withstand a series of political threats—from Milan, from Naples, from Milan again—which stretched out into the period when, after 1430, Cosimo de' Medici began to manage much of the political life of what remained, in a very important sense, a republic. These years witness an extraordinary flowering of humanist literature and of artistic achievement. It was perhaps natural that neighbouring states like Siena should react against Florentine manners and men. Other parts of the peninsula had little use for cultural accomplishments which were wrapped up in the envelope of republicanism. Yet in the 1440s and 1450s a bridge was being built between Florence and her neighbours. Cosimo de' Medici, the greatest patron of his dynasty as well as the shrewdest man of business, displayed the advantages of wealth and power by exhibiting his sympathy for books and ideas, for a new art and a new architecture. In his own day, as ever since, Florence laid claim to be the home of civilisation. This was a claim heard enviously by the other rulers of Italy. Medici power lay not only in a counting house and a vast commercial empire; it lay also with libraries and writers and with handsome new buildings. All of this could be readily adapted to bolster up the prestige and power of a prince as well as of a first citizen—indeed a prince had certain advantages in display over a Florentine subject who eschewed overt demonstrations of his magnificence. In 1450 Florence made peace with the Milanese. It was a sign perhaps that Florentine cultural primacy was coming to an end.

By the mid-fifteenth century the new art and the new humanities had begun to grow roots in the least propitious places. Small dynasties like the houses of Este and Gonzaga began to throw up great patrons and massive buildings. In Urbino, where a poor hill-top town in Umbria seemed to offer an inauspicious environment for advances in the arts, a successful *condottiere* Guidobaldo da Montefeltro built a superb modern palace and filled it with one of the most splendid collections of books and pictures. The papal court, meanwhile, was not only led by Nicholas V into plans for rebuilding St. Peter's and the Borgo, but heard the argument urged that the successor of St. Peter, far from being evangelically poor or stoically indifferent to riches, must himself be wealthy if he was to do proper justice to his role.

The final phase in Italian developments came with the penetration of humanist literature and (if the expression may be accepted) humanist art and architecture, into the great principalities of Italy—Milan, Naples and Venice. By now the doctrines of the active life and of service of the community had lost their republican overtones; even at Venice the Republic was a republic of 'nobles'. Now was the time when the ideas and the methods of the humanist, having penetrated Italy as a whole, could be more readily assimilated in neighbouring lands.

It has seemed desirable to take the broad outline of cultural development in Italy down to the end of the fifteenth century. It may be put in a few words as being centred in Florence, then in smaller courts, finally in larger ones; or as moving from a republican milieu to a princely one. We often still treat the Renaissance in Italy as a single movement, whereas it was diverse in both time and place. Diverse indeed far beyond what is revealed in the sketch offered above. Under Alfonso V, for instance, we find a king patronising some scholars, but as a centre of humanist activity with strong and continuous traditions Naples had to wait till the end of the century. Likewise (and this will be a factor to be encountered later in the evolution of the English scene) we must not regard Florence as dropping out of the race. Lorenzo de' Medici, while a lesser patron than his grandfather, was a lover of literature and continued to encourage the study and translation of Plato by Ficino and his friends. And far from slipping easily into a principate, after Lorenzo's death in 1492, Florence experienced a period of intense popular government: this was the age of Savonarola and Botticelli.

Before we turn to examine the situation in England we must identify the main features of the humanist programme. Expressed in a word this was (as we have seen the word itself implies) education.[20] It was a programme by which young men who would have public responsibilities were to be given training suited to their role in society. (This does not, of course, exclude a few prominent women being educated in this way, nor a large number of men who in the end became clergymen). The method of instruction was based on a thorough competence in Latin grammar and practice in using the language for speaking and writing. This last depended on an absorp-

---

[20] The works of W. H. Woodward remain basic expositions of the theory and (so far as we can assume it followed the methods of Guarino and Vittorino) the practice of the new curriculum: *Vittorino da Feltre and other Humanist Educators* (Cambridge, 1897); *Studies in Education during the Age of the Renaissance* (Cambridge, 1906). See also R. R. Bolgar, *The Classical Heritage and its Beneficiaries* (Cambridge, 1954).

tion of the precepts of the classical rhetorical writings of Cicero and Quintilian; the main rhetorical practices had, of course, been known and applied throughout the Middle Ages, but they were now studied in the original theorists and with a new fervour for civilised and stylish composition. All of this depended on a regular study of the Latin classics and an emphasis on the moral teaching of the philosophers, historians and poets. The prescription, it will be seen, was a hard one. Boys had learned Latin in earlier centuries, but only those destined for the Church had to take its study seriously and even they were supposed to apply it not to the cultivation of their moral or literary sensibilities but to the needs of devotion, of scriptural exegesis, of liturgical observance and the business of the Church. Now education was to be firmly structured in what were regarded as the interests of the laity and so firmly did a 'classical' curriculum become associated with the governing classes of Italy and later of Europe that it is only in our own day that it is ceasing to dominate the secondary schools. In my judgment there is no doubt that the 'political class' of Florence, in the decades pivoting on 1400, as later in the courtiers and gentlemen of Italy, took to the new education because it was based on assumptions regarding public and private morality more in keeping with their actual lives than the traditional renunciation of life preached by Christian teachers.[21] A sympathy, conscious with the clever and instinctive with the rest, drew more and more Italians of substance towards a plan of learning based ultimately on an ethos that was compatible with involvement in business public and private, and the rewards in wealth and temporal honour which went with such involvement. The world of Cicero and Livy, of Vergil and Ovid was an upper-class world; the Latin of the Golden Age was designed for and perfected by élites; all of this cemented the hold which the new schoolmaster acquired over the teaching of men who mattered.

It must not be supposed that the humanists took over all instruction. For long the novel attitudes to literature and moral philosophy made little impression on the university curriculum, although they were not actively repulsed. Hence Aristotle stood unchallenged in the universities, as he was to do until the seventeenth century. Side by side with the cultivation of the new humanities at Florence,

[21] I must refer here to the seminal studies on the active life and the problem of wealth contributed in 1938 by Hans Baron to *The Bulletin of the John Rylands Library*, XX, 72-97, and *Speculum*, XIII, 1-37.

Ferrara, Mantua, or Venice, we have the unchallenged place of Justinian's code and digest, and of the Greek medical texts at Bologna, Pavia, Padua, Pisa. But more and more of the doctors of law or medicine were also steeped in the humanities and, like the gentry who were their social equals, ensured that their children had a classical education.

This then, from the viewpoint of ideas and pedagogical methods, was what the Italy of the fifteenth century had to offer Europe. In the fine arts and architecture a classicism no less imposing manifested itself, which I am not competent to do more than allude to. What did Englishmen find in this splendour which they could admire and use?

In England between 1399 and 1500 we are at first sight presented by an almost uninterrupted period of war, internal and external. It is the internal war (the Wars of the Roses) which appears to have been more damaging than the external war with France. The deposition of Richard II by Henry Bolingbroke in 1399, of Henry VI by Edward of York in 1461 and 1471, the murder of Edward's children by Richard III and the latter's defeat at Bosworth by the rank outsider Henry Earl of Richmond in 1485, who was to have two serious rebellions in his reign, are merely the highlights in a gruesome story. The divisions at the centre, the struggle for the throne itself, enabled thugs of all kinds noble and non-noble to practise brutality at the perimeter. Compared with such divisive forces the war with France exercised, as we have seen, a certain cohesive pressure: Agincourt was a tonic for distracted Englishmen; Henry V could become a hero-king. In any event (and much to the grumbling discontent of those who had done well in France) the English were evicted from all their conquests save Calais and the war petered out in 1453. Yet for all the treasure and blood squandered in France, for all the ruthlessness of the civil war at home (where the gentler conventions of chivalry and ransoms did not apply) one's overall impression of fifteenth-century England is one of promise rather than prejudice, to adopt C. L. Kingsford's celebrated title.[22]

---

[22] *Prejudice and Promise in Fifteenth Century England* (Oxford, 1925); there are good things in the rather disjointed contents, but none as good as the title. Two recent short books are full of interesting ideas: F. R. H. Du Boulay, *An Age of Ambition* (London, 1970); and J. R. Lander, *Conflict and Stability in Fifteenth-Century England* (London, 1969). Short but reliable accounts of the political and social background will also be found in A. R. Myers, *England in the late Middle Ages* (Harmondsworth, 1952), and George Holmes, *The Later Middle Ages* (Edinburgh, 1962).

War and economic stagnation did not prevent Henry VII being a stronger, more effective king than any of his predecessors save perhaps William I and Edward I. And when Henry VII died in 1509 he bequeathed his son a greater fortune than had ever been at the disposal of an heir to the throne. The machinery of central government steadily went on during the turmoil of the fifteenth century. Parliament met with such regularity that constitutional historians used to refer admiringly to the 'Lancastrian experiment'. More local rivalries were settled by due process of law than were settled by violence, which in any case was endemic in every part of Europe until the eighteenth century. The country gentleman wrote his letters even in the darkest days of the mid-century knowing that they would be delivered, and his estates, however widely scattered, were managed by men who had evidently never heard of the Wars of the Roses.[23] If the lack of 'governance' had been as bad as used to be alleged one would hardly expect landowners to have squandered fortunes not on defensible fortresses but on those comfortable mansions where crenellation was merely a status symbol.

The vast majority of the middle group in society, the 'Commons' of well-to-do burgesses and country squires, pursued its way more or less untroubled, but the changes in the dynasty and the fortunes of the very great have considerable interest for the cultural historian. There were features of Italian humanist activity very relevant to princes and great men, whether falling or rising in power. Likewise the sentiments which attracted the burgesses and minor nobility of Italy towards the new educational plan were far from absent in England or any other country of North Europe. Before examining how far these forces led to a quickening interest in the civilization of *quattrocento* Italy we must first briefly examine the points of contact between the two countries—and in doing so recall that to all intents and purposes the Italy we are dealing with excludes the Kingdoms of Naples and the duchy of Savoy.

V. ANGLO-ITALIAN CONTACTS

In his study of *The English Traveller to Italy* George B. Parks listed the following categories of visitors: kings and diplomats, clerics and pilgrims, soldiers and merchants.[24] (These categories overlap,

---

[23] On this see Kingsford, *Prejudice and Promise*, 33-34, 67-73. Too much emphasis has been put on the exceptional circumstances of the Paston family.

[24] Pp. 276-494.

a man who figures early as a student may later reappear as an envoy). Few princes made the journey in the warring Middle Ages. Lionel duke of Clarence married Violante Visconti in 1368, and died soon afterwards. Bolingbroke, the future Henry IV, passed through North Italy on his way as a pilgrim to the Holy Land in 1392-93. Lord Rivers, Edward IV's brother-in-law, was in Italy, probably as a pilgrim during a year of Jubilee (1475), and Edward IV's sister, the dowager duchess of Suffolk, was in Rome in 1500, another year of Jubilee. Far more important as a source of fruitful contact than these episodic and aristocratic travellers were the professional diplomats who, now that the pope was again an Italian and (after 1420, and more permanently since 1443) resident in Rome, maintained English interests in the Curia. Many of these were Italians, as we shall see, but the well-trained, if traditionally trained, professionals, nearly all clerks with prelacies, listed by Parks contain the majority of Englishmen who figure in the reception of Italian humanism in fifteenth-century England.[25] To them must be added a small number of English members of the Curia, whose limited literacy in Latin and odd pronunciation aroused Flavio Biondo to adverse comment;[26] a list of them would not be long but it would be worth compiling.[27] Its most distinguished fifteenth-century member would be Adam Moleyns, D.U.J., who served under Eugenius IV for about five years (1430-1435). At any rate his written Latin passed muster.

If diplomacy took a fair number of distinguished men from England to Italy for longish periods, business traditionally associated with the Curia was drying up as a result of legislation against papal provisions and the legal jurisdiction of Rome. Provisors and Prae-munire were irregularly applied. Despite Provisors (1351 and later reenactments) prelates continued to be technically 'provided' by the pope and to pay common services; but they normally did this through agents in Rome and lesser fry were prohibited from seeking benefices through papal interventions. As for the Rota, a handful

---

[25] *Ibid.,* 301-303.

[26] F. Biondo, *Scritti inediti,* ed. B. Nogara (Città del Vaticano, 1927), 125, in the 'De verbis Romanae locutionis'. Other non-Italians are censured along with the 'Anglicos-Britannos ... qui etsi litteras sciunt, adeo tamen rudes et artis grammaticae aliarumque scientiarum aliquando ignari sunt....' Their defects are especially noticeable in 'latini sermonis ... practicam'.

[27] The main reason why there were relatively few English curialists was that there were no resident English cardinals before Bainbridge, and of course no English popes; for similar reasons there are few English curialists in the Avignon period: see the various tables in Guillemain, *La cour pontificale à Avignon.*

of English appeals are recorded (despite the statute of Praemunire) throughout the fifteenth century—and some few litigants travelled to Italy to supervise their Roman advocates.[28] Likewise a few English-men are found in the list of ordinations *apud sedem apostolicam*.[29] There is small reason to suppose that these intermittent associations with the learned *scriptores* had much cultural effect. Nor did the much larger number of pilgrims contain many whose intellectual formation was affected by a visit *ad limina*, though some of the agents and ambassadors whose influence we must discuss shortly were enrolled in the English college, the Hospice of the Holy Trinity and St. Thomas of Canterbury in via Monserrato and in the various fashionable confraternities patronised by foreign visitors.[30]

Mr. Parks's categories of soldiers and merchants are of small interest to us; Italian merchants were far more prominent in England than English merchants in Italy; English soldiers only figured to any extent in the Italian wars of the fourteenth century. But with students we deal with a group which was to prove much more alert to cultural change, much quicker to transmit new ideas, and where our information, although far from complete, is nevertheless based on surviving graduation and other registers from Bologna, Padua and other universities. There are gaps in these records but those for Bologna seem sufficiently full for the later fifteenth century for us to say with some confidence that English students were increasingly switching their interest to civil law. Between 1451 and 1475 only three Englishmen are recorded as graduating in civil law against nine canonists; in the last quarter of the fifteenth century we find thirteen civilians, fourteen canonists and four D.U.J.s.[31] A similar impression is gained from the more fragmentary records of other Italian universities.[32] On the other hand it will appear that the students who were to prove most friendly to the new humanities were not lawyers, but divines, so far as their training and qualifications were concerned.

---

[28] I owe this information to the kindness of Mr. James Robertson.

[29] I hope to publish a study of curial ordinations.

[30] Parks, *The English Traveller to Italy*, 358-382. On the hospice see now B. Newns, 'The hospice of St. Thomas and the English Crown', *The Venerabile*, XXI (1962).

[31] Parks, *The English Traveller to Italy*, 625-627.

[32] *Ibid.*, 628-640; R. J. Mitchell, 'English students at Padua 1460-1475', *Transactions of the Royal Historical Society*, 4th series, XIX (1936), 101-117; *id.*, 'English students at Ferrara in the fifteenth century', *Italian Studies*, I (1937), 74-82.

The traffic in Englishmen to Italy was balanced by visits of Italians to England. These Italians were fewer in number but perhaps overall more influential in stature. They have attracted much attention from historians of humanism in England but we should remember that most Italians who came to England came for professional reasons (trade, diplomacy, ecclesiastical business) rather than as students in search of learning or the support of cultivated patrons. However much English scholastics such as Scotus and Ockham were admired by Italian students of theology or philosophy, I cannot find that there were many Italians at Oxford or Cambridge in the fifteenth century;[33] the admiration felt for English scholastic thought, which is reflected in well-known humanist jibes about British sophists and so on [34] was nourished by books and not by the somewhat unimpressive lectures of the English universities.[35] The Italian merchant in England must have often been involved in the importation of books and perhaps other objects of Italian origin, but such trade is hard to document. What we do know is that the printed book trade, although it was dominated by foreigners for half a century after 1475, does not seem to have attracted Italian enterprise.[36] Secular diplomacy, if we may judge by the earliest (ca. 1500) Venetian *relazione*, was cool and calculating.[37] The ambassador made for the men who mattered and they were important because they were politicians, not because they were reputed to be intellectually eminent, at any rate before Thomas More became chancellor. Castiglione's visit of 1504 was, it appears, not a cultural occasion: [38] his influence was to date from 1528 with the publication of *Il Cortegiano*.

---

[33] I count about a dozen Italians among the 60 foreign Dominicans sent to study at Blackfriars in Oxford in the fourteenth and fifteenth centuries; see appendices to W. A. Hinnebusch's paper on the subject in *Oxford Studies Presented to Daniel Callus*, Oxford Historical Society, new series, XVI (1964), 101-134. A. B. Emden in the introduction to his *A Biographical Register of the University of Oxford to 1500*, 3 vols. (Oxford, 1957-59), I, xlii, says that only a few mendicants came from abroad.

[34] E.g., in *Prosatori latini del quattrocento*, ed. Eugenio Garin (Milan, 1952), 60: Bruni's reference to 'britannicis sophismatibus'.

[35] A brief but suggestive survey of English writings known to Italian scholars, a relatively unexplored field, in Parks, *The English Traveller to Italy*, 446-455.

[36] See below p. 214.

[37] *A Relation of . . . England*, ed. C. A. Sneyd (Camden Society, 1847).

[38] See the important revisions of Cecil B. Clough, 'Federigo Veterani, P. Vergil's Anglica Historia and B. Castiglione's Epistola . . . ad Henricum Angliae Regem', *English Historical Review*, LXXXII (1967), 772-783.

On the other hand, ecclesiastical diplomacy and the administrative business of the church did bring a number of persons to England who were humanists in the sense we have been using the term. None was a literary or scholarly figure of the first rank or even perhaps of the second. Poggio (if we may group him here), Piero del Monte, and lesser figures such as Simone da Teramo, Giuliano Cesarini and Gaspare da Verona; all these were in England in the early fifteenth century.[39] In the later fifteenth century papal emissaries were more important prelates as well as more thoroughly trained in the new educational manner of Italy: for example Giovanni and Silvestro Gigli, Adriano Castellesi, and (beyond 1500) Polydore Vergil and Piero Griffo.[40]

VI. ENGLISH PATRONS IN THE FIFTEENTH CENTURY

By the time we reach the reign of Henry VII it is evident that there is a change in the official climate of opinion regarding the humanities. Before this is considered we must revert to the fifteenth-century environment and those Anglo-Italian contacts which bore fruit, however meagre. There are two sides to the matter. On the one hand we have a small group of wealthy English patrons whose personal learning is of less moment than their admiration for the learning of other people. On the other we have a smaller group of men whose talents reflected the new learning and who were fired to some extent by the novelties in the Renaissance programme of scholarship.

The wealthy English patrons are headed by a royal duke. Why Humphrey duke of Gloucester became enamoured of the new learning, even the degree to which he properly realised its novelty, must remain in some doubt.[41] He was vain and ambitious, knew France and the Low Countries and (through Italians such as the bishop of Bayeux, Zenone di Castiglione) must have been aware of the new learning such as it had filtered into France by this time.[42] The effectiveness of up-to-date Latin propaganda might have attracted him to the new style, although there was plenty of old-fashioned Latin and vernacular propaganda circulating in the Anglo-French

---

[39] Weiss, *Humanism in England*, 23-24.

[40] See now Michele Monaco, ed., *De officio collectoris in regno Angliae di Pietro Griffo da Pisa* (Rome, 1973), esp. 171-222 of the introduction.

[41] Weiss, *Humanism in England*, 39-70 and addenda; also the Bodleian exhibition catalogue, *Duke Humphrey and English Humanism*.

[42] Cf. below p. 197.

ambience which, one might have thought, would have carried more influence than neo-classical panegyrics or hexameters.[43] At any rate Humphrey had two Latin secretaries and used them as an Italian prince would have done: for correspondence, administration and flattery of Humphrey and his causes. He also accumulated contacts with many important Italian scholars as well as a library containing many humanist works commissioned or solicited by him, or sent by hungry authors to the gullible Maecenas in faraway Britain. His principal literary dogsbody was Tito Livio Frulovisi and Professor Weiss regarded the life of Henry V written for Humphrey by Frulovisi as the most influential of his many writings—but an influence exerted rather in the sphere of historiography than in the classical revival as such.[44] Certainly the poem the 'Humproidos' exalting Humphrey himself passed at once into a deserved oblivion from which it has only recently been partially recovered.[45] A more permanent inspiration for future scholars lay in his library. This is forever commemorated by the name 'Duke Humphrey' for part of the Bodleian Library in Oxford. There is no doubt that Humphrey's collections were very remarkable. His books included not only the classics as known in the Middle Ages (and these were for the most part the ones that mattered in the Renaissance) in new modern editions, but also copies of recently discovered ancient texts. Even more significant, he had a fair sample of the writings of Petrarch and his successors. And he possessed not only the traditional Petrarch (*De remediis* and so forth) but the more original Petrarch of the letters and the *Rerum memorandarum libri*. He had Boccaccio's *De genealogiis deorum*, Salutati's *De laboribus Herculis*, and probably other humanist works of significance as well as a mountain of humanist trivia.[46] Humphrey intended all his books for Oxford, but in the end a number of them ended up in King's College Cambridge and many were dispersed. The university library suffered in proportion

---

[43] For instance *Le débat des herauts d'armes*, ed. L. Pannier and P. Meyer, Société des anciens textes français (Paris, 1877); A. Bossuat, 'La littérature de propagande au XVe siècle: le mémoire de Jean de Rinel ... contre le duc de Bourgogne', *Cahiers d'histoire*, I (Grenoble, 1956), 131-146.

[44] I paraphrase Weiss, *Humanism in England*, 44-45.

[45] Roberto Weiss, 'Humphrey duke of Gloucester and Tito Livio Frulovisi', in *Fritz Saxl. A Volume of Memorial Essays* (Edinburgh, 1957), 218-227.

[46] On Humphrey's collection, see Weiss, *Humanism in England*, 62-67, with related corrigenda and addenda, and the Bodley Library catalogue, *Duke Humphrey and English Humanism* (1970).

as the colleges became effective teaching units.[47] It is however indisputable that his gifts to Oxford provided for a time the nucleus of a collection of classical and neo-classical texts the like of which did not exist elsewhere outside Italy.

Another nobleman of markedly less august origins who collected books and obedient humanist dependents was John Tiptoft, created earl of Worcester in 1449.[48] Another ambitious man, he coincided with the upheaval in England of the late 1450s and escaped from them to pilgrimage in Palestine and a visit of rather more than two years to Italy whence he returned (some thought) with an Italianate relish for tyranny. His scholarly aims were more personal than those of Humphrey: he had read arts at Oxford and later tried to be a humanist himself, as well as a patron of the many Italian scholars he met and of a few Englishmen like Free. His patronage was probably more important than the large collection of texts he accumulated, for these were in the event scattered after his execution in 1470. This did not mean that all his books were lost to English readers but it frustrated his intention of endowing Oxford and Cambridge in the manner of Duke Humphrey. His own talents as a Latinist are judged to be mediocre. His own tastes as reflected in his translations of Cicero (*De amicitia, De senectute*) and Buonaccorso da Montemagno (*De nobilitate*) were conventional.

Descending a further rung in the hierarchy of nobility we encounter the more imposing figure of William Gray or Grey, son of a north country knight and a daughter of the first Neville earl of Westmorland, nephew of a man who was successively bishop of London and Lincoln. Gray was well-connected, rich with benefices and a graduate of Oxford. From Oxford he went to Cologne to read theology (1442) and thence to Italy (1445) where he finally became a graduate in theology at Padua. He visited Florence, spent a few months attending Guarino's course at Ferrara and was then appointed royal proctor in Rome where he remained, with short visits back to England, until his final return in 1453 shortly before being given the see of Ely. And all the time—in Oxford, in Cologne, in Padua, Ferrara and Rome, and through the Florentine bookseller Vespasiano —Gray was buying books and on his death in 1478 they came to

---

[47] See *Duke Humphrey and English Humanism* and also the catalogue of another Bodley exhibition, *Oxford College Libraries in 1556* (1956), with an introduction by Dr. Neil Ker.

[48] Weiss, *Humanism in England*, 112-122 and refs.

his old college Balliol.[49] The collection is not remarkable from the humanist point of view. Gray was a theologian by training and by interest. But he bought books wherever they were good and interesting and in this way, especially during his Italian sojourn, he acquired a few classical texts and some *quattrocento* Italian writings. More important in the long run for literature was Gray's patronage for a few years in Italy of Niccolò Perotti and his encouragement of John Free. There is no evidence that his munificence was extended to these men as a matter of policy; he was a far more frequent benefactor of clergy who were neither humanists nor scholars.

Gray's career is strikingly paralleled in that of Robert Flemmyng. Another rich bishop's rich nephew, an Oxford man who later studied divinity at Cologne and Padua, another serious collector of books (bequeathed in the end to Lincoln College) he nevertheless is in many ways to be distinguished from Gray. He was without question attracted to the new learning. His attendance at Guarino's lectures was longer and less perfunctory than Gray's and he attained some competence in Greek, which he was at pains to keep up. There were Greek manuscripts in the collection given to Lincoln College, as well as a number of modern Latin versions of Greek classics, and the spread of his classical Latin texts was more extensive than Gray's; he had a copy of Valla's *Elegantiae*; he could employ 'a neat italic handwriting'. Even his embarking on a poetical eulogy of Sixtus IV and his Rome in the *Lucubraciuncula tiburtinae* (ca. 1477), bad though the verse is 'by Italian standards', represents a gesture which none of the patrons of scholarship and collectors of books previously mentioned could have attempted.[50]

Yet we must remember that, as with Gray, so with Flemmyng, divinity and books of a theological or liturgical character remained the prime interest. Lincoln College was devoted to divinity and I do not clearly understand what Weiss has in mind when he says of Flemmyng: 'As a "Maecenas" he contributed to the introduction of humane standards into Oxford, and to the bringing of theology into contact with neo-classicism'.[51] The one young English scholar whom any of these eminent personages directed towards the human-

---

[49] *Ibid.*, 86-95, and now the admirable account by R. A. B. Mynors, *Catalogue of the Manuscripts of Balliol College Oxford* (Oxford, 1963), introduction, xxiv-xlv.

[50] Weiss, *Humanism in England*, 86-95. Parks, *The English Traveller to Italy*, 601-606, gives a literal version of part of the poem.

[51] Weiss, *Humanism in England*, 105.

ities (apart from putting books on library shelves) was John Free.[52] Free, after studying at Balliol, was sent by Gray, now bishop of Ely, to work under Guarino at Ferrara in 1456; later on he was secretary to Tiptoft. He undoubtedly became an accomplished scholar in both Latin and Greek. His achievements, according to Weiss, place him 'beyond all doubt above every fifteenth-century English humanist before the time of Grocyn and Linacre'.[53] While one cannot disagree with this it is hard to see what consequences his career had for literature and learning. He copied a few manuscripts (doubtless more than the handful which have survived). He wrote a few formal Latin letters and orations. He translated the Greek of Synesius's satirical essay *On Baldness* into Latin. It is impossible to attribute to him any lasting impression on the culture of his day in Italy or England. His death at Rome in 1465 was hardly an intellectual catastrophe. Weiss groups with 'the English pupils of Guarino' (Gray, Tiptoft, Free) a more interesting man, John Gunthorpe, about whom I shall say a word shortly.[54] For the rest the other 'English pupils of Guarino' seem to me somewhat idiosyncratic characters who were touched with a love of books, enjoyed to some extent the literary life, but in no sense were aware of the significance of what was happening in Italy. It seems to me that we can apply to all of them reflections similar to those of Sir Roger Mynors on Bishop Gray:

> If we try to summarise the impression left on us by Gray as a patron of learning and a book-collector, we see at once that he was no renaissance prelate-patron. He kept no tame humanists in his household, except Niccolò Perotti for a short time as a youth of eighteen. He received no dedications, except from the inexhaustible John Capgrave, who had been wooing Duke Humphrey a quarter of a century before. He was no great promotor of learning in others, except for his not very lavish support of John Free, whom he had decided to send to Italy as companion to one of his own nephews.... Nor was he specially devoted to the new learning.... It is the wide range and high standard of his original texts in philosophy and theology that is so impressive. . . . .[55]

It is hardly surprising that men brought up in the older mental traditions should find it easier to assimilate what was familiar to

---

[52] R. J. Mitchell, *John Free. From Bristol to Rome in the Fifteenth Century* (London, 1955).

[53] Weiss, *Humanism in England*, 111.

[54] See below, p. 204.

[55] Mynors, *Catalogue*, xlv.

them. It was the Petrarch of the *De remediis* not the Petrarch of the *Secretum* which proved immediately comprehensible. It was the traditional morality purveyed by Bruni's translation of Aristotle's *Ethics* or *Politics* not (perhaps understandably) the much more explosive but domestic works such as the *Dialogue* against Vergerio or the history of Florence. Exactly the same kind of filter operated in the reception of Italian humanist writings in France, as has been shown by Professor Franco Simone.[56] To the incomprehensions inherent in this situation we should add hesitations due to a more positive hostility to all things Italian. King, Lords, Commons and clergy were at one in a generalised suspicion of the Italian—papal fiscality, papal rascality and the clever bankers who were the agents of rapacious Rome. In so far as the common lawyers were aware of a threat they too were resentful: Wycliffe had urged the superiority of the common law over the Roman law and so, later on, did Fortescue; Tiptoft's high-handed behaviour as High Constable was attributed to his having been corrupted by the law of Padua.[57] What was essential for a change in this situation was a conviction of the relevance of Italian experience among not merely a handful of rich eccentrics but among a larger and more continuously important group, the 'political' class of fifteenth and sixteenth-century England. The beginning of such a change can in fact be discerned. Its effects become more noticeable as the fifteenth century draws to an end.

VII. THE RECEPTION OF THE RENAISSANCE IN ENGLAND: PRECONDITIONS

The traditional explanation for the spread of the Italian Renaissance to the rest of Europe is, of course, couched in terms of individual contacts, such as those alluded to in the previous pages. Gray and Flemmyng, later Linacre, Grocyn and Colet, brought back the humanities as though they were packets of seeds which had only to be scattered about in order to beautify England with peninsular pleasances. This seminal work was aided in the traditional tale by the diplomats (soldiers too in the case of France and Spain after the Italian wars began) who caught culture as others caught syphilis,

---

[56] For a synoptic and recent statement of his views, see *The French Renaissance* (London, 1961).

[57] Cf. H. D. Hazeltine's remarks in the introduction to S. B. Chrimes's edition of Sir John Fortescue, *De laudibus legum Anglie* (Cambridge, 1942), xvii-xviii.

that further contribution to western civilisation at this time which was attributed to Italy. Shirwood, Sellyng, Pace are cases in point of envoys and orators who spent time in Italy which they found congenial.[58] This old 'explanation' went with a general assumption that the Renaissance formed part of a period of human enlightenment—of exploration, intellectual adventure, religious reform—which needed little justification or analysis.

An extension of this older view, or an elaboration of it, is the emergence of the 'New Monarchy' and the 'Rising Middle Class'. These myths—or 'models' as myths are called nowadays—were part of the stock-in-trade of the first fifty years of this century and still pop up, especially in works written by literary historians. It is as though Henry VII (founder of the 'New Monarchy' in England) would have been a better king if he had read Machiavelli's *Prince*, as if the *Prince* contained information without which powerful government would have been more difficult. I have already pointed out that the early Tudors were extremely effective rulers, and no lively prince in Europe but knew all that Machiavelli had to tell him about winning friends and influencing people, about sweetness, brutality and *virtù*. Machiavelli differed from earlier writers *de regimine principum* only in analysing what princes had always done, not in inventing new ways of ruling. And in northern Europe, where princes were not hampered by the Italian urban complication of a communal tradition, kings had in fact even less to glean from Renaissance Italy than Italians themselves.[59] As for the 'middle class' this muzzy concept has been laughed out of court by Professor Hexter: historians in England have used the term to cover the urban bourgeoisie, the rural gentry (who were regarded as 'noble' in continental lands) or the amalgam of both in the Commons. Regarding their 'rise', they were rising (gentry and bourgeois) from as far back as one can see. At any rate the gentry were, and the 'rise of the gentry' is a kind of sentimental extension of the concept. They

---

[58] Cf. Weiss, *Humanism in England*, 149-159, and now the introduction by R. Sylvester and F. Manley to their edition and translation of the *De fructu qui ex doctrina percipitur* (New York, 1967). Pace awaits an adequate biography, but see Jervis Wegg, *Richard Pace* (London, 1932).

[59] Cf. Allan H. Gilbert, *Machiavelli's Prince and its Forerunners* (Durham, North Carolina, 1938), esp. 234; and the article by Felix Gilbert, 'The humanist concept of the prince and the "Prince" of Machiavelli', *Journal of Modern History*, XI (1939), 449-483.

were also falling. And bourgeois and gentlemen were to rise and fall for centuries to come.[60]

What indeed is certain is that the basic tenets of the humanist were as applicable north of the Alps as south. The doctrine that the men who mattered should serve their community, their city, their prince, and be properly educated with such service in mind, did not need a Mediterranean environment in order to flourish. But it did need a conviction that educated administrators and an educated group of 'governors', to use Elyot's word, were essential to efficient government at all levels. Of course educated administrators were no new thing in Northern Europe and kings in England had leaned heavily for many centuries on the clergy, the clerks, who had been the only fully literate members of a society in which Latin was used not only in the liturgy, not only in running the Church, not only in international relations, but in many of the basic documents of royal and noble life—the charters and other instruments conveying title to land and other properties and privileges. These 'clerical clerks' were rewarded by their masters with benefices as well as more intermittent stipends. Such benefices were not directly heritable since the clerks were technically celibate, although the greater prelacies carried with them a vast amount of patronage, perfectly legitimately exercised by bishop or abbot in the interest of members of his family. In England this clerical basis of royal administration, and of the administration of great and smaller lordships as well, began to crumble in the fifteenth century. The laity were called in to run the affairs of king, duke, great landowner, as well as of the towns. Administration thus steadily came under lay control. Such a process may be seen at work everywhere. It is one of the most momentous transformations in European government and society.

VIII. CLERICAL AND LAY ADMINISTRATORS

In the absence of detailed analysis of the process it seems likely that what happened first was the emergence of a highly literate group of nobles and gentlemen (or 'Commons', which included the bourgeoisie, since we are concerned with the development in England). These men were, at any rate from the thirteenth century, acutely aware of the need for good management of their estates (if they were landowners), of their business interests (if they were

[60] J. H. Hexter, *Reappraisals in History* (London, 1961), 26-44, 71-162.

merchants and tradesmen). It was the landlords who mattered
politically and socially and their literacy by the end of the fourteenth
century is hardly to be doubted, if by literacy we mean competence
in reading the vernacular, if not necessarily writing it. Some indeed
there surely were who neglected their stewards' accounts, who
rusticated in declining manors. But the men who got on, who were
active as sheriffs, commissioners for this and that, M.P.s and J.P.s,
were perfectly able to cope with the written word. So too, were
many of the women of this class, perhaps more so than some of the
men, for the women had often to manage the estates (or the businesses)
while the men were away for long periods. A smaller number consisted of men who had acquired some Latin: such a man was *bene
literatus* and indeed 'literacy', if the concept could have been conveyed
to the socially important men and women of the fourteenth and
fifteenth centuries, would have meant for them competence of some
sort in Latin grammar and the ability to read a Latin text. The late
K. B. McFarlane had an entertaining lecture on the education of the
nobility in the later Middle Ages.[61] He was certainly right in arguing
that a high proportion of them were very well educated. What he
wrote of the nobility can be applied *mutatis mutandis* at a considerably
lower social level,[62] even while admitting that the bulk of the population, consisting of peasants and artisans, had little need to read and
little or no ability to communicate in writing.

What then seems to have happened is that this educated lay group,
composed of rich and influential men, were anxious to have affairs
managed by men of their own sort, and so increasingly were princes.
Further, the aspiring man of business (in this slowly changing
climate of opinion) could make his way to the top without entering
the church. He could found a family and, with hard work and luck,
obtain lands in perpetuity rather than precarious prebends; in certain
circumstances he could become an earl, he and his descendants for
ever, rather than a bishop or even a cardinal for a life-time. Nor
should we ignore more honourable motives. A career and influence,
whether for the well-born or the relatively humble, had meant in
effect celibacy and some men who were otherwise gifted for public
life wanted to live honestly with the women they loved. The tension

[61] Printed posthumously in *The Nobility of Later Medieval England* (Oxford,
1972).
[62] See remarks on literacy in Sylvia Thrupp, *The Merchant Class of Medieval
London* (Chicago, 1948), 156-158, 161.

between the benefice and matrimony was a genuine one and we find traces of it in England at this time; the advance of lay administration removed it.[63] Without some such considerations it is, I believe, hard to account for the steady drift towards a new type of administration and, accompanying this change, towards a new type of education.

Why did the prince and the 'governors' further this steady change? At first sight it was hardly to their advantage. If one employed a clergyman he was in the main paid for out of the endowed income of the church, from the domestic chaplain and family 'clerk' who could hope for a family living or one solicited on his behalf by his master, up to the king's man who could in the end grow wealthy, even extremely wealthy (one thinks of William of Wykeham) out of royally-sponsored promotion in the church. Nor were such men inherently less able than their lay successors. Although their training was largely scholastic that discipline was in itself a rigorous exercise in marshalling arguments and remembering propositions: the syllogism had been perfected to a high degree, certainly being regarded as a more difficult exercise than the rules of rhetoric necessary only for polite letters and speeches. Moreover the clergyman-official could not treat his appointment as a property: he might feather his own nest but he could not transmit the nest to a legitimate son, or sell it to the highest bidder.

How able and alert such men could prove is illustrated from the careers of some of those reckoned by Professor Weiss as early 'humanists'. He discusses Thomas Bekynton, an Oxford don who became chancellor to Duke Humphrey, secretary to Henry VI, Keeper of the Privy Seal and bishop of Bath and Wells; this able man relished good Latin and acquired some humanist texts. Much the same can be said of Adam Moleyns; after his return from the papal Curia he became a busy servant of the Crown, clerk of the council, frequently on embassies, Keeper of the Privy Seal (1444), bishop of Chichester (1449).[64] At a much lower level Sir John Fastolf's secretary, William Worcester, had antiquarian leanings which faintly suggest those of Flavio Biondo; although there is no

---

[63] A good discussion of Italian material in Carlo Dionisotti, 'Chierici e laici', *Geografia e storia della letteratura italiana* (Turin, 1967), 47-63. On the English scene the careers of some men who in the end got wives and should be recalled: Lily and More. And so should the careers of some who remained 'celibate': Wolsey and Skelton.

[64] Weiss, *Humanism in England*, 71-75, 81-83, 189.

evidence that among the humanist texts he knew was the *Italia illustrata*, yet he indulged a taste for what would come to be called chorography, and he is not an entirely isolated figure as we can see if we recollect John Rous of Warwick.[65]

Such men, adaptable and intelligent though they were, had nevertheless grave disadvantages for their employers. As clergymen they were not readily pushed around or, when beneficed, stripped of their source of income. The parson had his freehold; the bishop might lose the Great Seal but not his see. I do not mean that in any significant sense the clergy had transcending loyalties to the Church, let alone to the pope. There are no Anselms or even Beckets in fifteenth-century Europe. The English clergy obeyed the king, in cathedral chapters they elected his nominee, in convocation they taxed themselves for his benefit. But while a peccant priest or bishop might be lynched (as Adam Moleyns was lynched by a mob of soldiers in 1450) you could not legally execute him save for treason: Archbishop Scrope of York had been so punished in 1405. The fall of Wolsey points a similar moral. He was replaced as chancellor by More but remained an extremely rich and powerful man, as cardinal archbishop of York, so powerful, indeed, that he proceeded secretly to continue with what was virtually his own foreign policy. This it was which led to his final arrest and presumably would have entailed a charge of treason. Yet if Wolsey had been less avid for power at the centre, less unable to relinquish his pivotal influence, he could well have remained an important, though not all-important, political personage.[66] Such protection and permanence was not afforded to a secular official. Wolsey's servant, Thomas Cromwell, a nobody like Wolsey, was a layman. He could become a millionaire earl. He could end up on the block, which terminated his political influence abruptly; but his son succeeded as Lord Cromwell. The trend towards the lay administration is slow in manifesting itself in the fifteenth century and its effects must not be exaggerated. Nevertheless we can point to the erosion of the clerical monopoly of administration from the fourteenth century, with its collegiate life

---

[65] K. B. McFarlane, 'William Worcester, a preliminary survey', *Essays presented to Sir Hilary Jenkinson* (London, 1957), 196-221; Worcester's *Itineraries* have recently been edited by John H. Harvey (Oxford, 1969). For Rous, see T. D. Kendrick, *British Antiquity* (London, 1950), 19-29; who also (pp. 29-33) discusses Worcester.

[66] A. F. Pollard, *Wolsey* (London, 1929), esp. chap. xii.

burdensome to men who were only technically clerks.[67] And in the new Signet Office we have a department which was staffed by laymen from the start.[68] Nor must it be thought that secular careers like this are novel in the fifteenth century. The fief in all its forms was the reward of military or administrative employment, even if by becoming hereditary the burdens of feudalism had become fiscal by the fifteenth century. Kings gave their intimates titles and (if they were poor) the wherewithall to maintain themselves. There are several social nonentities who became nobles as a result of their enterprise during the Hundred Years' War and related campaigns: there are the de La Poles of Hull, the earliest of the merchant magnates (and a rare enough breed for long enough). In short one climbed high by being an effective instrument of the Crown. 'The truth is', wrote K. B. McFarlane, 'that the aristocracy *was* in the main one of service, that it was entered by service and that acceptable service was the cause of promotion within it'.[69] The aristocracy, as another writer has recently pointed out, consisted in the main not of old families but of new families.[70] What I believe we find in the fifteenth century is a steady application of these pressures at a level lower than the peerage, and a consequent turning of the middle ranks of society to the acquisition of the means, mainly sound education, which enabled them to compete.

A quite different influence exerted itself, especially on the Crown and a few great men: competition with the administration and administrative techniques of Italy. When the Schism ended, especially from the mid-fifteenth century, Italy attracted intense diplomatic activity. In this England was naturally less concerned than the continental powers. But Rome was the diplomatic hub of Europe in the late fifteenth century, and we have seen how the King's proctors in the City were important men. This was to lead to even more

---

[67] Some interesting points bearing on this neglected problem in T. F. Tout, 'The English civil service in the fourteenth century', *Collected papers*, III (Manchester, 1934), 191-221. For the Statute 14 & 15 Henry VIII c.8, which permitted the six clerks in chancery to marry, cf. G. R. Elton, *The Tudor Revolution in Government* (Cambridge, 1953), 54, n. 1: 'a sign rather of the complete laicization of the secretarial offices than a beginning'.

[68] See my earlier essay, 'The Early Renaissance in England', *From the Renaissance to the Counter-Reformation . . . in honor of Garrett Mattingly*, ed. C. H. Carter (New York, 1965), 98-99 and refs; above, p. 154 and refs.

[69] McFarlane, *Nobility*, 233.

[70] Du Boulay, *Age of Ambition*, 68.

important agents being accredited to Rome, until from the 1470s
something like a permanent embassy was maintained there.[71] Regular
contact with the Curia meant regular contact with humanists, for a
large number were now employed by the pope in offices either
important or honorific or venal or all three. (And, we may add, a
fair number of them were laymen, including two well enough known
about in England—Poggio and Flavio Biondo. Rome was a pioneer in
selling offices and curialists, married or unmarried, lay or clerical,
expert at conveying them *in favorem*). The orator or ambassador
at Rome had to match in style, material and cultural, his hosts and
the other orators who were engaged in both a *concours d'élégance* and
a competition in eloquence; the rivalry sometimes reached the
length of fisticuffs. Keeping up with the humanist Jones became a
preoccupation of government not only in Rome but at home. The
pope had a librarian with Platina in 1475 and his successors.[72] Henry
VII had to have a librarian, and we find Latin secretaries in the
English court and laureate poets if not poets laureate at about the
same time.[73] If the prince was constrained to behave in the new
manner so were those of his advisers who met foreign envoys or
travelled on foreign missions. Henry VII employed John Gunthorpe
on diplomatic work as Edward IV had done earlier. Another and
more celebrated humanist ambassador was Richard Pace. Familiar
though it may be, and regarded by McFarlane as *ben trovato*, the
episode recounted in Pace's *De fructu* of the clodhopper gentleman,
rapidly declining into anachronism, must be quoted:

> About two years ago, more or less, when I returned to my country
> from the city of Rome, I was at a banquet where I was unknown to
> most of the guests. After we had drunk a sufficient amount, one of
> them (I don't know who, but, as you could tell from his speech and
> appearance, he was no fool) began to talk about the proper education

[71] B. Behrens, 'Origins of the office of English resident ambassador at Rome',
English Historical Review, XLIX (1934), 640-656; D. S. Chambers, *Cardinal
Bainbridge in the Court of Rome 1509-1514* (Oxford, 1965). The above was written
before I had seen William E. Wilkie, *The Cardinal Protectors of England. Rome and
the Tudors before the Reformation* (Cambridge, 1974), but this proved to be a survey
of the diplomatic policies of England with regard to the papacy from 1514 to
1534.
[72] The most recent and authoritative account is Jeanne Bignami Odier, *La
Bibliothèque Vaticane de Sixte IV à Pie IX* (Città del Vaticano, 1973), chap. iii
(pp. 20ff.). Chapter ii deals with the earlier and less permanent tenures of Giovanni
Tortelli and Giovanni Andrea Bussi (Aleriensis).
[73] Weiss, *Humanism in England*, 122-127.

for his children. He thought first of all that he should find them a good teacher and that they should by all means attend school and not have a tutor. Now there happened to be a certain person there, a nobleman, or so we call them, who always carry horns hanging down their backs as though they were going to hunt while they ate. When he heard us praise learning, he became wild, overwhelmed with an uncontrollable rage, and burst out, 'What's all this stuff, buddy? To hell with your stupid studies. Scholars are a bunch of beggars. Even Erasmus is a pauper, and I hear he's the smartest of them all. In one of his letters he calls *tên kataraton penian*, that is, goddamn poverty, his wife and complains bitterly that he's not able to get her off his back and throw her in the ocean, *bathykêtea ponton*. God damn it, I'd rather see my son hanged than be a student. Sons of the nobility ought to blow the horn properly, hunt like experts, and train and carry a hawk gracefully. Studies, by God, ought to be left to country boys'.

At that point I wasn't able to keep myself from making some reply to the loudmouth in defense of learning. I said, 'I don't think you're right, my good man. For if some foreigner came to the king, a royal ambassador, for example, and he had to be given an answer, your son, brought up as you suggest, would only blow on his horn, and the learned country boys would be called on to answer him. They would obviously be preferred to your son, the hunter or hawker, and using the freedom that learning gives, they would say to your face, "We would rather be learned, and thanks to learning no fools, than to be proud of our stupid nobility" '.

Then glancing about him on all sides, he said, 'Who's this, talking to me like that? I don't know the man'. And when someone whispered in his ear who I was, he mumbled something to himself—I don't know what—and finding a fool to listen to him, he snatched up a cup of wine. Since he had no answer to give, he started to drink, and the conversation passed on to other things. And so I was saved not by Apollo, who saved Horace from a blowhard, but by Bacchus, who saved me from an argument with a madman, which I was afraid would go on a lot longer.[74]

The anecdote also neatly illustrates the inevitability for the humanist of a career in the service of the great or the usually much less welcome alternative of educating children—children who would in turn become either 'governors' or educators. Another tale, later in the book, declares that princes care nothing for theologians, and that theologians know nothing of the world and its ways.[75]

---

[74] *De fructu qui ex doctrina percipitur*, ed. and trans. F. Manley and R. S. Sylvester, 23-25, quoted by permission; and cf. the introduction, p. xxi; also McFarlane, *Nobility*, 228-229.

[75] *Op. cit.*, 83-85. For 'beggars' on p. 85, read 'mendicants'; the theologian is obviously a Dominican.

IX. INNOVATIONS IN EDUCATION

The expansion in secondary and the changes in university education in northern Europe in the later Middle Ages are well-attested facts and the invention of printing in the 1440s in the Rhineland is the most impressive of the many evidences of rising lay literacy. If printing spread with amazing speed—prior to the nineteenth century it is the only important technical innovation to cover the continent within a generation—it was because people could read and wanted books. This was because schools were numerous by the fifteenth century in many parts of the Continent. England was only exceptional because it was less populous, and so was proportionately less well supplied than were certain other areas of Europe.

Nevertheless England's schools were relatively plentiful in 1400 and multiplied steadily through the century. On this subject there has, of course, been much debate over A. F. Leach's contention that a large number of grammar schools were destroyed during the English Reformation, in particular with the suppression of the chantries after 1545. If Leach's arguments were based on exaggerated assumptions regarding the quantity and quality of schools associated with convents and chantries or chantry priests, his critics have probably erred in attributing too few establishments to the Middle Ages, and in emphasising too much the progressive influence of the Reformation.[76] The most recent work, based on a carefully compiled list of schools, prints a series of maps of which that for fifteenth-century England shows a remarkable spread of endowed and 'public' schools.[77] Admittedly these were often small and often in small places. But such schools were usually supplemented by more precarious institutions. If (for instance) the county of Northumberland had schools at Alnwick, Hexham and Norham, it is reasonable to suppose that at Newcastle upon Tyne it was possible for the townsfolk to find education suited to their needs, even though the endowed and public school apparently did not emerge until late in the six-

---

[76] A. F. Leach's researches remain extremely important. His *English Schools at the Reformation* (1896) has been particularly attacked: see Joan Simon's articles of 1955 and later and now her *Education and Society in Tudor England* (Cambridge, 1966), where there is a full examination of mid-Tudor developments (pp. 223-244). The most recent investigation of English education (to 1530) is Nicholas Orme, *English Schools in the Middle Ages* (London, 1973), a balanced and thorough study from which I have greatly benefited.

[77] Orme, *English Schools*, 216: 'Endowed schools found in England 1330-1530 and open to the public'.

teenth century.[78] There seems no doubt that our documentation is very patchy, and that serious research may well multiply the number of firmly established schools as well as those of a more temporary character.

Expert opinion seems agreed that the fifteenth century sees a marked step forward. Mr. Orme writes:

> The fourteenth century had seen the origin of the endowed schools; in the fifteenth they became at last a widespread and popular form of charity. It is here, and not in the age of the Reformation, that the great movement really begins by which during five centuries hundreds of private benefactors founded hundreds of endowed schools all over England, and thus effected one of the principal achievements of English civilization.[79]

Mrs. Simon, while regarding the Reformation period as the watershed, nevertheless draws attention to 'the steady expansion of lay education at various levels' in the fifteenth century.[80] Instructing the ignorant was, after all, one of the traditional spiritual works of mercy and, in centuries when the laity were steadily taking over intellectual leadership, it was inevitable that schools should be an off-shoot of lay devotion, whether by direct and independent endowment or through gilds and chantries.[81] It is also highly significant that William of Wykeham's foundation at Winchester (1382) and Henry VI's at Eton (1440), while being initially intended to produce clergy soon became a preserve of the lay nobles and gentry: the 'commoners' began to take over before the Dissolution.

It is important to remember the developing provision of schools in the England of the later Middle Ages, for it was in the old schools that the new Renaissance educational methods were to take firmest root, offering a pattern to the many new foundations of the mid- and late sixteenth century. This was, of course, most plainly to be seen in the case of St. Paul's School in London. In answer to the chronic shortage of grammar schools in the capital, a concern which

---

[78] R. F. Tuck, 'The origins of the Royal Grammar School, Newcastle upon Tyne', *Archaeologia Aeliana*, 4th series, XLIV (1968), 229-271.

[79] Orme, *English Schools*, 194.

[80] Simon, *Education and Society*, 56.

[81] See in general W. K. Jordan's works on charitable bequests and especially the synoptic *Philanthropy in England 1480-1660* (London, 1959), 147, on the 'secularisation of the charitable impulse'. I am not convinced that the Protestant reformation had much to do with this development: cf. Brian Pullan's work on charity in an Italian town, *Rich and Poor in Renaissance Venice* (Oxford, 1971), and, for schools in Venice, pp. 404ff.

had agitated the citizens for a century and more, Dean Colet lavishly refounded St. Paul's in 1509. His aim was a devout laity; his prescription, while encouraging good Latin, retained the old-standing suspicions of the unsettling effects of reading the pagan classics, especially the poets; but it was at this school that the classics were first to come into their own.

There are several signs that the period sees a new and more professional attitude to education. In 1448 William Byngham established a college at Cambridge called Godshouse, which has not unfairly been regarded as a kind of teachers' training college. It was intended to ground twenty-five scholars in advanced grammar; when qualified they were to work in grammar schools. In fact Godshouse was never as flourishing as intended but some of its purposes were taken over when it was absorbed into the Lady Margaret's foundation of Christ's College. The teaching at Godshouse comprised study of some of the classical authors but was not in any sense educationally adventurous. For a newer approach we have to turn to Magdalen College at Oxford, where William Wainfleet, bishop of Winchester and formerly provost of Eton, in 1480 added a grammar school. The first master appointed here was John Anwykyll who started the slow revolution in the teaching of Latin in England which was to be continued by John Stanbridge and John Holt, who both began their teaching careers at Magdalen College School, and by Colet and his schoolmasters, notably William Lily.[82] Interest in the humanities is evident, as we have noted, among a few wealthy and well-travelled gentlemen. It is also observable in much humbler folk, such as those discussed by V. H. Galbraith in dealing with 'John Seward and his circle'. In this we are shown a group of London schoolmasters who, in the early fifteenth century, are meeting for literary jollifications, swapping verses with somewhat laborious classical allusions and (it may be suspected) using epigrams and adages in a somewhat novel manner for educational purposes. The master whom these obscure *literati* revered was John Leland, 'flos grammaticorum', an Oxford schoolmaster whose contemporary reputation seems excessive.[83] These men had all to some degree felt

---

[82] A survey of the teaching of grammar in Orme, *English Schools*, 106-115.

[83] 'John Seward and his circle', *Medieval and Renaissance Studies*, I (1941-43), 85-104; R. W. Hunt, 'Oxford grammar masters in the later Middle Ages', *Oxford Studies Presented to Daniel Callus* (see n. 33 above), 163-193, where a sober appraisal, concluding with Leland, does not suggest much enlightenment.

the influence of the new humanities, yet it is surely significant that (save for Lily) their direct contact with Italy was minimal or non-existent.[84] The introduction into the grammatical teaching of the influence of Valla and Perotti reflected a willing acceptance of new methods by a few English teachers who shared instinctively a desire for a fresh approach. The steady increase in schools, the switch in endowments to secular purposes were to find instruments at hand for the reception of the humanist educational curriculum.

These developments owed little to the two universities, despite Godshouse and Magdalen College School. Of course Latin was basic to the arts courses at the University, but, though it was therefore easy to learn elementary Latin at Oxford and Cambridge there was no academic interest in the teaching of Latin as such. There were no chairs in poetry or rhetoric, and the later hostility of the older establishments to the new humanities is well known. On the other hand the 'university' as such was losing ground in the later Middle Ages to the colleges and this was to prove a most important change, for it facilitated both the penetration by laymen into the groves of Academe and the slow transformation of college curricula in ways which would have been resisted at university level. The establishment of new colleges permitted a rapid increase in the number of non-clerical 'commoners', and founders could introduce limitations on the character of the studies to be encouraged by their foundations which sometimes indicate an interest in innovation. Like the schools alluded to in the previous paragraphs, colleges were endowed as an act of piety. 'To maintain or "exhibit" a scholar or two at a school or university was a recognised "good work" long before the age of colleges'.[85]

The founders of late medieval colleges at the two English universities were predominantly clergymen who had risen high in the royal administration and had reaped the reward of at least a bishopric. At Oxford this generalisation admits of only one exception—Bishop Fleming of Lincoln, who founded (1429) the college of that name, was an ecclesiastical but not a royal politician. At Cambridge there are more exceptions: the great ladies who endowed Clare and Pembroke, Gonville who was beneficed well in return for stewardship of the lands of great men, Byngham of Godshouse (already mentioned),

[84] See below, p. 225.
[85] Hastings Rashdall, *The Universities of Europe in the Middle Ages*, eds. F. M. Powicke and A. B. Emden, 3 vols. (Oxford, 1936), III, 175.

the remarkable establishments of Corpus Christi (gilds, 1352) and St. Catherines (a provost of King's, 1475); and the colleges created by Henry VI (Kings and Queens, 1441 and 1448).

If Cambridge offers many exceptions it also offers a most remarkable example of royal association with the university. This was the establishment of the King's Hall as an off-shoot of the Chapel Royal by Edward II in 1317; Edward III with an endowment made the society into a college but the link between it and the world of administration did not weaken. Even when the recruitment of scholars ceased to be exclusively from the children of the Chapel Royal 'throughout the fourteenth and early fifteenth centuries a varying percentage of Scholars was drawn directly from this source or from the court circle'. I quote from the admirable account of Dr. Cobban. He goes on:

> Even after direct recruitment from the chapel had apparently ceased, the connection with the court continued and the college became to an ever-increasing extent a base for graduate fellows, especially for civil lawyers, who were frequently non-resident and were employed in various capacities in ecclesiastical and secular business.[86]

The concern of founders with the provision of public servants is occasionally expressed elsewhere,[87] but this is the only establishment which in effect made a college an adjunct of the royal household— the solid basis 'of the university-court nexus throughout the medieval period'.[88] In a way the arrangement reminds one of Wykeham's Winchester-New College connection, or of the Eton-Kings link which was to bring another royal foundation to Cambridge, for 'the chapel royal incorporated what may best be described as a sort of independent grammar school' and it was from this school that a considerable number then went on to the King's Hall.[89] How did these potential officials prepare themselves? In the main by the study of civil law. Dr. Cobban enables us to construct the following statement concerning the second degrees of scholars at the King's Hall over two half-centuries:

---

[86] A. B. Cobban, *The King's Hall within the University of Cambridge in the Later Middle Ages* (Cambridge, 1969), 13, n. 4.

[87] *Ibid.*, 22.

[88] *Ibid.*, 60-65. Dr. Cobban suggests that Wykeham's 'principal English model' was this Court-Cambridge relationship.

[89] *Ibid.*, 54-55.

	Total	M.A.	Civil Law	Canon Law	Theology
1350-1400	51	22	23	6	—
1400-1450	54	22	25	4	3

Equally important, of those entering the college in the first period less than a third proceeded to higher degrees; in the second period the proportion has risen to 45%.[90] This prominence of civil law is remarkable evidence of a preference among the ambitious and their patrons for this kind of training. If we repeat for the fifteenth century the simple arithmetic regarding the qualifications of the archbishops of Canterbury and York which we did for the fourteenth, we find out of a total of eleven names that six were civilians, one was a D.U.J., two were theologians and one was M.A.[91]

The lawyers of England were, however, common lawyers and their education was at the Inns of Court, not at the university. The history of the Inns at this time remains to be written [92] but it was clearly highly professional and in many ways resembled the lectures and disputations of the contemporary university. The Benchers and Readers of the Inns 'trained the students of the law and called them to the bar', each of the four Inns of Court and the smaller Inns of Chancery being organised on a collegiate basis. The resemblance to the university extended to the panoply of the Judges and Sergeants-at-law, whose position was, in Fortescue's words, 'no less worshipful and solemn than the degree of doctors'. It was, says Holdsworth, a rigorous apprenticeship which 'no doubt kept the practical, the argumentative, the procedural side of law prominently to the front'.

At the same time we cannot say that it gave no opportunities for instruction in legal theory. It also produced Littleton and Fortescue. We may conjecture that the students had some opportunities for 'private reading', perhaps in the chambers of the elder lawyers; and to those whose minds are prepared by such reading suggestions thrown out in argument, and the quick play of mind upon mind, will often give hints as to the existence of difficult problems and clues to their solution. Moreover, we may remember that this mode of

[90] *Loc. cit.*

[91] And William Booth (York, 1452-64) is *magister*, which probably means an arts degree: Le Neve, *Fasti*, VI, 4.

[92] See Sir William Holdsworth, *A History of English Law*, 12 vols. (London, 1903-38), II, chap. V, II; and *Readings and Moots at the Inns of Court in the Fifteenth Century*, ed. Samuel E. Thorne, I (Selden Society, London, 1954); vol. II, in which fifteenth-century legal education is to be discussed is not yet published. An important contemporary witness is Sir John Fortescue, *De laudibus legum Anglie* (cf. above, n. 57).

instruction, if it began by making men pleaders, and continued by making them advocates and keen doctors, ended by making them judges.[93]

Nor was it the case that civil law was unknown to the young men in the Inns. Many of the better-off and the abler had read some law in the university before beginning their professional studies. The Inns had three further enormous advantages, which they only partially shared with Oxford and Cambridge. They were exclusively composed of laymen, whereas the undergraduate was still technically part of or associated with a clerical community. They accepted (as did the universities) students who did not intend to practise a profession but who stayed only for a portion of the course, who left (one might say) without graduating; but they gave such young men a smear or a deeper tincture of a subject which in a litigious age was of direct importance in everyday life to all men of any substance, and this could not be said of the traditional arts curriculum of the university. Finally the Inns had a location in the one big city in the land, the universities were tucked away in two little provincial centres. Doubtless the attractions of the capital were not all intellectual, but that probably mattered less than would appear; the boys at the university were far from all being swots. At London was the Court and the courts and the High Court of Parliament. When printing came it came to London first and foremost. Mrs. Simon may well be right to say

> It is usual to account the Elizabethan age as the time when the Inns of Court became leading educational establishments because they then attracted so many young gentlemen; but this influx and other pressures operated to undermine traditional forms of training, and it was rather before it took place, in the fifteenth century, that the Inns had their golden age as centres of legal education.[94]

At any rate, it was out of a spell at Oxford and professional training at Lincoln's Inn that there emerged the greatest English humanist, Thomas More.

X. LITERATURE: BOOKS AND LIBRARIES

If there are grounds in educational history for considering the pre-Reformation century as lively and receptive, so I believe there are in literature. Some aspects of literature are not impressive, it

---

[93] Holdsworth, *History of English Law*, II, 508.
[94] *Education and Society*, 55.

is true. Latin scholarship, before the last decade of the fifteenth century, when the new grammars and *vulgaria* began to appear, seem to have been in a low key, although until we have a history of English scholarship before the seventeenth century it is by no means certain what remains to be discovered and evaluated.[95] But one has the impression that literary historians are determined to regard the interval between Chaucer and Shakespeare as a period of almost unrelieved mediocrity in English. As a recent critic has neatly put it: 'it is possible to suggest that the "decline" of fifteenth-century literature is due to nothing so much as the historians' need for something of the sort between Chaucer and the Renaissance'.[96] It was part of C. S. Lewis's 'drab'; the Chaucerians were all in Scotland; the endless verses of Lydgate and Gower and the repetitive, slogging prose of Malory dominate the scene, relieved only by a handful of enchanting lyrics. 'The glory had departed'.[97] It is true that much fifteenth-century English prose and verse lacks sparkle, lacks the irony produced by the author regarding himself with interest: compare Malory's treatment of his heroes with Boiardo's or Ariosto's. But what the evidence does suggest is the rapidly growing public for books. In this England was on all fours with Germany and France. The scriveners were turning out manuscripts in the vernacular at an impressive rate. Some of the multiplying manuscripts were inherently fairly trivial, the *Brut* for example, (however important its continuations are for modern historians) or the works of John Shirley. But some were not. There are nearly 200 surviving manuscripts of the Bible in English (despite the slight danger that the possession of this could be awkward for anyone suspected of heresy) and over 80 manuscripts of all or part of Chaucer's *Canterbury Tales*. And how many copies of these popular works formerly existed but have now perished? Should not the quality of the reading public at any rate be partly judged on the older books

---

[95] For example, we have no adequate study of Reginald Pecock or Thomas Gascoigne; the *Loci e libro veritatis* of the latter was not published in its entirety by J. E. Thorold Rogers (1881). The only topic adequately covered is historiography in C. L. Kingsford's *English Historical Literature in the Fifteenth Century* (Oxford, 1913), which covers writings in both Latin and the vernaculars. It is a great pity that we do not have the revision of this which only K. B. McFarlane could have provided. There is an interesting comparison of two treatments of a critical question in J. M. Levine, 'Reginald Pecock and Lorenzo Valla on the Donation of Constantine', *Studies in the Renaissance*, XX (1973), 118-143.

[96] D. F. Pearsall, *John Lydgate* (London, 1974), 68.

[97] H. S. Bennett, *Chaucer and the Fifteenth Century* (Oxford, 1947), 96.

they read, as well as on current production? The production of the
press, once the art arrived in 1475, bears out the popularity of an
older literature. It also shows little or no humanist influence.

> Nearly half his (Caxton's) publications were of this [religious and
> didactic] kind (35 out of 77 original editions, or 56 out of 103 published
> items), and must have given him little anxiety. Indeed, nine of them
> ran into two or more editions—among them such substantial works as
> *The Golden Legend*, Maydeston's *Directorium Sacerdotum*, Mirk's *Liber
> Festivalis* and the pseudo-Bonaventura *The Life of Christ*. His other
> largest venture was the publication of various poetical works, but
> here again he ran only a small risk ... after Caxton had found a
> ready market for some of his little quartos of Chaucer or Lydgate's
> verses, he followed this up by the publication of *The Canterbury Tales*
> and the *Confessio Amantis* of Gower.[98]

Such a picture is more or less true of the first century of English
printing as a whole: the volume of publication increases every year,
but traditional tastes predominate.

Nevertheless the evolution of grammar school education noted
earlier is reflected in the output of the press. Much of the old continued—Donatus, Alexander of Villedieu, John of Garland. But
the new compilations of Anwykyll, Stanbridge and Whittinton
also figure prominently.[99] If there are only two editions of Anwykyll's
Compendium (1483), there are some fifty of Stanbridge's various
works before 1530 and about four times as many of Whittinton's.[100]
To this must be added a large importation of Latin educational
works from continental presses. The *Short Title Catalogue* includes
foreign-printed books designed for the English market. But it does
not, of course, cover the books imported into England as a venture
by merchants or booksellers, or at the request of a customer. From
the beginning, it seems, sizeable quantities of such books were
coming in, evidently mainly religious and educational.[101] An even
better indication of the early trade in learned literature is found
in early library catalogues, such as that for Syon Monastery, the
first version of which apparently dated from 1504. In the catalogue

----

[98] H. S. Bennett, *English Books and Readers 1475-1557* (Cambridge, 1952), 17.
Mr. Bennett in this work made good use of W. B. Crotch's edition of *The Prologues
and Epilogues of William Caxton*, E. E. T. S. (1928).

[99] Bennett, *English Books*, 86-87.

[100] See *S.T.C.*, Nos. 23140-23199, 25444-25581. Many undated editions survive
and exact figures are hardly worth attempting.

[101] Cf. H. R. Plomer, 'Importation of books into England in the fifteenth and
sixteenth centuries', *The Library*, 4th series, IV (1923-24), 146-150.

as a whole (it was not continued after 1526) there are entries for nine
printed items from England, and for 387 from the continent.[102]
As was proper in a strict house of the Bridgettine Order, the contents
(they are of the men's library, not the nuns') are predominantly
liturgical, theological and grammatical—good, traditional material,
although exhibiting, as will be noted, the influence of new ideas.

One can put a book in a library but one cannot ensure that anyone
reads it, although we can be more sure when we have registers of
the books lent out, such as the one Platina maintained for the library
in the Vatican.[103] Hence library catalogues are by themselves perhaps
a less certain guide to established taste than multiple copies for
publication and sale. Yet one of the momentous changes in the
laicization of literacy and life was not only the demand for books
but the altered conditions for their preservation. One can now
observe the creation of libraries of quite a novel kind. Great collections of manuscript books were nothing new. They are found in
dozens of abbeys and friaries, even (as at Syon) in well-endowed
nunneries; the two universities and their colleges had such collections, the latter becoming steadily more important, as already noted.[104]
But with a literate gentry the gentleman's libracry became a possibility. The magnate was treating his home as a pleasure ground
rather than as a centre of power: men of wealth made parks and
comfortable country palaces; the bourgeoisie who could afford
fresh air—'pastoralism' is Professor Du Boulay's word for it—had
modest country houses.[105] Part of all this comfort included books
and soon a library became part of a gentleman's equipment. When
the literate, book-accumulating members of society had been clergy

---

[102] Ed. by Mary Bateson (Cambridge, 1898). Cf. p. viii: 'The English presses
are very poorly represented'. On this library see further below, p. 229.

[103] E. Muntz and P. Fabvre, *La Bibliothèque du Vatican au XVe siècle* (Paris,
1887); Maria Bertola, *I due primi registri di prestito della Bibliotheca Apostolica
Vaticana* (Città del Vaticano, 1932). Our information for England at this time is
scanty. There is a register of borrowers (1440-1516) of the books bequeathed by
Thomas Markaunt (d. 1439) to Corpus Christi College Cambridge, cf. J. O.
Halliwell, in *Publications of the Cambridge Antiquarian Society*, quarto series, XIV,
part 1, 16-20; F. M. Powicke, *The Medieval Books of Merton College* (Oxford, 1931),
describes the system of *electio*, a distribution of books among members of the
society, on pp. 12-18, and prints the pretty uninformative *electiones* from the
fourteenth and fifteenth centuries (pp. 60-82). On borrowing see also Ernest
A. Savage, *Old English Libraries* (London, 1911), 98-103.

[104] F. Wormald and C. E. Wright, eds., *The English Library before 1700* (London,
1958), 1-147; *Oxford Libraries in 1556* (cf. above, n. 47).

[105] *An Age of Ambition*, 51.

there was an inevitable dispersal of possessions, including books, at death. In this way college, monastic and other corporate libraries, as well as the relatives of testators, benefitted. And the impulse to donate to such institutions remained very strong indeed during the fifteenth century and indeed for much longer; it is not yet dead. But a great man, or even a man who had some secure income, might now bequeath his books to a son who added to them. Or he bequeathed not to a corporation of clergy but to some kind of 'public' library. Donors to the Library of the University of Cambridge, even if it was very small, were giving in some sense to a 'public' library; Duke Humphrey's munificent gift to Oxford—neglected though it soon alas became—is another example of the awareness of the need for public libraries; and so was the Guildhall Library, although its purpose was basically theological.[106] Far more is known about the institutional libraries of medieval England than about private collections,[107] especially those of laymen.[108] It seems undeniable that there were not very many of them, although inventories in wills do not become obligatory until 1521. No English collection exists comparable to the library assembled at Urbino by Duke Federigo da Montefeltro and we do not know what books were to be found in the great houses built by successful administrative operators like Sir Roger Fiennes (Hurstmonceaux) and Sir Ralph Cromwell (Tattershall). In any case the two greatest book collectors could in the end not look to a future for their families. Duke Humphrey died suddenly in 1447 *sine proliis legitimis* and John Tiptoft earl of Worcester was attainted and executed in 1470—one reason why his library was dispersed.[109] All one can say therefore is that conditions were ripe for the establishment of private lay as well as public libraries and there are hints of it among modest enough families, such as the Pastons, who 'were accustomed to turn to books for relaxation'. Their rumbustious ally Sir John Fastolf may not

---

[106] The Guildhall Library was begun about 1425. Two other public libraries, also theological in intention, were established later in the century at Worcester and Bristol. Orme, *English Schools*, 83-85.

[107] For institutional libraries, see N. R. Ker, ed., *Medieval Libraries of Great Britain*, second ed., Royal Historical Society (London, 1964).

[108] See the list in Savage, *Old English Libraries*, 274-285; and cf. Raymond Irwin, *The English Library* (London, 1964), 207. For 'catalogues' based on wills see Sears Jayne, *Library Catalogues of the English Renaissance* (Berkeley, 1956), and for the legislation of 12 Henry VIII cap. 5, see his introduction, p. 9.

[109] Weiss, *Humanism in England*, 118.

have had a room designated as a library but he kept a collection in the Stewe House at Caister.[110]

Among these new buildings there is as yet no hint that Renaissance architectural styles were admired by lay patrons. In ecclesiastical buildings the final development of Gothic was reaching towards its most elaborate perpendicular triumphs. Foreign influences, such as they were, were Burgundian and German rather than Italian in art and architecture. Where flimsy materials were concerned, the decoration for *joyeuses entrées* and similar public displays, we deal with the impermanent and ill-documented. But here too the country was not without relevant experience.[111] In the limping meter of Lydgate's middle English the verses describing the pageant of Henry VI's entry into London in 1432 sound tawdry as well as clumsy in comparison with the descriptions of (for instance) the papal processions we find written up glowingly in Pius II's commentaries, or rehearsed efficiently in Burkard's *Diarium*, but the aim and effects were not so dissimilar.

> And in the Cornhill anoon at his komyng
> To done plesaunce to his magestee,
> A Tabernacle surmontyng off beaute,
> Ther was ordeyned, be fful ffresch entayle,
> Richely arrayed with Ryall Apparayle.

> This Tabernacle off moste magnyficence,
> Was off his byldyng verrey Imperyall,
> Made ffor the lady callyd Dame Sapience;
> To-fore whos fface moste statly and Ryall
> Weren the seven sciences callyd lyberall . . .

> ffirst there was Gramer, as I reherse gan,
> Chief ffounderesse and Roote off all konnyng
> Which hadde a-fforn hire olde Precian . . . .

And so on. The whole inserted in a city chronicle, rejoicing in this visible evidence that London was 'Citee of Cities, off noblesse precellyng, in they bygynnynge called newe Troye'.

> Suche Joye was neuer in the concistorie
> Made ffor the Tryumphe with all the surpluage,
> Whanne Sesar Julius kam home with his victorie;
> Ne ffor the conqueste off Sypion in Cartage . . . .[112]

---

[110] H. S. Bennett, *The Pastons and their England* (Cambridge, 1932), 112-113, and Appendix, pp. 261-262.

[111] Sydney Anglo, *Spectacle and Pageantry in Early Tudor Policy* (Oxford, 1969), 54-56, 191, 195, 284-289.

[112] C. L. Kingsford, ed., *Chronicles of London* (Oxford, 1905), 105, 115.

XI. THE CROWN AND THE NEW CULTURE

To compare the poor sickly child Henry VI to Julius Caesar
strikes one as absurd. The triumph of his entry into London after
Henry VII's victory at Bosworth might well have seemed premature
to contemporaries but we have no doubt that it was celebrated with
new poetry as well as traditional decorum. Henry's laureate, who
seems to have arrived in the country with him, tells us that, inspired
by poetical frenzy, he recited publicly the verses carefully transcribed
in his 'Vita Henrici VII'.

> Musa, praeclaros age dic triumphos,
> Regis Henrici decus ac trophaeum
> Septimi, lentis fidibus canora
>   Dic age, Clio
>
> Dicat arguta chorus ille sacro
> Voce cum Phaebo, cythara canente
> Grande certamen, ferat huncque regem
>   Semper ad astra

And much more besides.[113] That Henry's reign was inaugurated
with a 'Carmen Sapphicum' was an omen. For it was in his reign
that the humanities came to court and, equally important, began
to be naturalised.

One must admittedly avoid the fallacy of thinking that in 1485 the
'Middle Ages ended' or (to quote an authority) 'Modern times as
distinct from the middle ages had begun under the Tudors'.[114]
Caution is indeed needed since every survey of English history
makes a break in narrative or analysis at the accession of Henry
VII and it is extremely hard to detach oneself from the assumption
that with Henry and his successors we have a run up to, and then
the fulfilment of, the Reformation and the Renaissance, regarded
as conjoint moments of illumination. Sceptically though one must
regard these old but tenacious propositions, associated as they are
with other hoary absurdities I have mentioned earlier (New Monarchy,
Rising Middle Class), there is no doubt that Henry VII's rule saw
some remarkable innovations in English culture. That there had
been a long period of preparation I have tried to show; that in
concrete cases some positive developments antedate the Tudors
is true; but the sense of a new atmosphere of patronage and the

---

[113] James Gairdner, ed., *Memorials of King Henry VII*, Rolls Series (London,
1858), 35-36; cf. Anglo, *Spectacle and Pageantry*, 8-10.
[114] Godfrey Davies, *The Early Stuarts* (Oxford, 1938), xix.

knowledge that this patronage was to have permanent consequences
lends the decades on either side of 1500 a peculiar significance. Nor
was patronage alone responsible for change. We have solid evidence
for the spontaneous adoption of new ideas and new styles. Much of
this admittedly saw its flowering after Henry VII's death. Polydore
Vergil's *Anglica Historia*, for instance, was not published until
1534. But it had been commissioned by Henry VII.

The notion of Henry VII commissioning works of literature or
art is at first sight absurd, for another of the firm convictions of
scholarship, even fairly well-informed scholarship, is that the king
was the very model of parsimony. There has recently been considerable debate on this question, but the fact is that the king died
leaving both a fortune and a reputation for avariciousness.[115] His
adoption of foreign scholars was, in fact, an economical demonstration of taste compared with building, in which his activity was
modest—the Henry VI chapel at Westminster and continuing works
already begun at Windsor. Moreover the scholars were frequently
clergy who were rewarded, as of old, with benefices.

There was a purposefulness in the first Tudor's adoption of
Renaissance styles among his learned entourage which is not to be
accounted for in Henry's own upbringing. Princes had been well-
educated for long enough,[116] and it is perhaps indicative of the
hopes of his Tudor guardian, the earl of Pembroke, that some care
seems to have been taken over his training. Not a great deal seems
to be known about his tutors. Bernard André says that he heard
from one of them, Andrew Scott, since dead but then a student of
divinity at Oxford and a very well-trained scholar, that Henry's aptitude
for learning was remarkable. In his *Itinerary* Leland mentions in
passing the tomb in the collegiate church at Warwick of 'Hasely,
schole-mastar to Henry the 7 and Deane of Warwyke'. Edward
Hasely was, like Scott, an Oxford man.[117] After his accession their

[115] G. R. Elton, 'Henry VII: Rapacity and Remorse', *The Historical Journal*, I
(1958), 21-39; J. P. Cooper, 'Henry VII's Last Years Reconsidered', *ibid.*, II
(1959), 103-129; Elton, 'Henry VII: a restatement', *ibid.*, IV (1961), 1-29.
[116] An excellent short account in Orme, *English Schools*, 21-29.
[117] W. Busch, *England under the Tudors*, I (London, 1895), 319-320; André
'Vita', in Gairdner, *Memorials*, 13; John Leland, *Itinerary*, ed. Lucy Toulmin
Smith, 5 vols. (reprinted, London, 1964), V, 151, and cf. II, 42. Cf. also the
monumental work of A. B. Emden, *A Biographical Register* (above, n. 33), II,
883-884, and III, 1656.

pupil rapidly acquired those appurtenances of the princes who were his contemporaries which he lacked.

One office already existed, that of Secretary.[118] It had already attracted the services of some very well-trained scholars. Thomas Bekynton, royal secretary from 1438 to 1443, set the tone. This was *applied* learning, so to speak. In Professor Weiss's words, Bekynton 'conceived classical learning not only as an intellectual attainment but also as a thing of practical value'; and he attributes to Bekynton's influence the 'literary qualifications' of not fewer than six other royal servants and diplomats. Additional to Bekynton and his flock we find James Goldwell, a civil lawyer from All Souls who became Edward IV's secretary, proctor at Rome, bishop of Norwich (1472) and on his death (1499) bequeathed a remarkable collection of humanist books to All Souls. Under Edward IV the secretary becomes a very important person, and is a member of the Council. It was also Edward IV who appointed the first French secretary in the person of Oliver King. King was another lawyer: Eton and King's and later the university of Orleans. He was French secretary (1475-90) and then secretary to both Edward IV and his son (1480-83). Surviving Richard III's reign (uncomfortably) he became secretary once again with Henry VII, being rewarded successively with the bishoprics of Exeter and Bath and Wells. I have already alluded to the Signet Office, over which the secretary presided, and staffed by lay 'clerks' from its inception.[119]

On all this Henry VII built. The importance of the secretary steadily grew, though the mountainous *paperasserie* of his office has not survived as it was to do from the administration of Henry VIII's reign. (And doubtless Henry VIII's servants, and especially Thomas Cromwell, were a great deal more energetic and independent than his father's). The continuity of the Yorkist secretary King into the reign of the first Tudor is noteworthy. Councillors were

---

[118] See further my brief account , above, p. 154.

[119] Weiss, *Humanism in England*, 74, 176-177; J. Otway Ruthven, *The King's Secretary and the Signet Office in the Fifteenth Century* (Cambridge, 1939); J. F. Baldwin, *The King's Council in England during the Middle Ages* (Oxford, 1913); A. R. Myers, *The Household of Edward IV: the Black Book and the Ordinance of 1478* (Manchester, 1959); *Dictionary of National Biography*, *sub nomina*. In general for administrative developments at this time see S. B. Chrimes, *An Introduction to the Administrative History of England* (Oxford, 1952), 241 and refs.; and G. R. Elton, *The Tudor Revolution*, chap. 1.

too expert to be squandered in factious changes of government [120] and the secretary as a councillor had what had become in effect a career appointment. King is the first secretary to be made a bishop while in office. When he is succeeded in 1500 by Thomas Ruthall the secretaryship had become in some sense 'public' and we are looking forward to the Cecils and Walsingham, although the term principal secretary of state does not become official until 1540. Ruthall (bishop of Durham 1509) like his immediate successors was a lawyer.[121] Equally noteworthy is the appointment in 1496 of Pietro Carmeliano as the first Latin secretary. Carmeliano, who came from Brescia or its neighbourhood, had been in England since 1481, and was a royal pensioner as early as 1486, probably being in royal employment well before then.[122]

The secretary (and *a fortiori* the Latin and French secretaries) was closely associated with diplomatic activity and diplomatic correspondence. No wonder then that the offices involved education and acquaintance with the Italian diplomatic style. Hence it comes as no surprise that to Thomas Ruthall was dedicated the oration of Pietro Griffo designed to be delivered to Henry VII.[123] Carmeliano edited some Italian diplomatic exchanges in elegant epistular form published by Caxton in 1483 (*S.T.C.* 22588). He celebrated the solemnities of the betrothal of the Archduke Charles with Princess Mary in 1507 (*S.T.C.* 4659). More important, he is the author of verses in Anwykyll's grammatical *Compendium* of 1483 and lent his name poetically to the English version of Dominic Mancini's *De Quatuor virtutibus* (*S.T.C.* 17242, 1523?), a popular poem combining neo-classical Latin with conventional moral ideas.[124]

The king's library had probably been organised at the instigation of Edward IV and on Burgundian models rather than Italian ones.

---

[120] J. R. Lander, 'Council, administration and councillors 1461-85', *Bulletin of the Institute of Historical Research*, XXXII (1959), 138-180.

[121] Pace's education in Italian universities may have resulted in a doctorate but this is far from certain. Cf. Wegg, *Pace*, chap. 1; Parks, *The English Traveller to Italy*, 317-318.

[122] Weiss, *Humanism in England*, 170-173; C. A. J. Armstrong, *The Usurpation of Richard III*, second ed. (Oxford, 1969), 4.

[123] *S.T.C.*, No. 12413; Monaco, *De officio*, 60. For dedications see the very helpful work by Franklin B. Williams, Jr., *Index to Dedications and Commendatory verses in English books before 1641* (Bibliographical Society, 1962). Ruthall is listed under 'Rontal'.

[124] *D.N.B.*, *sub nomine*; Williams, *Index to Dedications*, 33; and Armstrong, *Usurpation*, 19, n., who dates the Mancini book to about 1520 and discusses it (pp. 11-13).

Certainly 'the king's stay at Bruges in 1470 and 1471 must have been of signal importance, for it is with the Bruges and Ghent illuminators that the Edward IV books now in the Royal collection ... are associated'.[125] Equally telling, the first known royal librarians were Flemings, Quentin Poulet, librarian in 1492, and Giles Duwes, whose name occurs in 1509.[126] Compared with some of the princely accumulations on the continent, it was a very small library. But a librarian implies permanence and what the prince did was to be imitated by others. Very considerable libraries were to found in some English country houses by the middle of the sixteenth century.[127]

As I have indicated, attention had for long been paid to the education of the children of the royal family. This now took on a markedly humanist tincture. Henry VII's eldest child Arthur had as his tutors John Reed (later Warden of New College), André and Linacre, the latter at any rate being an outstanding humanist. Henry, the second son, and in the event to succeed, had as his teacher John Skelton, whose fame was to survive as an English poet, but whom contemporaries regarded primarily as a scholar, the translator of Cicero and Diodorus Siculus, already one of Henry VII's 'laureates'. Henry VIII in his turn was to provide his children with humanist instruction, the only difference being that the quality of the royal tutors increased immeasurably as the sixteenth century advanced; it was to include Cheke and Ascham.[128] Again, what the sovereign did was to be emulated by his subjects, though most of them had to rely on a good school rather than a good tutor.

Another development of Henry VII's reign lay in public and court spectacle. Processions and revels were not new but there seems little doubt that the first Tudor encouraged the use of display with a careful eye to its effects. Dr. Anglo has admirably discussed this subject and it is only necessary here to draw attention to the evidence

[125] Wright, *English Library*, 163.
[126] Wright, *loc. cit.*; and G. F. Warner and J. P. Gilson, *Catalogue of Western MSS. in the Old Royal and King's Collections*, I (London, 1921), xiii.
[127] Jayne, *Library Catalogues*, 93-103. The bulk of these collections consists in a relatively small number of books, mostly the possession of clergy and dons. But there are considerable libraries in lay hands: cf. Andrew H. Anderson's publication of the inventory of the collection of Lord Stafford (1556), *The Library*, 5th series, XXI (1966), 87-114.
[128] For the extraordinary programme of reading which André claimed Prince Arthur was subjected to by the time he was sixteen, see Gairdner, *Memorials*, 143. The prominence of the new grammarians is noteworthy: Guarino, Perotti, Pomponio Leto, Sulpizio and Valla; but the list of classical authors is also long.

he has assembled.[129] The stately and expensive entries into London and other centres, with their elaborate decoration, with the music and acting and stiff symbolic figures, gradually permit the introduction of classical motifs, not least the use of 'Britain' and 'British' as the theme of so much pictorial propaganda. The Welsh background here was provoking memories of Cadwallader and King Arthur; it was the Britain of Geoffrey of Monmouth. But it lent itself nicely to the rhythms of the poetasters of the court. Such decorative ceremonies, even if planned with courtly advice, were paid for by loyal subjects. They were a distinctly economical way of advertising. Court revels on the other hand had to be paid for and Henry was prepared for that. It seems that William Cornish was at work at court as early as 1501. It was his achievement to have introduced 'a multiform spectacle, combining music, poetry, débat, combat, scenic display and dance'.

> This complex spectacle was adopted during the early years of Henry VIII's reign—when Cornish, as Master of the children of the Chapel Royal, came to the fore as deviser of court entertainments—and is the direct ancestor of the mask which reached its apogee at the courts of James I and his son Charles.[130]

Cornish was, of course, in no sense a humanist, and we must not try to discern Milton's *Comus* in the early sixteenth century.

Skelton *was* a native and a humanist, a grammarian and rhetorician from Cambridge and Oxford, although he strikes one as a somewhat strange and exceptional individual. It is remarkable that so many foreigners thronged Henry VII's court and the influence of a substantial scholar like Vergil needs no stressing. But it is important not to exaggerate the deliberation behind Henry VII's patronage. It so happened that the uncle and nephew Giovanni and Silvestro Gigli who successively held the see of Worcester were humanists as well as useful to Edward IV and Henry VII, but they were in England because they were servants of pope and king; there is no reason to suppose that, when nominating Vergil as papal sub-collector, Adriano Castellesi intended to produce the main propagandist of the new dynasty. Nevertheless the humanists at court, however casually they had come there, were quick to demonstrate the value of up-to-date Latinity, and not only in panegyrics to members of the royal family but in invectives against foreign calumnies, as when in 1490

---

[129] Anglo, *Spectacle and Pageantry*.
[130] *Ibid.*, 118.

André, Cornelio Vitelli and Giovanni Gigli replied in kind to Gaguin's attack on England and her sovereign.[131]

XII. THE NATIVE HUMANIST

Gradually however native scholars and 'poets' would make the services of imported visitors unnecessary. Once a group of able English humanists emerged they were, by and large, very much better than the somewhat fly-blown foreigners who had failed to make a career at home, or sometimes (like Vitelli) anywhere. The great names in the roll-call of English humanists—Grocyn, Linacre, Colet, More—need have felt no sense of inferiority in the company of their continental contemporaries and, when all is said and done, the debt they owed to direct contact with Italian practice has probably been overstated; in the case of More it was, as I have said, non-existent. Yet the future of the humanities was hardly to be established by a handful of scholars however able and however highly placed. The basic importance of Henry VII's reign is that it saw the emergence of a new kind of secondary education which was to impress itself on the grammar school curriculum until the end of the nineteenth century, and even perhaps later.

The process is clear in general outline. The details are often obscure. One small point may be cleared out of the way. Greek in England, so long and so often made the test of what constituted humanist education, made precious little advance at this time.[132] It was never regarded as comparable in importance to Latin in Italy, so far as school teaching was concerned, and the same is true of Renaissance England. Only a handful of scholars took the study of Greek seriously, and when it came into school teaching it tended to be for higher forms. I believe it is therefore less important than some would have it to trace early Greek manuscripts in English libraries or to identify competence in the language. It is obviously of great interest that John Free's mastery of Greek was far above the average, polished as it was by the teaching of Guarino,[133] and it is equally interesting

---

[131] H. L. R. Edwards, *Skelton* (London, 1949), 43-45; L. Thuasne, ed., *Roberti Gaguini epistole et orationes*, 2 vols. (Paris, 1903), I, 81-87; one is reminded of the Brice-More controversy of 1513-20.

[132] Note the absurd observation of the editors of *Skelton's Diodorus Siculus* (E.E.T.S., 1957), in their foreword: 'At least one of us, and probably both, would now use that term [humanist] in a more restricted sense, confining it to true Hellenists'. Ignorance of the meaning of the term *umanista* cannot go further.

[133] R. J. Mitchell, *John Free*; Weiss, *Humanism in England*, 106-112.

that Prior William Sellyng of Canterbury, having learnt or perfected his Greek on visits to Italy, should have taught it in the convent about 1470.[134] But neither man seems to have made disciples, so to speak, and it is symptomatic of the irrelevance of the discipline that the Greeks Andronicus Callistus, George Hermonymos and Demetrius Cantacuzenos seem to have excited little patronage on their visits in the 1470s. John Serbopoulos, on the other hand, seems to have survived as a copyist of Greek texts at Oxford and Reading in the next decade and the survival of three manuscript copies of Gaza's Greek grammar in his hand in British libraries suggests, as Roberto Weiss wrote, 'the presence of a public anxious to learn Greek'.[135] But not, one imagines, a very large public.

The foundation of the Renaissance in England, as elsewhere in Europe, rested on the teaching of classical Latin as a preparation for an active participation in public affairs. The rapid penetration of Latin into the school curriculum begins in Henry VII's reign. It is largely an Oxford phenomenon in its initiation and closely connected with Waynfleet's school attached to Magdalen College. Some earlier evidence there is of the humanities at Oxford. Stefano Surigone, a humanist from Milan, who later contributed verses to Caxton's edition of Chaucer's Boethius (*S.T.C.* 3199, 1478?), was it seems teaching in Oxford in the 1450s and after and may have had some hand in inspiring Sellyng's humanist inclinations.[136] But the story essentially begins with Magdalen College school and its grammarians. Fortunately the story has been well told and its main monuments, the *vulgaria* of the teachers, are readily accessible.[137] The pupils and teachers of Magdalen School leavened English education and their direct influence can be first traced when Colet appointed a former Magdalen Demi (scholar) as first master of his reformed St. Paul's. Together with Colet himself, and with Erasmus as a further contributor, Lily produced a Latin grammar which swept all before it. Henry VIII later ordered a version of it to be used in place of all other similar works. Whittinton's and Stanbridge's grammatical writings were forgotten.

---

[134] Weiss, *Humanism in England*, 153-159.

[135] *Ibid.*, 145-147.

[136] *Ibid.*, 138; cf. Josephine W. Bennett, in *Studies in the Renaissance*, XV (1968), 70-91.

[137] R. S. Stanier, *Magdalen School* (Oxford Historical Society, 1940), with an admirably lucid picture of the old grammatical manner and the new; *The Vulgaria of John Stanbridge and the Vulgaria of Robert Whittinton*, ed. Beatrice White (E.E.T.S., 1932); William Nelson, ed., *A Fifteenth Century School Book* (Oxford, 1956).

Colet's aims in establishing his new St. Paul's were pious, as were those of most benefactors of education. That he himself was a devout and influential theologian, whose humanist approach to the scriptures owes something to Erasmus and Ficino, and much to the spirit of the *Nova devotio*, leaves one wondering how far he could have anticipated what would happen at his foundation. He had prescribed the Christian 'classics'—Juvencus, Lactantius and so on, with one or two devout moderns (Baptista Mantuanus and Erasmus). But within a generation this was all forgotten. St. Paul's, Eton, Winchester, and scores of lesser grammar schools such as that at Ipswich (set up by Wolsey, another former Magdalen teacher) were basing their teaching on Terence, Virgil, Cicero (especially the letters), Horace and Ovid; and of course the writers of modern dialogues, especially Erasmus. The total victory of the Renaissance curriculum in the humanities was accomplished by the mid-sixteenth century, so far as the secondary school was concerned. There were still Trojans holding out in Oxford University, but their ultimate defeat was assured and it had been largely because of the activities of an Oxford grammar school. 'Small Latin and less Greek' might perhaps be the result in most cases: but Latin and a bit of Greek and virtually nothing else was to be the pabulum of the grammar school-boy for generations to come.

We cannot associate this remarkable transformation with religious motives, nor attribute as much as was done in the past to the coincidence of Colet with the time when Ficino was the main intellectual force in Florence; the two men never met, although we now know that Colet studied carefully some of Ficino's writings.[138] It seems, indeed, very dubious if Ficino, on whom Paul Oskar Kristeller has shed so much light, would pass his own test for what constituted a humanist! The traditional association of Greek scholarship with the reformers is not in question, although it is important to remember that most of the leading Northern humanists adhered to the old religion. What does seem to be mistaken is the view (I quote the words of a well-known authority) that 'the progress of learning was intimately connected with the progress of the reformation. The study of Greek was now encouraged, now suspected, according to the royal attitude in ecclesiastical affairs'.[139]

The two English universities were cowed clients of the Crown

---

[138] Sears Jayne, *John Colet and Marsilio Ficino* (Oxford, 1963).
[139] J. D. Mackie, *The Earlier Tudors 1485-1558* (Oxford, 1952), 271-272.

after Wycliffe and were never more subservient than in the Tudor period. But it proved difficult to prevent innovation since the life of the places no longer lay in the university corporations themselves, but in the colleges. Even if Henry VII and his contemporaries could have forseen the Lutheran revolt and associated it with Humanity or Greek, such subjects might enter by the back door, so to speak. We have seen the explosive consequences of Magdalen College School. At Cambridge Alcock's foundation of Jesus college (1496), and Christ's (1505) and St. John's (1511), both inspired by that conventionally devout figure Henry VII's mother, the Lady Margaret Beaufort, all pointed the way towards change. Alcock's college had a grammar school attached, grammar teaching was also important at Christ's, where the Lady Margaret's confessor, Bishop Richard Fisher, was the first Cambridge man profoundly to affect the progress of humanist studies there. He not only introduced humanity into the curriculum, he sponsored Erasmus and Greek. At St. John's Fisher followed a similarly original line.[140]

It would be good to be able to measure the effect of these changes on the vernacular for it was only when the humanities really influenced English literature that the Renaissance in England came to full flower. There are hints and anticipations not merely in the somewhat laboured classical themes of early Tudor writers like Skelton and Barclay; much of such matter is correctly described by C. S. Lewis as 'Late Medieval'.[141] But occasionally the manner becomes arrestingly sharp. This is most often found in the *vulgaria* where the rigour of Latin composition lies close at hand. I believe that the late Professor Lewis was totally misguided when, having argued that it was false to regard neo-latinists as 'somehow more enlightened, less remote, less limited by their age, than those who wrote English',[142] he went on (a *tour de force*) to translate quotations from humanist Latin into sixteenth-century English. This is to misconceive entirely why writers chose to compose in Latin. They liked Latin because it had rules for spelling and composition, because one could attain a perfection and exactitude of expression in it as yet

---

[140] A first-class survey in M. H. Curtis, *Oxford and Cambridge in Transition* (Oxford, 1959), with some retrospective coverage of the early Tudor period (e.g., pp. 70-71). A more recent, wider ranging survey in Hugh Keearney, *Scholars and Gentlemen, 1500-1700* (London, 1970).

[141] *English Literature in the Sixteenth century excluding Drama* (Oxford, 1954), 120-156.

[142] *Ibid.*, preface.

unapproachable by northern vernaculars; they liked it because it was glamorous; they liked it because it commanded an international public. Latin *was*, in short, 'more enlightened and less remote' than the angular and repetitive English of the time. In the end neo-classical Latin so worked on the vernacular that we reach the splendour of what Lewis called the 'golden English' of the later sixteenth century. Glimpses of it are found in the *vulgaria*. More's English prose points in the same direction. It seems to me that much remains to be done by scholars of English language and literature to enlighten us on the influence of Latin on English during the Renaissance.[143]

It is true that Professor Jones had displayed how competition with Latin led English writers to a profound dissatisfaction with their own 'uneloquent language',[144] but he does not discuss the pressure exerted by the new grammar school curriculum from the early sixteenth century. And the 'barrenness of the mother tongue' [145] was only partially fertilised merely by extending the vocabulary with new borrowings, the feature dealt with most thoroughly by students of English language in the late medieval, early modern period.[146] One book, however, does seem to me to touch on the heart of the matter. I quote Professor Ian A. Gordon:

> The effect of all this on the writing of English prose was everywhere apparent. One should perhaps speak of the effects in the plural, for the influence of humanist Latinity, though it was widespread and permanent, did not all tend in the same direction. At one end of the scale a fine classical Latinist like Sir Thomas More wrote English prose of Anglo-Saxon simplicity; at the other extreme the chronicler Edward Hall and Sir Thomas Elyot introduced Latinisms as strange as the Saxonisms that Pecock had unsuccessfully tried to naturalise.[147]

What is at issue is the whole swing, style and omnicompetence of a means of communication.

---

[143] Cf. my 'Early Renaissance', *ad fin.*, where I dig a 'couplet' of 'golden' English from a prose passage in the *vulgaria* edited by Professor Nelson ; above, p. 167.

[144] Richard Foster Jones, *The Triumph of the English Language* (London, 1953), esp. 3-31. My colleagues Mrs. V. Salmon and Professor Angus McIntosh kindly allowed me to consult them on this subject.

[145] Jones, *Triumph of the English Language*, 70.

[146] For instance in the useful works by J. A. Sheard, *The Words We Use* (London, 1954); and Mary S. Serjeantson, *A History of Foreign Words in English* (London, 1935), 259-266. But note in the former the jejune account of the Renaissance (p. 242).

[147] *The Movement of English Prose* (London, 1966), 74; and see the whole section on 'The impact of humanist latinity', pp. 73-83.

Of one thing we can be sure. At the level of the availability of the classics the Englishman in the early Tudor period had, thanks to the printing press on the Continent, almost everything he required of ancient and modern scholarship; and, for good measure, medieval as well—we must remember that some of the greatest monuments of ancient thought were familiar parts of the medieval intellectual landscape. If one compares the availability of the Latin classics in medieval libraries, as tabulated by Dom David Knowles and Sir Roger Mynors [148] with those at the disposal of the Bridgettine fathers at Syon (1504-1526) one sees the scale of the change. Greek may still be thin on the ground. Latin and neo-Latin are plentiful. Here is Miss Bateson's summary of the books at Syon:

> Its strength lay in the Latin translations of the Renaissance; for instance Argyropoulos, Hermolaus Barbarus, Gaza, Marsilius Ficinus, G. Trapezuntios and Erasmus are well represented as translated from the Greek. The monastery kept pace with the new learning in its Latin Renaissance literature; Coluccio, Leonardo Bruni, Poggio, Bessarion, Platina, Poliziano, Pico della Mirandola, are here, but there are no books in Italian. Petrarch appears as a Latin writer on the penitential psalms, Boccaccio as the author of a dictionary of classical antiquities. Savonarola, *De virtute fidei* is there. Reuchlin represents the German humanists, but there are no books in German. From the English Renaissance, Colet's sermon to the clergy of St. Pauls is here, and Linacre's translation of Proclus. More is represented by the translation of Lucian . . . which he wrote with Erasmus.[149]

The 'hard core' of authors inaccessible in the early fifteenth century (Catullus, Lucretius, Pliny's *Letters* and Statius's *Silvae*) is not represented,[150] but the collection is still impressive. After all, as I have just observed, most of the main Latin authors of antiquity were known, if in indifferent texts, well enough in the Middle Ages and they were at Syon too, often in improved printed versions. This, let it be recalled, was a *monastic* library. To see what an English humanist could assemble the books of Grocyn may be adduced—a very choice collection indeed.[151] And for a glimpse of the wealth

---

[148] M. D. Knowles, 'The preservation of the classics', *English Library before 1700*, 136-137; R. A. B. Mynors, 'The Latin classics known to Boston of Bury', *Fritz · Saxl . . . Essays*, 199-217 (an arrangement and commentary on material in the early fifteenth-century compilation of John Boston, monk of Bury St. Edmunds, *Cathologus de libris autenticis et apocrifis*).

[149] Edition cited above (n. 102), p. viii.

[150] Mynors, 'The Latin classics known to Boston of Bury', 217.

[151] Thomas Linacre's list, ed. Montagu Burrows in *Collectanea*, second series (Oxford Hist. Soc., 1890), 319-331; cf. Emden, *Biog. Reg. Oxford*, II, 828-830.

of material available to a man with money, a list of the books sold
by the Oxford bookseller John Dorne in 1520 (the year after Grocyn
died) has survived in his 'day-book'.[152] 'The English books are few
compared with the Latin . . . Latin theology forms the bulk of the
more important volumes sold, as might be expected, and next to
that Latin classics'.[153]

It seems to me that by this date the humanities in England had
reached the point of 'take-off', to use the economists' jargon. They
were beginning to be self-supporting, and no longer needed to be
propped up by royal or other high-level patronage. That such
developments were to be seen at work all over northern Europe
doubtless made Englishmen confident in the new ways they were
gradually learning to tread. And in saying this one must on no
account forget the Renaissance in Scotland.[154] England and Scotland
were locked in political rivalry, but linked in 1503 in a dynastic
marriage which was to lead a hundred years later to a Scottish king
and his courtiers taking over in England. Already by 1500 there
were three Scottish universities, each probably more in touch with
the exciting changes on the Continent than the two universities
(as opposed to their colleges) in England. At Aberdeen we have the
first Renaissance university in 'Britain', as continental humanists
indifferently called England or Scotland or both. The term 'humanity'
in Scotland was to adhere to the professor of Latin.[155] It is perhaps
equally important that in Scotland the early sixteenth century saw
the steady reception of Roman law, in line perhaps with what some
statesmen, including Henry VIII, may have wished to see south

---

[152] 'Day-book of John Dorn', ed. F. Madan, *Collectanea* (Oxford Hist. Soc.,
1885), 73-177; corrections and additions by F. Madan with notes by H. Bradshaw,
Collectanea, second series (cited above, n. 151), 463-517.

[153] 'Day-book', 75.

[154] Lewis, *English Literature in the Sixteenth century*, 66-119; J. Durkan, 'The
beginnings of humanism in Scotland', *Innes Review*, IV (1953), 5-24; John Mac-
Queen, *Robert Henryson* (Oxford, 1967), 1-23. None of these writers takes into
consideration the effects on Scottish culture of the contemporary reception
of Roman law, on which see Holdsworth, *History of English Law*, IV, 251, and, in
general disappointingly, *Introductory Survey of the Sources and Literature of Scots
Law*, Stair Society, I (1936). See also Lord Cooper, 'The central courts after
1532', *Stair Society*, XX (1958), 341-349. To an outsider it seems that the problem
deserves much more scholarly attention than it has so far received.

[155] But the earliest case of a written example is 1564, according to the *Dictionary of the Older Scottish Tongue*, III, 175. The earliest English case of 'humanity'
= Latin is 1483, according to the *O.E.D.*

of the Anglo-Scottish border.[156] When James VI became also James I he came from a country where the grammar school was an official educational ideal. In both countries the curriculum was broadly the same: the curriculum of the Italian humanist of the fifteenth century. By the seventeenth century 'Great Britain' was to be joined to the Continent by cultural links stronger than any forged before.

---

[156] I am by no means sure that Maitland's argument that the English common law was seriously threatened in the early sixteenth century is as easily disposed of as his later critics have supposed: Holdsworth, *History of English Law*, IV, 252-263, whose views are repeated by many others. The nature of the new prerogative courts and concepts of equity both marry in with the establishment of chairs of civil law in sixteenth-century Oxford and Cambridge, the prestige of Doctors' Commons and the whole contemporary spirit of intelligent and modern government.

10

THE CHURCH OF ENGLAND IN THE

LATER MIDDLE AGES

FACED with the general pre-eminence of the pope in the medieval Church and with the practical segregation of the clergy in England under the Crown, historians have naturally been brought to a consideration of the relationship between the two authorities. In its crudest form the problem may be stated as the way to translate the phrase *ecclesia anglicana* which begins to come into use in the twelfth century.[1] For the last two generations the established tradition has been to regard the phrase as meaning 'church *in* England' until the cataclysmic events of the 1530s, after which it may be translated as 'church *of* England', or even 'Church of England'. Such a view is to be found in the best authorities. For example in his recent book on *The English Reformation* Professor A. G. Dickens writes:

> Nationalism within the English Church grew in strength throughout the medieval centuries . . . All the same, the common medieval term *Ecclesia Anglicana* never meant 'Church of England' in the post-Reformation sense of an independent national Church claiming parity with that of Rome.[2]

Phrased as carefully as this the view is, perhaps, unexceptionable, though one must scrutinize carefully the notion of an English church 'claiming parity with that of Rome'. It is important, at any rate, not to read into 'parity' the notions that one Church had been abandoned after 1535, that men accepted in the modern way a plurality of churches. The title of the first Prayer Book of Edward VI (1549) runs: *The Booke of the Common Prayer and Administracion of the Sacramentes, and other rites and ceremonies of the Churche: after the use of the Churche of England*. It is true that the second Prayer Book (1552) drops the words 'of the Churche: after the use', thus leaving only 'the rites and ceremonies in the Churche of Englande', a gesture to the radical views then prevailing. But in both Prayer Books the faith of the Catholic Church is proclaimed, and by phrases such as 'the whole body of the Church' are to be understood the acceptance of a

[1] See the clear and useful account of Charles Duggan in *The English Church and the Papacy in the Middle Ages*, ed. C. H. Lawrence (London, 1965), hereafter *ECP*, pp. 107–8. There are some interesting and pertinent reflections in I. P. Shaw, *Nationality and the Western Church before the Reformation* (London, 1959).

[2] *Op. cit.* (London, 1964), p. 86.

Christian community which transcended national or geographical frontiers, transcended, in some sense, even doctrinal and certainly ceremonial frontiers. It was to the elucidation of this difficulty among others that Hooker devoted many pages of his *Ecclesiastical Polity*. He argued that there were many churches but only one Church; that Paul's dealings with Jerusalem, Corinth, Galatia make it very hard 'to conclude the duty of uniformity throughout all churches in all manner of indifferent ceremonies';[3] that, for all its faults, the Church of Rome was 'to be held and reputed a part of the house of God, a limb of the visible Church of Christ'.[4]

Now distinctions of this type had doubtless to be drawn more sharply in the second half of the sixteenth century, but they were not new. The word Church was rich in ambiguities from the start, as we can see from Hooker's use of the Pauline epistles. There were particular churches—attached to a town or village, there were larger ecclesiastical communities embraced within the bishoprics and provinces of Christendom, the Church of York, the Church of Rouen. The Church could mean simply all the clergy, and there were still larger congregations involving clergy and laity—the Church of Rome, the Church of God or of Christ, 'the whole community of the faithful', the Church militant and triumphant, the Church visible and invisible. Although these grand concepts lie behind all else, this essay is intended to deal primarily with something more limited. From the twelfth century churches are encountered which were associated with large political areas. Two of these were the Gallican Church and the Anglican Church. Both were members or aspects of the Roman Church, but were distinguished from the whole by growing national characteristics, the product of language, experience, government. In his *Constitutional History and Constitution of the Church of England* (1895) F. Makower was tempted to discuss the medieval Church in federal terms, as a way of recognizing the unity and the diversity which he encountered. Maitland, in his *Roman Canon Law in England* (1898) spoke forcibly against such a view and argued that the English clergy accepted the pope as universal ordinary. He was, of course, right in saying that there was no 'Anglican' Canon Law.[5] Yet it may be suspected that Canon Stubbs (as he then was) had reason on his side when he persuaded his brother commissioners considering

---

[3] *Of the Laws of Ecclesiastical Polity*, IV, xiii, 5; *Hooker's Works*, 2 vols. (1850), i, 401–2.

[4] *Ibid.*, V, lxviii, 9; *Works*, ii, 102. Cf. below p.234 for Pecock's anticipation of this sort of position.

[5] J. W. Gray, 'Canon Law in England: some reflections on the Stubbs–Maitland controversy', *Studies in Church History*, iii (1966), 48–68 (which I read after I had written the following pages) points out that practice in England must be examined as well as theory. The thirteenth-century attempts by the papacy to reform the clergy were frustrated by inaction on the part of the English hierarchy; Roman Canon Law was in this instance received but it was not applied. Mr. Gray further shows that English bishops were by no means unwilling to accept 'at least some of the restrictions which were placed upon papal sovereignty in England by crown policy and English custom'.

ecclesiastical courts that there had been a 'national church' before the Reformation.[6] Maitland himself was far too shrewd a historian to ignore the facts and played with the phrase 'liberties of the Anglican church', referring to the observation of the sixteenth-century French jurist Hotman 'that France, with all its Gallicanism, had allowed the clergy an immunity which England refused'.[7]

The following pages discuss the coherence of the Church in England, keeping in view the neighbouring Church in France. It will be necessary briefly to review the rise of Gallicanism, to examine the English situation in the period when Gallicanism was developing and to outline the reactions of the two ecclesiastical communities to the conciliar movement in the fifteenth century. In conclusion the question will be put: how did Englishmen in the later Middle Ages actually talk about the Church in their midst?

i

The word 'Anglicanism' is not, of course, used to mean the sum of privileges, peculiarities or separateness of the hierarchy and clergy in the medieval English Church. The word 'Gallicanism', which is used in this way, is itself a post-Reformation coinage, but the reality to which it refers had roots deep in the past and received full expression in the late fourteenth and fifteenth centuries. In essence the 'Liberties of the Gallican Church' were the product of an alliance between the French Crown, the French clergy, the *parlement* of Paris and the Sorbonne. This formidable conjunction resulted from a century during which the papacy was at Avignon and of the two decades when France, almost alone, supported the expensive intransigence of the schismatic Clement VII and Benedict XIII. Gallican sentiment—the conviction that in a certain sense the Church in France had its own momentum—was even older.[8] But its first categorical expression came with the decisions of Crown and clergy to withdraw obedience from Benedict XIII. This issue was debated in 1396 and the decision was taken in 1398. A declaration of neutrality was subsequently made in 1406. What was asserted on these occasions? What authority replaced that of the pope? To an English ear it all sounds mild enough —there is no rumbling of the thunder of a William I or Henry II. The councils of clergy in 1396 and 1398, afforced by councillors and royal princes, found against their own pope Benedict and were at pains to point out that they had never obeyed the 'intruder' at Rome. No taxes were to be paid to Benedict. No 'provisors' were to be admitted. Vacancies were to be supplied by canonical election; that is

---

[6] *Reports etc.*, 1883, vol. x, c. 3760.
[7] Op. cit., pp. 62–3. There is a dispassionate account of the Stubbs–Maitland debate in E. W. Kemp, *An Introduction to Canon Law in the Church of England* (London, 1959), pp. 11–16; see also the essay quoted above by J. L. Gray.
[8] Victor Martin, *Les Origines du Gallicanisme*, 2 vols. (Paris, 1939), i, *passim*.

to say, the 'ancient canons' were to govern the Church and not the new-fangled regulations of recent popes. The fundamental authority of general councils (whose powers were being currently debated at the Sorbonne) was insisted on at the debates of 1406: 'the Holy Spirit controls general councils'.[9] And so was the role of the king as custodian of the 'ancient liberties of the Gallican Church'. The assembly of 1406 was thus less concerned about ending the Schism, more concerned about defining the exact nature of the Church in France. Victor Martin summarizes the situation in these words:

> For the first time the French clergy openly turned to the king, inviting him, despite the pope, even against the pope, to re-establish the ancient liberties and to assure their maintenance; but the clergy remained anxious not to trespass beyond the limits imposed by the law as they understood it. They had evolved the concept of a national Church, autonomous in its actions, which yet remained in the bosom of the catholic faith.[10]

To the position thus attained the fifteenth century added the doctrine, established at Constance (1415) and reaffirmed at Basle (1433), of conciliar superiority to a pope; this was already implied in the transactions briefly described. The principle was adopted formally by another council of French clergy at Bourges in 1438 and was embodied in the famous Pragmatic Sanction.[11]

These momentous events in France have close parallels in England. What was the nature of the relations between pope and Church in the English context? There is no doubt that there was no 'English' Canon Law as such.[11a] The church courts in England applied the universal laws of Latin Christianity and this was accepted not only by the clergy but also by the laity in those fields where canon law touched them, notably matrimony and wills. It is true that the high-handed treatment of the Church by Norman kings and the restrictions on the admissions of papal bulls make it seem to foreign observers, like Victor Martin, that there was something less than a total acceptance by the English of the jurisdiction of the pope. This will be mentioned again shortly. It is also true that appeals to Rome were circumscribed by the Statute of Praemunire (1353), but this and its reenactment in Richard II's reign (1393) have to do mainly with provisions, to which it also will be necessary to return.[12] One gets the impression that the interest of English ecclesiastics in the curial courts declined somewhat in the fourteenth century, and that the standing

---

[9] Pierre Le Roy, quoted in Martin, *Gallicanisme*, i, 316.

[10] Martin, i, 325. Some of the administrative and legal results of the withdrawal of obedience are illustrated by G. Mollat, 'L'application en France de la soustraction d'obédience à Benoît XIII jusqu'au concile de Pise', *Revue du moyen âge latin*, i (1945), 149–63.

[11] Martin, ii, *passim*.

[11a] But see J. L. Gray's observations.

[12] W. T. Waugh, 'The Great Statute of Praemunire', *Eng. Hist. Rev.*, xxxvii (1922), 173–205, esp. pp. 174–5.

of English church courts rose, so that perhaps less business went to the papal tribunals.[13] But the *Provinciale* of William Lyndwood, completed by about 1433, which surveyed the legislation of the provincial synods of Canterbury, makes it clear that the doctrine remained unimpaired that the Canon Law applied in English church courts was dependent on the legislation of the popes and the Roman 'codes'.[13a]

As for the day-to-day activity of the pope and his officers in England, this was to be seen in three fields; the grant of dispensations and other privileges, taxation and church appointments. The papal registers are full of letters, many in favour of laymen, most in favour of clerks, permitting exceptions to the rules, conferring favours, regularizing a hundred and one awkward situations—of which bastardy is one of the commonest cases.[14] Indeed the late K. B. McFarlane, reviewing volume xiii of the *Calendar of Entries in the Papal Registers relating to Great Britain and Ireland (1471–84)*, wrote: 'As far as the English church was concerned the pope's authority was mainly an authority to dispense.'[15] The effects of the pervasive and continuous exercise of this power to dispense should not be minimized. Graces to hold incompatible benefices, annulling oaths or granting indulgences, cost money and were therefore showered by a complacent curia on the rich and the powerful rather than on men of modest means, let alone on the poor. But their remarkable range and frequency is evidence for the general acceptance of papal power in practical matters and for the penetration of that power into every part of the land.

Dispensations and privileges cost money and thus lead directly to the second aspect of papal activity, taxation. There seems no doubt that the liberality of the popes in granting graces of all kinds was provoked by their being a source of income, making up in some measure for the decline in other revenues; the sophisticated machinery of the papal chancery and the Apostolic Penitentiary made up for the contraction in the activities of the *camera apostolica*. As far as England was concerned the old papal taxes on the clergy were virtually a thing of the past. It remained a plank in papal policy to revive demands for Peter's Pence, and to ask for clerical subsidies. Such requests were refused by the king. Mr. Scarisbrick has reckoned that during the late fifteenth and early sixteenth centuries the clergy in England paid two and a half times as much to the Crown as they

---

[13] W. A. Pantin in *ECP*, pp. 175–8.

[13a] But cf. below p.235 Dr. Kemp, *op. cit.*, pp. 27–9 admirably illustrates the limitations imposed by English 'customs' on the operations of the Canon Law; and indeed reminds us of the extremely complicated nature of Canon Law itself.

[14] See the excellent survey by Professor R. H. Du Boulay, *ECP*, pp. 227–33.

[15] *Eng. Hist. Rev.*, lxxiii (1958), 677. On 'Church–State' relations in England in the later Middle Ages see Penry Williams and G. L. Harriss, 'A revolution in Tudor History?', *Past and Present*, 25 (1963), 3–58, esp. pp. 13–20; and G. R. Elton's 'Reply', *ibid.*, 29 (1964), 26–49, esp. pp. 28–36.

paid to the pope.[16] The bulk of what was paid to Rome[17] was, however, derived from the heavy chancery taxes (common services and related payments) levied when the pope provided men to consistorial benefices, that is (to simplify) bishoprics. This is, therefore, the heart of the matter: the pope's right to provide to vacant English livings.

Papal reservations and provisions are familiar enough to all historians. Starting in the thirteenth century popes claimed the right to nominate to ever wider categories of benefices. By the early fourteenth century the papacy had asserted its right to fill practically any benefice in Latin Christendom, vacant or to be vacated, and had succeeded in using this power to replenish its treasury. This 'papal fiscality' has attracted much attention among recent historians. At the time it attracted violent criticism everywhere in Europe. The reaction in England was particularly sharp; England was at war with France and fourteenth-century popes were Frenchmen. As is well known, protests began with the angry denunciation of the parliament of Carlisle in 1307 and continued throughout the fourteenth century. In 1351 parliament enacted the statute of Provisors, which was reissued in 1390.[18]

The first statute of Provisors was intended: (1) to secure free elections to all elective offices in the Church; (2) to guarantee to all prelates the right to present to benefices in their gift; (3) to give the king the right of appointment to all prelacies and other benefices illegally conferred by papal provision for that turn; (4) to punish recalcitrant provisors and their agents with arrest and imprisonment. These enactments were rehearsed in 1390, with the added penalty of banishment. The statute was reissued again by Henry IV.

The preamble to the first statute is worth pondering, for it makes the point that the Church of England (*Seinte Eglise Dengleterre*) was founded in 'an estate of prelacy' by the king and his ancestors, by the earls, barons and nobles and their ancestors, 'to instruct the people concerning the law of God, to provide hospitality, alms and other works of charity in the places where the churches were established for the souls of the founders and their heirs and of all Christians'. These churches were assigned lands and rents of great value by their founders to sustain these charges, and kings, earls, barons and nobles have and should have the right of presentation, for they are the 'lords and patrons' (*seigneurs et avowes*). The pope of Rome, seizing the lordship, gives these benefices away in despite of the law of England. The provisors, aliens or cardinals, or even natives, are not the men the patron would wish and soon there will follow the disinheritance

---

[16] J. J. Scarisbrick, 'Clerical taxation in England, 1485–1547', *Journ. of Eccles. Hist.*, xi (1960), 41–54; see p. 50. Mr. Scarisbrick makes it clear that his assumptions probably exaggerate the total payments to Rome.

[17] Not, of course, including the money sent for the graces, etc., referred to in the previous paragraph.

[18] *Select Documents of English Constitutional History 1307–1485*, ed. S. B. Chrimes and A. L. Brown (London, 1961), pp. 72–6, 155–7.

of the king and the great men, the subversion of the whole estate of the realm. Thus far the statute repeats the *gravamina* of the parliament of Carlisle. Parliament in 1351 added some interesting further points. It reminded the king of his coronation oath (*est tenuz par son serement*). And it described the king as being the 'paramount and immediate patron of all clergy', (. . . *des genz de Seinte Esglise, dont le roi est avowe paramount immediat*). Sentiments such as these, expressed as they had been in parliaments and royal letters before 1351,[19] deserve consideration. The acceptance of a proprietary attitude to the church is unmistakeable; the relative absence of concern for the bad spiritual consequences of papal provisions is also notable —the only reference to this being to undesirable aliens who have never lived in England and cardinals who cannot live in England. But above all it was the king whose interests were at stake. He was directly and indirectly a patron on a vast scale, his normal rights being extended whenever bishoprics and other great prelacies fell vacant.[20] It is well known that popes forbore from provision at the expense of lay patrons; but, however cautious, they could hardly avoid threatening the interests of the king.[21]

It is usually argued that parliament, rather than the king and his ministers, was responsible for the enactment of the statute of Provisors. The ground for this interpretation is the continuance afterwards of the old arrangement for appointing bishops whereby the king told the chapter whom to elect and at the same time nominated to the pope for provision. This certainly happened, right down to the reign of Henry VIII. It must, however, be observed that royal rights were carefully protected. A bishop was not granted his temporalities until he had expressly renounced 'all clauses and phrases in the bull' of provision 'which might be deemed prejudicial to the royal authority'.[22] More important still, with few exceptions popes did as they were told.[23] At a level below the episcopate papal provision seems to have declined steadily, especially after the re-enactment of 1390; for example it soon became extremely unusual for the *rotuli beneficiandorum* (the lists of graduates for whom papal provision was asked) to be submitted by English universities to the Curia,[24] and fewer foreigners were provided.[25]

[19] M. McKisack, *The Fourteenth Century* (Oxford History of England), pp. 272–3; W. A. Pantin, *The English Church in the Fourteenth Century* (Cambridge, 1955), pp. 76–102 gives a full and balanced account of Anglo-Papal relations in the period.

[20] R. A. R. Hartridge, 'Edward I's exercise of the right of presentation to benefices as shown by the Patent Rolls', *Camb. Hist. Journ.*, ii (1927), 171–7; and in general, K. L. Wood-Legh, *Church Life under Edward III* (Cambridge, 1934).

[21] Ann Deeley, 'Papal Provision and royal rights of patronage in the early fourteenth century', *Eng. Hist. Rev.*, xliii (1928), 497–527; and see McKisack, *op. cit.*, pp. 274–8.

[22] A. Hamilton Thompson, *English Clergy and their Organization in the Later Middle Ages* (Oxford, 1947), p. 22 and n. 4.

[23] *Ibid.*, pp. 18–24; Du Boulay, *ECP*, p. 226.

[24] E. F. Jacob, 'Petitions for benefices from the Universities', in *Essays in the Conciliar Epoch*, 2nd ed. (Manchester, 1953).

[25] Hamilton-Thompson, p. 11; cf. Pantin, *ECP*, p. 189.

In short it seems a fair summary of the position in England during the last two centuries before the Reformation to say that the king controlled the higher clergy and permitted papal influence only as far as it suited him. In these circumstances there was in effect a kind of concordat after 1351 and it is hardly surprising that two attempts were made formally to negotiate such treaties in the later fourteenth century onwards. The first of these transactions, between Edward III and Gregory XI, dragged on from 1372 to 1377, interrupted by the violent anti-papalism of the Good Parliament; some minor irritations were removed but nothing was achieved for the future.[26] The second episode produced a startling document, the fully-fledged concordat of 1398. By this Richard II and Boniface IX divided up between them the patronage of the English Church. Nomination to bishoprics was reserved to pope and king, the pope agreeing to confirm the man elected by the chapter unless he was unacceptable to the king in which case the pope would provide the nominee of the king. Of all vacant greater dignities of cathedrals and colleges the pope would nominate one in three, but no alien could be appointed in this way save a cardinal. With lesser dignities (i.e. those which were 'not in cathedral and collegiate churches'), the pope was to nominate every other time, at any rate for the following two years.[27] This remarkable document was doubtless the upshot of Richard II's frenzied and unrealistic ambitions and of the pope's vulnerability. But, so far as prelacies were concerned, it did no more than regularize what in fact had been happening. It also prefigures the whole course of concordats in centuries to come in countries which did not have kings as strong as those of England. If parallels are sought, there is no need to cast forward to arrangements like the Franco-papal concordat of Bologna in 1516. A similar division of ecclesiastical patronage is to be found in the Concordats with which the Council of Constance concluded its attempt at reform.[28] The German and the French[29] Concordats (1418) both have specific restrictions on papal reservations and provisions; this was to be achieved by a system of rationing which (roughly speaking) left the pope the liberty of nominating to benefices vacated at the Curia and about half of the lesser dignities. The English Concordat at Constance has nothing at all to say about provisions;[30] the English Crown had little incentive to pursue the matter, for it had all the control which it required.

It is obvious that the evolution of policy in the fourteenth century followed parallel lines in England and France. Victor Martin (following Haller) goes further and argues that the French were not merely

[26] E. Perroy, *L'Angleterre et le Grand Schisme* (Paris, 1933) pp. 27–50.
[27] *Ibid.*, p. 349 and appendix XVI (pp. 419–20); summarized in McKisack, p. 283.
[28] C. J. Hefele–H. Leclercq, *Historie des Conciles*, vii (1916), pp. 535–65.
[29] Which applied also in Italy and Spain, Hefele–Leclercq, vii. 549.
[30] Hefele–Leclercq, vii, 560–5; Du Boulay, *ECP*, pp. 212–13; E. F. Jacob, 'A note on the English Concordat of 1418' in *Medieval Studies Presented to Aubrey Gwynn S.J.* (Dublin, 1961), pp. 349–58.

aware in general terms of the ability of the English to rid themselves of the incubus of provisions, but had before them the text of English legislation. He points out the extraordinary verbal similarities and is able to quote from the French debate of 1398 observations which show that what the English had accomplished was in the forefront of Frenchmen's minds on the occasion.[31] Nevertheless, as he also shows, the situation in England was different, for there had been restrictions on papal action from the start. Whatever precise weight one gives to William I's introduction into England of the *coutumes Normandes* and their reiteration in the Constitutions of Clarendon, it is a fact that English kings made English bishops from the twelfth century onwards, and limited the entry of papal legates and bulls. As parliaments said again and again, as Edward III pointed out in a letter to the Curia in 1342, the English laws were an unalterable impediment to papal influence. 'The English', says Martin, 'had no need to look further for a juridical foundation for their resistance'[32] and he contrasts the 'limited acceptance of Canon Law' in England with France which 'lived under the rule of Canon Law pure and simple, recognized by the State'.[33] Hence the French had to construct their 'ancient liberties' and 'to oppose the canons to the decretals'.[33a] There was, however, another basic difference between Gallicanism and what may perhaps be called Anglicanism. The decisions arrived at in France resulted from deliberations of synods of clergy. Doubtless they were influenced by courtiers and councillors, but voting shows that nine out of ten of the clergy present favoured royal protection as a remedy against papal extortion. In England, whatever members of the hierarchy may have privately thought, they were far from taking a lead. This was provided by the Lords and the Commons. In Professor Du Boulay's words: 'the classes represented in parliament offered to papal policy a strong, clear and unending hostility'.[34]

ii

With the Council of Constance the whole picture looked for a time as though it might change. The Council declared its superiority to popes in the decree *Sacrosancta* of 1415. It deposed two of the rival

---

[31] Martin, i, 352–3; with reference to J. Haller, *Pappstum und Kirchenreform* i. Miss Deeley, *op. cit.*, p. 526, notes the adoption in France from 1334 of the English policy of trying disputed collations before the royal courts.

[32] Martin, i, 355.

[33] *Ibid.*, p. 353; 'L'Angleterre admettait sans doute le droit canonique, mais avec des reserves'; p. 355; 'En France, la situation était tout autre. L'Église y vivait sous le régime du droit canonique pur et simple, reconnu par l'État.'

[33a] French royal administrators (for example) made a fuss about their king's absolute right (*pleno jure*) to present to a great many benefices, especially in royal chapels: see G. Mollat, 'Le roi de France et la collation plénière (*pleno jure*) des bénéfices ecclésiastiques', *Mémoires présentés à l'Académie des Inscriptions*, xiv, pt. 2 (1951), 107–286. But in England the king exercised similar rights without feeling the need to justify them; cf. Hamilton Thompson, pp. 81–2 and n. 5 to p. 81.

[34] *ECP*, p. 206.

pontiffs and accepted the resignation of the third. It laid down in
the decree *Frequens* (1417) that in future general councils would
meet at regular intervals. In due course councils met at Pavia-Siena
(1423) and Basle (1431). The successful operation of the new
machinery, which would have made the pope a constitutional rather
than an absolute monarch, was, however, impeded by Martin V
(elected at Constance in 1417) and his successors. Eugenius IV (1431–
1447) was able to reduce the council of Basle to impotence and under
Pius II conciliarism received the shock of the bull *Execrabilis* (1460),
which anathematized appeals from the pope to a future council.
Though the English delegation had played a large part at Constance,
there was no effective English participation in the subsequent councils
and this has perhaps led historians to neglect the importance of
conciliarism in English relations with, and attitudes towards, the
papacy. There is no doubt about the importance of the councils and
conciliarism in France (or, for that matter, elsewhere on the Continent). The French played a large part in the Council of Basle,
almost as big (down to 1438) as the Germans. At that point, when
Council and pope reached their final rupture, the main anti-papal
legislation of the Council was reviewed by an assembly of French
clergy which gave its approval. As we have already noted, the king,
at the request of the clergy, embodied the substantive decisions of
Basle in the Pragmatic Sanction of Bourges. The main points were
these: the superiority of councils to popes and the summoning of
councils every ten years; free elections and suppression of reservations;
drastic restrictions on papal provision, appeals to the Curia and papal
taxation (annates). There were also other, less controversial, decisions
—for a college of cardinals broadly drawn from all the provinces of
the church, and for reforms in disciplinary and liturgical matters.[35]

It will be evident how unpalatable this was to the popes of the
later fifteenth century, victorious as they were over Basle and its
anti-pope Felix V, successful in negotiating Union with the Greek
church, busy pursuing their aim of recovering power in the Papal
States where conciliarism had legitimized anarchy. The Pragmatic
Sanction consolidated the effects, achieved in England over centuries,
of the Constitutions of Clarendon and the statutes of Provisors and
Praemunire. Popes were able to disentangle themselves gradually from
explicit recognition of the decree *Sacrosancta,* but never formally
abrogated' the degree *Frequens* (which, after all, implied conciliar
supremacy). They sought again and again to negotiate Concordats
with French kings from Charles VII onwards; and always when
French kings encountered papal obstinacy they invoked a future
council—even going to the length of sponsoring the *conciliabulum*
of Pisa in 1511. The upshot of this long duel was the Concordat of
1516. Pope Leo X abandoned the old papal claims in return for

[35] See Martin, *op. cit.,* ii, 282–91, 303–15.

Francis I's dropping the references in the Pragmatic Sanction to conciliar superiority; thereafter the king nominated to bishoprics and the pope provided his nominees. 'From this point', writes Monsieur Renaudet, 'the French monarchy had no interest or advantage in demanding church reform'.[36]

From its insistence on the validity of canonical practice (the 'ancient liberties') French kings and clergy had been led to accept in the fullest sense the authority of general councils over popes and only bartered this away for total royal control over the French hierarchy. Things fell out differently in England where kings already had *de facto* mastery of the clergy. But there too conciliarism had its attractions at moments when popes were completely obstructive. Such episodes were rare. The 'apostle', as the vicar of Peter is often called in English documents, was content to let well alone. His fault, in Dr Pantin's word, was 'compliance'.[37] The Crown got its nominees, elected by docile chapters, provided at the same time by an equally docile bishop of Rome, who got his chancery fees. What French kings did not securely enjoy until 1516 was already possessed by English sovereigns from the fourteenth century. One searches through the history of later medieval England for head-on confrontations between the king and the pope almost in vain. Almost but not quite. There was a crisis in 1427–8 and there was another in 1534–5. On both occasions men remembered the comfortable doctrine embodied in the decrees *Sacrosancta* and *Frequens*.

In the 1420s Martin V, elected by the extraordinary conclave at Constance, repeatedly attempted to secure the repeal of the statute of Provisors. The campaign he conducted, designed to play off against each other the factions at the court of Henry VI, is well-known.[38] What has missed recent observation[39] is that Archbishop Chichele, deprived by the pope of his legatine powers in an attempt to compel him to move the abrogation of the pernicious legislation, appealed from the pope to a future council. In this solemn protestation the archbishop began by defending himself and then proceeded to appeal 'to the holy general council, representing the universal church'.[40] In the event simpler and very English solutions were at hand. The bull of deprivation was impounded by royal officers and parliament refused

---

[36] H. Hauser and A. Renaudet, *Les débuts de l'âge moderne*, 'Peuples et civilisations' (Paris, 1929), p. 160.

[37] *ECP*, p. 182.

[38] E. F. Jacob, introduction to *Chichele's Register*, i (1941), pp. xlv–xlvii and for the chronology, id., *Trans. R. Hist. Soc.*, 4 ser., xv (1932), 112–13; id., *The Fifteenth Century*, 'Oxford History of England' (Oxford, 1961), pp. 234–6; id., *Archbishop Henry Chichele* (London, 1967), p. 52; Du Boulay, *ECP*, pp. 214–16. For Martin V's attempt to put the clock back in France at this time see Martin, *op. cit.*, ii, 255–68 (concordat of Genazzano).

[39] Although noted by Stubbs, *Constitutional History*, 3 vols. (Oxford, 1880), iii, 323, n. 1. To what extent did Chichele feel that the primacy of Canterbury was threatened? Cf. the episode of 1440 when Kemp was made a cardinal: W. Ullmann, 'Eugenius IV, Cardinal Kemp and Archbishop Chichele', *Studies to A. Gwynn*, pp. 359–83.

[40] D. Wilkins, *Concilia*, iii (1737), pp. 485–6. The finality of such an appeal may well have led Wilkins to a mistaken arrangement of the documents in the case.

to entertain any pleas for a mitigation of the law. Faced by the old combination of king and parliament, Martin climbed down and restored the archbishop's powers. But Chichele had not been alone in seeing in a council a way out of the impasse created by Martin V. In the letter written by the university of Oxford in support of Chichele the flowery sentences must occasionally have grated on the pope's ears. The dutiful dons reminded the pope that the unity of the church had only recently been re-established, and that he had been chosen as pope by the agency of the Council. The implication of this ornate obsequiousness was clear: another council lay ahead.[41] Thereafter for a hundred years popes avoided conflicts with England. And after Basle they avoided councils—a much more difficult task.

Englishmen did not entirely forget councils. Thomas Gascoigne in the 1440s frequently refers in his *Book of Truths* to the episode just touched on. His garbled version of it is worth repeating:

> Recently the Roman pope Martin V wrote to some bishops I know censuring certain evil customs and certain evil public statutes, inveighing against them and striving to secure that contrary statutes should be decreed in parliament. Because the bishops did not do this, nor indeed dared to do it, the same Pope Martin excommunicated them and suspended the archbishop of Canterbury from his legateship . . . so the bishops then openly said that the general council was above the pope and appealed from the pope to the general council next to be celebrated.

Gascoigne says some bishops changed their minds about this, but what ended the affair was the death of the pope.[42] There does seem to have been considerable confusion in England over the status of the conciliar legislation. There is no doubt that Lyndwood, who had been at Constance, was firmly opposed to the decrees *Sacrosancta* and *Frequens*. Since he was constructing his survey of canon law round the provincial legislation of Canterbury he does not discuss the matter outright; but incidental references make his view clear.[43] On the other hand the Carmelite Thomas Netter of Walden in his great *Doctrinale*[44] was unequivocally in sympathy with conciliar supremacy, and the important place Netter occupied at the English court from the reign of Henry IV to the reign of Henry VI should be remembered.[45] For those who were interested in the matter the facts of

[41] *Concilia*, iii, 477a.

[42] *Loci e Libro veritatum*, ed. J. E. Thorold Rogers (Oxford, 1881), p. 17; cf. Gascoigne's several references to a great book 'De gestis et actis concilii Pisani, et concilii Constanciensis, et concilii Basiliensis' in Durham College, Oxford, e.g. pp. 121, 164. On Gascoigne see Winifred A. Pronger, published in two parts in *Eng. Hist. Rev.*, liii (1938), 606–26 and liv (1939), 20–37.

[43] William Lyndwood, *Provinciale* (Oxford, 1679), pp. 16 (*Authoritatem concilii*), 284 (*Per Ecclesiam*).

[44] Thomae Waldensis *Doctrinale antiquitatum fidei*, ed. B. Blanciotti, 3 vols. (Venice, 1757–9), i, 385, 563. Netter's attitude embarrasses his editor.

[45] Was it Netter that Pierre Janelle thought of when he wrote 'la théorie conciliaire, restée vivante en Angleterre depuis le début du XVe siécle'? See *L'Angleterre catholique à la vielle du schisme* (Paris, 1935), p. 178.

the great debate were available. Gascoigne, like the early Tudor chroniclers,[46] rehearsed the succession of the popes during the Schism and described the deposition of Eugenius IV and the election of Felix V. Compared with the fervid conciliar propaganda to be found in France or Germany in the mid- and late fifteenth century this is not much. The point is simply that there was no advantage for the English kings to sponsor conciliar activity.

This can be clearly seen early in Henry VIII's reign. The English government, while naturally being opposed on political grounds to the French *conciliabulum* of Pisa in 1511, showed very little interest in the Fifth Lateran Council which immediately followed.[47] When the Council had served its purpose of thwarting French diplomacy, Henry was profoundly uninterested in the reforms which the Lateran turned to, profoundly hostile to its reassertion of papal rights. But the Council and its use as a bludgeon against recalcitrant popes were remembered promptly enough when Henry VIII encountered Clement VII's inability to grant him a divorce. It was then, of course, natural for Henry to appeal to a council and Cromwell's assiduous publicists got to work preparing the relevant material.[48] More surprisingly, the greatest of the king's opponents also urged a conciliar solution. Sir Thomas More wrote to Cromwell on 5 March 1534:

> As for the general councils assembled lawfully . . . the authority thereof ought to be taken for undoubtable, or else were there in nothing no certainty . . . For albeit that I have for mine own part such opinion of the pope's primacy as I have showed you, yet never thought I the pope above the general council.[49]

In fact the break with Rome proved to be permanent. Councils gradually receded to the domain of an ideal ever less attainable. More's fear was surely that matters of faith would be nationalized; that the 'common corps of Christendom' would be split into fractions. And this is what happened. After the Act of Supremacy, Christian doctrine 'received definition from the king as Supreme Head and later rested on the authority of the king-in-parliament'.[50]

iii

In the light of the foregoing observations it is useful in conclusion to ask again: how should one translate the phrase *ecclesia anglicana*

[46] E.g. R. Fabyan, *New Chronicles* (repr. 1811), pp. 578, 612–13; P. Vergil, *Anglica Historia* (Basle, 1534), p. 435; E. Hall, *Chronicle* (repr. 1809), pp. 47–8.

[47] I am indebted to Dr. D. S. Chambers for the loan of an unpublished article by him and Dr. M. J. Kelly on 'English Bishops and the Fifth Lateran Council'.

[48] For this see F. Le Van Baumer, *Early Tudor Theories of Kingship* (New Haven, 1940), pp. 49–56; W. Gordon Zeeveld, *Foundations of Tudor Policy* (Cambridge, Mass., 1948), pp. 88–9, 130–6, etc.; Lacey Baldwin Smith, *Tudor Prelates and Politics* (Princeton, 1953), p. 160; James K. McConica, *English Humanists and Reformation Politics* (Oxford, 1965), p. 181; P. A. Sawada, 'Two anonymous Tudor treatises on the General Council', *Journ. of Eccles. Hist.*, xii (1961), 197–214.

[49] *Correspondence of Sir Thomas More*, ed. Elizabeth F. Rogers (Princeton, 1947), pp. 498–9. I have drawn attention to the problem in a brief note in *Moreana* 15 (1967).

[50] Elton, *Past and Present*, 29 (1964), 33.

in the period prior to the Reformation? There can be no doubt about how Englishmen translated it in the fourteenth and fifteenth centuries. It will have been seen that in the statute of Provisors of 1351 the French text reads 'église d'Angleterre'. Now this is not an accident forced on the drafters of the bill by the exigencies of the Anglo-Norman language they were using. One can, if one wishes, say 'the Church *in* England' and one or two examples of such terminology are to be found: in 1376 the Rolls of Parliament have 'seinte Eglise en Angleterre'.[51] But there is no doubt at all that the normal translation is Church *of* England and this is documented from 1290 in Latin,[52] from 1341 in French[53] and from the later fourteenth century onwards frequently in English.[54] It is obvious that the phrase 'defensio ecclesiae et regni Angliae', which one meets in so many of the episcopal mandates of the period, can only be Englished as 'of the Church and realm of England'. These examples are necessarily drawn from written texts. One may be sure that long before they occurred in writing such expressions were used in spoken language.

This is not to suggest that the clergy and laymen who availed themselves of such plain words assumed that there was not a universal Church of which they formed a part. It is, however, to argue that they regarded the universal Church as being composed of a number of singular churches. We have their own authority that this was the case in the later Middle Ages. Chichele, writing in Latin in 1434, used the following words: 'Our holy mother church of England which used to be strong in her liberties, flourishing and *excelling other churches*, is now seriously fallen'.[55] A generation later his successor Thomas Bourgchier wrote in English 'sith the bountee of the grace and tendernesse of our said holy fadre is so amply shewed to the said chirch of England, *above the chirchis of any other Cristen region*'.[56] Language like this simply accepted the facts of life.[57] There was a universal

[51] *Rot. Parl.*, ii, 337; cf. 'seinte Eglise en Roialme' (1306), *ibid.*, i, 219, and again 'Seinte Esglise en le dit Roialme' (1378), *ibid.*, iii, 48b.

[52] This is in a Latin paraphrase of the expression 'ecclesia anglicana'. *Rot. Parl.*, i, 57b; 'Ecclesia de Regno Angliae'.

[53] *Rot. Parl.*, ii, 129b; cf. *ibid.*, iii, 26a (1377); iii, 583b (1406); iv, 94 (1416); iv, 175b (1422), etc.

[54] The earliest examples I have noted are Wyclifite: 'Myche more late the chirche of Engelond appreuve the trewe and hool translacioun of symple men . . .', Purvey's Prologue in *The Holy Bible . . . in the Earliest English Versions*, ed. J. Forshall and F. Madden, i (Oxford, 1850), p. 58; 'the reformation of holi chirche of England', H. S. Cronin, 'The xii conclusions of the Lollards', *Eng. Hist. Rev.*, xxii (1907), 295; and again *ibid.*, p. 296. But the usage is soon orthodox enough: *Rot. Parl.*, v, 281a: 'Fadir of the chirche of this land' (1455); cf. Edmund Dudley *Tree of Commonwealth*, ed. D. M. Brodie (Cambridge, 1948), p. 25.

[55] '. . . sicque sancta mater ecclesia anglicana quae in suis libertatibus olim pollebat, floruit et alias ecclesias antecellebat, nunc . . . non modicum est depressa', *Register*, ed. E. F. Jacob (Cant. & York Soc.), iii, 256.

[56] *Register*, ed. F. R. H. Du Boulay (Cant. & York Soc., liv), pp. 119–20.

[57] Cf. again Mr. Duggan on the twelfth century: 'Such phrases . . . certainly described with aptness the corporate sense and interests of the Churches of the various regions, but they were not designed or understood to imply a separateness from the *ecclesia Romana*', *ECP*, p. 108. I. P. Shaw uses the phrase 'churches in communion with Rome', *op. cit.*, p. 18.

Church—under councils and popes. But there was also a Church of England, a Church of France and others—the 'nations' who had deliberated at the Council of Constance were a tangible and a useful as well as an unavoidable way of looking at the Church universal. The ultra-orthodox Reginald Pecock in his *Book of Faith* (*c.* 1456?) refers to the Pauline 'one Lord, one faith, one baptism'. He then goes on:

> And ȝitt the baptim of this man, here in Ynglond, is not the same baptym in being, and in kinde, which is the baptym of another man in Fraunce; for ech man, as he is dyvers in being fro ech other man, so his baptim, and his sacramental waisching is dyvers in being fro ech other mannys baptim and waisching in water. Nevertheless, this baptim of this man in Ynglond is oon in significacioun, and in representacioun, with ech othere mannys baptim in Fraunse. Forwhi alle the baptymes signifien, representen and sacramenten oon thing, which is this, as Poul seith, Ro. vi⁰ c͏ʳ. that ech man owith be deed and biried to all synnys, and rise into a newe lyf in clennes of vertu. Also in lijk maner, the chirche of Ynglond is oon chirche with the chirche of Fraunce, but hou? Certis not in being, in kinde, and in substaunce; fforwhi the peple being here is not the peple being there; but thei ben oon in reputacioun of auctorite, of feith, of power, and of iuresdiccioun; that is to seie, for the oon of these chirchis hath lijk power and iuresdiccioun to the othere ȝoven to hem fro God.[57a]

The English clergy had a spiritual leader in the pope; they had a master in the king. In the late fourteenth century Wyclif said: 'For sith clerkis ben lege men to kingis in whos londis thei ben inne, kyngis han power of God to punishe hem in Goddis cause, bothe in bodi and in catel.'[58] A century and a half later another martyr accepted Wyclif's premise—and illustrated its conclusion by giving his life: in 1529 Thomas More asked, 'Hath his hyghnes of eny part of hys realm bene better obayd or more humbly served then of hys clergy?'[59] Marsilio of Padua had already made Wyclif's point in his *Defensor Pacis* of 1324. In this extraordinary book an Italian at Paris argued that in every State the clergy were subordinate to the civil authority; an English version of this appeared in the year of More's execution.[60] The theory was catching up with the facts in an uncomfortable way.

Historians (and others) should be less diffident in using the phrase 'Church of England' for the later medieval period. If one had lived then, that is what one would have said. There can have been little

---

[57a] *Book of Faith*, ed. J. L. Morison (Glasgow, 1909), pp. 273–4, quoted in part also by Arthur B. Ferguson in his valuable essay on 'Reginald Pecock and the Renaissance sense of history', *Studies in the Renaissance*, xiii (1966), 147–65. The striking parallels between the approaches of Pecock and Hooker have been noted: V. H. H. Green, *Bishop Reginald Pecock* (Cambridge, 1945), pp. 230–1; P. Munz, *The Place of Hooker in the History of Thought* (London, 1952), pp. 42–5.
[58] *Select English Works of J. Wyclif*, ed. T. Arnold, 3 vols. (Oxford, 1869–71), ii, 88–9.
[59] *Supplycacyon of Soulys* (London, 1529), fo. XVIIIᵛᵒ.
[60] *S.T.C.*, no. 17817.

surprise when in 1533 the statute in Restraint of Appeals observed
that the Spirituality was 'now being usually called the English
Church'.[61] To say this is not to assert that the events of the 1530s
were not momentous. Prior to the Henrician legislation the king,
whatever his practical powers, was not head of the Church; after it he
was. Before he could not decide doctrine; afterwards he could. Before
it his right to dispense from the Canon Law (and it should be
remembered that such dispensations were made)[62] was irregular;
after he had the power legally. All of this Thomas More saw clearly.
What he died for was the old, easy, undefined situation which had
worked well, where there was a Church of England within an unbroken Faith. Now Henry VIII and Cromwell had produced an
English Church apart, destined to go on its way. Yet even in the
post-Reformation church of England some of the old ambiguities
remained. Historians refer to them as the *via media*.

It seems very likely that in the sixteenth century there would have
arisen a doctrine of the 'liberties of the Anglican Church' if instead
there had not occurred a break with Rome. When the Commons in
1347 said 'Seinte Esglise doit estre fraunche' they no longer meant
free of the king, they meant free of the pope.[63] On the whole such a
freedom was conveyed by the operation of the law by strong kings.
But that would have had to be explicitly recognized in the post-
Tridentine church. The English might then have adopted the convenient doctrines of France just as in the fourteenth century French
clergy and kings had modelled their efforts at autonomy on the
practices of medieval England.[64]

[61] G. R. Elton, *The Tudor Constitution* (Cambridge, 1960), p. 344.
[62] See S. B. Chrimes, *English Constitutional Ideas in the Fifteenth Century* (Cambridge, 1936), p. 283; cf. p. 287.
[63] *Rot Parl.*, ii, 171.
[64] I have to thank Professor R. H. Du Boulay, Professor G. R. Elton, Professor V. H. Galbraith and Dr. Roger Highfield who were good enough to read and comment on a version of this paper. They are, of course, in no sense committed to what I say.

11

SIR THOMAS MORE'S *UTOPIA*: LITERATURE OR POLITICS?

I accepted your kind invitation to address the Accademia Nazionale dei Lincei and its guests on More's *Utopia* in the hope that a specialist in later medieval history might perhaps be able to comment usefully on a text normally discussed by specialists in 'early modern' history [1]. I chose the above title for my talk since there is still a temptation to regard *Utopia* as a *jeu d'esprit*, a mere literary exercise. Whatever the answer to the question I have posed, the book can still sometimes confuse the reader not alert to the assumptions of its author. This remains true despite the very fine and prolific scholarship devoted to More in recent years [2]. I shall begin by reminding you of the structure of the book and its contemporary influence, of the relationship of *Utopia* with the circumstances of More's own career. Second, I shall turn to *Utopia* in the perspective of the fourteenth and fifteenth centuries, dealing first with social and economic conditions, and then with some moral presuppositions underlying the book.

I.

It may seem unnecessary to ask–for this in a way is what I am doing– whether More is serious in *Utopia*, or whether the book is a brilliant intellectual creation, intended to amuse a small coterie of friends. This question has, of course, been much debated, and not only in his own day, when (as we shall see) the only comfortable way of looking at *Utopia* was to regard it as a joke. In the nineteenth century and after, when his works were more

---

(1) I have left the lecture in the form in which it was delivered, adding some references and amplifying one or two statements. I have to thank dott. Giuseppe Roglia, Vice–Cancelliere of the Academy, for much consideration and kindness.

(2) I signal out for mention the following, as especially relevant to this essay: The Yale University edition of the complete works, and especially vol. 4, *Utopia*, ed. and trans. by Edward Surtz S. J. and J. A. Hexter (New Haven and London, 1965), to which all my references will be made; R. W. GIBSON, *Sir Thomas More: a preliminary bibliography to...* *1750* (New Haven and London, 1961). Most recent work on More finds a reflection in *Moreana*, inspired, edited and sometimes largely written by the Abbé Germain Marc'hadour at Angers since 1963. See especially *Moreana* 15 (1967) where several papers, contributed in honour of Miss E. F. ROGERS, discuss *Utopia*; and cfr. below p.263 and nn. 52,53.

earnestly regarded, the purpose of *Utopia* was more urgently discussed. For some his book was one of the early calls to the realisation of socialism on earth. For others it advocated the re-establishment of a sober, sincere, Christian commonwealth, supposing that this had once existed before, in the Golden Days of the Golden Middle Ages. But for others the only way to avoid embarrassment in the book was still to regard it as a jest—for how could a sensible scholar and devout Catholic like More suppose either that you can change human nature or, in any fundamental way, change human society?

These are, in fact, important points and though much of the fire has gone out of the socialists (I will name Kautsky as an example) and of the neo–Catholics (I select R. W. Chambers as representative of the class) [3], there does remain a residual wonder at More's eccentric behaviour and it is that I should like to reflect on for a few preliminary moments.

I shall first remind you of some circumstances that lead one to feel that More had his tongue in his cheek. There is, first of all, the dialogue form in which the first book of *Utopia* is written, the part in which contemporary European governments and societies are held up to ridicule. Now it is notoriously difficult to know what an author is up to in a dialogue, more particularly the sort of dialogue where there is fierce give and take over genuine problems, as in the argument over whether giving honest advice to governments does any good, since governments act always in a selfish, short-term way. This problem of the dialogue is, in fact, a question which has bedevilled much Renaissance scholarship. The reputation (I mean the moral standing) of Lorenzo Valla, for instance, has fluctuated according to the stress his commentators have placed on this or that speaker in the dialogue *De voluptate* (De vero bono) as indubitably representating the author's views [4]. And there are other cases of this sort of thing. Now out of all the argument one thing does seem to be established with tolerable security: when the writer of a Renaissance dialogue used as his interlocutors real persons, not characters with invented names, then the views put into their mouths seem to correspond closely with what we know to have been the opinions of the men in question. (It was obviously difficult, if one made a prominent contemporary— whose attitudes were broadly familiar to his friends and enemies—express sentiments which he was known not to hold). Now in the case of the dialogue in *Utopia* book I there are two real people present, More and his friend Peter Gilles, though in fact Gilles takes little part in the conversation. And there is the remarkable figure invented by More, Raphael Hythlodaeus, the man who had lived among the Utopians, though they are hardly mentioned in book I. In which personage, Hythlodaeus or himself, did More express his

(3) KARL KAUTSKY, *Thomas More and his Utopia with a historical introduction* (London, 1927); R. W. CHAMBERS, *Thomas More* (London 1935), which remains the best biography.

(4) F. GAETA, *Lorenzo Valla – filologia e storia nell'umanesimo italiano* (Napoli, 1955), pp. 15–53; CHARLES TRINKAUS, "*In our Image and Likeness*". *Humanity and Divinity in Italian Humanist Thought*, 2 vols. (London, 1970), i. 103–170.

own views? In the remarks of the traveller Hythlodaeus, who speaks much more than More, or under his own name, Thomas More? There is at any rate a *prima facie* case that More was saying what he himself thought in those observations which he puts into his own mouth, especially perhaps those which in some important respects modify or contradict the opinions of the traveller.

That is the first point to bear in mind. The second is that, in fact, More's *Utopia* was addressed to a handful of *cognoscenti* and not to the masses, not even to the very small mass of his own educated countrymen. It was written in Latin, like most of More's earlier works (those written before he became a royal servant), and it was published on the Continent, as was the case with many other Latin works written by Englishmen in the sixteenth century and even in the seventeenth. And (though critics sometimes do not understand this) it was *not* a best-seller in sixteenth century terms. Erasmus's works really were best-sellers: the *Adagia* and the *Colloquia* went into hundreds of editions. And so did those of even a second rank humanist like Polidoro Vergilio (whom I recall this evening with pleasure since it was through him, just before the War, that I first became enamoured of the Renaissance and of Italy); his *De rerum inventoribus* went through fifty editions before he died in 1555 and it was early translated into English and other languages [5]. *Utopia* was not fated to be so immediately popular as the works of these two friends of More. First published at Louvain in 1516, at Paris in 1517, it was again reprinted at Basle twice in 1518, and at Florence in 1519. More died (1535) before another edition appeared. There follow editions at Louvain and Cologne, in 1548 and 1555 respectively, and, with other works, at Basle in 1563. In 1565 *Utopia* was published in each of the two editions of the *opera* published in Louvain in that year, and reprinted twice in 1566. The last sixteenth-century Latin edition was at Wittenberg in 1591. As for translations published in the sixteenth century, the following are recorded: French 1550 and 1559; English 1551, twice in 1556, 1597; German 1524; Italian 1548 [6]; Dutch 1553, 1562. These dates can be summarised briefly. By 1600 *Utopia* in its original Latin form had appeared thirteen times, if we include the *Works*; and by the same terminal date it had come out in five vernaculars on ten occasions. Between 1516 and 1600 there were thus, in some form or other, twenty three issues [7]. Yet by the end of the sixteenth century Polidoro Vergilio's *De rerum inventoribus* [8] had appeared about ninety times

(5) See my *Polydore Vergil* (Oxford, 1952), pp. 52, 70.

(6) I have to thank Professor Rodolfo de Mattei for his kindness in presenting me with a copy of *Utopia*, ed. by Luigi Firpo, published by Utet (Turin) for Christmas 1970.

(7) This is a very generous allowance, based on Gibson, pp. 3–57, which counts the two ' imprints' of the 1565 and 1566 editions of the *Opera* separately; in fact two printers were involved but in all probability only one real impression; the English editions of 1556 are also really only one.

(8) Cf. J. FERGUSON, ' Notes on the work of Polydore Vergil " de inventoribus rerum " ', *Isis* xvii (1932), 71–93. In 1944 the Historical Library of Yale University School of Medicine issued a useful Handlist of editions and locations of this work.

and Erasmus's *Colloquia* at least 150 times in Latin alone [9]. I do not mean that *Utopia* did not have admirers at the time or lack a certain amount of influence on contemporaries. Among More's close friends like Erasmus the book was widely known and regarded highly—a group fairly represented by the dedicatory and other letters attached to the earliest editions of *Utopia*: the best known of them today are Guillaume Budé, Jerome Busleyden and, of course, Peter Gilles. Beyond this small coterie. Rabelais was influenced by *Utopia* a little and Tomasso Campanella a lot. But by Campanella's time we are entering into the seventeenth century, when the nature of interest in More began its change. It is, I suspect, not till the nineteenth century that More began to assume a really commanding position mainly, though of course not exclusively, by reason of *Utopia*. Prior to that time, while known to an enlarging public, *Utopia* had given rise to a concept and a technique, but these were often put to trivial purposes [10]. In the atmosphere of social reform after 1789 ' Utopias ' had new value, and the critics of change could also use the idea as a symbol of all they disliked. Is it a coincidence that apparently the first Englishman to use the abstraction Utopian*ism* was the utilitarian Jeremy Bentham in 1802?

Here, then, we have a book which, in its Latin form, was not a great success with *le grand public*, and in which More's personal views to some extent contradict those of Raphael Hythlodaeus, who argues vehemently (and, from the point of view of the people likely to read the book, unfashionably) that a wise man and a scholar would not counsel princes. Hythlodaeus's attitude of contempt for princes is not only contradicted by More's *Utopia* [11]. It is contradicted by More in life itself. Two years after his character Hythlodaeus had delivered a diatribe against the cunning and corruption of all rulers More became the king's ' good servant ', and the king was that shabby character Henry VIII. Are there not therefore solid grounds for regarding More's book as a delicious satirical exercise? The attacks on the law, on wealth, on the gentry, the picture of the virtuous hard–working Utopians— is all this not just a firework display to amuse the intellectual élite of Western Europe? Can More not have known that it would be distasteful to the kings, councillors and gentry of the whole Continent? And yet it is difficult to think of More being so acidly contemptuous of the institutions and assumptions of

---

(9) ' Sans compter les extraits et les traductions ': LUCIEN FEBVRE et H.J. MARTIN, *L'apparition du livre*, Paris 1958, p. 414; and on the complicated problems of the early editions see CRAIG R. THOMPSON, *The Colloquies of Erasmus*, a new translation (Chicago and London, 1965), intro. pp. xxii–xxvii.

(10) An analysis of the material listed in Gibson pp. 291–413 would be interesting. My impression seems to be borne out at any rate by *Les Utopies à la Renaissance*, Bruxelles: Université Libre, Colloque international, avril 1961 (Presses Universitaires, 1963). There are some interesting papers in this volume but several of them have small connection with More or his *Utopia*.

(11) *Utopia*, pp. 55–7, 87, 97–103 for the debate on Counsel; see also Hexter's introduction, lxxxi–xcii.

the contemporary world if he was genuinely indifferent to its fate. We should remember his background: his London patrician stock, his eminent father judge, his love of learning and his yearning for the cloister. It is difficult at any rate for me to see young Thomas living with the Carthusians at the Charterhouse when reading for the law at the Inns of Court if he was really alienated from the world around him or unconcerned with its fate. Attendance at the Inns of Court in the capital city was a far more joyous and culturally exciting thing in More's day than the experience of being an undergraduate at Oxford if what he wanted was wit and entertainment. And one cannot forget his end, twenty years after entering Henry's service, four years after leaving it, a martyr to his own conscience and the king's imperious will. I am not suggesting that one should look in the author of *Utopia* as he was at the date of composition (1515–6) for the martyr (1535). Yet the ultimate composition of the man remains a constant. In his last years he still displayed a gaiety of disposition. In *Utopia* there were sober undertones which make it absurd to regard the book as basically frivolous.

The two books of *Utopia* were written at two different times. The *Discourse of Utopia* (book II) was written first, while More found himself with some unexpected leisure when representing London merchant interests on a visit to the Netherlands in 1515. The *Dialogue of Counsel* (book I) was written, much more quickly, about a year after his return to England. These terms, *Discourse of Utopia* and *Dialogue of Counsel*, are those of Professor Jack Hexter whose *Utopia: The Biography of an Idea* came out nearly twenty years ago and, short though it is, still remains by far the best introduction to the subject [12]. (In his introduction to the Yale edition of *Utopia* in the *Complete Works*—with Father Edward Surtz S. J.— an elaboration of the same material can be found) [13]. Now if the purpose of *Utopia* was to entertain or—in an academic sort of way—to edify, with a model community described as a reproach to the actual world, why on earth does More later on spoil the joke by making book I a savage and penetrating attack on his grasping, ruthless, short-sighted, bloated English neighbours, living on the backs of the indigent since, without injustice on this monumental scale, the rich could not be rich and powerful? The Dialogue of Counsel is far from being amusing. In it More attacks not just vague evils, but indicates specific horrors: men are executed for stealing, sheep are eating up men, the nobility hunt like butchers, aided and abetted by most clergy who are as hypocritical and as greedy as their lay kinsfolk [14]. It is a devastating picture, and the sharpness of More's observation, the violence of his analysis, without a doubt contributed to the distrust of the book among the landed classes and the *haute bourgeoisie*, the two groups which more or less had things their own way in the sixteenth and seventeenth centuries.

(12) Princeton, New Jersey, 1952.
(13) See above n. 2.
(14) *Utopia*, pp. 59–87.

You will see that I have no doubt that *Utopia* is really a serious book, intended to have some influence on this sublunary world. This does not, of course, imply that I think More has any connection with Karl Marx. More's communism had a much more obvious source than Plato's *Republic* or the Fathers of the Church. His communism was based on those angular precepts in the New Testament which still make some men sell all that they have, and which, down the ages, have had their reflections in St. Benedict and all the other monks (including More's Carthusians) and in St. Francis and all the other friars. *Utopia* is, in this sense, another hymn to Lady Poverty.

Clearly, in the end, he decided that it was his duty to give advice to Henry VIII. Hexter supposes that this was due to the hopeful way More regarded Wolsey's efforts to attack enclosures, to limit royal extravagances, to reform law by means of the prerogative courts with their emphasis on equity, to pursue peace abroad and economy at home. Perhaps these optimistic thoughts did occur to More, though one should recall his references in *Utopia* to original sin [15]. I suspect that what influenced More to a greater extent was in the last resort the ingrained respect for legally constituted authority, for the King, which was part of the Teutonic (but not the Latin) way of life. He may have disliked the law as it was practised. (What humanist from Petrarch to Calvin did like it?). But he came out of a world in which even the Statutes of the Realm were signed: *Le roi le veult*. For a London lawyer, as More was, order and the king were synonymous. The witty Thomas was even prepared to spend evenings of excruciating boredom when he entered the court of Henry VIII, while Henry expected entertainment as well as counsel: *Le roi s'amuse*. I wonder when Henry's amusements began to trouble the failed Carthusian?

At any rate we can see the moment when More realised that Hythlodaeus's pessimism in the Dialogue of Counsel had been justified. In that discussion More's reply had been to refer the traveller to Hythlodaens's favourite author Plato, who had seen good government as depending on philosophers becoming kings or kings becoming philosophers. 'What a distant prospect of happiness there will be', adds More, ' if philosophers will not condescend even to impart their counsel to kings '. Hythlodaeus then illustrates his disillusion with counsellors and kings by supposing he had been present at a discussion before the French king in his privy council as to the correct policy to follow in his Italian wars; his own advice, ' to stay at home before France is ruined ', is not well received. To this and further argument More replies by admitting that ' academic philosophy ' has no place at court but that there is ' another philosophy more practical for statesmen '. It is an imperfect world.

> If you cannot pluck up wrongheaded opinions by the root... yet
> you must not on that account desert the commonwealth. You

---

(15) ' Nam ut omnia bene sint, fieri non potest, nisi omnes boni sint, quod ad aliquot abhinc annos adhunc non expecto ', *Utopia*, p. 100.

must not abandon the ship in a storm because you cannot control the winds... what you cannot turn to good you must make as little bad as you can [16].

I am irresistably reminded of Francesco Guicciardini—and indeed all statesmen who, if they are honest, know that whatever they do will prove to be wrong [17].

II

Most discussions of More are in the Renaissance–Reformation context. In the second half of my talk I shall look at *Utopia* as a reflection of an earlier day rather than as a product of the years when it was written.

Yet it is important to remember the context. More's *Utopia* was written at almost exactly the same time as Machiavelli's *Prince*. Machiavelli wrote his book in 1513. More wrote his in 1515 and 1516. There is probably a closer affinity between the minds of the two men than might be supposed. They both wrote their main works in periods of enforced retirement from active affairs: More in a gap during his diplomatic work in the Netherlands and Machiavelli wrote the *Prince* and the *Discourses on Livy* when he had been ruined by the return of the Medici to Florence in 1512. And More had, in his way, a capacity for political analysis which is astonishingly similar to Machiavelli's: read in book I his imaginary debate in the French King's council on the Italian wars—an exact analysis of French policy, hinting shrewdly at its outcome twenty years later, at a time when the French cause was finally lost and the Hapsburgs mastered the Peninsula [18]. Which was to be the year when More was executed.

But the connection between Machiavelli and More is largely one of coincidence. A more important feature of the years when they wrote was that it was the last hopeful moment before the Lutheran bomb exploded. After 1517, when the reformer challenged the Church, or at any rate after 1520 when he burned the bull of excommunication or 1521 when he defied Charles V and appealed to the German people, it is hard to see either Machiavelli or More writing their books—or at any rate writing the sort of books they did write. Certainly for More, *Utopia* represents—for all its acceptance of Christian pessimism—a sense of hope for human society, a conviction that if reason will not prevail it will nevertheless make a difference. Such convictions were shaken by the upheaval in Germany. After Luther's gesture would Erasmus have translated the Greek Testament or Cardinal Jiminez de

(16) *Utopia*, pp. 99–101; and the whole discussion, pp. 87–103.

(17) GUICCIARDINI, *Ricordi*, ed. Canestrini (Florence, 1857), p. 195: ' Se bene gli uomini deliberano con buono consiglio, gli effetti però sono spesso contrarii; tanto è incerto il futuro. Nondimanco non è da darsi come bestia in preda della fortuna ma come uomo andare con la ragione; e chi è bene savio ha da contentarsi più di essersi mosso con buono consiglio, ancora che lo effetto sia stato malo, che se in un consiglio cattivo avessi avuto lo effetto buono '.

(18) *Utopia*, pp. 87–9.

Cisneros have promoted the Complutensian Polygot? Would More have advocated toleration of religious diversity of a profound kind—as he does in *Utopia* [19] if he had written the book five or ten years later? It seems unlikely. Before that fateful year one could still believe in scholarship as a bulwark of Christian understanding, of what Erasmus and his friends called the ' philosophy of Christ '. This was certainly not what was meant by ' philosophy ' in the writings of either Thomas Aquinas or Descartes.

One would like to know if More realised how totally the old public relationships and conventions were going to collapse. Perhaps when he was in the Tower he may have done. But what strikes me when I look at *Utopia* is its bland assumption that the old ways were the best ways, and that where they were threatened they should be bolstered up, where lost they should somehow be recovered. This assumption is prominent in the first book; but it lies behind the second book as well. I shall try to explain what I mean at the risk of boring you with some medieval history.

III

The economic proposals of More in *Utopia* are in line with those of other writers of his own and an earlier day who deplored two things: first, the enclosure of arable land for sheep and the manufacture of woollen cloth as a main source of wealth; second, the high rate and capricious nature of royal taxation. ' The sheep are eating the men ', says More bitterly. And ' The king should live of his own ' [20].

Now More was wrong about the sheep. English wool had been famous for centuries as the raw material from which the best grade of luxury cloth was manufactured at Bruges and Ghent and in Florence. It was derived, this fine short wool, from sheep grazing not on good land but in poor parts of the country—in the moors of Yorkshire and on the borders of Wales and Scotland, on the Lincolnshire fens. The flocks were grazed in vast sheep runs controlled— owned in effect—by great lords and above all by great monasteries, Cistercians for the most part. The income to be got from taxing wool tempted English kings and led as a result to the decline in the export of the raw material and the (very slow) rise in exports in English cloth [21]. Now all of this is affected by an overall economic recession in the later Middle Ages: population fell after 1300, there was endemic famine and the undernourished Continent

(19) *Utopia*, pp, 217–37. And see HEXTER, *More's Utopia—the biography of an idea*, pp. 49, 51 where he rightly denies the possibility of inferring from this section what More's own convictions were. My point is not that More necessarily believed in toleration in 1515-6, but that he would not have written about religion as he does in *Utopia* if the book had been published in the mid–1520s when ambiguity on this issue became undesirable.

(20) *Utopia*, pp. 65–7 (sheep), 95–7 (taxation, when the phrase used is ' uiuat innocuus de suo ').

(21) EILEEN POWER, *Medieval English Wool Trade* (Oxford, 1941); E. CARUS WILSON in *Cambridge Economic History* ii (Cambridge, 1952), pp. 413–28.

fell victim to that terrible disease of the poor which at this stage became pandemic, killing the rich as well; I mean the bubonic Plague, the Black Death. From 1348 the economic recession was intensified in most parts of Europe [22]. The consequences in England were manifold. One of them was the failure of farmers to attract labourers and there is no doubt that one reason at any rate for hedging in the open fields, for enclosing land for sheep, was the inability of farmers to resume their old traditional arable farming [23]. But it is worth while pointing out that enclosure in the fifteenth and sixteenth centuries was on a modest scale; the process had begun in the twelfth and was not to reach its height until the eighteenth. It is also worth pointing out that sheep reared on lush land, formerly arable, had long coarse hair. This was quite unsuitable for fine broadcloth, which was the luxury cloth of the Middle Ages, although satisfactory for the manufacture of cheaper worsted, which became an important export of England in the sixteenth century [24]. Landlords were therefore moving from arable to sheep because they were unable sometimes to do anything else. But the shortage of labourers, and this means of dealing with the situation, nevertheless were both causing outcry: there was dearth of grain from time to time, there was (paradoxically) unemployment, the military manpower of the country was weakened—these are some of the points made in the preamble to the first general statute of 1489. More would, we may assume, have been indifferent to the needs of the army but his attitude to underpopulation and unemployment is as inconsequential as the Act: like all sensible men, he wanted it both ways [25]. And, again like a sensible man, his criticism is tinged with nostalgia, for a world that

(22) There is a rapidly developing literature on the recession of the later Middle Ages. For a recent overall view see HARRY A. MISKIMIN, *The Economy of Early Renaissance Europe 1300–1460* (Englewood Cliffs, New Jersey, 1969); a recent popular but useful book on the Plague is *The Black Death* by PHILIP ZIEGLER, London, 1969.

(23) See, for instance, M. D. BERESFORD, *The Lost Villages of England*, London 1954; and H. P. R. FINBERG, *Agrarian History of England and Wales*, IV, *1500–1640* (Cambridge 1967), where Mrs. JOAN THIRSK, editor of the vol., discusses 'Enclosing and Engrossing', pp. 200–255. Since my lecture was written I have read with interest the article ' Population Change, Enclosures and the early Tudor Economy', *Economic History Review*, ser. 2, XXII (1970), 427–445 by Dr. IAN BLANCHARD. In this he argues that the English population did not rise, and the economy remained stagnant until the 1520 s. On enclosures he points out that ' the evicting landlord, intent on converting arable to pasture, was probably as rare a phenomenon in 1520 as he had been in 1420. The land was in the lord's hands because he could find no one to take it . . . It indeed seems improbable that conversion of holdings [of arable to grazing] was in the economic interest of the lord between 1485 and 1547 . . . If the land could be let, it probably returned more to the lord from rents ' (pp. 437–8). It was only in the 1530 s that legislation tried to reduce the size of herds, and limit enclosure; only then that land hunger reached crisis (Ket's Rebellion, 1549).

(24) See P. J. BOWDEN, ' Wool supply and the woollen industry ', *Economic History Review*, ser. 2, IX (1956), 44–58, and esp. pp. 46–9.

(25) I am thinking of the way in which idle gentlemen are reproved in *Utopia* p. 63 (cfr. p. 320) for employing idle servants; this ostentation leads in turn to poverty and the servants, then dismissed, swell the numbers of unemployed.

had probably never existed. There was, incidentally, a shortage of corn in London in 1515, the year of *Utopia* [26].

Another consequence of regression and the Black Death was the virtual disappearance of the serf or—as More would have called him—the bondman. The 'commutation of labour services' is the grand way to describe this process by which the peasant farmer lost his obligations to render specified labour services to his landlord in return for paying a money rent. Like enclosures this had a very long history and was not invented in the later Middle Ages. But in the fourteenth century the demand for freedom—*legal* freedom— increased and the lords of land were in no position to resist it. They could put down the Peasants' Revolt in 1381; they could not reverse the economic pressures which compelled them—if they were to get labour—to offer tenancies for rent instead of for labour services [27]. And so by More's day there were virtually no bondmen left; practically all peasants were legally free men, to be judged only in the king's courts. I have stressed 'legally' because, as we all know, to possess legal freedom does not mean to possess economic freedom. Remember how in Utopia bondmen form an important element in society. These bondmen are either Utopians who are being punished by semi-servitude for the offences they have committed; they are 'poor labourers' imported from other countries who prefer being bondmen in Utopia to misery in their own lands; and, finally, they are criminals from other lands condemned to death there for 'heinous crimes' [28]. A jolly crew. Some of them must have resembled the negro and slavonic slaves in Renaissance Italy (save that the latter were all employed on domestic duties) [29]. I believe commentators on *Utopia* would do well to ponder the bondmen of the blessed island. Professor Hexter says they were not essential to the economy of the island since other sources existed for persons to do the dirty work [30]. Then why did More explicitly give the dirtiest of the dirty work to *serui*? They work in slaughter houses (and for Utopians butchery was a very unwholesome occupation), and they work as scullions in kitchens (not, of course, as cooks) [31]. Professor Hexter and Father Surtz usually translate *seruus* as 'slave', though the first English translator Robinson (1551) rendered it as 'bondman'. I am not sure that I do not prefer bondman; there are some passages in Utopia where it makes better sense to think of the *seruus* as a serf. For example when faced with the phrase 'ascriptios seruos' the Yale editors translate 'serf

(26) Mrs. THIRSK in *Agrarian History*, IV. 214–5.

(27) A recent and authoritative brief account with bibliography is R.H. HILTON, *The Decline of Serfdom in Medieval England*, Economic History Society' Studies in Economic History' (London, 1969).

(28) *Utopia*, p. 185.

(29) C. VANDERLINDEN, *L'esclavage dans l'Europe médiévale* i (Bruges, 1955); IRIS ORIGO, 'The domestic enemy: the Eastern slaves in Tuscany in the XIV and XV Centuries', *Speculum*, 30 (1955), 321–66.

(30) *Biography of an idea*, p. 68.

(31) *Utopia*, pp. 139, 141, 171.

attached to the soil ' [32]. Indeed here they had no alternative and they seem to me not entirely to come to grips with the problem in their commentary on More's passage ' De seruis ' [33]. More talks of different kinds of slaves (' seruorum genera ') [34] and I suspect (agreeing with the learned editors that one cannot be sure) that the fast disappearing serf, as well as the new captive caught in colonial expansion, is in More's mind: ' the hardworking and proverty stricken drudge ' from another land who, though otherwise well treated, is set to work harder because ' he is used to it ' suggests a nice patrician attitude on More's part [35]. If so we see More again looking back nostalgically at a world where the sheep were out of sight in the hills and fens, and where ' honest drudges ' tilled the fields.

With this concept of a Merry England that had never really existed went More's third specific for economic happiness: no more taxes. That the ' king should live of his own ' had been the monotonous refrain of parliaments for two generations and more [36]. And it had become clear to all sensible kings that the only way they could even pretend to do that was to keep out of war—which Henry VII did and which, in 1516, it looked as though Henry VIII would do as well [37]. But, while grumbling about taxation and complaining of royal extravagance and mismanagement, in fact men at the same time wanted the king to be prodigal and to be protective. Only if he had money could he give some of it to courtiers and dependents, and to landowners who were not enjoying as much prosperity as they wished. The direct taxes he could levy (with the consent of parliament), the famous ' tenths and fifteenths ', produced a derisory sum when compared with the taxes raised in Venice or Florence, let alone in a large monarchy like France [38]. So the king of England made the most of indirect taxes (the customs); in combination with the pope he creamed the Church (as he had always done); and in old and new ways he tried to get money from the landed rich—a process aptly named ' fiscal feudalism ' by Professor Hurstfield [39]. There was absolutely no alternative in the sixteenth century. If you were to be an effective ruler you had to be

(32) *Ib.*, p. 114 (cfr. p. 389).

(33) *Ib.*, pp. 184–6; cfr. pp. 473–7.

(34) *Ib.*, p. 184.

(35) *Loc. cit.*

(36) B. P. WOLFE in various articles and recently in the introduction to *The Crown Lands 1461–1436* (London 1970) has produced a major reinterpretation of the role of royal lands in English constitutional history; see esp. pp. 15–28. The notion that the king's principal source of revenue in normal times should be his own estates begins in the early years of Henry IV's reign but was systematically operated by Edward IV, who declared to parliament in 1467 ' I purpose to live upon mine own ' (*op. cit.*, p. 102).

(37) Cfr. HEXTER, *Biography of an Idea*, p. 154: ' Wolsey was ready to wage peace '.

(38) A ' tenth and fifteenth ' produced some £ 36,000, not a twentieth part of what Louis XI got from the *taille*.

(39) JOEL HURSTFIELD, *The Queens Wards* (London, 1958). In *Utopia*, p. 93 Henry VII's efforts to mulct the rich are criticised. More himself profited from royal grants of wardship; Hurstfield, pp. 143–4.

rich—even at the risk of being unpopular with those of your subjects who did not share in the booty.

Here again in his refusal to admit the inevitability of taxation and other revenue devices I believe More was looking back to a time when there had been a simpler economy—an economy a little more like the one in Utopia, perhaps. There the solemn Utopians labour themselves and consume their own, jointly owned, produce as and when they need it. Now it is clear that More did not think this had ever fully been the case, save (I suppose) in the prelapsarian idyll of Adam and Eve. But it is a further indication of a deep nostalgia for a world that had irrevocably passed away, if it had ever really existed at all.

Some of the moral assumptions of *Utopia* also look backwards.

It has, of course, been evident to all discriminating readers that the themes of both book I and book II turn on contempt for wealth. It is because some men are greedy and acquisitive, More says, that others of them are poor and driven to crime. This is the prelude to that violent attack (by Hythlodaeus not More, be it noted) on idle gentlemen with idle servants; on the professional soldier; and finally on the landlords who employ shepherds and not ploughmen [40]. Now all of this is familiar enough to all students of the later Middle Ages. It was the basic teaching of the mendicant Orders, based on the doctrines in the Gospels; ' Beati pauperes ' occurs twice in the New Testament [41]. It is the matter of countless sermons—' pulpit commonplaces ', as they have been called [42], with which More and his contemporaries must have been familiar from childhood, they and their forefathers before them [43]. This is, of course, not to say that More's diatribes on wealth and the attitude he displayed to riches are not expressions of deeply-felt concern. Nor does More adopt a facile or conventional position. His views on poverty assume that in *Utopia* no one starves. The Utopians make gold into chamber-pots and into chains for criminals [44]. That is, their contempt for riches is a contempt felt by rich people for their possessions. Like St. Bernardino, More's message is not that possessions in themselves are bad but only *love* of possessions [45]. It was in this way that the staggering austerity of Christ and St. Francis was made liveable with. If we recall these antecedents, is it a surprise to read in *Utopia* of *beata illa pecunia* which Robinson reads as ' that same worthye princesse Lady Money' [46]. Robinson's version

(40) *Utopia*, pp. 63–9.

(41) Mat. v. 3 (' pauperes spiritu'); Luke vi. 20.

(42) G. R. Owst, *Literature and Pulpit in Medieval England* (Cambridge, 1933), p. 289 n.

(43) *Ibid.*, pp. 287–374; *id.*, *Preaching in Medieval England* (Cambridge, 1926), pp. 88–91.

(44) *Utopia*, p. 153.

(45) Bernardino, *Opera Omnia*, 9 vols. (Quaracchi—Firenze, 1950-65), vi. 348-64 (Tractatus de octo beatitudinibus evangelicis, sermo ii).

(46) *Utopia*, p. 242; Robinson's version, Everyman ed., p. 113.

has its propriety: Lady Money is, after all, the opposite of *domina Paupertas*, Lady Poverty. Religious sentiment in England was (and is) tepid compared with the ardours and exaltations of the Mediterranean lands; and More's own devotional attitudes sound in a minor key and echo this muted music. Yet the two groups of regular clergy which still attracted some popular respect in the England of the fifteenth century were the Observant Franciscans and the Carthusians, both (in their different ways) advocating a contempt for worldly success and for worldly wealth.

The Carthusians, it will be recalled, were the monks whom More most admired, to whom he nearly united himself in life and with whom he will always be associated in death [47]. Now is not Utopia like a monastery? There is the same insistence on order and a rhythmical life. There is the same solemn dedication of oneself to the community. There is the same emphasis on labour—how the Utopians worked!—a labour, too, of love. Does not one remember the old Benedictine ideal—*Laborare est orare*? Of course this is a 'mixed' monastery. It is peopled by families. This had been More's own personal crisis—to become a monk or a father, and Utopia would have suited his private problems excellently: he could have been both a monk and a married man.

Behind avariciousness in More's hierarchy of the sins lay pride. This was at the root of the obtuseness of the great and of their lust for honour and outward display. Here again, I need hardly say, we have a doctrine, founded on both Old and New Testaments, which had been enormously developed by the moral theology of a thousand years. Pride is the first of the seven deadly sins and it is contrasted with humility in countless homilies [48]. When Hythlodaeus concludes his account of the Utopians it is to point out how they have by their wise constitutional arrangements achieved what Christian doctrine demanded: the shackling of property and thus the control of pride, 'the chief and progenitor of all plagues' [49]. This attack on pride is, as I indicated, completely traditional. But seldom has the old sermon been preached with such vehemence, a vehemence which would have had to be damped down (we may suspect) after 1520. Nor should we forget that this sharp reiteration of an old theme was this time couched in stylish Latin addressed to those humanists, alas not entirely themselves devoid of *superbia*, who, as counsellors, secretaries and ambassadors, managed the affairs of nations: men like Busleyden and Gilles. Much of *Utopia* reads as though it was one of the Contemporary Venetian *relazioni* which offered such crystal-clear comments on society. But Venetian ambassadors described countries and identified centres of power. They did not indict sins, pillory the rich or write in good Latin.

(47) CHAMBERS pp. 77-8, 320-6. For More's attraction to the Franciscans of the Strict Observance cf. CHAMBERS, p. 77.
(48) E. g. BERNARDINO'S, *Opera Omnia*, vi. 208, vii. 577-18; OWST, *Literature and Pulpit*, pp. 293, 440-1 etc.
(49) *Utopia*, pp, 242–4.

After what I have said you may feel that the Latin in which More wrote was the only humanist aspect of his work. This is not true. I have mentioned his optimism in feeling that men could be influenced for good by rational arguments. I have mentioned his advocacy of tolerance in matters of religion. Much could be said about this aspect of Utopian religion, with its enjoyment of the satisfactions of ritual combined with a realization that they are of indifferent significance—a sort of adiaphorism, as it was to be called in the debates between Protestants and Catholics. All of this is the more impressive because More had no doubt about man's sinful nature.

Above all, I believe we can see More's humanist inclinations in the high place he accords to education in his ideal commonwealth. Indeed his whole approach to the description of the Island is didactic. Hythlodaeus's relation has no meretricious attractions (*omissa interim inquisitione monstrorum*) [50]. The whole aim of the Utopian is moral and intellectual improvement. Their constitution aimed principally to one end:

> ut quoad per publicas necessitates licet, quam plurimum temporis ab servitio corporis ad animi libertatem cultumque civibus universis asseratur. In eo enim sitam uitae felicitatem putant [51].

'The freedom and culture of the mind' as the *summum bonum* of, need it be said, only of those Utopians worthy of the fullest development, not of the slaves or bondmen, not of those whose wits turned to more practical employment. Thus limited to the people who mattered, self-improvement in knowledge and wisdom is the highest Utopian activity. Such a view expresses the essence of Renaissance educational theory as preached and practiced by the great teachers from Guarino da Verona to Roger Ascham. And in some ways it remains the greatest contribution of the Renaissance to the world.

So More's Utopians eat their communal meals like monks or like school boys, presided over by the Syphogrant and his wife, while improving passages are read aloud. One is back in a monastery again. Utopians assemble at dawn to hear daily lectures before they go to work. One might be in the great piazza at Siena when it was filled in the early hours by the crowds who hung on St. Bernardino's words. As I have said, the Utopians who go to lectures are already selected. There are bondmen already at work when the masters indulge their intellectual appetites. In *Utopia* More was, unlike Bernardino, not speaking to all men but only to some men, those educated in the humanities. More, redolent as he is of the religious attitudes of the later Middle Ages as well as of the educational

---

(50) *Utopia*, p. 52; cfr. ROBINSON: 'monsters be no news'.
(51) *Utopia*, p, 134. Cfr. p. 414, where *in eo* is appositely glossed.

principles of the humanities, had, perhaps for those very reasons, a hankering for an aristocratic world and an aristocracy of the intellect.

IV

May I summarise in conclusion? In his social and economic thought (as we have it in *Utopia*) I regard More as old fashioned and somewhat unpractical, though much of his approach derives ultimately from bedrock Christian doctrine. In his explicitly moral and educational views he is much nearer to the heart of Renaissance theory and looks forward to assumptions which grammar schools, academies, gymnasia were to take for granted for centuries. That is to say More, like a good humanist, accepted the following propositions: Latin (plus a smear of Greek) makes men better able to take a full part in the running of their communities. Some men, but not all. For More, as for his contemporaries, political egalitarianism was frightening, democracy was still a dirty word.

I entitled these reflections ' Utopia—Literature or Politics? '? The most novel aspect of the book is that More would have regarded the antithesis as absurd. For a humanist, literature and politics, learning and action were not opposed, but complementary. ' There is ', wrote R. J. Schoeck, ' no conflict between the *jeu d'esprit* and the sense of urgency, provided that we do not exaggerate either or insist on the one to the exclusion of the other ' (52). *Utopia* was indeed a tract for the times, the ' times ' being the years before Christendom was driven into disarray by the Reformation. The continuing attraction of *Utopia* lies in its extraordinary combination of ' *Angst* ' and ' *festivitas* ' (53), of idealism and shrewdness, of Platonism and good, old-fashioned Christianity, of the new and the old. This Janus-book deserves all the questions we can put to it.

---

(52) R.J. SCHOECK, ' " A nursery of correct and useful institutions ": On reading More's Utopia as a dialogue ', *Moreana*, 22 (1969), 19-32, at p. 27. After this lecture was printed *Moreana* 31–32 (1971) was published as a ' Festschrift on More's *Utopia* in honour of Edward Surtz S. J. '.

(53) *Ibid.*, p. 19.

12

THE DIVISION OF THE SPOILS OF WAR
IN FOURTEENTH-CENTURY ENGLAND

THE desire for booty was a motive in all medieval warfare. The preoccupation of the soldier with spoils, with prisoners, horses, equipment and movable wealth in general, is, however, less evident in the surviving sources of early medieval history than in the records of the fourteenth and fifteenth centuries. Even a cursory knowledge of the period of Anglo-French hostilities between 1337 and 1453 leaves one under no illusions as to the overriding importance to the combatants of the winnings of war. Spoils mattered equally to the rank and file soldier, to the magnate and to the crown. The depredations of the *chevauchée* in Languedoc in 1355 benefited everyone in the Black Prince's army. 'Chevaliers, escuiers, brigants, garchons' were loaded with 'leurs prisonniers et leurs richesses'.[1] Froissart makes Gloucester in 1390 object to a peace with France because of the ensuing discouragement of the 'poor knights and squires and archers of England whose comforts and station in society depend upon war'.[2] And he tells us also how the Sire d'Albret looked back over his military career and regretted the peace which alliance with France had given him. 'I'm well enough,' he told an enquirer, 'but I had more money, and so did my retinue, when I fought for the king of England.' An army on the move, he explained, often gave the chance of capturing a rich merchant; hardly a day passed without its prize; thus one could afford the 'superfluitez et jolitez. . . . Maintenant nous est mort.'[3] The

[1] Jean le Bel, *Chronique*, ed. J. Viard and E. Déprez (Société de l'histoire de France, 1904–5), ii. 222.

[2] 'Aussi s'enclinoient à la guerre povres chevalliers et escuiers et archers d'Angleterre, qui avoient aprins les oiseuses [*var.* aises] et soustenoient leur estat sur la guerre', *Œuvres*, ed. Kervyn de Lettenhove (Brussels, 1867–79), xiv. 314.

[3] Froissart, ed. S. Luce and others (Soc. d'hist. de France, Paris, 1869 ff.), xii. 205; cf. Robert Boutruche, *La Crise d'une Société* (Paris, 1947), p. 348. Further references to Froissart are to the Paris edition unless the contrary is stated.

progress in acquisitiveness can be measured in terms of ransoms, which steadily mounted as the war with France went on. By the end of the reign of Edward III the convention that a gentleman would not unduly embarrass his captive[1] was somewhat strained: the ransom of 200,000 nobles asked of Charles of Blois thirty years before then seemed modest enough.[2] Contemporaries accepted without repugnance the most brutal consequences of this warfare for gain: the losing party could console itself on saving the wages—always in arrears—of its captured or slaughtered troops[3]; a bloody battle, it was argued, at any rate left more in the way of pickings to the survivors.[4] The slaughter was, of course, usually restricted to the common soldier. The gentlemen participating were too valuable to be killed, and in fourteenth-century campaigns in the West we normally find the destruction of considerable numbers of potential prisoners only in conditions of civil war, as in Brittany and Castile.[5] Even then one can apprehend the lively sense of wasted opportunity. When the English side at Aljubarotta (1385) had to kill their prisoners, Froissart notes not only that this was pitiful (*pitié*) but also that it was a disaster (*mesaventure*), 'because that day they killed good prisoners from whom they could have had 400,000 francs'.[6]

For no one were the profits of war more valuable than for

[1] Cf. the 'finanche raisonnable, enssi que on doit mettre ung gentil homme sans lui trop presser' (Froissart, ii. 345).

[2] 'Qui estoit moult grande a payer (mais non seroit à présent pour ung duc de Bretaigne, car les seigneurs se fourment maintenant sur autre condition et manière que ils ne faisoient pour lors, et treuvent plus tost une finance [*var.* chevance] que ne firent jamais leurs prédécesseurs ou temps passé, mais du temps passé ils ne usoient fors de leurs rentes et revenues, et à present la Duchié de Bretaigne sur ung an ou sur deux, pour aidier à leur seigneur, très bien se tailleroient à deux cens mille nobles)' (Froissart, ed. Kervyn, xii. 55). In fact, Charles of Blois did call on his subjects: S. Luce, *Bertrand du Guesclin* (Paris, 1876), p. 226; cf. Jean le Bel, ii. 243; Robert of Avesbury, *De gestis mirabilibus regis Edwardi III* (Rolls Series), pp. 418–20; Rymer, *Foedera*, iii (1). 336.

[3] Concerning French losses at Sluys: 'Li rois de France a à lor mort gaegniet deux cens mille florins. On lor devoit lors gages de quatre mois, et si en est la mer delivrée' (Froissart, ii. 226).

[4] So Cuvelier makes Bertrand du Guesclin talk of the war of Breton succession (Luce, *op. cit.*, p. 208).

[5] Cf. Luce, *op. cit.*, p. 51 (Roche-Derrein, 1347); Froissart, vi. 168 (Auvray, 1364).

[6] Froissart, xii. 162–3.

Edward III, who had the good fortune to take prisoner a king of Scotland and a king of France, besides many other magnates only slightly less illustrious and remunerative. Doubtless the sums actually paid by the Scots and the French after Neville's Cross and Poitiers were considerably smaller than the amounts agreed on in the instruments of ransom, and doubtless much of the money was already spent before it arrived.[1] Nevertheless it has been reckoned by Professor Perroy[2] that between 1360 and 1370 Edward III received the enormous sum of about £268,000 from three major ransoms. Much of royal income from war was directly or indirectly devoted to war[3]: it soon became a criticism of the crown that war did not pay for itself as it seemed that it should be easy for it to do.[4] For the crown obtained ransoms and spoils not only from princes and a couple of great battles, but from a continuous series of smaller men and on less dramatic occasions. It is the purpose of this paper to examine how, within the framework of the general desire for spoils, the profits of war were distributed between the crown and its soldiers.

Given the naked greed of many of the troops, if not of all of them, one might assume that victory in any military engagement would at once result in the victors fighting each other for the rewards of their success, unless appetite was restrained by an accepted convention. And in fact a few instances of such sordid disputes come before us. Once, we read, the commander of a French fortress surrendered to the attacking English; but the latter disputed over the ransom and murdered the enemy captain in the ensuing brawl.[5] Such cases must have occurred from time to time, but it is significant that they are not often recorded. For we must not regard as coming within this category the more frequent occasions when a prosperous or famous prisoner was claimed by rival captors. Of such cases the most celebrated is

[1] The assignments on these ransoms make it difficult to compute with certainty what was in fact paid. See D. M. Broome, 'The Ransom of John II' (*Camden Miscellany*, xiv. 1926).

[2] E. Perroy, 'L'affaire du comte de Denia', *Mélanges Halphen* (Paris, 1951), pp. 573–80.

[3] '...et envoyèrent tout leur butin et grand foison de prissoniers en Angleterre, dont grand trésor issi, dont le roy Edowart paya largement ses souldoiers', Jean le Bel, ii. 74 (1346).

[4] *Rot. Parl.*, ii. 323a, iii. 57b, 74a.

[5] Thomas Gray, *Scalacronica*, ed. H. Maxwell (Glasgow, 1907), pp. 140–1.

King John II of France, the most romantic that of John Jewel and the most interesting that of Olivier du Guesclin.[1] These are examples not of rapacity as such, but of rapacity working through well-organized legal channels, where titles to property depended on interpretation of the law of arms. Evidently the desire to take prisoners rather than fight was something of a problem for army commanders, and a proclamation was made by the Black Prince immediately prior to Poitiers that no man should linger over his prisoner on pain of forfeiting him, a rule repeated on later occasions.[2] But even legal disputes over prisoners seem to be rare enough, and on most occasions when men were made prisoners and booty was taken, we must assume that the spoils were divided fairly peaceably according to well-understood rules. What do we know of these rules?

The only statement I know of by a competent authority is by Professor A. E. Prince in his most useful survey of 'The indenture system under Edward III'.[3]

> All the 'advantages of war' were usually granted by the king to the other indenting party. To this rule there were two main exceptions, for the king reserved for himself the most important castles and lands, and, secondly, the most influential prisoners of war ... [for whom] the king promised, however, to pay the actual captors 'a reasonable reward' ... In subcontracts, both parties seem to have shared in the spoils of capture. Ralph Stafford and Hugh FitzSimon in 1347 agreed to divide equally the proceeds, but the more normal practice was for the superior contracting party to take a third only.[4]

Mr. Prince's remarks on the crown's right to the main enemy

---

[1] For the dispute about John II, see Froissart, v. 55, 57 (and ed. Kervyn, xviii. 394–6); Rymer, iii (1), 385, 467, 706; *Cal. Pat. Rolls 1358–61*, p. 320. Jewel was taken at Cocherel, 16 May 1364, wearing a helmet engraved 'Qui Jehan prendra, cent mille frans aura', and died soon after his capture, but not before there was a dispute (Froissart, vi. 129–30, 310; Luce, *Bertrand du Guesclin*, p. 445). O. du Guesclin was taken during the second half of 1378 and his ownership was disputed by Charles of Navarre and Sir John d'Arundel, while further litigation arose between Arundel's heirs and other interested parties (Froissart, ix. 98 and introd., p. lvi, n. 1; Rymer, iv. 72; *Calendar of London Plea and Mem. Rolls, 1364–81*, pp. 297–300; *1381–1412*, pp. 8–9).   [2] *Black Prince's Register*, iv. 338; below, p 271.
[3] *Historical Essays in Honour of James Tait*, ed. J. G. Edwards and others (Manchester, 1933), pp. 283–97.   [4] *Op. cit.*, p. 295.

prisoners seem to me to be completely correct and in this matter we need only enquire into the antiquity of the right, a subject I shall mention shortly. But on spoils apart from ransoms, and the ransoms of the lesser enemy captives, his observations seem to me less self-evident. His authorities for the subcontractual arrangements are a contract of 1347 in which the winnings are equally divided,[1] and an indenture of 1372, between John of Gaunt and Sir Richard Whitefield,[2] which, as we shall see in a moment,[3] is one of the first surviving instruments in which the claim to a third of the booty is specifically mentioned. Is it therefore the case that 'the superior normally took a third only' in the central period of Edward III's reign? And what of the crown's position? For in the indenture armies of Edward's foreign wars the crown was ultimately the 'superior contracting party' of practically all the soldiers under its control. Mr. Prince, we may note, makes no reference to the sharing of spoils in his later essay on the army and navy in the first decade of Edward III's reign, which perhaps indicates that he then felt less sure of the matter than in his earlier essay[4]; though prior to 1337 the indentured retinue was presumably a minor element in the English army. In view of the volume and value of the winnings of war it seems sensible to sift what evidence there is for the sharing of those 'advantages of war' which we regularly encounter in the commissions and contracts of the first half of the Hundred Years War.[5]

It will be safest to begin with a firm point, although it lies beyond Edward III's reign. In 1385 were issued the first of the general 'Ordinances of War', which regulated discipline in the royal army. Issued for the forces advancing against Scotland,

[1] G. Wrottesley, *Crécy and Calais* (1898), p. 192.

[2] *John of Gaunt's Register*, ed. S. Armitage-Smith, i (Camden Third Series, xx. 1911), 293.

[3] Below, p. 272.

[4] 'The army and navy', in J. F. Willard and W. A. Morris, *The English Government at work 1327–1336*, i (1940), 332–93.

[5] 'Qil puisse avoir toutes autres avauntages de guerre', Commission of Henry of Lancaster as Lieutenant in Gascony, 13 March 1345, Pub. Rec. Off. K.R. Mem. Roll E 159/123, m. 254. I have to thank Mr. Pierre Chaplais for drawing my attention to this. Cf. *Black Prince's Register*, iv. 143–5 (10 July 1355); 'Et avera le dit M. Henri [de Scrop] les gains de guerre... comme autres capitains ant euz, par vertue de leur commissions ou endentures, en temps passez'; John duke of Lancaster appointing a captain of the town and castle of Calais, 1369 (Rymer, iii (2). 881–2).

the 'Ordinances of Durham', as we may call them, have survived in a considerable number of manuscripts.[1] The sixteenth clause runs as follows:

> Item, qe chescun paie le tierce a son seignur ou mestre, de toute manere de gaigne darmes, et ce auxi bien ceux qe ne sont point a soulde, mes tant soulement herbergent desouz banere ou pennon daucun capitaigne.[2]

Here we have the arithmetic authoritatively set down. Each man will pay one third of his winnings of war to his lord or master. The retained soldier thus pays a third to his captain, and the captain pays a third of this, together with a third of his own winnings, to the crown. The crown is thus entitled to the 'thirds and thirds of thirds' of all the spoils of war. While we have no earlier statement of similar general bearing, there are several grounds for regarding the Durham Ordinances as a statement of existing practice rather than an innovation.

To start with, the document as a whole undoubtedly represents the military practice, in discipline and control, which was observed in the English armies of Edward III's reign. It would take too long to establish this in detail, but we may note that the arrangements laid down for taking the surrender of a defeated opponent (clause 22) have many parallels in the narratives of actual fighting half a century earlier.[3] The arrangements for pre-

[1] 'Ceux sont les estatutz, ordenances, et coustumes a tenir en lost... a Duresme, le xvij jour du Moys de Juyl, lan du regne nostre seignur le Roy Richard second noefisme', printed accurately by Travers Twist, *Black Book of the Admiralty* (Rolls Series), i. 453–8, from Brit. Mus. Cotton MS. Nero D. vi, fos. 89v–90. Other early MSS. in the British Museum are Add. 32097, fos. 42–4, Domitian A. xviii, fos. 30v–32 (dates 27 July). Another French version in Stowe 140, fos. 148–50, and English versions in Harley 369, Harley 1309, Egerton 2342, Add. 6297. There are late copies in the Bodleian, MSS. Rawlinson B. 131, B. 491, Ashmole 856, 863. There is a copy in the College of Arms (according to F. Grose, *Military Antiquities*, ii (1788), 60), and doubtless there are others. The date of 27 July looks more plausible than the generally accepted 17 July: *Cal. Pat. Rolls 1385–9*, pp. 7, 10; *Cal. Close Rolls, 1385–9*, p. 83.

[2] The thirds are also mentioned in clause 19, where penalties are laid down for not taking prisoners promptly to king, constable and marshal and for failing to guard prisoners properly. The *Black Book* makes two words of *hostyant*, in error.

[3] E.g. Froissart *passim*, and the count of Dammartin's narrative of his surrender at Poitiers in *Black Prince's Register*, iv. 339.

venting interruption of the action through anxiety to control prisoners are essentially the same as those laid down by the Black Prince in 1356.[1] Moreover, the clause itself laying down the payment of thirds is curiously matter-of-fact and seems more concerned to point out the duties of the non-retained men than those of the soldiers in the indentured retinues: all must pay thirds, it says in effect, not only the men with formal contracts. If there was doubt at all, in other words, there was doubt only about the winnings of those in the field who were not bound by the strict relationship of the indenture army. That Richard II could have invented a claim to so large a share as a third without arousing protest is on the face of it highly improbable. His magnates were to be all too anxious to find sticks to beat him with, and this seizure of a third of their profits would have been a spectacular grievance which would not have escaped both the chroniclers and the Rolls of Parliament. Nor would such an innovation have remained unmodified by the Lancastrian, Yorkist and Tudor successors of Richard, who duly repeated his claim 'that everyman pay his thirdes to his capitayne, lorde, or master, of all maner wynyng by wares',[2] and some of whom, notably Henry V, sedulously sought to collect the thirds from their troops.[3]

An even more telling argument against the sudden imposition by king and council of a division of the spoil by three in 1385 is

---

[1] Above, p. 268.

[2] 'Statutes and Ordenances made by . . . Henry the Fifft at . . . Maunt', Nicholas Harris Nicolas, *History of the Battle of Agincourt* (2nd ed. 1832), appendix, pp. 31–40, from a MS. in the College of Heralds; a Latin paraphrase will be found in Nicholas Upton, *De studio militari*, ed. E. Bysshe (London, 1654), pp. 133–45, and other English versions in *Black Book of the Admiralty*, i. 282–95, 459–72. In general see *Short Title Catalogue*, nos. 9332–9336; Grose, *Military Antiquities*, ii. 66–106; C. G. Cruickshank, *Elizabeth's Army* (Oxford, 1946), pp. 112, 149–50.

[3] Prohibition of unauthorized ransoms, 20 May 1416, *Cal. Close Rolls Henry V*, i. 355; cf. R. A. Newhall, *English Conquest of Normandy* (New Haven, 1924), pp. 285–6. For instances of the thirds and thirds of thirds being collected see Newhall, *op. cit.*, pp. 156–7, and also Pub. Rec. Office E. 101/46/4 (bond to pay a third to the crown, 3 Henry V), E. 101/48/2 (file of 47 bonds, 3 and 4 Henry V), E. 101/53/7 (receipt for 96 bonds to Henry V, 19 October 13 Henry VI); cf. *Rot. Parl.* iv. 178a, petition (1422) for a settlement between crown and the lords and captains of the late Henry V, taking account of the 'tierces et tierce de tierce de tout manere de gaignes, gaigneez par voie de guerre'.

the existence of such a fraction in documents of the preceding decade. Early indentures of retinue very seldom make mention of any proportion of spoils,[1] but I have found several which do so after 1370. Of these one is the document referred to by Mr. Prince.[2] It states that 'en droit des prisoners et autres profitz de guerre prises ou gaynez par le dit Richard [Whytefeld] ou nulle de ses gentz l'avant dit Duc [de Lancastre] avera la tierce partie'. This indenture was drawn up on 3 January 1372. Other indentures in similar terms are found in the duke's *Register* for 1374[3]; others hardly less significantly say that in respect of prisoners the duke will treat his retainer 'comme il ferra as autres de sa condicion',[4] a pretty clear indication that in the ducal household there was an accepted convention in this matter. Next we have a series of indentures between Sir Thomas Felton and a number of captains, in which Felton, acting as a royal lieutenant, reserves to the crown the thirds and thirds of thirds. These documents[5] are dated in 1381. Finally we have in April 1386 a royal indenture in which a captain is exempted from paying the magical third.[6] But this was after the Ordinance of 1385, and from then

---

[1] References to most printed indentures will be found in N. B. Lewis, 'The organization of indentured retinues in fourteenth-century England', *Trans. Roy. Hist. Soc.*, 4th ser., xxvii (1945); K. B. McFarlane, 'Bastard Feudalism', *Bulletin of the Inst. of Hist. Research*, xx (1943–5); and in Mr. Prince's articles quoted above, pp. 268-9. The biggest MS. collection of them is at the Public Record Office, in the Exchequer series 101/68, use of which is made below.

[2] See above, p.269 and n. 2. For an example from 1370 see below, p.273, n. 2.

[3] *John of Gaunt's Register*, ii. 5–6.

[4] *Ibid.*, i. 294–5, ii. 4; *John of Gaunt's Register 1379–1383*, ed. Eleanor C. Lodge and R. Somerville, i (Camden Third Series, lvi. 1937), 16–26; cf. a similar indenture between the Earl of Warwick and John Russell, 29 March 1383, Thomas Blount, *Nomo-Lexicon* (London, 1670), sig L [2v] *s.v.* 'Bouche of Court'. Much the same language ('come il ferra as autres banretz deson estat et solonc le manere de pais') is found in the enrolled copy of the contract of 1370 between Lancaster and Nevill (which Mr. H. C. Johnson kindly consulted for me) summarized in *Cal. Pat. Rolls 1370–74*, p. 46. Mr. K. B. McFarlane directed my attention to this document; I owe him further thanks for discussing with me some of the general problems examined in this paper.

[5] P.R.O., E 101/68/8–9. The phrase is 'la tierce partz de touz les prouffis gaignez par la personne du dit [captain's name] et la tierce part du tiers du prouffit de sa retenue'.

[6] P.R.O., E 101/68/10, between the king and Sir Thomas Abberbury.

onwards thirds and the thirds of thirds figure regularly in in-dentures.[1]

It is thus pretty clear that in the 1370's the practice in the Lan-castrian household and in the royal household was the same, viz. to demand for the superior a third part of the winnings of war of soldiers serving under contract. While at an earlier date it is more than likely that the methods of dividing the spoil varied from magnate to magnate, the recruitment of the indenture army of the French wars may well have led to the widespread, if not to the exclusive, adoption of the royal third, for the indenture army meant that, through contracts and sub-contracts, a high propor-tion of troops were in a sense in the royal household or working to its rules and conventions. The obligation which lay on royal captains to pay a third of their winnings logically involved the crown in a claim to a third of the third[2] the captains themselves gained from their companies. The ordinance of 1385 is accord-ingly not an innovation when compared with actual practice to-wards the end of Edward III's reign. We are left none the less with the question of how the division was made during the earlier decades of Edward III's reign, and the evidence for this must now be examined.

There was, as already stated, no doubt of the crown's right to dispose of all prisoners. This was, in fact, a very ancient right,[3] but it is sufficient here to note that it was the understanding lying behind the money feofs created in the Low Countries for military purposes by Edward III in the late 1330's. From our point of view the general characteristic of many of these instruments, so feudal in language and so unfeudal in spirit, is that the king of England promises to indemnify the vassal in the event of losses and claims all the prisoners taken by him in the event of gains.[4] The most

---

[1] N. H. Nicolas, *Agincourt*, app., pp. 8–10; Rymer, ix. 230–2, x. 392–4; S. Lysons in *Archaeologia*, xvii (1814), 214–16; A. Abram, *Social England in the Fifteenth Century* (1909), pp. 227–8; cf. the royal pardon in John Whetamstede, *Registrum* (Rolls Series), i. 89.

[2] The first 'thirds of thirds' I have found explicitly referred to occurs in 1370; J. Bain, *Calendar of docs. relating to Scotland*, iv. 178.

[3] See the references in Alwyn Schultz, *Das höfische Leben zur Zeit der Minnisinger* (2nd ed. Leipzig, 1889), ii. 298–305; L. Gautier, *La chevallerie* (3rd ed. Paris, 1895), pp. 699–700; P. Meyer's note to *Guillaume le Maréchal* iii (Paris, 1901), 39; refs. quoted by F. M. Powicke, *Loss of Normandy*, cited below, p. 282.   [4] Rymer, ii (2). 970, 984, 992.

interesting of them relates to Henry of Flanders, count of Lodi.[1] In it Henry agrees to hand over all prisoners to the king's marshal, 'as other lords do' (*en manere que autres seignurs ferront*), that the king may have his will of them.[2] That 'other lords' were expected or required to do so may, indeed, be implicit in the omission of such stipulations in other similar contracts[3] as well as in more positive statements which show that the king or his representative had a right to prisoners.[4] It was this right which enabled the king to prohibit the release of prisoners[5]; it was this right which was frequently conveyed to royal lieutenants, usually with the reservation to the crown of prisoners of the highest rank and over a certain value, generally £500.[6] But the exercise of the royal monopoly was tempered by the distribution to the actual captor of some of his gains. The best known of such gifts were the 'rewards' for the capture of David II of Scotland and John II of France. But the practice was general and was reinforced by older traditions of largesse.[7] It was, perhaps, positively incumbent on the king. At any rate in 1340 Edward III stated that one of his commanders should be compensated for prisoners taken over by the king or released by royal order, because this was only reasonable,[8] and this notion of reasonable compensation for the prisoners

[1] Cf. *Cal. Pat. Rolls 1338–40*, p. 370; H. S. Lucas, *The Low Countries and the Hundred Years War* (Ann Arbor, 1929), p. 330.

[2] P.R.O., E 101/68/3, 26 February 1339.

[3] E.g. Guy count of Namur (1335) (Rymer, ii (2). 921).

[4] Bartholomew Burghersh to Stratford, July 1346: 'et le chambelen de Tankerville fust pris dun bacheler monseignur le prince, si qil est le prison moun seignur', Adam Murimuth, *Continuatio Chronicorum* (Rolls Series), p. 203.

[5] Murimuth, *loc. cit.*; Rymer, iii (1). 98; Henry Knighton, *Chronicon* (Rolls Series), ii. 44; *Cal. Pat. Rolls Ed. III 1348–50*, pp. 60–1, 312.

[6] P.R.O., E 101/68/4 (1355): Northampton as 'chevetein et gardein' of Brittany (cf. Rymer iii (1). 37, a similar commission of 1345). The Black Prince as lieutenant in Gascony (1355) was to have all prisoners, except the chief of the enemy (*Black Prince's Register*, iv. 143–5). Cf. A. E. Prince, 'Strength of English armies in the reign of Edward III', *Eng. Hist. Review*, xlvi (1931), 370–1.

[7] Cf. McFarlane, 'Bastard Feudalism', pp. 177–8.

[8] 'Et quia est consonum rationi quod praedicto Waltero [de Manny], ... satisfactionem competentem a nobis habeat pro prisonibus supradictis', Rymer, ii (2). 1123; *Cal. Pat. Rolls, 1338–40*, p. 479. Cf. Rymer, ii. 304 (*Cal. Pat. Rolls, 1313–17*, p. 602), licence to David earl of Atholl to plunder the Scots, 1316: he is to hand over any prisoners whom the king wishes to have, in return for 100 marks.

claimed by the crown is a regular feature of later commissions. The frequent exercise of this royal right to have prisoners against 'reasonable compensation' makes it hard to distinguish the king's privilege from mere participation by the crown in the well-known traffic which took place in enemy captives. If Edward III often gave 'rewards' for the 'free surrender' of prisoners taken in war, he or his clerks often refer to his purchase of prisoners, more particularly in the later part of the reign.[1]

The notion that the crown must share the profits is also clearly revealed in the practice of naval warfare at this time. The king had a right to all prisoners taken at sea if he chose to exercise it, but habitually he conceded a proportion of the spoils, usually half, to the crew of the victorious ship. When the ship was not a royal vessel the king only got a quarter, the other quarter going to the owner.[2] The admiral's share in prizes crystallized as a tenth[3] and the whole matter remained very lively for centuries to come.[4] One's impression of the proportions used in the distribution of the winnings of war at sea is that there was some slight variation, the crown occasionally being prepared to increase the proportion as an incentive, particularly to the early type of privateer; and this certainly happened later.[5]

If we may thus assume with some confidence that the crown had the right to prisoners whom it thought it desirable to take over on economic or political grounds, and the right to a definite share in booty and prisoners taken at sea, we are still left with

---

[1] Cf. *Cal. Pat. Rolls Ed. III*, *1345–8*, pp. 225 (William Douglas), 285 (W. de Haliburton), 337, 538, 550 (count of Eu); *1358–61*, pp. 63 (royal purchase of a share in a French prisoner), 300 (purchase of Black Prince's prisoners).

[2] *Black Book of the Admiralty* (Rolls Series), i. 20–2, 30, 145–7, 223; R. G. Marsden, *Law and Custom of the Sea* (Navy Record Society), i. 1–2, 66–74, 169n. In E 101/68/7 there is a damaged indenture in which the crown reserves a quarter of spoils taken at sea, 10 April 1 Richard II; cf. Rymer, iii (2). 970, indenture of 1373 with two Genoese captains for service at sea, the crown reserving a half of the spoils.

[3] *Black Book*, i. 150, 247, 399; Marsden, 'Early prize jurisdiction', *Eng. Hist. Review*, xxiv (1909), 675–97, esp. pp. 675–6; G. Schwarzenberger, 'International law in early English practice', *Brit. Year Book of International Law*, xxv (1948), 81–2.

[4] See Richard Pares, *Colonial Blockade and Neutral Rights*, *1739–63* (Oxford, 1938), pp. 5–20, and the literature there quoted.

[5] Pares, *op. cit.*, p. 6.

the question of the division of the spoil, including those prisoners not taken over by the crown, prior to the period, roughly after 1370, when the third seems to have been generally accepted. We may survey the evidence chronologically.

Early indentures of retinue, as already stated, do not contain references to prisoners and spoils being shared.[1] A knowledge of the principles upon which the division was made was assumed by the contracting parties. But as the war in France gathered momentum we find the matter more or less fully dealt with in a special clause. The earliest precise information which I have come upon is the indenture, quoted by Mr. Prince, and drawn up on 16 March 1347, in which Ralph, Lord Stafford, retains Hugh Fitz Symond, reserving to himself 'la moytie des proffitz' of any ransoms of captives.[2] Next we have an indenture of 1 May 1347 recorded in the *Black Prince's Register*; in it the Prince retains Sir Thomas Furnival and ten men-at-arms. The important feature of the document is that it is laid down that if Furnival takes a prisoner, the ransom shall be halved with the prince. There is another indenture in identical terms and of the same date for Sir John Willoughby.[3] In 1348 occurs a sinister contract between Edward III and Raoul de Caours, to which Luce drew attention in his unfinished life of Bertrand du Guesclin. In this the mercenary is granted £1,000 worth of lands in Poitou to be conquered by him and all the advantages of war, Edward reserving to himself a half of ransoms and the right to determine whether or not prisoners of rank should be released.[4] On 5 March 1350 Sir Gerard de Lisle contracted to serve the earl of Arundel on the basis of an equal share in captured prisoners.[5] From these examples one might be inclined to infer that the normal procedure in the 1340's, at any rate in continental campaigns, was for the spoils to be divided by half. Such a judgment is, I suggest, premature and may well be upset as fresh evidence turns up. A more likely explanation is that we are here dealing with arrangements for sharing the profits of war which depend on a wide variety of

[1] Above, p. 272.
[2] G. Wrottesley, *Crécy and Calais* (cited above, p. 269, n. 1).
[3] *Register*, i. 128–9.
[4] 4 July 1348, Rymer, iii. 164, 168; Luce, pp. 89–90.
[5] Berkeley Castle, Select Charters. I owe this information to Dr. N. B. Lewis.

considerations: there is the possibility that on land, as later at sea, the crown and its servants needed to increase rewards in order to enlist support; there is a positive likelihood that traditions in this respect varied from the household of one magnate to another. This last point is important and can be amplified, for as we shall see, the Black Prince continued to demand a moiety when there was in other households, and notably in the royal household, a demand for a third only.

The evidence for the 1350's and 1360's is fortunately fairly plentiful. An entry in the Patent Roll for 10 December 1351 orders the arrest of John de Staunton and others, lately staying in Brittany at the king's wages, who have taken prisoners divers of the king's enemies. Walter Bentley, keeper of the land of Brittany, ought to have a part of these ransoms; but, after receiving such ransoms as well as their wages from the king, the men have left Brittany without royal permission and without satisfying Bentley of what pertains to him in respect of the prisoners.[1] By itself this tells us only that Bentley as royal captain, and possibly also the crown, had a claim to part of these ransoms. Light is, however, thrown on the matter by the survival of a series of questions put to the king and council by Bentley in the following year, together with the answers given him.[2] The English captain asked for authority to place all soldiers under royal command, 'and those who do not wish to be paid (*engagés*) should hand over the thirds of their prisoners (*les tersages des prisoniers*)'. This was approved by the crown: 'le roi voet que de ceux qui ne voillent demorer à ses gages en Bretayn, que le capitayn illoeque eit le tiersage de lour gain et de lour prisoniers'; and Edward also ruled that the captain in Brittany should be informed by all troops of the capture of any duke, count or other great lord so that if the ransom exceeded 4,000 crowns the prisoner might be handed over to the captain in Brittany for the king (*au noun du roi*) against reasonable compensation (*le roi en fera convenable grée*). Taken together the commission of 1351 and the council's rulings of 1352 leave us in no doubt that soldiers in royal employment in Brittany, those directly or indirectly

[1] *Cal. Pat. Rolls, Ed. III, 1350–54*, p. 205.

[2] Printed from Bréquigny's collections (who, so I am told by Professor Le Patourel, got it from the French Roll), by Kervyn de Lettenhove in the supplementary volume of his edition of Froissart, xviii. 339–43.

contracted to the crown, were required to hand over one third of their winnings of war. Indeed the terms of the Durham Ordinance of 1385 are practically anticipated, for as then, so thirty-odd years earlier the crown is at pains to stress that all, not only contracted soldiers, are liable to surrender a third.

At some point between 1356 and 1359 another royal officer on the continent sought advice from the government in England. This was Philip of Navarre, Edward's lieutenant in Normandy, and the royal replies to his enquiries are similar in form to those given to Bentley a little before. Edward is insistent that the forces under his lieutenant are *not* in royal control. This is a substantial point, for England and France were technically not at war and the Navarrese command was over soldiers of fortune fighting for themselves. Their actions damaged France, as Edward no doubt wished them to, but it would clearly have been highly embarrassing for him to have done anything to turn the ravaging of freebooters into an official and overt act of war. Hence to Philip of Navarre's enquiry as to whether he was to exact the third the king replied negatively:

> Item, au quart point du tierz du gaign de guerre, semble qe mons' Philippe ne poet cela demander si les gentz ne feussient a ses custages, et aussint le Roi ne le prent nulle foiz de ses [Philip's] gentz, ne aussint ne les poet il charger de le doner a nul autre contre lour gree.[1]

Here we have again proof that troops in royal pay were liable to surrender a third: the forces in Normandy are not and so do not pay it, though had the fighting been formal war doubtless the king would have demanded it as he had done in 1352.

In the 1350's we thus have the crown reserving not a half but a third of the winnings of war, and there seems no reason to suppose there is any interruption in this practice before the 1370's when, as I have tried to show, we are on firm ground.[2] Yet during the late 1350's we have conclusive proof that Edward the Black Prince was maintaining his claim to one half. In 1357 the prince ordered the arrest of two brothers who had defaulted

[1] Mr. Le Patourel kindly communicated this document (from Caligula D III) to me; he is inclined to date it 1358.
[2] Cf. above, p. 272, and below, p. 280 and n. 5.

in the payment of the duke's half in a prisoner captured at Poitiers.[1] And in 1358 the prince is found making an assignment on his moiety of the 500 marks ransom to which one of his knights, Sir Warin de Bassyngbourne, had put a prisoner, Sir John de Sentri.[2] This is Jean de Saintré, claimed by some as the prototype of the hero in the later romance by Antoine de la Sale: he was taken in 1356.[3] Yet if in one great magnate's following the half was still customary in the 1350's, there is some indication that during the 1360's the third gained ground even there. This seems to be the inference we must draw from the copy of a document, unfortunately not dated, which refers to the division of the spoil at the battle of Najera in 1367. It forms part of the *dossier* in the famous case of the count of Denia and recounts the transfer by the Black Prince to the king of his rights in the Spanish nobleman, apart from the prince's third (*sauvant et reservant a nostre dit filʒ son tierʒ*).[4] Later this third was separately conveyed to Robert Hawley.[5] The prince's third at Najera indeed throws light on more than this one battle. By the treaty drawn up the year before between him and King Peter, Prince Edward was promised that portion of ransoms 'which was customary in the French wars'.[6]

Summarizing, we may say that there is every appearance of a variety of usages prevailing in the disposal of booty and ransoms of prisoners not claimed outright by crown, superior lord or captain in the first decades of Edward III's reign. The references we find to royal practice suggest that the third was of old standing in the royal household; yet the persistence of the half in the following of a royal duke and prince precludes any certainty that in general the larger fraction was exceptional. There does, however, seem to be every likelihood that the royal system of taking only a third was gradually adopted during the period after the Peace of Brétigny, and was pretty universal by the last decade

[1] *Register*, iii. 251–2, 294–5.   [2] *Ibid.*, iv. 249.

[3] Froissart, iv. 105; A. Coville, *Le Petit Jehan de Saintré: recherches complémentaires* (Paris, 1937), p. 64. Saintré had been captured before in 1351.

[4] Brit. Mus. Add. MS. 24062, f. 162. For a discussion of it see E. Perroy in *Mélanges Halphen* (cited above, p. 267, n.2). Professor Perroy uses the old foliation (172).

[5] *Cal. Close Rolls Edward III, 1374–7*, pp. 337–8 (13 March 1375).

[6] Rymer, iii (2). 800 (Sept. 1366).

of the reign. The reason for this lies doubtless in the growth of the indentured army. 'The king's army was essentially the household in arms', to quote Professor Tout.[1] As the tradition of separate feudal contingents declined, uniformity spread in all military relationships, including the one under discussion.

It would be satisfactory if we could trace in detail the payments made, to king or captain, under the terms of the conventions which prevailed from time to time during the fourteenth century. This seems, however, unlikely to be feasible. The money paid in as the royal share of ransoms or booty went into the private treasure of the king and is lost in the recesses of the privy purse.[2] The Exchequer had no say in such adventitious and personal income. Though at a time of financial crisis ransoms which had swollen the resources of the Chamber found their way, by means of a loan, to the central financial department, this seems to have been exceptional[3]; the enquiry into the breaking of Exchequer rules in 1364 which arose over an instalment of King John of France's ransom was not an attempt by the Exchequer to secure control of the money, but to regularize its temporary custody of funds which properly belonged to the Chamber.[4] We may none the less hope for accidental record of such income, such as we have in the quittances given in 1361 to two men for thirds of ransoms pertaining to their commands in France.[5]

In the commission of 1351 quoted above, it is stated that the soldiers concerned absconded with *both* their wages *and* their ransom profits.[6] This suggests that the profits of war were deducted from wages. This procedure we know to have been applied in Henry V's campaigns in France[7] and it seems a logical extension of the sharing of spoils which we have been considering. The earliest explicit reference to such a method of accounting which I have come upon is in an indenture dated 1 March 1373 between the king and Robert, Lord Willoughby. After outlining

---

[1] *Chapters*, ii. 133.   [2] Cf. *ibid.*, iv. 317, n. 5.
[3] *Ibid.*, iv. 329–30.   [4] *Ibid.*, iii. 245–8.
[5] Robert de Eves and Thomas Fogg, *Cal. Pat. Rolls Ed. III, 1361–4*, pp. 122, 126; cf. the charges against Lord Latimer in 1376, *Cal. Pat. Rolls Ed. III, 1374–7*, p. 353; and the quittance to the bishop of Lincoln in 1365, Rymer, iii (2). 776.
[6] Above, p. 277.
[7] R. A. Newhall, *English Conquest of Normandy*, pp. 156–7; *Muster and Review* (Cambridge, Mass., 1940), pp. 83–4.

the terms on which Lord Willoughby will serve with 30 men-at-arms and 30 archers, the contract goes on:

> Rebatant toutes voies en descharge nostre dit seignur le Roi des ditz gages et regard du dit Robert et de sa dite retenue pour le second demy an lavauntage et profit qil et meisme sa retenue prenderont des ranceons en chivauchant et osteyant et par constreint du plat paiis parmi les chasteux et fforteressces si aucuns soient pris et tenuz par le dit Robert et sa dite retenue es parties du France durant le dit an si avant.[1]

One can hardly conceive of a scheme more likely to ensure damage to the enemy, granted the erratic and dilatory payment of wages.

No adequate survey of the division of the spoils in earlier times can be given here, but a brief glance at this topic will not be out of place. It is clear that the spoils were of immense importance in the Dark Ages, as in all 'heroic' periods of history.[2] It is also clear that from Clovis sharing the booty at Soissons, down to William the Marshal and on to the heroes of the Hundred Years War, the gambling element was closely associated with the sharing of the winnings of war.[3] Definite principles of division are also discernible, varying from area to area, from the fifth, which we find in Spain from the eleventh century to the sixteenth,[4] to the half, which was the fraction adopted in the

[1] P.R.O., E 101/68/6, with others of the same date in similar terms.

[2] A useful collection of references in Jakob Grimm, *Deutsche Rechtsalter-tümer*, ed. A. Heusler and R. Hübner, i (Leipzig, 1912), 343–4; cf. H. M. Chadwick, *The Heroic Age* (Cambridge, 1922), pp. 340–2.

[3] For Clovis, Gregory of Tours, *Historia Francorum*, ii. 27; *Guillaume le Maréchal*, ed. P. Meyer, lines 4177–4196, cf. 11,310: 'Li uns desuz, l'autre desoz'; Froissart, ed. Kervyn de Lettenhove, xii. 6: 'A ce coup serons-nous tous mors ou tous riches. Il en faut attendre l'aventure'; appendix to Muri-muth (Rolls Series), p. 247, on pillaging after Crécy: 'spolia dividebant, sortem mittentes inter se quis quid tolleret.' See, too, the 'belle aventure de bons prisonniers' in Froissart, iii. 144, and cf. the 'adventuras quaerere' of official documents, N. Denholm Young, 'The tournament in the thirteenth century', in *Studies . . . presented to F. M. Powicke* (1948), pp. 252, n. 3, 267.

[4] R. Menendez Pidal, *Cantar del mio Cid*, ii (Madrid, 1911), 816–17, 887; an instance in 1520 will be found in the forthcoming *Calendar of Letters of James V of Scotland*, pp. 428–9.

crusading states and the Latin kingdom of Jerusalem.[1] Compared with our certainty in these countries we are more in the dark with regard to England and France.[2] There is, however, one country where we are well informed, namely Wales.

Here, from early times, the division of plunder was regulated by elaborate rules and the basis of the division was the third. This proportion of the winnings of war of the royal war band (*teulu*) was given to the king, as we may read in the Ancient Laws of Wales.[3] The booty was, of course, mainly in captured animals and there is every reason to suppose that Welsh princes were as rigorous in demanding their thirds of the valley sheep in the thirteenth century as they had been earlier.[4] This is not an academic point, for among the regalian rights which the English marcher lords claimed to have derived from their penetration into Wales[5] was the prerogative of the thirds of the winnings of their men in border war. This emerges during the celebrated quarrel between Gloucester and Hereford in 1290, in which Edward I intervened and details of which are to be found in the records. It was stated during these proceedings that Gloucester, whose men had invaded Hereford's lands, had been well aware of what was going on 'and that he had a third part of the goods thus taken as spoils, as was proper for the lord to have in time of war, according to the use and custom of the March' (*et quod habuit tertiam partem bonorum sic depredatorum, prout decet*

[1] P. W. Topping, *Feudal Institutions . . . In the Assizes of Romania* (Philadelphia, 1949), pp. 81–2; J. La Monte, *Feudal Monarchy in the Kingdom of Jerusalem, 1100–1291* (Cambridge, Mass., 1932), pp. 120, 163.

[2] F. M. Powicke, *The Loss of Normandy* (Manchester, 1913), pp. 358–63, 438, and references is the most explicit discussion. For France, see the despairing note by Professor Fawtier in F. Lot and R. Fawtier, *Le premier budget de la monarchie française: 1202–3* (Paris, 1932), p. 216.

[3] A. W. Wade Evans, *Welsh Medieval Law* (1909), pp. 154, 158, 165. This is an edition of the misnamed 'Gwentian code' of Aneurin Owen's *Ancient Laws and Institutes of Wales* (Record Commission, 1841), where other references to the king's third are encountered *passim*. T. P. Ellis, *Welsh Tribal Law and Custom* (1926), i. 339, notices these without comment; cf. J. E. Lloyd, *A History of Wales* (1948), i. 317.

[4] *Mabinogion*, trans. E. Jones and G. Jones (Everyman's Library), pp. 196–7.

[5] W. Rees, *South Wales and the March 1284–1415* (Oxford, 1924), pp. 43–4; A. H. Williams, *An Introduction to the History of Wales*. ii. *The Middle Ages*, pt. i (Cardiff, 1948), pp. 167–73.

dominum tempore guerre habere, secundum usum et consuetudinem Marchie).[1] It is also known that on the Scottish side of the other border the lord was entitled to a third of the winnings of his men, but the evidence for this is derived from a later date and it would not assist the present enquiry to consider it here.[2]

It is tempting to connect the royal third of the mid-fourteenth century with the Principality of Wales, with the marcher lords and the mists of Celtic antiquity. We are told that the Spaniards got their fifth from their Moslem opponents.[3] Why should not a similar borrowing have occurred in the military contacts of England and Wales? But this is pure guesswork and results from an attempt to achieve a precision and a chain of causation which are alike beyond our grasp. Our information is largely restricted to the indenture armies of the fourteenth century. To go behind them we must enter a feudal world. When we know so little for certain of the exact obligations of knight service,[4] how may we expect to ascertain with exactitude the perquisites of that service on the field of battle?

There is one line of enquiry that would, I think, throw much light on the problem in the fourteenth century and probably on earlier centuries as well. That is an investigation of the obscure subject of the law of arms and of the neglected offices of the marshal and the constable. These two officers had certain rights to plunder which I have not discussed here, but which are strictly germane to any larger enquiry into the subject. And the law of arms, which is so inadequately treated by the works on chivalry, governed the day-to-day relationships of the soldiers whose 'abominable mélange de mercantilisme et de prouesse, de coups de lance et de coups de bourse' we have been discussing.[5] It is to be hoped that in these and other ways we may have better knowledge of that fourteenth- and fifteenth-century no-man's-land between public policy and private profit and loss.

[1] *Rot. Parl.*, i. 72a; cf. W. A. Morris, *Welsh Wars of Edward I* (1901), p. 231.

[2] Cf. R. C. Reid, 'Merkland Cross', *Transactions of the Dumfriesshire and Galloway Natural History Society*, xxi (1939), 6–16. I hope to deal with the Scottish evidence elsewhere.

[3] Menendez Pidal, *loc. cit.*

[4] F. M. Stenton, *First Century of English Feudalism* (Oxford, 1932), pp. 168–9.

[5] L. Gautier, *La chevallerie*, p. 700.

5 Hermitage Castle, Liddesdale, from the South West *(Crown Copyright)*

13

BOOTY IN BORDER WARFARE

The subject of my paper sounds modest enough.[1] In
reality it is, I believe, very large in scope, touching on a
wide range of problems not only of Scottish and English
history, but of European history at large. Until almost our
own day the spoils of war have been a not inconsiderable inducement to martial ardour. Doubtless the national armies
of the French Revolutionary wars and the latter-day development of conscription have reduced the importance of the
winnings of war to negligible proportions; but many of us must
have met soldiers in the last ten years who brought home
with them from Italy or Germany articles which (in what
the dictionary calls " euphemistic " army slang) had been
" won." Prior to the eighteenth century, when an army
literally lived on the land, this element played a correspondingly greater part. And the further we go back towards
the Dark Ages the bigger we find to have been the influence
of booty in warfare. The impulse to make war profitable
was, indeed, entirely responsible for the wars of the little
kings of Christendom at the outset: among the German tribes
settled in the Western Empire each spring saw the warriors
assembled for aggressive war; how else could a non-commercial
economy sustain itself? In our own island there is evidence
of such an attitude in the Celtic peoples, in the Germans who
displaced them, and in the Norsemen—Danes and Normans
—who followed after. Of the activities of the Norsemen we
are particularly well-informed in the *Sagas* where we read
the tale of brutal assault and ruthless acquisitiveness year
by year, reign by reign, until something like monotony

[1] My acknowledgments are due to Mr R. C. Reid, who placed at my
disposal his notes on early XVI. century records of the Lords of
Council and was kind in many other ways. I have also had help
from Professor W. Croft Dickinson, Dr Gordon Donaldson and Mr
A. A. M. Duncan.

obscures for us the ugly incentive behind the barbaric virtues of the heroes.

Nothing is more revealing in this universal itch to ravage and to spoil than the traces we find in the sources of rules for the sharing of the plunder. Clearly such rules must have played a big part in preventing disputes about the booty which would otherwise have arisen when a war band was victorious and marched or sailed home with the gold vessels, the arms and armour, the maidens, the young warriors and the chieftains, of the vanquished and despoiled enemy. Our knowledge of these rules is tantalisingly meagre in the early days. Compounded of traditions stretching back into the remotest periods, modified by contact with Rome, with Christianity, with Islam, for long no one felt it necessary to set down precisely how for any people at any time the spoils were divided. In Britain it is not until we come to the Ancient Laws of Wales that we find a systematic codification of practice. In this remarkable collection of laws (some of which date back to the tenth century) the sharing of the prisoners and the plunder is accounted for meticulously. We meet, for instance, this sort of regulation: " The captain of the royal war-band is entitled to two men's portions of the spoils acquired out of the country; and of the king's third he is to have a third. He is the third person who is to have a third with the king: the other two are the queen and the chief falconer." The mention of the chief falconer is significant. The division of the winnings of war, not only in Wales, but in all other areas, seems to have been closely related to the division of the spoils of the chase. Nimrod has always had a somewhat ambiguous character.[2]

It is within this larger framework that I invite you to survey the question of plunder in the Borders. The matter is somewhat intricate. For one thing our records, particularly at first, have little explicit light to shed on the

2 Some references to works bearing on the division of the spoils in the Dark Ages and in early mediæval Wales will be found in my paper, "Division of the spoils of war in Fourteenth-Century England, above, pp. 265-84.

question: there must have been plunder and arrangements for disposing of it equitably from the start (whenever that was), but we cannot profitably trace it beyond the fourteenth century, while most of our information is later even than that. We are dealing with an area where Marcher Law (whatever that was) serves as an additional complication. And, finally, the Anglo-Scottish border is, for much of its length, a waste of high moorland where reiving and rapine can frequently not be separated neatly into international and domestic incidents, where the stout borderers were (on both sides of the frontier) often interested in making ends more than meet at the expense of their neighbours whether Scottish or English, and in farming an area which is an economic unit—farming it, moreover, by grazing animals which were no respecters of treaties, truces, or national boundaries.

Though some of these complications will have to be touched on in what follows, I propose to limit myself as far as possible to the question of plunder in the narrowest sense. I shall begin by surveying the types of booty involved, go on to discuss attempts to regulate Border aggression, and conclude by discussing the evidence for the sharing of the spoils. The period I shall be covering is roughly from 1314 to 1542—from Bannockburn to Solway Moss.

The Borderers or men of the Marches[3] took to plundering on a variety of occasions, which must be distinguished. There were long periods of overt war. Then the frontier was crossed by armed bands, organised and directed — though often imperfectly controlled—by the governments of Scotland and England. Plundering at such a time was military duty; rapine was licensed; and damage to the enemy was not only profitable but also patriotic. In this connection we must remember that the Anglo-Scottish wars of the period are closely related to the phases in the hostility of England and

---

[3] In general Border is commoner in English, March in Scotland; the " March " *tout court* in England meant the Welsh March. The Scottish humanist historians refer to Borderers as " Marciani " (Buchanan, *Opera*, Leyden, 1725, i. 352) or " limitanei " (Major, *Historia*, Edinburgh, 1740, p. 323).

France.[4]   But there were also periods of truce and even
periods of so-called peace; from the mid-fourteenth century to
the mid-sixteenth there are literally dozens of such arrangements. Some were for only a few months' duration, some were
intended to be practically indefinite, like those of November,
1449, and July, 1499; some even aimed (like the treaty of
1502) at a perpetual peace. In practice, however, the truces
were short; a three or five-year truce was often followed the
year after it was made by a fresh agreement to suspend
hostilities.[5] The reasons why the truces were abandoned were
only partly due to the policies of kings and magnates; often
the explanation is the rapacity of the Borderers themselves,
and there is no doubt that the signing of a truce often made
little difference to the behaviour of the fighting men of the
Marches, though it had a bearing on the geographical extent
of their raids and on the legitimacy of their plunder, and
must therefore be regarded as a distinct type of border aggression. In this respect it is interesting to note that it was
argued more than once that when " lawful " war broke out
it automatically legitimised booty captured in earlier
" unlawful " attacks.[6] The third type is the raiding, not of
Scots on English or vice versa, but of Scots on Scots and of
English on English. Sometimes one must regard this last
brand of rapacity with charity: it was often not clear to the
participants whether they were the lieges of the Scottish or
the English king; the " Debatable Land " continued far
into the sixteenth century as a source of equivocation;[7] there
were Graemes, Armstrongs, Nixons, and Waughs on both

4 Scots and English preyed on each other in France before the
   campaigns of Henry V.: cf. the supposed capture of Archibald
   Douglas at Poitiers, when he wriggled out of ransom as a gentleman
   and paid only 40s as a servant (*Scalacron.*, ed. Maxwell, 1907, p. 125,
   n. 2 and refs.); Bain, IV., No. 709—Scots captured by Calais garrison
   1405.
5 A catalogue of these documents would be worth compiling. Most
   (but not all) are in Rymer's *Foedera* and were extracted for his
   chronological survey by G. Ridpath, *Border History*, 2nd ed.,
   London, 1810.
6 James Balfour, *Practicks*, Edinburgh, 1754, p. 596; *Acts of the
   Lords in Council in Civil Affairs*, 1501-1554, p. 534.
7 W. Mackay Mackenzie, "The Debatable Land," *Scottish Hist.
   Rev.*, XXX. (1951), 109-125; D. L. W. Tough, *The Last Days of a
   Frontier*, 1928.

sides of the Border.[8] But sometimes there is little excuse for the brutality and greed with which neighbouring families of the same nationality preyed on one another. These cases hardly fall within the purview of this paper, for they are criminal acts by any definition and were prosecuted as such whenever the Scottish or English governments were strong. But their frequency through two centuries is worth remembering here, for it suggests that reiving, cattle-lifting, brigandage, and theft were endemic on both sides of the Border.[9] That such activities assumed the forms of war is pretty clear, but it is equally clear (to quote a Scottish case of 1537) that it was prohibited by common law for any Scot to take another prisoner, let alone rifle his possessions and hold him to ransom.[10]

What kind of plunder was sought for in Border warfare between England and Scotland? Scarcely anything came amiss to the raiding party or the advancing army; money and precious metals, cattle, goods and equipment of all descriptions, prisoners. At sea the captured ship—like the pillaged town or village—provided a convenient amalgam of all these spoils. Of this mass of winnings of war we know most about prisoners, for in this case the value of the capture depended on fairly elaborate negotiations, often involving documents which have fortunately survived. Of other booty we hear much, but not so often in precise terms; the

[8] W. Mackay Mackenzie, *op. cit.* Annandale also suffered: Rot. Scot., i. 887-8 (1364).

[9] It is easy to document this type of lawlessness from the English records: Bain, *Calendar of Documents relating to Scotland*, iii., iv. (1887-8) contain many examples: iii., 948 (1328), 1334 (1340), 1454 (1346), 1555 (1351), iv., 128 (1366), 180 (1371), 230 (1376), 1312 (1442-60), 1556 (1490); see also *Cal. Close.*, Rolls Ed., III., 1348-50, p. 60-1; *Pat. Rolls*, 1358-61, p. 167. The capture of Louis of Beaumont and two cardinals in 1317 by Gilbert Middleton is a related case, T. F. Tout, *Place of Edward II. in English History*, 2nd ed., p. 103 and refs. Scottish material is fullest for a later period: R. Pitcairn, *Criminal Trials in Scotland*, Maitland Club, 3 vols. in 4, 1883, I. (1) 18+, 31+, 351+ (1493-1550); *Acts of the Lords in Council*, 1501-54, p. 604.

[10] Patrick and Alexander Murray, with Alexander Armstrong took prisoner Archibald Douglas of Cowschogill. They took his money (£12), his horse and equipment (30 merks) and ransomed him for 1000 nobles, for which Lord Maxwell stood surety, Reg. Ho., Acta Dom. Con. and Sess., ix., f. 25v.

Scots returned home with a vast quantity of cattle in a raid after Bannockburn,[11] and a few years later the English gain " prædas animalium " ;[12] the inhabitants of a pillaged area petition for exemption from taxes because their stock has been completely carried off.[13]   Wyntoun rejoices in the " catale and powndis " of the successful foray, and on one occasion lists the products :

> Wessayle, and apparylle off halle
> And off Chamoure, thare tane war all.[14]

Sir Thomas Gray, at just about the time Wyntoun was writing, estimated that when his castle of Wark was despoiled by the Scots he lost goods to the value of 2000 marcs.[15] Occasionally a more concrete picture emerges. The Scots in 1316 were delighted to capture iron on a raid into England on the west side, " because iron is scarce in Scotland " ;[16] while a great bell taken from an English raid on Dundee was sold at Newcastle to the Dominicans of Carlisle.[17] The frequent capture of horses doubtless made opportune the capture of three cartloads of harness in 1322.[18] and the rifling of the treasure chest sometimes gave the raider plunder which was of somewhat academic interest—like the muniments of a Yorkshire priory taken off by the Scots in the mid-fourteenth century.[19] Sometimes our information is so precise as to raise doubts about its veracity, as when we read that the only plunder Edward II.'s army took in the Lothians was one cow at Tranent.[20] In particular it is hard to trace the minor acquisitions of the victors in a pitched battle. Ancient Pistol at Agincourt is, we may guess, typical enough in this respect:

11 *Lanercost Chronicle*, ed. Joseph Stevenson, Bannatyne Club, 1839, p. 230; cf. 239-40 (1319), 246-7 (1322), 341 (1344).

12 *Ibid.*, p. 291 (1337).

13 24 Parishes in Northumberland, 1440, Bain, iii., 1441.

14 Ed. Laing, iii.: Book IX., i. 45-8, v. 343 (1371, 1384).

15 Bain, iv., 542 (May, 1400).

16 *Lanercost*, 233.

17 *Lanercost*, 282 (1335).

18 Bain, iii., 791.

19 *Ibid.*, 1509.

20 W. Fraser: *Douglas Book*, 1885, i. 151 and n.

Owy, cuppele gorge, permafoy,
Peasant, unless thou give me crowns, brave crowns;
Or mangled shalt thou be by this my sword.[21]

At Flodden King James IV.'s chief cook, Thomas Shaw, lost £20 in an encounter with such a captor; but we only know about it because it was not his money, but the king's.[22]

Of plunder taken at sea much might be written.[23] I will content myself with a reference to a case from the West of Scotland, partly because it is more appropriate in this gathering and partly because most of our evidence comes from the east coast, where merchant shipping was much more numerous. In the winter of 1387-8 a Liverpool merchant, John Hall, was sailing to Ireland when he was captured by men of the Earl of Douglas on the high seas and "beyond the bounds and limits of the truce." He, his ship, and his men were all taken to the "Isle of Galloway" and there he agreed to a ransom of £100. To pay this he was authorised to export to Scotland beans, peas, oats, malt, flour, mulse (or mead), cloth, muslin, knives, belts, and various other *minuta mercimonia*, but not arms or military equipment.[24]

One type of aggressive act is perhaps worth a moment's attention, the exaction from a community of a money payment in return for not being burnt and ravaged. This seems to have occurred in the fourteenth century campaigns and to have been practised by the Scots rather than the English, though it regularly formed a part of English chevauchées in the wars in France, where a special term (pactise) was applied to the action. The procedure seems to have been for the raiding Scots to move elsewhere if they were adequately bribed to do so, as in 1322 when the Abbot of Furnes "made a ransom for the land of Furnes."[25] Sometimes, as at Ripon in 1318, the town could not produce outright the

21 *Henry V.*, IV., iv. 36-8.
22 *Exchequer Rolls, Scot.*, xiv. 53.
23 Bain, iii. 888-9 (1326), 1345 (1340), 1427 (1344), iv. 10 (1358), 23 (1359), 16ᵈ (1370), 250 (1377), 283 (1379), 564, 573 (1400), 623 (1402), 789 (1410), 830 (1412), 1039 (1431). *Rot. Scot.*, ii. 31 (1380), etc.
24 *Rot. Scot.*, ii. 91-2 (28th February, 1388).
25 "Fecit redemptionem pro patria de Furneys," *Lanercost*, 246; cf. *ib.*, 248 where Beverley does the same.

sum demanded, and gave hostages for the balance of the sum.[26] At the other end of the fourteenth century the Abbot of Holmcultram in 1385 paid £200 to the Earl of Douglas and his men to avoid being burned.[27] There was clearly in this situation a danger that Border strongholds would be ransomed by their owners rather than used in active defence: a number of pardons have survived for the loss of such fortresses.[28]

Rapid and tangible gains in cattle, cash, and gear were then the constant preoccupation of the combatants. Ransoms, about which we know most, are just a special case of booty, but, since large sums were at stake, they are worth considering separately. What happened was this. During an engagement, and particularly in the pursuit of vanquished by victors after an engagement, the defeated soldier surrendered as an individual to an individual soldier of the winning party. The captor might at once take his prisoner into captivity; or he might agree then and there to an exchange against prisoners on his own side in the hands of his prisoner's party; or he might allow his prisoner to go on parole for a specified period, on a promise to appear at a stated place later. At a later time the captive was required by his master to agree to a ransom, often (but not always) by subscribing a formal deed in which the terms of payment, and the securities for it, are set down. The securities were usually either other prisoners of substance, local men of wealth on the captor's side, or else members of the captive's own kith and kin, who came as hostages while the principal departed to raise his ransom. The ransom having been paid, the securities were discharged and the prisoner was a free man. It is perhaps worth noting that prisoners very often paid their ransoms by exporting commodities to the country in which they were

26 Bain, iii. 858, petition by six poor women of the town whose husbands are hostages in Scotland; *Cal. Close Rolls*, Ed. II., 1318-23, p. 274 (Rymer ii. 437); the Vale of Pickering also gave £400, secured by hostages, to obtain " salvation," *Rot. Parl.*, i. 422.

27 Bain, iv. 343; *Rot. Parl.*, iii. 181b.

28 Bain, iv. 542 (Gray at Wark, 1400), 585 (Middleton at Bewcastle, 1401).

imprisoned, so that in this way trade was stimulated by war-fare.[29]

These processes are well known and can all be illustrated from the Anglo-Scottish campaigns under review. It is, in fact, impossible even summarily to list the hundreds of names of prisoners on the two sides involved in two centuries of pretty steady hostility. We do not always know a great deal about the ransom transactions, but we know many of the names of captives, both from chronicles listing particularly the many captured men at Bannockburn, Neville's Cross, Otterburn, and Homildon Hill, and from a steady stream of safe conducts and other documents in the Scottish Rolls, Exchequer Rolls, and in Bain's collection. The only side of the matter which is not so well recorded is the exchange of prisoners. This is a pity, for presumably a large number of the smaller men were released in this way. There are some notable cases where we have many particulars, like the exchange of the Earl of Hereford taken after Bannockburn and exchanged for Bruce's wife and others;[30] and the con-temporary exchange of Segrave against seven Scottish prisoners.[31] But there must have been many exchanges which have left no traces on the records.[32] As Barbour writes of the fighting in 1327:

> And thai that tane war on a day
> On ane othir changit war thai.[33]

This was especially true of the minor Border forays where in all respects less ceremony was used.

The formalities of capture, ransom, and payment were all intensified when a great man was captured, not only be-cause of his rank but because of the money at stake. When

29 E.g., *Rot. Scot.*, ii. 31, 35a, 52b, 83a, 85a, 109-10 (1380-91), etc.; *Ex. Rolls Scot.*, ix. 145, 146, xii. 473, xiv. 49, 56 (1481-1514).
30 Barbour, *Bruce* (ed. W. M. Mackenzie), 1909, xiii. 670-87 and notes; cf. exchange of Murdoch Stewart and Henry Percy, Bain, iv. 895 (1419).
31 *Rot. Scot.*, i. 134b.
32 *Close Rolls*, 1354-60, p. 288: Beaumont is to return to Scotland where he is a prisoner, and Scottish prisoners whom he has released by standing surety, must return. He had no business to make this arrangement for an exchange.
33 *Bruce*, XIX., 522-3; cf. 379-80.

the Scots took a Percy or the English a Douglas we find usually the most elaborate documentation; and the capture of David II. and James I. leave their memorials in page after page of Rymer's *Foedera*. A king's ransom was, however, not merely large, it was complicated by political considerations, and we will not consider it now. Nor was the redemption of one of the great Border earls free of repercussions, as the events after Homildon Hill testify, for the Earl of Douglas, taken by the Percies, became a bone of contention between the latter and Henry IV., and was finally re-taken at the battle of Shrewsbury fighting side by side with his former captor.

More typical are the smaller gentlemen who are taken prisoner in the two centuries under review, whose ransom is not measured in thousands of pounds like a Percy[34] but in hundreds[35] or in tens.[36] For the early sixteenth century, when Scottish litigation brings into view a mass of ransoms, some of the sums involved are very small indeed.[37] Of course the cumulative effect could be impressive. A Border magnate looked upon such spoliation as an act against himself, and Douglas in 1357 complained that Sir Robert Tilliol had plundered Eskdale of not only 1000 oxen and other beasts, 1000 sheep and horses, and goods from houses to the tune of £20, but also that many of his people had been ransomed to a total of £5000.[38] Half a century later Sir Thomas Gray claimed that the Scots had ransomed his children and people for £1000.[39] These, of course, are claims by interested parties and do no more than give us an order of magnitude. But Froissart, who was a neutral in the Anglo-Scottish war, was informed that the captives at Otterburn in 1388 paid

34 Hotspur's ransom was aided by a royal grant of £1000.

35 E.g., Bain, iv. 358, 409, 1379; *Ex. Rolls Scot.*, xiv. 80.

36 E.g, Bain, iv. 424, 563, 566; *Ex. Rolls Scot.*, iii. 212, vi. 128, ix. 145, 146, xii. 473, xiv. 49, 56.

37 A.D.C., xx., f. 44v., xxii., f. 48 (1509); xxvi., f. 146, xxvii., ff. 4, 45v., 163v., 234 (1514-6); xxviii.., ff. 5-6, 23v., 25 (1516); xxxv., f. 165v. (2524); *Acts of the Lords of Council in Civil Affairs*, 1501-54, pp. 305, 539, 546 (bis), 602, etc.

38 Bain, iii., 1664.

39 *Ibid.*, iv. 542.

more than 100,000 francs in ransoms, more (he adds) than the Scots gained at Bannockburn.[40]

Faced with a heavy ransom, many men changed sides:

> O yield the, Pearcye! Douglas sayd,
> And in faith I will thee bringe
> Where thou shall high advanced bee
> By James our Scottish king.

The invitation to be a turn-coat was listened to by many illustrious captains and noblemen: it would be distasteful to rehearse their names, though in many cases we could advance political as well as financial reasons for their treachery. How many of the smaller men pocketed their pride and changed sides we cannot even guess: they figure in the records as rebels, though the embarrassment of governments often made subsequent reconciliation possible, as it did in the debatable lands on the perimeter of the English province of Gascony.

In the long-standing conflict between the two countries the influence of March Law affected the mechanics of plunder. With the antiquity of the customs of the March we cannot concern ourselves, although it is significant that on the English side they have been shown to have analogies with laws of the tenth century.[41] From the present point of view it is sufficient to remark the curious double nature of March Law: it was both a special custom for the subjects of each kingdom within each kingdom, and a custom governing the relations of the lieges of Scotland and the lieges of England. Both countries, that is to say, recognised that the Border lands represented a special area for domestic jurisdiction, as well as one in which it was essential to codify certain practices of international law. It is a matter for astonishment that this fascinating problem has received virtually no attention from legal historians, although from at any rate

---

40 *Chroniques*, ed. Kervyn de Lettenhove, xiii. 257 (on Froissart's veracity as a neutral see J. Major, *Greater Britain*, Scot. Hist. Soc., 1892, 256-7). Fordun is emphatic about the value of the spoils after Bannockburn, " Annals," cxxxi.; Barbour describes the pillaging, *Bruce*, xiii. 443-64.

41 T. Hodgkin, *Wardens of the Northern March*, 1908, pp. 15-6.

the end of the thirteenth century[42] there is a good deal of material awaiting study. Here we cannot do more than indicate very summarily some of the conventions which had a bearing on plunder.[43]

From an original interest in the legal position of lieges with lands and loyalties on both sides of the Border, the governments of the two countries soon concentrated on the related problems of malefactors who escaped punishment by crossing the frontier, and redress of injuries done during periods of truce. Wardens of the Marches on both sides gradually acquired powers for transacting business at March Days or Days of Truce. Essentially the customs, and the written conventions which set them down and modified them, established that the old right of pursuit of raiders by a victim and his neighbours should be under legal safeguards, and that as far as possible the redress of injuries should be effected not by individuals but by negotiation between the wardens or special commissioners.[44] That much of this diplomacy was wasted is evident from the failure of treaties and truces to survive more than a few years at a time; and certain of the agreements—like that of 1398 which provided for an exchange of prisoners and a repayment of ransoms by each side[45]—are positively Utopian in their optimism. But there is considerable evidence that from time to time the machinery of the warden's meetings did effect redress, and therefore, presumably, that they minimised the normal vendetta procedure of the Border. We find attempts made to restore prisoners made in violation of the truce,[46] the

---

42 The status of the "recognition" of border laws made in 1249 *Acts Parl. Scot.*, i. (83+ - 86+) is disputed: D. L. W. Tough, *op. cit.*, 96-7; it is treated as genuine by Sir F. M. Powicke, *The Thirteenth Century*, 1953, p. 588.

43 See for a brief discussion of some of these problems D. L. W. Tough, *op. cit.*, 95-171, whose list of border conventions, however, does not include many of the formal treaties and agreements drawn up in the fifteenth century. Most of these are in *Foedera*, paraphrased in Ridpath.

44 Wardens were usually also conservators of the numerous truces and treaties. Of particular importance are the arrangements of 1424, 1429, 1438: Rymer, *Foedera*, x. 323, 428, 688.

45 Rymer, *Foedera*, viii. 54-61; Bain, iv. 510.

46 Bain, iii. 1062 (1332), 1550 (1350), iv. 235 (1376), 1050 (1431).

formal presentation of claims for damages by one side to the other,[47] and the actual payment of money by one warden to his opposite number of sums in respect of damages.[48] Even in formal war an attempt was made by both sides to prevent prisoners being illegally abused. In 1348 the English government appointed commissioners to enquire into the complaint by a Scottish knight that he was forced to pay ransom twice before release;[49] and in 1535 the Lords of Council in Scotland heard a case in which the complainer, William Woodhouse, an Englishman taken at sea, accused Robert Fogo and others of agreeing to a ransom of 100 crowns and then later insisting on 500 crowns.[50] This maritime case should remind us of the numerous attempts to deal with damages inflicted at sea or on wrecked shipping on the coast, by the governments of the two countries,[51] though the developing theory of maritime reprisals led also to authorised acts of aggression.[52]

I turn now to what is for me the most interesting aspect of Border warfare, namely, the arrangements which prevailed from time to time for the sharing of plunder. I began by indicating the general importance of this subject, and it might perhaps be helpful if I sketched very rapidly the English practices in this respect before turning to Scottish evidence.[53] It seems likely that the feudal lord had a right to the prisoners taken by his men, while they enjoyed a right to horses and equipment. By the fourteenth century more elaborate rules emerge. The magnates who contract with the king to provide his army, and the king himself in his contracts with captains, explicitly reserve rights to prisoners and plun-

---

47 *Ibid.*, iii. 1664 (1357), iv. 318 (1383); and in many of the negotiated truces and treaties.
48 *Ibid.*, iv. 192 (1371), 308 (1382), 375 (1388), 924 (1423); *Acts of the Lords in Council in Civil Causes*, 1478-95, p. 49 (1480).
49 *Cal. Pat. Rolls Ed. III.*, 1348-50, p. 152.
50 A.D.C. and S., vi., fo. 58, 65v., 86. Norroy herald appeared for Woodhouse; the Lords dismissed the complaint, on failure of proof. Cf. *Acts of the Lords in Council in Civil Causes*, 1496-1501, pp. 68-9.
51 Bain, iii. 883-9 (1326) 1345 (1340), iv. 10 (1358), 23, 26, (1359), 164 (1370), 1115 (1438), 1121 (1438), 1303 (1442-59), 1414 (1474), 1429 (1475), 1443 (1476).
52 *Ibid.*, iv. 250 (1377), 283 (1379), 789 (1410).
53 For what follows see above, pp. 265-84.

der: sometimes prisoners above a certain value or of a certain rank are reserved by the superior; sometimes the booty is to be halved between the two parties. By the 1360's we see more and more uniformity in such contracts. The captain has a third of the winnings of war of his men; the king has a third of his captains' winnings and a third of the third which the captain derived from his retinue. Always the royal right to prisoners is apparent. These developments may be illustrated from Anglo-Scottish wars. The king's right to prisoners was rigidly insisted on after Neville's Cross, for example.[54] And the emergence of the third is clearly revealed by the history of Lochmaben and Annandale: English custodians of the castle from 1346 agreed to pay their superior, the Earl of Northampton, two-thirds of all " advantages ";[55] but from 1371 this proportion is reversed and the warden of Lochmaben had then to pay his master a third of the " gayne," a third of the third of prisoners made by the garrison and to surrender any prisoner above £100 in value for whom the superior promised to pay £100.[56] " Thirds and thirds of thirds " survived in English usage well beyond the limits of the period we are here concerned with. They are formally expressed in the " Ordinances of War " which ran from 1385 onwards in a fairly regular series.

When we turn to Scotland we find a singular paucity of direct evidence. The Scottish army was, practically speaking, unpaid during the fourteenth and fifteenth centuries.[57] The host was summoned usually for fifteen or twenty days' service, and only in exceptional cases for as much as forty, and there was a distinct unwillingness to serve.[58] Since the army was unpaid we may expect the

---

54 *Rot. Scot.*, i. 675-706, *passim; Cal. Pat. Ed. III.*, 1345-8, pp. 225-6, 285, 363.
55 Bain, iii., 1459; cf. iv. 98, 109, 144, 161.
56 *Ibid.*, iv. 178; cf. 224 and Lancaster's indenture of 1403 as warden of the marches, quoted by Dr Chrimes (see below p. 304, n. 94).
57 See John Major's discussions of this, *Greater Britain* (Scot. Hist. Soc.), pp. 265, 346.
58 Gladys Dickinson, " Some notes on the Scottish army in the first half of the XVI. century," *Scot. Hist. Rev.*, XXVIII. (1949), p. 144 and n.

Scottish crown to have had small interest in, or right to, the spoils of war; it is the English king's rights which lead in part to the fuller English documentation. Equally the contingents in the Scottish host, unlike their English contemporaries, were not paid by their leaders, and so provisions regarding the divisions of the spoil do not survive in indentures.[59] A Scottish magnate in war was accompanied, not by professional soldiers as such, but by his kinsmen and '' allies.''[60]

Nevertheless from the beginning of our period we may trace the importance attached to the division of the spoils. In Barbour's *Bruce*, for instance, we read how Sir James Douglas, by a timely show of force, relieved Earl Randolph, but would not let his men participate in the actual fighting lest

> Men suld say we thame raschit had . . .
> He sule haf that he wonnyn has.[61]

While Bruce exhorts his men to fight well because they shall enrich themselves:

> That the pouerest of yhou sall be
> Bath rych and mychty thar-with-all.[62]

Later in the same poem we read of the Black Douglas defeating Neville and dividing the spoil among his followers:

> The pray soyne emang his manyhe
> Eftir thar meritis, delit he.[63]

And the chronicles contain other references to the sharing of plunder at a later date.[64]

There are no Scottish ordinances for war in the fourteenth and fifteenth century which have survived as such. The nearest equivalent is the list of articles drawn up for the Franco-Scottish attack of 1385, but this is mainly con-

---

59 Sometimes bonds of manrent are called indentures (Spalding Club *Miscellany* V. (1842), p. 251). But these documents, in certain respects comparable to indentures of retinue, do not seem to contain provisions for sharing the spoil.

60 See Barbour, *Bruce*, xvii. 316-9, on the Stewart defenders of Berwick, 1319.

61 See Barbour, *Bruce*, xii. 105-29.

62 *Ibid.*, xii. 242-3.

63 *Ibid.*, xv. 515-9.

64 E.g., *Pluscarden* (ed. Skene), ii. (1830), 236, in 1370.

cerned with the relations between Jean de Vienne's men and the Scots.[65] But there are traces in the Laws of the Marches of such general rules: after all the English Border was for all practical purposes the only place on which Scottish armies regularly operated. These traces of military orders governing the discipline of an army are quite distinct from the arrangements for law on the Marches, but they have been hopelessly confused with them. The confusion is not only the product of Bishop Nicolson in his *Leges Marchiarum*[66] and of earlier codifiers, like Balfour,[67] it is inherent in our earliest compilation, the " Statutis and use of Merchis in tym of were " of 1448.[68] In this document we have an amalgam of " statutis, ordinances, and punctis of weir " and other matters pertaining to Border jurisdiction in a narrower sense, such as the powers of the warden of the Marches. A not dissimilar obscurity hangs over later documents of this kind[69] and even seems to have worried the Scottish Parliament.[70]

Nonetheless these " ordinances and statutes " tell us something about the spoils of war. Aside from provisions as to disputed prisoners[71]—parallel to those found in English ordinances—there is a reference in the collection of 1448 to the punishment of men who do not fight dismounted when ordered to do so: they will be fined by handing over two-thirds of their prisoner's ransom and their booty to their master and one-third to the " chiftane of the oistis "; this suggests that, if any share at all went to the master and the chieftain, it was smaller than that here laid down. Further at the same time we have this article:

> Item, quhatever thei be that cumis to the oist bot in sensable maner with bow or speir and ther be ony deperting of gudis, tua of tha salbe put til ane bowis part.

65 *A.P.S.*, i. 554-555.
66 London, 1747.
67 *Practicks*, Edinburgh, 1754, especially pp. 590-613.
68 *A.P.S.*, i. 714-6.
69 *A.P.S.*, ii. 44-5 (1455).
70 *Ibid.*, c.l.: " Item as to the first artikyll quhare it speke of the deliverance and decret that the King sulde gif anentes debates betwix diverse personnis of the Realme of the taking of presonaris . . . that artikill is referryt to the baronys . . . . for thai haif experience thareof."
71 *A.P.S.*, i. 554-5, 714-6, ii. 44-5.

This clearly suggests that in the rank and file division was somehow based on the individual's equipment.[72]   The most illuminating point comes, however, in the Acts of the Scots Parliament for 1455 (chap. 9):

> Quen the wardan rides or onyuther chiftane and with him gret falloschip or small, that na man gang away with na maner or gudes quhill it be thriddyt and partyt before the chiftane as use and custom is of the Merchis, under the payne of tresone to be hangyt and drawin and his gudes eschet.[73]

Here we have the division of the booty into thirds, although there is no statement of how the thirds were distributed.

Here and there in the Scottish records there are, fortunately, documents which give us a little more information.   The earliest case that has come to my notice is concerned with the ransom of Sir Ralph Percy, taken at Otterburn in 1388.   Percy's captor was Sir Henry Preston, and Preston's master was presumably the Earl of Mar.   At all events King Robert III. in 1390 granted lands to Sir Henry Preston " pro redemptione " of Percy, and to the Earl of Mar a pension of £20 " in recompense and satisfaction of the third part of the ransom " of the English Knight."[74] This looks as though the king had bought Percy from the two men who had an interest in his ransom; such transactions were common enough in fourteenth- and fifteenth-century usage and are well attested for a later period of Scottish history.[75]   The important point is that Preston, the captor, owed a third to Mar, the " chieftain."   A century later we have more evidence.   In 1478 Lord Carlile went to law with the laird of Mousewold over £20, " for the

---

72 *A.P.S.*, i. 716b.
73 *A.P.S.*, ii. 44-5
74 *Reg. Mag. Sig. Scot.*, i. 801 and app. 2, p. 631: cf. *A.P.S.*, i. 581b. Froissart gives the captor's name as Makyrell and says he was handed over to the Earl of Moray. Even if this is the case, and the parties had sold their rights in the captive, the case none-the-less illustrates the existence of the third.   See E. Barrington de Fonblanque, *Annals of the House of Percy*, 2 vols., 1887, i. 150-1, 515.
75 For instance the sale by David Hoppringle of his prisoner Thomas Naill to George Towris, which led to litigation in 1548: A.D.C. and S., vol. XXIV., fos. 142, 16lv.; cf. *Accts. of the Lord High Treasurer*, iv. 300.

ransom of Robert Simson," an Englishman.[76]   Was this a
question of a third?   We might guess so, as five years later
Lord Carlile and his son were proceeded against by Cuthbert
Murray anent the third of the ransom of Clement Skelton.[77]
And in the next year, 1484, there seems little doubt that
when the Earl of Douglas was captured by Alexander Kirk-
patrick, a third of the price which had been put on Douglas's
head went to his master, Robert Charteris.[78] Two unequivocal cases occur in the 1550's, just after the limit set for
this paper : in the first a litigant claimed he had a decreet
from the " merchell and his deputies " authorising his right
to the third of a captured man's ransom.[79]   In the second
the Lords of Session assigned two-thirds of the ransom of a
prisoner taken at Ancrum Moor (1545) by a household man
of Cardinal Beaton to his actual captor and one-third to the
Cardinal, " according to border usage."[80]   The reference
to the Marshal in the earlier of these two cases suggests that
he had jurisdiction of cases involving disputes over the spoils
of war, as he had in England.   There is, however, no indication in the surviving memorials of his office,[81] as there is
in England,[82] that (like the constable) he had independent
rights to spoil—aside from his having certain privileges to
the equipment of the tournament.[83]

To sum up this discussion, we may say that there is
evidence from the early fourteenth century that in Scotland
spoils were divided systematically, and from the late fourteenth and fifteenth century that the proportion was one-
third to the chieftain (to use Scots terminology) and two-
thirds to the man.   In all this I find no indication that the
Scottish King had any rights to the spoils of war, unless, we

76 *Acts of the Lords Auditors*, 1466-94, p. 72b.
77 Ibid., p. 112+b; R. C Reid, " Merkland Cross," D. and G. Trans.,
   Vol. XXI., 3rd series, p. 216.
78 R. C. Reid, *op. cit.*. p. 222; *Acts of the Lords Auditors*, p. 95+.
79 *Acts of the Lords Auditors in Civil Causes*, 1501-54, p. 602.
80 *Ibid.*, p. 639.
81 Spalding Club *Miscellany* V. (ed. J. Stuart, 1842), pp. 211-50; M.
   Bateson, in Scot Hist. Soc. *Miscellany*, ii. (1904).
82 *Rot. Scot.*, i. 208a (1327); F. Grose, *Military Antiquities*, 2 vols.,
   1786-8, i. 216, 226-9.
83 Spalding *Miscellany* V., 212; G. Neilson, *Trial by Combat*, 1890, pp.
   271-2.

may suppose, his own direct retainers gained any.[84]   And
this inference is borne out by looking at the customs observed
in sea warfare.   This may be done by consulting the Stair
Society volume which prints proceedings in the Admiralty
court from 1557-62.[85]   Here we find elaborate rules for the
division of captured ships, equipment, merchandise, and
prisoners according to the rank of the members of the ship's
crew and the shares of the owners.[86]   And we find that the
Lord High Admiral was entitled to a tenth of the plunder.[87]
These rules are of considerable antiquity; at any rate they
are very similar to English provisions going back to the
fourteenth century.[88]   But in England the crown claimed
and frequently exacted a proportion of the winnings of its
mariners in time of war: this proportion was sometimes half,
sometimes a quarter.[89]

Superficially the paid English army was clearly a more
reliable instrument than the Scottish host, the English crown
with its right to thirds and thirds of thirds and all enemy
prisoners of substance was better off than the impecunious
and more retiring crown of Scotland.   These differences
account, perhaps, for the severity of the raids made by Scots
on northern England, for the moderation displayed by Lancaster and his men in their half-hearted attack of 1384 which
so astonished Scots at the time.   But we should beware of
over-emphasising the difference.   There are some savage
documents dating from Edward II.'s reign and early in
Edward III.'s in which an invitation is extended, sometimes
to a named individual,[90] sometimes to allcomers,[91] to attack
Scotland in return for the possession of anything that can

---

84 We are tantalisingly near a statement of principle in the articles
   sent in 1489 to James IV. by supporters of the dead James III.
   (Fraser, *Lennox*, 2 vols., 1874, pp. 128-9) where the critical passage
   is torn: " Alsua, that al ransoms takin be ony of our souerane . . .
   be restorit and gevin agane."
85 Ed. T. C. Wade, 1937.
86 E.g., pp. 111-2 and introduction, p. xxvii.
87 E.g., pp. 32, 56-8.
88 See above, p. 275 and refs.
89 *Ibid.*
90 Rymer, ii. 304 (David Earl of Atholl); *Rot. Scot.*, i. 166b (Fulk
   Fitz Warin); *ibid.*, 187a (William le Scryveyn).   These are in 1316-8.
91 Rot. Scot., i. 208a, 283-4 (1327-34).

be taken—though the king's rights to prisoners of substance and the customary fees of constable and marshal seem usually to be reserved.[92] This may perhaps be looked on as to some extent Scottish rapacity and revenge: it is the era of the disinherited. No such excuse can be offered for turning the sanctuary men of Beverley and other liberties against the Scots, as was done in 1342.[93] But later on different causes sometimes gave a harsher colour to English warfare on the Border. As is well known, the Percies in 1402 rebelled partly at least because their claims for payment for the defence of the northern marches were not met. We now know that their claim was true: under Henry IV., Henry V., and Henry VI. the highest proportion of dishonoured tallies went to the Scottish wardens and to other officers in the north, like the warden of Roxburgh.[94] The English magnates and their men were thus presumably often just as inclined to unbridled rapacity as their opponents in the Scots side of the boundary; certainly morale was very low at times and captains threatened to abandon their duties.[95] The Percies and Nevilles thus had almost as much interest in the spoils as the Douglases; and as late as the mid-sixteenth century we find a record being kept at Alnwick of captured plunder.[96]

May I conclude with one or two general points which to my mind emerge from the foregoing discussion? One point is the impossibility of running a frontier through the

92 Prisoners are reserved in the licenses to the Earl of Athol and to Fitz Warin. In the proclamation ordered by a writ of 1327 prisoners, goods, cattle and movables may be taken without hindrance from royal officers, "saving the due and customary fees of constable and marshal," *Rot. Scot.*, i. 208a. Other references to marshal and constable, ibid., 249a, 252.
93 *Rot. Scot.*, i. 629-30.
94 S. B. Chrimes, "Letters of John of Lancaster as Warden of the East Marches," *Speculum*, XIV. (1939), pp. 6-7, 11; A. B. Steel, "English Government Finance, 1377-1413," *Eng. Hist. Rev.*, LI. (1936), 577-97. Bain, iv. pp. 200-268 *passim* for returned tallies, 1424-61.
95 Bain, iii. 1338 (1340), 1463 (1346).
96 Duke of Northumberland's MSS., Alnwick. Hist. MSS. Comm., 3rd *Report* (1872) appendix, p. 113a; cf. Barrington de Fonblanque, *Annals*, ii. 128: a spoil recorded of 280 cattle, 1000 sheep, and horses and prisoners (1557).

Marches of England and Scotland. The whole economy of
the area militated against this. We read again and again of
attempts by the two sides to prevent smuggling, particularly
of wool ;[97] we read again and again of the impossible task set
the wardens on each side to prevent sheep from wandering.
At one stage the English complain that 10,000 Scottish sheep
daily graze in England.[98] And we even have a fantastic safe
conduct issued in 1389 for 1600 sheep belonging to the Countess
of March and Lady Hering to graze daily within five leagues
of Cockburnspath for three years or the duration of the
truce.[99] To the unity of the pastoral economy we might add
the unity of the warlike economy of the region. The borderers liked warfare: at all events Sir Thomas Gray in the
Scalacronica argues that the onus of proving that peace will
bring advantages lies on the peacemaker.[100] The nefarious
behaviour of Scots who betrayed brither Scots into English
hands and of English borderers who did likewise needs no
elaboration.[101] In peace and war the men of the marcher
counties were like minded.

The area has one other characteristic deriving from
matters touched on here. That is the way it bred, on both
sides, the magnate described in Fortescue's influential phrase
as " the overmighty subject." The way in which their
custody of the Marches led to the swelling of Percy power
has been examined in detail by Miss Reid.[102] Much the same
story is true of the Douglas power in the area where we are
meeting to-night. Indeed, the reward given to the Earl in
1324, known as the Emerald Charter, which conferred such
a massive liberty, was granted because Douglas surrendered
to the king some French prisoners.[103] The two families,

97 *Ex. Rolls Scot.*, ii. 51, 78 (1360-61); Bain, iii. 1625, iv. 117, 200, 444,
486, 572 (1356-1401).
98 *Hamilton Papers*, i. 81-2.
99 At the request of Hotspur: presumably as part of the price of
his release after Otterburn. Bain, iv. 392; Rot. Scot., ii. 99a.
100 Ed. Maxwell, pp. 164-6; ed. Stevenson, pp. 197-8.
101 Cf. R. C. Reid, " Littlegill Murders," *D. and G. Trans.*, 3rd
series, XXIV., p. 83.
102 R. R. Reid, " Office of Warden of the Marches," *Eng. Hist. Rev.*,
XXXII. (1917), 479-496.
103 W. Fraser, *The Douglas Book*, 4 vols., 1885, iii. 11-2 (cf. i. 154-5
for commentary).

traditional enemies on a heroic scale, who dominate the lands
of the Border, were perpetually jealous of the encroachments
on their independence by the kings of England and Scotland.
So that even in their leaders the men of the Marches in each
country found a similarity of purpose which further encouraged the homogeneous character of the Anglo-Scottish
Border.

14

ENGLAND, SCOTLAND AND EUROPE:
THE PROBLEM OF THE FRONTIER

IN what follows I propose to discuss certain questions concerning frontiers as they affect historians. Most of my time will be devoted to the Anglo-Scottish frontier, for the reason that it displays phenomena much more easily identified and documented than those associated with the frontiers of Europe. Some of the lessons one may draw from Anglo-Scottish frontier history are, moreover, of relevance elsewhere within the Continent, not only between countries but in some instances inside countries.

Our present concern with sharp lines on maps conditions us in all sorts of ways which may interrupt a clear view of political and cultural contacts in earlier times. For a century and a half statesmen have been trying to solve international conflicts of all kinds— political, economic, religious and sentimental—by adjusting boundaries between areas of sovereignty. Never has such activity been more intense than in the last ten years. Indeed at the very moment when I write, in Asia, in the Middle East and on our own doorstep in Ireland frontiers and the hopes and fears attached to them obtrude themselves daily and tragically on public attention. In our present troubles divisions are due to ethnic, religious and ideological conflict. But it is reasonable to suppose that awareness of such antitheses is never far from the surface anywhere. It is a curious commentary on the Enlightenment that it has proved so feeble a constituent in later attitudes among intellectuals, let alone in the public at large, even in regions of high literacy. As the nine-teenth century progressed it became more and more difficult to become a member of the 'Heavenly City of the Eighteenth Century Philosophers', to use the title of Carl Becker's famous book.[1] What intelligent man today could describe himself as a 'citizen of the world'? We can, of course, console ourselves to some extent by our modern acceptance of the reasonableness of unreason and by pretending that one can scientifically study the dark irrational forces within each of us.

[1] New Haven, 1932.

I venture to mention these imponderables at the outset because we should remember that behind most political tensions lie assumptions which (for want of a better word) might be called moral. These are to be found whenever a man enters an unfamiliar environment—when the poor man crosses the threshold of a rich man, even more perhaps when the rich man crosses the threshold of the poor. At a higher point of social organization come the distinctions between larger groups. The earliest of these was surely the town-country dichotomy and I cannot do better than quote a few lines by Carlo Cipolla:

> The city represented for people in Europe during the eleventh, twelfth and thirteenth centuries what America was for nineteenth-century Europeans. The city was 'the frontier': a dynamic and new world in which men had the power to break the shackles of the past, where people saw or thought they saw new opportunities for economic and social success, where the old institutions and old prejudices no longer counted, where institutions and fortunes were all to be made or moulded as a reward for initiative, boldness and risk.[2]

One is reminded here, of course, of Marc Bloch's famous description of the chasm which separated the bourgeoisie from the feudal society around them, symbolized by the sworn commune between equals.[3] One is also reminded of the equally celebrated discussion by Braudel of the mountain and the plain in Mediterranean history.[4] For my purposes, in fact, Braudel's *montagnards* and agriculturists are more to the point than the townsmen of Bloch or Cipolla. Cipolla's city 'frontier' is obviously an application of Frederick J. Turner's interpretation of the American experience, where the frontier was on the move for generations and the type of society associated with it conditioned the whole development of United States history. Such a view does not have much if any relevance in the continent of Europe, where the concept of the frontier was very different. Nor is it applicable in the context of England and Scotland.

The Anglo-Scottish frontier was long in establishing itself. For centuries after the departure of the Romans the island they had called Britain was divided and subdivided into clans and petty kingdoms. After the English invasions some of these divisions were

---

[2] Carlo M. Cipolla, *Storia economica dell' Europa pre-industriale* (Bologna, 1974), p. 200.

[3] *Feudal Society*, trans. L. A. Manyon (London, 1961), p. 355.

[4] F. Braudel, *La Mediterranée et le monde mediterranéen à l'époque de Philippe II* (Paris, 1949), esp. part I, chap. I.

modified but the future boundary between the two kingdoms was overlaid by Celtic peoples in Cumbria (later Cumberland and Westmorland with S. W. Scotland) and English tribes in the North East—a Northumbria which stretched from the Firth of Forth to the Humber. Subsequently the Scots were compelled to recognize a single king. By the time of the Norman conquest the Scots not only exercised some control over Cumbria but had conquered that part of Northumbria which lay north of the Tweed. When William Rufus made good his recognition in Cumberland and Westmorland something like the later frontier had emerged. It was not until the Treaty of York in 1237 that these *ad hoc* arrangements were in some sense recognized, although the armed incursions of one country with the other were, of course, to continue for centuries. The Treaty of York was, it has been said, 'an incident' in the process of Scottish unification, part of the 'southern phase of the process'.[5] It should be stressed that 1237 was not in any way a deliberate delimitation of territories. It is simply the case that, in subsequent wars between England and Scotland, the border then accepted was not subsequently greatly modified, save by the incorporation in England of Berwick and its 'bounds', permanently after 1482. The chronology of the establishment of a firm ecclesiastical frontier between the two countries was somewhat different, but the archbishop of York's claims to metropolitan jurisdiction in Scotland were not seriously pressed after the thirteenth century.

I have set out in brief these developments because, and this is surprising, there is very little discussion of the frontier in ordinary surveys of Scottish or English history.[6] Books there are which do discuss the frontier, but they do not seem to have attracted much attention, since major conflicts between the two countries were affected only marginally by the ambiguities of the Tweed-Solway line.[7] In the long tally of wars and treaties, of dynastic claims and dynastic marriages, the details of demarcation are certainly not negligible (witness the Debateable Land); but they are subsidiary to wider international issues, and notably the relationships of each country with France. However, the prolonged hostilities meant that the frontier had to be guarded and Wardens of the Marches were appointed on each side and to them was committed not only the defence of the respective kingdoms, but also the much more

[5] F. M. Powicke, *The Thirteenth Century*, 2nd edn. (Oxford, 1962), p. 574.

[6] Powicke, *op. cit.*, is exceptional; now see Geoffrey Barrow, 'The Anglo-Scottish Border', *Northern History*, i (1966), pp. 21–42.

[7] James Logan Mack, *The Border Line* (Edinburgh, 1924), is a careful account of earlier descriptions and maps, together with an on-the-ground perambulation. The standard narrative remains George Ridpath, *The Border History of England and Scotland* (Berwick, 1776; revd. edn., Berwick, 1848).

difficult task of managing the Borders in time of official peace. They have been well studied,[8] and, if the establishment of a fixed boundary has been somewhat taken for granted, this has not been the case with the Marches as two areas to be administered. One in England, the other in Scotland. For the Border was not merely a line, notionally following rivers and burns and leaping to standing stones and ditches or dykes. It was a tract of territory separated in some senses from the countries on either side of it. It was thus a frontier of a peculiar kind.

This was evident to any sharp observer. Here is Polydore Vergil writing in the early sixteenth century. Having given some information regarding the dimensions of Scotland (grotesquely distorted because seen in the shape of a contemporary map) he goes on: 'Beside the Tweed, which rises from the hills not far from Roxburgh, a region lies to the South which they call the March, that is the frontier of the kingdoms of the English and the Scots. The Tweed separates this from Northumberland, the last region of England, which faces on to the German ocean and whose main town is Berwick'. He then turns to the *Scotiae limes* in Cumbria and the Solway. 'Between these two regions Mount Cheviot rises in the heart of the land'.[9] For Vergil—this is the point I am making—the Anglo-Scottish *limes* is the centre of a *regio*.

It is not entirely true, of course. The bounds of Berwick were clear enough, and the great medieval and early modern fortifications a permanent reminder that near the town the Tweed began the frontier. But it was then readily fordable even near Berwick and soon ceased to be more than an occasion for irritating riparian quarrels over fishing rights; these were the limits of the East March. In the West the great tidal estuary of the Solway was also fordable at several points and so were the rivers north and west of Carlisle; the West March in Scotland comprised modern Dumfriesshire and Kirkcudbrightshire and in England the counties of Cumberland and Westmorland. As for the central section, the Middle March in each country, the great rolling masses of the Cheviot Hills were traversed by many well-worn cattle roads. On this large extent of moorland agriculture was only possible in the lower valleys and, in the east, in the level Merse. The agricultural areas were more extensive nearer to the line of the frontier on the Scottish than on the English side. In the moorland proper there was only grazing

[8] R. R. Reid, 'Office of Warden of the Marches', *Eng. Hist. Rev.*, xxxii (1917), pp. 479–96; D. L. W. Tough, *The Last Years of a Frontier* (Oxford, 1928); Thomas I. Rae, *The Administration of the Scottish Frontier 1513–1603* (Edinburgh, 1966).

[9] *Anglica historia*, ed. Thysius (Leyden, 1651), p. 12; cf. the anonymous English version, ed. H. Ellis (Camden Soc., 1846), p. 6.

and sheep and cattle were allowed, by consent, to pasture in-differently on either side. To the activities of the shepherd, rein-forced where conditions permitted by some crops, the land afforded one other economic activity: banditry or, in the local expression, reiving. Reiving was hunting for booty or 'prey', a word which fairly catches the grim overtones of *praeda*. Throughout its history down to and even after the Union of the Crowns, 'prey' was sought by borderers from both sides of the boundary. It was, perhaps, commoner for Scots to raid English and English to raid Scots, but the English and Scots also preyed on their own countrymen. Prey meant, especially before the sixteenth century, absolutely anything: men for the ransoms they would fetch, or pay to avoid destruction (let us remember the Border origin of the expression 'blackmail'), money and articles of value but above all moveable wealth on the hoof—sheep, cattle, horses.[10] These last commodities had one enormous attraction: they were self-propelling. A few men and a few dogs on a drove road with a days' start took a great deal of catching before the beasts were safely away.

All of this led to vendettas and rapine, to burnt farmsteads and castles and even churches. Policing the area was virtually impossible and however carefully international agreements were reached for Wardens to apply the 'Law of the March', its official application was always retrospective. Border law was, in its essentials and in so far as it was effective, a law of self-help. It was a primitive law, matching the primitive conditions of the area. It deserves study, and so do the social habits—not so different, it seems—in the south of Scotland and the north of England. Dr Rae has recently reminded us how clans or 'surnames', under one or more leaders, emerged in the later Middle Ages to exist beside the old 'feudal' tenurial dependents of the greater families, or even to develop at the expense of the older nobles[11]. It was a world in which gangs and gang warfare could flower and even seem patriotic. This structure of society was paralleled south of the border and in both countries great magnates found the office of Warden a useful adjunct to tenurial resources and family loyalties. The Douglasses and the Percies and Nevilles are not just story-book figures. They stain the pages of history as well as glorify those of romance.

It is not my purpose to display how nasty, brutish and short life was in and near the wide swathe of the Marches between England

---

[10] Hay, 'Booty in Border warfare', *Trans. Dumfriesshire and Galloway Nat. Hist. and Antiquarian Society*, xxxi (1954 for 1952–53), pp. 148–66; see above, 285-306.

[11] Rae, *Administration of the Scottish Frontier*, pp. 5–7; for the English side *cf.* J. A. Tuck, 'Northumbrian society in the fourteenth century', *Northern History*, vi (1971), pp. 22–39, esp. pp. 27–28 and refs.

and Scotland[12] but to add one or two complications to the picture I have sketched and then to put before you some observations regarding the confrontations of the two countries separated as they were by a human undergrowth (if this word may be applied to an area which observers agreed was singularly treeless) of gentry and shepherds, lords and men accepting mutual violence not as an exceptional occurrence but as a way of life.

First of all, the complication of the Debateable Land, or rather Lands. These tracts lay between the English West March and the confines of the Middle and West Marches of Scotland and (two smaller areas) between the two Middle Marches. They were for long a monument to the intractable character of the natives, for while it was agreed that one might by day graze them, no one might live there. Any habitation erected by Scots could be destroyed legally by English; and *vice versa*. These absurdities were partially removed in 1552, when the main disputed area was successfully partitioned. Second, even without violence, it was manifestly absurd to operate in any meaningful way a frontier crossing wild hills which gave a livelihood to men only by being grazed by beasts. The very pattern of transhumance, which was followed in parts of the Borders, stressed this. The high shielings at heads of valleys were found everywhere and survive widely, if only in little ruins, as evidence of this activity which persisted, of course, well beyond 1603 or 1707.[13] The present shared grazing of all our northern moorland shows that even today, with our acuter sense of property and territorial rights, the highlands of Cumberland or North Northumberland are indivisible. This is clearly seen in countless ways in the years before the Union. At one stage the English complained that 10,000 Scottish sheep daily grazed in England. And we have a safe-conduct issued in 1389 for 1,600 sheep belonging to the countess of March and Lady Hering to graze daily within five leagues of Cockburnspath for three years or the duration of the truce.[14]

A third consideration. It was the case, it seems, that many of the indwellers in the north of England were in fact Scots. This would be proved alone by the distrust of Scottish servants and the punishment of men of substance for having Scottish dependents. Lord

[12] A fine brief picture of this in Edward Miller, *War in the North* (St John's College Cambridge lecture 1959–60 . . . at the University of Hull. Hull, 1960). An older but equally unromantic picture in G. M. Trevelyan's essay, 'The Middle Marches', best read in the reprint published at Newcastle in 1934 for the Northumberland and Newcastle Society.

[13] H. G. Ramm, R. W. McDowall, Eric Mercer, *Sheilings and Bastles* (H.M.S.O., 1970).

[14] See above, p. 305 and refs.

Hunsdon estimated that '2500 Scots, few of them denizens, lived in the East March in 1569; later on English estimates put the number of Scots within ten miles of the frontier as one in three'.[15] There was also a fair amount of intermarriage,[16] so it was not only banditry and the hostility of the rugged reivers to pressure from either Edinburgh or London which gave the region its coherence. It was the economic pressure of a pastoral economy, which made the borderers suspicious and alien to their more civilized neighbours and drove them in on themselves and out against everyone else.[17] This coherence may, perhaps, be reflected in the language used. To a southern Englishman the English borderers even in the sixteenth century sounded Scottish.[18] And in the modern and highly technical linguistic studies which have been made of this area there are some traces of a spill southward, especially in the East March, of words associated in recent times with the south of Scotland rather than the north of England.[19] But this evidence from today or even yesterday tells us little for sure about the sixteenth or seventeenth centuries let alone earlier times. We can however say with confidence that there was no linguistic frontier such as that which separated Romance and Teutonic areas in continental Europe. Here we have at any rate a further reason for some unity within the region. Shepherds and lords could communicate across the frontier which separated and united them in their ambiguous relationship. The pastoral economy itself meant that for months at a time men whose permanent dwellings were perhaps twenty miles apart came together on one sheiling ground during the summer months.[20] It was much more difficult for a burgess of Edinburgh and a Londoner to communicate by word of mouth.

Nor was living in the Border region without its compensations. In a cruel age it offered shelter to men on the run. Some were doubtless malefactors who sought the sanctuary of the hills in order not only to avoid harsh justice but to make a living by the wicked ways they knew—thieving, murdering, counterfeiting the coins of either realm. But the misty moors and their remote farms and castles offered sanctuary to religious refugees: I am thinking of catholics, presbyterians and even Anglicans, trying to exercise

[15] Tough, *Last Years of a Frontier*, p. 179.
[16] Rae, *Administration of the Scottish Frontier*, pp. 10–11.
[17] *Cf.* Braudel, *La Mediterranée*, pp. 650–52.
[18] Tough, *Last Years of a Frontier*, pp. 34–35.
[19] See Beat Glauser, *The Scottish-English Linguistic Border. Lexical Aspects* (Bern, 1974); Hans-Hennig Speitel, 'An areal typology of isoglosses: isoglosses near the Scottish-English Border', *Zeitschrift für Dialektologie und Linguistik*, xxxvi (1969), pp. 49–66. I have to thank Dr Speitel for allowing me to consult him.
[20] P. W. Dixon in *Archaeologia Aeliana*, 4th ser., I (1952), p. 251.

liberty of conscience. This was all the easier since changes in religious policy arrived at by central governments left many leading families in the Border region for long unaffected.[21]

Another curious compensation for occasional war and endemic freebooting was the money it brought to a poor region.[22] The provision for wardens and supporting troops in each of the three Marches produced fair sums of money even on the Scottish side, where stipends were small and the notion of a paid soldiery was not yet established by the sixteenth century. On the English side large retainers were paid and some garrisons (such as that at Berwick) were substantial. It is of course true that the cash did not always arrive: the famous episode of the dishonoured tallies in Henry IV's reign was among the factors which led the Percies to revolt.[23] But overall a very considerable amount must have been spent locally on troops and by the troops on victuals and other goods. Here again was a bond between Borderers. The garrison at Berwick was largely fed by the provender purchased in the Merse.[24] Building of fortifications obviously gave employment, especially at seasons when normal reiving was difficult, as in long summer days. Such building was by no means restricted to castles for the rich or for agents of the government such as the Wardens. One of the characteristic features of the whole Border area, from Firth to Tyne, was the construction of fortified farms or 'bastles' 'fortalices', towers and churches—places where men and cattle might seek safety against raiders and their swords and torches. These buildings were by the sixteenth century, it seems, frequently erected by tenant farmers. Rents were low in the Borders, especially on Crown land which gradually controlled 'the whole of the upland border by the later sixteenth century'[25]

Finally it would be absurd to omit among the more creative side of Border life the emergence of a ballad literature which bears comparison with any such elsewhere.[26] The heroic element in the life of the Marches was paid for, we may think, at a terrible price in brutality and boorishness. But it was based on concepts of undying and unquestioning loyalty, reflected in ballad after ballad. The propriety of singing the praises of *Outlaw Murray* or *Johnny Armstrong* may be questioned: they were sung at the time, and

[21] 'The religion of the Borderers' in Tough, *Last Years of a Frontier*, pp. 61–75.
[22] Hay, 'Booty', p. 13. Was the general decline in the later medieval economy intensified or retarded in the Borders by war and reiving? I understand from Dr. Tuck that there is debate on the question.
[23] J. M. W. Bean, 'Henry IV and the Percies', *History*, xliv (1959), pp. 212–27.
[24] Tough, pp. 45–46.
[25] Dixon, *loc. cit.*, pp. 254–55, an extended assessment and supplement to *Shielings and Bastles*, above, p. 82, n. 13.
[26] An excellent recent book is by James Reed, *The Border Ballads* (London, 1973).

Bishop John Leslie, writing about 1570, describes this musical activity as spontaneous and moving.[27] Moving it still is, but also extraordinarily revealing of all aspects of border life—resistance to central authority, lust for prey, kinship ties and so on. The Scottish ballads are truer, less sophisticated than the English ones, perhaps because the ethos of the frontier area lingered longer in southern Scotland.

If the borderers may sometimes seem enviable, that was hardly how they struck contemporaries, especially by the sixteenth century. The gentry of southern England who visited the North as soldiers, merchants or missionaries were appalled at the bestial lives of the upper valleys and the hills. Feuds and violence made any regular life a mockery, and not least the regular life of the Church.[28] As a boy born in Cumberland the situation must have been well-known to Bernard Gilpin; later, a saintly don and archdeacon of Durham, he took his duties seriously, pastoralism of a different sort. He found churches desolate, parsons ignorant, the people divided by hate. The Prayer Book calls to Communion those who are 'in love and charity with their neighbours', an echo of the Pax which had latterly become a favourite part of the old Mass. It was difficult in small neighbourhoods for feuding families to love neighbours they were at odds with. They either lost face, or provoked a fracas, or they stayed away from church.[29] They usually stayed away.

The perpetual disturbances on the Border were intensified by weak or divided government in England and Scotland. On balance the Scottish government was less capable of managing its border region and the traditional families maintained their independence with considerable success. On the English side central government was stronger and, as Mr James has demonstrated, 'the values of lineage, good lordship and fidelity' on the English March were perceptibly dissolving in the later sixteenth century.[30] There were regular attempts at government level to iron out differences[31] and the Border itself was the subject of serious negotiation. I have mentioned the division of the main debateable area in 1552; for the rest it is clear that in 1552, and perhaps earlier, the watershed was regarded as determining the boundary in the wastes of the Cheviot

[27] Tough, *Last Years of a Frontier*, p. 36; again *cf.* Braudel, *La Mediterranée*, p. 651.
[28] Tough, *op. cit.*, p. 64.
[29] *Northumberland County History*, xv (Newcastle upon Tyne, 1940), p. 312 (Gilpin at Rothbury). *Cf.* John Bossy, 'The Reformation and the people of Catholic Europe', *Past and Present*, 47 (1970), p. 55.
[30] M. E. James, 'The first earl of Cumberland and the decline of northern feudalism', *Northern History*, i (1966), pp. 43–69; *id.*, 'The concept of order and the Northern Rising of 1569', *Past & Present*, 60 (1973), pp. 49–63.
[31] Tough, *Last Years of a Frontier*, pp. 175–77, 187–278.

hills in the Middle March.[32] This was certainly the case in the abortive memorandum submitted to Elizabeth in 1580. The phrase is clumsy but its meaning is inescapable: 'the height whereof (in the forest of Cheviot) as the water falleth, is the march of England and Scotland'.[33] But the long tale of war and rapine was in theory brought to an end by the accession to the English throne of King James VI of Scotland. The repeated attempts at a dynastic solution had finally paid off.

The learned monarch attempted at once to ordain a union of the two realms under the title 'Great Britain'. Professor Bindoff has shown how futile such a gesture proved at the time and for long after.[34] This was despite the precedents for such a usage which, as I have explained elsewhere, were indeed plentiful through the later Middle Ages and which became even more intense under the influence of humanist secretaries, ambassadors and men of letters.[35] James VI and I even had designs prepared for a flag which combined the crosses of St Andrew and St George; and a proclamation set out the manner in which British ships were to show the flag.[36] But all of this was part of a programme which was far from being effective. James as king of Scotland had made fruitless and some- times bloody efforts to enforce his authority in southern Scotland. 'Of the nine judicial raids which took place, James VI attended seven in person . . .'.[37] After 1603 the problem changed. As Dr Rae says, 'the international aspects of the problem had been eliminated, and a problem of frontier control involving two states became a domestic problem of administering the unruly Middle shires of King James's "united kingdoms"'.[38] It was far from easy to ad- minister these unruly shires, and the desire to make money out of the customs levied on border traffic was a strong incentive to

[32] Bowes' survey of 1550 is reprinted in Mack, *The Border Line*, pp. 32–40.

[33] *Calendar of Letters and Papers relating . . . to the Borders . . .* , ed. J. Bain, 2 vols. (Edinburgh, 1894–96), i, p. 31. *O.E.D.* gives the first use of 'water-shed' as 1803.

[34] S. T. Bindoff, 'The Stuarts and their style', *Eng. Hist. Rev.*, lx(1945), pp. 192–216.

[35] 'Great Britain in the Middle Ages', *Proc. Soc. Antiquaries of Scotland*, lxxxix (1955–56); I published a revised version of this as an appendix to the second edn. of my *Europe—the Emergence of an Idea* (Edinburgh, 1968). Much additional material could be adduced.

[36] National Library of Scotland MS. 2517 (a miscellany of heraldic papers), fos. 67–68, consist of a folded sheet of designs for a union 'jack'. Four of these are designs in colour; a further monochrome sketch displays a fifth way of combining the two national crosses. The earl of Nottingham (Charles Howard) signs, indi- cating his preference for a design where the colours will not run, presumably in his capacity as Admiral. None of these was the pappern adopted in 1606, on which see Sir W. L. Clowes, *The Royal Navy. A History*, ii (London, 1898), p. 25 and n.

[37] Rae, *Administration of the Scottish Frontier*, p. 212 and pp. 206–22, *passim*.

[38] *Ibid.*, p. 233.

maintain economic separation.[39] There was also regular pressure from over-mighty subjects on both sides which led, *inter alia,* to the attempt virtually to eliminate the Grahams (Graemes) of Eskdale early in James I's reign, the subject of the *saeva indignatio* of a descendant of the surname writing only fifty years ago.[40] Other similar barbarities were only slowly abandoned and when the mid-seventeenth century revived in effect a state of war between the two countries principles could again shelter factions. But unhappily the history of the Borders after 1603 remains to be written. All one can be sure of is that the sheep and cattle went on grazing; that more agriculture came to be practised; that more Scottish farmers drifted southward into Northumberland and the Lake counties, bringing with them industrious ways and the reformed religion,[41] a process which was still going on in the eighteenth and nineteenth centuries. This process of eroding ancient ways had at any rate reached the point when in 1707 the bad habits, or the old habits, were no impediment to the legislative Union which in the end brought the Britain of James VI and I to something like a reality.

The Borders were a region and remain a region: the sheep have seen to that, and until a century ago not just the border sheep but the cattle from further north which followed drove roads over the Cheviots to feed the hungry industrial towns of England, until the railways completely took over the job.[42] Berwick was and is a shopping centre for Berwickshire as well as north Northumberland; the Scottish border towns have long had markets which attract southern farmers just as more recently the licensing laws brought droves of thirsty Scots into England on a Sunday. Much of this, as can readily be imagined, is reflected in the current speech of the area.[43] I do not wish to evoke the modern Border as to some extent still a self-contained social entity, although as I have remarked its history in such a context deserves to be written, especially for the period after 1603. My point is that we have not merely a region with a surviving life of its own (based to some degree on its history); there are, after all, many such territorial groupings in Britain—especially those where linguistic differences invoke old ethnic patterns, as on the edges of the Highlands and Islands of Scotland, Wales, and perhaps even the South West of England, where we

[39] A. R. B. Haldane, *The Drove Roads of Scotland* (Edinburgh, 1952), pp. 16–19. The drovers of course did not find it hard to avoid such taxes.

[40] John Graham, *The Condition of the Border at the Union: Destruction of the Graham Clan,* 2nd edn., (London, 1907).

[41] Trevelyan, *The Middle Marches,* p. 29; I wish I could agree that 'vulgarity has not invaded from the cities', for it has since 1950.

[42] Haldane, *The Drove Roads of Scotland,* pp. 168–86.

[43] *Cf.* above p. 313, n. 19.

are meeting this evening. In all such regions, and indeed throughout
the land, moss-trooping and reiving, piracy, highway robbery,
blackmail, murder and rapine were endemic in the Middle Ages
and the early modern period[44]. But none of such regions constitutes
historical let alone present-day frontiers. The Welsh Marcher
counties were not in any sense a frontier zone surviving the thirteenth
century, although up till then it is true that the great Marcher lords
claimed a right of private war in terms not dissimilar to those
liberties arrogated to themselves by border magnates. Outlaw
Murray in the ballad that bears his name made his position clear
to an officious king:

> 'These lands are mine', the Outlaw said,
> 'I ken nae king in Christentie;
> Frae Soudron I this Foreste wan,
> When the King nor his Knightis were not to see'.

Just as Murray had 'won' his lands from the southerner, so
Gloucester and Hereford in 1920 based their privileges on right of
conquest of Welsh lands. Edward I effectively killed that,[45] even if
the valley sheep, being fatter, still attracted the hillsmen.

In the United Kingdom of England and Scotland the Border
region remained distinct from the others because it continued to
mark an administrative division, as in certain respects it still does,
while existing within a larger political entity. Here again I do not
wish to imply that the Anglo-Scottish border has no parallels in
other parts of Europe. What were the county (later duchy) of
Piedmont and the kingdom of Navarre but marcher lordships,
straggling across mountains? The count of Armagnac held his fief
'of the eagle', as many a border lord could have claimed to hold his of
the buzzard or the falcon. There were debateable lands inside
France and everywhere there were liberties where asylum could be
found, and sub-frontiers where jurisdictions changed and the original
writ had to be replaced by some new authorisation if a criminal was
to be punished.[46] Banditry was worst, as Braudel says, where
governments were weakest, in mountainous areas and in frontier
zones; and he instances the Dalmatian uplands between Venice
and Turkey, the Hungarian frontier, Catalonia and the Pyrenees,
Messina, Benevento, the boundary of the Papal States and Tuscany,

[44] *Cf.* B. W. Beckingsale, 'The characteristics of the Tudor North', *Northern History*, iv (1969), pp. 67–83.

[45] Powicke, *The Thirteenth Century*, pp. 329–30; Hay, 'The divisions of the spoils of war in fourteenth-century England', *Trans. Royal Hist. Soc.*, 5th ser., 4 (1954), 108–9 and refs; see above, 282-3.

[46] Hay, 'Geographical abstractions and the historian', [*Irish*] *Historical Studies*, ii (London, 1959), p. 12 and refs.

and those between Milan and Venice, Venice and Austria.[47] One could make a longer list if one left the Mediterranean countries.

Borders represent divisions. But the tension of division forges bonds at the same time. The inter-feuding and intermarriage already mentioned as a unifying feature of Border life existed from the Normans onwards as between England and Scotland. Apart from Celtic areas in Wales and the Highlands, the two countries shared common linguistic backgrounds (Latin, Teutonic and French), a common religious tradition (Catholic and then, in broad terms, reformed), and a common literature. Differences remained after 1707, even after the spate of nineteenth-century Westminster legislation; education, law, the official relationship of Church to State. These however were not enough to nullify the basis of Union, which in the end offered opportunities especially to Scots, comparable in some sense to those in the Empire they helped so vigorously to create. In such circumstances the Border ceased by the eighteenth century to have any disruptive effect. On the contrary, it became an area of romance which the sophisticated of both countries could enjoy. Walter Scott published the *Minstrelsy of the Scottish Border* in 1802–3; James Hogg, the Ettrick Shepherd, was already producing verses and gathering material for his stories.[48]

You may have noticed that in the ballad I quoted the bard refers to 'Christentie' or Christendom as the widest area he and his listeners could know. Christendom (perhaps this was its main weakness) can have no conceivable frontiers: this would be a contradiction in terms. But Christendom bequeathed to Europe a large part of its ideological content, and I conclude with a few, I fear fairly obvious, reflections on the frontier of Europe, that area whose history has been as full of wars as has that of our own island. My first and most banal observation is that Europe has only one certain frontier—the seas which bound it to west and south. To the east it has only artificial limits, marks on a map which, as I have pointed out elsewhere, are now made entirely by Soviet administrators and geographers.[49]

[47] I paraphrase Braudel, *La Mediterranée*, p. 651; but the whole section, pp. 643–59, on poverty and banditry and the role of the noble malefactor, is relevant to Border conditions. *Cf.* also Braudel's comparison, p. 534, between well-governed Castile and anarchic Aragon, with its semi-independent lords, which can be applied more or less to the Anglo-Scottish scene.

[48] *E.g. The Brownie of Bodsbeck* (1817). *The Confessions of a Justified sinner* is by no means typical of James Hogg's work, as Professor William Beattie rightly points out in his introduction to the Penguin *Border Ballads* (Harmondsworth, 1952), p. 25. For the change in fashion which made popular ballads so appealing see Reed, *The Border Ballads*, pp. 1–8.

[49] For this paragraph and for what follows see my *Europe—The Emergence of an*

I confess that whenever I consider Europe as a political or cultural abstraction I realize that I am at the mercy of public pressures which I find it hard to resist, or if I resist I suspect that I over-react to them, to use current cant. When I began collecting material for the book I wrote on the idea of Europe it was 1950 and I was drenched in pro-European sentiment. This sentimental affection distorted my approach, or so I felt when I came to prepare a new edition in the mid-sixties. Now, when the selfishness and stupidity of the countries constituting the Community have all but destroyed its credibility, my heart again is stirred as I remember the inheritance by Europeans of Greece and Rome, of Christianity and Judaism, of an ideal of tolerance and material comfort which distinguishes the Continent from its neighbours in Asia and Africa. Apologies are due for such a series of personal revelations, although I daresay some of you may find echoes of current preoccupations affecting your work, especially if it lies in the very modern field.

Especially, but not entirely. In the last resort I suspect every topic in which we interest ourselves has its origins in some external suggestion and usually reflects contemporary interests. In any event it is the historian's job to destroy legends and if he is aware that he does this by creating new ones (they are called 'models' nowadays) than that is no bad thing. To understand how Britain as an abstraction survived from antiquity to become politically useful in the seventeenth century is to realize the power of a word. And when *Europe*, after centuries as a geographers' term, assumes a new role in the years after the Second World War we witness a similar phenomenon. Even 'Western Europe' can seem to have a role of its own, as it did to Yves Renouard in 1958—I suppose as a consequence of his being moved by the negotiations leading to the Treaty of Rome.[50]

What I suspect we will all do well to heed is the vulnerability of such abstractions. Europe, with or without frontiers, comprising only western Europe (and how western is western?), contains only so much meaning as its inhabitants and the outside world put into it, which at the moment is very little. And I venture to suggest that we should treat the concept Britain with similar reserve. Nothing is permanent in the no-man's-land where political relationships reflect patriotic sentiment. We were brought up—it is implicit in

---

idea (cited above, n. 35). In that edition there is a new preface and a new conclusion. 'Christentie' = Christendom, *ibid.*, pp. 22–23 and refs; this is a Middle English usage, not specifically southern Scottish or Border.

[50] Treaty of Rome, 1957; Yves Renouard, '1212–1216. Comment les traits durables de L'Europe se sont définis au début du XIIIᵉ siècle', *Annales de l'Université de Paris*, xxviii (1958), pp. 5–21.

Renouard's 1958 article—on the assumption that there were great verities—France, Spain, Britain—which were the product of thirteenth-century settlements, bloody at the time but in the end sealed by the inexorable physical facts of the Pyrenees and the Alps and the English Channel. We were brought up to believe that after Ferdinand and Isabella, or at any rate after Charles V, Spain was 'unified' just as England and Scotland were after 1603 and 1707. Can any one of us be so sure today that even France, where the very word patriotism was born,[51] may not embark on processes of devolution which may go far, as may those, more obviously, in Spain and perhaps in the United Kingdom? If such developments do occur it will bring the old 'nation states' of Europe into line with the fractionalized systems that have returned to Germany and from which Italy has never departed.

My remarks about the frontier lead me to a hopeful generalization: frontiers are man-made and therefore admirable subjects for an historical approach. The absurd concern with natural features, above all the terrible effects of using watersheds to carve up peoples, display an approach to political predicaments which has done terrible damage, at any rate within the European area. Let us remind our students and our readers that the future is what we make it, just as were all the futures which lay in front of our forefathers. Nothing is inevitable, not even patriotism, not even a frontier.[52]

[51] For some relevant considerations see Jean Lestocquoy, *Histoire du patriotisme* (Paris, 1968).

[52] This lecture was delivered before I had the advantage of reading Mr A. C. Goodman's paper, 'Reformation and society in the Scottish Marches', delivered to the Second International Colloquium in Ecclesiastical History organized by the British Sub-Commission for the Comparative Study of Ecclesiastical History, Oxford, September 1974. I understand that this will be published. I have also now seen a useful summary by Dr D. P. Kirby, 'The evolution of the frontier, Part II, 1018–1237', contributed to the forthcoming *An Historical Atlas of Scotland*, edited by Peter McNeill and Ranald Nicholson.

15

SCOTLAND AND THE ITALIAN RENAISSANCE

The Italian Renaissance may conveniently be summarised under three or four heads: a new style in painting, sculpture and architecture: a new educational pattern based on the ancient, and especially the Latin, classics and which stressed, as medieval literature had done to a minor degree only, the moral content of the authors studied; a conviction that education was just as important for the laity who were in positions of importance as it had earlier been for clerks; and – perhaps this is implied in the last point – a reverence for eloquence and the power of effective communication, whether in Latin (the model) or in the vernaculars of Europe. The latter, so far as Scotland was concerned, was by the sixteenth century rapidly becoming English, however it might differ in vocabulary, orthography and pronunciation.

If these matters are considered in turn the influence of Italy at first seems fairly remote in the Scotland of the century which ended in 1603.[1] Certainly in the fine arts it seems hard to trace more than very marginal Italian effects, whether arrived at directly by imported craftsmen or indirectly through travellers and books. As in England, the period sees the slow, slower than south of the Border, admiration of decorative details – the finish of a mantelpiece, the turn of a door-post or the decoration of a ceiling.[2] There is seldom anything large, dramatic, or unquestionably in the new manner. When James VI had the Half-Moon battery erected in Edinburgh Castle in 1573 there is no evidence (as there is for the even more impressive ramparts of Berwick) of Italian workmen or workmanship. Perhaps the most impressive innovation of this nature is the remarkable north range at Crichton Castle, built by the earl of Bothwell after his return from Italy in 1581. The architect who designed the diamond rustication and other details which seem unquestionably of direct Italian inspiration is not apparently known and the innovations introduced by Bothwell had no immediate influence.[3]

[1] I am much indebted to the advice of Dr John Durkan as well as to his paper 'The beginnings of humanism in Scotland', *Innes Review* iv (1953), 5-24. Among many people who have tried to plug gaps in my knowledge I must first of all thank Professor William Beattie, who was good enough to read an early draft of this essay.

[2] On the *Painted Ceilings of Scotland* see the book of that title by M. R. Apted (Edinburgh 1966).

[3] Colin McWilliam, *Lothian except Edinburgh* (The Buildings of Scotland, Harmondsworth 1978), 146.

What prompted this extravaganza in a building which in other respects had all four feet on the ground is far from obvious and remains mysterious insofar as the older style of fortified nobleman's house covered the country. Even less can be said for painting. It is true that the Trinity College altar-piece brought something of the new manner into Scotland. The four beautiful panels, perhaps by Hugo van der Goes and to be dated to the 1470s and 1480s, are nevertheless unquestionably northern in manner, however much Italians at the time admired such work. Again the work seems to have had no native emulators.[4] Native Scottish painters of a sort there were soon in plenty, 'but none of their surviving work suggests any first-hand knowledge of the continental traditions of painting'. The great wall of (imaginary) portraits of Scottish kings in Holyrood palace is late seventeenth century, but clearly by the end of the previous century there were a good number of uninspired likenesses being made of famous men, mainly reformers.[5]

As for sculpture, no evidence is to be found in the authorities of any sixteenth-century work carrying an Italian or even an Italianate flavour before the tomb of George Home, who was Chancellor of the (English) Exchequer when he died in 1611. His tomb in Dunbar parish church is perhaps better described as Jacobean than Renaissance as such; it is certainly not in the least medieval and was probably made in London, where Home died.[6]

If the Italian arts had to wait for their full-scale reception in Scotland, this is much less true of educational and moral attitudes. There is no doubt that confessional controversies seriously interrupted the peaceable introduction of the new methods of teaching and learning, but in Scotland, as elsewhere in Europe, the worst violences of the Reformation did not prevent fundamental if episodic changes in schools and universities.

There was much educational activity in sixteenth-century Scotland. There was certainly much need for it. The three universities of St Andrews, Glasgow and Aberdeen were at a low ebb;[7] this in turn affected the provision

[4] Stanley Cursiter in Roy. Comm. on the Ancient Monuments of Scotland, *Inventory of the . . . Monuments of the City of Edinburgh* (Edinburgh 1951), 38-40.

[5] Duncan Thomson, *Painting in Scotland 1550-1650* (Scottish National Portrait Gallery, 1975), 10; cf. the same author's *Life and Art of George Jamesone* (Oxford 1974), 44-50.

[6] McWilliam, *Lothian except Edinburgh*, 161-2.

[7] Hastings Rashdall, *Universities of Europe in the Middle Ages* second ed., revised by F. M. Powicke and A. B. Emden, ii (Oxford 1936), 301-24 are virtually unrevised), see also G. D. Henderson, *Founding of Marischal College, Aberdeen* (Aberdeen 1946) and the attractive *mise au point* by Leslie Macfarlane in *Aberdeen University Review* xlviii (1979), 2-17. John Durkan and James Kirk, *The University of Glasgow 1451-1577* (Glasgow 1977) has a wide-ranging bibliography. James K. Cameron's work on the early history of St Mary's College, St Andrews, is awaited with interest and Edinburgh University is planning a celebratory volume in the near future. For George Buchanan's influence on later sixteenth-century changes, see *Buchanan* (London, 1981) by I. D. MacFarlane and also the interesting early biography by David Irving, *Memoirs of the Life and Writings of George Buchanan* (Edinburgh 1807) and the biography by P. Hume Brown (Edinburgh 1890).

of schoolmasters and (at a later stage) ministers for the reformed kirk as well as lawyers to staff the courts at Edinburgh, although the need for the latter was felt more by the judges than the advocates. Lack of endowment accounts for some of the troubles at St Andrews and Glasgow but the three older Scottish universities had, in fact, little occasion to influence Scottish education along Italian lines. The Italian universities, while not as hostile to the new learning as were some northern institutions like Oxford, Paris and Louvain, had been successful and significant partly because they were involved in the training of the many men who became notaries,[8] but mainly because of their training of professional men of higher legal status, especially civil and canon lawyers. It is significant that this need for legal instruction was especially emphasised by Bishop Elphinstone at Aberdeen, who had studied law at Paris and taught it at Orleans. The French background was to be typical of early Scottish universities, together with an admixture of German academic influence. Nevertheless, it is advisable not to depreciate the value of the Aristotelianism prevalent in the older European universities, where original ideas were not necessarily inhibited, whatever critics like Erasmus might say.[9] And we may perhaps interpolate here Elphinstone's supposed connection with the act of the Scottish Parliament of 1496 'which required all barons and freeholders to have their eldest sons instructed in "Arts and Jure"'. This sentiment expressed the essence of Renaissance educational principles as stated by writers in Italy like Vittorino, or elsewhere by, for instance, Elyot in the *Governor* (1531).[10]

Nonetheless, the future of the humanities owed little to the Italian or northern universities, despite a few with 'trilingual colleges' such as Busleyden's foundation at Louvain, or Corpus Christi College, Oxford, despite the accommodation which some of the old practitioners were prepared to afford to Latin and Greek and the moral imperatives of Cicero.[11] The real roots of what was novel lay outside the old centres of scholarship, where a doctorate in divinity was as good as a doctorate in canon and civil law

[8] For notaries public in Scotland see, *The Renaissance and Reformation in Scotland*, edited by I.B. Cowan & D. Shaw (Edinburgh, 1983), pp. 22-40.

[9] See *Studies in the Renaissance* (1974–80) in which Charles H. Lohr surveys *seriatim* Renaissance Aristotelian commentaries, the latest instalment reaching authors whose names begin with Sm; cf. also James McConica, 'Aristotle and Humanism in Tudor Oxford', *EHR* xcv (1979), 291–317, in which he argues for the compatibility of Aristotelian teaching with concepts which can be termed 'Christian humanism'. Euan Cameron's lecture, 'Archibald Hay and the Paduan Aristotelians at Paris, 1530–45', delivered at the Fourth Neo-Latin Conference at Bologna (1979), shows Euhemerism surprisingly making an appearance in this context; it was Archibald Hay who urged the teaching of classical languages at St Mary's College, St Andrews. For the background see many works of P. O. Kristeller, e.g. 'Platonism and Aristotelianism' in *Renaissance Thought* II (New York 1965), 89–118.

[10] W. H. Woodward, *Vittorino da Feltre and other Humanist Educators* (Cambridge 1897); Stanford E. Lehmberg, *Sir Thomas Elyot: Tudor Humanist* (Austin 1960), chaps. 3–5.

[11] Not the totality of intellectual activity between, say, 1450 and 1650, but the concept as defined by Kristeller.

for purposes of promotion in church or state. It is to the extra-university establishments that we should look, to the 'Academies' of which the earliest and for a time the most influential was that associated with Ficino at Florence. In sixteenth-century Europe such bodies both multiplied and became formalised. It is in this intellectual climate that Edinburgh steps upon the Renaissance scene.

The new university had, to begin with, a chequered career. Dogged by the meanness of the burgesses and the crown, the actual foundation is doubtless to be dated to 1583, but it is of the greatest interest that a generation earlier the Regent Mary of Guise had established Alexander Sym in the name of the infant Queen Mary 'lector and reader in the laws or any other sciences at our burgh of Edinburgh or where he shall be required by our said dearest mother thereto; and also to give all other young men of fresh and quick ingynis occasion to apply their whole minds to study for like reward to be had of us in time coming'. In 1556, a similar appointment was made of Edward Henderson, LLD. In both cases a pension of £100 p.a. was to be involved. These steps have reasonably been compared with the establishment by Francis I of 'lecteurs royaux' in the 1530s (a development which Mary of Guise must have known about) which was ultimately to develop into the Collège de France, the present highest French academic institution. [12] Francis I was bypassing the Sorbonne and its generally sullen resistance to the new humanities. This was not paralleled in Edinburgh, where there was as yet no university to offer resistance, although Robert Reid, bishop of Orkney, had already in mind the endowment of legal, literary and philosophical studies. The bishop's main aim was to encourage the study of law, but it was to be long before any of Reid's money was to be applied to academic purposes. Likewise the Regent's appointments of two scholars who could fairly be termed 'lecteurs royaux' did not last long nor lead to the evolution of a new centre of higher education similar to the Collège de France. But there does seem every reason to believe that Reid, in an old-fashioned way, and Mary of Guise in a much more adventurous and up-to-date way, were aiming to redress the odd position which left the premier city without any centre of higher learning. [13] After all, it was not to be long before the *First Book of Discipline* (1560) was to lay down, in a protestant milieu this time, the need for parish schools, grammar schools in towns, and universities. [14] The aim of the reformers was, of course, to establish the means for producing a godly laity and a learned ministry. But then this had been the aim of John Colet in re-establishing St Paul's school in London, which almost at once became one of the focal points of the new learning south of the Border. An even more

[12] The Collegium Trilingue at Louvain was not part of the (fairly recent) university; see the study in English by Henry de Vocht, 4 vols. (Louvain 1951–55).

[13] The best account of these developments and of the establishment of the university is D. B. Horn, 'The Origins of the University of Edinburgh', University of Edinburgh *Journal*, spring and autumn 1966, 213–25, 297–312.

[14] *First Book of Discipline*, ed. J. K. Cameron (Edinburgh 1972), 128–55; in the section regarding schools there are curious reminiscences of *Utopia*.

important reflection of the Collège de France is probably to be seen in the *nova erectio* of Glasgow University in 1577. Here the influence was Andrew Melville's, who had studied in the new French institution and who was successful in introducing a system of scholarly instruction, abrogating the old regent arrangement and making provision in the Arts for three professional experts respectively in Greek and rhetoric; dialectic and logic together with moral philosophy and arithmetic and geometry; and natural philosophy and astronomy 'and likewise general chronology and history'. The principal, Melville himself, was in charge of theology and biblical languages.[15]

The most impressive display of innovation along humanist lines, or at least on Italian precedents, in sixteenth-century Scotland was, however, in the field of legal reform. There was something very like a 'reception' of Roman law, in marked contrast to what, in the end of the day, was to happen in England. The outward symbol of the process, which was to be a long one, was the establishment, with papal connivance, of the erection from church income, of the College of Justice. The term covered the institutionalisation of the court known earlier as the 'session' and it seems likely that the expression 'college of justice' was derived from the name used in Pavia.[16]

Education was also to the fore; provision for teaching at parish and burgh level was laid down in the *First Book of Discipline*. In theory there was to be an elementary school in every parish and a grammar school in every town. If this fell short of the mark, it was not altogether without effect.[17]

The extent to which new principles were put into effect in any European country may be partly measured by the attention paid to the education of the Prince. Here James V's education seems to mark the beginning of a serious effort to produce learning and morality. Certainly his tutors – Dunbar, Bellenden, Lindsay and Inglis – were intellectually superior to the men who had taught James IV and his predecessors. But a really great man was the chief instructor of James VI – the historian and poet George Buchanan, not the only scholarly tutor allotted to the child but potentially far and away the most influential, if only because his pupil was to rule England as well as Scotland.[18]

James V, despite his familiars including literary figures, was not himself a man of learning or aptitude in letters and doubts have been expressed about the degree of his Latin literacy. But there seems certainty that Gavin Dunbar was mainly responsible for such competence as he had and there is no doubt that James V's reign witnessed the most remarkable collection of

---

[15] See the very complete survey in Durkan and Kirk, *University of Glasgow*. I leave aside the question of Ramist humanism, as it is now often termed. The influence of Ramus on Scottish scholars is certainly important, not least on Buchanan. This remarkable scheme was to last until 1640, and, if it then petered out at Glasgow in favour of regenting, by then its innovatory effects were being experienced elsewhere in Scotland.

[16] The standard work remains R. K. Hannay, *The College of Justice* (Edinburgh and Glasgow 1933); 49–50 on the putative Pavian model.

[17] Cameron, *Book of Discipline*.

[18] For the tutors of James VI and I see the biography by D. H. Willson (London 1956), chaps. 1 and 2.

writers. They owed little to Renaissance Italy, though Gavin Douglas's translation of the Aeneid has been described as one of the high points in 'British' literature. 'To read the Latin again with Douglas's version fresh in our minds is like seeing a favourite picture after it has been cleaned . . . the fine flower of medieval Vergilianism.'[19] Douglas and Dunbar should not be labelled 'Scottish Chaucerians'; they write in a strong native tradition on which Vergil impinges, so to say, as a traditional heroic poet.

Earlier there seems little doubt that Henryson at the end of the fifteenth century came under the influence of Italian vernacular poets, as did later Gavin Douglas. Italian (as opposed to Latin humanist writings) from time to time continued to have direct influence on Scottish writers, though the main route by which new styles and techniques reached Scotland was normally France or England.[20] In consequence much more would have emerged on the literary front in a theme not confined to 'Renaissance' unqualified by 'Italian' and not limited in range to the sixteenth century. From the mid-sixteenth century onwards the Italian poets and novelists, direct or via France, exercise a fascination for many Scots including writers as famous as Sir David Lyndsay (though hardly in his masterpiece, *Ane Satyre of the Thrie Estaits*). Some of this cultural contact was to produce very impressive results: the sonnet was acclimatised and there were major adaptions of Italian works, most notably perhaps the *Roland Furious* of John Stewart of Baldynneis; it has been noted that Stewart derived some of his inspiration from the 'wider Scottish literacy tradition he inherited.[21] On the other hand, it must be remembered that much of this writing was not published and that it was therefore influential if at all at a remove. The same remark applies to William Fowler's partial translation of Machiavelli's *Prince.*[22]

With Machiavelli the influence of the humanities on Scottish literature is manifest. Argument there may be over the degree to which the *Prince* reflects ancient models, but it certainly was in the Florentine tradition, stemming from Leonardo Bruni and the republican period; after all there is no doubt that by predilection Machiavelli was a republican. Fowler's version is, it seems, the first in English so that, even if his translation circulated only

[19] *Oxford History of English Literature* (1954), 66–119; quotations 86–7.

[20] Aside from Durkan's essay, above n. 1, see the full treatment of the second half of the sixteenth century by R. D. S. Jack, *The Italian Influence on Scottish Literature* (Edinburgh 1972), especially 29–143. On Henryson cf. the more cautious approach of John MacQueen (Oxford 1967), who nevertheless sees Italian influences at work.

[21] Introduction to *A Choice of Scottish Verse, 1560–1660* (London 1978), 15. Dr Jack discusses Stewart's use of Ariosto (with some French intermediaries present) and of Petrarch in *Italian Influence*, 57–74. There is little doubt of the Italian competence of William Fowler, living at the turn of the century; on him see Jack, *Italian Influence*, 74–86 and next n.

[22] On Machiavelli see the lecture by Mario Praz (British Academy 1928), reprinted in *Machiavelli in Inghilterra* (Florence 1962), 97–151, especially at 100, quoting the Introduction by John Purves to the Scottish Text Society's edition of *Fowler's Works*, iii (Edinburgh 1940); see also Jack, *Italian Influence*, 87–8 and the essay by Nicolai Rubinstein in *Il Rinascimento: interpretazioni e problemi* (Laterza, Rome-Bari 1979), especially 227–35 and references.

among a restricted court circle, it is perhaps the most telling evidence of Italian vernacular influence in Stuart Scotland. The rest (save a letter derived from the *Decameron*) was from the Italian poets. Poetry is easier to emulate, if not to excel in, than prose. And it is easier, in a sense, to cheat at this time by the use of aureate English, the equivalent of the style of the *grands rhétoriqueurs*. It should, incidentally, be remembered that 'aureation', making three long words do the work of one, is also found in the Latin of the period.

In the Machiavellian era prose with both an Italianate and Renaissance tinge was found in Scotland. In this respect a change had overtaken the prose writers of medieval Scotland, where no strong native tradition existed to sustain them in an independent course, and brought them in the sixteenth-century into a much more renaissance-dominated world. It was, after all, a world of books and if few English or Scottish publishers ventured into publishing works in Latin, they (hardly as yet to be regularly distinguished from booksellers) sold those imported from continental centres such as Venice, Lyons, Basle and Paris. In consequence there was a good deal of intellectual traffic between Scotland and the continent. But the greatest bridge which joined both halves of Britain to their neighbours was built of printed books.

Our initial guide here are the surviving books from Scottish libraries down to about 1560, when the Reformation did so much damage to the older collections.[23] These supply a very impressive picture of what the Scottish scholar acquired: virtually all of the main classical authors are represented, with Latin and Greek, and, equally important as transmitters of the ideas of classical antiquity, the patristic and early Christian writers.[24] The extant volumes are necessarily selective; there is no clue to what is missing, nor of course what was actually read and regarded as important. But something of this is revealed in the prose writers of Jacobean Scotland, and especially the historians, traditionally the purveyors of moral precepts, 'teaching by example' as men had said in antiquity and as they went on saying all through the Middle Ages and repeated with a new urgency during the Renaissance in Italy and, as it spread, everywhere in Europe.

Scotland, unlike England and France, did not import her humanist historians: 'from the start it was in the hands of natives'.[25] They are a

---

[23] John Durkan and Anthony Ross O.P., *Early Scottish Libraries* (Glasgow 1961), in effect reprinted from the *Innes Review*. See also Sears Jayne, *Library Catalogues of the English Renaissance* (Berkeley 1956), 23 and notes. Although it deals with a collection later than 1603 attention must also be drawn to the catalogue of books of Drummond of Hawthornden compiled by R. H. Macdonald (Edinburgh 1971). See also C. P. Finlayson, 'Clement Littill and his Library: The origins of Edinburgh University Library' in *Edinburgh Bibliographical Society and Friends of Edinburgh University Library*, Edinburgh 1980.

[24] Durkan and Ross, *Early Scottish Libraries*, Introduction, 12–13. This is reminiscent of the books recorded in the *Library Catalogue of Syon College*, ed. Mary Bateson (Cambridge 1898).

[25] E. Futer, *Geschichte der neueren Historiographie* (1911), best read in the only revised edition, the French translation (Paris 1914), used here; for quotation see 209.

remarkable lot, even if John Major's *Historia majoris Britanniae tam Angliae quam Scotiae* (Paris 1521), with its punning title, may be regarded as the product of an old-fashioned Parisian schoolman. His aim, as one might have expected, was to provide his patron James V with lessons of a practical sort and to do this with all the freedom of a scholastic disputant.[26] Hector Boece, another theologian, may be characterised as a humanist on the strength of his *Scotorum historiae a prima gentis origine libri XIX*. This came out, incomplete, at Paris in 1526, although it is hard to see why it was not finished. His book was completed by Ferrerio and is chiefly remarkable for its invention of the myth of the 'jus primae noctis' and the lists of mythical kings of early Scotland.[27] So far the clouds of religious discussion had not crossed the horizon. The subsequent historians reflect the religious storm. John Lesley's *De origine, moribus et rebus gestis Scotorum* was explicitly defending the old church; the first edition of his history came out in Rome in 1578.[28]

Much the greatest and most influential of the Jacobean historians was in the end a protestant and his works were among the most influential in the whole field of European neo-Latin scholarship. George Buchanan's career was not unlike that of Major's at the beginning, but he was primarily a writer and in the new manner. His experience as a professor at Bordeaux and Coimbra took him for a time away from letters and instruction; later he was tutor to James VI, which led directly into his involvement in politics.[29] He was unquestionably the most influential Scottish writer of the sixteenth century in Europe at large. As a historian his version of the events of the Reformation period was taken over by De Thou (Thuanus); his *Rerum Scoticarum historia*, published in Edinburgh in 1582, took the story down to

[26] Most accessible now as *A History of Greater Britain as well England as Scotland . . .*, trans. Archibald Constable with a life by Aeneas J. G. Mackay (Scottish History Society, Edinburgh 1982); cf. Fueter *loc. cit.*

[27] Boece's book ends with the accession of James III; it was reprinted by the Bannatyne Club in 1825 and by the New Spalding Club in 1894. On the nonsense about the 'jus Primae noctis' see Fueter; not only were contemporaries gulled (e.g. Polydore Vergil, *Anglica Historia*, Basel 1534, 167–8) but it continues to lead a shady journalistic life, as on p. 1 of the *Guardian* for 15 September 1979: 'Ancient right to a profitable gift shop'.

[28] A vernacular version written in Mary's reign and covering the period 1436–1561 was reprinted by the Bannatyne Club in 1830. It is hard (as Fueter acknowledges, 319–20) to regard John Knox's *History of the Reformation in Scotland* as history in the same sense as the others mentioned here; it is polemics, with an historical preface added later as book i; but see ed. W. Croft Dickinson, 2 vols (Edinburgh 1949), intro. lxxx–lxxxi.

[29] For the older studies of Irving and Hume Brown and the recent work by I. D. McFarlane, see above n. 7. An admirable paper on the composition of his dramatic verse was read at Bologna (above n. 9) by Dr Peter Sharratt. A recent study of the *History* and the *De jure regni* was published by H. R. Trevor-Roper, *George Buchanan and the Ancient Scottish Constitution*, third supplement to the EHR (London 1966), which is entertainingly cut down to size by G. W. S. Barrow in a review in *Annali della Fondazione per la storia amministrativa* 4 (1967), 635–5. And see now Quentin Skinner, *The Foundations of Modern Political Thought*, 2 vols (Cambridge 1978), ii 340–5 with references.

1571 and had enormous authority not least because of the author's deserved reputation as a Latinist.[30] He was, of all the persons mentioned here, the most 'humanist' and, though the inspiration of his interpretation of events was Calvinist and not in any sense Italian, the notion of the ex-statesman writing history in his latter days cannot fail to evoke Machiavelli and Guicciardini. His poetry, his grammar, even his variety of republican sentiment may convey more than is just an echo of a 'renaissance' element. But the influences which were most important to him were French, as with so many Scots referred to above, and of the historians he regrettably paid exaggerated attention to Boece.

If France bulks much larger than Italy in the cultural contacts of Scotland and Scots, there were steady and regular visitors from Scotland to the Peninsula and in the other direction. Of Scottish connections down to the Reformation the most productive occasions were due to membership of the Roman Church. The petitions flew from Scotland to Rome under James IV and James V, especially after 1517 when the king could threaten the pope that his country would desert orthodoxy until his insatiable demands were met.[31] For the most part the royal (and noble) demands were met and it was a financially denuded kirk which moved into the Reformation. Popes, of course, occasionally tried to see that their beneficence reached the right channels; such was a task performed for the last time by Pietro Lippomano, bishop of Verona, in 1548. These political and administrative contacts between the Scottish Crown, Scottish clergy and the curia have been much studied.[32] They had few detectable cultural consequences (or even for that matter spiritual ones). To this there is one exception in the activities of Giovanni Ferrerio, a Piedmontese who was indisputably an 'Italian humanist' and who taught for a few years at the abbey of Kinloss in the 1530s and 1540s. He also continued the history of Hector Boece, this work being published in Lausanne in 1574. He was involved in the diplomacy of Lippomano's nunciature and if his stature as a humanist is modest there is no doubt that he played an important role, more cultural than that of most Italians, among Scots in Paris.[33]

[30] Subsequent editions in the *Opera omnia*, ed. T. Ruddiman (Edinburgh 1715, repr. Leiden 1725). For some pertinent remarks on Scottish sixteenth-century historiography see Thomas I. Rae, 'The historical writing of Drummond of Hawthornden', SHR liv (1975), 22–62.

[31] Documented in R. K Hannay's two posthumous collections: *Letters of James IV*, ed. R. L. Mackie and Anne Spillman (Scottish History Society, Edinburgh 1953) and *Letters of James V*, ed. Denys Hay (Edinburgh 1954).

[32] For these diplomatic contacts see W. J. Anderson, 'Rome and Scotland' in *Essays on the Scottish Reformation*, ed. David McRoberts (Glasgow 1962), 463–83 with an important correction at 468 n. of Hannay ed. Hay (see previous n.). On Grimani and Lippomano see the recent study of John E. Law and John M. Manion, 'The nunciature to Scotland of Pietro Lippomano, bishop of Verona', *Atti e memorie della Accademia di Agricoltura, Scienze e Lettere di Verona*, ser. vi, xxii (1970–71), 403–48.

[33] John Durkan, 'Giovanni Ferrerio and religious humanism in sixteenth-century Scotland' in *Studies in Church History*, 17 (Oxford, 1981). I have to thank him for letting me read the text of this and also of his essay on 'Giovanni Ferrerio, Gesner and French Affairs'.

Ferrerio left no account of his experience as such, but only incidental allusions and impressions. Indeed the only Italian who did so was Pius II (as Aeneas Sylvius Piccolomini) whose contribution to Scottish cultural life was nil; true, an idealised picture of the future prelate figures among the paintings in the Piccolomini Library in Siena Cathedral. But Pinturicchio just painted an imaginary sylvan scene in which to place king and future pope.

Two other indices of Italian influence may be pointers to a change in the intellectual climate – the introduction of italic and roman in printing and of humanist script in writing. Roman and italic type penetrated into the few books published in Scotland during the mid-sixteenth century.[34] This is to some extent an unreal point, since Latin-reading scholars in both England and Scotland habitually bought their books from the great continental centres. Handwriting is complicated by another consideration; there is no fixed time when italic or roman scripts replaced the older native chancery or court hands. It was a gradual process but as and when humanist secretaries were employed by popes and Italian princes the practice of writing in the new manner (*cancelleresca*) began to spread. For long, however, a scholar, even a dyed-in-the-wool humanist, often used both hands – a stylish italic or the traditional book or court hand of his neighbourhood, or a mixture of the two. In general it was, once again, not till the seventeenth century that the new manner became an essential sign of learning, or at any rate a pretence to good breeding.[35] This transition remains unstudied, but examples of the new way

[34] H. G. Aldis, *List of Books published in Scotland before 1700* (rev. ed. Edinburgh 1970). The National Library of Scotland maintains a copy in which additions are recorded. Some 400 books were printed in Scotland before 1603. William Beattie, 'Some early Scottish books', in *The Scottish Tradition* ed. G. W. S. Barrow (Edinburgh 1974), 107–20, esp. at 116. Professor Beattie tells me that 'the first printer in Scotland to use Roman and italic' was Thomas Davidson, 1541; sparingly to begin with, e.g. for chapter headings.

[35] Above n. 23. The complications explain why the subject has not been definitively studied and perhaps cannot be. A perusal of the copies of James V's Letters in NLS MSS 35 5 9 A, B, C, D, shows that, although there are occasional words in italic even in the 1520s, the royal secretaries did their business in a good traditional hand; italic influences manifest themselves regularly only at a later date, in the 1560s and 1570s; cf. the last folios of MS 35 5 9 D. Mr J. F. Hudson of the British Library, who kindly consulted two similar volumes, Royal MSS 13 B II and 18 B VI, on my behalf reached a similar conclusion. For the other collections see Hannay's brief survey (ed. Hay, xi–xiii, above n. 31). These are of course copies kept for the record and not the originals as despatched, which Hannay did not chase up: it would have been an enormous task, though essential for a true answer to the problem posed. Two other points may be made. It seems almost certain that many men of learning and or of public importance *signed* their names in italic, while habitually employing an old-fashioned hand, a point to be remembered in considering the book inscriptions mentioned above and the author's observations in *The Italian Renaissance in its Historical Background* (rev. ed., Cambridge, 1977), 202 and plate XXIV. Finally it should be remembered that manuals of the new art (*cancelleresca*) began to be published in Italy in and after 1520s: *Three Classics of Italian Calligraphy*, ed. Oscar Ogg (New York, 1953). For *cancelleresca corsiva* and the books based on it, see James Wardrop, *The Script of Humanism* (Oxford 1963), chap. iii and references. Pertinent remarks on the Scottish scene appear in the very useful work of Grant Simpson, *Scottish Handwriting 1150–1650* (Edinburgh 1973), 19–31.

of writing in early sixteenth-century Scotland are represented by two beautiful italic signatures of Bishop Chisholm of Dunblane.[36] George Buchanan likewise seems to have written habitually a fine italic.[37]

In conclusion, the Italian Renaissance as such made a relatively delayed appearance in Scotland and it was in general transmitted by Scots and Italians based in France. The Reformation of 1560 unquestionably interrupted this process, but the influence of new ideas can be seen in the steady growth of libraries (containing for the most part books printed on the Continent) and in a strong historiographical tradition, notably represented by George Buchanan. He, too, may reflect some part of Renaissance Italian republican sentiment, though Calvinist theology had a more powerful influence on his thought. Nor were the Scottish historians, or other writers, affected much by the rhetorical temptations which are so marked a feature of much humanist historiography.[38]

[36] Durkan and Ross, *Early Scottish Libraries*, plates XXXA, XXXVI.

[37] Those examples of his undoubted hand which I have seen are all in impeccable italic: the Lisbon inquisition of 1550, to be found, aside from other reproductions, in plates II and III of D. A. Millar, ed., *George Buchanan: a Memorial 1506-1906* (St Andrews and London, n.d.) and NLS Adv. MS. 15.1.6, fos. 18, 49, the former in French, the latter a Latin Testimonial addressed to Beza, dated respectively 1574 and 1581). The only oddity is that in the same MS, fos. 3–11 there are Buchanan's proposals for university reform at St Andrews, written in a traditional court hand; on fo. 12[vo] someone (perhaps the clerk who copied the document?) has written the foregoing 'pages are in Buchanan's own hand'. Dr T. I. Rae of the National Library of Scotland was good enough to look at this piece and confirms what I have said.

[38] Cf. Dr Rae's remarks on Drummond in art. cited above n. 30, at 47–49.

16

RELIGION NORTH AND SOUTH: CHRISTENDOM
AND THE ALPS ON THE EVE OF THE REFORMATION

Many of us who did university courses in history at school and university before the war, and a fair number after the war, concentrated on the period of the Renaissance and Reformation, the 'Ren. and Ref.' of British schoolboy slang, while in British history we covered the era of the Tudors and the Stuarts. So far as the Continent is concerned this meant that, broadly speaking, the Renaissance was treated as a kind of curtain-raiser (to use a theatrical analogy) to the Reformation. The Renaissance, a kind of Enlightenment *avant le jour*, blew away the cobwebs of medieval obscurantism, barbarous theology, corrupt practices in the religious life of Christendom, and heralded in a period of religious clarity together with repeated and diffused attempts at Reformation. Now it is the case, or so we thought, that while the Renaissance *began* as an Italian phenomenon, the earthquake of the Reformation found its epicentre in Germany. Here, by way of illustration, let me quote from a work still worth consulting, T.M. Lindsay's *History of the Reformation* (1906). In Chapter III he begins by declaring that 'the Movement called the Renaissance in its widest extent may be described as the transition from the medieval to the modern world. All our present conceptions of life and thought find their roots in this period'. His authorities are, of course, Burckhardt, Geiger, Symonds *et al.*; with obviously the old *Cambridge Modern History*, volumes i and ii, titled respectively 'Renaissance' and 'Reformation', as they still are in the *New Cambridge Modern History*. Later, Lindsay writes, 'Italy was the first land to become free from the conditions of medieval life, and ready to enter on the new life which was awaiting Europe'. The connecting links between Renaissance and Reformation, in this view, were multiple but most directly witnessed, I suppose, in the field of philology, from Valla to Erasmus and Reuchlin, and Luther's conviction of the need to translate *poenitentia* by 'repentance' rather than penance. One of the seminal and serious books on these lines was by the Unitarian Charles Beard, *The Reformation of the Sixteenth Century with Relation to Modern Thought and Knowledge*; this came out in 1883 and greatly excited me as a teenager; I am sorry it seems to have dropped out of the student bibliographies, though it remains of interest to the many scholars today interested in the socinian antecedents of Unitarianism.

Put in a word, the traditional picture of the first decades of the sixteenth century is religious ferment in the North, religious torpor in Italy. The northern upheavals had a longish history and many forms. The most advanced spirits of the late fourteenth century, Wycliffe and Huss, failed to consolidate their religious positions; they are therefore the losers and we are right to call them heretics, which is another name for an unsuccessful ideological minority. True, a handful of men followed in some sense along the paths charted by Wycliffe in his later years, but no one would now argue that they were to lead to the break with Rome in 1535. As for Huss, his condemnation at Constance led to rebellion in Bohemia and, in the fullness of time, to the development of a religious group which was separate from Catholicism, the quietist church of the Bohemian Brethren which was to survive to influence Wesley and Goethe. But at the time and for long after these heresiarchs were not founders of churches, and in the customary and conventional picture I have been painting they were termed 'morning stars' of the Reformation. They herald the Dawn but are not themselves the Dawn itself.

Such violence (and in England it was not so very violent) was, however, far from being the only ingredient in the northern religious scene. We have among intellectuals the *Nova Devotio* and among simpler souls the connected phenomenon of the béguines and beghards. Found in the Low Countries and the Rhineland, these groups were fundamentally informal; but they also affected organised religion and semi-organised religion. Of

the latter, the semi-organised religions, the outstanding example is offered by the Brethren of the Common Life, at whose
school at Deventer Cusa and later Erasmus were to be pupils.
Of the former, the intellectuals like Groote, the effects on the
regular clergy can best be illustrated by the Augustinian canons'
house at Agnietenberg where Thomas à Kempis composed the
Imitatio Christi, and indeed the *Nova Devotio* affected the
whole so-called 'Congregation' of Windesheim of which Thomas's house was a member.

To these narrowly spiritual evidences of religious activity
we may add the activity of the theological faculties in Continental universities north of the Alps. Often these were cantankerous and provided self-indulgent training in mental gym-
nastics, as some one has said, but they were immensely stimulating to many scholars as the *via moderna* or Occamism gradually obtained an ascendancy over the *via antiqua*. This observation has of course received recent confirmation in the important work of Heiko Oberman on Luther's intellectual roots
in his book on Gabriel Biel; this admittedly had long been
familiar to Luther scholars and Oberman, in a sense, is merely expanding the knowledge of its long term effects.

Religious art in the North was, so it seems to an ignoramus
like me, distinctly more religious in spirit than the contemporary fifteenth century work in Italy. The Italians admired it on
aesthetic as well as technical grounds, so far as painting is concerned. In architecture Northern styles had made striking
inroads in Piedmont and the Milanese. The character of popular
art was, one might guess, more diffused and accessible in Germany and northern France, even perhaps in England, than in
Italy. I am thinking of the way that the work of Alberto Tenenti reinforces to some extent the old assumption that Italian
quattrocento art has a realistic quality totally different from
that found in the Flemish primitives: the Dance of Death is
not found as a motif in Italy.

Moreover, so runs the old argument, printing is not an Italian invention. It was certainly adopted in Italy with astonishing
rapidity but so it was nearly everywhere. It is the only invention
before the nineteenth century to spread so quickly in the whole

history of western civilization. Now books, like the *Nova Devotio*, come out of western Germany in the mid-fifteenth century. Can it be that the demand for them was occasioned by the
rise of literacy? Can it be that the peoples North of the Alps
were already better educated, or at least that more of them
could read than in Italy? Georg Voigt in his *Wiederbelebung*
(1859) crowed over this German innovation which certainly
fits very neatly into a North-South antithesis, especially if we
remember that the Brethren of the Common Life were leaving
copying for printing as early as 1476 and that the *Imitatio
Christi* was printed 99 times by the end of the fifteenth century.

Nor do these matters which I have discussed lack the support
of reasonable explanation. Consciousness of national sentiment
had undoubtedly been accelerated in the North by the Great
Schism of 1378 and its aftermath. The international Orders,
already breaking into units which more or less corresponded
with political entities, were shattered still further by the emergence of rival obediences; and one Order, the Franciscans, already had the Alps as a demarcation line for both the Con-
ventuals and the Observants. In so far as Italy was almost
totally insulated from these consequences (though not from
others) we can understand the character of, for example, the
heresies of Wycliffe and Huss: we now know (thanks to the
late Reginald Betts and Dom De Vooght) that they had little
direct connection with each other; they were also most certainly
severely limited in their range of influence. Perhaps with this
we should stress the political aspect to which I have just alluded: the rise of strong monarchy outside Italy – in France,
the Germany of the Princes, England and the Spanish Kingdoms. Such developments in various ways inhibited where they
did not totally preclude the inquisitorial controls of the *curia
romana*. There were virtually no papal inquisitors in northern
Europe by the fifteenth century; Ferdinand and Isabella managed to get their own private (and profitable) organisation.
But the English Lollards had to be handled by a set of puzzled
bishops, lacking training, for the most part, in theology, who
found their background, usually canon and civil law, quite ir-

relevant to the situation.

Wycliffe and Huss did not share a common platform in the ideas they espoused (save in metaphysics), but they shared with each other a growing conviction that papal autocracy was unjustified and the source of much other evil. Indeed a denial of papal infallibility was, Dom De Vooght argues, the only position Huss adopted that makes it possible to regard him truly as a heretic; and even that did not become a dogma until 1870. But in their regarding the pope as a source of corruption the Englishman and the Czech were expressing in their own ecclesiastical ways a violent antipapalism which had persisted in northern Europe since when? Perhaps since the Investiture contest or even earlier; certainly from the thirteenth century, an antipapalism which grew rapidly in the Avignon period, and was intensified by the sordid events of the Great Schism; and an antipapalism which was fed by a more widespread and unsophisticated anticlericalism.

If what I have said goes some way to describe and partly account for the storm slowly gathering force North of the Alps. what account can we give of the sinister inertia of Italy, which was to survive 1517 and 1527? In some ways the situation in the peninsula was surely almost directly opposite to that of Germany, France and the other ultramontane countries. Take the question of the Inquisition. It was doubtless disliked by the governments of Italy and by the people in general too, but in general it was active and effective. Despite hindrances the surveillance of heretics was not relaxed; in 1376 the papal interdict on Florence (which led to the war of the 8 Saints) was based by the pope on (among other things) the legislation of the commune which interfered with the operation of the Holy Office. Yet it was in Florence that the Inquisition dealt with the last remnants of the Fraticelli in the 1470s and it was in Florence that Savonarola was burned in 1498. Heretics were also denounced by the great Observant preachers of the fifteenth century and intermittently the machinery for enforcing orthodoxy is found at work in Venice and the Veneto. Whether or not we should give the credit for this to the curial suppression of error, the fact is that there are very few heretics in pre-Reformation Italy at all comparable with those whom we find in the North of Europe. Now that heresy is a much more popular subject than it used to be with Italian church historians we have had elaborate investigations into the Brethren of the Free Spirit and the Waldensians. But these have not succeeded (in my judgement) in modifying the situation sketched above at the end of the Middle Ages.

A further feature of the Italian scene is the quite remarkable survival of the papacy as a viable political and financial entity. Even in the XIV century 'Through its rise as a major territorial power, the Church had thus become *ipso facto* a subversive force in Central Italy' (Brucker, 281). Later, and despite the lamentable effects of the Schism, especially damaging to popes and prelates after 1409 (the Council of Pisa, which added a third Italian pope to the already existing Italian and Aragonese), despite a Rome which was not tamed until the later fifteenth century, the popes of the period from about 1450 to 1520 intrigued, often successfully, to get their way with the other princes of Italy and they continued to gather in revenues from the Papal States and the clergy of Christendom which kept them about the middle of the Italian power league. As has been pointed out more than once, northern princes, hostile as they were to the papal attempts to extract money from their clerical subjects, nevertheless tolerated this practice in the shape of common services, the tax a prelate paid for being provided by the pope after his nomination by his prince; common services, a very large tax as far as England was concerned, were paid to the Camera Apostolica by prelates in England down to the break with Rome, despite the fourteenth century statute of *provisors* (1351), which expressly forbade papal reservation and provision, on which the system rested.

This papal finance was often strained to breaking point by war and the fifteenth century sees the augmentation of papal cash by the ingenious if corrupt practice (to be adopted by lay princes everywhere before long) of selling offices. But the sale of offices, the creation of bureaucracies for Romans and other Italians to invest in, even occasionally the auctioning of cardinal's hats, was not only the result of political and military pressures. The popes by the third quarter of the fifteenth century were spending lavishly on Rome, on the Vatican, on their library and their jewels. If anything could have been riskier than this, more provocative of criticism, more liable to casuistical defences, it is hard to know what it might be. These undesirable consequences did occasionally manifest themselves, as when in 1466 a Spiritual Franciscan, one of the few still left, preached a sermon on Paul II's tiara (which one, one might ask, since he ran through four of them, all richly decorated with the gems he liked so much?). To this a defence of the papal panoply was provided by (surprisingly) Cardinal Jouffroy. He argued that the pope had the right to behave imperially, so to speak, because of the authority of scripture and the powers conveyed by the Donation of Constantine; because jewels were full of an inherent spiritual virtue; and because a monumental crown exalted the pope and the Church. And this argument could, of course, justify the glory and grandeur that Renaissance popes and cardinals gave to Rome. If their moral leadership of Christendom had been eroded, it has often been said, they could claim an aesthetic domination in its place.

And I suppose the rapid sketch I have provided of the absence of Italian 'enthusiasm', so to speak, is connected with those movements and new attitudes that we summarise in the term Renaissance. It is true that there were no great powers in Italy until Charles V establishes his grip in the mid-sixteenth century, so that there was no inducement, or very little, for the dukes and marquises of the peninsula, or the harassed king of Naples, to encourage or even tolerate dissident religious elements: they had a better way of squeezing the pope by direct action against their clergy – taxing them, limiting the *privilegium fori*, and normally getting their way over episcopal appointments and appointments to the few big abbeys. In any case these princes by the late fifteenth century not only had their agents at the curia, they had a relative in the college of cardinals and – who knew? – he might be a future pope. It is true that this last only came off in the early sixteenth century and then only with the Medici popes; but what a marvellous success they had in reestablishing their family in Florence!

The embellishment of Rome during the decades turning on the year 1500 is the most dramatic example of religious fervour becoming exteriorised, one might say. There was hardly a town in Italy which did not turn its local church into a Renaissance building, if only by clothing it in a mantle of fashionable design, as the Malatesta treated the duomo at Rimini. It is hard to evaluate the precise sentimental or spiritual significance of this transformation of the ecclesiastical landscape, which is not found in North Europe (or for that matter in some parts of north Italy); there the old Gothic buildings stood on and were only very gradually replaced by smarter and more up-to-date edifices as fire and subsidence rendered rebuilding necessary – often not till the seventeenth century, and sometimes these old churches survive still. But there does seem to be a reasonable sense in which one can attribute to this building, and the commissioning of religious paintings and sculpture in the new manner, a serious drain on church finance and on church energy. The same could be true also of the literary Renaissance. Higher clergy who might have tried to catch a glimpse of their evangelical mission were all too often polishing their hexameters instead of preaching or praying, or even over-administering an Italian church where there were hundreds of unnecessary prelates. To the splendour of the static, even shrinking, cities we should perhaps add the splendour of public display at all levels from the papal processions downwards, a topic which is now attracting a much overdue attention. The amount of time, thought, energy and cash these elaborate spectacles must have taken is staggering to contemplate although, of course, they brought together the dazzling talents of the humanist and the artist.

I have tried very rapidly to offer what, in broad lines, we might regard as the traditional diptych of Christendom in the period of two or three generations before Luther. 'Look here upon this picture and on this.' In what follows I should like to blurr these images and to point out how strong are the links that bind North and South together. There remains a difference, I think we shall see, but we must not exaggerate it. That we have a tendency to do so is, I suspect, engrained in a Protestant or ex-protestant society, such as Britain. It affects not only historians and critics who are active Protestants or who came out of that tradition but also Roman Catholic writers who often view Rome and Italy with despair, as so many of them did at the time of Vatican I and as so many do in the wake of Vatican II.

Such tacit assumptions coloured the views of an Acton or a Stubbs, as they coloured the attitudes of Jacob Burckhardt: with these men we run over the whole gamut of Northern religious attitudes from Roman Catholic to sceptic, with an Anglican in the middle (and what is Anglicanism save Roman Catholicism without Rome?). But are we not, with such assumptions, reading history backwards? We all know that this is the historian's temptation and, when succumbed to, his greatest sin, although I am coming to believe that 'futurology' comes close to it nowadays; a new sin but really old positivism in new terminology.

One basic fact should be recalled. Those profound cultural changes which occurred first in Italy – a new art and architecture, a new educational programme, a reasoned defence of the *vita activa* and of the compatibility of wealth with virtue – were steadily to spread over most of Western Europe (and the New World) in the sixteenth and seventeenth centuries. By 1600 we have nearly everywhere except in Teutonic and Slavonic Europe the adoption of the italic and roman styles of writing and printing; the grammar school and lycée are even more widespread; and there is a slow and steady acceptance that the grand manner in the arts has Italian preceptors. This surely suggests that, whatever differences there are between Italy and her neighbours in the cultural field, and however important they may seem, these elements common to Europe as a whole made the reception of Renaissance values relatively simple once the process had begun. The Italians (or to be more accurate some Italians in some centres) had evolved principles and practices which met not only their own needs but those of Christendom as a whole. The republicanism of Florence in the age of Bruni was an integument readily shed and which did not preclude active citizens from being active subjects and from deploying their new energies in the service of king or prince. Lutheran and Anglican schools shared with Roman Catholic schools the same curriculum; and the Jesuit and Calvinist academies were to have more in common than they had differences. That this was the case need hardly surprise us. The Western European experience during the Middle Ages had been essentially similar in all countries. If the Italians 'were the first-born among the sons of Europe', to use Burckhardt's phrase, the point I am trying to stress is that they *were* sons of Europe.

One may therefore wonder whether we have not over-emphasised the uniqueness of the Italian experience. The Alps are high, but they were hardly an adequate barrier to the passage of men and ideas. Let us recall that over the centuries both men and ideas had crossed the mountains, rising gently from the north to the watershed, and then tumbling headlong down into the Po valley. The linguistic frontier is a reminder of this centuries-long process by which barbarians penetrated Upper Italy to the extent that French is spoken in Piedmont and German in parts of the Veneto, leaving ugly and still contentious no-mans-lands in some of the valleys. But if Turin and other towns recall France, let us remember the traffic in the other direction, and not least by merchants, which moved quicker when the bridge was built over the St. Gothard in the early thirteenth century and when a century later the Septimer pass had a road for not only pack animals but light carts. Later still the galleys from Venice and Genoa traversed the straits of Gibraltar and made for the ports of the North Sea. In this commercial activity there is no doubt that the Italians were the aggressive initiators — exporting the rarities of the Orient and the Levant, and later establishing enclaves in the bigger cities of the North where their banking and credit facilities vastly increased Italian influence and aided in the operation of international exchange of money and goods.

For our purposes, however, we should perhaps stress rather the interchange of intellectuals, or at any rate the educated.

This was very much a two-way traffic, and had been long before the fifteenth century. The great educational centres, manly Bologna and Padua, drew English, French, Germans and the rest to their law schools. This is admirably illustrated by S. Stelling Michaud, Agostino Sottili in a recent study, and forms a substantial part of the only published volume to appear of *The English Traveller to Italy* by George B. Parks. Hundreds of northern scholars were laureated in canon or civil law or both, the last emerging as *Doctores utriusque juris,* with an infinite world of advancement before them in Church and State. Alas, we cannot trace the Italians in the north before 1500. Apart from the new and as yet small and unprestigious German universities, there is a dearth of matriculation registers for Paris, Oxford and Cambridge. It is guesswork who went to Paris or Oxford or Cambridge, though Dr. Emden has made a series of indispensible guesses with regard to the last-named places and is doubtless right to minimise the foreigners who were so numerous in the greater Italian centres. But we know of a chain of Italian theologians who went north, to Paris above all (and to a lesser extent Cologne) to learn theology, virtually untaught in the Peninsula outside Dominician convents before the Reformation. The chain begins with Aquinas and Bonaventure and goes on to Pico della Mirandola and beyond; I have elsewhere drawn attention to Bandello identifying an Italian Sorbonista in his *Novelle* in order to indicate his status.

In this mingling of scholars we are told that the Council of Constance and (to a lesser degree) the Council of Basel played a seminal role. It was as a result of the troubles in the church that Poggio Bracciolini, Pietro del Monte and Aeneas Sylvius Piccolomini made their well-publicised descents on Britain; Roberto Weiss has collected the names of a dozen more Italians in England and traced the (admittedly rather mediocre) careers of Englishmen in Italy, although we could do with more on this, I believe, and might get it if we had a full study of some of the diplomats as yet undiscussed: I am thinking in particular of Richard Pace for whom we have a meritorious but totally inadequate biography by Jervis Wegg.

Mention of a diplomatic envoy like Pace should remind us

of the curious century between 1450 or so until Cateau Cambrésis, during which Rome was the centre of European diplomacy, so that a man like Cardinal Bainbridge was to be found actually living in the *curia*. For every Cardinal Bainbridge there were scores more Englishmen, Scots and other barbarous races who went to Rome on business with the officials of chancery, *camera* and even the *Rota*. And there were literally hundreds who went on pilgrimages, especially on the by now 25-year Jubilee, a time of piety and junketing and of prosperity for the hospices and inns of Rome, when some who went to the Basilicas also went to see the sights of ancient Rome.

Nor would it be right to associate religious fervour mainly with the lands which were to experience violently the Reformation. Although the subject has not, I think, been much studied, we may doubt whether there were preachers in the North comparable in magnetism with the Observantine Franciscans like Bernardino da Siena, Giovanni della Marca, Bernardino da Feltre, or Savonarola; the only non-Italians of comparable stature who come to mind are the Catalan St. Vincent Ferrer (d. 1419 in N. France) and the German Cardinal Nicholas of Cusa (d. 1464) and we think of the latter rather as a philosopher than as a fisher of souls. His name, however, suggests reform and we should remember that reform, the Councils having in effect failed to circumscribe the alleged plenitude of papal power, now fell back on the shoulders of the popes. We know that they too failed. Yet they tried once or twice. It was to Pius II that Domenico de' Domenichi and Nicholas of Cusa submitted their reform memoranda; Sixtus IV contemplated reform and so, in a mad moment of folly, did the reprobate Alexander VI. Finally, scholars nowadays are paying far more attention to the Fifth Lateran Council, summoned by Julius II and meeting in 1512 under Leo X. One of the documents presented to it was the *libellus* of two Venetians, Giustiniani and Quirini, who have no comparable predecessors north or south of the Alps in their bitter denunciations of abuse and corruption. What is more, unlike earlier Italian reform documents so called, they (like Cusa) were aiming at a reformation of Christendom as a whole and not just the papacy and its administrative departments, which is what 'head and members' had come by now to mean.

All of this is paper work, you may well say, and that is true, but it is also true that in all sorts of other ways the quattrocento Italian was by no means last in displaying genuine religious sentiment. I am thinking, for example, of the extraordinary number of confraternities in Italian towns. Of course confraternities are found everywhere and fulfil not only religious but social functions, social functions which are both charitable, charitable, indeed, in a precise way: let us remember that they covered effectively the seven acts of corporal mercy. They were also opportunities for good fellowship, for the 'cakes and ale' which Shakespeare offered to Malvolio's dour puritanical virtue in *Twelfth Night*. These Italian confraternities are a much studied subject today and perhaps this has led me to overstress their significance, but what is indisputable is that some of them lead on to the oratories of divine love, to *the* Oratory and to those new Orders of Clerks Regular of whom the smallest group were the Barnabites and the greatest the Society of Jesus, whose activities spread into every corner of the world, including Protestant corners. Other features of Italian devotion worth remembering also spread outside Italy in the last centuries of the Middle Ages – the Rosary, the Stations of the Cross, the Angelus and the Pax. The preaching of sermons in the vernacular and the devotional devices I have just mentioned are in a true sense *popular*, and (apart from Cusa) the names of preachers I have mentioned are not those of intellectuals.

Nor were Italians slower in moving towards what later generations were to regard as more essential aspects of religion. If the Dance of Death has a more aristocratic equivalent in Italy, the *ars moriendi* literature spread there as did the mystical writings of men like Thomas à Kempis; almost the earliest translation of the *Imitatio* was into Italian; and there are a dozen editions of the Bible in Italian in the incunable period. Moreover the practice of more frequent communion (say four times a year) as opposed to the more perfunctory, if more regular, attendance at Mass was certainly proceeding quicker south than north of the Alps. True, the laity in Italy did not clamour for the cup as they did in Bohemia while Huss lay in prison in Constance. But, as John Bossy and others have pointed out, the practice of giving the faithful the (unconsecrated) rinsing wine after the wafer, which to simple people must have seemed in effect a communion in both kinds, is found in fifteenth century Italy as well as in the North.

Nor did the North have in any sense a monopoly of ignorant parochial clergy, unbridled lasciviousness in convents of men and women and attempts by some enlightened laymen, mostly nobles and princes and prelates, to do something about it. Perhaps in England, where the peccadilos of the nuns at Godstow, tempted as they were by the young men in the adjacent university of Oxford, are more typical of error and slackness than are the few bold bad monks and friars, it is unlikely that at any time we will find either saints or real sinners. But the corruptions of politically divided Germany, among the religious Orders in particular, are parallel in Italy in dozens of ways, as one may read in G.G. Coulton's *Five Centuries of Religion*, vol. iv. And so are attempts to correct the abusive immunities which lay behind much licentiousness. The chief corrective device of these evils was the 'Congregation', or group of houses belonging to the same Order, combining together for purposes of mutual reform and discipline. I have mentioned that the Augustinian canons, of which Thomas à Kempis was a member, belonged to such a Congregation and there were scores more, ranging up to the great Benedictine battleship in the Danube which formed the heart of the congregation of Melk. Similar groupings existed in Italy, and out of one of them was to come that unusual group, the Lateran Congregation (which was not in the end based on the Lateran) whose early sixteenth century history has been so well written about by Professor McNair in his book on Peter Martyr Vermigli.

Now this Peter Martyr *did* become a heretic, like a few other Italians of all classes and kinds, so that we are brought back to the point from which I started. There *was* a Reformation in the North; there was *not* a Reformation in Italy, despite the Waldensians, despite a few parishes in the North of Italy electing protestant pastors. (In passing one might add that this almost universal Italian practice of electing the parish priest offered a surprisingly easy way for reformers to come in, especially in north Italy, had there been much support for innovation among the patricians of the towns. There are some examples of it happening, but not, I believe, very many). Of course the matter is not so cut and dried as all that. Very large areas of Catholic Europe remained Roman Catholic when the dust settled. In Spain, indeed, there was hardly any dust raised at all.

I conclude with a few trite observations. One is that in my judgment the religious barometer stays fairly steady at 'changeable', at any rate until scepticism starts its erosion of intellectual acceptance of Christianity in the Enlightenment. I can see no real evidence that, overall, the twelfth or thirteenth centuries were more 'devout' than the Dark Ages or the period of the Renaissance. The second observation is perhaps better put as a question. Just what did the Reformation reform? If one looks at the state of the generality of clergy and laity in the late sixteenth and seventeenth centuries, their state after the event seems much as it had been before. We can point to Calvin, Knox and a few other eminent protestants; the Society of Jesus is sowing its martyrs 'from China to Peru'. But what does it all add up to? Scottish presbyterianism in the eighteenth century was a cover sometimes for the most disgusting debauches called communion services; and suspicious governments found it easy to persuade a vulnerable papacy to dissolve the Society of Jesus in 1773; earlier than that the Jesuits had been suppressed in Portugal, France and Spain. Paradoxically it was in Protestant Prussia and Orthodox Russia that they legally survived.

It seems to me that *if* the Reformation and the Catholic Reformation aimed at an educated clergy and a pure clergy (or at any rate a clergy really expected to be pure) then, in Protestant as in Roman Catholic areas, we have to wait until the nineteenth century. It is the case that a few Catholics worried by the state of the priesthood established in Rome before 1500 two training colleges for priests. But seminaries for Roman

Catholics, while legislated for by Lateran III and Lateran IV and the Council of Trent, hardly emerge before the early nineteenth century, when, as a somewhat comic coincidence, the Church of England felt that its parochial clergy should have a smattering of Greek, Latin and Hebrew – as a preparation for their parochial duties.

My final point. Compared with the *Sturm und Drang* provoked by Luther, the quiet revolution of the humanist seems to me to have had much deeper and longer lasting effects. By the mid-seventeenth century we have a society in Europe committed (I refer, of course, to the social and intellectual élites) to accepting the truth of the Bible and the necessity of a classical education. This amalgam was to pervade the Western world until almost our own day, for it was to prove, if only momentarily, in the last century liberal enough to accommodate the march of positivism and the rise of the natural sciences. In brief, I consider the Renaissance a much more significant group of ideas, events and influences than the Reformation.

SHORT BIBLIOGRAPHY

In lieu of heavy annotation of the above remarks I append the following selection of works, which in the main attempts to follow the exposition above.

J. BURCKHARDT, *Civilization of the Renaissance in Italy* (many eds. and trans. since original ed. in 1860); J. HUIZINGA, *The Waning of the Middle Ages* (again many versions since original, 1919); J. DELARUELLE and others, in FLICHE and MARTIN (eds.), *Histoire de l'église*, vol. 14; *L'église au temps du Grand Schisme et de la croise conciliaire*, in two parts (1962-4), and in the same series, R. AUBENAS and R. RICARD, *L'église et la Renaissance* (1951); *New Cambridge Modern History*, vols i, ii (1957, 1958); D. KNOWLES, O.S.B., *The Religious Orders in England*, vols. ii, iii (1955, 1959); CHARLES BEARD, *The Reformation in the Light of Modern Knowledge* (1883); K.B. McFAR-LANE, *John Wycliffe and the Beginnings of English Nonconformity* (1960); J. DE VOOGHT, O.S.B., *L'hérésie de Jean Huss* (1960); A. HYMA, *The Christian Renaissance* (1924; extended ed. 1965); HEIKO OBERMAN, *The Harvest of Medieval Theology* (1963, and many of the vols. in Oberman's series 'Studies in Medieval and Renaissance Thought' contain much material pertinent to this brief talk); ÉMILE MÂLE, *Religious Art in France: the XIII century* (first in French, 1910, and in English 1913); E. PANOFSKY, *Renaissance and Renascences in Western Art* (1960); E. CASTELNUOVO, *Un pittore italiano alla corte di Avignone* (1962); M. MEISS, *Painting in Florence and Siena after the Black Death* (1951); L.H. HEYDENRICH and W. COTZ, *Architecture in Italy 1400-1600* (1974); A. TENENTI, *Il senso della morte e l'amore della vita nel Rinascimento* (1957); H.C. LEA, *A History of the Inquisition in the Middle Ages*, 3 vols. (1888); DENYS HAY, *The Church in Italy in the Fifteenth Century* (1977, with an Italian version which is now published, containing bibliographies which will not be repeated here); JOHN N. STEPHENS, *Heresy in Medieval and Renaissance Florence*, « Past and Present », 54 (1972), 25-60; PETER PARTNER, *Papal State under Martin V* (1958); GENE A. BRUCKER, *Florentine Politics and Society 1343-1378* (1962); A. GOTTLOB, *Aus der Camera Apostolica des 15. Jahrhundert* (1889); W.E. LUNT, *Papal Revenues in the Middle Ages*, 2 vols. (1934); J. DELUMEAU, *Vie économique et sociale de Rome dans le seconde moitié du XVIᵉ siècle*, 2 vols. (1957-9); L. VON PASTOR, *Storia dei papi* (trans. MERCATI and CENCI, 1942-); G. TOFFANIN, *Storia letteraria d'Italia, Il Cinquecento* (1938); S. STELLING MICHAUD, *L'université de Bologne et la pénétration des droits romain et canonique en Suisse aux XIIIᵉ et XIVᵉ siècles* (1955); G.B. PARKS, *The English Traveller to Italy*, i (all published, 1954); A.B. EMDEN, *A Biographical Register of the University of Oxford to 1500*, 3 vols. (1957-9); DENYS HAY, *Profilo storico del Rinascimento Italiano*, second ed. revised (1978); ROBERTO WEISS, *Humanism in England during the Fifteenth Century*, third ed. with additions (1967); DAVID CHAMBERS, *Cardinal Bainbridge at the Court of Rome* (1965); JERVIS WEGG, *Richard Pace* (1932); LÉONCE CÉLIER, *L'idée de réforme à la cour pontificale du concile de Bâle au concile du Latran*, « Revue des questions historiques », lxxxvi (1909), 418-35; E. DELARUELLE, *La pietà popolare alla fine del Medio Evo*, in *X Congresso internazionale di scienze storiche, Relazioni*, iii (1955),

515-37; JOHN BOSSY, *The Counter Reformation and the peoples of Northern Europe*, « Past and Present », 47 (1970), 51-70; G.G. COULTON, *Five Centuries of Religion*, iv (1950); PHILIP MCNAIR, *Peter Martyr in Italy* (1967); G.B. BURNET, *The Holy Communion in the Reformed Church of Scotland* (1960).

17

ITALY AND BARBARIAN EUROPE

The French attack of 1494 was regarded by many Italians at the time and shortly after as a 'barbarian' invasion—the first of a fresh series. The purpose of the following pages is to ask with what justification the Italians regarded the situation in this light, to examine briefly the political and cultural relations of the peninsula and the rest of Europe, and to survey some of the evidence for the use and significance of the term 'barbarian' in the Renaissance period.

The catalogue of the invasions of Italy is a long one. In historical times it starts with the Gauls, whose sack of Rome in 390 B.C. was often remembered by the French and Italians of the fifteenth and sixteenth centuries. The third century B.C. saw the Punic wars, culminating in Hannibal's descent on north Italy. There then ensued some centuries when Italy was free from outside attack, at the enormous price of devoting most of her energy to containing the turbulent migratory peoples of the north.

The collapse of the Empire under the pressure of attack from German and Slav tribes was, of course, the barbarian invasion *par excellence*. In the fourth and fifth centuries the peninsula succumbed to the invading Goths and Vandals. Italy was for a time divided between German masters and Greek governors, responsible to the emperor at Constantinople. And then, after the Lombard influx of the sixth century and the failure of the Greeks to make good their reconquest, the peninsula finally entered on its career as a group of distinct territories, bound only by history to the universal state which had once been centred on Rome.

The Italian Middle Ages are remarkable for the repeated invasions of the peninsula by outside princes and peoples—

remarkable, that is to say, by comparison with other regions of the Continent. The Moslems, it is true, conquered much of Spain and invaded France; Hungarian horsemen ravaged Germany and occasionally terrorized more distant areas; the Danes conquered half of England and the Normans all of it. But when all is said and done the subsequent history of Spain, Germany, France and England is remarkably self-contained. Spain admittedly had her *Reconquista*: but this was mainly an internal affair. Germany spread slowly east and north; and subsequently some German areas were lost in the later Middle Ages—but they were lost spontaneously and not by foreign attack. France and England may seem exceptional, for a French prince led French forces on English soil in the early thirteenth century and in the later Middle Ages Edward III and Henry V successfully invaded France. Yet the French attack on England was negligible and the Hundred Years War in the event was to give the English only a fugitive superiority in France: only for some thirty years in the fourteenth century and for about as long in the fifteenth century was France seriously debilitated by invasion: civil war was another matter in both France and England, and, indeed, explains in each country the foreign invasions to which we have referred.

Very different was the experience of the principalities which emerged from the Dark Ages in Italy. Carolingian intervention culminated in the assumption of the imperial title by Charle-magne in 800: thereafter the Franks and later the Germans had a constitutional interest in the politics of the peninsula. Italy was the *regnum Italicum*, her crown the diadem on the head of an emperor who was king of Germany. The eleventh and twelfth centuries witnessed the repeated attempts of German monarchs to make good their claims south of the Alps, and of popes to frustrate the effective power of rulers whom they rightly considered to be their principal rivals: in the process the south of Italy and Sicily were conquered by Norman knights. From this competition between pope and emperor for the political control of Italy other princes acquired an interest in intervention. The Hohenstaufen, rulers of south Italy in the early thirteenth century, were so great a threat to the papacy that the Angevins were encouraged to undertake the destruction of Frederick II and his descendants. In their turn the Aragonese ousted the Angevins from Sicily and aimed intermittently at securing Naples as well. By the end of the thirteenth century Germans, French and Spaniards all had ambitions, fortified by what they considered to be legal rights, in the divided and subdivided peninsula.

To this tale of invasions the fourteenth and fifteenth centuries were to add others. Imperial pretensions were, it is true, of less moment than they had been: the Italian expeditions of Henry VII (1310–13) and Lewis IV (1327–30) cannot be regarded as constituting a threat comparable to the interventions of Barbarossa; and the later appearances of emperors south of the Alps were even less pretentious. But north of Rome republics and tyrants still looked to the emperor as a source of *de jure* authority, south of Rome the Aragonese dynasty strove to extend its control from Sicily to Naples and a fresh generation of Angevins was prepared to pledge its resources, and at times the resources of the French king, in an effort to oust the Spaniards from the *Regno*. The popes continued their policy of enlisting foreign support to resist all native attempts at a general superiority in Italy. Established as they were at Avignon during most of the fourteenth century, and then weakened by two generations of bitter schism, the popes were, indeed, more prone than ever they had been to sacrifice Italy to the conquests of non-Italian princes. The French pope, Clement VII, in 1379 constituted the bulk of the Papal States into the 'kingdom of Adria' and granted it to Louis of Anjou. Earlier popes had been willing to bribe non-Italian princes to protect the lands and power of the Church in Italy by grants and privileges elsewhere in the peninsula: the dismemberment of these very lands was a much more radical step.

Clement VII was a Frenchman, whose only hope of obtaining control in Italy was by force of French arms; his 'kingdom of Adria' proved a chimaera. But the Italian popes who opposed him, and their successors after the schism ended in 1417, maintained the old policy of dividing in order to rule, and of alliance with foreign kings. What was different about the fifteenth century was that a number of powerful Italian princes were now on the scene—bigger figures than their fourteenth-century prototypes, with the prospect of longer tenure of power, with larger resources and a correspondingly advanced sense of political opportunity and even of political responsibility. Cosimo and Lorenzo de' Medici, Filippo Maria Visconti and Lodovico Sforza, Alfonso V and Ferrante may not have disposed of the same wealth as Venice, but for decades at a time they enjoyed a stability of power not unlike that of the Republic of St. Mark.

Yet the existence of principalities on this scale of course carried with it the association of Italian rulers with contemporary princes outside Italy. The Aragonese were in any event tied to Sicily and later to Naples; Florence had her traditional association with France; the Visconti and the Sforza looked at both Aragon and France with apprehension, and were even concerned to keep when possible on good terms with the Empire. In view of all this the events of 1494 are something of an anticlimax, for the upheaval had nearly occurred more than once already. In 1447, when Filippo Maria Visconti died, the Milanese inheritance lay open to attack: and attack came. Alfonso V moved north, Charles VII east and Frederick III, though in no state to move anywhere, asserted his claim as overlord: that Sforza was victorious in 1450 in large part because he deflected French activity towards Naples is a further anticipation of 1494. Alfonso's death in 1458 was productive of further moves similar to those that occurred when Ferrante died, for Alfonso was followed in Naples only by Ferrante; Sicily was linked to Aragon and the Spaniards were once more an outside power so far as the south of the peninsula was concerned. From this point onwards French and Spanish intrigue in Italy mounted in intensity and effectiveness: at any moment general war might have resulted; 'only deliberate avoidance of armed intervention on the part of Louis XI and Anne of Beaujeu had prevented any one of the quarrels of the last twenty years from culminating in a French invasion'.[1]

[1] C. M. Ady, 'Florence and North Italy', *Cambridge Medieval History*, viii, 218.

The invasion of 1494 and the ensuing wars in Italy were admittedly a formidable change from the intermittent support given earlier by the French crown to the Italian claims of Orleans and Anjou. But this should not blind us to the constant activity of foreign troops in fifteenth-century Italy. The soldiers of France, Spain and Germany were no strangers to Italy long before 1494. The predatory actions of the Swiss in the Milanese date from 1412 and were regularly renewed: it was no accident that after Lodi the Swiss were included in the Italian League of 1455. As for France the catalogue of Angevin expeditions is long and only broken in the 1480's when the claims of René passed to the French crown: the political revolutions at Genoa are a measure of this French participation in Italian warfare. Alfonso V's control in Naples had been backed by military forces which were predominantly Catalan.

War had thus involved Italy deeply with her neighbours, and over the centuries had united the fortunes of the states of the peninsula with the fortunes of the rest of Europe. Italy's indebtedness to her neighbours in a more general sense are no less striking, although the convention that Italy in the Renaissance was the benefactress of mankind tends to make them seem less important.

Socially, the structure of the Italian commune was undoubtedly an original creation. But the bulk of the land was, even in the later Middle Ages, organized on a predominantly rural plane, revolving round, not cities, but lords of land. In all that pertained to feudalism and monarchy Italians were pupils of the Franks and not their masters. Gothic and Lombard invaders doubtless laid the foundations of the Italian feudal world, but the bonds thus created were renewed and extended by the activities of the German emperors in the north and in the south by the Normans and Angevins. A confused memory of these influences lingers on in Machiavelli:

'E la Italia, poi che la fu in mano de' Franciosi, mutò in parte forma e ordine, per avere preso il papa nel temporale più autorità, e avendo quegli condotto in essa il nome de' conti e de' marchesi, come prima da Longino, esarco di Ravenna, vi erano stati posti i nomi de' duchi.'[1]

This exotic terminology, indeed, gained ground as time went on: however bourgeois they sometimes were by origin, the counts and marquises of Renaissance Italy pay unconscious tribute to the unity of Italy and the rest of medieval Christendom.

Italy was even more indebted in the cultural field. For the two centuries running from Abelard to Ockham, France was the mother of scholarship and letters. From France radiated out that interest in literature which has been called the twelfth-century Renaissance. In France developed philosophical and theological studies which culminated in the thirteenth-century enthronement of rational speculation as the highest form of university activity. To this Italy contributed little but Italians much. Save for Bologna, the story of the Italian universities in the central Middle Ages is not of much moment and it is hard to see how Aquinas, or Bonaventure, or Marsilio of Padua, could have displayed their talents in their homeland as well as they did in Paris. And Bologna, where civil law was the one great achievement of higher education in Italy, was a centre from which northern Europe learned, at the least, as much as Italy.

In no field was northern influence more marked in Italy than in vernacular literature. Italy could boast no native Italian literature as old as French, German or Spanish. The court of the German Frederick II was the first centre of Italian poetry, the poetry of the 'Sicilian School'; the great fructifier of Italian genius was French, and more particularly Provençal. In a very real sense Italian literature was provoked by the more mature linguistic development of the north. The debt was not merely linguistic but extended to style and subject-matter. A great range of Italian literature, from lyrics to *novelle*, bears the imprint of French inspiration; Boiardo, Ariosto, Folengo, Tasso were all poets of stories which had been born and developed in France, in the period when France could claim to be the medium of the *gesta*

---

[1] *Istorie Fiorentine*, i, xi (ed. Carli, i, 29).

Dei, when her kings, dukes and counts were the ideal types of Christian secular society.[1]

In the field of the fine arts Italy was also extraordinarily indebted to her neighbours. Sixteenth-century Italians readily conceded both the superior religious sentiment and the technical innovations of Flemish painters. This, however, is only a small part of northern influences which, in and after the thirteenth century, began powerfully to affect peninsular art and architecture, hitherto dominated by Byzantium. From this bondage Italian genius was released by the Gothic. The road which was to lead, through Giotto and Masaccio, to Leonardo and Michelangelo, begins in France.

In war and in peace the peoples of Italy had thus been, more perhaps than other countries of Europe, moulded by contact with their neighbours.[2] Yet these neighbouring peoples were described as 'barbarians' by many Italians at the end of the fifteenth century. What is the history of the term 'barbarian'? What did it imply for an Italian at this time?

Barbarian to a Greek signified one whose culture and language were not Greek. As taken over by the Romans the exclusive term was given a somewhat wider meaning: it was applied to those who dwelt beyond the bounds of Roman society, beyond the frontiers of the Empire; in a narrower sense it was applied to grammatical error.

These concepts had an extraordinarily prolonged career. In the Eastern Empire the contempt for all that was non-Greek survived the barbarian invasions, the loss of the Greek provinces in the west, and the shrinkage of Byzantine power in the Balkans and Asia Minor. Anna Commena in the eleventh century still treats the Franks contemptuously as barbarians[3] and so describes on one occasion the spiritual leader of the west, the pope.[4] This

[1] Cf. P. O. Kristeller's remarks in *Studies in Renaissance Thought and Letters* (Rome, 1956), pp. 553-83, and especially pp. 555-6, 575-6.

[2] Cf. G. Volpe, *Momenti di Storia Italiana* (Florence, 1925), pp. 303 ff.

[3] See G. Buckler, *Anna Commena* (London, 1929), pp. 440-1.

[4] Ibid., p. 308, n. 2.

arrogant superiority was one of the minor symptoms of the ten⁄
sions which divided the Christian world into two.

In the west the influence of Christianity made inroads on the
simple antithesis, Roman or Italian and Barbarian.[1] The pressure
of the German and Slav tribes in the third, fourth and fifth cen⁄
turies was at first capable of being viewed in these terms, for it was
the Roman world which was Christian: the barbarians were
pretty much the same as non⁄Christians at this stage. But it was
a stage which did not last. Soon the barbarians of the north were
converted and, conscious of their own barbarism, tended to
weaken or extend the expression to mean, not only non⁄Italian,
but also non⁄Christian. By the tenth century the chancery of the
German kings was regularly issuing charters which referred to
the *Christian* and *Barbarian* parts of the kingdom; thus Otto III
made a grant to the merchants of Magdeburg allowing them to
traffic *ubique in nostro regno, non solummodo Christianis, sed etiam
barbaricis regionibus.*[2] William of Malmesbury can even make the
pope at the Council of Clermont deny Christianity to the
barbarous peoples of Europe: 'Who could term Christian
those barbarians who in their distant islands dwell in the frozen
ocean, living like beasts?'[3] And Roger Bacon goes even further
and makes barbarian and rational the poles of opposition—a

[1] See the article 'Barbari' in *Enciclopedia Italiana*, vi, 123–4.

[2] See article cit. for reference. The thesis of this article is disputed by Rodolfo de
Mattei, 'Sul concetto di barbaro e barbarie nel medio evo', *Studi de Storia e Diritto
in onore di Enrico Besta*, iv (Milan, 1939), 483–501, who tries to prove that for all
practical purposes the Roman distinction between Italian and barbarian survived
and was current throughout the medieval period. He shows, indeed, that all the
citations of the *Enciclopedia* author are equivocal save those referring to the German
kings; but he shows that in Germany, where the distinction mattered, it was
almost common form (p. 497), a point which goes against him. But the *Enciclo⁄
pedia* writer and his critic have by no means surveyed all the evidence—and it
cannot be presented here in any detail. A point to be remembered is the existence
of Barbary—a geographical reminder of ethnical barbarism. Another development
of significance is the word 'brave', *bravus, bravo*. It seems likely that this derives
ultimately from *barbarus*. See W. Meyer⁄Lübke, *Romanisches etymologisches Wörter⁄
buch*, 3rd ed. (Heidelberg, 1935), p. 78.

[3] Malmesbury, Rolls Ser. ii, 395.

reasonable extension of meaning to be made in the thirteenth century when rationalism and Christianity were more closely bound together than ever before or since.[1] The Italian Balbi in his dictionary (1286) defines *barbarus* as *crudelis, incultus, austerus, stolidus, et est nomen crudelitatis et austeritatis.* 'Formerly,' he goes on, 'all races were termed barbarous save the Greeks and Latins.'[2]

Admittedly an equation of Christianity with civilization or rationality on the one hand and an assumption that it is opposed to barbarism on the other, brings the use of the term barbarian very close in spirit to the original sense which it had for the classical world. And that sense was far from being neglected in the Middle Ages. In the patristic period the concept was naturally kept alive, and it is also found in many Dark Age writers.[3] Among the texts of the schoolmasters Roman literary values were remembered, and many a clerk must have re-echoed Einhard's modest self-description: *homo barbarus, et in Romana locutione perparum exercitatus.*[4] The grammarians, indeed, developed still further the ancient literary usage of 'barbarism'. For the Roman a literary barbarism was essentially a spoken error; *barbarolexis* an error in the form of a word. Very early in the Middle Ages these meanings shift and Isidore of Seville can explain that 'barbarism is the wrong spelling or pronunciation of a word', *barbarolexis* 'when a word of a barbarian language is introduced into Latin'.[5] These terms become firmly embedded in medieval grammatical theory and are repeated down the centuries by educationists:[6] Balbi naturally devotes far more space in the *Catholicon* to *barbarismus* and derivative critical words than he does to *barbarus*. *Latinitas* remained the opposite of literary barbarism, as it had been for the Romans.[7]

[1] *Opus Majus,* ed. Bridges, 1, 301.
[2] *Catholicon* Johannis Januensis (Lyons, 1489), s.v.
[3] See R. de Mattei's very useful survey, quoted above.
[4] *Vita Karoli,* proem.
[5] *Etymologiarum,* ed. W. M. Lindsay (Oxford, 1911), lib. i, xxxii, 1, 2.
[6] John of Salisbury, *Metalogicon,* trans. D. D. McGarry (Berkeley, 1955), p. 52.
[7] C. S. Baldwin, *Medieval Rhetoric and Poetic* (New York, 1928), p. 216.

By the fourteenth century barbarian had thus come to mean someone who was non-Christian (with an associated lack of civilization and rationality), at another level, a writer of bad Latin, and, also an ancient sense, one who was outside the cultural world of Rome. In the Italy of the fourteenth century this last meaning, the original sense of the word, was to be given again its full weight. The Italian patriot of the period was taught by Petrarch to view his northern neighbours under a rubric to which the worst associations were conveyed. For Petrarch in poetry, and briefly and uncomfortably in practice for Cola di Rienzo, *Italia* emerged as the ultimate terrestrial loyalty. The peninsula, cut off by God from the *rabies barbarica* of the north by the *Alpes aerias*, *barbarico oppositas furori*, was the home of all that made life kind, the heart of a Church which was literally Roman.[1] This attitude was not only displayed by Petrarch in his Latin writings: it was also Petrarch in glowing vernacular indignation—a more potent and influential matter altogether. The famous canzone 'Italia mia' is a hymn to the concept of an Italy which needs only domestic peace for the release of ancient valour, the expulsion of foreign barbarians. Written in the mid-1340's,[2] these verses expressed a position which only strengthened as time went on and as the scholarly discipline of the humanists was diffused through Italy.

In the next generation we find Guelf Florence at war with a papacy still absent from Italy. According to the Florentines, the French pope was now flooding the peninsula with foreign mercenary soldiers as well as with brutal and grasping French priests. The war of the 'Otto Santi' went far to precipitating a general use of barbarian for the foreigner in current Florentine political jargon and the pages of the official letters written in 1376 by Coluccio Salutati, who had just become chancellor, are full of a spirit which identified Florence with Italy, Italy with

[1] To Urban V, 1366, *Sen.* vii, 1; *Epistolae Selectae*, ed. A. F. Johnson (Oxford, 1923), pp. 165–6.

[2] For the date of 'Italia mia' see *Rime*, ed. G. Carducci and S. Ferrari (Florence, 1924), pp. 202–3.

Latinitas and barbarism with the French and the English mercenaries.[1]

'Italy', Florence informed the Romans, 'by the efforts of your ancestors was mistress of the world: we shall not tolerate her being subdued by foreigners and barbarians.'[2] The Italian company of St. George was thanked by the *signoria* a little later: 'God made the barbarians cowardly and you bold and strong . . . you deserve to be called the liberators of Italy.'[3] Despite a very different viewpoint, much the same attitude is displayed by Pier Paolo Vergerio: 'There is no room in Italy for barbarians'—'Italy which in reputation and in fact stands out above all other nations.'[4]

This view of the Italian past was confirmed by the sober scholarship of Flavio Biondo, whose *Roma instaurata* and *Roma triumphans* were supplemented by his *Italia illustrata* of 1453 and who viewed the whole of Christendom from an Italian standpoint in his history of the Middle Ages, the *Decades* (1440–52, first edition 1483). From these works later Italian historians drew the material for a view of the past which constantly harked back to the golden days of Rome. This is what lies behind the analysis by Machiavelli of Italy's disunity—both in early times when popes caused the attacks of barbarians[5] and in the fifteenth century when the hordes again devastate the land;[6] it was for a redeemer, *un suo redentore*, who would liberate Italy from *questo barbaro dominio*, that Machiavelli wrote his *Prince*.[7] This is what lies behind the sad description

[1] Cf. E. Duprè Theseider, *I papi di Avignone e la questione Romana* (Florence, 1939), pp. 178–9.

[2] M. Gherardi, 'La guerra dei Fiorentini con Papa Gregorio XI, detta la Guerra degli Otto Santi', *Archivio Storico Italiano*, 3rd series, V, pt. ii (Florence, 1867), 35–131; appendix of documents, no. 140, in VII, pt. i (1868), 223.

[3] 11 May 1379. Printed in the appendix to F. T. Perrens, *Histoire de Florence*, v, 473–4.

[4] 22 January 1391. P. P. Vergerio, *Epistolario*, ed. L. Smith, Fonti per la storia d'Italia (Rome, 1934), pp. 46, 53: 'Quanto enim et nomine et re ceteris nationibus clarior extat Italia, tanto magis, etc. . . .' 'Indignetur et obstrepat quantumlibet despecta barbaries: illi in Italia nullus locus est.'

[5] *Istorie Fiorentine*, ed. cit., i, 26.   [6] Ibid., ii, 4.

[7] Ed. L. A. Burd, p. 371; cf. F. Ercole, *Da Carlo VIII a Carlo V. La crisi della libertà Italiana*, especially pp. 217–22.

by Guicciardini of the year 1494—*anno infelicissimo all' Italia, e in verità anno primo degli anni miserabili, perchè aperse la porta a innumerabili e oribili calamità.*[1] And this is why Guicciardini listed the expulsion from Italy of all the barbarians as one of the (probably unattainable) desires of his life—

'Tre cose desidero vedere innanzi alla mia morte; ma dubito, ancora che io vivessi molto, non ne vedere alcuna: uno vivere di republica bene ordinato nella città nostra, Italia liberata da tutti e Barbari, e liberato il mondo dalla tirannide di questi scelerati preti.'[2]

The resulting picture, idealizing not only the place of Roman antiquity but the balance of power in Italy after the Peace of Lodi, entered the canon of Italian historical mythology. Over a century later Muratori practically repeats Guicciardini;[3] modern writers mostly follow the same pattern.

It is important to remember, on the other hand, that the Italian contemporaries of Biondo and Guicciardini did not all view Italy as a haven of culture threatened by a barbarous trans-Alpine world. If they had done so no French king, however powerful, could have made headway for a moment. On the contrary, Italian politics were and remained essentially centred on local issues, and Italian political speculation thus remained, for all its penetration, curiously divorced from the 'Italia' to which so much lip service was paid. Of all the powers in the peninsula only the papacy could have been expected to take a broad view. And it would have been strange if the papal curia, traditionally bound to the service of Christendom, not of Italy, staffed as it still was with a fair number of 'barbarian' officials, had taken a consistently anti-barbarian line. This was, of course, changing and by the time of Leo X the curia was more homogeneously Italian: Paris de Grassis *does* use the term barbarian,[4] for example, while his

---

[1] *Storia d'Italia* (Paris, 1837), i, 127.

[2] *Ricordi*, no. 236: *Opere inedite*, ed. G. Canestrini (Florence, 1857), p. 154.

[3] *Annali d'Italia*, IX, 570: 'Cominciarono in quest' Anno i guai dell' Italia, guai di lunga durata', etc.

[4] Quoted Pastor, *History of the Popes*, trans. and ed. Antrobus, vi, 345.

predecessor as master of ceremonies, the Strassburger John Bur-
chard, does not—though violently hostile to the French.[1] And the
pope who bore the brunt of the first French attack was himself a
barbarian, the Borgia Alexander VI. Some small use does seem
to have been made of the concept of barbarian-Italian antithesis in
practical politics. Giovanni Bentivoglio in March 1494 urged
Ludovico Sforza's envoy to tell his master that 'we Italians should
not allow barbarian peoples to come between us especially as their
claws and teeth are long'.[2] Another occasion when practical men
put their thoughts and policies forward in this way was in the
debate at Venice in 1498 when Guicciardini reports Trevisan as
foreshadowing a possible alliance between the *casa di Austria*
and the French, 'a union of barbarians, eternal enemies of Italy'.[3]
Above all, for Julius II the notion of barbarian hostility seems to
have been a genuine inspiration. His 'Fuori i Barbari' was probably never spoken in so many words.[4] But he undoubtedly said
as much on more than one occasion[5] and when Guicciardini
analysed Julius's aims he made the same point: the pope's desire
di cacciare il re di Francia di tutto quello possedeva in Italia derived, he
wrote, either from the pope's harbouring an ancient grudge
against them, or because over the years his suspicions grew into
hate, or because he desired 'the glory of being the man who
liberated Italy from the barbarians'—*la cupidità della gloria di
essere stato, come diceva poi, liberatore d'Italia dai barbari.*[6] The same
desire (according to the same authority) inspired Leo X.[7]

But these examples are not impressive when set beside the
general indifference not only of Italian princes and governments,

---

[1] RR. II. SS., ed. Celani, p. 541: the Cardinal of Gurk has a lily carved in
his heart. Latin continued to be the language used within the Curia till 1480,
Pastor, i, 242 n.

[2] Quoted C. M. Ady, *The Bentivoglio of Bologna* (London, 1937), p. 114.

[3] *Storia d'Italia*, ed. cit., ii, 48; the basis of the hostility is 'la diversità degli
animi tra i Barbari e gl'Italiani', p. 49.

[4] Pastor, vi, 322 n.

[5] Pastor, loc. cit.; Creighton, *History of the Papacy*, v, 76–7.

[6] *Storia d'Italia*, iii, 159; note the qualification of 'poi'.

[7] Ibid., iv, 354.

but of many of the humanists themselves. Bernardo Rucellai's *De bello italico*, completed between 1506 and 1509,[1] does occasion-ally make play with Italy's *barbarus hostis*,[2] but this is not in any sense important for his frigid and efficient analysis of Charles VIII's relations with Italy. It is also salutary to remember that older usages of 'barbarian' were not entirely swept out in Renais-sance Italy. Giovanni Rucellai, the father of Bernardo, used the word in a sense essentially opposed, not to Italian values, but to non-Christian values: he thanks God that he has made him 'a rational creature, a Christian, and not a Turk, a Moor or a barbarian'.[3] Marsilio Ficino's *exhortatio ad bellum contra barbaros* was intended to stir up resistance to the Turks.[4] The defence of Christendom was, in fact, in the hands of Balkan 'barbarians'.

In Italy, too, the technical, literary meaning of 'barbarous', noticed as a feature of medieval rhetorical teaching, was positively encouraged by the humanists. For them there was, it is true, a close association between the notion of linguistic propriety and general civility: the Romans' greatest achievement, said Valla, was their language.[5] As time went on there was an ever-closer connection between *Latinitas* in its grammatical sense and Italian culture. Politian could urge a lively and living attitude to Latin composition: only slavish copying of a model author saved some little men from barbarism.[6] But within a generation Ciceroni-anism was all but triumphant in Italy, and the papacy encouraged this in its efforts to use scholarship as a prop for the Church.[7]

Fierce indeed were the diatribes launched against the defenders

[1] F. Gilbert, 'Bernardo Rucellai and the Orti Oricellari', *Journ. Warb. and Court. Institutes*, xii (1949), 111–12, note.

[2] B. Oricellarii, *De Bello Italico* (London, 1724), p. 3; cf. p. 100, 'barbari externique principes, quorum finibus Gallia continenter cingitur'.

[3] *Zibaldone* (1466), quoted W. H. Woodward, *Studies in Education during the age of the Renaissance* (Cambridge, 1906), p. 78.

[4] Kristeller, op. cit., p. 112 and n.

[5] Preface to the *Elegantiae, Prosatori Latini del Quattrocento,* ed. E. Garin (Milan-Naples, 1952), pp. 594–601.

[6] Ibid., p. 902.

[7] G. Toffanin, *Storia Letteraria d'Italia: Il Cinquecento* (Milan, 1945), p. 16.

of the vernacular by those, like Lazzaro Bonamico, who regarded it as a barbarous corruption of Latin. Violent were the recrimina-tions against Longolius (Christophe Longueuil), the stranger from Malines who humbly sought Ciceronian perfection in Rome.[1] The papal plan to grant him official Roman citizenship provoked a storm against him which in 1519 drove him from the city in shame and despair: he was accused of having dared to compare Italy with France in an early work; of having praised Erasmus and Budé, who were barbarians; of having been bribed into visiting Italy in order to acquire the best books to take back to the barbarians, so that they could dispute Italian primacy; above all he was regarded in Rome of being guilty of being a barbarian himself. But the chief indignation of the poetasters and literary politicians was reserved for Erasmus, whose *Ciceronianus*, poking fun at the whole idea of an absolute Latin in the current Roman manner, was published in 1528. Erasmus's views were no secret before this: he had meditated his position from at least 1516,[2] and his argument that exaggerated Ciceronian diction was pagan and irreligious gave the ensuing debate added bitterness; for Italians it tended to put the author even more clearly in the Lutheran camp.[3]

The Italian *questione della lingua* in fact soon abandoned the sterile problem of whether Latin should be the sole vehicle of literature. Ciceronianism won, inside and outside Italy, but was confined to the limited field of Latin: Petrarchism played a similar role in the vernacular. This changed the conventional picture of Latin's unique place in the linguistic hierarchy. One finds, as early as the *Ercolano* of Benedetto Varchi (1560), an analysis of the term barbarian which is entirely devoid of the emotional over-tones to which the events of 1494 and later might have been supposed to contribute. In the dialogue Varchi divides all languages into certain basic categories and his interlocutor asks

---

[1] Ibid., pp. 22-5; R. Sabbadini, *Storia del Ciceronianismo* (Turin, 1885), pp. 52-7.

[2] Angiolo Gambaro, *Il Ciceronianus di Erasmo* (Turin, 1950), pp. 2-6.

[3] Ibid., pp. 41-7; Sabbadini, pp. 59-66.

why one of these divisions is not between barbarous tongues and the rest. Varchi replies:

'This word *barbaro* is equivocal and can signify more than one thing. Thus, when it refers to the spirit, a "barbarous man" means a "cruel man", a "brute of a man", with savage habits. When it refers to variations between regions, or their remoteness, *barbaro* means any one who is not of your own country, and is practically equivalent to "strange", or "foreign". But when it refers to speech, which was its first and proper meaning, *barbaro* is applied to all those who do not speak one of the "noble" languages, or who, though using one of them, do not obey the rules and instructions of the grammarians.'[1]

And Varchi adds that he could not exclude Hebrew, French, Spanish, German, *e molte altre* from the list of languages in which style was possible.

With all of this the barbarians could agree. Were they not being told by Italians, who presumably should know, that as a result of the wars 'good literature, both Latin and Greek, was emptied out of Italy, and poured across the Alps into Germany, France, England and Scotland'?[2] Had they not embarked on their own campaign against barbarism? Erasmus had printed his *Antibarbarorum Libri* in 1520: but this, like the *Ciceronianus*, was an old story, going back to 1495.[3] In it Erasmus defended good literature as a worthy human purpose; the rest of his life was a

[1] *L'Ercolano* (ed. Milan, n.d.), pp. 111-12: 'Questo nome *barbaro* è voce equivoca, cioè significa più cose, perciocchè, quando si riferisce all' animo, un uomo barbaro vuol dire un uomo crudele, un uomo bestiale e di costumi efferati; quando si riferisce alla diversità, o lontananza delle regioni, barbaro si chiama chiunque non è del tuo paese, ed è quasi quel medesimo che strano, o straniero; ma quando si riferisce al favellare, che fu il suo primo e proprio significato, barbaro si dice di tutti coloro, i quali non favellano in alcuna delle lingue nobili, o se pure favellano in alcuna d'esse, non favellano correttamente, non osservando le regole e gli ammaestramenti de' grammatici.'

[2] P. Vergil, *Anglica Historia*, ed. Hay (Camden Series, 1950), p. 145: 'Iisdem temporibus perfectae literae similiter latinae atque graecae ex Italia bellis nefariis exclusae, exterminatae, expulsae, sese trans Alpes per omnem Germaniam, Galliam, Angliam, Scotiamque effuderunt.'

[3] *Opus epistolarum*, ed. Allen, i, 121 note.

commentary on the thesis that scholarship should be pure and compatible with a devout Christianity; barbarism for Erasmus was thus opposed to reason and Christianity, as we have met it already.[1]

In every northern country a campaign to secure a new curriculum, an attitude to letters comparable with that of the Italian humanist, was being waged in the sixteenth century.

'Emulate, noble men, the ancient nobility of Rome, which after taking over the empire of the Greeks, assimilated all their wisdom and eloquence, so much so that it is hard to decide whether it has equalled all the Greek discoveries and equipment of learning or surpassed them. In the same way you who have taken over the empire of the Italians should cast off repulsive barbarism and seek to acquire Roman culture.'[2]

Thus Conrad Celtis (Pickel) at Ingolstadt in 1492, speaking, as he said himself, as a 'manikin born as some say in the midst of barbarians and drunkards'[3] to an audience whose leaders the Italians would describe 'merely as the barbarians'. National sentiment doubtless helps to explain the vehemence with which the new programme was adovcated in the north.[4] But it spread because it answered other needs than a petty desire to score off the Italians. Its success was remarkable. In every northern country the victory of the humanist schoolmaster was complete, and, though there were few Guarinos or Vittorinos, Italy had no scholar of the stature of Erasmus. Even more significant, the main counter-attack to Erasmus's *Ciceronianus* was conducted by a Frenchman, Etienne Dolet, and a Frenchman by adoption, Julius Caesar Scaliger.[5]

.   .   .

[1] Above, p. 361.
[2] Conrad Celtis, *Selections*, ed. and trans. L. Forster (Cambridge, 1948), p. 43.
[3] Ibid., p. 37.
[4] See P. S. Allen, *The Age of Erasmus* (Oxford, 1914), pp. 264-8, and the collection of references to German-Italian hostility in the correspondence of Erasmus, *Opus Epist.*, iv, 280, line 67 note.
[5] Sabbadini, pp. 68-71.

For an honest Frenchman or Englishman the superiority of the Italian was far from evident, but Italian consciousness of superi⁄ ority was not the only unpleasant feature of peninsular society. Lemaire de Belges (for example) found much to admire in Italian literature while thinking French literature just as good in different ways:[1] but he could not find Italian republicanism palatable, and hated the 'tyrants' at Venice.[2] No right⁄thinking barbarian in the north could find himself fond of the papacy, at all events until it had been crushed politically and rent by the Reformation, and the Leonine identification of civilization with papal Rome undoubtedly exacerbated an already tender situation. Yet the fact remains that, despite such antagonisms, we witness in the sixteenth century the adoption in the north, not only of an educational reform of Italian origin, but also an acceptance of those deeper changes in moral outlook which are coincident with humanism—the new attitude to the active life and to wealth which were hammered out in *Quattrocento* Italy.

The diffusion of the cultural achievements of Renaissance Italy thus proceeded in two ways: on the one hand the new pedantry spread among schoolmasters and scholars; on the other hand a new view of social obligations and rewards spread among the ruling classes.

As for the first, it needs little elaboration, save to point out that the process (somewhat as in Italy) moved from a Latin basis to a basis in both Latin and the vernaculars. The poets and dramatists learned humanity (or Latin) at school: they wrote in French or English. From the *rinascita del vero testo classico* the French movement, for instance, proceeded to the *culto del volgare*.[3] Joachim du Bellay argued in his *Deffence et illustration de la Langue Francoyse*, 'that the French language should not be called bar⁄ barous.'[4] There were contemporaries of du Bellay who went so

---

[1] *Concorde des deux Languages*, ed. Frappier, pp. 4–5; *Illustrations de Gaule*, ed. Stecher, i, 11.   [2] *Illustrations*, i, 7.

[3] See the admirable chapter in Franco Simone, *La Conscienza della rinascita negli humanisti Francesi* (Rome, 1949), pp. 91–157.

[4] Edited H. Chamard (1948), pp. 15–21.

far as to describe as 'barbarians' ink-horn terms', some of the neologisms involved in the latinized vernaculars. Montaigne, the best possible example of the effects of the new humanist education, brings us back to the sound moral division between civilized people and all the rest when in his *Essais* he reflects on cannibals.[1]

Montaigne was a burgess turned gentleman: it was through this mixture, and rather through the gentleman part of it than through the burgess part of it, that the essential changes in moral values referred to above were passed from Italy to the north. The most important single contribution to a diffusion of Italian values was Castiglione's *Courtier*. This is seen not merely in the translations which appeared (for example the French versions of 1537 and 1538, Hoby's English of 1561), or the printing outside Italy of the Italian text, or the turning of it into Latin for pedagogical purposes, but above all by the way in which it stimulated other countries to produce similar studies. Claude Chappuys and Philibert de Vienne in France, Sir Thomas Elyot and Roger Ascham in England (to name only a few) vulgarized and made local application of Castiglione and other Italian writers on education and manners.[2] Renaissance Italy, destroyed by the Barbarians politically and economically, was the victor in letters, social values, and, though it has not seen touched on here, the fine arts.

Yet the paradoxical truth is that what made possible in the first place the elaboration of the new Italian attitudes, just as what made possible later the transmission of these attitudes across the Alps, was precisely the divisions of Italian society which had provoked in the peninsula the use of the concept of *Italia* and the related idea of barbarism. The Tuscan and Lombard communities which produced a self-conscious bourgeois society, the small courts where Vittorino and Guarino taught, the Urbino of Castiglione are all peculiar to the Italian scene, and cannot be exactly paralleled elsewhere. Had Italian unity been accomplished in the fourteenth century as Dante and Petrarch hoped and had

[1] Ed. M. Rat, i, 234.
[2] Cf. A. Tilley, *Literature of the French Renaissance*, i, 48-9; W. H. Woodward, *Education during the Renaissance*, pp. 269-322.

the peninsula then embarked on the centralizing path of France, Spain and England, it is hard to see how the crystallization of the new moral and political values could have happened. The crisis of liberty so well analysed by Dr. Hans Baron[1] derived from a situation in which Florence was pitted against Milan, where what was viewed as politically and culturally essential reposed in a multiplicity of governments. It is equally evident that, had a congeries of genuine republics survived in fifteenth-century Italy, the Italian message would have penetrated much slower than it did among the French, the English and the rest. The Italian prince as patron of fine art and literature, as the centre of political and social activity, as the fount of a courtesy which could be readily adapted to chivalric traditions, was himself in every sense a product of the bourgeois environment: but he acted as a bridge over which ideas and attitudes could pass to the kings and gentry of the north. The price of the victory of the Italian Renaissance in European civilization was the existence in Italy of a variety of states: in helping to maintain such a situation by intervention and intrigue the 'barbarians' thus contributed directly to their ultimate absorption of new ways of thought and action.

As far as the antithesis between Italy and barbarism was concerned, the sixteenth century saw its end. It lingered on as an irritation to foreigners; but the foreigner was too firmly established in the peninsula, the political nullity of the country too self-evident, for Italian superiority to have genuine meaning. The 'Italianate' Englishman or Frenchman might be an object of fun or exasperation to his compatriots, but already in the pages of the *Courtier* Castiglione has to castigate Italians who ape the ways of France and Spain.[2] By a fresh *translatio litterarum* the home of literature and art was again to be France. And there Montesquieu calmly summarized the matters touched on in the preceding pages. Of the barbarians who had engulfed the Roman empire

[1] Hans Baron, *The Crisis of the Early Italian Renaissance*, 2 vols. (Princeton, 1955).

[2] *Il Cortegiano*, ed. Cian (1947), pp. 69–70, 174–5, 193.

he states: *ces peuples n'étaient point proprement barbares, puisqu'ils étaient libres.* Italy he describes as *une nation autrefois maîtresse du Monde, aujourd'hui esclave de toutes les autres.*[1] French *civilisation* is to replace Italian *civiltà.*[2] Barbarism is to become a necessary stage in the evolution of all mankind.

[1] *Lettres persanes*, no. cxxxvi.
[2] E. Benveniste, 'Civilisation: Contribution à l'histoire du mot', *Éventail de l'histoire vivante. Offert . . . à Lucien Febvre*, i, 47–54.

6 La Piazza del Popolo, Rome, after Blaeu, *c.* 1724

18

THE ITALIAN VIEW OF RENAISSANCE ITALY

A me piace abitar la mia contrada,
Visto ho Toscana, Lombardia, Romagna,
Quel monte che divide e quel che serra
Italia, e un mare e l'altro che la bagna.
Ariosto, *Satira*, III, 57-60

I must begin this brief essay with an apology for a title which may mislead. 'Renaissance,' as here used, is intended to cover a particular period of time – roughly the period between 1300 and 1550. In what follows I shall not be much concerned with the Italian awareness of the cultural innovations which took place in Italy at this time, a subject which has often been discussed and which forms a significant element of such fundamental books as *The Renaissance in Historical Thought*. My theme is different. I propose to examine the way in which some Italians looked at the geographical area in which they lived, at their *patria* in the largest sense of that term.

For most Italians, *patria* meant, not the entire peninsula, but those narrower localities with which they had immediate sentimental and political ties. Yet, however oblivious in practice to the demands of larger loyalties, literate Italians were forever referring to the land as a whole. It is hard to find a poet or historian, or writer of any kind, who does not offer observations or reflections which might be used to illustrate a view of Italy. During the Risorgimento the scholars who promoted unification ransacked earlier literature to demonstrate that there had always been an Italy. And in the Renaissance they found much material. It was, of course, particularly noticeable in the sources for the late fifteenth and early sixteenth centuries, the years of the French invasion of 1494 and the subsequent Italian wars when 'liberty' was destroyed in Italy and many Italians were conscious of this. There is much recent work on this period, and on the reactions of (for example) Machiavelli and Guicciardini to the tortured choices before them, the safety of Florence against the safety of Italy, and how the individual could survive to influence events in those cruel days.[1] But the contemporary material is nearly all polemical. From Petrarch, in *Italia mia*, to the anguished writers who witnessed the campaigns of Charles VIII, Francis I, and Charles V, the picture of Italy as struggling against barbarism is distorted by immediate political purposes, which in the event were to be frustrated. What I intend to present in the following pages are the opinions of a few Italians who considered the land with no such urgency, who were anxious to display Italy without political overtones, Italy as such and not as an ideal or as a programme. I shall summon three witnesses: Dante (writing in the early fourteenth century), Flavio Biondo (mid-fifteenth), Leandro Alberti (mid-sixteenth). I shall indicate summarily their varying approaches and then attempt a few conclusions.

By way of preface we should recall the main features of the public scene in Italy during the two hundred and fifty years spanned by the lives of these men. At the beginning of the period, Italy was emerging from the chaos which had engulfed her with the fall of the Hohenstaufen in 1250; at the end, the country was entering the exhausted peace which followed the domination of the peninsula by Spanish armies. In the interval the emperors had lost all effective power and – after residence at Avignon, after the schism, the councils and Luther – so had the popes, save precariously in the states of the Church where they reigned like princes. From a peak of commercial wealth attained in Dante's day, Italian prosperity had generally and steadily declined until in 1550 it was a shadow of what it had been. But these too are the centuries of the Renaissance in Italy, one aspect of which was a heightened understanding of *Italianità*, of the uniqueness and value of Italy. The authors discussed below were not directly concerned to promote such an understanding but their works contributed to its development and reflect changes in cultural emphasis.

The work of Dante is rich in Italian reflections, not least in the *La divina commedia*, where there are many glancing references to the land, both affectionate and contemptuous. In one of his Latin works, the *De vulgari eloquentia* (c. 1305), he deliberately surveyed the scene in a dispassionate fashion, giving us a personal view of the map of Italy.[2] This work was, of course, intended not as a geographical or chorographical manual, but as a survey of the Romance languages and a guide to writers in 'il bel paese là dove il sì suono.' In the course of his remarkable analysis, the earliest and for ages the only scientific treatise on linguistics, Dante made several observations which reveal his way of apprehending Italy.

1 A useful recent survey is provided by V. Illardi, 'Italianità,' *Traditio* XII (1956), 339-67.
2 I am grateful to Mr Colin Hardie for a note on the date of the work.

In reading these portions of the *De vulgari eloquentia* it is important to remember that the author had before him, perhaps literally but most certainly in his mind, a map of the kind associated with Pietro Vesconte.[3] This displayed the peninsula as part of a circular world-map, with Jerusalem in the centre and Asia in the top half. Europe was depicted in the lower quarter on the left, separated by the Mediterranean from Africa in the lower quarter on the right. This arrangement – deriving from ancient sources and reflected in the medieval 'T & O' diagrams – meant that Italy was drawn with the Alps at the bottom left and the toe at the upper right. Dante's references to left and right are accordingly the reverse of later practice.

In discussing the Italian language Dante touches twice on the peninsula as a whole, in chapters ix and x of book i. To illustrate the linguistic variations of Italy he compares:

> the speech of the right side of Italy with that of the left: the Paduans talk differently from the Pisans. Neighbours have different speech: the Milanese differ from the Veronese, the Romans from the Florentines. Even peoples who are of one race are disparate: the Neapolitans and the men of Gaeta, for instance, or the people of Ravenna and those of Faenza.[4]

In a later passage he surveys the peninsula more systematically:

> Italy is divided into two parts, a right side and a left. If you ask about the dividing line I will briefly reply that this is the range of the Appenines, which, like the sloping ridge of a roof,[5] divides the waters running down, channelling them now to one shore and now to the other, as Lucan describes in the second book [of the *Pharsalia*]. The right side drains into the Tyrrhenian sea, the left into the Adriatic. The regions of the right are: Apulia (though not all of it), Rome, the duchy of Spoleto, Tuscany, the March of Genoa. Those of the left are: part of Apulia, the March of Ancona, Romagna, Lombardy, the March of

---

3 See *De vulgari eloquentia* (hereafter DVE), ed. A. Marigo (Florence 1938), pp. 47 and 82, notes: cf. P. Revelli, *L'Italia nella Divina Commedia* (Milan 1922), esp. pp. 59-73 on the 'confini e regioni d'Italia.' For a recent discussion of Dante's geography, see G. Vinay, 'Ricerche sul *De vulgari eloquentia*: iii Apenini devexione clauduntur,' *Giornale storico della litteratura italiana*, cxxxvi (1959), 367-82. I have to thank Professor Cecil Grayson for this reference.

4 DVE, I,ix,4-5 (Marigo, p. 66)

5 Cf. 'Si come neve tra le vive travi/per lo dosso d'Italia si congela ...' *Purg.* xxx. 85-6

Treviso with Venice. Friuli and Istria thus have to belong to the left of
Italy and the Tyrrhenian islands, Sicily and Sardinia, belong to or
rather are naturally to be associated with the right of Italy.[6]

Dante goes on to point out that each of these regions had a distinct language; there were at least fourteen. But, in addition to that, in Tuscany,
men from Siena spoke differently from those of Arezzo; in Lombardy, the
men of Ferrara and those of Piacenza had their own languages. And he
refers to an earlier passage in which he had shown that even in a single
town there could be more than one vernacular. In Bologna the men of
Borgo San Felice, just outside the wall, had a tongue differing from that
of the inhabitants of the centre, of 'strada maggiore.'[7] All in all, Dante
concludes, 'if one wanted to count the main and the secondary vernaculars
of Italy, together with their further divisions, in this small corner of the
world the number of linguistic varieties would reach not merely a thousand but even more.'[8]

For centuries no subsequent writer looked at Italy so coolly as Dante
did in this extraordinary book. But the realities pointed to in the *De vulgari eloquentia*, like the book itself, were to be ignored. The book, which
remained half-finished, was not influential. An Italian translation appeared in 1529 but the Latin original was not published until 1577 when,
amid the growing assertiveness of Tuscan, it was felt that Dante's strictures on that species of the vernacular betrayed the cause; it was even
argued that the work was not an authentic writing of the poet.[9] Yet Dante's
aim had been to advocate a 'courtly' Italian which would unify the land
and encourage the fundamental cultural unity he discerned behind all the
divisions.

No such ambition lay behind Flavio Biondo's *Italia illustrata*. Biondo,
in the papal secretariate from 1434, came from Forlì in the Romagna, and
is best known for his *Historiarum ab inclinatione Romanorum imperii
decades*, a history of Europe from the fall of Rome to his own day. He
also wrote two archaeological works, the *Roma instaurata* and the *Roma
triumphans*. The *Italia illustrata* was composed between 1448 and 1453,
but it is likely that the author had been collecting materials for some time
earlier. It is not a long book, but it is an important one. Dante's description was incidental to his linguistic purposes; Biondo's was the first work
expressly devoted to Italy as a whole. It was published (in October 1453)

6 DVE, I,x,6-7 (Marigo, pp. 80-6)
7 DVE, I,ix,4 (Marigo, p. 66)
8 DVE, I,x,9 (Marigo, p. 88). It is difficult to put neatly into English the phrase
    'primas et secundarias et subsecundarias vulgaris Ytalie variationes.'
9 See Marigo's introduction, pp. xliii-xlviii

before it was completed, in order to frustrate the circulation of unauthorized copies, and Biondo tinkered with it thereafter almost till his death (in 1463).[10] What was Biondo's purpose in writing this unusual work? The inspiration for it came, it seems, from Alfonso v who asked for a 'description of Italy in which the ancient names were to be related to their modern equivalents.'[11] And this is what Biondo set out to do, basing his account as far as possible on classical authorities, but adding details of men famous for valour and letters so that (in his own words) he provided 'not just a description of Italy ... but a sort of summary of Italian history.'[12]

The book begins with a general discussion of Italy, eschewing praises of the land – which have been sufficiently provided by Vergil, Pliny, and Petrarch – but giving its over-all dimensions. Biondo then writes:

> Italy has a back-bone, the sort we see in fish, and this is the Appenines, a mountain range which begins at the end of the Alps nearest the Tyrrhenian sea, goes straight down towards Ancona and seems about to end there; but it starts off again and goes through the middle of Italy, ending in Calabria ... Having displayed the site and the size of Italy, we must now divide up the land and describe in detail the places in it.[13]

He bemoans the difficulties of this task. Places have changed their names and Roman Italy is no more. Where of old there were seven hundred cities the Roman curia now counts only two hundred and sixty-four with bishoprics. Of the ancient regions only one has not significantly changed: ancient Etruria had the same boundaries as modern Tuscany; the other ancient regions have changed their names and limits several times. He accordingly divides his survey into eighteen regions (not including the islands), making use in general of those names best known in his own day. His regions are: Liguria or the Genoese (p. 295); Etruria (p. 299); Latium or the Campagna and Maritima of Rome (p. 313); Umbria or the duchy of Spoleto (p. 328); Picenum or the March of Ancona (p. 334); Romagna, or Flaminia and Emilia (p. 342); Gallia Cisalpina or Lombardy (p. 356); the Veneto (p. 369); Italia Transpadana or the March of

10 See the account by B. Nogara, *Scritti inediti e rari di Biondo Flavio, Studi e Testi*, 48 (Rome 1927), pp. cxxi-cxxvi; the editor prints, pp. 215-39, some of the later additions. A critical study of the *Italia illustrata*, and an authoritative text, would be welcome.

11 Nogara, *Scritti inediti*, pp. 163-4

12 I quote from the Basel edition of 1531, p. 295

13 *Italia illustrata*, p. 294

Treviso (p. 374); Aquileia or Forum Julii (p. 384); Istria (p. 386); Samnium or the Abbruzzi (p. 389); Old Campania or Terra di Lavoro (p. 406); Lucania; Apulia (p. 421); Salentini or Terra d'Otranto; Calabria; Brutii.[14] These divisions Biondo derived ultimately from Pliny;[15] they bore little relation to the political facts of his day, save that Venice – by the mid-fifteenth century a major territorial power in Italy – was recognized as a separate region, and the existence of the *Regno*, conquered by his patron Alfonso v, was accepted by Biondo, in grouping at the end the provinces south of Rome. In fact, not only did Biondo omit the islands, he also omitted the last four regions, having been disappointed of help from Neapolitan scholars,[16] so that his survey is very defective.

Biondo begins each description of a region by listing its boundaries, and then proceeds to deal *seriatim* with towns, castles, rivers. In all this he follows wherever possible the ancient authorities, and never forgets that his aim is to relate ancient names with modern. But he regularly intersperses brief indications of scenery and notes the occasions when small places have momentarily had historical importance. When he discusses larger towns a succinct account is given of origins, of subsequent history, of the current situation, including the names of celebrated writers, and of families who have produced popes. All in all the work is an impressive attempt to come to terms with the history, geography, and monuments of divided Italy.

Yet the book is very unbalanced. Apart from the defective treatment of the south of the peninsula and the omission of the islands, the amount of space allocated to the regions of central and northern Italy is hardly what one would expect. The account of the Romagna is the most glaring example of this. It is as long as the sections on Tuscany or Rome and twice as long as the section on the Veneto. But then the Romagna was Biondo's native land. It was the home of the revival of letters and the birth-place of the Italian general Alberigo da Barbiano, whose indigenous militarism seemed to Biondo to point to a happier political future.[17]

The *Italia illustrata* was the first of the chorographical works of the

---

14 The places are listed as on p. 293 of *Italia illustrata*, the page references are to the beginnings of the completed sections.

15 *Historia Naturalis*, iii,v,45 – iii,xx. Pliny's description is based on the eleven regions of Augustus. For these, and later modification, see R. Thomsen, *The Italic Regions* (Copenhagen 1947).

16 Nogara, *Scritti inediti*, cxxiv

17 *Italia illustrata*, p. 350. Cf. D. Hay, 'Flavio Biondo and the Middle Ages,' above, chapter 3, pp. 35-66.

Renaissance, and it deservedly attracted attention.[18] It circulated widely in manuscript form. It was printed at Rome in 1474 and (with other works) by Froben at Basle in 1531. In 1548 Lucio Fauno (who had earlier translated Pius II's abbreviation of the *Decades*) issued an Italian version of the *Roma triumphans* and of the *Italia illustrata* at Venice. This vernacular recension might well have been much to the taste of the public but, in the event, it was to be overtaken by another similar but more elaborate survey, the *Descrittione* of Leandro Alberti.

Leandro Alberti is much less well known than Dante or Biondo. He was born in 1479 and died probably in 1552. He came from Bologna and, though as a Dominican friar and provincial he travelled extensively in Italy, he spent much of his time in his native town. He wrote the history of the town and made a *tavola* of its leading families and he wrote of the great men of the Dominican order.[19] His chief claim to fame, however, was his *Descrittione di tutta Italia,* first printed at Bologna in 1550.[20]

The handsomely printed volume was five times longer than Biondo's but had the same general aim; in the author's words it was 'a work of a geographer, a topographer, and an historian all together.'[21] He began by cataloguing all other descriptions of the peninsula and explained that for moderns it resembled a human leg, beginning with the thickness of the thigh and descending down to the extremity of the foot. 'In fact,' he wrote, 'this seems to me a very helpful concept,' and he or his printer put in the margin at this point. 'Bella simiglianza.'[22] Then he explained that he planned to describe the boundaries of each region, to give the ancient and modern names not only of the regions but of towns, castles, mountains, rivers, lakes, and springs, narrating the marvels of nature, celebrating the famous deeds of those associated with these places; 'in a word I promise to record (as far as I may) the notable and commemorable things of this

18 R. Weiss, 'Lineamenti per una storia degli studi antiquari in Italia,' *Rinascimento,* IX (1960 for 1958), 141-201.

   Since my essay was written the late Roberto Weiss' *The Renaissance Discovery of Classical Antiquity* has appeared (Oxford 1969).

19 A brief life and bibliography by A.L. Redigonda is found in *Dizionario biografico degli italiani,* I (1950) (DBI). A study of Alberti and his *Descrittione* has been undertaken as a doctoral dissertation at Edinburgh by Miss Rosemary Austin, to whom I am obliged for checking the above account. I am also grateful to Dr Esmond de Beer for allowing me to consult his collection of editions of the *Descrittione.*

20 There are two versions of the first pages of the *editio princeps,* one with and one without the engraved portrait of Alberti.

21 Quoted Redigonda, DBI

22 *Descrittione,* p. iii^v

our Italy.'[23] And then (like Biondo) he urged the difficulties.

Biondo was his immediate model. The eighteen regions of the *Italia illustrata* were broadly followed, though Alberti sometimes defined their boundaries differently and, in all, identified nineteen regions. For the rest his book is more elaborate partly because he could not resist catalogues of ancient authorities. Where Biondo was content with one name, Alberti puts in half a dozen. It was, of course, the case that by the mid-sixteenth century a good many towns and localities had been written about by humanist scholars and topography, particularly in relation to ancient survivals, was establishing itself as a genre. Biondo had pioneered such studies and Alberti was able to make use of a wide range of secondary material which had not existed a century earlier.[24] The larger scale of the work also encouraged more detailed descriptions. These are sometimes extensive and evocative: for example, Lodi, which was discussed in a few lines by Biondo, occupies three pages or so of Alberti and we are told not only of its history but of the cheeses in the market and the irrigation of the countryside.[25] In general a great deal of geographical detail is provided. The *Descrittione* is also easier to follow because, unlike Biondo, Alberti moves systematically down one side of the peninsula and up the other.

There is, however, the same lack of proportion that we have noticed in Biondo though not to so marked an extent. This time the south is fairly discussed but Alberti, like his predecessor, came from Romagna and that province is given elaborate attention; it occupies, in fact, more space than the Campagna. Although under Rome are listed all the emperors and all the popes as well as the main monuments and a potted history, under Bologna there are catalogues of saints, prelates, professors, artists, and so on, in addition to a description of events and buildings.[26] The islands do not figure in the first edition though Alberti explained that he had written about them and if his work was well received, he would add them subsequently.[27] And not all of the recent authorities to which Alberti turned were reliable. He was a victim of the forgeries of his fellow Dominican Annius (Nanni) of Viterbo who died in 1502 and his pages contain many references to the (spurious) writings of Berosus the Chaldaean.

The elaboration and the completeness of the *Descrittione* nevertheless command respect and this was immediately recognized. In 1551 a second

23 *Descrittione*, pp. vi^v-vii
24 R. Weiss, '*Lineamenti*'
25 *Italia illustrata*, p. 362; *Descrittione*, pp. 370^v-3
26 *Descrittione*, pp. 96^v-141, 263-316^v
27 *Ibid.*, p. 469^v. Venice is listed as an island (p. vii^v) but is in fact dealt with in the first edition, pp. 450^v-67^v, as are the 'Isole intorno Vinegia,' pp. 467^v-9

edition appeared at Venice[28] and down to 1631 there were a further nine Venetian editions. The promised additional section on the islands appeared in 1561 and in the edition of 1568 each island was accompanied by a map. Two editions of a Latin translation were issued at Cologne in 1566 and 1567, curious tribute to the European appeal of a book which was being used as the *vade mecum* of the northern visitor to Italy. Montaigne apparently had it with him on his celebrated journey,[29] but so had many other travellers down to the eighteenth century, as one can see from the inscriptions in the surviving copies.[30] Alberti's work is, in fact, a step towards the later guide book, destined to be made otiose only as and when that new type of travel literature made its appearance with the *Itinerarium Italiae* of François Schott (1600), another work which in various forms was to have a long life.[31] But this, as they say, is another story.

What small sustenance can one derive from these sketchy indications? Obviously the map of Italy has been turned the right way up, at least for those of us accustomed to having the north at the top. Dante's cartography was necessarily schematic and literary. Biondo and Alberti were looking at the country much as we look at it: the *portolano* had done its work and by Alberti's day Italy was rapidly moving into the first great age of systematic cartography. There can be no doubt that Alberti used maps and that the cartographers of his day and later used his book in making theirs.[32] The geographical unity of Italy is pronounced and through the centuries this is reflected in descriptive works.

28 This includes in the preliminaries the portrait of Alberti which is found in some issues of the first edition but which was omitted in later reprints. In some of the latter a certain amount of additional material is provided in the text.

29 E.S. de Beer, 'The Development of the Guide-book until the early Nineteenth Century,' *Journal of the British Architectural Association*, 3rd ser., xv (1952), 36n. Dr de Beer has kindly indicated to me a number of parallel passages which are conclusive. Alberti is not referred to by C. Dédéyan, *Essai sur le Journal de Voyage de Montaigne* (Paris, n.d.), whose discussion of 'les sources livresques,' pp. 155-9, is, however, perfunctory.

30 In 1778 W. Minto had a copy of the Venice edition of 1553 with him in Rome. A few years later he urged his executors to give it to the university library at Edinburgh when he died, writing in it: 'This valuable work is very scarce. It is the best Classical Description of Italy. Addison has taken a great many things from it.'

31 See E.S. de Beer, 'François Schott's *Itinerario d'Italia*,' *Library*, 4th ser., XXIII (1942), 57-83

32 R. Almagià, *L'Italia di G.A. Magnini e la cartografia dell' Italia nei secoli* XVI *e* XVII (Naples 1922)

Yet there are some curious discrepancies. All our witnesses testify to the Alps being the northern boundary: they had no geographical or historical alternative. Yet, in practice, they neglect the northern fringe of Italy. Dante said that Trent and Turin were on the frontier but, more surprisingly, also says this of Alessandria.[33] Biondo's discussion of the northern fringe of Lombardy is very scant and, by the time of Alberti, Piedmont, as he noted, was ruled by the king of France, Henry II, to whom (with his consort Catherine de' Medici) the *Descrittione* was dedicated.[34] Even odder is the neglect of the islands. Dante greatly admired the dialect of the Sicilian nobles of an earlier day, and admitted that Sicily and Sardinia were part of Italy; but in his survey he was contemptuous of Sardinian speech and did not mention Corsica.[35] In the *Italia illustrata* Biondo has no place at all for the islands, and no explanation for their absence. The work is admittedly defective in its discussion of the southern portions of the peninsula; it is hard to see how the author could have avoided Sicily if he had dealt at all adequately with the provinces comprised in the *Regno,* though in his request for information in December 1450 he does not mention the island from which Alfonso v had conquered the mainland.[36] There are fleeting references to Corsica and Sardinia in connection with Genoese activity overseas, almost as though they were simple colonies.[37] Alberti's approach to this matter is thus a marked change, for he firmly states in his introduction[38] that Corsica and Sardinia are part of Italy and from the start he had included the islands in his survey, although (as we have observed) these sections did not appear in the earlier editions.

What of the images which the three authors invoke to convey a picture of the peninsula? For Dante (and Lucan) the Appenines are, in a curious way, a unifying element in divided Italy. The rain rattles on the tiles and runs off east and west, but one roof shelters the chattering and quarrelling peoples. Biondo likens the structure of the land to a fish with a long spine and Alberti admires this: 'Veramente pare questo Monte un dorso ò sia schiena d'Italia.' [39] But his own preference, as we have seen, is for Italy

33 DVE, I,xv,8 (Marigo, p. 132) ; for the limits of the area of 'sì' in Dante, see Vinay's article, note 3 above
34 *Descrittione*, sig.* ij and p. 408
35 DVE, I,xi,7; I,xxii,2,4 (Marigo, pp. 94, 96-8)
36 Nogara, *Scritti inediti*, p. 163: '... ea Italiae pars, quam regnum Siciliae appellamus, in aliquot divisa regiones, Campaniam scilicet veterem, Samnium ... Aprutium, Apuliam, Lucaniam, Calabros, Bruttios et Salentinos.'
37 *Italia illustrata*, p. 298, and Nogara, *Scritti inediti*, p. 229
38 *Descrittione*, p. vi^v
39 *Descrittione*, p. iii; earlier classical 'figures' are listed

as a leg; he elaborates the anatomical correspondence at wearisome length.[40] To some degree these inventions reflect the increasing precision of the maps which were available. It was only when representations of the peninsula became fairly accurate that the resemblance to a leg was evident. Alberti's 'bella simiglianza' also suggests the personified maps of Europe which were shortly to be made, such as that in Sebastian Münster's *Cosmographia* (1588).[41]

In more general terms the three texts adduced in these pages underline the peculiar provincialism of Italy. And by 'provincialism' I do not mean the 'Italic' provinces or regions into which the country was divided;[42] I mean those urban units to which real attachment was felt. Dante's analysis is town-based, though sometimes he was thinking also of the *contado*.[43] Biondo, like Alberti, measures the prosperity of the land by the number of its towns. In ancient times, Biondo pointed out, there were 700; Alberti increases this number to 1,166. In Biondo's day there were only 264 and Alberti could count only 300. The view which emerges is one of small urban units, town-based governments, overlaid from time to time (especially in Alberti's discussion) by larger but somehow irrelevant controls.

This impression is encouraged by the arbitrary names of provinces which Biondo adopted and which were carried on and elaborated by Alberti. True, these ancient names were to the taste of classically educated readers, and they had, like the bishoprics of Italy which had boundaries which often still fitted neatly into the old provinces,[44] a kind of permanence amid the perpetual fluctuations of the Italian political scene. Originally, after all, they had to some extent reflected permanent geographical features, not least the Appenines. Yet certain broad political entities were firmly established by the fourteenth century, not least the states of the Church and the kingdom of Sicily. By Biondo's day a large hereditary duchy of Milan might reasonably have figured as a permanent part of his world, though he was writing just after the attempt to establish the Ambrosian republic had failed. And Venice was likewise mistress of the north-eastern provinces. It is not that Biondo or Alberti entirely ignore these features. Biondo (for instance) mentions that the Genoese have really dominated

40 *Descrittione*, pp. iii^v-iv
41 Reproduced in my *Europe: the Emergence of an Idea* (rev. ed., Edinburgh 1968), frontispiece. But in this Italy appears as an arm, not a leg.
42 In fact, *provincia* is normally used by these writers to mean Italy itself, *regio* or *regione* its larger parts.
43 Cf. Marigo, p. 132n
44 Thomsen, *The Italic Regions*, p. 316; cf. the areas of the *Rationes decimarum* (thirteenth and fourteenth centuries) used in papal taxation in Italy; cf. Revelli, *L'Italia*, p.73.

most of Liguria[45] and Alberti writes of the 'great empire and lordship which the gentlemen of Venice have had and still have both by sea and on *terra ferma.*'[46] But they did not see the country organized in such units; they avoided the basic issues of their day. No one concerned with the urgent pressures of politics could have afforded to do this. It is salutary to compare with Biondo his contemporary Pius II who was under no illusions about the state of Italy. This might be illustrated from many of his writings, and not least from the *Commentarii,* but it is displayed most succinctly in his section on the *novitates Italiae* in *De Europa,*[47] written when he was Cardinal Aeneas Sylvius Piccolomini. His chapters are devoted to Genoa, 'mistress and queen of the Ligurians,' Milan, Venice, Mantua, Ferrara, Bologna, Florence, Siena, Rome, Umbria, and the kingdom of Naples – this the longest section in the book.[48] Here again we are presented with towns: but it is those towns which were of general significance in mid-fifteenth century Italian politics. For the foreigners, looking at Italy from outside, the bigger units naturally obtruded; this is evident enough in diplomatic sources, but may be even more tellingly seen in the *History of Italy* compiled by the relatively unenlightened Welsh visitor, William Thomas.[49] Thomas certainly gives the old names of the provinces (he had beside him the *Italia illustrata* of Biondo), but he places them under their present rulers.[50] After reading Alberti it is refreshing to begin Thomas' book with: 'The greatest prince of dominion there at this present time is Charles the Fifth, Emperor of Almain, who for his part hath the realm of Naples and the duchy of Milan.'[51]

Dante's linguistic treatise was designed to promote Italian unity. It is clear also from his other writings, and especially from the *Monarchia,* that this was his aim. However, he accepted political diversities and had no desire that the emperor should obliterate the liberties of Italy. Biondo's *Italia illustrata* is a political morass, perhaps a reflection of the atmosphere of the curia in his day. For Alberti, division has come to stay – or so one feels. His artificial provinces dominate even the index to his work. Each letter of the alphabet is subdivided into nineteen sections, corre-

45 *Italia illustrata*, p. 298
46 *Descrittione*, p. 452ᵛ
47 *Opera Omnia* (Basle 1551), pp. 445-71
48 As it was to prove to be one of the biggest problems of his pontificate.
   There are a few briefer chapters in the book, which is composed of collections intended to be used in a later expanded form.
49 William Thomas, *The History of Italy* (1549), ed. George B. Parkes, (Ithaca, 1963)
50 *Ibid.*, pp. 16-19
51 *Ibid.*, p. 16

sponding to each of the *regioni* of the *Descrittione* – a nightmare indeed for the user who did not know which of the ancient territories contained the place about which he sought information. Despite the general confusion Biondo is optimistic; a new day has dawned. This is far from being the sentiment to be distilled from Alberti. In the detailed descriptions of a good many places in the *Descrittione* cheerfulness and pride are evident, but in the introductory section on Italy as a whole he is gloomy enough. 'Evil, envy and unrestrained appetite for power are dominant in Italy and have led her to such misery that from being a lady and a queen she has become worse than a slave girl. One cannot think of this without great grief.'[52] Yet a curious absence of resentment is found in Alberti: he does not revile the French and Spanish barbarians. Biondo had been bitterly critical of the foreign mercenaries of trecento Italy.[53] Alberti accepts a situation which, at the price of foreign occupation, was to give the urban units of the peninsula a peace such as they had not known for three centuries.

Finally one must recognize a steady decline in the originality of the scholarship of the books we have glanced at. Perhaps it is unfair to compare Dante's *De vulgari eloquentia* with the others, for it was a work of rare genius which had few competitors and was, in any case, intended to explore problems to which the geography and history of Italy were in a sense peripheral. Yet his firm and angular Latin, precise and economical, compares favourably with the smooth Latin prose of Biondo, himself no stylist. In turn Biondo's style strikes one as clear and well-structured compared with the flaccid Italian of Alberti, whose sentences limp along with a mixture of Latinizing and vernacular phrases; reading him is a somewhat laborious business. With Alberti one is conscious too that the outpouring of the classical scholarship of the Renaissance can have a stultifying effect. He is besotted with his authorities, and his exposition becomes muscle-bound through over-exercise in name-dropping.

Yet Alberti in Italian was to reach a public infinitely wider than Biondo in Latin. This public was at first largely composed of his own countrymen but, as we have seen, soon the regular visitors to Italy from beyond the Alps were to find him a useful companion. The *Descrittione* overtook the *Italia illustrata*, even in Fauno's Italian version. The *Descrittione* itself, by the end of the sixteenth century, was gradually to be replaced by guide books on the one hand and by more scholarly works on individual towns on the other, a process with which successive publish-

52 *Descrittione*, p. vi
53 *Italia illustrata*, p. 349

ers of the book strove to cope by revision.[54] Works of this kind, unlike the pilgrim literature of an earlier day, were in constant need of *aggiornamento*, were constantly in danger of becoming obsolete.

In their attempts to convey a total picture of Italy, Biondo and Alberti were thus bound to become outmoded. But one may suspect that in their quiet fashion they (and the men who in different ways were to succeed them – men like Ludovico Guicciardini, Ughelli, Muratori) were to do more by patient description and collection of materials than were the wilder enthusiasts from Dante down to Machiavelli. Biondo and Alberti were also to transmit to the rest of Europe the ambition to describe countries exactly, and to relate the ancient places to the modern names. Both the *Italia illustrata* and the *Descrittione di tutta Italia* have been undeservedly neglected. They expressed an important Italian mood and helped to construct a permanent awareness, at levels deeper than politics and war, of the underlying unity of Italy. They conveyed such an appreciation of Italy among foreign visitors. And they precipated similar national self-consciousness elsewhere.

54 This is an aspect of the later editions of the *Descrittione* which merits study, though revision does not seem to have been very thorough-going. In the 1558 Venice edition of Fauno's translation of Biondo's work there are 'Annotationi,' sig. HH6-II 3ᵛ.

19

RENAISSANCE EDUCATION AND ITS INFLUENCE
ON THE "GOVERNORS"

European nations governed the colonial worlds they had conquered in the eighteenth and nineteenth centuries by men who had been educated almost exclusively in the humanities. I had better begin by asserting that it was the educational background initiated in fifteenth-century Italy which was the main contribution of the Renaissance to government. One has, of course, a fleeting temptation to drag in the few humanists (mainly in Florence and later in Venice) who speculated on political theory. But I am, in the first place, not sure that they were in any sense humanists. Certainly Sir John Fortescue in England was not; nor, despite the dedicatory letter to his *Mémoires,* was Philippe Commynes. And, despite his Florentine ambience and his *Discorsi,* nor am I convinced that the author of *Il Principe* was in any meaningful sense a product of the humanities. In short I am not intending to argue that the *humanitas* which inspired the reflections of Salutati and Bruni, and others of lesser note, when they looked at programmes for human public activity was the most important element in the contribution of the Renaissance to political practice. And it is practice, government, which I wish to put at the forefront of the following brief essay.

My assumption is based on one certainty. By the middle of the fifteenth century Italians of prominence had been exposed to the experience of a humanist educational discipline; and that this was true of the rest of Western Europe by the middle or at any rate by the end of the sixteenth century.

I have said « one certainty », yet how uncertain is this certainty, as are so many others. I am often astonished, in the case in point, at the gaps in our knowledge of the role and the character of education in Renaissance Italy. There are several aspects of this about which we are unfortunately ignorant. In the first place we know little about educational practice in the period from (say) 1400 to 1650. Only in one or two areas are we relatively well-informed.

The first is educational theory as applied by certain celebrated teachers. It is this which has attracted the attention of scholars. The two most famous are, of course, Vittorino da Feltre and Guarino da Verona, studied for the most part through treatises on education by Vergerio, Leonardo Bruni, Aeneas Sylvius and others, available in English notably in those remarkable studies by W. A. Woodward which came out in 1905 and 1906 and which have weathered so well [1]. To these may be added a new and indeed very recent work, also in

---

[1] *Vittorino da Feltre and other Humanist Educators* and *Studies in Education during*

English, by R. G. G. Mercer on Barzizza [2]. Although Dr. Mercer claims to treat Barzizza in the same way as Sabbadini and Woodward treated earlier educators he stresses two points which we shall have to bear in mind : the blurred distinction between school and university teaching as well as their connection with private tutoring; and the close connection between traditional, medieval grammar and rhetoric, and the fresh emphasis put upon it by humanists rather than the total innovation that humanists are supposed to have effected in the teaching. To repeat Paul Oskar Kristeller, « ...the eloquence of the humanists was the continuation of the medieval *ars arengandi* just as their epistolography continued the tradition of the *ars dictaminis* » [3].

Our knowledge of educational practice as opposed to pedagogic doctrine, so to speak, is sketchy, with one notable exception. To the best of my belief we have no general discussion of « secondary » or grammar *school* education in France and Spain or most of the other countries of Europe before the Reformation hardened. At that point we have elaborate studies of protestant education in Germany (associated with Philip Melanchthon) and of Roman Catholic schools (the concentration here being upon Jesuit establishments). It is true that to the canonical writings discussed by Woodward and others [4] we have the handful of other treatises coming from outside Italy in the early sixteenth century. Of these the most important are by Erasmus, Budé and Juan Luis Vives.

Erasmus's essays *De ratione studii* (1511) and *De Pueris* (1529) are readily accessible, not least in the translation in Woodward's own book on Erasmus (1904); we may look forward to their appearing in the astonishing Toronto series, as they have in the new Latin opus at Amsterdam [4a]. Of these authors we may note that two themes were held in common : the desirability of a good tutor, which failing a good school; and the importance of educating the prince [5]. This in fact is a variant of the first theme, for only princes could afford the sort of high level teacher who alone sufficed. The scholar-ruler was, of course, not a Renaissance discovery; and in the first book of More's *Utopia* we find a scathing commentary on the real power-grasping, cynical and ruthless king, whom no humanist-trained man should serve — though, as we all know, Thomas More did so within a few months of writing his diatribe.

In practical terms, of course, command of Latin was first of all to be inculcated in the home and only later in the public or town school. The lengths

---

the Age of the Renaissance, and in Italian in E. Garin, *L'educazione umanistica in Italia,* Bari, 1949 and a number of reprints.

[2] *The Teaching of Gaspardino Barzizza with special reference to his place in Paduan Humanism,* London, Modern Humanities Research Association, 1979.

[3] P. O. KRISTELLER, *Studies in Renaissance Thought and Letters,* Rome, 1956, p. 566. Kristeller has made the same point in other, later essays.

[4] Notably E. GARIN, *L'educazione in Europa,* Bari, 1957 and his anthology referred to above, n. 1. There are later theoretical works by one or two Italians, notably Sadoleto's *De liberis recte instituendis* (1531).

[4a] *De pueris instituendis* and *De ratione Institutis principis Christiani,* ed. O. Harding, *ibidem,* IV. 1, 1974.

[5] ERASMUS, *Institutio principis Christiani* (1516), G. BUDÉ, *L'institution du prince* (also 1516) are good examples.

were remarkable to which a few families went to surround the child from his earliest days with the Latin, if not of the classical writers, then at least with those multiplying conversational works which were produced for the purpose, such as Mathurin Cordier's *Colloquies* (1564)[6]. Latin had been spoken in the household of the child Thomas More, of the Estiennes, and, most celebrated of all, in that of the young Michel Montaigne, a pupil perhaps and certainly a contemporary of the Scottish « poet » George Buchanan at the Collège de Guyenne[7]. For his essay on education Montaigne chose the title, redolent of the Latin works already alluded to, *De l'institution des enfans*. As many have pointed out, it is a paradox that Montaigne, who had this profound education in Latin, in the event wrote his wonderful introspective essays in French.

By the later half of the sixteenth century our knowledge of continental schools has improved. But for earlier periods the exception, to which I have referred earlier, to our knowledge of secondary educational practice as opposed to theory is England. For long English historical educational records have yielded a rich harvest. One has only to think of the works of A. F. Leach, Mrs. Joan Simon, the twin studies of Shakespeare's *Petty School* (Urbana, 1943) and « Grammar School » entitled *Shakespeare's small Latine and less Greek* (Urbana, 1944) by T. W. Baldwin, and most recently the remarkable studies of Nicholas Orme, *English Schools in the Middle Ages* (London, 1973) which show the extraordinary number of *endowed* (i. e. permanent) grammar schools in England and long before the sixteenth century, when they multiplied exceedingly. Some of them have been studied in depth, as with John Colet's St. Paul's, and it is instructive to witness how this foundation, or refoundation, of 1510 soon left the study of Christian works for the entertaining and better written « classics » of pagan antiquity. Exactly the same trend is to be observed at earlier foundations such as Winchester and Eton. Far from producing free or reasonably priced education which would produce clergy or devout laymen, such schools and dozens less distinguished were populated by gentlemen, or by the burgesses who wanted to be gentlemen.

We have no reason to suppose the situation as different in continental countries, or that, so far as educational practice was concerned, the Reformations, Protestant and Catholic, made little if any difference. Education was provided for those who were, or wanted to be, « governors », to adopt the title of Sir Thomas Elyot's influential work on education[8].

In turning to the governors and their interest in Latin education, I believe that with the Italian Renaissance we witness the introduction of a « model » educational curriculum which was, let us say by 1600 at the latest, to dominate the middle and upper ranks of government until after 1900. Put in a cruder way,

---

[6] Erasmus's more celebrated *Colloquies* started off with the same intention, a point somewhat lost in the recent translation by Craig R. Thompson, Chicago and London, 1965.

[7] For More see R. W. CHAMBERS, *Thomas More,* 1935; for Estienne, E. ARMSTONG, *Robert Estienne, Royal Printer,* 1954, pp. 15-16; for Montaigne, essai xxxvi of Book I, ed. M. Rat, i. 187-8. Buchanan, like Cordier, ended up as a Calvinist. A major study of Buchanan by I. D. McFarlane is in the press.

[8] *The Governors* (1531) has been frequently reprinted. For its author see Stamford E. LEHMBERG, *Sir Thomas Elyot, Tudor Humanist* Austin, 1960; there were eight sixteenth-century editions, Lehmberg p. 197; se also his general discussion in chapters 3-5.

if one wanted to get on in the world, or even cope with the higher reaches of power, one had to have a classical education. The princely pupils of Guarino and Vittorino were not restricted to the Este and the Montefeltro and the other lords of the peninsula. From the later fifteenth century onwards the princes who, however remotely, might become kings or queens of England were given the very best Latin tutors available, culminating in Robert Ascham's responsibility for Queen Elizabeth and George Buchanan's (cantankerous) supervision of James VI of Scotland who was to become James I of England in 1603 [9].

The *locus classicus* always advanced to justify the submission of the future civil servant or administrator to the whip of the schoolmaster (for neo-Latin was hard) is, of course, the passage in Richard Pace's *De Fructu* (1517) where the scholarly ambassador of a prince in his travels has an uncouth nobleman as a dinner companion. The ambassador sharply shows that, confronted with the elegant Latin allocution of a visiting diplomat, the prince for a suitable reply has no use for a hick who can only serve him in the vernacular and whose talent is restricted to blowing his hunting horn [10].

To a large extent the princes of Europe were keeping up with their neighbours. If Leo X's secretary wrote a letter to Henry VIII Henry needed someone trained in the new style, and equipped with the new italic handwriting, to reply. And so « Latin secretaries » abound in the Europe of Henry VIII and Francis I. If you wished to be a governor, a magistrate or royal counsellor or secretary, the new manner was essential. Of course with this came in other things; the Rhenish *sodalitas,* the Vienna of Conrad Celtis, the France of Gaguin and Du Bellay and Ronsard, like the England of More, Ascham, Wyatt and others, did not only import Latin. They imported Italian values in literature at large and, in due course, Italian patterns of art and architecture. All of these « importations » would have meant little if the harbour had not been ready to receive them, if the importers had not already been tuned to the overtones of a new cultural world.

But our concern in this essay is with *government* values, or Renaissance values, and general practice is less easy to establish, however one may instinctively feel it to be true. The princes of Europe did not need the optimism of *Il Principe* or the pessimism of Guicciardini's numerous writings to learn how to manage men and societies. As I have said before, Edward I of England and Philip IV of France, around the year 1300, were much tougher characters, much better able to get their way, than Francis I or Henri II, than Henry VIII or Queen Elizabeth. But undoubtedly a massive change occurred. By the late XV century in Italy, by the mid-XVI century in Northern Europe we have moved into a world of *cortesia*. However beastly you were, if you were ambitious you remained a well-educated gentleman. I am not sure that these developments are not best expressed musically, in the stately *pavanes* performed by courtiers who would without much compunction slit a throat, let alone ruin a reputation. And if my phrase « a world of *cortesia* » is not quite right it does at least suggest the

9 See above, chapter 9, pp. 169-231.

10 *De Fructu,* trans. and ed. Frank Manley and Richard W. Sylvester, New York, 1967.

undoubted truth that, in all countries big and little, the nobles and gentry were flocking to court.

Of course these men had their share, perhaps more than their share, of fops and dandies. Their *humanitas* (in the sense of mastery of Latin) was perhaps skin deep, and deserves the criticisms of the sharp observers described by Anglo and Grendler [11]. But they had all been well-tutored, if very rich, or well-schooled if from the middle ranks of the gentry. And out of them were drawn the royal administrators, diplomats, clergy, functionaries of all kinds until the nineteenth century.

What effects did the training of this source of manpower have on government ? Some continuities of course there were. For centuries kings had depended for advice and action on the best-trained men to hand. These were often clergy, and the qualification of an M. A. or better still a doctorate in law, especially civil law, was a sure way to rise in public importance. This went on being the case, just as the « anti-curialists », the mockers at the make-believe of the grandly brought-up, continue through the Middle Ages and Renaissance. But, if men trained in law had the edge over others in the way of promotion, we must remember that they too had by the fifteenth century in Italy and the sixteenth century elsewhere come out of a basic training in the humanities; in turn this was during the sixteenth century to change the course and alter the character of the law, especially on the continent where Roman law was « received » in a way it was not in common law England.

Some silly consequences of the new respect for the ancient world there were, for sure. One thinks of Bandello's account of Machiavelli trying to apply to his so-called citizen army the tactics of antiquity, or of the comical consequences of a Venetian attempt to reconstruct a Roman trireme [12]. Rulers wanted real soldiers and sailors, not classical simulacra, to fight and to command their armies and fleets. The change here was produced in quite another way, by the introduction of gunpowder which steadily raised mathematics from the marginal and speculative place it had occupied in the educational curriculum of the middle ages to an important place in the intellectual world.

Nor, I believe, did an education based practically entirely on the Latin (with some Greek) classics lead, at any rate quickly or directly, to a new type of political thought. I have always regarded the chapter by Burckhardt on « The State as a Work of Art » as puzzling and rather aimless. For a start we are faced with the paradox, ignored by Burckhardt, that the Florentine « Enlightenment », to quote George Holmes's title [13], took place in a republican ambience although it was soon adopted by princes in Italy and elsewhere to whom republicanism was anathema. Then we have the casual way that there are glancing references to the divine right of kings in Aeneas Sylvius Piccolomini, before he was pope, and in the Castilian Cortes of Olmedo — both in the mid-fifteenth century before the total failure (at any rate until our own day) to

[11] S. ANGLO, *The Courtier : the Renaissance and changing ideals*, in *The Courts of Europe,* ed. A. G. Dickens, London, 1977; PAUL F. GRENDLER, *Critics of the Italian World,* Madison, 1969.
[12] Such instances could be multiplied.
[13] *The Florentine Enlightenment, 1400-1450,* London, 1969.

establish the doctrine that popes were subordinate to councils and, by inference, kings to their subjects [14]. In any event doctrines, probably derived from civil law, that the king was an emperor in his own land and that Italian communes were in fact sovereign bodies, go back to the early fourteenth century. *Salus populi suprema lex* can fortify an autocrat as well as a republican oligarchy, and that tag was being bandied about in the thirteenth century.

Nor must we forget the expressed contempt of leading humanists like Erasmus and More for kings and courts, for aggression of all kinds, nor the profoundly Christian basis on which society had been, at any rate ostensibly, based for fifteen hundred years. « Love thy neighbour » does not exactly tally with Justinian and his *codex*. Popes were regularly preached at but the advice thus proffered seems to have had little effect, although it introduced a new type of rhetoric into the sermon [15].

But a new type or rhetoric had arrived and not only in preaching to popes. Kings everywhere had to have representatives trained in the new discipline, as we have seen in the Pace anecdote. They had to have clerks who could both compose stately and correct Latin missives in reply to those they received from other princes and also write in the cursive italic which begins in the papal chancery and soon spreads over most of Europe, as the « good » hand if not the common hand of correspondence between governments.

I dare say one could argue that the use of good Latin made for more secure communications in that it was not liable to misunderstanding, was more precise. But this is hardly a major effect on political activity although it is not to be questioned that steadily rising literacy and the printing press did permit government by ordinance and proclamation on a scale unattainable in an age of hand-writing and shouting at market crosses and in pulpits.

There also seems little doubt that the old nobility (say the generation of the mid-fifteenth century in Northern Europe, earlier in Italy) consciously strove to master the new technique, linguistic and oratorical, in order to serve their commonwealth, usually under a prince. There are not many discussions of the process but we have a valuable essay, to which I shall return, by J. H. Hexter on « The Education of the Aristocracy in the Renaissance »; and, for later medieval England, suggestive passages by the late K. B. McFarlane [16]. Two propositions emerge. The dutiful subject (or citizen) should be as well-educated as possible in order to serve his prince or his community; and that education should be based on Latin. In this we have, *in parvo*, the explanation of the government of the British Empire. May I remind you of persons like Leonard Woolf emerging from Cambridge in 1904 to run about a third of Ceylon with nothing to help him save a couple of policemen and a tin trunk full of the classics of the Enlightenment ? [17].

You will see how circumspectly I approach in conclusion the centre of

---

[14] R. W. and A. J. CARLYLE, *A History of Medieval Political Theory in the West*, VI, Edinburgh and London, 1950, pp. 185-191.

[15] J. W. O'MALLEY, *Praise and Blame in Renaissance Rome*, Durham, N. Carolina, 1979.

[16] Hexter's essay in reprinted in *Reappraisals in History*, 1961, pp. 45-70; For K. B. McFarlane, see refs. in my survey above n. 9.

[17] L. WOOLF, *Growing*, London, 1961.

my subject : « the new humanities and the governors » ? It is in fact a question which has been avoided, even evaded, by historians of ideas, let alone those strange characters among whom I number myself, the « straight historians ». In fact I can think of only one major historian who considered the matter deliberately, so to speak. I refer to that remarkable Italian, Federico Chabod, in whose memory these volumes have been put together. He touched on the relationship of culture and the state, and more particularly the Renaissance and the Renaissance State, several times in his prodigious output, just as he dealt repeatedly with the problem of religion and the Renaissance, a subject which I have avoided in this paper [18].

Chabod characterised Burckhardt's « State as a work of art » as « an elegant formula..., but quite superficial ». He emphasised the existence of a strong link between prince and people based for centuries on mutual self-interest and noting that « patriotism » owed nothing to the Renaissance, in Italy or anywhere else. What he did note was that in the fifteenth and sixteenth centuries we enter a world where the Prince is surrounded by bureaucrats, by officials who buy their offices often, who certainly reckon to profit from them, whose loyalties are thus somewhat different from the vassal and lord relationship which had long ceased to be a reality, though ceremonial vestiges remained.

And where did these bureaucrats come from ? Here we have admirable guidance in J. H. Hexter's essay, to which I have already referred, « The education of the aristocracy in the Renaissance » reprinted in his *Reappraisals in History* [19]. Hexter's survey is valuable because he surveys French and Burgundian material as well as the better known English field where Sir Thomas Elyot's *Boke named the Governor* (1531) was to be followed in due course by Sir Roger Ascham's *Schoolmaster* (1570). By now, the early sixteenth century princes practically everywhere were extremely well taught; I have already instanced Ascham who was tutor to Elizabeth of England, and George Buchanan to James of Scotland. More significant is the way in which the gentry and nobles were everywhere flocking to grammar school and university. Their aim, in Elyot's words, was to acquire « the education... of the child of a gentleman, which is to have authority in a public weal » [20].

In this general pattern Hexter sees the well-born French as exceptional. Their aim was to command armies and head (but not more than picturesquely) pompous embassies. It is perhaps not unimportant that Michel Montaigne, whose ambitious parents had given the infant and the child the full humanist treatment, later retreated into scholarly gentility; but I think we must make

[18] Most directly in *Y a-t-il un état de la Renaissance ?*, in *Actes du colloque sur la Renaissance,* 1956, Paris, 1958; an Italian version in *Alle origini dello Stato moderno,* Rome, 1957. For Chabod and religious change see his *Machiavelli and the Renaissance,* 1958, *passim, Scritti su Machiavelli,* Turin, 1964, *Per la storia religiosa dello Stato di Milano durante il dominio di Carlo V,* Roma, 1962; and the essay by Delio Cantimori in the memorial issue of the « Rivista Storica Italiana », LXXII, 1960, pp. 687-711.
[19] 1961; an earlier version in « Journal of Modern History », 1950. See too my remarks in *Itinerarium Italicum,* ed. Oberman and Brady, above n. 9, for the education of the English gentry and nobility.
[20] Quoted Hexter, p. 65. See too W. GORDON ZEEVELD, *Foundations of Tudor Policy,* Cambridge, Mass., 1948.

allowance for the bleak influence on him of the wars of religion. We should also remember the influence of the clerks in the *parlements* who frequently entered French royal service.

In short I believe we have in the remarkably consistent evidence for an educated gentry and bourgeoisie, committed to serve the commonwealth, the main contribution of the Renaissance to the political activity of Italy and Europe in the fifteenth and sixteenth centuries. One must, nevertheless, be careful. Kings had for long depended on clerks, whose activities often made their cloth a mere outer uniform. It is the *style* that has changed. The councillors of the Medici dukes who went to their Academies [21], the sort of badinage-cum-learning that Ascham describes among the courtiers at Windsor in the early pages of the *Schoolmaster* [22] — these are providing the prince (or the town, or the church even) with a new and secular-based group. So well did they fulfill their functions as administrators and executives that the curriculum of humanist design through which they had passed was to last for centuries.

The cement which set in this mould was at any rate in large measure provided by those Academies to which I have alluded in Florence, but which are, of course, found everywhere and not least in the France whose lack of culture was deplored by Montaigne and Hexter [23]. Now membership of a literary club is a *voluntary* activity. Unlike the school child who has no choice in the matter, the pullulating academies of France and Italy, and indeed the continent as a whole, are supported by men who were not conscripts for the new learning, so to speak, but volunteers. England comes rather badly out of the volunteers for (before the Royal Society of 1660) we can only trace the fugitive activities of what has been called the « Elizabethan Society of antiquaries » [24]. But we have noted a remarkable enforcement in England, indeed in Britain, of the conscript element, the schoolboys. So perhaps the various bits of the Continent were culturally marching together, although by slightly different routes, to that extraordinary seventeenth century when the basis of civilization lay conjointly on the Latin classics and the Bible.

---

[21] Cfr. ERIC COCHRANE, *Florence in the Forgotten Centuries*, Chicago, 1973.
[22] Ed. by L. V. Ryan, Ithaca, 1967, pp. 5-12.
[23] F. YATES, *French Academies of the XVI Century*, London, 1947.
[24] M. McKISSACK, *Medieval History in the Tudor Age*, Oxford, 1971, pp. 155-169.

20

DID POLITICS CHANGE
IN THE LATE MIDDLE AGES AND RENAISSANCE?

May I begin the following brief reflections by glossing my title? 'Politics', I presume is self-evident in its meaning, but 'late Middle Ages and Renaissance' is a clumsy attempt to deal with the chronological problems thrown up by these two unavoidable expressions which are, to add to the confusion, often used to refer to periods contrasting with each other. In the north of Europe the Middle Ages are traditionally regarded as coming to an end about 1500, when they are followed by a period commonly termed Renaissance, except in Italy where the features of the new cultural attitudes manifest themselves in the course of the fourteenth century and dominate the Peninsula in the fifteenth. The Renaissance is reasonably applied to the rest of continental Europe, including the countries generally called Britain, in the sixteenth century. Hence if these terms are used to delimit epochs, what is medieval in the North corresponds with the Renaissance south of the Alps. The matter is further complicated since for many non-Italian scholars and students the northern Renaissance is treated as a sort of curtain-raiser to the Reformation, and in Germany a very short curtain-raiser. Such assumptions directly invite the pursuit in pre-sixteenth- century times of predecessors, of 'morning stars', of the Renaissance, such as may be seen in the writings of Franco Simone on France and Roberto Weiss on England. None of these terminological abstractions posed obtrusive problems so long as historical narrative stuck to politics, narrowly defined. There is nothing about cultural change in the old Longmans History of England in the volumes contributed by Sir Charles Oman and H. A. L. Fisher (both published in 1906), although the latter has a brief chapter, not integrated into the rest of the book. Even more surprising is the virtually total absence of any reference to Italian literary and artistic innovations in the standard and valuable *Le signorie*, Luigi Simeoni's two volume contribution to the 'Storia politica d'Italia' which came out in 1950. True, like the Italian series, the Longmans' volumes were explicitly political. So long as one adheres to *l'histoire événementielle*, it might be thought, the rest of human activity can remain marginal.

Burckhardt inserted political history into his great survey of the Renaissance in Italy as early as 1860. In the last half-century the moral aspects of humanist thought, the concept of 'civic humanism' as elaborated by Hans Baron and Eugenio Garin and others seem to make it inevitable that the divorce between cultural aspects and the hunt for power, which is what politics is about, should be annulled and I believe most historians would feel that all activities of a period should be related to one another. I certainly accept such a point of view, and I am aware that it presents many dangers.[1] It would be tempting to deal with civilization fractionalised into the compartments of familiar states, towns, dynasties, and such work is indeed being pursued. Perhaps one should wait until more of this has been finished before venturing on generalizations. What I have tried to do below is to see some of the ways in which recent scholarship has related in concrete fashion trends and tastes which would have seemed peripheral to political narrative a century ago, or even later; when I suggested at Oxford in 1935 I might read for the 'Special Subject' the Renaissance my tutor V. H. Galbraith vetoed the idea by remarking that only girls did such options: I must do 'Church and State under Edward I' with F. M. Powicke. I leave to the concluding lines of my short essay an indication of my view regarding the connection of culture and politics and will begin by reminding the reader of much stimulating research recently devoted to patronage of the arts or literature, painting, sculpture and architecture, and the integration of all these arts in public display. This 'interdisciplinary' study brings together in a way which seems to me extremely significant both the attitude of men and women in all ranks of society and the few creative authors and artists who were caught up in gestures big and small organised by communities and 'governors' – town councils, princes, kings, popes and cardinals.[2]

There are elements in some manifestations of this interreaction which look backwards in time. Florence's unavailing efforts to secure the relics of Dante (buried in Ravenna) and Petrarch (buried at Arquà in the Euganean hills) recall the ruthless way in which saints' bones were subject to theft in an earlier period and were trafficked in by the Vatican in the early twentieth century (on this last I refer the reader to R. Peyrefitte's entertaining but alas mainly accurate book *Les clefs de Saint*

---

[1] A very different version of this brief essay was originally delivered in French at the twenty-fifth anniversary of the Centre d'Études Supérieures de la Renaissance at the University of Tours in December 1981: 'La Renaissance et la politique, hier et aujourd'hui'. I must here thank Professor J. C. Margolin for many kindnesses on this occasion. In re-writing it for Ralph Davis's *Festschrift* I repay inadequately a debt to an old friend who taught me a lot as my first pupil. The annotation in what follows is highly selective and mainly restricted to recent literature.

[2] There has been much research recently into public display and government. Cf. the bibliographies in A. G. Dickens (ed.) *The Courts of Europe* (London, 1977) to his own chapter and the chapter by Dr Sydney Anglo; a recent work of relevance is Gordon Kipling, *The Triumph of Honour. Burgundian Origins of the Elizabethan Renaissance* (Leiden, 1977). I have to thank Professor André Chastel for drawing my attention to this book.

Pierre, 1955). We may dismiss this latest, perhaps last, úse of relics as totems or bread-winners, and remember that we do not know the splendour which might have attended the reception in Florence of those two laureates Dante and Petrarch. But we do know the panoply which attended the reception in Rome of the head of St Andrew, for we have the description from the pope himself who received it in 1462: Pius II.[3] There is little doubt that this event was orchestrated to appeal not just to clergy but to the people of Rome, as were the regular events associated with the *possesso*, the ritual procession of a new pope from the Vatican to the Lateran. And we may be certain that Paul II's reorganisation of the carnival in Rome in 1465 was designed to please the populace as well as the Curia, the senior members of which delighted in it in later times; indeed Paul's carnival was designed to replace other even less respectable festivities in the City.[4]

Such demonstrations of the arts and literature in the service of a government are of course found all over Europe in the majestic ceremonies of the marriages and deaths of the great and especially of monarchs. And every country witnessed the *joyeuses entrées* into large cities. These spectacular displays were often garnished with literary allusions which must have been mysterious even to many tolerably well educated courtiers let alone the majestic personages, whose advisers contrived to mount them in conjunction with local councils which also often had to foot the bill. And not only for princes but for all the great and well-endowed birth, marriage and death were occasions for parties in which the generality participated. If the Latin inscriptions and Latin orations were beyond them, every one would enjoy the music which from the fifteenth century began to figure largely in such festivities in most European cities.

As for the Latin oration, it became *de rigueur* in the Italy of the fifteenth century, and the propaganda value of the modern good style begins really earlier in Florence with Coluccio Salutati, chancellor of the Republic from 1375. One of the interesting features of this literary development is that Italy was prolific in its public use of notaries. Notaries, indeed, were found everywhere although more numerously in the regions of Europe bordering on the Mediterranean, a result of the Roman inheritance, doubtless. The notaries of Italy and their cultural influence deserve more attention than they have as yet received. The small Tuscan town of Arezzo, which produced so many of them, is a case in point: it would not be going too far to say that the grammarians of Arezzo had more influence on the literary Renaissance in Italy, at any rate down to the mid-fifteenth century than all the splendid legists, doctors of civil law or of canon law or, the cream, *Doctores utriusque iuris*

---

[3] The whole affair is described in book VIII of Pius's *Commentaries*, ed. Gragg and Gabel, *Smith College Studies in History*, xxxv (1951), 523–542.
[4] L. Pastor, *History of the Popes*, trans. Antrobus, iv. 31–2.

from Bologna, Padua and elsewhere.[5] Salutati had fulfilled a number of unimportant administrative posts in small communes before his Latin talent caused him to be made chancellor or secretary of the Signoria at Florence. It is true, one may admit, that no one involved in his appointment realised that his cultural influence was to become so great by his death in 1406 that the republic found it desirable to have further humanist chancellors, including the great Leonardo Bruni, down to the point where the Medici moved to the front of the political stage with Lorenzo after the Pazzi conspiracy.[6] But if the Florentine businessmen, hard-headed, jealous, politicians in all the bad senses as well as the good, did not realise that with Salutati they were inaugurating cultural innovation, nor, we must suppose, did the Pazzi who commissioned Brunelleschi to build a chapel for them at Sa. Croce, nor the Brancaci when they employed Masaccio for their chapel in Sa. Maria del Carmine. These gestures may have been incidental but they were to change the whole direction of architecture and art, just as Bruni and his contemporaries in Italian courts and communes, and the papal Curia also (where Bruni had previously worked) were to make it essential for governments everywhere to employ 'Latin secretaries' (i.e. Latin of the new sort, including the new scripts) in order to deal with Italian and international affairs. Later the royal library needed a librarian. Sometimes we find a historiographer with an official appointment, the equivalent of the poets laureate and propagandists for the governments who employed them.

This was not, we should remember, the innovation solely of the Italian humanists. The intense patriotic rivalries in northern Europe also threw up their share of propagandists. A signal example was the famous *Débat des Héraults d'Armes* in which a French apologist, writing about 1460, castigated English pretensions; the episode is interesting because a century later the whole argument was stood on its head in a pro-English version which was printed in London in 1550.[7] And similar broadsides were delivered at the Council of Constance where the traditional four nations of the medieval university formed the sub-divisions and were thrown into disarray by the arrival of a fifth nation, the Spanish. This well known episode is obviously less surprising in a collection of clergy who were educated both in debate and Latin, *literati* in the good and the bad sense, one might say, rather like the deliberative bodies of a modern university. What is new about the *Débat* and propagandists like Gaguin in France or Polydore Vergil in

[5] I understand that Dr Robert Black will discuss the schools of Arezzo in his forthcoming *Benedetto Accolti and the Florentine Renaissance*; he plans further studies on Aretine learning.

[6] See E. Garin's essay, 'I cancellieri umanisti della repubblica fiorentini', now reprinted in his *Scienze e vita civile nel Rinascimento Italiano* (Bari, 1965) pp. 1–21.

[7] Both the French and English texts in *Le Débat des Héraults d'Armes*, ed. L. Pannier, Societé des Ancien Textes Français (Paris, 1877).

England, the Latin secretaries, the pompous speeches and diplomatic exchanges, is that by the early sixteenth century the way to get on in the world of politics was to have an education in grammar, i.e. Latin. One recalls the famous story of Richard Pace in his *De fructu* where the 'huntin' and shootin'' gentlemen are shown to be useless to a prince, who did not want a visiting ambassador greeted by a hunting horn but by eloquence in the approved style.[8]

It was indeed from about this time and very generally all over western Europe that the grammar schools began to be endowed to which young men were sent by families who could not afford to employ, as the very rich did, a private tutor. So deeply ingrained did this education at *gymnasia, lycées,* academies and grammar schools become that it was to last into the nineteenth century, and become part of the process of growing up rather than the preparation for a public career, although it was the essential hurdle to be cleared by those anxious for state promotion.[9]

There are indeed some curious paradoxes in the process. Castiglione in his *Courtier* described in detail the humanist servants of a prince and their importance in enhancing the reputation of his court. Yet at much the same time that Castiglione was recalling the wit and wisdom of Montefeltro Urbino, Thomas More compiled the *Utopia.* This work is curious in two ways. It criticised everything that Castiglione had admired, and especially in its first book (clearly the second to be written) arrived at the conclusion that no wise man should serve a prince. Yet not only is this written in Latin by the greatest English humanist (who, incidentally, had never visited Italy) but by a man who was shortly to do the opposite of what he had prescribed in the book.[10] Thomas More was to climb steadily to the top of the conciliar structure almost until his execution, when he did give sincere advice to Henry VIII and refused to retract it.

If More remains unique and, to the end of his days, enigmatic, his life does display the conjunction between a new educational programme and a steady increase in the number of laity in all countries of Europe who attained positions of importance in government. This was a

[8] *De Fructu qui ex Doctrina Percipitur*, ed. and trans. F. Manley and R. S. Sylvester (New York, 1967) pp. 23–5. The original and only earlier edition of Pace's work itself was printed by Froben at Basel in 1517.

[9] Curiously enough very little systematic work has been done on these developments, so far as I am aware, in Italy or France; England has been well served, latterly by Nicholas Orme, e.g. in *The English School in the Middle Ages* (London, 1973).

[10] For the composition of Utopia see J. H. Hexter, *More's Utopia: the Biography of an Idea* (London, 1952) and at greater length in his share of the introduction to the edition with Edward Surtz, S. J. of *Utopia* in the Yale 'Complete Works' (New Haven and London, 1968). A splendid catalogue of an exhibition (1977–8) in the National Portrait Gallery, London, '*The King's Good Servant*'. *Sir Thomas More*, ed. by J. B. Trapp and Hubertus Schulte Herbruggen, contains many recent references.

development full of contradictions. On balance the universities took small part in it, either in Italy or the North; in Italy the law (and not the mastery of Latin which notaries acquired at grammar schools and from *artes dictaminis*) and in the great centres of the North such as Paris, Oxford, Cologne, divinity and above all theology were senior and dominant. There were pockets of novelty such as Busleyden's Trilingual college at Louvain[11] where the University itself was the home of rigid orthodoxy and censorship as ruthless as was the Sorbonne's. In France the Crown had later to establish the Collège de France to give the new humanist disciplines a platform; and in Oxford the idiosyncratic foundation of Corpus Christi College – not by a civil servant like Busleyden but by a bishop (Richard Fox, who had, not surprisingly, been a royal administrator too) which was in its way a kind of mini-Trilingual – had to be bolstered up by More and Henry VIII against the attacks of the Oxford conservatives, who were against Greek on principle one might say, and hostile to 'literature' in its new and growing sense, a sense which also appealed to the butcher's son Wolsey, apparently a reader of Machiavelli's *Prince*.

It is tempting to see these European developments as part of the victory of laity over clergy. In some ways they were. In Herbert Butterfield's phrase 'there was a wind blowing on the side of kings' and kings wanted to demonstrate their ability to keep up with the sophisticated Italians; rulers in the north were much richer and more powerful, but they found it desirable to play the international game according to Italian rules. Why was it so desirable? There is a big unanswered question here, but part of the answer may lie in the development of the papal Curia at this time. For although popes were pitifully lacking in muscle, Rome was to remain, until the Reformation finally obliterated its influence in the later sixteenth century, the sounding board of European political activity and, so long as the Roman church remained undivided, Rome was necessary for the senior clergy in all principalities as the tree on which the sweetest plums grew.

If a secular spirit was evidently developing in normal circumstances, it may be harder to discern in the abnormal 'state' of the church, not only in the 'States of the Church' but also in the Christendom of which the pope claimed to be, and, however little it helped the holders of the office, was accepted as being a different and superior ruler. The Curia was, however, changing and helping the wind in the world. This is not easily discernible because the upper rungs of papal administration were composed of men who were, at any rate technically, celibate, and who looked towards ecclesiastical rewards of a rich kind: commendams of wealthy abbeys, archdeaconries and canonries of substance, bishoprics and even cardinalates. It is true that in the midst of this great company

[11] For Jerome de Busleyden (1470–1517) and his Trilingue see Henry de Vocht, *History of the Foundation . . . of the Collegium Trilingue Lovaniense*, vol. i (Louvain, 1951).

the highest officers, the cardinals were often the least influential. The pope was not saddled, or aided, by the sort of council to whom princes turned; for one thing the pope was normally a compromise candidate, disliked and distrusted by the men who had elected him, anxious to appoint others, including some relatives, on whom he felt he could depend. But the consistory, when the pope presided over the cardinals, and which was often attended by other and perhaps more influential curialists, was seldom asked for its advice in any meaningful sense. The pope may have been a puny figure among the rulers of Christendom but in his own narrow territory he was in theory an absolute monarch. He had no need himself to invoke those comfortable civilian doctrines that the will of the prince has the force of law, *salus populi suprema lex, rex imperator in regno suo*. Powerless many popes were, their anathemas ignored, their funds small even compared with those of other Italian rulers, but they clung to the shreds of spiritual sovereignty. Powerless occasionally even in Rome itself[12] they could sometimes strike a bargain with noble families to benefit their own kinsfolk, and play tricks of a cynical kind such as freeing Cesare Borgia from his clerical status as a cardinal so that he might become a prince in central Italy. The strongest, almost the only, lever the cardinals had at their disposal was the threat of another schism – and here again the lay rulers of Europe behaved in similar fashion. In short the clergy in the Curia may have been ordained, and some even well-educated in the older disciplines of theology and canon law, but they were virtually indistinguishable in attitudes, in morals, in style of life, from the courtiers elsewhere in Italy and in Christendom.

Nevertheless celibacy is an important feature of the administrators in many parts of Europe in the medieval period and after. It was not only popes who promoted clerks, but civil governments as well. In practice a king made (as he had for centuries) bishops of whom he pleased; so did dukes of Burgundy or of Brittany (the latter styling himself *dux dei gratia*); and one of the bribes popes offered in their negotiations was the right to nominate for a period to a certain number of benefices, which might be very large. It was bargaining like this that enabled the pope to detach the emperor from the council of Basel. Thus the wealth of the church largely financed the administration of the state and this posed problems, especially in Protestant areas after the Reformation, when crown servants expected to have 'tenure' and, indeed, like their clerical predecessors, the right of handing on their offices to children or other relatives. But this was a problem which had hardly emerged by the mid-sixteenth century. Purchase of office, initiated by the popes at Avignon, was no new thing. In northern Europe it went side by side

---

[12] That the pope could not always get his way, even in Rome itself, see the extraordinary account of the so-called Lateran Canons in Philip McNair, *Peter Martyr in Italy* (Oxford, 1967).

with purchase of titles of honour. But the lesser men climbing the ladder by service were hardly affected (until they made their pile) by such procedures.

Did these developments affect the character of government, of politics? One may feel that, though the changes are important, they hardly affected the structure of power. Senior clergy had looked to their lay masters to protect them if possible from the predatory claims of the *Camera Apostolica*, common services and annates. The clergy hoped, despite frequent deceptions, that the lay power's rapacity would be tempered by the pope. In the end the sixteenth century was to see a division of the cake, an illustrious example being the Concordat of Bologna in 1516. It remained for the clergy almost everywhere to use their cloth in a more discreet way – to avoid tiresome legal process, or even lynching. But the *privilegium fori* was everywhere in decline. It is fascinating to see this dilemma in the heart of the Papal States, where a papally appointed bishop had to face another notable clerk, who was governor in temporalities, over the question of the rights of the clergy and the punishment of their wrongs. The case of Bologna has been the subject of just such a study.[13]

The steady change towards a lay administration paid by the state brought in its train various consequences. The lay purchaser of office felt a proprietory interest in it, felt that he should be able to transmit it to an heir. This proprietorial sentiment was deeply ingrained in medieval habits and it seemed entirely reasonable that a man should do his best for his relatives. Hence the fourteenth and fifteenth centuries saw the mechanism of the *resignationes in favorem* and the *regressio* develop, permitting a prelate to hand on his benefices to a successor chosen by himself; contemporaries regarded this (despite its perilous proximity to simony and its undoubted encouragement of corruption in the administration of diocesan and monastic clergy) as a perfectly understandable practice.[14] Here again the similarity of clergy to laity is evident. Just as a barony descended for generations in the same family, so did many a bishopric.

None of all this was in any way directly attributable to the changing educational patterns so pronounced in Italy by about 1400 and influential everywhere a century later. It meant that money to pay for administration had to come (from the church, where else?) by a different route, even if that involved a dissolution of the monasteries or parallel acts of a draconian kind. The new style of public splendour did however make for heavy charges falling on lay princes and their lay subjects. Here the Italians were unquestionably leading the fashion, with palaces dressed, one might say, overall, like the ducal palace at Urbino or the ceremonial rooms at the Vatican. The tournament and jousting in cities

---

[13] In the admirable study of Paolo Prodi, *Il sovrano pontefice*, (Bologna, 1982).
[14] A. Clergeac, *La Curie et les bénéfices concistoriaux* (Paris, 1911).

to entertain gentlemen participating also served to please the plebs (and let us remember jousting was found in all the bigger Italian towns during the Renaissance); even an artistically unimportant centre like London had by the sixteenth century its band of musicians, although they could not compare with the choirs of foundling children for whom Venetian composers were creating masterpieces in the sixteenth century. By 1500 Rome and Venice had parallels in the grandeurs of Mantua and Ferrara.[15] It was to be long before northern Europe created spaces for urban pomp to be fully displayed just as one did not (outside Italy) deliberately build new cathedrals to replace the old ones. A new St Paul's in London had to await the Great Fire of 1666, and the Sack of Rome in 1527 doubtless encouraged the construction of new *piazze*, and straight thoroughfares, the destruction of the old streets where porticos invited crime: but St Peter's was being rebuilt well before 1527.[16]

But we may wonder if the Italy of the time of Leonardo da Vinci and Michelangelo did not witness the introduction of a new and sharper attitude in government. This, I suppose, is the traditional defence of regarding the changes in the state around 1500 as constituting a watershed. Had not the political speculation of the Middle Ages been expressed in treatises which aimed to set out what princes and governors should do to be good, to obey, and cause to be obeyed, the laws of God? The *de regimine principum* of Aquinas and other similar works were now challenged by a more pragmatic theory, whose most illustrious example was Machiavelli, especially in *The Prince*. Of course there had been earlier attempts to define sovereign power and the power of the executive. Marsiglio of Padua was groping towards this in his difficult *Defensor Pacis*; as we have noted above, Fortescue in England, with his analysis of the problems posed by the over-mighty subject, was edging towards greater political realism; and in France Commynes in several reflective passages in his *Mémoires* ventured beyond narrative into precepts to secure effective government. There is an astringency in Machiavelli which some contemporaries found shocking. Yet the former chancellor of Florence longed to have a post under the re-established Medici and it is clear that *The Prince* is not advocating a general political programme but dealing with a particular situation. Machiavelli was a Florentine republican as we can see in his *Discourse on the First Decade of Livy*, and a Florentine republican meant an advocate of the mixed balance of forces which precariously survived in the city till the re-introduction of the Medici in 1512.[17] The rich

[15] Cf. *Splendours of the Gonzaga*, catalogue ed. by David Chambers and Jane Martineau of the Exhibition at the Victoria and Albert Museum, London, 1981–2.

[16] On the Sack of Rome see now André Chastel's Mellon Lectures for 1977, with that title (Princeton, 1983).

[17] The last stages of the Republic are now analysed by J. N. Stephens, *The Fall of the Florentine Republic* (Oxford, 1983).

bourgeoisie were in control of the tortuous administration. Much the same was the viewpoint of the rich bourgeois Guicciardini, who, like Machiavelli, lost power with the advancing autocracy of the Medici, who in his day really did become princes. The two men were of course very differently composed. Machiavelli was an optimist, and envisaged a society which could be remade along sensible lines if men would only follow good principles of government – a citizen army rather than mercenaries and so on. Guicciardini was a pessimist. He knew that the basis of life, and especially of political action, was that whatever a statesman did was bound to prove mistaken in the end. 'Nevertheless one must do one's best'. A truly patrician view.

Does any of this matter, save to students of ideas? Did men of power wait to exercise it until their theorists could produce moral or any justification? That they did not was precisely the reason for Thomas More's criticisms in Book 1 of *Utopia*, referred to earlier in this paper. Charles V, Henry VIII, Francis I acted first and then, if it was unavoidable, argued later; as the scope of national governments widened, so principles tended to dwindle. The famous debate between Sepulveda and Las Casas in Valladolid in 1550, even if it produced official sympathy for the Dominican case, did not have much effect on the aggressive settlers, remote as they were from Spain. Both in Germany and in America the emperor pursued what were normally pragmatic policies. And so (when he could bring himself to action) did Pope Clement VII. Earlier we may wonder if Edward I of England waited to obliterate an independent Scotland till he had collected from the monastic chronicles the justification of his annexation. And, at about the same time, Pierre Flotte (speaking for his master King Philip IV) told Pope Boniface VIII, 'You have verbal power, we have real power'. And so it was. Kings (and in certain circumstances urban authorities) made and if necessary broke clergy. Even an archbishop could be executed for treason; even a cardinal could end his days in the Castel S. Angelo. Everywhere at the lower level there was *peine forte et dure*, and the threat of employment of popular violence. Everywhere in vernacular tales the clergy are treated with contempt, sometimes all the ruder from being humorous. So it is in the *Fabliaux*, in Boccaccio, in Chaucer, and a little later in Scotland in *Ane Satyre of the Thrie Estaites*. No one dared to write of kings or town councils in such a contemptuous manner. There is no anti-laicism to balance the anti-clericalism. Was there a 'Renaissance State'? Federico Chabod asked himself, and concluded that there was not.[18]

---

[18] Federico Chabod, 'Y-a t'il un état de la Renaissance?' in *Actes du Colloque de la Renaissance 1958* (Paris, 1962); cf. my 'Renaissance education and its influence on the "Gouernours"', in *Per Federico Chabod, 1901–1960*, atti del seminario internazionale, ed. Sergio Bertelli, Annali della Facoltà di Scienze Politiche, Perugia 1980–1 (Perugia, 1982) ; see above, pp. 389-96.

Referring to Burckhardt's celebrated section on 'The State as a work of art', Chabod described it as 'an elegant formula . . . but quite superficial'. Much criticism could be levelled at Burckhardt's treatment of the subject. Its chief significance, in my view, is that it completed the slow progress of the concept of the Renaissance from literature, to art, to politics. But on the main issue, Chabod, who (be it remembered) was a formidable politician as well as a formidable historian, was surely right. The style and manifestation of politics were altered. The bureaucrats, even when still clergy, were by the mid-sixteenth century educated in the new manner. The humanities all over Europe, and in the seventeenth century in North America too, were the way in which one was trained to run the world. 'Floreat domus de Balliolo' is ugly Latin, but its disciples (among whom Ralph Davis and I must be numbered) encouraged public service as a function or justification of education. Humanists, if I may quote myself, are all educators. I do not believe there is a nobler calling.

La Historia

DI ITALIA

DI M· FRANCESCO
GVICCIARDINI

GENTIL' HVOMO
FIORENTINO

Con i Priuilegi di Pio IIII. Sommo Pont. Di Ferdinando I. Imp.
Del Re Cattolico, & di Cosimo Medici II.
Duca di Firenze, & di Siena.

IN FIORENZA,
Appresso Lorenzo Torrentino Impressor Ducale.
M D L X I.

7 Title page of Guicciardini's *La Historia di Italia* (Florence, 1561)

21

FIAT LUX

In principio creavit Deus caelum et terram. These are the first words of the text of the first book to be printed with movable metal type, the great 42-line Bible that came out at Mainz about 1455. In Genesis that beginning was followed by others. Immediately after heaven and earth came light. 'And God said: Let there be light.' On the sixth day God created man in his own image: 'male and female created he them'.

The earliest men and women communicated with each other (it must be supposed) by making noises. Grunts and screams, ejaculations prompted by pain, fear, hunger and desire, the smoother tones of momentary comfort and warmth, these were intelligible in a given situation when eked out by gesture and mime. Groups of men were small and their material equipment was scanty. The family and the tribe responded instinctively to the rhythmical demands of the seasons and met the slow changes in climate and geography with a dogged love of life which made them move their hunting grounds in the face of ice or drought. One can capture still this inarticulate but expressive atmosphere in moments of panic, in grief and in laughter and in the obscure but telling sounds made by babies and lovers.

Yet the passing millennia brought words, and this command of language was probably the most important single instrument which primitive peoples were able to use in the compli-cated game of survival. Particular noises became attached to particular actions and objects. It became possible to describe absent things and to construct future relationships. The tribe could debate its problems and plan concerted action. The powerful could exert their wills in relatively distant places by servants carrying messages; and one way of winning and consoli-dating power was the exercise of oratory, the construction of arguments, the pronouncement of effective verbal threats and promises. The leader of men, though tongue-tied himself, might yet have fluent spokesmen and such men were at hand in the priests. With words came the magic of words, the power to identify gods and to offer them prayer and praise. And with words came poetry. The bard who recited the deeds of the heroes of the tribe and the dynasty passed on his talents and his stories to other bards, as the priests trained other priests to recite the hallowed incantations. Memories were acute and tradition strong, for the lines spoken by bard and priest, like the commands borne by the courier of a king, had to be exactly reproduced. Curiously enough it is more difficult for people living in advanced societies to recapture this phase of speech than the earlier phase of sounds and signs. The glimpses one can get of it suggest languages (there were many of them) of repetitious formulae. For those members of society for whom words had public importance it must have been like the game 'I packed my bag and in it I put'; if one forgot one's sequences one was out of the game, perhaps painfully or utterly out of the game. In a world of speech words could become shackles.

II

The bondage of words was broken by writing them down. This stage seems to have been first reached in Mesopotamia between about 4000 and 3000 B.C. From a large number of conventional pictorial signs marked on clay tablets, symbols for things and numerals, writing arrived at a point where abstractions could be conveyed. It could further use the symbols to represent not only things and the actions or abstractions associated with them, but also phonetic qualities—a step towards the transcription of actual speech which the Sumerians had evidently reached at the time the earliest surviving examples of their cuneiform script were made. A little later writing roughly similar in accomplishment was evolved in the so-called hieroglyphics of Egypt and the 'characters' of Chinese. Sumerian cuneiform and Egyptian hieroglyphics perished in the course of time; Chinese has survived, a living fossil, so to speak, among the great scripts of the world.

Almost as important as the achievement of pictorial abstractions was the invention of a purely phonetic alphabet. This is known to have existed in Syria from at least the sixteenth or fifteenth century B.C. and there is now strong evidence of an alphabetical script being used in Canaan one or two centuries earlier than that. 'Of all the areas of the Near East', writes David Diringer, 'the region of Palestine and Syria provides the most likely source for the invention of the Alphabet.' The antecedents of 'Northern-Semitic' may be obscure. It can however be shown that from Canaanite, through Greek, were to descend the European alphabets, destined to overrun most of the world.

Writing and literature developed in every part of the globe. They were to have the greatest extension in Europe because there writing was practised in an alphabet composed of a very small number of letters. Latin, which had originally only twenty-one characters (derived from Etruscan and Greek) and the alphabets derived from it (such as modern English with its twenty-six), should be compared with the enormous numbers of characters of Chinese; some 5,000 to 6,000 are regularly used. Moreover the materials used for writing in Europe also changed. From carvings or incisions on wood, stone and clay, and marks on bark, leather and cloth, scribes adopted first of all papyrus and then prepared skins marked with ink. Papyrus, fibre from a marsh plant found in the Nile valley and in the East Mediterranean area, was formed into sheets which could be used separately or glued together lengthways to make a continuous writing surface which was rolled up for storage. In the fourth century A.D. these rolls of papyrus came to be replaced by books made from sheets of vellum or parchment, in which the material was folded and sewn, in much the same manner as a modern book. Papyrus books are found, but the material was less robust and did not lend itself to this format. The paged book made of skins was also easier to handle than a roll on which the columns of writing succeeded each other continuously, and the surface of parchment lent itself to more rapid cursive writing.

The availability of the written word conditioned the whole development of civilization. A new dimension was given to the mind of man: he could afford to forget since he could store his information outside himself. The priest could list his temple-dues, assemble the canon of his scriptures and preserve the details of the liturgy. The prince could have his rights listed and transmit his orders with a new precision and authority. In both religion and politics the written word encouraged larger unities. In place of the fugitive contacts of speech the written word remained: *littera scripta manet*. The seeds of an advanced civilization could thus scatter themselves and the dominant position in the Mediterranean area and the southern half of Europe acquired successively by Greek and then by Latin culture was due principally to writing. These seeds could, moreover, lie dormant for centuries and yet spring to life, as did the literature and learning of the Greeks and Romans in the European Middle Ages and Renaissance.

The literature of the written word was not only religious and political. The bard gave way to the poet and in its turn imaginative prose found a place beside older epic and newer lyric. Men could and did play with their pens, and more subtly than they could play with their tongues: the crude pun and spoonerism could be matched by complicated acrostic and ana-gram, meaningless until seen in black and white. The simple arithmetic of addition and subtraction could give rise to the abstractions of pure mathematics. Language and literature acquired norms preserved in the certainties of grammar and orthography. The scriptures of religion could have secular parallels, 'classics' as they were later to be called, to which the grammarians turned as models of style.

These changes occurred in all regions where writing developed. They were probably carried furthest and fastest in Christian Europe. The 'third portion of the inhabited world', peopled by the sons of Japhet, inherited the simplified alphabet of the Graeco-Roman Mediterranean tradition and acquired a religion based on written scriptures, old and new. Christianity was thus pledged to the promotion of reading and writing. Its Bible or book bred other books. Its priests were committed to an educational programme which in the end was to make so many men clerkly that the demand for the written word could not be met by conventional methods. The pressures thus built up in Europe resulted in the invention of printing.

The growth of literacy in the Middle Ages is imperfectly documented. Broadly speaking the education of priests was the main aim of formal instruction until the thirteenth century, and the curriculum was geared to the acquisition of a mastery of Latin, both written and spoken. The grammar school and the university remained throughout the period coloured by this original purpose; but by the later Middle Ages large numbers of laymen were attending both types of institution with no intention of following either a career in the Church or in one of the professions (law and medicine) for which the universities also catered. Secondary schools began to multiply in all European countries in the fourteenth and fifteenth centuries. They were most common in the bigger towns but gradually the gentry also sent their sons to be educated. Laymen in public positions in the tenth or eleventh centuries were usually illiterate. By the fifteenth century a nobleman and his steward could read and write, so could many of the ladies in the landed classes, and so of course could the merchants and shopkeepers in the towns. Doubtless by 1400 the illiterate still formed the large majority of the population; but it is certain that by then the clergy formed a minority of those who could read and write.

This transformation of society was accompanied by a transformation in the character of the book. In the so-called Dark Ages a book was a rarity. Produced in a sheltered corner of culture, a monastery in Ireland or Italy, it was usually connected with the Church and was treated with the reverence accorded to sacred things. With the spread of parishes over Christendom and the rising number of monasteries (in England convents increased from about sixty in the early eleventh century to just over 1,000 at the beginning of the fourteenth century) books ceased to be so precious. They were needed as Bibles and service books, they were needed as grammars to instruct clergy, they were needed for the religious who were transcribing old commentaries and works of devotion and composing new works of their own. Education by the twelfth century was entirely dependent on books. At school and even more at the university 'authors', prescribed and approved, were read and glossed and considerable numbers of texts were required.

By this time the monasteries, which had earlier been the main centres of book-production in western Europe, could not meet the demand and their monks were, in any case, not particularly involved in the education of the secular community or even of the clergy, except their own monks. Hence the market was supplied by professional scriveners, men who made a career as book-producers. In Barbarian Europe author and scribe were often the same person. By the thirteenth century there began to be a difference between them. In and after the thirteenth century one could rely on there being a bookshop in a university town. Furthermore a big step had been taken to increase production of books, and lower the costs of producing them, by the use of paper. Parchment, it is true, had by the end of the Middle Ages become very fine and light and until the mid-fifteenth century there seems to have been enough of it. But by then the use of paper was widespread. Paper had first entered Europe from China by way of Muslim countries in the twelfth century. By the early fourteenth century rag paper was manufactured on a considerable scale both in Spain and in Italy and from Italy its manufacture spread north of the Alps. This does not mean that by about 1400, with an important manufacture of books (many made of paper), in all essentials the situation as we know it today had been reached. There were big differences and to appreciate the influence of printing one must look carefully at the manuscript book in the last two centuries before Gutenberg's invention.

The handwritten book was a separate unit unlike any other. This is true not only of original works, written *ab initio*. It is almost as true of books of which very large numbers of copies were made, works like the Bible itself, or the dozens of approved authors read by students at school or university. The very greatest care was certainly taken to secure authentic texts.

Rules for copyists in the *scriptoria* of monasteries were strict and universities laid down the most stringent regulations for the *stationarii* who supplied texts. Yet the transcribers each wrote a distinct hand, conforming certainly with the accepted style of their time and place but permitting themselves endless variations in the formation of letters and in methods of abbreviating words or shortening them by other conventions, such as suspension of final syllables. Even when a work was copied quire by quire with gatherings of parchment or paper of the same length as the gatherings of the *exemplar* (the *pecia* system), the resulting manuscript was still distinguishable from its exemplar by infinite if subtle or minor variations. If the text of no two books was exactly alike, it can be imagined how much greater differences there were in apparatus—contents, index, glosses. The index in particular tended to be a highly particularized exercise and when found was the work of an owner rather than of a copyist. In such a situation the identification of books was frequently less by the general description afforded by a title, and more often by the precise indications afforded by their opening words (*incipits*) and concluding words (*explicits*) together with the number of the first and last folio. This is how books were usually catalogued in the public libraries which were beginning to be found in universities at the end of the Middle Ages, as in the collections formed earlier by great monasteries and cathedrals.

When books were made by hand errors were thus bound to occur and they naturally had a cumulative effect. In the case of fundamental texts like the Bible repeated efforts at emendment were made and a general correctness was maintained. In service books knowledge of the liturgy secured correct copies. But in a wide range of writing a manuscript book tended to become less authentic the more it was copied. This deterioration was intensified when the main source of supply was no longer the clergy, especially the regular clergy, but lay scriveners. Writing often under great pressure, for a steady and known market, the professional scribe was often careless and incompetent. At the same time the handwriting itself became poorer in quality. Though there were splendid manuscripts produced by proud calligraphers in fifteenth-century Italy, and even some noble volumes made in the north of Europe, the average manuscript book of the later Middle Ages was slovenly, unattractive to look at and difficult to read when compared with similar works of the eleventh and twelfth centuries. Writing and reading were, as has been observed already, much commoner by the later date, and familiarity bred contempt.

The book trade existed. It was, however, essentially dealing in well-known works, and it did not have much if any influence on the composition of new books, which entered the dealer's regular stock only when there was a large and certain demand. An author as such (as in the days of Greece and Rome) thus needed to support himself by means other than his pen; he was a monk, a beneficed clerk, a university professor or the familiar protégé of a prince or great man, occasionally an official in the employment of a city. His writing could redound to the honour and prestige of his patron, and occasionally he might be rewarded by some extraneous Maecenas to whom he dedicated a work; but he was in no sense paid for writing. Above all he had no right in his book, no copyright. If it proved popular and began to figure regularly on the stalls of Paris or Cologne, he had no royalties.

In these circumstances publication was effected in one of two ways. The writer could deliberately send a fair copy of his completed manuscript to a friend or patron, usually with a letter of dedication. Or he might lend his work, perhaps in an unfinished state, to a colleague and find later that copies of it were circulating without his prior agreement. Further, the author often dedicated the same work to different patrons, perhaps revising the text to suit them; in this way arose the four main recensions of Froissart's *Chronicle*. Or he might keep the original manuscript beside him, constantly tinkering with it but allowing portions of it or the whole of it to be transcribed from time to time; this explains the complicated textual history of Thomas à Kempis's *De imitatione Christi*. Here again a vast range of variables distinguishes copies of the same work. Which is the 'true' text of Froissart or the *Imitation of Christ*?

If publication was erratic, suppression of manuscript books could be much more systematic. Nothing offers better evidence of the rapid spread of books than the repeated attempts made to stifle the use of some of them. From the early thirteenth century (and there are cases even before that) works by theologians and philosophers were from time to time proscribed by other, more powerfully placed theologians and philosophers. Sometimes such attempts were in vain, as was the hierarchy's condemnation of Aristotle in the schools of Paris in the early thirteenth century; in the next generation a new race of Aristotelians had secured acceptance for his doctrines. Marsilio of Padua and William of Occam encountered papal censure; they and their works survived unscathed. A more concerted attack, in which the popes concerned had the support of most responsible theologians, was made on the teaching of Wycliffe, though he was burned as a heretic only many years after his death. John Huss's writings brought him to the pyre at Constance in 1415. The condemnation of a man carried with it the condemnation of his books and they too were destroyed. Clearly it was easier for bishops and inquisitors to obliterate heretical works when they had just been written and before they had attained a wide circulation, and this in fact happened: many a minor heretic's writings have survived only in the indictment of his crimes. Yet the circulation of books was such that not only did Wycliffe's theology easily move from Oxford to Prague, but the writings of Wycliffe and Huss (wrongly accused of being a disciple of Wycliffe) in large measure survived the official holocaust.

An author might not be able to control the publication of his book or ensure in all cases that it survived unmutilated or at all, and he could not derive an income from it even if it was successful. But by the later Middle Ages he had readers beyond his own immediate circle and, if the work was non-technical and in the vernacular, he had a public in the modern sense of the term. Dante's *Divine Comedy*, Petrarch's lyrics, the *Decameron* of Boccaccio and Chaucer's *Canterbury Tales* were written not to entertain one man or even a court or a coterie but to be enjoyed by all who had the ability to read. The fourteenth or fifteenth-century author had linguistic difficulties. There was no one French or English or Italian. Significant creative writing in the vernacular did, however, promote the emergence of dominant literary languages as the works of Dante, Petrarch and Boccaccio stimulated the later importance of what might be called 'courtly Tuscan'.

The rising literacy of the fifteenth century was to make many more readers, so many more that the printing press was invented. At that critical moment, what was the intellectual stock of Europe? What books existed for the early printers to print? The list is formidably long. It contains the main writers of classical antiquity, including by 1450 all the main Roman writers save Tacitus, and (in Latin translation as well as in the original) most of Aristotle and some Plato, as well as Homer. From these works there had already stemmed a vast literature of commentary and creation as Roman and Greek ideas mingled with and challenged the most revolutionary corpus of writing inherited from the past—the Hebrew Scriptures and the Christian New Testament. With these Greek, Roman and Hebrew ingredients were mixed the scholarship and science of the Arab world—Rhases, Averroes and the rest. Like their Hellenistic predecessors, medieval scholars and men of letters often channelled their vast reservoirs of ideas into digests, anthologies and *florilegia*. They had developed to a fine art, again repeating the pattern of an older day, the habit of glossing and expounding a text, aided by the conviction that dialectic was a way of approaching the truth and that the written word of an *auctor*, an authority, was at any rate the beginning of wisdom.

The plenitude of ideas generated by medieval books defies simple analysis. One finds in the millennium between the fall of Rome in 410 and the fall of Constantinople in 1453 the expression of practically every imaginable opinion. There are monarchists, republicans, and communists. There are philosophers who bound man and the created world in a net of rational causation and others who denied this legalism in favour of a subjective approach to the mysteries and a pragmatic attitude to the language of metaphysics. There are cynics and mystics, and many who are a bit of both. There are chroniclers and memorialists, and scholars whose computations of chronology formed the basis for such narrators. There are tellers of stories, of lives of the saints and of great men, and there are even a few introspective writers (like Petrarch) who display their souls with pen and ink. And there are poets. The poets in Latin sometimes aped the classical writers they had learned at school—with happy results in a few cases. But they had a better chance when they let their fancy wander, even in Latin, to the rhythmical and rhymed verse of the vernacular as in the goliardic songs, full of a casual gusto and sometimes of a carnal pathos which should have been foreign to the 'clergy' who wrote them.

One important distinction must be made. With few exceptions, writing on serious subjects was in Latin and the vernaculars were the vehicles of written compositions only in what at the time were regarded as frivolous and secular fields. Dante's scholarship, like Petrarch's and Boccaccio's, was in Latin: like theirs his Italian writings were reserved for more popular themes. Latin was the language of cultivated men, understood universally and taught in every part of Christendom. It was the only language which was regularly taught beyond the elementary stage. Italian did not exist: there were a dozen Italians; and so it was with French, German, English and the languages of Spain. In France and England the court and the capital were giving one particular kind of French and English a predominance over the others. By the early fifteenth century there was no similar incipient unity in other parts of Europe save what was being imposed (as observed earlier) by the great vernacular writers themselves.

Yet even in the dialects, as the regional languages would later become, there was a remarkable sharing of cultural trends. Arthurian romance penetrated everywhere, and so did many of the Latin classics, translated into North German or Catalan. The really literate were still the clerks and the men (often laymen now) who had acquired some Latin at a grammar school or university primarily designed for clerks. But for those who were not able to read Latin there was also much to hand. Among the works generally available in a vernacular version by the end of the Middle Ages was the Vulgate Bible.

III

At the entrance to the 1963 Exhibition, of which this volume is an outcome, there was an enlarged reproduction of the first page of Gutenberg's Bible, on which a spotlight picked out the words *fiat lux*; 'Let there be light'. The vast increase in the accessibility of books which resulted from printing may suitably be illustrated by the example of the Bible itself. The Latin Vulgate had been printed ninety-four times by 1500; vernacular translations were in print for virtually every European language by 1600. By the latter date a press was to be found in nearly every town of any size. Some inventions (the water mill, for example) have taken centuries to be widely adopted and even more have taken several generations. Printing was an exception. It spread at a phenomenal speed from Mainz and by the 1490s each of the major states had one important publishing centre and some had several.

The world of books had been transformed and it is impossible to exaggerate the rapidity of the transformation. It is all too easy to exaggerate the consequences and to credit printing as such with occasioning as rapid a change in the mind of man. When Bacon listed the printing press along with gunpowder and the compass as ushering in the modern world he sadly oversimplified the realities. A closer examination of the first age of printing, from Gutenberg in the 1450s to the early nineteenth century, reveals many and profound continuities with the old manuscript-bound Middle Ages.

The early printed book physically resembled the manuscript book. The latter had been made up of gatherings of parchment or paper, sewn and bound between covers. On a shelf a row of medieval manuscripts does not look different from a row of early printed books. Nor does a manuscript look different from an early printed book when taken off the shelf and opened. The printer aimed his wares at the existing book-buying public and he did his best to provide an article with which his customers were familiar. In the Rhineland Gutenberg had used type designed to look like the best local book hands. In the Low Countries a 'bastard' hand was imitated and this Caxton used for the first works for the English market. In Italy 'humanist' hands, to settle down as 'Italic' and 'Roman', were being used, especially for the copying of texts in the humanities. These were the models followed by the printers of Rome, Venice, Milan, Naples and Florence; printers were at work at all of these places by the early 1470s. Nor did the first printers venture often to display their capacity for large-scale production. Editions seldom consisted of more than 1,000 copies and 200 seems to have been a common figure. There were technical and financial reasons for this, and not least the difficulty of raising capital to be tied up in large stocks of paper, metal and finished books. Yet the main explanation lay in the dependence of the printer-publisher on a market which was not unlimited. He could rely on a steady sale only of established works like the Bible, Donatus's grammar, prayer books and so on. The bulk of the works printed in the first century of printing were the old works, familiar to the region where the printer was at work. Fairly soon a degree of specialization developed and the volumes produced by some printers established themselves as articles of long-distance commerce and formed the staple of special markets or book fairs, such as the celebrated ones at Frankfurt and Leipzig.

Nor was there any change in the position of the author, who was not paid for the sales of his work on any pro rata basis. Many new books, perhaps most, were printed at the cost of the author or his patron. If the author was becoming well known the printer might share the costs. If the author was famous—Erasmus or Luther, for example—the printer might bear the entire cost and even allow the author some copies to give away. But nothing prevented a popular book being reprinted dozens of times and in dozens of places without the knowledge of the author. Men like Erasmus and Luther could thus make a fortune for a printer; the reverse was not true. It was only in the course of the seventeenth century that authors began to be paid in cash and not until the early eighteenth that they were given big sums of money. Finally, beginning with England, the state gave copyright to the author. By 1800 the process had been more or less completed. Authors could, if successful, live directly from their pens and not indirectly through a proliferation of dedications to rich and powerful men or by enjoying sinecures in Church or State. One of the fundamental characteristics of the first three centuries of printing is that the creative writer, the man of ideas and inspiration, wrote his books because he wished to express himself and not to make money. Erasmus with his well-placed friends was comfortably off, but his enormous output of best sellers, the *Praise of Folly*, the *Adagia*, the *Colloquies*, the long series of volumes of educational and moral works, the massive erudition of his classical and patristic editions, were the product of a man who researched and wrote compulsively and not for cash. Milton did not write *Paradise Lost* for the £5 paid for the manuscript by his publisher (or the further £5 which was to follow if a reprint was needed).

In many respects books and authors were thus not materially affected by printing, save that larger numbers of a work could now be rapidly made. Yet this multiplication of books was itself a very remarkable change. Coinciding, as the invention and spread of printing did, with the further development of the rising literacy which had provoked it, the increasing consumption of books undeniably meant that more persons wanted to read, just as it facilitated their acquiring the ability: a *virtuous* circle had been set up. In the sixteeenth and later centuries it became almost impossible for a man to attain positions of wealth or influence if he was illiterate. The well-to-do in every European country knew that to survive here below, and even to spend their money in fashionable ways, education was necessary; the ambitious knew that education opened a well-paved road to success. All gentlemen's sons and the sons of most of the urban bourgeoisie went to grammar school, *lycée* or *gymnasium*. The crofter's son in Scotland who sought his M.A. to become a minister or a dominie, the sons of *contadini* in the Romagna and the Abruzzi who entered religious orders, caused (in the seventeenth and early eighteenth centuries) what would be termed, in the jargon of the modern economist, 'a crisis of overproduction'. The curriculum of secondary education was remarkably similar in all European countries. Roman and Teuton, Roman Catholic and Protestant, were given a lot of Latin grammar and a little Greek. The texts they read furnished their masters with moral aphorisms and the subjects pursued were those which could be illustrated by the ancient classics: the history of antiquity, rhetoric, poetry—in a word, the humanities. Education was literary and mathematics had small part in it. At a level below this children could learn their letters and some arithmetic in the sporadic schools run by a parson or his clerk or by a literate 'dame', and the craftsman and the merchant picked up their skills, including the ability to read and write, mainly through apprenticeship or its equivalent. The grammar school was, however, the main regular source of education for those who could afford it and it covered the gentry and upper bourgeoisie of Europe with a patina of Latin-based culture.

The books used by the schoolmaster and his pupils, and those written and read by the handful of *literati* and scholars, were also technically improved compared with those of the later Middle Ages. When a volume was printed instead of being copied by hand it became worth while to take pains, infinite pains, to get the text right. In the manuscript accuracy was highly desirable but in practice hardly attainable; in print, with careful composition, with careful proof-reading, with the *corrigenda* published at once and then incorporated in later reprints, something like perfection seemed in sight and was certainly aimed at by the great printers of the sixteenth century (Aldus, Froben, the Estiennes and others) and by their successors. Further, when there were more books than before it became necessary to identify them precisely and quickly. The title of a book, obscurely found (if at all) in the colophons of manuscripts and early incunables, came to figure prominently at the beginning of the printed work and soon occupied a full preliminary page—an advertisement for the work which followed. The clumsy gloss gradually gave way to the footnote, permitting author and reader to avoid tiresome interruptions of the text by learned references or lengthy asides. The index was perfected and the alphabet took a further big step forward as an instrument of enlightenment and erudition.

Libraries became more plentiful and much bigger. The library of the Sorbonne in the early fourteenth century numbered fewer than 2,000 volumes and at Cambridge in the fifteenth century there were only 500 or so books in the University collection. By the seventeenth century the picture had altered. Princely patrons and great men were competing to establish great public libraries, such as that formed by Cardinal Mazarin with its 40,000 volumes. England lagged behind as far as noble or princely patronage was concerned, but the Bodleian Library at Oxford at this time became a national institution and led the way with its printed catalogues, as the Library of the British Museum, founded in the mid-eighteenth century, still does in the mid-twentieth. More significant, perhaps, was the spread of private libraries. In the course of the sixteenth century the main purchasers of books ceased to be the clergy: between 1557 and 1600 surviving inventories of books in France show that for every collection made by an ecclesiastic (prelate, priest or don) there were more than three made by lawyers and administrators, the lay 'aristocracy' of the *gens de robe*. 'In 1500' (Mr Sears Jayne tells us in his *Library Catalogues of the English Renaissance*) 'the principal owners of books in England were ecclesiastical institutions...By 1640...both Universities boasted many fine libraries of thousands of volumes each, there were several private collections of more than a thousand volumes, and there was not a single important ecclesiastical library in the country.' By the early eighteenth century a gentleman's house of any size had a room called the library. With this development went a new system in library management and in biblio-graphical expertise. Lists of books on a subject basis begin almost with printing. Johann Tritheim, who became abbot of Spanheim (not far from Mainz), published a *Liber de scriptoribus ecclesiasticis* in 1494. In 1545 the Swiss physician and naturalist Conrad Gesner published his *Bibliotheca Universalis* 'or complete catalogue of all writers in Latin, Greek and Hebrew, surviving and perished, old and modern up to the present...A new work necessary not only for the formation of public and private libraries but for all students...'. The science of bibliography had been established. By the mid-seventeenth century it was relatively easy to find out what books had been published on any topic. The purchaser was already able to turn to catalogues produced regularly by the biggest printing houses. The annual lists of the Frankfurt book fair began in 1564. More or less full lists of books published in France were issued from 1648 to 1654; a similar English catalogue appeared first in 1657. Even more important for the dissemination of information about new books and the ideas in them was the review-journal. This started with the French *Journal des Savants* (1665) which was followed by the *Philosophical Transactions* of the Royal Society of London (1675). By the early eighteenth century this process had been internationalized by translations of such periodicals and by the group of scholars, of whom Pierre Bayle was the most important, who diffused the intellectual novelties circulating in Europe from their asylum in the United Provinces where they published *Nouvelles de la République des lettres* and similar reviews.

One other list of publications was also published from time to time, but with the object of warning readers against the books it named. This was the *Index Librorum Prohibitorum*, issued under papal authority from 1559. The papal inquisitor or, in areas where there was no papal Inquisition (England was one), the local bishop had been responsible in the later Middle Ages for the suppression of heretical and erroneous writings. The printing press made such super-vision of books of even greater concern not only to the prelates or the pope, but also to governments. Two generations after Gutenberg Luther roused Germany and a horrified orthodoxy tried to identify the sources of Lutheran doctrine and prevent such influences continuing to be effective; not only were earlier prohibitions of the books of Wycliffe and Huss repeated, but at the same time Erasmus's writings were attacked and condemned. Equally the hierarchy and its theologians attempted to suppress Luther's writings and those of his disciples. At first the attempts at censorship were localized, as described below at p. 49. The centralization of Roman Catholic censorship in the Roman *Index* was effected after the Council of Trent. Frequently issued in revised editions, the *Index* undoubtedly impeded the free circulation of books in countries where there was a vigilant bishop or inquisitor, and it continued to do so for centuries, though signs of increasing tolerance became apparent in the year of grace 1966. But it entirely failed to prevent the books which it condemned from penetrating even areas obedient to Rome. Elsewhere, among Protestants or (later) among *libres penseurs* or 'progressives', the knowledge that a book was in the *Index* constituted a positive reason for reading it. Nor were princes and town magistrates much more successful in suppressing books which they judged to be seditious or immoral; it should be remembered here that with printing came pornography. There were many attempts at state supervision of unwelcome works. The wary, ingenious and covetous printer defeated them all, though not without occasional danger to himself and not without leaving behind some bibliographical puzzles. It had not been easy to burke a manuscript book. It was impossible to stifle print. In Milton's *Areopagitica* the doctrine of freedom of publication was given canonical form.

The printed book thus differed from the manuscript book by appearing in numbers so large that suppression was in practice impossible, by presenting in general a more reliable text (supported when appropriate by footnotes, indices and other apparatus), by lending itself easily to collection in public and private libraries and to access through bibliographies and periodical reviews. In all these ways printing made book-learning, and book-pleasures of other kinds, much more accessible. It also promoted changes in style and presentation which caused the printed book to become inherently more attractive, more attractive as a physical object, than earlier manuscripts. It is, of course, true that all through the Middle Ages beautiful books were made by hand, from the glorious manuscripts made in Charlemagne's day down to the glorious manuscripts collected by Guidobaldo Montefeltre at Urbino in the fifteenth century; it was said that he would not tolerate a printed volume in his library. But the general level of ordinary manuscript books, the workaday tools of teacher or researcher, were unpleasant to look at by the fourteenth and fifteenth centuries. Bibles could be made sufficiently neat and small, but at the price of writing them in a hand so minute as to be almost indecipherable. Early printing, aimed at a mass market, at first copied locally prevailing book hands. This however changed as printers and typographers accustomed themselves to the new medium. Everywhere the trend was away from heavy black pages towards lighter pages, which gave an overall impression of grey. This was achieved mainly by adopting a lettering which was lighter, finer, better spaced and arranged. In this steady transition Italian printers provided in their italic and roman faces a model which was generally followed in Europe, save in Germany and in Slavonic lands. The victory of Italian typography was the last, but by no means the least, stage in the conquest of the rest of Europe by the values and methods evolved in the peninsula during the Renaissance. Associated at first with the texts of Latin classics and the humanists of Italy, these agreeable and economical founts acquired general prestige by being used by the Venetian printer Aldus Manutius. That they were steadily adopted all over Europe is a tribute to the key position of the grammar-school master and his high-born and influential pupils. Even in Germany roman type was used for classical or humanist texts. At the same time books began to be smaller. Great folios still abounded in the seventeenth and eighteenth centuries, but there were more quartos, octavos and duodecimos.

It has been observed earlier that the advent of printing had no immediate effect on the material circumstances of the author. As the printed book slowly evolved and perfected itself, consequences for authorship nevertheless slowly followed.

It is impossible to believe that the writers of the sixteenth and seventeenth centuries did not feel sensuous pleasure at the sight of their work in print, as their twentieth-century successors do. The smell of the paper, the ink and the glue have not (thank heavens) been distilled and bottled in Paris or New York and one can still discriminate between the scent of a woman and the perfume of a new book: yet the ensuing sensations can be of the same invading wholeness. The authors of an earlier day would, it is true, have titivated their noses with vellum and leather, odours which can nowadays only be savoured among the aromatic shelves of a great library where the gold and the calf exude incense, even if it is only saddle-soap and insecticide. They too would view a dozen crisp copies of one of their books with astonished pride: not everyone can father such multiplicity, nor send into the unknown so many heralds and hawkers.

Composition of a book which was to be 'published' in manuscript meant that the writer knew who would read it, at any rate initially. With a printed work publication meant something different. Automatically it was offered to a number, perhaps a very large number, of purchasers and readers with whose background and tastes the author could not be familiar. In the case of some specialized works, for instance in medicine and law, a professional audience could be anticipated. But in more general fields, history, literary criticism, philosophy, natural philosophy and even theology, as well of course as imaginative prose and verse, there was no telling in advance who precisely would be attracted. It is true that the medieval writer was aware that he could often expect ultimately to have unknown readers, but the degree of anonymity in his public to which an author was committed by printing was of a different order. New inducements existed to make one's writing intelligible and its presentation agreeable. Where appropriate, the author must now avoid plunging *in medias res*; he must rather set the scene and provide an introductory summary, explaining himself and his subject. (Compare the preliminary pages of the fourteenth-century Florentine *Chronicle* of Giovanni Villani with the beginning of Machiavelli's *Istorie Fiorentine*, which was designed for publication though it appeared after the author's death.) Moreover an attractively written book was much more likely to be published, for—from the mid-sixteenth century onwards—it was booksellers rather than printers who put up the capital for a new work and they knew, or thought they knew, what the public wanted.

From the sixteenth century there arose one basic change in the public for books which conditioned authorship: Latin gradually ceased to be the only or even the main vehicle for serious writing. It has already been pointed out that the vernaculars were used in the Middle Ages, broadly speaking, only for ephemeral works, even if a later age was to regard the *Romance of the Rose* and the *Divine Comedy* as immortal. This attitude persisted in the first century of printing, but gradually the vernaculars (under the pervasive influence of Latin) acquired a maturity which enabled English, French and the others to carry with confidence and efficiency the most sophisticated thoughts. Prudent and far-sighted men might question whether professional knowledge (in medicine, physical science or theology) should thus be made available on the market-place; certainly there were meaner experts who resented their *arcana* being exposed to the light of common day. But the process was irreversible. Latin scholarship in all subjects was turned into English and French and Castilian, and in the same languages scholars now began to compose. By the end of the seventeenth century Latin was no longer indispensable to the learned *writer*, even though as a *scholar* he still found it indispensable. At the Frankfurt book fair the proportion of Latin to German books was two to one in the decades between 1560 and 1630; by the 1680s more books were for sale in German than in Latin.

In English the appearance of Richard Hooker's *Of the Laws of Ecclesiastical Polity* (1594–7) marks the emancipation of English as an autonomous medium. Fifty years earlier such a book would have been written in Latin or else would have appeared in the clumsy obscurity of what C. S. Lewis called 'drab'. Yet Hooker paid a penalty for his achievement. His remarkable theological work remained virtually unknown to continental scholars. Isaak Walton in his life of Hooker (1664) described how he had been told 'more than forty years past' that the attention of Pope Clement VIII was drawn to the book by 'either Cardinal Allen, or learned Dr Stapleton'. The pope was informed that 'though he [the pope] had lately said he never met with an English book whose writer deserved the name of an author; yet there now appeared a wonder to them, and it would be to his Holiness, if it were in Latin; for a poor obscure English priest had writ four such books of Laws and Church-Polity, and in a style that expressed such a grave and so humble a majesty, with such clear demonstration of reason, that in all their readings they had not met with any that exceeded him'. With this view Clement concurred when Dr Stapleton read him the first part in an extempore Latin translation.

Across the linguistic frontiers of Europe scholars continued to communicate in Latin even when they ceased to publish in it. One must remember that many original Latin works were being printed until well on in the eighteenth century, and that many writers (Galileo, Descartes and scores more) published works with equal fluency in Latin and a vernacular. Latin remained the normal language for international correspondence between scholars in different countries, only slowly being replaced by Italian and then by French. Translation was also able to diffuse knowledge originally available only in vernacular writing and was undertaken with an increasing care for accuracy. Latin translations were even published of periodicals such as the French *Journal des Savants* and the English *Philosophical Transactions*. Translation was, moreover, facilitated by the nature of vernacular prose and poetry down to the end of the eighteenth century. Heavily influenced everywhere by Latin grammar and syntax, vernacular writers shared a common attitude to style. They had also been brought up on a classical pabulum which ensured that their allusions and points of reference were readily understood everywhere. There was nevertheless now a choice before an educated author, whether to address himself first or mainly to an international audience in Latin or to a national audience in his mother-tongue.

The choice of such a writer was often determined by his purposes. The moralist and above all the church reformer naturally sought to address large numbers. This was not a new situation. Huss preaching in Czech, Bernardino in Italian, were doing what Luther and others were to do in print—going to the masses. Indeed the sermon-hungry audiences of the fifteenth century often represented the whole population of a town, whereas the printed word immediately reached only those who could read, though they in turn might speak out the message. But the vast quantities of pamphlets issued in Germany (630 have been listed from the years 1520 to 1530) leave no doubt that without the printing press the course of the German Reformation might have been different. Luther's own writings constitute a third of the German books printed in the first four decades of the sixteenth century; his address *To the Christian Nobility of the German Nation* (August 1520) was reprinted thirteen times in two years; *Concerning Christian Liberty* (September 1520) came out eighteen times before 1526; as for his translation of the Bible, Dr Steinberg summarizes the complicated bibliographical story thus—'All in all, 430 editions of the whole Bible or parts of it appeared during Luther's lifetime'. Polemical literature was also naturally put to the service of governments. Here again the propagandist had predecessors, as can be seen in the chauvinist pamphleteering provoked by Anglo-French hostilities during the Hundred Years War or by the respect accorded by other courts in Italy to the Florentine scholar-chancellors from Salutati onwards. But the government which sponsored manuscript warfare was trying merely to influence other chanceries and the councillors of princes. Printed polemics were designed to interest large and influential sections of public opinion. Hence the retained men who wrote for kings and ministers from the days of Henry VIII, Francis I and Charles V down to the hacks operating official journalism in the eighteenth century. Hence the 'historiographers royal' who spread from the French court to other countries in the seventeenth century. Hence, too, the counter-government publications of critics and rebels, the object of censorship and persecution, which reached behind the police to the man in the study, if not the man in the street.

Much, perhaps most, of what was printed in the centuries which followed the invention was to be of no lasting interest, save when digested statistically: the mounting number of royal proclamations, the emergence and diffusion of the periodical press, the very numbers of books published themselves. What is of interest is the growing enlargement of the human spirit which is recalled in the pages of this book. By 1600 the whole range of ancient thought was available to the curious, and much of it was accessible in vernacular versions. The main philosophers, scientists and historians of the Middle Ages had been printed, though as yet without the critical care that was beginning to be lavished on the writings of antiquity. And to this inherited knowledge and reflexion the Renaissance added its own contributions, which germinated rapidly and which thus could rival the influence of the works by those established *auctores* of the ancient and medieval periods. The pace of intellectual change quickened and the notion of *auctoritas* was challenged by novelty. The excitement of the new began to act as a leaven. There are no medieval Utopias. From More onwards the world has never been without them, and it was by printed books that moralists, scientists, philosophers and critics of art and literature mapped out fresh paths.

Prior to the French Revolution the audience for serious writing was composed of all educated men and women and learning was, at any rate in principle, undivided. The rigid academic distinctions which were later to impose themselves were absent. Galileo regarded himself not only as a scientist but as a philosopher and a man of letters and he did in fact write good Latin and good Italian. The cultivated public was able to understand, even if it disapproved of, the current advances in natural philosophy and technology, let alone the more familiar subjects of ethics and theology. Difficult some of the ideas were, but good writing and the device of correspondence or dialogue facilitated attractive exposition; when a physicist like Newton was too austere to do this for himself a writer like Fontenelle was available to undertake the necessary *haute vulgarisation*. Even reference books could be idiosyncratic, witty and stylish, as Bayle and Johnson showed. The existence of a wide reading public turned publication itself into a gesture of some significance and the writer, even if unrewarded as such until the eighteenth century, had emerged as a distinct species. And some writers had *genius* 'as opposed' (says the dictionary) 'to *talent*'. Genius in this sense apparently comes into English in 1759.

Printers were responsible not only for issuing books and pamphlets of temporary significance and for works of genius or at least talent. They also published an increasing number of books which, by adding to the conveniences of the scholar and man of affairs, saved his time for more important things. Dictionaries are the most obvious instance of this and the student who had a printed *Thesaurus* should be compared with the medieval scholar who had to make his own or depend on a tatty copy of the *Catholicon*. The published tables of logarithms and other tabulated mathematical and astronomical material not only speeded up scientific calculation but put reliable instruments into the hands of ships' navigators.

Besides the utilities the press encouraged the graces of life. The printing of music disseminated the latest songs and compositions among the gentry who were often still themselves performers. Hand-copied music depended on skills which the amateur could scarcely be expected to possess; the engraved music of the printer provided the equivalent in accurate, legible and convenient form. Engraving also speeded up the knowledge of the pictorial art of distant centres. Long before the young painter or architect had visited Italy he could study the masters in albums and absorb the principles of Palladio. His patron came back from the Grand Tour provided, if he could afford it, with some original canvases but certainly with engravings by Piranesi.

With music and the fine arts the function of printing was, so to say, ancillary. With imaginative literature it had by the seventeenth century become an essential part of composition. Though the bard lingered on in the Balkans and Finland until the twentieth century, though ballads were composed in industrial Britain and in America during the nineteenth, oral literature was in effect displaced by print, and the poetry of the later Renaissance has a quality it could not otherwise have possessed; it was meant to be read, not recited. Read aloud it often was, and so were the prose romances and the elegant essays (of indescribable dullness for the most part), on wet days when hunting was impossible, or by the ladies after dinner while the men sobered up. But it was designed by the writer for the reader. Both saw it silently on a printed page.

IV

With the nineteenth century the pace of communication speeded up, at first with books themselves and later with the invention of other devices. The more rapid production of books was made possible by the perfection of various technical improvements—stereotyping, then mechanical type-setting and machine binding—which enabled steam and other forms of power to be applied to printing so that what had remained for centuries a craft was steadily transformed into an industrial enterprise. Publishers, who had by the end of the eighteenth century become largely separated from the printers who made books and the shopkeepers who sold them, were often now large companies of influential businessmen, keen to supply the widening market for print.

That market increased rapidly. The men who came to power in Europe in the generation after the French Revolution can be described, in a phrase which came to be generally adopted at the time, as middle class. At one end of the spectrum they were promoters of industrialization, of international commerce and banking, and at the other they were middlemen and retailers. Their prescription for the world's woes was the diffusion of their own values as the wealth of the community increased. Those of their critics who deplored the passing of the golden age of an educated *élite* were powerless to resist the march of bourgeois egalitarianism. Their other adversaries, who challenged capitalism and foretold its doom, shared to the full the optimism of the age. Both capitalists and socialists advocated universal literacy to be achieved by compulsory education. They were pushing at an open door. A predominantly agrarian community can dispense with reading and writing: the farmer's education is (or perhaps was) provided through an apprenticeship with nature. The industrial revolution brought in its wake the necessity for a lettered population. In the world of nineteenth-century machinery the illiterate not only went to the wall; they could be dangerous in a big factory and were useless as shop assistants in a big store.

The Revolution in France had led to the enunciation of the principles of free and compulsory education at the primary level, and this was incorporated in the constitution of 1791. On the Continent the early nineteenth century saw the general adoption of state schools for all. In Britain progress was, as usual, much slower, save in Scotland where effective parish schools were already in existence. Yet even in Britain the provision of public schools (as opposed to Public Schools) came hesitantly in the mid-century although, before that, there was an amazing degree of self-improvement: Mechanics' Institutes, the *Penny Cyclopaedia*, and so forth. Nor was self-improvement restricted to the working class. In the early decades of the nineteenth century a big town usually acquired an institution—the one at Newcastle upon Tyne is called the Literary and Philosophical Society—which organized lectures and maintained a library of serious books. At the same time the intelligent reader could now turn to an intelligent journalism, of which the *Edinburgh Review* was the first great example.

The idealization of literacy and the remarkably quick progress which literacy made, at any rate in Western Europe and North America, were further encouraged by more rapid transport. The isolated parts of great countries were penetrated by better roads, by canals and, even more important, by railway lines, which drove first from one big centre to another and then curved through tunnels and over viaducts into mountain and moor. One could now travel through the Apennines, the Massif Central and the Scottish Highlands in hours instead of days. Pockets of traditional life were eliminated. The language (and the books and ideas) of Paris and London began to erode ever more quickly the frontiers, already in retreat, of Catalan, Provençal and Breton, of Welsh and Gaelic. The schoolmasters in highland areas had been trained in the big towns and their pupils were brought up to feel that culture went with capital cities. The demand for books was stimulated by these enlargements of the market. Railways also affected publisher and author by providing tranquil hours of dis-occupation. The railway bookstall supplied the necessary distraction. The yellowbacks of early Victorian England, the sophisticated publications of Tauchnitz (designed for the English-speaking visitor to the Continent) and serious magazines like *Blackwood's*, *The Atlantic Monthly* and so on, were direct results of the new world of steam.

'World' is the right word. Just as the railway made for rapid and certain travel on land, so did the steamboat at sea. Here, too, there were *longueurs* to be sweetened by print and here too there were markets to be exploited. The English publisher now had vast English-speaking areas overseas at his disposal—North America, where the population was quickly augmented by immigrants from all over the world, Australia, India and a wide network of smaller colonies where literacy was largely confined to the white administrators, the settlers and missionaries, who did their best to spread a reading knowledge of the Word.

Until the early twentieth century the overseas conquests of English might have been paralleled, though not equalled, by German, French and Spanish. In the event, although Spanish has still a huge currency in South and Central America, English is now unrivalled as a world language, and it is surely not fanciful to foresee the day when it will be universally known. This is a factor which weighs heavily with contemporary publishers and authors and which will undoubtedly weigh much more heavily in years to come.

The scholarship and the science of nineteenth-century Europe were, however, far from being determined by the British. The leadership in letters, the arts and academic subjects had moved at the Renaissance from France to Italy. In the nineteenth century a much more complicated *translatio litterarum* came about. Cultural primacy was shared by Germany and France, and to some extent the division was one between the 'two cultures' about which so much has been written in recent years. The German university recovered first from the dol-drums in which higher education had been becalmed and it was in the German university that a new science and a new scholarship emerged in the post-Napoleonic period to set their seal on advanced teaching elsewhere in Europe and in North America. The German pro-fessor, with his disciples in a seminar or laboratory, was interested in furthering the know-ledge of his subject, not in turning out gentlemen or even men of affairs. France, on the other hand, with romantic literature and later with realism, with the impressionists and the post-impressionists, acted as a magnet for poets, novelists and painters. There were, of course, great French scientists; Darwin was an Englishman educated in Scotland. But the pacemaking in nineteenth century history, philology, physics and chemistry was by Germans and there is no British Stendhal or Flaubert, no Spanish or Italian Cézanne. The decision to exclude from the 1963 Exhibition works of imaginative literature (though some squeezed themselves in) means that this French monopoly is not reflected in this book. But it is noticeable that, of the scholarly works described below which were published in the century and a half after 1800, a third are from German-speaking Europe, mostly from Germany itself.

As for the attitudes to books themselves which developed by 1900, one finds a curious contradiction. On the one hand old books are cherished with care, and on the other new books are generally regarded as expendable. The collecting of books, which had originally been restricted to incunables and editions of celebrated authors, has been enlarged in the last two generations to cover every variety of printing and every type of writer. Bibliographical expertise has increased and a tender concern watches for minute variants. This, reflected in sale-room prices, has led to the amassing of collections by men who regard books as an investment rather than as reading matter, and among the connoisseurs and the Ph.D. students it has given enormous prestige to libraries lucky enough to possess or acquire numbers of rarities. The days are over when the Bodleian Library could eject its first folio of Shakespeare when the third edition was printed in 1664.

At the same time the paperback, starting slowly in the early decades of this century, has now taken over much of the market in books. The strident display at a shop like Brentano's Basement in New York is totally different from the quiet of even the pre-Second World War bookshops and this brittle assertiveness seems to be the pattern for the future. Who does not see his local bookshop being slowly engulfed by the lava from the paperback volcanoes? The issue of a serious work in paper covers apparently for many readers confers on it the hallmark of the classical. Such books do not last physically; they are as flesh, all too easily assimilated to the lascivious-seeming works of fiction which are sold beside them. The reader buys the solid product as an instrument of entertainment or ambitious self-improvement. My own shelves are clogged with the detritus of thirty years of casual buying of paperbacks on all sorts of subjects, kept because I am an old-fashioned book-keeper and these belong to the genus *book*; but not kept in my study. Yet there, too, I have paperbacks—some of them, it is true, are in French and Italian (for publishers of serious and even expensive books in continental countries still tend to assume that their readers will have them bound) but some of them are editions of important works of scholarship in English which one might hunt for too long in a bound edition.

The multiplication of books in our own day is only one aspect of the changes which have recently occurred in communications. Far more important has been the advance of radio—first sound and then television. Like printing, radio is a technical innovation which has spread with extraordinary rapidity. And it represents a further stage not only in the diffusion of news and knowledge, but in the scope of political and cultural organization. Writing, it will be remembered, enabled government to increase in range and efficiency, and printing furthered the process. With radio the reach of political power is in principle almost boundless in our small universe. If the nineteenth century experienced a quickening pace in the penetration of more isolated areas by the central culture of bigger countries, radio is in a fair way to obliterating entirely the locally rooted community and the values that went with it.

It is, of course, conceivable that radio might replace the world of books. If this were to happen man might find himself back again in square two—not square one, that environment of gesture and emotive sound, but the next stage, the use of speech without writing. The invulnerability of the book must certainly not be taken for granted. Man has been reading now for something like six thousand years, a short enough space in the whole span of his development. He has been speaking for a far longer period than that and even before he spoke he had developed those activities of feeding and fighting and making love which still give him his deepest satisfactions. Reading and writing are relatively recent accomplishments and for that reason may suffer: 'last in, first out', as they say. There are, indeed, forces within scholarship itself which militate against the book. Advances in some of the sciences mean that a book on the subject is out of date almost as soon as it is printed. The biologist, the physicist and the medical researcher depend on periodical literature to keep in touch with their fields of interest. Even that is less satisfactory to them than direct contact and so they turn to the spoken word at congresses, conferences and colloquies. In the old humanist arts' subjects, where tradition might seem most deeply entrenched, the language laboratory is making otiose the familiar grammars and texts. Will radio, the acceleration of scientific discovery and new techniques of instruction mean that the book as we have known it will pass away?

Littera scripta manet: let us give the adage in its entirety—*Vox audita perit, littera scripta manet.* 'The spoken word passes away, the written word remains.' It is appropriate that the tag seems to have appeared first in one of the earliest printed books, Caxton's *Mirrour of the World* (1481). It is surely inconceivable that the impresarios of the future will succeed entirely in persuading the creators, the makers, to consign their inspiration to the ether, to be bounced about between the earth and the Heaviside Layer until the waves peter out in inaudible murmurs. Authors are not like children, content to see their beautiful pebbles flung into the pool of eternity. The student and the scholar, at any rate in many fields of human learning, will also want a measure of continuity. They will want shoulders to stand on as they peer at the past and future, and will not want to revert to the age when memory counted for everything. Equally the endless varieties of individual research and enjoyment could never be adequately reflected in the choices broadcast by Public Authority or Private Enterprise, however enlightened. Perhaps some day it may be possible to devise ways of recapturing the flying words and images of the past. Until that happens there will be no substitute for print and the book will remain the only way by which one age can speak to another.

This essay is entitled 'Let there be light'. This may seem a paradoxical way of describing printer's ink and the art of putting it on paper which was discovered by Gutenberg five hundred years ago: it is the dark letters we look at, not the white paper. But it may be justified. The printed page illuminates the mind of man and defies, in so far as anything sublunary can, the corrosive hand of Time.

INDEX